Information Systems Development

Chris Barry • Kieran Conboy • Michael Lang
Gregory Wojtkowski • Wita Wojtkowski

Editors

Information Systems Development

Challenges in Practice, Theory
and Education

Volume 2

 Springer

Editors

Chris Barry
Business Information Systems Group
J.E. Cairnes School of Business & Economics
National University of Ireland, Galway
University Road
Galway
Ireland

Kieran Conboy
Business Information Systems Group
J.E. Cairnes School of Business & Economics
National University of Ireland, Galway
University Road
Galway
Ireland

Michael Lang
Business Information Systems Group
J.E. Cairnes School of Business & Economics
National University of Ireland, Galway
University Road
Galway
Ireland

Gregory Wojtkowski
Boise State University
Department of Electrical & Computer
    Engineering
1910 University Dr.
MEC 202C
Boise, ID 83725-2075
USA

Wita Wojtkowski
Boise State University
Department of Electrical & Computer
    Engineering
1910 University Dr.
MEC 202C
Boise, ID 83725-2075
USA

ISBN: 978-0-387-78577-6   e-ISBN: 978-0-387-78578-3
DOI: 10.1007/978-0-387-78578-3

Library of Congress Control Number: 2008928765

Printed on acid-free paper

springer.com

Preface

This two-volume book is the published proceedings of the 16th International Conference on Information Systems Development (ISD2007) that was hosted by the Cairnes Graduate School of Business & Public Policy at National University of Ireland, Galway, from 29–31 August 2007. The theme of the conference was "Challenges in Practice, Theory and Education." The theme is not a new one – we chose to reproduce that used in Lithuania in 2004 because it encapsulates our ideals for the profession we are in: Teaching ISD practice and theory is what we all must aspire to achieve.

In total, 120 delegates from 27 different countries registered for the conference, making it a truly international event. Papers presented at the conference strongly reflected the three pillars of our conference theme. Of 131 papers submitted, 84 were presented at the conference, representing an acceptance rate of ~64%. All papers were double-blind, peer reviewed by at least two referees. Over the course of 3 days, 29 sessions were held, covering a range of areas such as agile methods, usage of systems development methods, method tailoring, users and usability, web development methods, requirements analysis, business process modelling, systems analysis and design, ISD in developing nations, ISD in public sector organisations, socio-technical aspects of ISD, human resources issues in ISD, knowledge management in ISD, ERP systems development and implementation, legal and ethical dimensions of ISD, management of ISD, information systems security, ISD education and training, e-learning technologies, project and requirements management, data quality and integrity, database design, practical applications of database technologies, Web services, automation of software development, and information systems engineering. The book is organised by the order of the conference sessions.

Reviewing papers, which is key to ensuring quality and fairness, is not generally a task that is acknowledged at a conference. It is done as part of a sense of collegiality and duty. At our conference a remarkable 95% of reviews were completed. In recognition of the reviewer who applied the most diligence and penned the most extensive review with both critical and constructive feedback, a *Best Reviewer Award* was given. Of course, a *Best Paper Award* was given as well. Details of these awards can be found on the conference Web site at http://isd2007.nuigalway.ie.

Our gratitude is extended first to all those who attended and authored work for the conference. The contribution of the International Program Committee was invaluable in identifying track chairs and reviewers to commit to doing vital work. Although volunteering to host a conference is a highly personal undertaking, without institutional support it would be impossible. Thus, a special thanks to Professor Jim Browne, the Registrar and Deputy-President of NUI, Galway, who opened the conference and welcomed the delegates to the Cairnes Graduate School. Our local organising committee laboured industriously to make the conference a success, especially Laura Regan, our conference secretary, who worked tirelessly to ensure harmony in all affairs. We also received invaluable advice from our conference office and assistance from the Centre for Education and Learning Technologies (CELT). Our sincere thanks are also extended to Mike Roche of IBM Dublin Software Laboratory and Professor Stefan Decker of the Digital Enterprise Research Institute (DERI) in Galway, who delivered the keynote addresses. Finally, we thank our sponsors for their financial support and other aid.

The ISD conference community has developed over the years a real sense of collegiality and friendliness, perhaps unusually so for a conference. At the same time it has been a stimulating forum where a free exchange of views and perspectives is encouraged. Perhaps what brings the community together is a belief that the process of systems development is important; whether it is systematic or structured or improvised or spontaneous, there is something about the process and the outcomes that excites us. We form a spectrum of thought from those who see the activity as somewhat scientific to others that see it as wholly sociological; we span a divide between abstract and conceptual, to hard code and artefacts – somewhere in-between lies the truth. If our work is to make a meaningful contribution to both practice (by teaching students) and research (by sharing our experiences and studies with others), then hopefully this conference will have done a little of the former and much for the latter.

Chris Barry and Michael Lang
ISD2007 Programme Chairs

Kieran Conboy
ISD2007 Organising Chair

Conference Organisation

The 16th International Conference on Information Systems Development was hosted by the Business Information Systems Group, Cairnes Graduate School of Business & Public Policy, National University of Ireland, Galway, from 29 to 31 August 2007. The organisation and management of such a major international conference requires the collaboration and dedication of very many people. We are especially grateful to our international programme committee who voluntarily gave their time to review the submissions. The excellent standard of papers contained within this volume bears testimony to the diligence and rigour of the peer review process. We are also very appreciative of the efforts of all the conference officers and the tremendous support provided by the local organising committee.

Programme Chairs

Chris Barry	National University of Ireland, Galway	Ireland
Michael Lang	National University of Ireland, Galway	Ireland

Organising Chair

Kieran Conboy	National University of Ireland, Galway	Ireland

International Advisory Committee

Gregory Wojtkowski	Boise State University	USA
Wita Wojtkowski	Boise State University	USA
Stanislaw Wrycza	University of Gdansk	Poland
Joze Zupancic	University of Maribor	Slovenia

Local Organising Committee

Tom Acton	National University of Ireland, Galway	Ireland
Annmarie Curran	National University of Ireland, Galway	Ireland
Brian Donnellan	National University of Ireland, Galway	Ireland
Willie Golden	National University of Ireland, Galway	Ireland
Mairéad Hogan	National University of Ireland, Galway	Ireland
Martin Hughes	National University of Ireland, Galway	Ireland
Séamus Hill	National University of Ireland, Galway	Ireland
Orla McHugh	National University of Ireland, Galway	Ireland

Anatoli Nachev	National University of Ireland, Galway	Ireland
Laura Regan	National University of Ireland, Galway	Ireland
Murray Scott	National University of Ireland, Galway	Ireland
Patricia Walsh	National University of Ireland, Galway	Ireland
Eoin Whelan	National University of Ireland, Galway	Ireland

Track Chairs

Managing Information Systems Development

| Brian O'Flaherty | University College Cork | Ireland |
| Gaye Kiely | University College Cork | Ireland |

Innovation in Information Systems Development

| Brian Donnellan | National University of Ireland, Galway | Ireland |
| Séamas Kelly | University College Dublin | Ireland |

Enterprise Systems Development & Adoption

| Anders G. Nilsson | Karlstad University | Sweden |
| Odd Fredriksson | Karlstad University | Sweden |

Public Information Systems Development

| Michael Lang | National University of Ireland, Galway | Ireland |

Agile and High-Speed Systems Development Methods

| Pär Ågerfalk | University of Limerick | Ireland |
| Kieran Conboy | National University of Ireland, Galway | Ireland |

Information Systems Engineering

| Norah Power | University of Limerick | Ireland |

Business Systems Analysis & Design

| Larry Stapleton | Waterford Institute of Technology | Ireland |
| Chris Barry | National University of Ireland, Galway | Ireland |

Data and Information Modelling

Markus Helfert	Dublin City University	Ireland

ISD Education

Lorraine Fisher	University College Dublin	Ireland
Murray Scott	National University of Ireland, Galway	Ireland

ISD in Developing Nations

John Traxler	University of Wolverhampton	UK

Legal and Administrative Aspects of ISD

Rónán Kennedy	National University of Ireland, Galway	Ireland

Service Oriented Modelling and Semantic Web Technologies

William Song	University of Durham	UK
Remigijus Gustas	Karlstad University	Sweden
Yuansheng Zhong	Jiangxi University of Finance & Economy	China

International Programme Committee

Witold Abramowicz	Economic University, Poznan	Poland
Tom Acton	National University of Ireland, Galway	Ireland
Pär Ågerfalk	University of Limerick	Ireland
Majed Al-Mashari	King Saud University	Saudi Arabia
Scott W. Ambler	IBM Rational	Canada
Viveca Asproth	Mid Sweden University	Sweden
David Avison	ESSEC Business School	France
Karin Axelsson	Linköping University	Sweden
Per Backlund	University of Skovde	Sweden
Akhilesh Bajaj	The University of Tulsa	USA
Chris Barry	National University of Ireland, Galway	Ireland
Janis Barzdins	University of Latvia, Riga	Latvia
Richard Baskerville	Georgia State University	USA
Dinesh Batra	Florida International University	USA
Frances Bell	University of Salford	UK
Paul Beynon-Davies	Cardiff Business School	UK
Juris Borzovs	Information Technology Institute	Latvia
Deborah Bunker	University of New South Wales	Australia
Adriana Schiopiu Burlea	University of Craiova	Romania
Dave Bustard	University of Ulster, Jordanstown	UK

Tom Butler	University College Cork	Ireland
Rimantas Butleris	Kaunas University of Technology	Lithuania
Albertas Caplinskas	Institute of Mathematics and Informatics	Lithuania
Sven Carlsson	Lund University	Sweden
Michael Cavanagh	Balmoral Consulting	UK
Antanas Cenys	Semiconductor Physics Institute, Vilnius	Lithuania
Des Chambers	National University of Ireland, Galway	Ireland
Deren Chen	Zhejiang University	China
Rodney Clarke	University of Wollongong	Australia
Jenny Coady	Heriot-Watt University	UK
Gerry Coleman	Dundalk Institute of Technology	Ireland
Kieran Conboy	National University of Ireland, Galway	Ireland
Heitor Augustus Xavier Costa	Universidade Federal de Lavras	Brazil
Darren Dalcher	Middlesex University	UK
Gert-Jan de Vreede	University of Nebraska at Omaha	USA
Brian Donnellan	National University of Ireland, Galway	Ireland
Liam Doyle	Waterford Institute of Technology	Ireland
Jim Duggan	National University of Ireland, Galway	Ireland
Seán Duignan	Galway-Mayo Institute of Technology	Ireland
Dalé Dzemydiené	Law University, Vilnius	Lithuania
Phillip Ein-Dor	Tel-Aviv University	Israel
Owen Eriksson	Dalarna University College, Borlänge	Sweden
Chris Exton	University of Limerick	Ireland
Joe Feller	University College Cork	Ireland
Pat Finnegan	University College Cork	Ireland
Julie Fisher	Monash University, Melbourne	Australia
Lorraine Fisher	University College Dublin	Ireland
Brian Fitzgerald	University of Limerick	Ireland
Guy Fitzgerald	Brunel University	UK
Owen Foley	Galway-Mayo Institute of Technology	Ireland
Marko Forsell	SESCA Technologies Oy	Finland
Odd Fredriksson	Karlstad University	Sweden
Chris Freyberg	Massey University	New Zealand
Matt Glowatz	University College Dublin	Ireland
Goran Goldkuhl	Linköping University	Sweden
Gary Griffiths	University of Teesside	UK
Janis Grundspenkis	Riga Technical University	Latvia
Remigijus Gustas	Karlstad University	Sweden
Hele-Mai Haav	Tallinn Technical University	Estonia
G. Harindranath	University of London	UK
Igor Hawryszkiewycz	University of Technology, Sydney	Australia
John Healy	Galway-Mayo Institute of Technology	Ireland
Kevin Heffernan	Galway-Mayo Institute of Technology	Ireland
Markus Helfert	Dublin City University	Ireland
Brian Henderson-Sellers	University of Technology, Sydney	Australia
Ola Henfriddson	Viktoria Institute	Sweden

Alan Hevner	University of South Florida	USA
Séamus Hill	National University of Ireland, Galway	Ireland
Mairéad Hogan	National University of Ireland, Galway	Ireland
Jesper Holck	Copenhagen Business School	Denmark
Helena Holmstrom	University of Limerick	Ireland
Debra Howcroft	Manchester Business School	UK
Joshua Huang	E-Business Technology Institute, Hong Kong	China
Magda Huisman	North-West University	South Africa
Sergey Ivanov	George Washington University	USA
Mirjana Ivanovic	University of Novi Sad	Serbia and Montenegro
Letizia Jaccheri	Norwegian University of Science and Technology	Norway
Marius A. Janson	University of Missouri – St. Louis	USA
Sherif Kamel	American University in Cairo	Egypt
Roland Kaschek	Massey University	New Zealand
Karlheinz Kautz	Copenhagen Business School	Denmark
Felicity Kelleher	Waterford Institute of Technology	Ireland
Séamas Kelly	University College Dublin	Ireland
Rónán Kennedy	National University of Ireland, Galway	Ireland
Gaye Kiely	University College Cork	Ireland
Marite Kirikova	Riga Technical University	Latvia
Gábor Knapp	Budapest University of Technology and Economics	Hungary
John Krogstie	Norwegian University of Science and Technology	Norway
Rein Kuusik	Tallinn University of Technology	Estonia
Sergei Kuznetsow	Russian Academy of Science	Russia
Michael Lane	University of Southern Queensland	Australia
Michael Lang	National University of Ireland, Galway	Ireland
John Lannon	University of Limerick	Ireland
Mauri Leppänen	University of Jyväskylä	Finland
Xia Li	Shenzhen University	China
Mikael Lind	University of Borås	Sweden
Henry Linger	Monash University	Australia
Steven Little	Open University Business School	UK
Jan Ljungberg	Göteborg University	Sweden
Jo Lee Loveland Link	Volvox Inc.	USA
David Lowe	University of Technology, Sydney	Australia
Audrone Lupeikiene	Institute of Mathematics and Informatics	Lithuania
Leszek A. Maciaszek	Macquarie University	Australia
Lars Mathiassen	Georgia State University	USA
Orla McHugh	National University of Ireland, Galway	Ireland
Ulf Melin	Linköping University	Sweden
Elisabeth Métais	CNAM University, Paris	France

Peter Middleton	Queen's University Belfast	UK
Owen Molloy	National University of Ireland, Galway	Ireland
Robert Moreton	University of Wolverhampton	UK
Phelim Murnion	Galway-Mayo Institute of Technology	Ireland
Anatoli Nachev	National University of Ireland, Galway	Ireland
Lina Nemuraite	Kaunas Technical University	Lithuania
Peter Axel Nielsen	Aalborg University	Denmark
Anders G. Nilsson	Karlstad University	Sweden
Ovidiu Noran	Griffith University	Australia
Jacob Nørbjerg	Copenhagen Business School	Denmark
Briony Oates	University of Teesside	UK
Mel Ó Cinnéide	University College Dublin	Ireland
Gerard O'Donovan	Cork Institute of Technology	Ireland
Brian O'Flaherty	University College Cork	Ireland
Lorne Olfman	Claremont Graduate University	USA
Phil O'Reilly	University College Cork	Ireland
Malgorzata Pankowska	University of Economics in Katowice	Poland
George A. Papadopoulos	University of Cyprus	Cyprus
Jeff Parsons	Memorial University of Newfoundland	Canada
Oscar Pastor	University of Valencia	Spain
Anne Persson	University of Skövde	Sweden
Graham Pervan	Curtin University	Australia
John Sören Pettersson	Karlstad University	Sweden
Alain Pirotte	University of Louvain	Belgium
Jaroslav Pokorny	Charles University, Prague	Czech Republic
Norah Power	University of Limerick	Ireland
Jan Pries-Heje	The IT University of Copenhagen	USA
Boris Rachev	Technical University of Varna	Bulgaria
Vaclav Repa	Prague University of Economics	Czech Republic
Karel Richta	Czech Technical University	Czech Republic
Kamel Rouibah	Kuwait University	Kuwait
Alice Rupe	AR IT Solutions	USA
Steve Sawyer	Pennsylvania State University	USA
Murray Scott	National University of Ireland, Galway	Ireland
Keng Siau	University of Nebraska – Lincoln	USA
Klaas Sikkel	University of Twente	Netherlands
Guttorm Sindre	Norwegian University of Science and Technology	Norway
Piotr Soja	Cracow University of Economics	Poland
William Song	University of Durham	UK
Carsten Sorensen	London School of Economics	UK

Tor Stålhane	Norwegian University of Science and Technology	Norway
Ioannis Stamelos	Aristotle University	Greece
Larry Stapleton	Waterford Institute of Technology	Ireland
Uldis Sukovskis	Riga Technical University	Latvia
Håkan Sundberg	Mid Sweden University	Sweden
Bo Sundgren	Mid Sweden University	Sweden
Witold Suryn	Université du Québec	Canada
István Szakadát	Budapest University of Technology & Economics	Hungary
Janis Tenteris	Riga Technical University	Latvia
John Traxler	University of Wolverhampton	UK
Tuure Tuunanen	The University of Auckland	New Zealand
Olegas Vasilecas	Vilnius Gediminas Technical University	Lithuania
Ramesh Venkataraman	Indiana University	USA
Richard Veryard	Veryard Projects	UK
Richard Vidgen	University of Bath	UK
Jiri Vorisek	Prague University of Economics	Czech Republic
Gottfried Vossen	University of Münster	Germany
David Wainwright	University of Northumbria	UK
Hongbing Wang	Southeast University	China
Leoni Warne	Defence Science and Technology Organisation	Australia
Dave Wastell	University of Salford	UK
Brian Webb	Queen's University Belfast	UK
Eoin Whelan	National University of Ireland, Galway	Ireland
Edgar Whitley	London School of Economics	UK
Roel Wieringa	University of Twente	Netherlands
Gregory Wojtkowski	Boise State University	USA
Wita Wojtkowski	Boise State University	USA
Carson C. Woo	University of British Columbia	Canada
Stanislaw Wrycza	University of Gdansk	Poland
Judy Wynekoop	Florida Gulf Coast University	USA
Karen Young	National University of Ireland, Galway	Ireland
Yuansheng Zhong	Jiangxi University of Finance and Economy	China
Jozef Zurada	University of Louisville	USA

Contents

Morally Successful IT Projects

Tero Vartiainen[1] and Maritta Pirhonen[2]

[1] Turku School of Economics, Pori Unit, tero.vartiainen@tse.fi

[2] University of Jyväskylä, Department of Computer Science and Information Systems, maritta.pirhonen@jyu.fi

Abstract   Little attention has been given in the literature to the moral aspects of IT projects. The concept of moral success applied in this exploratory study derives from moral psychology theory, and experienced project managers' perceptions of a morally successful project are gathered and analyzed. The results show that a project may morally succeed or fail in the initiation phase (choosing clients, making the proposal), in the execution phase (meeting the objectives, ensuring the well-being of the team), and in relating to the context (laws and regulations, the effects on the stakeholders). These issues are reflected through the literature on project success, and implications for research and practice are presented.

1 Introduction

Projects are created in order to accomplish organizational changes such as the development of an information system (IS) (Boddy 2002). Boddy suggests that they share three common features. Firstly, each project is unique and it happens once at a particular time and with a unique set of players: it is expected to achieve something new or different. Secondly, projects depend on people, and project managers need to influence other people (such as the members of the project team). Thirdly, each project takes place in a context in which people work, and which is expected to change in the process. Furthermore, projects affect the stakeholders involved. A typical project goes through an initiation, a planning, an execution, and a closing phase (Rakos et al. 2005). Given the turbulent business climate in the IT field and the complexity of information systems development (ISD) projects, not to mention the effects of failed projects on stakeholders (e.g., low usability of an IS), the moral aspects matter in ISD projects. Indeed, questions concerning professional ethics have puzzled researchers in both applied ethics and professions such as health care and the military. Given the impacts of an ISD project process on the project team, organization, and stakeholders, we need research on ethics, or morals, of ISD projects. Taking moral psychology as our theoretical basis, we introduce the concept of a morally successful project. Moral psychology is a subfield of psychology dealing with the development of moral reasoning and opinions in individuals (Audi 1995, p. 510), and thus ISs research could benefit from the theories and frameworks it encompasses. Our assumption is that project managers are capable of producing perceptions using the concept of what is moral in the context of project success. We interviewed experienced managers of IS projects about their concepts of a morally successful project, and we then analyzed their perceptions and related them to the literature. In the following we briefly review the existing research on project success, and then derive our concept of moral success in the context of moral psychology theory.

2 Project Success

Project success is multidimensional and different stakeholders measure it in different ways at different times (see e.g., Larson and Gobeli 1989; Pinto and Pinto 1991). Given the complexity involved in measuring project success or failure, the research has spanned the fields of IS in the work of a number of scholars including Lyytinen and Hirschheim (1987), and management in studies conducted by Shenhar and Levy (1997), and Westerveld (2003), for example.

Lyytinen and Hirschheim (1987) defined four major categories of IS failure: correspondence failure (systems-design objectives are not met); process failure (the IS cannot be developed within the allocated budget and/or time schedule); interaction failure (the level of end-user usage); and expectation failure (the system does not correspond with its stakeholders' requirements, expectations, or values).

Shenhar and Levy (1997) conducted a study on project success by surveying managers in product-development projects, and identified the following four dimensions: project efficiency (was the project completed on time and within budget?); the impact on the customer (does the project meet performance and functional specifications, and is the customer satisfied?); business and direct success (is the project providing the sales, income, profits, and other benefits?); and preparing for the future (is the firm more prepared for the future?).

Westerveld (2003) reviewed the literature on project management and constructed a "Project Excellence Model" comprising six results areas and six organizational areas (Fig. 1). The results areas concern project-success criteria and the organizational areas concern critical success factors. The choices made in the organizational areas have to match the project goals in the results areas. The results areas cover the project outcomes (budget, schedule, quality), and the level of appreciation of the client (e.g., customer benefit), the project personnel (e.g., the team is happy), the users (e.g., their needs are satisfied), the contracting partners (e.g., the project is profitable for contractors), and the stakeholders (e.g., their needs are satisfied). The organizational areas include leadership and team spirit (e.g., how the project manager runs the project), policy and strategy (e.g., the project goals), stakeholder management (e.g., cooperation with external parties), resources, contracting (e.g., the choice of contracts and partners), and project management (e.g., scheduling, budget). The following external factors also have to be taken into account: the project manager and the team members (skills, background), the project itself (size, uniqueness, and urgency), the parent organization (management support, structure), and the external environment (political, technological).

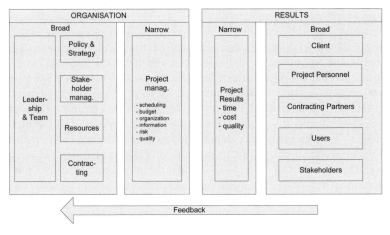

Fig. 1. Project Excellence Model (Westerveld 2003, p. 414)

3 The Concept of Moral Success

The concept of moral success applied in this paper derives from the field of moral psychology, and particularly the work of James Rest (1984). He categorized the existing research into four processes: moral sensitivity, judgment, motivation, and character. An individual may morally fail in her actions within these processes, or, if we take the opposite view adopted in this study, morally succeed (cf. morally successful industry-academia collaboration; Vartiainen 2005). The aim of these processes is to answer the question: "What must we suppose happens psychologically in order for moral behavior to take place?" Rest (1984) showed that a moral agent might perceive having failed morally in her acts if she concludes that her deliberation might have been deficient. The processes describe logical order in moral behavior, albeit there are complex interdependencies between them.

Moral sensitivity implies awareness of how our actions affect other people. It also implies being aware of alternative actions and of how those actions may affect other parties. For example, a project manager in an ISD project may not notice that the software produced weakens the users' capabilities in terms of carrying out their work tasks, but if someone points this out to the manager and the project team, they may begin to see their software solutions in a new light and take users better into account in their professional practice. However, being aware of morally significant issues is not enough: when confronting decision-making situations one needs to make decisions.

Moral judgment is about judging which courses of action are the most justified, and as it develops, a person's problem-solving strategies become more in tune with those of others, and more principled in nature. Kohlberg's (1981) six stages of moral development are based on the theory that people change their moral problem-solving strategies as they grow. As a brief example, stage 3 in Kohlberg's theory relates to maintaining good relations with others and stage 4 to maintaining law and order. An individual representing stage 5, social contract legalistic orientation, has an attitude of "society-creation." This means she bases her argumentation on a critical analysis of what kinds of individual rights and standards should stand for the whole society. In the above example of the project manager, if she thinks it important to maintain good relations with the users, the deliberation would be immature compared to the conviction that computer users in our society have the right to usable software that does not lessen the quality of working life. The project manager adopting the more mature decision-making strategy may affect users' lives in a more positive way on the whole. We could thus conclude that if a more mature approach to the problem at hand is available, which is possible for human beings to comprehend, but is not realized because of immature deliberation, the decision-making fails.

Moral motivation, in other words the prioritizing of moral values over non-moral values, like moral character, connects knowledge to action. Here a moral agent asks: "Why be moral?" She may be aware of an ethical issue (moral sensitivity), and may know what should be done (moral judgment), but is not fully motivated to do what she considers right. Again in the above example, taking users more into account might involve the allocation of more financial resources in order to produce more usable software. If the decision-makers in the project know the effects of the nonusable software and there are financial resources at hand but the decision is based on saving money, the decision-maker fails in terms of moral motivation.

Moral character refers to the psychological strength to carry out a plan of action. A person may be weak-willed, and if others put enough pressure on her to act immorally, she may fail in this component. In the example, if the project is under pressure from client representatives to cut costs and to leave the software in a nonusable state, for example, the project manager who gives in fails in the area of moral character.

4 Research Design

In order to increase understanding about the phenomenon of the moral success of IS projects we started an exploratory study. Given that the concept of success or failure in projects is assumed to be familiar to IT professionals, we added a moral perspective, ending up with the phrase "morally successful project." We refrained from educating the subjects on the theory developed by James Rest as we considered it too complicated for laymen not familiar with the concepts of moral psychology. Furthermore, given the exploratory nature of our research we were aiming at open-ended perceptions. We therefore asked the subjects to "describe what a morally successful IT project is."

Project managers with considerable working experience (5–10 years) in software projects were interviewed during the years 2005 and 2006. The companies they worked for mostly represent large enterprises located in the regions around Tampere, Turku, Pori, and Jyväskylä, in Finland. The interviews were conducted in two phases. Firstly, the first author conducted a group-discussion exercise with five IT project managers in a large manufacturing enterprise (in 2005). He presented the interview task at the start and asked prompting questions in order to move the discussion along. Secondly, ten IT project managers from software houses were interviewed and asked the same question (spring 2006). The first author interviewed five subjects and the second author five subjects. The age and gender profiles of the project managers, coded PM1...PM15, were (na = not available; F = female, M = male): na/M, na/M, na/F, na/M, na/F, 41/M, 42/M, 42/F, 59/M, 46/F, 50/M, 38/M, 35/M, 43/M, and 41/M.

All the discussions and the interviews were recorded and transcribed. Interpretive content analysis as developed by Lacity and Janson (1994, p. 148) was then applied to the interview data. This is an approach that takes into account the contextual circumstances in which the respondents frame their answers and the circumstances that influence the researchers' interpretations. The analysis proceeded as follows: the first author produced a preliminary classification of the issues that emerged from the interviews, which the second author then reviewed. We found that there were similarities between the issues and were therefore able to produce categories covering them. After much discussion we ended up with the final classification presented in the next section.

Krippendorff (1980) defined the validity criteria for content analysis: internal validity means that the research procedure yields the same results regardless of the circumstances of application. External validity assesses whether the findings represent the real phenomena in the context of the data as claimed. Krippendorff's (1980) external validity resembles, in some respects, the validity criterion for interpretive studies proposed by Lacity and Janson (1994, p. 149): they see validity in interpretive research in terms of its acceptance by the scientific community. In other words, if fellow scholars find the research meaningful, the results can be considered valid and worthwhile.

5 Results

Figure 2 shows the categories and the issues found in the perceptions of the project managers. The boxes indicate the three categories that were identified: initiation, execution, and context. The first two refer to the phases of the project (the arrow means transfer from initiation to execution), and the last to its surroundings. The

subjects described perceptions identified as both moral success and moral failure; thus both viewpoints are represented in the issues described next.

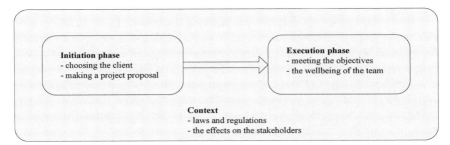

Fig. 2. Project managers' perceptions of morally successful projects

Choosing the client – profit vs. immorality. The morality of the client organization was a concern for some project managers. They expressed their willingness to avoid collaboration with a client whose values they perceived as immoral. The line of business as such was also described as potentially morally problematic. In sum, moral success means collaboration with clients with morally acceptable objectives and moral failure means that one agrees to collaborate with a client whose objectives are immoral. An exemplary extract follows:

> PM2: "Of course, the source of the morality is based on the client. Are the workings of the firm as a whole moral? … [I]f you carry out a project for a firm that produces pornographic films I wouldn't call it moral. … But in the commercial world today you're forced to lead such projects as it's be the only way to get any income."

Making a project proposal – upholding honesty. To what extent is a project proposal based on realism and the real capability of the vendor organization to implement it? The inclination to overplay one's hand in order to secure the project emerged in the subjects' perceptions. Moral success relates to upholding honesty and, in some cases, to having the mental capacity to maintain honesty in describing frankly the real capabilities of the vendor. Moral failure relates to situations in which personal interests are prioritized above the interest of the vendor organization or when the proposal is not based on honest assessments. Exemplary extracts follow:

> PM13: "…if you don't have the courage to tell the client that you can't allocate so many working hours … although you know yourself that you're not able to complete the project with the resources that the client assumes that it needs …"
>
> PM 6: "Or you won't order from the firm that provides the best but from [the firm] that is the most advantageous. … In our firm the ethical guidelines for purchasing, for example, define this…"

Meeting the project objectives – upholding honesty and integrity. In a morally successful project the objectives are met and it is delivered on schedule and within budget. The participants are able to stand behind the results, the work is based on lasting solutions, and the project team is not forced to take part in something that cannot, in reality, be implemented as promised to the client. On the other hand, a morally failed project does not meet the objectives set, it is late, and it overruns on costs. An example follows:

> PM8: "[T]he people truly understand what the successful result is and they really seek the successful result, not just because of the fear of failure or directed by the indicator [of the success] and then trying to explain everything best … and then the projects that everyone knows are completely crackbrained, and will never succeed. … Everybody is heavy-hearted in situations like that. You have to go through with it even if you know that it will flop."

The well-being of the team – taking care of people. Issues to do with the team members' well-being and their ethical treatment emerged very clearly from the interviews. Morally successful projects are those that take the team members into account, ensure their well-being, and foster motivation. The avoidance of work overload was mentioned. Two examples follow:

> PM1: "That is, the project isn't run so that the people involved are overburdened with work … in other words, nobody goes on sick leave during it or afterwards. … That happens often particularly in projects ... with a tight schedule you have to work overtime."
> PM10: "Somehow, I think what's moral is that people aren't mistreated during the project."

Effects on the stakeholders. A project affects the surrounding context in which it is being carried out – the workers and/or structure of the organization for which the IS is being developed, for example. Understanding the overall effect of the project relates to being morally successful. As an example, the five project managers in the group discussion raised the problem of the automation of work processes resulting in redundancies. On the one hand, changes in working life are perceived as unavoidable, but on the other hand, the affected parties should be taken care of in some way:

> PM1: "It's a good question if it's a moral project when we produce IT, well, if it relates to an IT system that reduces the workforce in the end."
> PM3: "Is it morally wrong if it [the system] changes the work so that it increases work in another profession? If it [the system] abolishes routine work tasks and increases technological planning tasks?"

Laws and regulations. Laws and regulations are upheld in morally successful projects. An example follows:

> PM12: "Morally successful also means that the working methods are in accordance with the law and people comply with the rules and adhere to agreements … all the taxes are paid and legal working hours are followed."

6 Discussion

Based on the 15 project managers' perceptions three categories and their underlying issues emerged as follows:

- Initiation (choosing the client, making a project proposal)
- Execution (meeting the objectives, ensuring the well-being of the team)
- Context (laws and regulations, effects on the stakeholders)

This collective description of a morally successful project makes sense as an ideal. It is nonetheless prone to moral failure.

The first sign of moral failure is to fail to recognize a significant issue as a moral one, and as a consequence to act in the particular situation in a way that harms someone. In our view this includes the issues reported in Fig. 2. Given the arguments put forward in the IS literature that IS professionals, for example, ignore social, political, and psychological aspects in their work (Jiang et al. 1999), they may well be deficient in acknowledging the well-being of their team members and the potential effects of the project. The affected parties, termed penumbra by Collins et al. (1994), have the least to do with the software process as such, but they are among the users of the developed IS and are thus affected by the software provider. Distance between the IS professionals and users/penumbra may cause deficient moral sensitivity (cf. moral distance in Rubin 1994).

After recognition and decision-making the course of action is prone to prioritization between moral and nonmoral values (moral motivation), and to the mental weakness of the moral agent (moral character). Major determinants of moral failure included economic reasons for securing a client or a project and the determination to get the most out of the project team. The incidence of moral failure should not surprise us as there are conflicting moral requirements in business. Carroll (1999) summarized these as the following four responsibilities: profitability, legal obedience, engaging in ethical practices, and philanthropy. According to the subjects' perceptions, profitability may be prioritized over moral values, meaning failure in moral motivation in Rest's (1984) terms. It seems that honesty is at stake (cf. dishonesty in small business reported by Vitell et al. 2000). The case of a professional adopting a neutral attitude to the objectives of his clients and being "a-gun-for-hire," thereby totally ignoring the question of "choosing the client" emerged as problematic in this study: the professional consciously makes a value decision that may be interpreted by others as morally flawed.

A comparison of the issues that emerged with previous studies on project success, such as Westerveld's (2003) Project Excellence Model, reveals straightforward similarities: results, and appreciation of the client, the project personnel, the users, and the stakeholders have their counterparts in Fig. 2. Choosing the client and making a project proposal could be interpreted as matching Westerveld's policy and strategy because client selection is based on organizational strategy. Issues in the execution category (meeting objectives, the well-being of the team) resemble Blake and Mouton's (1978) managerial grid with its management (concern for production) and leadership (concern for people) orientations.

6.1 Implications for Research and Practice

By applying a moral psychological theory in this study, we arrived at a description of idealistic objectives for moral success as well as real-life descriptions of moral failure. This experience shows that research on project management could benefit from research adopting a moral psychological perspective. Furthermore, the Project Excellence Model reveals significant areas of research interest in the context of the Four Component Model (Rest 1984). For example, studies on the ability of project managers to identify human-related moral conflicts might reveal targets for the development of leadership education. Research on project managers' decision-making strategies in Kohlbergian terms might reveal a need to train IS professionals to adopt more mature deliberation strategies. The occurrence of moral failure in IS projects should be investigated in order to produce in-depth understanding of the phenomenon (e.g., in accordance with the description of the generic phases of projects; Rakos et al. 2005).

6.2 Evaluation of the Study

The problems with interviewing include interviewee attempts at rationalization and the fact that the interviewees may fear being exposed (Fielding 1993). This may have been the case for some of the subjects in this study as morality may be a sensitive issue to discuss. Relating to this, Mattson (1998) argues that studying the morality of individuals must take place in various situations because when approaching people one may only get a picture of their moral ideology formed for the interview situation. On the one hand, Mattson's critique is relevant for this study since we do not know what the subjects left untold due to fear of being exposed. On the other hand, although the subjects did not confess their own moral failures, they described those of others. Regarding the analysis, as we were able to agree on the final version, and given the fact that we both have considerable experience of teaching project management in collaboration with IT firms, we believe that the results are valid. We have reported the data-gathering process and cited verbatim from the subjects' expressions to provide evidence for our claims.

References

Audi, R. (ed.) (1995) *The Cambridge Dictionary of Philosophy*. Cambridge: Cambridge University Press.

Blake, R.R., Mouton, J.S. (1978) The New Managerial Grid. Houston: Gulf Publishing Company. Referenced in F.E. Kast, J.E., Rosenzweig (1985). *Organization and Management, A Systems and Contingency Approach*. New York: McGraw-Hill.

Boddy, D. (2002) *Managing Projects: Building and Leading the Team*. Harlow, Essex: Prentice Hall.

Carroll, A.B. (1999) Ethics in Management. In R.E. Frederick (ed.) *A Companion to Business Ethics*. Oxford: Blackwell, pp. 141–152.

Collins, W.R., Miller, K.W., Spielman, B.J. and Wherry, P. (1994) How Good Is Good Enough? *Communications of ACM* 37(1), January, 81–91.

Fielding, N. (1993) Qualitative Interviewing. In N. Gilbert (ed.) *Researching Social Life*. London: Sage, pp. 135–153.

Jiang, J.J., Klein, G. and Means, T. (1999) The Missing Link between Systems Analysts' Actions and Skills. *Information Systems Journal* 9(1), 21–33.

Kohlberg, L. (1981) *The Philosophy of Moral Development, Moral Stages and the Idea of Justice*. San Francisco: Harper & Row.

Krippendorff, K. (1980) *Content Analysis, an Introduction to Its Methodology*. Beverly Hills: Sage.

Lacity, M.C. and Janson, M.A. (1994) Understanding Qualitative Data: A Framework of Text Analysis Methods. *Journal of Management Information Systems* 11(2), 137–155.

Larson, E. and Gobeli, D. (1989) Significance of Project Management Structure on Development Success. *IEEE Transactions on Engineering Management* 36(2), 119–125.

Lyytinen, K., Hirschheim, R. (1987) Information Systems Failures - A Survey and Classification of the Empirical Literature. *Oxford Surveys in Information Technology* 4, 257–309.

Mattson, M. (1998) *Pahanteon psykologia*. Helsinki: Tietosanoma. (Psychology of Perpetration; In Finnish).

Pinto, M., Pinto, J. (1991) Determinants of Cross-Functional Cooperation in the Project Implementation Process. *Project Management Journal* 20(4), 13–20.

Rakos, J., Dhanraj, K., Fleck, L., Harris, J., Jackson, S., Kennedy, S. (2005) *The Practical Guide to Project Management Documentation*. Hoboken, NJ: Wiley.

Rest, J. (1984) The Major Components of Morality. In W.M. Kurtines, J.L. Gewirtz (eds.) *Morality, Moral Behavior, and Moral Development*. New York: Wiley-Interscience, pp. 24–38.

Rubin, R. (1994) Moral Distancing and the Use of Information Technologies: The Seven Temptations. Ethics in the Computer Age Conference Proceedings, Gatlinburg, Tennessee, November 11–13, pp. 151–155.

Shenhar, A.J., Levy, O. (1997) Mapping the Dimensions of Project Success. *Project Management Journal*, 28(2), 5–13.

Vartiainen, T. (2005) Morally Successful Collaboration Between Academia and Industry – A Case of a Project Course. Proceedings of Fourteenth International Conference on Information Systems Development (ISD´2005), Karlstad, Sweden, August 15–17, pp. 459–470.

Vitell, S.J., Dickerson, E.B., Festervand, T.A. (2000) Ethical Problems, Conflicts and Beliefs of Small Business Professionals. *Journal of Business Ethics* 28(1), 15–24.

Westerveld, E. (2003) The Project Excellence Model: linking success criteria and critical success factors. *International Journal of Project Management* 21(6), 411–418.

The Risks of User-Supplied Content Online

Rónán Kennedy

National University of Ireland, Galway Law Faculty, ronan.m.kennedy@nuigalway.ie

Abstract Websites which rely on user-generated or user-supplied content (USC) run a variety of legal risks, as innocent, uninformed or malicious users may post material which infringes copyright, is defamatory, obscene or otherwise illegal. Amongst the strategies which developers might use to mitigate these risks are indemnities, moderation of content and designing systems in order to avail of the various 'safe harbours' which have been developed specifically for online service providers. As the first two strategies have a number of legal and practical drawbacks, the primary protection must be the safe harbours. In an increasingly globalised world, it is unsafe to ignore foreign laws and therefore USC sites should employ a robust but measured notice-and-takedown procedure.

1 Introduction

1.1 The Phenomenon of User-Supplied Content

One particular type of Internet information system which is becoming increasingly prevalent is the website which relies on users to supply a good deal of its content. Notable examples include Wikipedia, which is an attempt to create a free and open encyclopedia, YouTube, which is a video-sharing site, and MySpace, which is a social networking site that also allows users to post images, audio and video for playback and download. Users also provide reviews for the online bookseller Amazon, blog postings on a variety of hosting sites, and commentary on those blogs and many publicly-accessible mailing lists. Here, membership of the user base is open to all. Other sites may restrict membership, perhaps requiring the payment of a fee (e.g. genealogy sites), membership of an organisation (e.g. a distributed non-governmental organization) or participation in a marketplace (e.g. auction sites such as eBay).

This phenomenon is often known as 'user-generated content' (UGC) but is often, in fact, simply 'user-supplied content' (USC), as it is not the result of the independent creative work of the users but is copied from some other source, such as television broadcasts. Peer-to-peer file-sharing services for audio and video content, such as Napster, Grokster and KaZaa, have become well known, even infamous, as although they do carry legitimate content, much of what is provided by users for download is, in fact, copyrighted material and as a result, many have been shut down.

Information systems developers who are taking advantage of new business and content provision models, such as UGC/USC, need proper awareness of the legal pitfalls involved and how to avoid these where possible. Although the legal liabilities of online service providers (OSPs), particularly Internet service providers (ISPs), have received significant consideration in recent years and legislation has been enacted in order to clarify their position, much of this discussion has proceeded on the basis that they are simple conduits, indifferent to and unaware of the content which flows through their systems. USC sites are different as they actively encourage users to provide particular types of content, often as the foundation of their business model. They must therefore take care to ensure that they fit properly into the existing models. This paper considers some of the legal risks which information systems developers should consider when designing these types of systems. It makes some suggestions for reducing or minimising the risks involved, particularly how to ensure that the system fits into the various 'safe harbours' in American and European law.

2 Possible Legal Issues

2.1 Copyright Infringement

In general, if content has been genuinely generated by individual users of the site, then they will have the right to upload it to a public website for distribution. However, in many cases, the content will have been created by a third party and simply appropriated by the user, perhaps with either no understanding or a mistaken understanding of any risk of copyright infringement, and often with no malicious intent. Sometimes, also, UGC will contain both original work and content copyrighted by third parties.

Nonetheless, even if the purpose of the user is innocent, the legal liability remains the same. Therefore, perhaps the most important risk which operators of a user-supplied site must manage is from copyright infringement. A prominent current example is Viacom's allegation that copyrighted material often appears on the video-sharing site, YouTube (Computer and Telecommunications Law Review 2007), but this is an issue which pre-dates the widespread use of the Internet.

In *Playboy v. Frena*, a bulletin board system operator was held liable for the copying of images from the plaintiff's magazines although the uploading and downloading was in fact carried out by users. However, later courts refused to follow this precedent and in *Religious Technology Centre v. Netcom*, the Church of Scientology was unable to obtain damages from an ISP for infringing copies uploaded to USENET by a customer of the ISP (Reed 2004, pp. 96–97).

In these types of situation, there is little doubt that the user of the site is liable for copying the copyrighted work and making it available to the public (Clark and

Smyth 2005, pp. 333–337). The liability of the administrators of the site is less clear (Clark et al. 2005, p. 339). The most significant precedent on the issue in these islands is *CBS v. Amstrad*, where the defendant sold dual-tape cassette systems with an advertising campaign that emphasised how they facilitated copying of tapes through high-speed dubbing. The House of Lords held that they could not be held responsible for what consumers did with their equipment after purchase.

In the US, the recent Supreme Court decision in the *Grokster* case clarified that although the *Sony* rule which protects technology with both infringing and significant non-infringing purposes still stands, indirect liability for copyright infringement may attach to a defendant who actively induces users of technology to infringe.

Elsewhere, the Australian Federal Court found the operators of the Kazaa file-sharing network liable for facilitating copyright infringement (Williams and Seet 2006), while the Supreme Court of Holland upheld a decision of the Court of Appeals that Kazaa were not liable because the network operated independently of the company, it was not possible to identify copyrighted content, the company was not responsible for the acts of its users and some of the files shared were legitimate (Akester 2005).

2.2 Defamation

Defamation is 'the wrongful publication of a false statement about a person, which tends to lower that person in the eyes of right-thinking members of society or tends to hold that person up to hatred, ridicule or contempt, or causes that person to be shunned or avoided by right-thinking members of society' (McMahon and Binchy 2000, p. 882). The potential for such statements on a website that allows the general public to post information and commentary is obvious, although proving where and when publication took place can be difficult (McGonagle 2003, p. 74).

There is a defence of innocent dissemination, open to (for example) newspaper vendors and booksellers, but as it only applies to those who neither knew nor ought to have known of the defamation, it will only rarely apply to those administering UGC sites, particularly if the subject matter is contentious.

One notable recent Irish example of possibly defamatory USC involved the Rate-Your-Solicitor.com website. A barrister claimed that material posted on the website about her was defamatory and the President of the High Court threatened to jail the person who was alleged to have made the comments in question. The defendant claimed that he had not made these comments and had no control over the content of the website, which was hosted in the US. However, the material was removed before the deadline set by the judge (Carolan 2006; Collins 2006).

2.3 Other Contentious Forms of Speech

While these forms of conduct should be the primary concern of the administrators of a USC site, users may also post material that is pornographic or obscene, or that is prohibited on political grounds, perhaps as hate speech or sedition. However, these are probably less important in practice. In Ireland, there are few prosecutions for the publication of indecent and obscene material, even in print, and less under the Prohibition of Incitement to Hatred Act 1989 (McGonagle 2003, pp. 281–282), although prosecutions for obscene sexual material do occur in the US (Reed 2004, p. 106). Prosecutions for blasphemy are almost unknown (McGonagle 2003, p. 303).

However, Yahoo! was ordered by a court in France to remove all Nazi memorabilia from its auction website and, although it obtained a declaration from an American court that the French order was unenforceable in the US, it did ban all such material (Reed 2004, p. 95). Child pornography may be a particular concern (Reed 2004, p. 107) and so administrators should take care to remove it immediately if it is discovered on their systems. Finally, there may be concerns about users posting material which breaches the privacy of others (Holmes and Ganley 2007, 343).

3 Minimizing the Risks

When planning and designing an information system that uses USC, either as a main or subsidiary source of content, developers will want to reduce or remove the risk of legal difficulties. There are a number of strategies which they might adopt.

3.1 Indemnities from Users

The first possible line of defense is to require users to provide some form of indemnity. This will take the form of a legal agreement which users have to agree to before they upload content, either when they apply for membership of the site or each time they add more content, wherein they warrant that the material uploaded does not infringe copyright or contravene any other law (Miles and Caunt 2007, p. 25). Sometimes, these agreements go so far as to transfer legal ownership of any intellectual property in the uploaded content to the operator of the site (Holmes et al. 2007, p. 338). This can be controversial – the musician Billy Bragg removed all of his music from MySpace when he discovered that he was transferring all rights in the process (Levine 2006), forcing a revision of the terms and conditions (Orlowski 2006) and it may not be wise to go so far.

Indemnities can be useful, if only as a way of focusing the minds of users on whether they are willing to take responsibility for the content they are making public, and some sites go so far as to outline what those responsibilities are (Miles et al. 2007, p. 25). However, they have limitations, both legal and practical.

From a legal point of view, a point of controversy in the early days of contracting online was whether what are known as 'click-wrap' contracts are valid. These are generally licences for the use of software which the user agrees to when an application is used for the first time. Indemnities would present similar issues. Although their validity is not entirely clear, a clear and reasonable contract will probably be accepted by the courts (Johnson 2003). However, consumers still do not seem to regard them as constituting a valid contract (Gatt 2002), which raises the question of how carefully they will be read and whether they will act as a proper deterrent to risky or illegal conduct.

In addition, if the user is under the age of 18, the contract may not be enforceable. For adult users, the Unfair Contract Terms Directive (Directive 93/13/EEC) provides that unfair terms in standard form contracts involving consumers will not be binding on the consumer. A term will be held to be unfair if 'it causes a significant imbalance in the parties' rights and obligations arising under the contract, to the detriment of the consumer' (Article 3(2)). An indemnity which imposes too much liability on a consumer might be challenged on this basis.

From a practical point of view, the user may not be easily traceable. They may not provide sufficient or accurate information on their identity or location. They may, of course, be traceable by IP address, but this is a slow and cumbersome process which may involve protracted negotiations or litigation with their ISP (McIntyre 2004). Even if they can be located, they may be located in another jurisdiction, making enforcing the indemnity difficult, or they may not have very many assets, making enforcing the indemnity pointless.

3.2 Moderation of Content

Another potential defence is to employ humans to moderate content which is posted by users. However, in addition to the obvious resource implications, this may be a bad rather than a good idea from the perspective of legal liability. Early American cases involving online defamation made bulletin boards that exercised editorial control over content liable for defamatory content (*Stratton Oakmont v. Prodigy*), whereas those that did not were treated as a common carrier and thus immune from suit (*Cubby v. Compuserve*). While these cases have been superseded by the Communications Decency Act (CDA), which we will consider shortly, the risk is clear: operating a moderation system may, in fact, remove the immunities enjoyed by the ignorant and opens the service provider to liability if it fails.

Automated moderation, or filtering, is touted as an appropriate solution, particularly for copyrighted content, but despite asides to this effect in the US Supreme Court's decision in the *Grokster* case, difficulties in implementing, updating and mandating the use of such technology on a global scale make it impractical (Samuelson 2006).

3.3 Issues of International Jurisdiction

The Internet is, of course, international in scope. Those operating websites will often focus solely on legal liability under their local laws and will not be concerned about possible breaches of foreign laws. However, this may prove to be a short-sighted policy. The rhetoric of the Web as an untameable new frontier for the human mind is giving way to the more prosaic realisation that Internet traffic and content can be controlled (Goldsmith and Wu 2006). With increased globalization, the notion that individuals can ignore the laws of major world powers and trading powers, particularly the US, becomes increasingly untenable. This is perhaps most clearly illustrated by the impact which an American crackdown on Internet gambling has had on the industry worldwide, including the recent arrests of foreign CEOs of gambling websites for alleged breaches of American law while transiting through the US (Timmons and Pfanner 2006).

3.4 Availing of Safe Harbours

As the Internet developed, so did the understanding that OSPs were a new type of content provider and that applying the existing models of liability to them risked stunting or stifling a new industry. Many jurisdictions enacted legislation to give OSPs legal immunity for content which they carried on behalf of their users, on the basis that they could not realistically monitor or control the flow of information which governments wanted to facilitate. The shape of these 'safe harbours' differs; we will consider only the two most important, the American and the European, each of which is informed by different freedom of speech traditions.

American legislation creates two primary safe harbours for OSPs. One is § 512 of the Digital Millennium Copyright Act, 17 U.S.C. § 512, which provides that service providers shall not be liable to pay damages or be subject to an injunction for copyright infringement if the infringement occurs due to routing of material through their systems, caching, storage of information on their systems by users or providing links to infringing material. These immunities apply

'only if the service provider—

(A) has adopted and reasonably implemented, and informs subscribers and account holders of the service provider's system or network of, a policy that provides for the termination in appropriate circumstances of subscribers and account holders of the service provider's system or network who are repeat infringers; and

(B) accommodates and does not interfere with standard technical measures' (in other words, digital rights management systems).

In addition, to benefit from § 512 (c), which provides immunity for 'the storage at the direction of a user of material that resides on a system or network controlled or operated by or for the service provider,' the service provider must 'not receive a financial benefit directly attributable to the infringing activity, in a case in which the service provider has the right and ability to control such activity;' and 'upon notification of claimed infringement … respond[] expeditiously to remove, or disable access to, the material that is claimed to be infringing or to be the subject of infringing activity.' This is commonly called a 'notice-and-takedown' procedure; there is provision for a counter-notification which allows the user to rebut the claim of infringement.

In *Ellison v. AOL*, a user posted copies of the plaintiff author's books on USENET without authorization. Copies were stored on AOL's servers for 14 days, as was their standard policy. The author's email complaint to AOL went unanswered, probably because AOL changed its copyright notification email address without registering the change with the US Copyright Office and without automatically forwarding email from the old address. When he began a legal action, AOL blocked access to the USENET group. On appeal, the Ninth Circuit held that the confusion regarding copyright notifications probably made it impossible for AOL to benefit from the safe harbour and remanded the matter for further consideration.

In *CoStar v. LoopNet*, the plaintiff provided commercial real estate information. LoopNet allowed real estate brokers to post listings on its website. Users warranted that they had all necessary 'rights and authorizations' to post material. LoopNet employees cursorily reviewed photographs. Photographs copyrighted by CoStar were posted on LoopNet's website. The Fourth Circuit concluded that even if LoopNet could not benefit from the DMCA safe harbour, it could still benefit from the *Netcom* ruling and the screening of photographs by LoopNet was not significant enough to make them liable for copyright infringement.

Another safe harbour is the Communications Decency Act, 47 U.S.C. § 230, which gives providers and users of an 'interactive computer service' nigh-complete immunity for the re-publication of the content provided by others. For example, in *Zeran v. AOL*, an advertisement for tasteless t-shirts was posted on AOL with the plaintiff's telephone number and he received threatening calls as a result. AOL eventually removed the advertisement but Zeran filed suit, claiming that there was unreasonable delay in removing defamatory material. AOL successfully pleaded § 230 of the CDA as a defense. The court felt that the intention of Congress was to free OSPs from the impossible burden of having to check each individual message.

In *Batzel v. Cremers*, an email which was alleged to contain defamatory statements about the plaintiff was sent to the defendant by a third party. The defendant modified it slightly and forwarded it to a mailing list, something which was not intended by the original author. When the plaintiff sued for defamation, the defendant raised § 230 as a defence. However, the court held that this would only apply if the defendant had reason to believe that the original author was submitting the message in order to have it published online; otherwise, the protection would spread too widely.

What this means, then, is that in the US, the level of protection which an OSP has is relatively high. In general, there is no obligation to read and investigate every piece of information distributed or published through a website. Even if the information is edited and redistributed, such as through a mailing list, § 230 may still apply. Thus, for example, a blogger is not subject to liability for comments on their blog – although they remain liable for what they themselves publish on the blog.

In Europe, the relevant legislation is the Electronic Commerce Directive (Directive 2000/31/EC). This applies to those providing an 'Information Society service,' defined in Directive 98/48/EC as 'any service normally provided for remuneration, at a distance, by electronic means and at the individual request of a recipient of services,' a definition that is sufficiently broad to encompass most, if not all, USC sites.

Article 12 of the Directive exempts OSPs from liability when they act as a 'mere conduit':

'Where an information society service is provided that consists of the transmission in a communication network of information provided by a recipient of the service, or the provision of access to a communication network, Member States shall ensure that the service provider is not liable for the information transmitted, on condition that the provider:

(a) does not initiate the transmission;
(b) does not select the receiver of the transmission; and
(c) does not select or modify the information contained in the transmission.'

Article 14 exempts service providers from liability for hosting content:

'Where an information society service is provided that consists of the storage of information provided by a recipient of the service, Member States shall ensure that the service provider is not liable for the information stored at the request of a recipient of the service, on condition that:

(a) the provider does not have actual knowledge of illegal activity or information and, as regards claims for damages, is not aware of facts or circumstances from which the illegal activity or information is apparent; or
(b) the provider, upon obtaining such knowledge or awareness, acts expeditiously to remove or to disable access to the information.'

In light of the *Godfrey v. Demon* case, where an ISP was unable to plead the defence of innocent dissemination (which is on a statutory basis in the UK) because they had not acted in response to a complaint from the plaintiff, there remains uncertainty about what constitutes acting 'expeditiously to remove or to disable access to the information' complained of (Lloyd 2004, pp. 692–699). Unfortunately, there is a dearth of case law on the Directive which makes it difficult, as yet, to see how far it differs from the American situation.

Similar to the US position, Article 15 makes it clear that there is no obligation on service providers to monitor content on their systems:

'Member States shall not impose a general obligation on providers, when providing the services covered by Articles 12, 13 and 14, to monitor the information which they transmit or store, nor a general obligation actively to seek facts or circumstances indicating illegal activity.'

If one does choose to monitor, while *Batzel* makes it clear that the level of intervention which one may undertake while retaining protection under American law is high, the risk of losing immunity under Articles 12 and 14 of the Electronic

Commerce Directive is obvious. This is a strong argument against monitoring content posted by users.

Internationally, the general trend is that intermediaries are not absolutely liable for the actions of users unless they know or should know of illegal activity or they derive a direct benefit from it, although some jurisdictions, such as Singapore, do not extend this as far as hosted content (Reed 2004, Chapter 4). In order to avail of immunity, the OSP must have some procedure for dealing with complaints regarding material available on their systems and that this should operate without undue delay.

A solid notice-and-takedown procedure is therefore essential. This compromise between monitoring and lack of control is good for OSPs but it should be balanced with an awareness of the risks of overuse. The norm for UK ISPs seems to be automatic removal of material complained of (Lloyd 2004, 695–696), even though this is likely to lead to further difficulties with the user who posted the original content, who may be able to sue for breach of contract. From a broader perspective, abuse of notice-and-takedown procedures can have a chilling effect on speech on a global scale (Urban and Quilter 2006).

4 Conclusion

User-supplied or UGC websites are another iteration in the continued and always surprising development of the Internet as a global communications medium. As this technology develops, information systems developers should be conscious of the legal risks involved. This raises different challenges for different members of the ISD community. Educators must ensure that their students have a proper awareness of the interaction between laws and new technologies and the gaps that can be created by the pace of change. Practitioners must bear the legal framework within which their finished product will be used in mind when designing it. Researchers must attempt to bridge the gap between the worlds of law and technology so that each can communicate with the other.

The immediate challenge is dealing with the reality that users may post material which infringes copyright, is defamatory or otherwise objectionable. Relying solely on indemnities or ignoring risks by complying only with local laws are probably inadequate strategies in the long term. Moderating content is too resource-intensive and filtering technologies are not yet, and may never be, practical.

Developers should therefore ensure that new sites and services can avail of the safe harbours in the countries which are their primary focus. This will generally involve a robust but balanced notice-and-takedown procedure.

References

Akester, P. (2005). Copyright and the P2P Challenge. *European Intellectual Property Review* 27, 106–112.

Batzel v. Kremers 333 F.3d 1018 (9th Cir. 2003).

Carolan, M. (2006) Man avoids jail after material about barrister removed from website. *Irish Times*, November 24, 2006.

CBS Songs v. Amstrad Consumer Electronics [1988] AC 1013.

Clark, R. and Smyth, S. (2005) *Intellectual Property Law in Ireland*. Tottel, Haywards Heath.

Collins, J. (2006) When online gets out of line. *Irish Times*, November 25, 2006.

Computer and Telecommunications Law Review (2007). Case Comment. Computer and Telecommunications Law Review 13, N115.

fCubby Inc. v. CompuServe Inc. 776 F Suppl. 135 (SDNY 1991).

Gatt, A. (2002) Electronic Commerce — Click-Wrap Agreements. Computer Law and Security Report 18, 404–410.

Godfrey v. Demon (1999) EMLR 542.

Goldsmith, J. and Wu, T. (2006) *Who Controls the Internet? Illusions of a Borderless World*. Oxford University Press, Oxford.

Holmes, S. and Ganley, P. (2007) User-generated Content and the Law. Journal of Intellectual Property Law and Practice 2, 338–344.

Johnson, P. (2003) All Wrapped Up? A Review Of The Enforceability Of "Shrink-Wrap" and "Click-Wrap" Licences in the United Kingdom and the United States. European Intellectual Property Review 25, 98–102.

Levine, R. (2006) Billy Bragg's MySpace Protest Movement. *New York Times*, July 31, 2006.

Lloyd, I. (2004) *Information Technology Law*. Oxford University Press, Oxford.

McGonagle, M. (2003) *Media Law*. Round Hall, Dublin.

McIntyre, T.J. (2004) Online Anonymity: Some Legal Issues. Commercial Law Practitioner 11, 90–95.

McMahon, B. and Binchy, W. (2000) *Law of Torts*. LexisNexis, Dublin.

Metro-Goldwyn-Mayer Inc. v. Grokster Inc. 545 U.S. 913 (2005).

Miles, J. and Caunt, D. (2007) Brave New World. Copyright World 168, 24–26.

Orlowski, A. (2006) Billy Bragg prompts Myspace rethink. *The Register*, June 8, 2006, available at http://www.theregister.co.uk/2006/06/08/blly_bragg_myspace/.

Playboy v. Frena 839 F Suppl 1552 (MD FL, 1993).

Reed, C. (2004) *Internet Law*. Cambridge University Press, Cambridge.

Religious Technology Centre v. Netcom On-line Communications Services Inc. 907 F Suppl. 1361 (ND Cal.1995).

Samuelson, P. (2006). Three Reactions to *MGM v. Grokster*. Michigan Telecommunications Technology Law Review, 13, 177–196.

Sony Corporation of America v. Universal Studios 464 U.S. 417 (1984).

Stratton Oakmont Inc. v. Prodigy Services Co. 23 Media Law Reports 1794 (NY Sup. Ct. 1995).

Timmons, H. and Pfanner, E. (2006) U.S. Law Causing Turmoil in Online Gambling Industry. *New York Times*, November 1, 2006.

Urban, J.M. and Quilter, L. (2006). Efficient Process or "Chilling Effects"? Takedown Notices Under Section 512 of the Digital Millennium Copyright Act. Santa Clara Computer and High Technology Law Journal, 22, 621–693.

Williams, M. and Seet, S. (2006) Authorisation in the Digital Age: Copyright Liability in Australia after *Cooper* and *Kazaa*. Computer and Telecommunications Law Review 12, 74–77.

Zeran v. America Online Inc. 129 F.3d 327 (4th Cir. 1997).

Evaluating Online Human Rights Resource Centres

John Lannon

University of Limerick, AIB Centre for Information and Knowledge Management,
john.lannon@ul.ie

Abstract Online human rights resource centres (OHRRCs) serve a variety of information and communication needs for grassroots activists, policy formulators, researchers, advocates and others within the human rights and development movements. However, there are no effective models with which to evaluate the impact of these systems, or to determine how they support their 'business' objective which is the promotion and protection of human rights. Drawing on three areas of literature, namely information systems evaluation (ISE), evaluation of information and communications technologies in non-profit organisations and human rights impact assessment (HRIA), this paper proposes a framework to address the problem. The model focuses on the need for stakeholder participation, and for ongoing evaluation triggered at key points in an iterative development life cycle.

1 Introduction

The number of online resource centres servicing the needs of human rights workers and activists has been increasing over the last number of years. This has been facilitated by technological developments, donor willingness to invest in such systems, the professionalisation of international non-governmental organisations (INGOs) and an increase in the number of service providers meeting the needs of civil society organisations. INGOs, intergovernmental agencies, governmental bodies, grassroots groups and human rights networks are now all using information and communications technologies (ICTs) to collaborate, organise and manage information. In this the Internet has become an effective, and in some cases indispensable, tool.

Nowadays, intergovernmental agencies, non-governmental organizations (NGOs) and even governmental bodies charged with promoting and protecting human rights are putting legislative texts, reports, educational material, case studies, testimonies and other digital resources in online publicly accessible repositories. They are also using their own Intranets to make sensitive or internal material

C. Barry et al. (eds.), *Information Systems Development: Challenges in Practice, Theory, and Education, Vol.2*, doi: 10.1007/978-0-387-78578-3_3,
© Springer Science+Business Media, LLC 2009

available to a limited audience. As a result, online resource centres are becoming a more significant source of human rights information for researchers, advocates and community workers around the world.

Given the importance of information to human rights work in general (Metzl 1996; Brophy and Halpin 1999) and to NGOs in particular (Weyker 2002), it follows that Internet-based tools and resources should have a positive impact on the human rights movement. There is plenty of case study evidence to indicate that this is so – see, for example, the use of the Internet by the International Campaign to Ban Landmines (Rutherford 2000), the campaign for an International Criminal Court (Pace and Panganiban 2002) and the Child Rights Information Network (CRIN) (Halpin 2003a, b). These show that the Internet has a wide range of benefits for the human rights movement: it strengthens the cases being made by advocates and empowers community activists; it reduces the costs associated with campaigning, particularly at international level; it speeds up the response time to crisis situations; and it leads to more effective and efficient collaboration between organisations working in the same area and with the same objectives.

Online human rights resource centres (OHRRCs), which are web-based systems that provide information management and communication services relating to an aspect of human rights to interested organisations and individuals, serve a variety of needs within the human rights and other related movements. Some serve the needs of formal networks like CRIN, others are targeted at experts working on a thematic area such as business and human rights and still others concentrate on a specific region or territory. In almost all cases they provide more than a catalogue of resources and are what Vasconcelos et al. (2005) determine to be a knowledge management framework as they reflect the underlying objectives, entities, activities, workflow and processes of the organisation behind them.

There is ample literature describing and analysing the use of the Internet and other ICTs in support of human rights (Brophy et al. 1999; Hick et al. 2000; Selian 2002; Weyker 2002; Lannon and Halpin 2006, etc.). However, no attempts have been made to evaluate the impact of online resource centres. There is no model to apply to this task, and as a result, human rights organisations have no standard way of measuring the merits or value of an OHRRC programme. For INGOs in particular this presents an emerging set of difficulties. Given the importance of information to what they do, most of them now see online resource centres as essential to their effective operation, and to the achievement of their overall goals. Consequently, INGO management and boards are now making decisions to allocate a significant amount of general income to the development of new resource centres or are seeking targeted funding for such projects.

The aim of this paper is to provide a nascent solution to the evaluation problem by designing a framework for INGOs to use when evaluating OHRRC programmes and projects. The OHRRC 'customers' are primarily, though not exclusively, within the human rights regime, which is a constituency encompassing a wide range of institutional actors including the United Nations; national legal systems and human rights bodies; criminal tribunals; quasi-governmental truth commissions; international, regional, national and grassroots NGOs; academics; lawyers; educators; and activists all over the world (Ball et al. 1997).

The paper begins by giving a contextual overview of human rights information management and the information management challenges in OHRRC development. Following this, it reviews key areas of literature that are likely to shed light on the problem of OHRRC evaluation. The proposed evaluation framework is then described, and the next steps in this ongoing research effort, including framework testing, are outlined.

2 Managing Human Rights Information

INGOs typically have a number of different audiences or stakeholders, all of whom have different information needs. Amnesty International, for example, provides information to individual letter-writing members around the world, as well as to coalition partners, the media, and intergovernmental agencies like the United Nations Human Rights Commission. The Treatment Action Campaign (TAC), which campaigns for greater access to AIDS treatment for all South Africans, provides information for the poor communities in which it raises public awareness about issues relating to the availability, affordability and use of HIV treatments. It also appeals to a more affluent group of professional people for voluntary effort and support, and delivers statements and important news to influential people locally and abroad (Wasserman 2005). These target audiences have information needs that differ in terms of timing, content, form and communication.

Since most human rights actors now use ICTs to communicate and share information (Selian 2002), ICT-based systems are playing an increasing role in human rights information management. In this context, OHRRCs meet a variety of needs. For example, they make new tools and tactics available to grassroots activists and NGOs; they present comprehensive guides on the human rights situation in a geographic region; they bring together a wide range of expertise on human rights issues; they facilitate access to legal and other resource material; and they disseminate campaigning material. Lawyers, policy makers, journalists, researchers, activists and others who have traditionally relied on public libraries and specialist documentation centres now prefer to find what they need online. Despite problems of affordability, skills shortage, language, censorship, regulation and other Internet access problems, the Internet makes human rights documentation available to a wider audience than ever before.

2.1 Information Management Challenges in OHRRC Development

Despite their value to the human rights movement, there are a number of problems relating to the development and maintenance of OHRRCs. Many of these problems apply to human rights websites in general, but are worth noting in the context of information centres.

The first problem is that human rights workers, operating with limited resources and often responding to crisis or opportunity may have little time or motivation to adopt new tools, despite their value. While some in an organisation or network may appropriate ICT-based systems, others may lag behind in terms of their use.

Reluctance to use new tools amongst human rights workers may also be linked to a lack of trust or confidence. The Internet environment lends itself particularly well to sabotage, distortion of information and even fabrication of whole organisations (Warnick 1998; Dahlberg 2001). Within the human rights movement the authenticity of a network, organization or report can usually be verified through association with others in the movement or through past record. However, the potential for actors to undermine the work of the movement by producing hoax or badly researched reports is significant. By unwittingly providing links to misleading websites or information, well-meaning initiatives can undermine the good work they set out to do.

Another problem is that information centres sometimes appear and disappear as the associated projects and human rights initiatives come and go. This is reasonable to expect in the case of websites associated with campaigns that run their course. However human rights websites disappear abruptly and without trace in many cases, because of increasing service provider fees, other technical costs, security problems or changes in organizational personnel or priorities. OHRRCs created by large well-resourced organisations are less likely to suffer such a fate, but if they do, it can create problems – particularly for organisations that have been using the centre and do not have the skills or capacity to find an alternative information source.

Static content is also a problem with many OHRRCs. Continuous effort is required to maintain public human rights information online (Chabanov 2004), and OHRRCs that are not updated regularly can be frustrating and sometimes even misleading. Initial enthusiasm can wane as staff and human rights activists return to dealing with human rights crises, campaigning demands and so on after deploying their online system. As a result, the latest information may not get added as quickly as it should.

Another challenge for OHRRCs is getting and maintaining visibility. Quite often a very useful human rights information source may exist, but is not known. This effectively renders the source as useless, and opens the possibility of other organisations replicating the work. Conferences, mailing lists, links on other websites and other promotional activities within networks are important for OHRRC promotion, as are technological design features to increase visibility.

Inaccessibility is always a problem with technology-based systems in the human rights movement. Even with Internet connectivity, OHRRCs, like all websites, can be inaccessible to many of the intended or potential users. Furthermore, if the information is misleading or confusing its utility for the human rights movement is reduced (Weyker 2002). Language can also be a barrier, as can the lack of conceptual clarity; in other words, content needs to be culturally aware and sensitive to the context of the disparate users.

Finally, attempts to avoid exclusivity and to design an OHRRC that meets a wide spectrum of user demands and needs can often result in it becoming too broad. In particular, information streams that are not directed towards a specific target group can lose focus (Joshi 2004), if suitable filtering mechanisms are not provided.

3 Literature Review

OHRRCs are intended for use in an environment that is complex and fluid. The human rights movement has extended, evolved and diversified over the last 50 years and the lines between it and other civil society movements have blurred. For example, most development actors are now taking cognisance of their human rights responsibilities and are looking towards human rights NGOs for expertise and advice.

OHRRC evaluation must recognise the complexities of this target audience. If a resource centre is developed for use within a small, focused organisation, a single method approach might be sufficient to predict and measure success or failure. But as Westbrook et al. (2004) who studied ICT evaluation in health care organisations showed, many of the behaviours one is interested in measuring in complex organisational structures emerge out of the interaction of multiple variables. OHRRCs therefore require multi-method approaches to first determine the variables that are relevant, and then to determine the ways in which these interrelate.

Three areas of literature are reviewed for insight into the approaches that might prove useful for OHRRC evaluation. One of these, the evaluation of ICTs in non-profit organisations, provides surprisingly little direction; the other two – information systems evaluation (ISE) and human rights impact assessment (HRIA) – are more helpful in addressing the problem presented.

3.1 Evaluation of ICTs in Non-profit Organisations

Very little academic or applied work has been done on formally assessing the impact of ICTs on non-profit activities. There are studies that assess the technical capacities and capabilities of selected civil society organisations and there are narratives describing the impact of new ICTs on specific voluntary and NGOs. However, research into the design of evaluation frameworks for ICTs in the non-profit sector is rare. Even the works that analyse and assess the impact of NGO activities, such as Landman and Abraham (2004)'s evaluation of nine human rights NGOs, give little or no coverage to their use of ICTs.

The model designed and used by Landman et al. (2004) does offer some useful pointers however. It emphasises the links between the activities of a human rights NGO and the realisation of the organisation's aims and objectives, and identifies three categories of questions which it claims cover the key dimensions of any assessment and evaluation framework; these are efficiency, effectiveness and relevance. Efficiency can be addressed, they say, through summaries of how work is carried out and how the organisation's aims and objectives are realised. Effectiveness is addressed through documentation and evidence that activities have achieved their aims and objectives. The third, relevance, is the hardest for organisations to answer.

One notable example of work relating to the evaluation of ICTs in non-profit organisations is Dameri (2005)'s outline of the balanced scorecard to evaluate ICT investments in non-profit organisations. He bases his work on the primacy of the mission in these organisations, and the importance of the short and long-term goals derived from this mission. ICTs contribute to the achievement of these objectives, he concludes, 'by means of its role in processes automation and services effectiveness, absorbing resources but also releasing qualitative benefits' (Dameri 2005, p. 113).

The weakness of this framework from an OHRRC perspective is that it sees ICTs entirely as *indirect* contributors to the organisation's objectives and mission. However, OHRRCs provide a service to the human rights movement and other movements, and as such they have direct value. It is therefore important to evaluate the effectiveness of these systems in relation to the organisation's objectives as well as evaluating their efficiency.

3.2 Information Systems Evaluation

ISE is defined as 'the assessment or appraisal of the value, worth or usefulness of an information system' (Smithson and Hirschheim 1998, p. 160). It is a widely researched area, but it is still regarded as a difficult and confusing problem for most organisations. Despite, or perhaps because of this, most of the research is highly anecdotal or case study based (Irani and Love 2001).

Traditionally, ISE has focused on benchmarking and the definition of costs, benefits, risks and, in some cases, implications, of capital expenditure in a business environment. For the most part these approaches have relied on financial appraisal techniques such as net present value, return on investment, internal rate of return and so on (Ballantine et al. 1998; Milis and Mercken 2004; Irani et al. 2005). However, these positivist approaches do not take account of the human, organisational or social components of information systems (Serafeimidis and Smithson 2003), or the manner in which they affect decision-making. Smithson et al. (1998) note that any of these aspects can improve or deteriorate, and that it is often problematic to isolate the factors that cause particular costs and benefits.

The need to consider the intangible costs and benefits of information systems has resulted in a wider approach to evaluation than a simple summing up of costs and benefits. Consequently, multi-criteria, interpretive frameworks that look beyond technological and accounting/financial aspects have emerged (Serafeimidis et al. 2003). Formal finance-based evaluation techniques are still useful for information systems that are implemented to make a process or task more efficient, but they are inadequate for systems that seek to improve organisational effectiveness (Fitzgerald 1998; Smithson et al. 1998), as OHRRCs do. For these, it is not sufficient to identify the benefits, it is also necessary that 'the recipients of those benefits will recognise and value the improvement and change their behaviour in some positive way as a result' (Fitzgerald 1998, p. 18). Customers or potential customers (other human rights actors in the case of an OHRRC) must not only be aware of the change; they must also perceive it as an improvement over the service they currently use – which may be no service at all.

Fitzgerald (1998) defines two stages in the benefits realisation process for IS projects. Firstly there is the provision or implementation of a project to provide benefit, and secondly there is the effect of that benefit on the wider environment and any resultant behaviour change. He describes the first of these two stages as internally controllable by the organisation and usually not dependent on any interaction with the outside environment. For efficiency projects the process ends here, after the gain has been accrued (or possibly not). Effectiveness projects move on to where resultant changes in external behaviour should lead to stage two benefits. The organisation has less control over these.

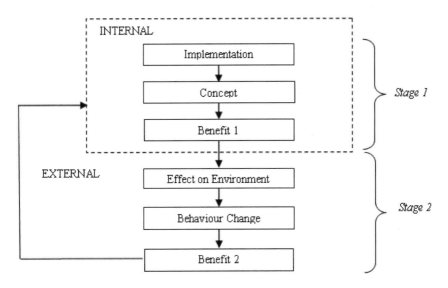

Fig. 1. Benefit realization process for IS projects (Fitzgerald 1998, p. 18)

Fitzgerald (1998)'s analysis of effectiveness projects takes a perspective that is organisation-centred and not entirely suited to OHRRC programmes. However it does provide useful insight into OHRRC development. He recognises that evaluation is an on-going activity that continues throughout the lifetime of a project, and that the results of evaluation at various stages of the process may trigger changes to the project. The approach must therefore be iterative, he concludes.

An organisation's size has a major influence on the choice of methods used for IS evaluation (Ballantine et al. 1998). So too does the culture, structure and strategy of the organisation (Irani et al. 2001) and the type and scope of the system. Indeed, Wilson and Howcroft (2004)'s social shaping of technology approach to evaluation suggests that the evaluation of information systems is always patterned by the conditions of creation and use. It can become a highly political activity (Smithson et al. 1998); not only can information itself have political implications in some organisational situations (Davenport et al. 1992), but even the costs and benefits of how it is managed can become politically charged.

A number of other ISE problems also exist. Firstly, the life-cycle of information systems are becoming more blurred (Irani et al. 2001) as they tend to evolve over time rather than having a clearly identifiable project start and end, and this makes it more difficult to know when an evaluation should be carried out. Secondly, it is difficult to know what to measure (Smithson et al. 1998) as there are often unplanned consequences from the introduction of a new system. Thirdly, there is usually a lag in delivering the benefits of an information system (Milis et al. 2004) – often due to learning difficulties or negativity amongst users. Fourthly there may be a lack of understanding of the human and organizational costs involved in evaluation, and of the time required to carry out an effective evaluation study (Smithson et al. 1998). Fifthly there can be a lack of commitment and involvement in system adoption. When this happens evaluations are often used to enroll users in the IS, to encourage a more positive perspective or to justify organisational decision-making through the presentation of organisational benefits in the evaluation exercise (Wilson et al. 2004). And finally there is the related problem that ISE, and particularly evaluation that takes place post-implementation, is often too close to the project and emphasises the value of the system rather than its improvement (Hedman and Borell 2005).

Serafeimidis and Smithson (2000) see information systems as 'complex socio-technical entities, inseparable from the organisational context within which they are situated and interact, as well as being products of history and human agency' (p93). Evaluation frameworks should be organised around the concerns, issues and actions of the stakeholders, they claim – a view supported by Brown (2005) who says that the tools and methods used should be aligned with cultural and organisational aims.

| | | Impact of information systems on organisation | |
		Tactical	Strategic
Perception of objectives	*Concensus / Clarity*	Control	Social Learning
	Nonconcensus / Ambiguity	Sense-making	Exploratory

Fig. 2. Four orientations to ISE (Serafeimidis et al. 2003, p. 256)

The importance of context in the perception and performance of IS evaluation is the basis for a definition of four different ISE orientations proposed by Serafeimidis et al. (2003). Their model is based on two dimensions; the horizontal axis refers to the impact on the organisation of a proposed IS investment; the vertical refers to the clarity and attainability of the objectives of the IS and their evaluation.

Given that human rights NGOs generally have clear objectives for OHRRC development and use but that there is uncertainty about the expected outcomes (i.e. the achievement of the objectives), they tend to fit into the social learning quadrant. Here evaluation facilitates learning through feedback mechanisms, providing a necessary increase in experience by applying critical input on actions taken and results achieved. Experimental actions such as prototypes can provide a source of knowledge throughout the system life cycle, with the learning orientation potentially contributing to organisational learning and understanding.

In looking at the organisational integration of ISE, (Serafeimidis et al. 2003) identify critical success factors for each orientation. Social learning evaluation, they say, requires a trigger to operate, and should be facilitated by formal processes as well as informal reasoning. Learning can be achieved in part through sense making, which requires communication between different evaluation and stakeholder groups to achieve consensus, and experimentation.

Hedman et al. (2005) describe organisational sense-making as an ongoing chain of four activities: act, measure, interpret, decision. This links into the increasing awareness of the importance of ongoing evaluation and the need to focus on how systems support businesses (Remenyi and Sherwood-Smith 1999; Hedman et al. 2005). It is a formative approach, which, in the case of OHRRCs means that ISE should always focus on how the system or project helps an organisation to fulfill its human rights objectives.

3.3 Human Rights Impact Assessment

Impact assessment (IA) is a term normally used in relation to development intervention. It refers to the process of identifying anticipated or actual impacts of an intervention on the factors that it is designed to affect or may inadvertently affect. It can take place before approval of the intervention (*ex ante*), after completion (*ex post*), or at any stage in between. Ex ante assessment forecasts potential impacts as part of the planning, design and approval phases; ex post assessment identifies actual impacts during and after implementation. IA is designed to enable corrective action to be taken if necessary and to provide information for improving future interventions (Kirkpatrick and Hulme 2001).

HRIA identifies consequences of interventions on human rights. It is generally used for actions that are specifically designed to have an impact on human rights, although it can also be used for other interventions that could impact on them indirectly. Interventions can impact on human rights by facilitating or strengthening the capability of an individual rights-holder to claim his or her rights (first-order impact) or it may enhance the capacity of human rights organisations and institutions to respond to individual petitions (second-order impact). NGOs are often effective mechanisms for the realisation of sustainable second-order human rights impact (Andreassen and Sano 2004), and OHRRCs are one way for them to achieve this.

It is reasonable, therefore, to apply the principles of HRIA to OHRRC IA. The process draws on information from the project itself, but it also uses knowledge about the environment before and after a project. Indicators, defined by Andersen and Sano (2006) as 'data used by analysts or institutions and organisations to describe situations that exist or to measure changes or trends over a period of time,' and described by them as 'communicative descriptions of conditions or of performance that may provide insight into matters of larger significance beyond that which is actually measured' (p11) are a key tool in the process. Indicators can be used to define programme or project objectives, to verify positive impact, and to document failures in achieving expected impact. They can describe situations or measure changes, and can be qualitative or quantitative.

Andersen et al. (2006) draw a distinction between effectiveness and impact. The former, the say, focuses on measuring the achievement of planned objectives and identifying target group achievements. The latter involves evaluation of how projects may contribute to broader societal goals such as strengthening the rule of law. The key issues when measuring effectiveness are the extent to which the agreed objectives have been reached, and whether activities are sufficient to reach these objectives. With IA it is necessary to look at the wider positive and negative effects, and whether the positive ones outweigh the negative. The main difficulty with the latter is determining what contributed to causing the impact.

The definition of evaluation used by Andersen et al. (2006) covers efficiency, effectiveness, impact, relevance and sustainability. Sustainability, which is the only criteria not identified already in the reviewed literature, assesses the likelihood that project benefits will continue beyond the lifetime of a project. It deals with predictive assessments, but since the overriding concern of human rights work is to achieve immediate results, historically it has not been given as much attention in human rights projects as the other evaluation criteria.

The terms of reference of evaluation can emphasise the five criteria to varying degrees, according to Andersen et al. (2006), but questions of efficiency and effectiveness should always be included.

Evaluation frameworks for human rights (and development) are generally based on the logical framework approach. This is a rigorous process that begins with an analysis of the current (pre-intervention or project) situation and the people, organisations or groups who might influence or be influenced by the problem or the potential solution. During the planning stage consensus is sought on the problem by bringing together many different stakeholders. This leads to a concrete definition of project goals and activities, which are combined with indicators of success, information about the indicators (the means of verification) and external factors that might impact on the project. These are usually presented in a logical framework matrix.

The logical framework's value as both a planning tool and a monitoring and evaluation (M&E) tool means that it is widely favoured by donors working with human rights organisations. In most cases HRIA has to be done by the organisation or institution itself because of resource constraints, even though assessments by external (independent) teams would add greatly to the credibility of an evaluation (Andreassen et al. 2004). It is the norm, therefore for human rights organisations to have expertise in the use of the logical framework approach, as they use it to report on their programmes.

4 OHRRC Evaluation Framework

Based on the review of literature, a number of important principles can be identified in relation to OHRRC evaluation. These are necessary in order to address the unique nature of the systems and their development – the fact that it is developed for and used within the non-profit sector; the difficulties in obtaining funds for development and maintenance; the divergent expectations of its users; and the difficulties faced in convincing some stakeholders of the value of technology-based solutions:

- The evaluation should, at a minimum, address efficiency and effectiveness criteria. Relevance, impact and sustainability criteria should, where possible, also be built into the evaluation.
- The evaluation should focus on second-order human rights impact, meaning the way it enhances the capacity of other human rights organisations and institutions to promote and protect human rights.
- The evaluation should be formative – in other words it should be undertaken during implementation so that changes can be made if necessary.
- The extent to which the system and the organisation's objectives are been achieved should be demonstrated using quantitative and qualitative indicators. These indicators should be identified early in a project life cycle, and should be practical and objective.
- Stakeholder participation is critical to the success of OHRRC evaluation, starting with initial needs assessment and continuing throughout the programme's lifetime.
- There should be regular feedback to OHRRC programme managers in relation to the achievement of intended results.
- Because of resource constraints, OHRRC evaluation must take advantage of the expertise that exists within the human rights organisation itself.

The proposed evaluation framework is a two-stage process covering goals definition, planning, benefits realisation and verification. It is intended for use at programme and project level, meaning it can be used to evaluate an OHRRC over a longer period than a single project life cycle. The stakeholders involved are the existing system users, target audiences for new services or content, experts in the particular area of human rights work being addressed by the system, and information specialists within the human rights regime. The tool used to plan and manage the process is the logical framework.

The first stage of the framework consists of the identification and exploration of initial needs, alignment with the organisation's mission, and an analysis of how the needs can be met by the organisation. The programme's intended impact and outcomes are documented, and concrete evidence is produced of the organisation's ability to deliver the expected benefit through proof of concept. This is done by building a prototype of the resource centre and seeking feedback on its likely impact from stakeholders. These steps provide the organisation with an assessment of how practical the system is, as well as its flexibility. They also help to determine the efficiency of the programme by identifying costs and resource requirements, they deliver an early evaluation of risks, and they provide an opportunity to enrol stakeholders (such as contributors of content).

The second stage is predicated on a decision to proceed at the end of the first stage. It begins with stakeholder consultation through questionnaires, interviews and other techniques, all of which lead to a definition of project outputs and activities. Following this there is a planning activity, leading to implementation of the current phase of the OHRRC. Once this is built and made available to stakeholders (users), monitoring and evaluation, based on the pre-defined indicators, begins.

Monitoring involves the periodic collection of information or feedback on the system's usage. Evaluation, defined in this context as the systematic collection and/or use of data to judge the merit and significance of an initiative, can use the monitoring information and should occur outside of and in addition to normal management activities. M&E activities performed in this way will result in a decision on whether to maintain, improve or extend the OHRRC. Extending means another phase of development and another cycle of stakeholder consultation, implementation and release; in other words, the *act – measure – interpret – decision* cycle that is needed for organisational sense-making.

If OHRRC programme objectives have been achieved, and feedback from the M&E activities confirms programme effectiveness, no action is required. However M&E should continue, and when realignment is shown to be necessary – either to improve effectiveness or relevance, or to maintain efficient use of the INGO's resources – then corrective action should be taken. OHRRCs are only useful if new content is being added constantly and the services made available (such as collaborative spaces, RSS feeds, etc.) are being used. Ongoing monitoring and the use of relevant indicators should indicate when programme modifications become necessary.

Indicators relating to effectiveness – i.e. the achievement of objectives – measure external factors such as the number of external organisations downloading content or the number of new resources/publications added each week. Efficiency indicators, which are addressed primarily though not exclusively in the first stage, are based on internally controlled variables such as cost. The definition of both sets of indicators and the successful management of stakeholder participation are vital to the success of the evaluation process.

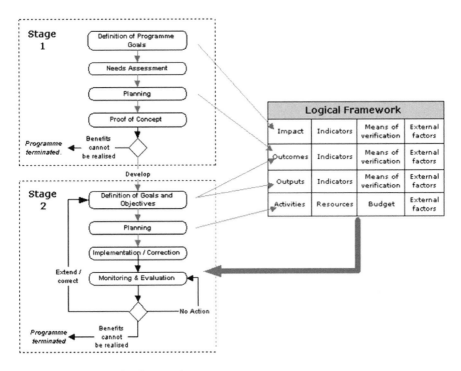

Fig. 3. OHRRC evaluation framework

4.1 Addressing the Information Management Challenges

The challenges identified earlier for OHRRC development and maintenance (transience, static content, etc.) need to be addressed in the evaluation framework. As most of these relate to effectiveness, this is done primarily at Stage 2. However they must also be considered in Stage 1, particularly in the planning activities.

When determining the programme goals and how they will be achieved, each of the key challenges needs to be considered. Indicators should be identified to ensure that they do not affect the outcomes negatively. This is also important in Stage 2; here, once again, the definition of goals and objectives and the planning activities need to take cognisance of impediments to OHRRC success.

For M&E to contribute to programme and project learning and improvement, it must be based on indicators that are meaningful and relevant to the overall goals of the OHRRC initiative. Very often success or failure is determined by the synergy (or lack thereof) among a variety of contributing factors, actors and circumstances. Instead of it being perceived as an annoying imposition, geared exclusively towards reporting progress and/or accountability, M&E should be used to get feedback for improvement, to avoid potential pitfalls and to contribute to organisational learning.

5 Summary and Next Steps

The approach proposed for the evaluation of OHRRCs is based on the concept of organisational learning through feedback mechanisms. The main sources of knowledge are consultative needs assessments, system prototyping and ongoing monitoring and evaluation – in other words a combination of experimentation and sense-making. The proposed framework provides a formative approach to evaluation, focusing on organisational human rights objectives and the second-order impact of an OHRRC programme or project.

OHRRC evaluation looks at if and how planned objectives are achieved. It is an ongoing process that continues beyond the development life cycle of an OHRRC project in order to ensure that a programme can, if necessary, be re-aligned in order to ensure its effectiveness and relevance, as well as the efficient use of an INGO's scarce resources. Even if there is a lag before planned objectives are achieved, ongoing monitoring and evaluation will ensure that progress towards achieving them is measured and recorded.

The OHRRC evaluation process is a two-stage one. The first stage focuses on the efficient implementation of a project to provide benefit. The second looks at its impact on the wider environment. The intended impact is increased capacity within the human rights movement, as well as governmental bodies, inter-governmental agencies, businesses and a range of other actors whose work is related to development and good governance. The framework can be used to evaluate the contribution that OHRRCs make towards this increased capacity, but it does not look at the resultant impact on how individual rights holders claim their rights. In other words, it relies on indicators designed to evaluate second-order human rights impact.

Work has already begun on testing the proposed framework, using an online resource centre being developed by a Dutch NGO. The organisation has completed its proof of concept and first phase of system development using a process that included most, but not all, of the components of the proposed framework and it is now ready to begin another phase in the development of its OHRRC. Using unstructured interviews and focus group discussion to examine the system development to date, and action research to apply the framework to the next phase of development, the suitability and shortcomings of the framework will be tested in practice.

In terms of the framework itself, further work is required to look at the first-order impact, and also to identify unintended consequences of OHRRC use. Nonetheless it is hoped that the next steps will show that it can provide international human rights NGOs with a useful tool for the evaluation of their online resource centres.

References

Andersen, E. A. and Sano, H.-O. (2006) *Human Rights Indicators at Programme and Project Level*, The Danish Institute for Human Rights, Denmark.

Andreassen, B. A. and Sano, H.-O. (2004) *What's the Goal? What's the Purpose? Observations on Human Rights Impact Assessment*, Norwegian Centre for Human Rights, University of Oslo, Norway.

Ball, P., Girouard, M. and Chapman, A. (1997) Information technology, information management, and human rights: a response to Metzl. *Human Rights Quarterly* 19(4), 836–859.

Ballantine, J., Levy, M. and Powell, P. (1998) Evaluating information systems in small and medium-sized enterprises: issues and evidence. *European Journal of Information Systems* 7, 241–251.

Brophy, P. and Halpin, E. F. (1999) Through the Net to Freedom: information, the Internet and human rights. *Journal of Information Science* 25(5), 351–364.

Brown, A. (2005) IS Evaluation in Practice. *The Electronic Journal of Information Systems Evaluation.* 8(3), 169–178.

Chabanov, S. (2004) *Information: an obstacle for human rights?*, eumap.org. Available from: http://www.eumap.org/journal/features/2004/infohr1/infohr2/.

Dahlberg, L. (2001) Computer-mediated communications and the public sphere: a critical analysis. *Journal of Computer-Mediated Communication* 7(1). Available from: http://www.ascusc.org/jcmc/vol7/issue1/dahlberg.html

Dameri, R. P. (2005) Using the balanced scorecard to evaluate ICT investments in non profit organisations. *The Electronic Journal of Information Systems Evaluation* 8(2), 107–114.

Davenport, T. H., Eccles, R. G. and Prusak, L. (1992) Information politics. *Sloan Management Review* 34(1), 53–65.

Fitzgerald, G. (1998) Evaluating information systems projects: a multidimensional approach. *Journal of Information Technology* 13, 15–27.

Halpin, E. F. (2003a) An evaluation of the child rights information network: examining information management in a global NGO-Part 1. *Canadian Journal of Library and Information Science* 27(3), 25–39.

Halpin, E. F. (2003b) An evaluation of the child rights information network: examining information management in a global NGO-Part 2. *Canadian Journal of Library and Information Science* 27(4), 31–54.

Hedman, J. and Borell, A. (2005) Broadening information systems evaluation through narratives. *The Electronic Journal of Information Systems Evaluation* 8(2), 115–122.

Hick, S., Halpin, E. F. and Hoskins, E. (eds.) (2000) *Human Rights and the Internet*, MacMillan, Houndmills.

Irani, Z. and Love, P. E. D. (2001) Information systems evaluation: past, present and future. *European Journal of Information Systems* 10, 183–188.

Irani, Z., Sharif, A. M. and Love, P. E. D. (2005) Linking knowledge transformation to information systems evaluation. *European Journal of Information Systems* 14, 213–228.

Joshi, S. (2004) *Towards A Global Network of Rights: The Experience of Nepal,* eumap.org. Available from: http://www.eumap.org/journal/features/2004/infohr1/infohr2/

Kirkpatrick, C. and Hulme, D. (2001) *Basic Impact Assessment at Project Level*, Enterprise Development Impact Assessment Information Service (DFID).

Landman, T. and Abraham, M. (2004) *Evaluation of Nine Non-governmental Human Rights Organisations*, Ministry of Foreign Affairs, The Netherlands.

Lannon, J. and Halpin, E. F. (2006) Human rights movements and the Internet: from local contexts to global engagement. In: Gascó-Hernández, M., Equiza-López, F. and Acevedo-Ruiz, M. (eds.) *Information Communication Technologies and Human Development: Opportunities and Challenges*, pp. 182–209. Idea Group Publishing, Hershey.

Metzl, J. F. (1996) Information technology and human rights. *Human Rights Quarterly* 18(4), 705–746.

Milis, K. and Mercken, R. (2004) The use of the balanced scorecard for the evaluation of Information and communication technology projects. *International Journal of Project Management* 22, 87–97.

Pace, W. R. and Panganiban, R. (2002) The power of global activist networks: the campaign for an international criminal court. In: Hajnal, P. I. (ed.), *Civil Society in the Information Age*, pp. 109–125. Ashgate, Hampshire.

Remenyi, D. and Sherwood-Smith, M. (1999) Maximise information systems value by continuous participative evaluation. *Logistics Information Management* 12(1), 14–31.

Rutherford, K. R. (2000) Internet activism: NGOs and the Mine Ban Treaty. *The International Journal on Grey Literature*. 1(3), 99–105.

Selian, A. N. (2002) *ICTs in Support of Human Rights, Democracy and Good Governance*, International Telecommunications Union, Paris.

Serafeimidis, V. and Smithson, S. (2000) Information systems evaluation in practice: a case study of organisational change. *Journal of Information Technology* 15, 93–105.

Serafeimidis, V. and Smithson, S. (2003) Information systems evaluation as an organisational institution - experience from a case study. *Information Systems Journal* 13, 251–274.

Smithson, S. and Hirschheim, R. (1998) Analysing information systems evaluation: another look at an old problem. *European Journal of Information Systems* 7, 158–174.

Vasconcelos, J. B. d., Seixas, P. C. and Lemos, P. G. (2005) Knowledge management in nongovernmental organisations. In: *Proceedings of 7th International Conference on Enterprise Information Systems (ICEIS 2005)*, Miami.

Warnick, B. (1998) Appearance or reality? Political parody on the Web in campaign '96. *Critical Studies in Mass Communication* 15(3), 306–324.

Wasserman, H. (2005) Connecting African activism with global networks: ICTs and South African social movements. *Africa Development*. XXX(1 & 2), 163–182.

Westbrook, J. I., Braithwaite, J., Iedema, R. and Coiera, E. W. (2004) Evaluating the impact of information communication technologies on complex organisational systems: a multi-disciplinary, multi-method framework. In: Fieschi, M., Coiera, E. and Li, Y.-C. (eds.) *MEDINFO*, pp. 1323–1327. IOS Press, Washington.

Weyker, S. (2002) The ironies of information technology. In: Brysk, A. (ed.), *Globalization and Human Rights*, pp. 115–132. University of California Press, Berkeley.

Wilson, M. and Howcroft, D. (2004) The politics of IS evaluation: a social shaping perspective. In: *Proceedings of Twenty First International Conference on Information Systems, December 2000*, pp. 94–103. Brisbane, Queensland, Australia.

'Calling Passengers' - An Ethical Problem in the Design of Self-Service Web Sites Amongst Low-Cost Airlines in Ireland

Chris Barry[1] and Ann Torres[2]

[1] National University of Ireland, Galway, Department of Accountancy and Finance,
chris.barry@nuigalway.ie

[2] National University of Ireland, Galway, Department of Marketing, ann.torres@nuigalway.ie

Abstract   Ethics on the Internet has been a widely debated topic in recent years covering issues that range from privacy to security to fraud. Little, however, has been written on more subtle ethical questions such as the exploitation of Web technologies to inhibit or avoid customer service. Increasingly, it would appear, some firms are using Web sites to create distance between them and their customer base in specific areas of their operations, while simultaneously developing excellence in sales transaction completion via self-service. This chapter takes a magnifying glass with an ethical lens to just one sector – the low-cost, Web-based self-service airline industry, specifically in Ireland. The chapter notes the teaching of information systems development (ISD) and, for the most part, its practice assumes ethicality. Similarly, marketing courses focus on satisfying customer needs more effectively and efficiently within the confines of an acceptable ethos. This chapter observes that while these business disciplines are central to the success of self-service Web sites, there seems to be a disconnection between the normative view and the actuality of practice. What follows begins with an analysis of the normative approach to information systems (IS) design and marketing. A review of questionable ethical practices used by low-cost carriers (LCCs) is then conducted, followed by a discussion on the phenomena. The chapter concludes with a look at the implications for research, teaching and practice.

1 The Success of Low-Cost Carriers

Traditionally, air travel succeeded by offering a premium service and through the protection of government regulation, cartels of established airlines flourished and easily drove out competition (de Neufville 2006). The advent of economic deregulation of the US airline industry in 1978 followed by the UK (1987), Canada (1988), Australia (1990), the EU (1992) and Japan (2000) meant legacy airlines

C. Barry et al. (eds.), *Information Systems Development: Challenges in Practice, Theory, and Education, Vol.2*, doi: 10.1007/978-0-387-78578-3_4,
© Springer Science+Business Media, LLC 2009

had to consider carefully their cost of operations. The most important consequences associated with the progressive deregulation of markets are lower fares and higher productivity (Kahn 2002). Although the average yields per passenger mile (i.e. the average of the fares that passengers actually paid) were declining prior to deregulation, between 1976 and 1990, average yields declined 30% in real, inflation-adjusted terms, which translated into an estimated savings to travellers of $5–$10 billion per year (Kahn 2002). Deregulation also fostered higher levels of productivity by removing the airlines' restriction on pricing and destinations. Without these restrictions, intense price competition ensued, which spurred airlines to seek improvements in efficiency (Kahn 2002).

The low-cost operation has been a highly successful model in the airline industry over the last decade (Alamdari and Fagan 2005). In Europe, LCCs are growing 20–40% annually (Alamdari et al. 2005) and currently hold 33% of the overall market (de Neufville 2006). Although there are variations in strategy among carriers, the basic LCC model is to achieve cost leadership to allow for flexibility in pricing and achieve higher operating margins. Typically, this strategy requires the carrier to examine every function and service they perform and either to eliminate those considered as superfluous frills or to charge for them separately as an addition to the basic fare. The sophisticated information systems (IS) LCCs employ for dynamic pricing and revenue management have contributed substantially to their healthy profit margins. However, in their focussed pursuit to eliminate frills, customer service is one function that has declined in importance. Among some LCCs, the justification given for neglecting meaningful customer service (i.e. managing complaints and concerns) are the very low air fares they offer customers.

2 The Normative Approach to Systems Development

The dominant approach used in developing systems for several decades has been structured methods. Their origins are in scientific research and they are of a positivist tradition. The normative approach is explicit in the more popular structured systems analysis methods (Constantine and Yourdon 1979; DeMarco 1979; Martin and Finkelstein 1981), and is widely used by practitioners. Human–computer interaction (HCI) has long held that its basic goal is to improve the interaction between users and computer systems by making them more usable and amenable to the user's needs (Dix et al. 2004). These fields are taught with the aid of popular texts on virtually every IS/IT undergraduate programme as the way in which information systems should be developed.

Within these methods there is a near-universal supposition that a key goal of information systems development (ISD) is to improve usability and deliver a satisfying user experience. The authors would argue that this supposition has become unsafe. To borrow the language of Argyris (1980), the 'espoused theory' of how IS should be developed is, for some, quite different to the 'theory-in-use.'

An examination of widely used texts on the principles of Web design (Nielsen 1999; Sklar 2006; Sharp et al. 2007) supports the hypothesis that IS professionals should adopt a benign and moral posture in designing and developing information systems. It fails to uncover any instruction on design strategies that inhibit customer response or retard interaction. Indeed, such texts ordinarily implore designers to, for example, include contact links on the home page that contain address, phone numbers and email (Nielsen and Tahir 2001).

3 The Normative Approach in Marketing

Marketing's central premise is to satisfy customer needs and wants more effectively and efficiently than the competition, as a means to achieving organizational success (Boone and Kurtz 2004; Brassington and Pettit 2006; Jobber 2007; Kotler and Armstrong 2007). This marketing management philosophy, also known as the marketing concept, clearly distinguishes between those firms which merely have forms of marketing, such as the presence of a marketing or customer service department, from those firms which are market-focused and customer-driven in implementing their strategies. Firms successfully employing the marketing concept pursue a delicate balance between satisfying customers' needs by creating more value, while simultaneously achieving organizational objectives by accruing profits.

An effective interaction between a buyer and seller may result in a satisfied customer, but to retain customers over the long-term means managing customer relationships consistently. In today's technology-rich environment, marketers facilitate their individual interactions with customers through customer relationship management (CRM) systems. Other terms for CRM are relationship marketing and customer intimacy; these terms reflect CRM's strategic intent – focusing on satisfying individual customers meaningfully as well as profitably for the firm (Wagner and Zubey 2007). Through the systematic combination of people, process and technology, CRM enables firms to find, acquire and retain customers. Finding and acquiring customers costs firms money, but retaining existing customers is substantially more profitable than seeking fresh customers for new transactions. On average, the cost of acquiring new customers is five times more than servicing existing customers (Keaveney 1995). Furthermore, the marginal cost of servicing existing clients declines over time, whereas the cost of attracting new customers typically increases over time.

In CRM 'meaningfully satisfying customers' refers to facilitating the full spectrum of customer interactions, including complaints. Marketers view customer complaints as opportunities for service recovery that can turn angry, disgruntled customers into loyal, vocal advocates for the firm. Indeed, good service recovery typically translates into higher sales than if all had gone well initially (Smith et al. 1999). Ultimately, poor service recovery translates into lost customers that migrate, often permanently, to competing firms (Keaveney 1995). Because many firms handle customer complaints poorly, those firms that do succeed in offering excellent service recovery, secure an unrivalled source of competitive advantage.

4 LCCs' Lack of Application of a Normative Approach in Marketing

LCCs offer value to customers through their low fares, and achieve profits by calibrating costs carefully to achieve attractive margins. A number of LCCs use their information systems in a conflicting manner when managing customer interactions. The Web sites for these LCCs smoothly engage and facilitate customers through the self-service process to purchase tickets and ancillary products, such as insurance, accommodation and car rental. However, the Web sites are 'gummy,' awkward and sluggish in facilitating customer complaints and concerns. The Web sites do not readily display contact details, such as telephone numbers, email addresses to register complaints and concerns. Customers are given only a postal address and, on occasion, a fax number, which delay the customers' opportunity for a timely response. This gumminess is an intentional design feature and is contrary to the ethos of designing a 'good system' to facilitate the full spectrum of customer service. These LCCs are exhibiting the classic strategic flaw of having the trappings of marketing without offering substantive marketing practices (Ames 1970; Peattie 1999). That is, LCCs offer superficial customer service on their Web sites, but do not make meaningful efforts to address customer complaints and concerns, resulting in service failures, poor service recovery, and ultimately, the loss of future revenue from these disappointed customers.

In employing these gummy features, LCCs are pursing a transactional rather than a relational model of marketing behaviour. They are seeking a high volume of discrete, profitable transactions rather than a high volume of profitable customer relationships enduring over time. That is, the airlines are pursuing short-term profitability through generating high-volume transactions, rather than pursing long-term profitability through the development of a loyal customer base. The loss of existing customers does not appear to be a concern for many LCCs; they believe their low fares compensate for poor service or justify the lack of service recovery efforts. Ultimately, these LCCs are increasing their operating costs in the search for new customers. Moreover, they appear to manage their business as if there were an infinite supply of new customers. In time, the most successful LCCs may be those who offer customers competitive pricing policies and high levels of service recovery.

5 Reviewing Ethically Questionable 'Gummy' Practices

5.1 Heuristic Evaluation

The authors conducted an exploratory study to evaluate the usability and functional design of six LCC Web sites used in Ireland; four of these carriers (Aer Lingus, Aer Arann, bmibaby and Ryanair) operate out of the Republic of Ireland and two carriers (easyJet and Jet2.com) out of Northern Ireland. The methodology used was heuristic evaluation, well established within the HCI field. It is a usability inspection technique that systematically assesses a user interface design for usability (Nielsen 1994). Heuristic evaluation is guided by usability principles (i.e. heuristics) that examine if interface elements conform in practice to those principles. The technique is adjusted for evaluating Web sites (Sharp et al., 2007). The heuristics were customized for identifying usability issues for the low-cost airline industry based partly on Nielsen's set and the authors' knowledge of issues, as well as ethical problems emerging from the sector (Alter 2003; Clark 2006; ECC Network 2006). The analysis, however, goes beyond the assessment of the 'goodness' or otherwise of usability and makes judgements on the concordance of Web site features with broader expectations of IS design and marketing principles. The heuristics developed are shown in Table 1.

Table 1. Evaluation heuristics

Heuristic	Description
Aesthetic and minimalist design	• *The Web site should not contain unnecessary or rarely needed clutter*
Navigation design	• *The means by which users navigate their way around the information structure should be clear*
Internal consistency	• *Users should not have to ponder whether different terms or actions have the same meaning* • *The language should be that of the user where possible and information should appear in a natural and logical order*
Depth of navigation menu	• *The Web site should be designed so that it is shallow rather than deep*
Completion of tasks	• *The system should be designed so that users are able to efficiently and effectively complete a task to their expectations.* • *Are there features that accelerate functionality for expert users but remaining flexible enough for novice users?*
Clarity of feature functionality	• *A feature should fulfil the function implied by the dialog* • *Dialog should be simple with no irrelevant or unnecessary information*
Minimizing the user's memory load	• *The interface should not require users to remember information between one part of the system and the next*
Help users recognize, diagnose and recover from errors or unintended actions	• *Careful design that prevents a problem from ever happening is better than good error or warning messages*

5.2 Task Construction

Given the heuristics in Table 1, a number of tasks were established (see Table 2) to gauge the effectiveness of each of the LCC Web sites. These tasks are commonly conducted activities that users would be expected to use as part of an online, self-service Web site. They are representative pre-sale, sale and post-sale activities.

Table 2. Analysis tasks

	Task
1.	Get a quote for a specified flight
2.	Book a specified flight
3.	Find an advertised 'cheap' flight
4.	Reserve (or get a referral) for a car for a specified trip
5.	Find and establish the nature of the firms 'About Us' details
6.	Find and establish the nature of the firms 'Contact Us' details
7.	Find and establish the nature of the firms 'Customer Feedback' details
8.	Complain to the LCC about a negative experience you had with hygiene on a recent flight
9.	Change a misspelled passenger name
10.	An impulse task that arises in situ

6 Web site Evaluations

6.1 Quotes, Bookings and Referrals

Getting a quote for a specified flight is probably the most common task carried out on every LCC Web site. Pricing is achieved by using the booking systems of all airlines, rather than a separate quote facility. Overall, the LCCs' Web sites afford a high level of usability, assisting the user to complete the task quickly and effectively. There are many design features that accelerate the process, from giving users the closest dates around the selected date (by default and when that date is unavailable) to retaining user dates and details, presumably in cookies. For example, Aer Lingus even allow the consumer to select departure and return flights for specific dates, where a screen is presented for which the priced flight is, in fact, the cheapest of a selection of other flights. Additionally, all of the LCCs afford advanced design features such as 'hub and spoke' route maps that superbly assist users in visualizing what would otherwise be complex flat information.

A uniquely useful feature on Jet2.com is a 'low fare finder' that allows a customer to play with available flight for a month at a glance. The available flights, all priced, can be seen for both flight segments on one screen. This feature contrasts markedly with other carriers which make it very difficult to find the cheapest combination of flights for customers who have date flexibility.

However, each LCC have design features that adversely affect usability and trust. There is significant uncertainty as to what constitutes a 'final price,' baggage allowance, taxes and fees; and a plethora of 'services' for which extra charges are levied; and for what are opt-in or opt-out choices. All airlines quote a price that suggests it is either 'Final…' or 'Total…' whereas, in fact, it is neither. Some airlines are more transparent than others; bmibaby is the only airline that includes taxes and charges, but they appear very high and are not explained to the user during the booking process. The taxes and charges that each airline applies subsequent to the first quoted price, except for bmibaby, are all substantial and generally unavoidable. Most LCCs (i.e. Aer Lingus, Aer Arann, easyJet and Jet2.com) do not break down the cost during the quote or booking process. While Ryanair does provide a 'details' link, it is a pop-up alert box that does not fully break down the charges and does not display the charges as text, so that a customer could print or even highlight and copy the charges. Such charges are often significantly different for each leg and little effort is made to explain the differential. A somewhat similar technique is used by Aer Arann, which use pop-up alert boxes to display different fare types denoted as 'E', 'K', 'V', 'W' and so on. This type of fare designation is wholly confusing, difficult to understand and the evaluation found no definition on the Web site of what differentiates these fare types. Such lack of clarity in design camouflages the nature of the real price of a flight for users.

Ryanair is the airline with the most extensive and perhaps contentious set of unavoidable additional charges. They include Duty Tax, Government Tax, a Passenger Service Charge/Airport Tax, Aviation Insurance Levy and a Wheelchair Levy. The strangest of these is the Passenger Service Charge/Airport Tax, which is "a charge made by the airport authority to an airline for the use of the terminal, runway, emergency services, security facilities etc." One would wonder how fair it is to publish prices for flights that do not include the use of an airport terminal.

The main difference between getting a quote and booking the flight is the imposition of credit or debit card 'handling' charges and negotiating a series of opt-in and opt-out services. These handling charges are for the most part unavoidable and inconsistently levied by the LCCs. For example, Aer Lingus charges by each passenger, Ryanair charges for each passenger for each flight segment, while Jet2.com has already included it as part of the taxes and charges.

Perhaps the feature that violates the most heuristics during the analysis was the decision on checked-in baggage with Ryanair. When entering passenger details, the number of bags is chosen from the drop down box where it would appear a charge is unavoidable, even if no bag is required, since it automatically suggests the user is choosing "0 bags - Online Check-in/Priority Boarding". A user is led to believe they must choose the priority check-in option if they carry hand baggage only. However, when this option is selected some text then appears beneath the drop down box that allows the user to 'remove' this option (after a pop-up a message box seeks confirmation) and an entry in the drop down list now appears that read '0 bags,' Such a deliberate design feature makes the completion of the task difficult and ambiguous. Another notable feature that limits the 'completion of tasks' heuristic is Aer Lingus's timing out of a user's session after a few minutes, thus all flight quote and users details disappear. Overall, the gumminess in the reservation process makes it ambiguous and lacking clarity for users.

In the past, many consumers find some of those advertised cheap fare to be 'elusive' (Whitehouse 2001). This evaluation discovered that generally advertised 'cheap' flights can be found. However, the process may involve considerable time as well as some trail and error. Most LCCs have headline offers with the usual charges added on. Of the LCCs evaluated, easyJet's Web site is the most straightforward and transparent. Prices are quoted as return flights per person with all taxes included except for final card charges. Generally, easyJet's Web site has internal consistency, is welcoming and easy to use. Moreover, most features in its Web site work in the manner they appear to suggest.

When tasked with getting a quote or a referral for a car for a specified trip all the airlines have partnership relationships with firms such as Hertz and Avis. Direct links are available on all the main pages and once in the booking screen the steps are generally quite clear and, in contrast with the LCCs, with few hidden or additional costs.

6.2 'About Us'

For many of the airline Web sites, the 'About Us' link was easy to find, as it was usually located at the top of the home page as at tab on a prominent navigation bar, or at the bottom of the page. As expected, 'About Us' offered a variety of information ranging from the airline's mission, its history and fleet, milestones in its operations, opportunities for employment and recruitment, its partnerships with other organizations (e.g. airlines, tourism boards, car rental agencies, hoteliers and media partners), to news worthy information on the airline's activities, such as business awards and charitable efforts. In the case of bmibaby, the 'About Us' information was found under the link 'Corporate', which may not be as immediately intuitive to users looking for information about the airline. In the case of Aer Lingus, the 'About Us' link led to the firm's contact details, while other company information was found in a menu located on the left of the page.

6.3 'Contact Us', Compliments, Complaints and Changes

Locating information to contact the airline, was relative easy in some Web sites, but could be highly problematic in others. In a couple of Web sites, the 'Contact Us' information could be found through links on the navigation bar, as well as within the site map. For example, on the Aer Lingus Web site contact information is found through the 'About Us' and 'Need Help' links at the top of the home page's navigational bar, as well as the site map. The contact details for Aer

Lingus's reservation desks and pre-flight help desks are organized by country and include phone numbers, opening hours, and in some cases include fax numbers, postal addresses and email addresses. The level of contact information is not consistent across Aer Lingus offices. Moreover, if consumers want to compliment or complain about an Aer Lingus flight (i.e. post-flight assistance), they are asked to write to the nearest Aer Lingus office and to include a copy of their ticket or boarding card. No telephone numbers or email addresses are provided for post-flight assistance. Jet2.com and bmibaby follow the same policy as Aer Lingus when it comes to pre-flight assistance, which are sales related inquiries and post-flight assistance, which relates to complaints.

Among the six airlines reviewed, Aer Arann provided the most complete contact information. Not only were there complete contact details for the head office in Dublin airport, but also contact information for Aer Arann's reservations desks across Europe, where in each instance, an address, phone number, fax number and email address was included. Moreover, Aer Arann uniquely facilitated post-flight assistance by offering email addresses for feedback, customer relations and refund queries.

With easyJet, although the 'Contact Us' link was easy to find at the top of the home page, it led to a list of FAQs with a search option. Thus, in searching for contact details consumers are directed to a list of premium-rated telephone numbers for Web support, customer services as well as sales and changes to existing bookings. As well, national premium telephone numbers are given for other countries. It was not possible to contact the airline by email or fax, but a postal address is given for easyJet's headquarters in Luton Airport.

Ryanair proved to be the most challenging in locating the 'Contact Us' link, as none was found on the home page. The most direct way to find contact information is through the site map, where 'Contact Us' is listed under 'About Us'. Indeed, if a consumer clicks on the 'About Us' link on the home page's navigational bar, the main horizontal navigational bar changes to include 'Contact Us'. The page cites 'Reservation Contact Numbers', but on the left panel a different 'Contact Us' link appears. When this link is selected a user finally gets 'real' contact details from 'Contacting Customer Service', which is nestled in between 'Contact for Disability Requirements' and 'How do I register with Ryanair for special offers?'. There is no order or apparent logic to this design; it is either exceptionally poor design or deliberately gummy. The heuristic that Web sites should be designed so they are shallow rather than deep (Larson and Czerwinski 1998; Shneiderman and Plaisant 2004) is clearly violated in this instance.

Similar to easyJet, the Ryanair Web site provides a list of FAQ links. Thus, for pre-flight assistance consumers may find the relevant information through the 'Reservation Contact Numbers' and the 'Internet Support' links, which list premium telephone numbers by country. For 'Contacting Customer Service', the link directs users to a series of postal addresses according the nature of the issue, such as complaints, EU 261 cancellation and delay complaints,[1] refunds for cancelled

---

[1] "In February 2005 a new European Regulation (261/04) came into effect which gives consumers rights when denied boarding or when a flight is delayed or cancelled. In June of 2004 the Montreal

flights and baggage claims. Complaints must be written in English and provide full flight details (e.g. dates and routes) and passenger names. A keyword search on the Web site for customer service provides another link for 'How can I contact Ryanair' where a fax number is given for post-flight assistance. Again, faxed letters must be written in English and full flight and passenger details must be provided.

According to Ryanair's Passenger Charter, the airline will respond to written complaints within seven days from the date of its receipt. It is interesting to note that Ryanair will respond to these written complaints to the email address provided at the time of reservation, but this specific detail is not outlined in Ryanair's Passenger Charter, but is given elsewhere on the Web site under 'Contacting Customer Service.'[2] It is baffling that Ryanair can respond to complaints by email, but it cannot receive complaints by email. Additionally, the Web page incorrectly refers to Ryanair's 'Customer Charter'; a key word search for either 'customer charter' or 'passenger charter' does not elicit any results. The 'Passenger Charter' exists, but is not easily found; it can be located under the 'About Us' link, where in the left hand panel there is a link to the 'Passenger Charter.'[3] Although, it is common sense that making Web sites gummy when consumers have complaints or concerns will increase the level of customer dissatisfaction, most LCCs are prepared to take such risks in what is a race to the bottom. While Ryanair claims on its Web site to have the fewest complaints in the industry, a 2006 study by the European Consumer Centre Network (ECC Network 2006), found Ryanair was the subject of a five-fold increase in complaints over the last two years.

Most of the LCCs have a facility to 'Manage Booking' or 'Change Booking,' where dates and destinations may be changed. However, in all LCCs, changing a misspelled passenger name is the same as changing a passenger name, so there was virtually no flexibility in accommodating minor errors. Although during the booking process, many LCC Web sites highlight that passenger names must be the same as they appear on passports. Name changes on tickets are a pre-flight form of assistance, where users are directed to contact sales desks, which are often premium telephone numbers. Although the per minute charges for these premium telephone lines are typically given, it is more difficult to find out the charge incurred for changing a name on a ticket. In the case of some airlines (e.g. Aer Arann and bmibaby), at the time of booking the user is notified that name changes are possible for €40 per person. On the easyJet and Jet2.com Web sites, the FAQ link provides users with the information for how to change a name and the associ-

---

Convention replaced the existing Warsaw Convention, which introduced new rules on compensation for loss, damage or delay to baggage or persons. At the same time, ECCs [European Consumer Centres] reported an increase in requests for information on the new rights and an increase in complaints and disputes. This increase continued throughout 2005 and air passenger rights continue to be one of the biggest areas of complaints handled by the ECC Net in 2006." European Consumer Centre Network (2006) Air Passenger Rights: Consumer Complaints 2005 A Summary and Analysis of Consumer Complaints to the European Consumer Centre Network. October 2006, p. 4.

[2] See http://www.ryanair.com/site/EN/faqs.php?sect=cnt&quest=custserv

[3] See Item 6 in Ryanair's Passenger Charter at:
http://www.ryanair.com/site/EN/about.php?page=About&sec=charter

ated cost; however, easyJet is the only LCC that allows name changes online, provided the user is a registered member.

6.4 Impulse Task

The tasks prompted to perform in situ were either to check-in online or book a specific seat, depending on which task was perceived as being given more emphasis on the LCC Web site. All the LCCs, except for easyJet, advertise online check-in on their home page; it is possible to find easyJet's online check-in under the 'Contact Us' FAQs. Typically, online check-in is reserved for those passengers who are only carrying hand baggage.

For most LCCs (Aer Lingus, Aer Arann, Jet2.com, bmibaby) online check-in and seat selection are parts of the same process, where the user may avail of online check-in usually a day or two prior to a flight departure and closes two or three hours before scheduled departures. The user goes online, enters their reservation number and departure city, selects a seat, and prints their boarding pass. For these carriers there does not appear to be any charges associated with this facility.

Other LCCs, Ryanair and easyJet, offer priority boarding for an extra charge, to facilitate passengers who want to sit together, or prefer a specific seating area. However, these LCCs do not appear to allow the user to select a specific seat. Aer Lingus is the only LCC that allows customers to select a specific seat, as a premium service at the time of booking. The Web site provides a demonstration video on how this is done, but the fee is only advertised within the video or whilst booking.

7 Discussion

For LCCs, it would appear that many non-sales-related activities are simply removed or distanced from the operations of the organization. This deconstructed, 'no-frills' business model is reflected in the design of the supporting IS. That the IS should reflect the business model is precisely how a 'good' IS should be designed. LCC self-service Web sites are thus primarily aimed at capturing revenues and appear highly effective, as they focus on sales completion and minimizing effort on the part of the customer. However, there remains a gap between the functionality one would expect to find in sophisticated, Web-based IS and what they actually offer. Similarly, some of the features are unorthodox in their design. The differential cannot be explained by Ogburn's cultural lag thesis which proposes that material culture generally advances more rapidly than nonmaterial culture. Thus, physical and operational systems first appear while ethics, philosophy and belief systems surface much later (Marshall 1999). Certain questions arise from this analysis.

How is one to interpret these design strategies? They are not accidental; the clear focus on assisting users in closing sales contrasts radically with strangely ineffective, poorly accessible or completely missing functionality. It is evident that some firms are quite deliberately using Web technologies to design out features one might expect in 'traditional' information systems and to obfuscate or complicate others. To cite the most obvious examples: why do LCC firms not use email or web forms to facilitate customer communications; why is it so difficult to quickly find contact details; and why are the structures of additional charges so fragmented?

What is it about self-service Web sites that lend themselves to this type of customer service? Such Web sites have certain unique characteristics that are different to bricks and mortar operations. The channel is indirect and certain features can be designed in (or out) in a way that would not be tolerated with face-to-face or telephone-based models. It is possible to de-market the business model far more effectively when direct contact is avoided. Self-service Web sites also devolve tasks to customers, delegating responsibility for accurate data entry and the initiation of remedial procedures when things go wrong.

Is the Web any less ethical than business practices elsewhere? Probably not; the practices outlined here are not illegal or, apparently, subject to regulatory sanction. Also, corporate codes of ethics have been widely adopted in ways that range from moderating business practices to guaranteeing the principles of fair trade in the supply chain. However, new Web technologies allow firms to develop obstacles and barriers that a bricks and mortar model would not facilitate.

Are ethics of IS and marketing professionals of any relevance? In a highly competitive industry that thrives on a low-cost strategy, simplicity and limited functionality are natural consequences for the design of IS. However, some IS/IT practitioners must be acutely aware that they are guilty of, at the very least, sins of omission in IS design practice. Furthermore it is, without evidence of disparity, reasonable to assume there is a congruence of values between management and IS practitioners. While there are well-established, if dissimilar, professional codes of ethics in the IS/IT field (Oz 1993), the notion of emancipatory ideals (Hirschheim and Klein, 1994), once feted in the IS literature, finding a role in the design of low-cost airline Web sites would appear to have found little resonance in this area of practice.

8 Conclusions

There are a number of implications of this study. While many business ethics issues are not manifestly new in Web-based IS, it is "becoming apparent that the ethical dimensions of IS-related business decisions cannot be safely ignored" (Smith and Hasnas 1999, p. 111). It is necessary to renew the articulation of ethics in view of the capacity of new technologies to affect dubious practice. Perhaps ethical guidelines and frameworks in IS design; corporate codes of ethics; professional

IS/IT and marketing codes of ethics; and ethic in the IS and marketing curricula, also need to be revisited.

There is assumed ethicality in how IS are designed and how marketing practice is conducted; such assumptions need to be challenged. Writers have advised practitioners and teachers to be worried if there is a 'complete absence' of contact information (Kassler 2002). This concern is largely focussed on the potential for deceit and fraud. It is not normally directed at 'reputable' firms who, for example, obscure contact details to reduce interaction and dialogue. This oversight too demands some revision in how information systems and marketing are taught. Do teachers make students aware of gummy practices or should they demonstrate how they can be achieved to match the demands of business practice?

Social responsibility in corporate governance has become an imperative for many firms. Do LCCs using self-service delivery demand different standards because they are low-cost? Is there a layer of insulation that such operators enjoy because, to many non-technical observers, the nuances of intentional design practices remain unclear? The lowering of customer expectations that de-marketing has brought about has also lowered the threshold of systems design. Is this benchmark acceptable? While all of these questions involve a much broader social discourse, it is timely to debate them.

References

Alamdari, F. and Fagan, S. (2005) Impact of the adherence to the original low-cost model on the profitability of low-cost airlines. Transport Reviews. 25(3), 377–392.

Alter, S. (2003) Customer service, responsibility, and systems in international e-commerce: should a major airline reissue a stolen ticket? Communications of the Association for Information Systems. 12(10), 146–154.

Ames, C. (1970) Trappings vs. substance in industrial marketing. Harvard Business Review. 48(4), 93–102.

Argyris, C. (1980) *Inner Contradictions of Rigorous Research*. Academic Press, New York.

Boone, L. and Kurtz, D. (2004) *Contemporary Marketing*. 11th Edition. South Western-Thomson Learning, New York.

Brassington, F. and Pettit, S. (2006) *Principles of Marketing*. 4th Edition. Pearson Education, New York.

Clark, A. (2006) Ryanair ... the low-fare airline with the sky-high insurance levy. *Guardian*. URL: http://business.guardian.co.uk/story/0,,1769707,00.html, accessed 5 April 2007.

Constantine, E. and Yourdon, E. (1979) *Structured Design*. Prentice-Hall, New York.

DeMarco, T. (1979) *Structured Analysis and Systems Specification*. Yourdon Press, New York.

de Neufville R. (2006) Planning Airport Access in an Era of Low-Cost Airlines. Journal of American Planning Association. 72(3), 347–356.

Dix, A., Finlay, J., Abowd, G. and Beale, R. (2004) *Human-Computer Interaction*. 3rd Edition. Pearson/Prentice Hall, New York.

ECC Network (2006) *Report on Air Passenger Rights: Consumer Complaints 2005*. European Consumer Centre Network: 1–46.

Hirschheim, R. and Klein, H. (1994) Realizing emancipatory principles in information systems development: the case for ETHICS. MIS Quarterly. 18(1), 83–109.

Jobber, D. (2007) *Principles and Practice of Marketing*. 5th Edition. McGraw Hill, London.

Kahn, A. (2002) Airline Deregulation. *The Concise Encyclopedia of Economics.* The Library of Economics and Liberty. URL: http://www.econlib.org/LIBRARY/Enc/AirlineDeregulation. html, accessed 10 April 2007.

Kassler, H. (2002) It's a Dangerous World Out There: Misinformation in the Corporate Universe. In Mintz, A. (Ed.), *Web of Deception: Misinformation on the Internet*, pp. 51–74. CyberAge Books, New York.

Keaveney, S. (1995) Customer switching behavior in service industries: an exploratory study. Journal of Marketing. 59(2), 71–82.

Kotler, P. and Armstrong, G. (2007) *Principles of Marketing.* 12th Edition. Pearson/Prentice Hall, London.

Larson, K. and Czerwinski, M. (1998) Web Page Design: Implications of Memory, Structure and Scent for Information Retrieval. ACM CHI 98 Conference on Human Factors in Computing Systems. Los Angeles, April 21–23.

Marshall, K. P. (1999) Has technology introduced new ethical problems? Journal of Business Ethics. 19(1), 81–90.

Martin, J. and Finkelstein, C. (1981) *Information Engineering.* Savant Institute, UK.

Nielsen, J. (1994) Heuristic Evaluation. In Nielsen, J. and Mack, R. (Eds.), *Usability Inspection Methods*, pp. 25–64. Wiley, New York.

Nielsen, J. (1999) *Designing Web Usability: The Practice of Simplicity.* New Riders Publishing, San Diego, CA.

Nielsen, J. and Tahir, M. (2001) *Homepage Usability: 50 Websites Deconstructed.* New Riders Publishing, San Diego, CA.

Oz, E. (1993) Ethical standards for computer professionals: a comparative analysis of four major codes. Journal of Business Ethics. 12(9), 709–726.

Peattie, K. (1999) Trappings versus substance in the greening of marketing planning. Journal of Strategic Marketing. 7(2), 131–148.

Sharp, H., Rogers, Y. and Preece, J. (2007) *Interaction Design: Beyond Human-Computer Interaction.* 2nd Edition. Wiley, New York.

Shneiderman, B. and Plaisant, C. (2004) *Designing the User Interface: Strategies for Effective Human-Computer Interaction.* Addison-Wesley, London.

Sklar, J. (2006) *Principles of Web Design.* Thomson Learning, London.

Smith, H. J. and Hasnas, J. (1999) Ethics and information systems: the corporate domain. MIS Quarterly. 23(1), 109–127.

Smith, A., Bolton R. and. Wagner, J. (1999) A model of customer satisfaction with service encounters involving failure and recovery. Journal of Marketing Research. 36(3), 356–372.

Wagner, W. and Zubey, M. (2007) *Customer Relationship Management: A People, Process and Technology Approach.* Thomson Course Technology, London.

Whitehouse, C. (2001) Fare and Square. *Time Europe.* 157(10): 49. URL: http://search.ebscohost. com/login.aspx?direct=true&db=aph&AN=4181067&site=ehost-live, accessed 5 April 2007.

Counterfactuals and Hybrid Reasoning
in an Ontology of Law Articles

El Hassan Bezzazi

IREENAT, University of Lille 2, bezzazi@univ-lille2.fr

Abstract   In this paper, we present a formal legal cybercrime ontology using concrete tools. The purpose is to show how law articles and legal cases could be formally defined so that the problem of case resolution is reduced to a classification problem as long as cases are seen as subclasses of articles. Secondly, we show how counterfactual reasoning may be held over it within the framework of Description Logic. Lastly, we investigate the implementation of a hybrid system which is based both on this ontology and on a non-monotonic rule-based system which is used to execute an external ontology dealing with a technical domain in order to clarify some of the technical concepts.

1 Introduction

We investigate in this paper the implementation of a formal ontology for criminal law dealing with cybercrime which is both functional and applicative. Our objective is twofold. First, we wish to present the ontology and an example of counterfactual reasoning it would use for its definition in a less abstract way than usual by using concrete tools. We use Protégé (2007), which is an ontology editor supporting the OWL language, and Racer (2007), which is a reasoning system based on Description Logics. We wish also to depict, in the case of an interdisciplinary collaboration, the clarification of some technical concepts through the use of a non-monotonic inference engine. This clarification brings to the ontology new information that may have consequences in the judge's decision. Having worked on law texts related to computer security, we have chosen cybercrime as a subfield of criminal law as long as it constitutes a relatively small closed field. This paper is structured as follows. In Section 2, we recall some of the basic ideas related to formal ontologies, typically Protégé ontologies, and to Description Logics. In Section 3, the corpus of interest is described and structured into classes. Section 4 is devoted to the reasoning mechanism that allows us to solve a case by identifying the law articles covering it. Issues related to concept fitting are pointed out in Section 5 and a technique to achieve such an operation is presented in Section 6.

2 Formal Ontologies

The use of ontologies in legal domains is an issue which has been intensively investigated (Asaro et al. 2003; Bench-Capon and Visser 1997; Breuker et al. 2002; Valente 1995). A formal ontology describes the concepts and the relations by relating them in a given domain. The relations define the semantics. Building a formal ontology is especially recommended for domains expressed in natural language as documents and corpora. An immediate benefit from the definition of such a formal ontology is the normalization of the semantics materialized by a structured terminology. This normalization is most relevant in the case of an interdisciplinary collaboration, where a given term may carry real ambiguity according to one field or another. Indeed, natural language is characterized by its contextual nature, which may lead to different interpretations. Think, in a forensic context, of how computer data suppression might be understood by a judge with no special knowledge in computer science. Expressing the concepts in a formal language such as OWL helps stabilizing the interpretation of these terms. Besides, expressing a formal ontology in OWL makes it machine-consumable. In computer science, at least three kinds of ontologies are to be distinguished (Sowa 2007). Terminological ontologies, in which concepts are named and structured using mainly relations of the sub-type/super-type kind. As a matter of fact, such an ontology, which is sometimes referred to as taxonomy, can be expressed by using rules as we will further do in the case of the ontology of computer data suppression. Ontologies of the second kind are those in which the concepts are built by enumerating the instances which compose them on the basis of some metric that defines their similarity. These concepts come usually as a result of a classification and are not named beforehand. The third type of ontology is the most sophisticated. The concepts are defined by axioms generally expressed in a decidable fragment of first-order logic, namely Description Logic. Logical inferences can then be implemented for the classification of new instances. Incontestably, Description Logic is currently the standard for expressing formal ontologies on the basis of the OWL language, for example. Efforts are carried out to extend it to a system that would be able to handle knowledge expressed in the form of rules. This way, requests could be sent to existing rule bases within the semantic Web (Eiter et al. 2004). Another advantage that we outline in this extension is the possibility of supplementing a knowledge representation based on Description Logic by a rule-based representation when this is more adequate. The use of rules is all the more relevant when it comes to taking into account certain exceptions which characterize non-monotonic reasoning.

2.1 Classes and Properties

Classes are a concrete representation for concepts. Different classes may be identified for representing a given domain of knowledge. They must afterwards be structured by linking them with relations. These can be subsumption relations or Protégé–OWL relations called properties. Properties are relationships between individuals, and an inverse property may be defined for a given property. Classes are interpreted as sets of individuals of similar structure. These can be organized in subclass–superclass hierarchy. The graphical representation of a hierarchy uses nodes for concepts and arcs for subsumption relations. Concretely, a class is defined by describing the conditions to be satisfied by individuals in order to belong to the class. Note that classes may overlap and can be made explicitly distinct.

2.2 Description Logics

A knowledge base using Description Logic as a knowledge representation tool has two components:

- TBox, which contains the terminology of the domain of interest
- ABox, which contains assertions on individuals named through the defined terminology

The vocabulary is composed of concepts which denote sets of individuals and roles that denote binary relations between individuals. The description language which is specific to each Description Logic system has a well-defined semantic: each TBox or ABox declaration may be identified to a formula of first-order logic or a slight extension of it. Description Logic provides also reasoning tools to decide, for example, if a description is consistent or not, or if it is more general than another. Elementary descriptions are atomic concepts and atomic roles. These allow more complex descriptions to be built with concept constructors. The Description Logic language we shall use is defined by the following assertions where C and D are concepts, A an atomic concept and R a role.

A	Atomic concept
T et $\perp$	Universal concept and empty concept
$\neg C$	Concept negation
$C \cap D$ et $C \cup D$	Concept intersection and union
$\forall R.C$ et $\exists R.C$	Value restriction and limited existential quantification

A formal ontology is defined by a set of structured concepts and a number of inclusions between these concepts. The semantics of the concepts and roles is defined with respect to a domain of interpretation O which defines the interpretation of each constant A: $\iota(A) = a$. Concepts are interpreted as subsets of O and roles are interpreted as binary relations over O satisfying:

$\iota(T) = O, \iota(\perp) = \varnothing$
$\iota(\neg C) = O - \iota(C)$
$\iota(C \cap D) = \iota(C) \cap \iota(D), \iota(C \cup D) = \iota(C) \cup \iota(D)$

$\iota(\forall R.C) = \{d \in O | (d,e) \in \iota(R) \Rightarrow e \in \iota(C)$ for all e in $O\}$
$\iota(\exists R.T) = \{d \in O |$ there exists e in O s.t. $(d,e) \in \iota(R)$ and $e \in \iota(C)\}$

Two frameworks are mainly referred to in practical logics: logic programming and first-order logic. An important difference between these two is the close world assumption (CWA) admitted in the former and the open world assumption (OWA) admitted in the latter. Even if OWL primarily admits OWA, CWA may be admitted if stated explicitly. CWA is very useful for dealing, for example, with the application of forward chaining. If in a rule base, only the rule 'IF offence OR crime THEN infringement' infers the fact infringement, CWA allows inferring that there is no infringement if none of the facts, offence or crime, is established.

3 The Corpus

We list in this section the French criminal law articles that are of interest to us and from which irrelevant metadata has been removed (Légifrance 2007).

Article 323-1: *Fraudulently accessing or remaining within all or part of an automated data processing system is punished by one year's imprisonment and a fine of € 15,000. Where this behaviour causes the suppression or modification of data contained in that system, or any alteration of the functioning of that system, the sentence is two years' imprisonment and a fine of € 30,000.*

Article 323-2: Obstruction or interference with the functioning of an automated data processing system is punished by three years' imprisonment and a fine of € 45,000.

Article 323-3: The fraudulent introduction of data into an automated data processing system or the fraudulent suppression or modification of the data that it contains is punished by three years' imprisonment and a fine of € 45,000.

Article 323-4: The participation in a group or conspiracy established with a view to the preparation of one or more offences set out under articles 323-1 to 323-3, and demonstrated by one or more material actions, is punished by the penalties prescribed for offence in preparation or the one that carries the heaviest penalty.

We shall consider in what follows three concepts (Figs. 1–3): malicious actions which are punished by criminal law, responsibilities related to an action and the criminal law articles. Other classes of our ontology such as Sanction and Infringement are of less interest in what we shall expose.

Several actions may be qualified as being malicious in computer security and put in classes like privacy or hacking which in its turn cover classes like intrusion, denial of service, etc.

The class Malicious_Act depicts a classification for a sample of malicious actions:

Fig. 1. The class of malicious actions   **Fig. 2.** The class of responsibilities

Fig. 3. The class of articles

Criminal law makes a distinction between two types of responsibilities: objective responsibility, which may be commission, omission or attempt, and subjective responsibility, which describes the intentional nature of the action. Of course the classes and subclasses defining these concepts are exclusives.

Criminal law articles which are of interest to us are grouped in the class Articles. As a matter of fact there are so far only six articles that deal directly with cybercrime. Among these, for our purpose, we shall consider in particular four articles. It should be outlined that the conception that we make of a law article makes of it a class which groups all the cases it allows to characterize, that is to say the cases which fall under this article! In this respect, our model is different from that of Asaro et al. (2003). The rationale behind this conceptualization is that the concept of case inherits the same characteristics and properties as the concept of article. Henceforth, the application of our ontology consists in classifying, if possible, each case of interest as a subclass of one or more subclasses of Articles.

Listed in Fig. 4 are some of the relations of interest we shall use here. In particular, between the two classes Articles and Responsibility, the relation has Responsibility specifies the nature of the responsibility handled in the article which may be commission, omission or attempt in the case of objective responsibility or which may be intentional or unintentional in the case of subjective responsibility. For each relation its inverse relation is given. Inverse relations are very useful and enhance the way of expressing axioms as we shall see below.

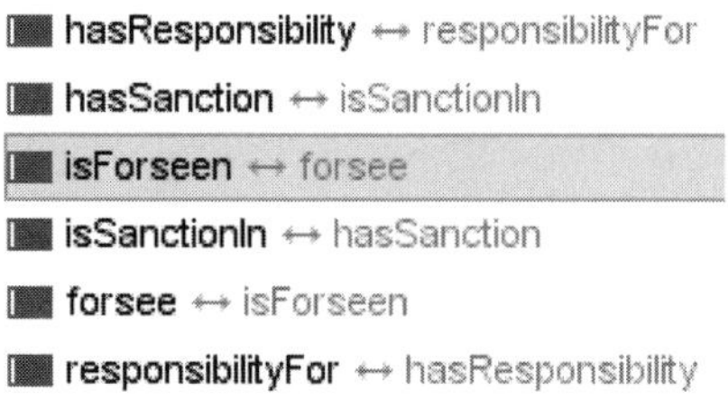

■ hasResponsibility ↔ responsibilityFor

■ hasSanction ↔ isSanctionIn

■ isForseen ↔ forsee

■ isSanctionIn ↔ hasSanction

■ forsee ↔ isForseen

■ responsibilityFor ↔ hasResponsibility

Fig. 4. Ontology properties

4 Using A Reasoner

The possibility of using a reasoner to infer automatically the hierarchy of classes is one of the major advantages in using OWL-DL. Indeed, in the case of important ontologies containing hundreds of classes the use of a reasoner is crucial, in particular when dealing with multiple inheritance. Thus the designer will focus on logical description which is hierarchical, flexible and consequently easy to maintain.

4.1 Articles Conceptualization

Ontologies which are described in OWL-DL may be processed by a reasoner. One of the main tasks handled by a reasoner is to check if a given class is a subclass of another class. Another task is to check consistency, the reasoner can check on the basis of the class conditions if the class may have instances or not. A class which has no instances is inconsistent. Thus a class which is defined to be a subclass of both classes A and B which are disjoint will be detected as inconsistent by the reasoner. Necessary conditions are used to express 'if an object is in this class it necessarily must satisfy these conditions'. A class which uses only necessary conditions is called partial. Necessary and sufficient conditions are used to express 'if an object is in this class it necessarily must satisfy these conditions and if an individual satisfy these conditions then it necessarily belongs to this class'. Such a class is said to be complete and allows a CAW reasoning. All the classes we shall deal with in this paper are complete. The axioms defining the classes Art_323-1, Art_323-2, Art_323-3 and Art_323-4 are shown in Protégé screenshots given in Figs. 5–8.

Several actions may be qualified as being malicious in computer security and put in classes like privacy or hacking which in its turn covers classes like intrusion, denial of service, etc. The class Malicious_Act depicts a classification for a sample of malicious actions. Criminal law makes a distinction between two types of responsibilities: objective responsibility, which may be commission, omission or attempt, and subjective responsibility, which describes the intentional nature of the action.

⬤ Articles
⬒ forsee ∃ intrusion
⬒ hasResponsibility ∃ Commission

Fig. 5. The class Art_323-1

⬤ Articles
⬒ forsee ∃ blocking
⬒ hasResponsibility ∃ Commission

Fig. 6. The class Art_323-2

⬤ Articles
⬒ forsee ∃ (Data_modification ⊔ Data_suppression)
⬒ hasResponsibility ∃ Commission

Fig. 7. The class Art_323-3

⬤ Articles
⬒ forsee ∃ (isForseen ∃ (¬(hasResponsibility ∃ Commission) ⊔ (Art_323-1 ⊔ Art_323-2 ⊔ Art_323-3)))
⬒ hasResponsibility ∃ Attempt

Fig. 8. The class Art_323-4

4.2 Reasoning with Counterfactuals

We are going to depict the expressive power of Description Logics through an example where an assumption is made that contradicts reality. This kind of reasoning is called counterfactual reasoning (Ginsberg 1986). It allows reasoning on abstract facts which are inconsistent with actual facts. From the point of view of logical semantics, a counterfactual is always true. However, in common-sense reasoning the truth value assigned to a counterfactual depends on the meaning it carries and on the current context. In Ginsberg (1986) the author gives an account of counterfactuals in terms of possible worlds initiated by Lewis (1973) and identifies some of the domains where counterfactuals have application such as planning, diagnosis and natural language understanding. In this chapter, we are considering this form of reasoning when writing and using law articles while thinking at the same time of cases to which these articles do apply. Typically, in criminal law, an article describes the conditions for which, if satisfied by a given case, a sanction is entailed. It may also happen that the definition of another article is made by reference to other articles possibly by relaxing or even contradicting some of their conditions. We shall consider in what follows an approach we propose for representing these mental constructions in Description Logics. It is based on the fact that in propositional logics the formula $X \Rightarrow Y$ is equivalent to $\neg X \vee Y$ on the one hand and on the fact that proving a disjunction comes to prove one of its disjuncts. Let B and D be the conditions that characterize a case falling under article A, $A = B \cap D$. On the other hand, article A' is literally defined by requiring instead of B a condition B' and keeping D. B' may contradict B. Of course we could simply write $A' = B' \cap D$, but what we wish to do is to stick as much as possible to the literal expression of the article A', which would not mention D but mentions A as in Art_323-4. We write $A' = B' \cap (B \Rightarrow A)$ to express that A' applies when the case is characterized by B' and if we suppose that B holds (even if it actually does not) the case falls under A. Therefore, we have:

$A' = B' \cap (\neg B \cup A) = B' \cap (\neg B \cup B \cap D) = B' \cap (\neg B \cup D) = B' \cap \neg B \cup B' \cap D$

To prove that a given case C falls under A', one should prove that either $C \subseteq B' \cap \neg B$ or $C \subseteq B' \cap D$. If the ontology definition is made in such a way that it is not possible for the reasoner to infer $C \subseteq B' \cap \neg B$, then the only way to prove $C \subseteq A'$ through the definition of A' is by proving $C \subseteq B' \cap D$.

The key point here is that we have succeeded this way of expressing A', $A' = B' \cap (B \Rightarrow A)$, in a manner which is close to its textual definition by not mentioning D, while proving that a case C falls under A' comes to proving that $C \subseteq B' \cap D$.

For example, solving a case which falls under article Art_323-4 needs, as stated even by this article, to compare the case to articles Art_323-1, Art_323-2 and Art_323-3. Solving the case is made possible by making an assumption in the definition of Art_323-4 which is contrary to what is stated in it. Indeed, think of a case defined by Attempt and Intrusion. To realize that this case falls under article_323-4, one should first assume that in case the responsibility was Commission, then the case would have fallen under Art_323-1. This is a counterfactual reasoning as long as the assumption Commission is contrary to the Attempt responsibility which characterizes the case at hand.

$\exists$forsee.$\exists$isForseen.($\neg$($\exists$hasResponsibility.Commission)$\cup$(Art_323-1$\cup$Art_323-2$\cup$Art_323-3)))

According to the interpretation rules given above, this is to be understood as the class of articles that foresee malicious actions that are foreseen in Art_323-1, Art_323-2 or Art_323-3, by assuming Commission responsibility. Rewritten as:
$\exists$f.$\exists$i.($\neg$C$\cup$(A1$\cup$A2$\cup$A3))

A1, A2 and A3 are the axioms defining the first three articles. A and C stand respectively for articles stating Attempt and Commission responsibility. To isolate within the articles the stated malicious actions from the responsibility, axioms A1, A2, A3 are rewritten as:

A1$\equiv$C$\cap$D1
A2$\equiv$C$\cap$D2
A3$\equiv$C$\cap$D3

On the other hand:

A4 = C$\cap$D4 with

$$D4 = \exists f.\exists i.(\neg C \cup (C \cap D1 \cup C \cap D2 \cup C \cap D3))$$

Thus:

$$\exists f.\exists i.(\neg C \cup (C \cap (D1 \cup D2 \cup D3)))$$

It is easy to prove in propositional logic:

$$\neg C \cup (C \cap X) = \neg C \cup (\neg C \cap X) \cup (C \cap X) = \neg C \cup ((\neg C \cup C) \cap X) = \neg C \cup X$$

Therefore, we have:

$$\exists f.\exists i.(\neg C \cup D1 \cup D2 \cup D3)$$

Note, as we have seen earlier, that we have managed this way to evacuate from Art_323-1, Art_323-2 and Art_323-3 the Commission responsibility to make things consistent. Figure 9 shows the resolution of three cases. Case_1 consists in both system blocking and data modification which have been committed, thanks to multiple inheritance, and Case_2 is a case where an intrusion attempt has been stated. Case_3 is an example of a case that might not be resolved, for example, a case referring to data theft, which does not appear explicitly in the corpus.

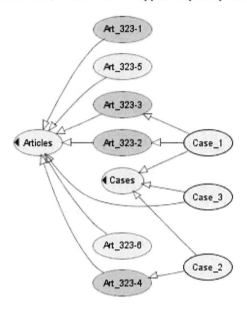

Fig. 9. The inferred hierarchy

5 Fitting Technical Concepts and Legal Concepts

Mismatching between legal concepts and technical concepts constitutes a serious issue (De Lamberterie and Videau 2006). In van Laarschot et al. (2005) the

authors address a similar topic where the issue is about making layman's terminology fit a legal terminology when describing their case. In our case, consider,
for example, computer data suppression happens to be mentioned in some of the
criminal law articles. With no explicit legal definition, this naturally leads the
judge to adopt the natural language definition for suppression. The common understanding of the term suppression is physical suppression where a thing which is
suppressed merely stops existing. However, in the computer world, suppressing
data means very often logical suppression where data could be restored with adequate tools. In addition, even in the case of a physical suppression, computer data
could be restored when a back-up or archiving politic is observed by the data
processor. This semantic difference should be definitely specified because the pe-
nal consequences for fraudulent computer data suppression may vary according to
the possibility of recovering the data. This means that although the action is con-
demnable in both cases, the sanction might be worsened or attenuated depending
on the type of suppression. To make the common understanding of the term suppression fit the effective definition of the term computer data suppression, one
solution consists in 'connecting' its concept in a legal ontology to its concept in a
computer ontology. This connection may need some new concepts and new relations be added to the two already existing ontologies. New concepts may also be
needed to summarize or to extract from the second ontology that information
which is readily of interest for a legal reasoning. For example, in the case we are
dealing with, such new concepts are 'restorable data' and 'unrestorable data'.
These ontological adjustments may prove to be disproportionate in case where the
relevant information is well defined. It is indeed sufficient to compute this information by using a rule-based inference engine. As a matter of fact, the second ontology is principally used to deduce facts rather than for classification.

6 Hybrid Reasoning

In a case where only the subsumption relation is used to deduce relevant facts, it is
sufficient to use the second ontology in a rule-based form within a propositional
logic framework (Fig. 10). However, the inference engine to be used should allow
non-monotonic reasoning if we wish the ontology preserve its structure in this
translation and in the same time manage conflicting facts. The use of defeasible
reasoning in ontology integration is depicted through scenarios in Bassiliades et al.
(2006). We have chosen to use an inference engine based on stratified forward
chaining which, through an adequate backward chaining (Bezzazi 2006), sends
questions to the user to compute which of the facts 'existing data' or 'non-existing
data' holds for the suppressed data. It should be noticed that the concept of legal
suppression and that of computer data suppression both inherit somehow the
French language concept of the term suppression which normally entails the no
more existence of the suppressed object. Indeed, according to the French definition, to suppress something is to be understood as putting an end to the existence
of something.

French_suppression > !Existence
Legal_suppression > French_suppression
Data_suppression > French_suppression.

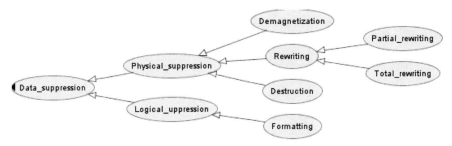

Fig. 10. The taxonomy of data suppression

The translation of this ontology fragment as a rule base yields:

Logical_suppression > Data_suppression
Physical_suppression > Data_suppression
Formatting > Logical_suppression
Destruction > Physical_suppression
Demagnetization > Physical_suppression
Rewriting > Physical_suppression
Partial_rewriting > Rewriting
Total_rewriting > Rewriting

We add a rule which expresses that data which have been logically suppressed may still exist.

Logical_suppression > Existence

If logical suppression is established, the stratified forward chaining will, like an inheritance system with exceptions, give priority to the application of this last rule with respect to the more general rule:

French_suppression > !Existence

Therefore, this rule base should help the lawyer or the judge make their decisions or instruct a case by shedding light on a technical concept lacking a legal definition. The explanation process is done through a question–response procedure.

7 Conclusion

The framework we have presented in this chapter is based on the idea of considering cases as being, by their structure, subclasses of articles. Therefore, the problem of solving a case is the same as that of classifying it. With such a system at work, all one has to do is to implement articles as classes, which should not be a difficult task at least manually. Doing this in a semi-automatic or automatic way constitutes an interesting topic for investigation. On the other hand, we have shown, in a rather practical way, how counterfactual reasoning and non-monotonic reasoning which are naturally used in legal reasoning may be performed in our system. As a matter of fact, the cybercrime ontology and the non-monotonic inference engine are both implemented, but interfacing these to achieve the so-called hybrid reasoning is only projected and further work need to be done on this topic.

References

Asaro, C., Biasiotti, M.A., Guidotti, P., Papini, M., Sagri, M.T., Tiscornia, D.A (2003) Domain Ontology: Italian Crime Ontology, ICAIL 2003 Workshop on Legal Ontologies, Springer Berlin/Heidelberg, Edinburgh, UK.

Bassiliades, N., Antoniou, G. and Vlahavas, I. (2006) A Defeasible Logic Reasoner for the Semantic Web, 2006, International Journal on Semantic Web and Information Systems 2:1.

Bench-Capon, T.J.M. and Visser, P.R.S. (1997) Ontologies in Legal Information Systems: The Need for Explicit Specifications of Domain Conceptualisations. In Proceedings of the Sixth International Conference on AI and Law. ACM Press, New York.

Bezzazi, H. (2006). On some inferences based on stratified forward chaining: an application to e-Government. Proc 15th Intl Conf on Information System Development, Springer Verlag, London.

Breuker, J., Elhag, L., Petkov, E. and Winkels, R. (2002). Ontologies for legal information serving and knowledge management. In Legal Knowledge and Information Systems. Jurix 2002: The Fifteenth Annual Conference. IOS Press, Amsterdam, The Netherlands.

De Lamberterie, I. and Videau, M. (2006). Regards croisés de juristes et d'informaticiens sur la sécurité informatique. In Symposium sur la Sécurité des Technologies de l'Information et des Communications. Rennes, mai-juin.

Eiter, T., Lukasiewicz, T., Schindlauer, R. and Tompits, H. (2004) Combining answer set programming with description logics for the semantic web. In D. Dubois, C Welty, and M.-A. Williams, editors, Proceedings 9th International Conference on Principles of Knowledge Representation and Reasoning, Whistler, British, Columbia, Canada, 141–151. Morgan Kaufmann.

Ginsberg, M.L. (1986) Counterfactuals. Artificial Intelligence 30:35–79.

Légifrance (2007) Retrieved February 4, 2007, from Web site http://www.legifrance.gouv.fr/html/codes_traduits/code_penal_textan.htm

Lewis, D. (1973) Counterfactuals. Harvard University Press, Cambridge.

Protégé (2007) Retrieved February 4, 2007, from Web site http://protege.stanford.edu

Racer (2007) Retrieved February 4, 2007, from Web site http://www.racer-systems.com

Sowa, J.F. (2007) Ontology. Retrieved February 4, 2007, from Web site http://www.jfsowa.com/ontology

Valente, A. (1995) Legal Knowledge Engineering: A Modelling Approach. IOS Press, Amsterdam, The Netherlands.

van Laarschot, R., van Steenbergen, W., Stuckenschmidt, H., Lodder, A. and van Harmelen, F. (2005) The Legal Concepts and the Layman's Terms. Proceedings of the 18th International JURIX conference. IOS Press, Amsterdam, The Netherlands.

Holistic Project Management Guidelines for Information Systems Evaluation

Lorraine Galvin

Waterford Institute of Technology, lgalvin@wit.ie

Abstract This chapter investigates current practice of Information Systems (IS) investment evaluation and proposes holistic guidelines for management. Qualitative research was undertaken through interpretive case studies of three Irish organisations on the evaluation context (life cycle stages, stakeholder and purpose). The guidelines proposed in this chapter include an eight-stage life cycle model, which details the purpose of evaluation, stakeholders' governance, benefits and measures at each stage.

1 Introduction

The past two decades have seen the role of Information System (IS) change, from traditional back-office automation to more strategic roles, resulting from competitive pressure, technological advances that promote greater communication through data networks and reduction in Information Technology (IT) hardware costs (Serafeimidis and Smithson 1999; Farbey et al. 1993; Doherty et al. 2003).

The introduction of new strategic applications saw many organisations investing large amounts in IS, with many resulting in well-publicised failures such as Taurus and the London Ambulance Service (Goulielmos 2003; Drummond 1999). These failures, along with the lack of understanding in measuring strategic benefits, and the rate of technological change have portrayed IS as a high-risk investment. However, in order for organisations to sustain competitive advantage they often must invest in IS; therefore there is a need to control the IS investment and to decrease these uncertainty-associated project failures. Reports from projects such as Year 2000, the Euro conversion, Pulse and the Credit Unions financial system showed that better project management could result in a decrease in project overruns and failures (Naughton 2004; Mangan and Stahl 2002). The high level of IS failures saw an increased activity in the research of this field (Remenyi et al. 2000; Farbey et al. 1999).

Despite this increased activity, Serafeimidis and Smithson (1999) note that the focus of evaluation, influenced by the financial paradigms, has generally been too narrow, concentrating only on tangible benefits and measurement with little attention

paid to organisational impacts. Silvius (2004) observed that this traditional financial perspective is only suitable for cost-saving investments and that the changing
role of IS has to be reflected in the way investments are evaluated. Serafeimidis
and Smithson (1999) support this perspective and propose that the organisational
context must be incorporated into the evaluation process.

This chapter examines the organisational elements of evaluation in practice,
interpreting evidence from three case studies. The discussion section presents
management guidelines on the evaluation of IS investments, which were consolidated from practice and current evaluation models. Section 5 outlines the main research findings and theoretical contributions.

2 Issues in the Organisational Context of Evaluation

Many authors have reported the narrow focus on the evaluation content and the
neglect of the organisational context. This section considers the main issues of the
evaluation context, which are examined in the case studies. The context of evaluation has been described as the purpose of evaluation, the stages of evaluation and
the stakeholders involved (Nijland 2004; Farbey et al. 1999; Remenyi 1999;
Serafeimidis and Smithson 1999).

Farbey et al. (1999) note that organisations are often unsure of the purposes of
evaluation, with most evaluations taking place before the system is implemented
(ex ante) to justify the investment, using financial measures. Where evaluation
only takes place as a financial activity, the organisational elements that are affected by the investment are not managed (Serafeimidis and Smithson 1999).
Evaluation should not be considered as an isolated activity, but an organisational
activity that can facilitate decision making, change management, organisational
learning, benefit realisation and maintain stakeholder interest (Remenyi 1999;
Al-Shehab et al. 2004; Nijland 2004).

Abma (2000) and Remenyi (1999) describe evaluation as a social system incorporating different stakeholder groups with different roles, interests, attitudes
and assumptions that often resulted in conflict. Many IS investments failures were
not related to the technical development of the system, but rather the social and
culture variables as stakeholders were often not involved in the decision-making
process and therefore lacked understanding of the system (Remenyi et al. 2000;
Serafeimidis and Smithson 1999).

Many researchers (e.g. Serafeimidis and Smithson 1999; Eason 1998; Ashurst
and Doherty 2003) have observed that organisations are unsure of the stages of
evaluation in the project life cycle and those that do evaluate use life cycle models
that are only suitable for the technical development of the system, which lacks organisational considerations and project management. Organisations seldom evaluate at other stages, as they perceive the time and cost involved too great. However,
without continuous evaluation across the project life cycle, change cannot be managed, stakeholders are not kept informed and many unexpected and unplanned
benefits that may arise are not identified (Remenyi et al. 2000; Farbey et al. 1999).

Various authors have developed evaluation life cycle models which incorporate ideas of stakeholder involvement, change and benefits management. These include Active Benefit Realisation (Remenyi 2000), IT Evaluation Life Cycle (Willcocks and Lester 1997), Decision Making (Hogbin and Thomas 1994) and and the Evaluation Life Cycle (Farbey et al. 1999).

Researchers (Deschoolmeester et al. 2004; Iraniet al. 2002; Serafeimidis and Smithson 1999; Farbey et al. 1999; Galliers and Leidner 1995) have called for a more holistic project management approach to evaluation that considers the organisational setting. Serafeimidis and Smithson (1999) suggest that guidelines and models for management must address these organisational issues through a holistic project management approach. Frisk and Planten (2004) support this suggestion and note that there is a need for research to improve current methods and models. Deschoslmeester et al. (2004) suggest that managers should receive a more knowledge-based education helping them to find out the combinations of IS evaluation techniques that can be put together in a more practical and holistic framework. Ballentine and Stray (1999) found that although organisations evaluate IS investments, few had formal procedures in place. Farbey et al. (1999) note that poor evaluation procedures restrict project selection, control and benefit realisation and that although much literature has focused on the problem of IS evaluation, few have provided guidelines for managers who wish to address the problem.

The main aim of this chapter, therefore, is to address the need for a practical holistic evaluation approach through the development of management guidelines. Such guidelines should incorporate the contextual aspects of evaluation in an attempt to overcome previous neglect and insufficient understanding of these issues.

3 Case Studies

This section reports a study of three organisations on the organisational context of evaluation that attempted to address the need for more holistic developments in practice. The qualitative approach adopted for this study allowed the contextual aspects of evaluation to be analysed and interpreted. Case studies therefore enabled in-depth research into the organisation practices in a natural setting (Denzin and Lincoln 2005; Patton 2001).

Organisations selected for this study were targeted using Patton's (2001) purposive sampling strategy, which specifies certain criteria to be used for the sample frame. The principle criterion for the selection of cases was the organisational expertise on IS evaluation that contributed both to the theoretical and practical aspects of this research. Organisations selected were also Irish indigenous, in the private sector, medium to large sized and had previously developed IS systems. The private sector was selected for research originality as Bannister (2001) had conducted a similar study of the public sector in Ireland.

During the study, four interviews in each organisation took place. In the Voluntary Health Insurance (VHI), the IT manager, business area manager and senior managers (2) were interviewed. In the Bank of Ireland (BOI), the IT manager, finance manager and senior managers (2) were interviewed. In Celtic Linen, the IT manager, finance manager, executive director and a business area manager were interviewed. The interviews were structured in nature, using a framework of questions based on the research issues identified. For each stage of the project life cycle, the following questions were asked:

What do you consider the purposes of evaluation to be at this stage?
What benefits (tangible/intangible) do you measure?
What techniques do you use to evaluate?
Who is involved in the evaluation?

These questions were designed to allow the natural progression along the evaluation life cycle to be interpreted, enabling a holistic understanding. Evidence in the form of methodology documentation, templates and standards were also collected and were particularly applicable in the development of project management guidelines.

For each case study, background information is initially provided, followed by an overview of their evaluation practices.

3.1 Voluntary Health Insurance

VHI Healthcare is Ireland's largest provider of healthcare services, with an 80% share of the Irish private health insurance market and over 1.55 million members representing 40% of the Irish population (VHI 2005).

The Executive Management Committee (EMC) in VHI developed a central Programme Office (PO), which provides project management support through project management procedures, project life cycles, standards and templates. The primary objective of the PO is to develop good project management practices through providing a framework for new projects on all stages of the project life cycle, ensuring consistent planning and control by supporting a reporting mechanism.

The VHI have developed a five-stage project life cycle model, which is based on good practice project management. The PO provides support on these stages in the form of detailed descriptions of each stage, report structures and the roles and responsibilities involved. The stages include the initial project proposal, a detailed business case, planning the project, running the project and closing/reviewing the project.

3.2 Bank of Ireland

Bank of Ireland (BOI) is a diversified Financial Services group and employs over 17,000 personnel in eight countries worldwide. Established in 1783, BOI is the largest Irish bank by total assets and the highest rated Irish listed financial institution, with a gross profit of €676 million in the first half of 2004 (Bank of Ireland 2005).

The Office of the Chief Information Officer (OCIO) in conjunction with the finance committee, operational risk unit, informational security unit and regulatory/compliance unit, developed the methodology and the supporting documentation templates, standards and criteria for the evaluation of investments in BOI.

The methodology includes the programme governance structure where the roles and responsibilities of the management stakeholders are defined, and a life-cycle approach to the tracking of objectives, benefits, costs, risks and issues. The methodology is owned at a centralised level in the organisation, not under the direct management of any particular function.

BOI evaluation methodology includes seven life cycle stages: feasibility, business case, development, testing, project closure review, operations and maintenance and system retirement.

3.3 Celtic

Celtic Laundry is a family-owned business (Scallan family) established in 1925, now known as the Celtic Group which encompasses three separate businesses: Celtic Linen, Trepan Hawke and Morris IT. Celtic Linen provides goods and services to the non-consumer market: hospitality, healthcare and industrial/commercial/education sectors (Celtic Linen 2005). Celtic is the largest family-owned business in the linen and garment rental sector. Its turnover was €26 million in 2003 and it employs 481 staff.

Celtic Linen's evaluation procedures include stages where evaluation takes place with identified stakeholders, benefits and measures. These stages include the project proposal stage, the business case stage, the development stage, the testing stage, the ex post stage, the maintenance stage and the end of system life stage.

The findings uncovered from these three case studies are now explored through practical and theoretical implications. Section 4 presents guidelines for the management of IS evaluation drawn from the case study findings and contributes the practical implications of this study. Section 5 analyses the findings under the main research issues and contributes the theoretical implications.

4 Discussion

Numerous authors (Deschoolmeester et al. 2004; Farbey et al. 1999; Frisk and Planten 2004; Serafeimidis and Smithson 1999; Ballentine and Stray 1999) have called for the need to develop holistic evaluation guidelines. The proposed guidelines in this chapter are based on good practice consolidated from the case studies and existing evaluation life cycle models. The aim of these guidelines is to provide a holistic approach to project management by focusing on the organisational context and content of evaluation. An evaluation life cycle model for the project management is presented and details the purpose of evaluation, stakeholders' governance and benefits and measures at each stage of the life cycle.

Both summative and formative evaluations are incorporated in these guidelines. Summative evaluations assess the impact of the investment and are used at stages of decision making to provide a yes/no answer. Formative evaluations take place throughout the life cycle and promote organisational learning, change management, benefit realisation, decision making and stakeholder participation through the continuous formulation of project objectives. Organisational learning is facilitated through the evaluation results, which indicate changes required and keep stakeholder informed on the project progress. Changes to the benefits of the investment are managed through benefits realisation, where the expected benefits are continuously assessed. Stakeholders are involved in the life cycle stages and develop an understanding of the project objectives, maintaining their interest and minimising conflict.

4.1 Evaluation Life Cycle Model for Project Management

The Evaluation Life Cycle Model for Project Management (Fig. 1) aims to provide an understandable and holistic approach to the evaluation of IS investments. The model defines eight stages of evaluation along the project life cycle and indicates the stakeholder involved at each stage through lettered circle (note: please refer to key stakeholder grid for stakeholder groups and corresponding lettering). The stages are consecutive, but also include feedback loops where changes identified in the evaluation results can be managed.

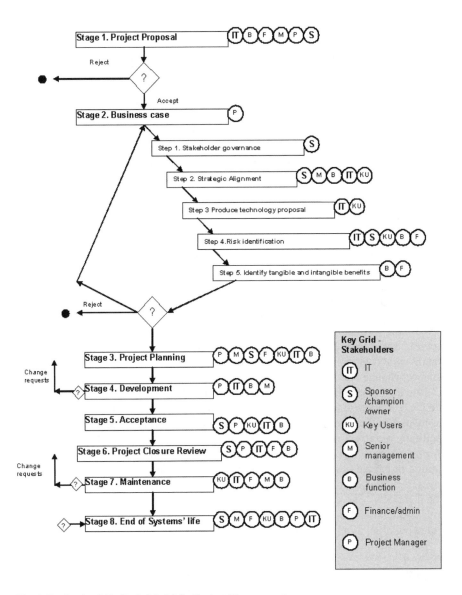

Fig. 1. Evaluation Life Cycle Model for Project Management

5 Conclusion

Deschoolmeester et al. (2004), Irani et al. (2002), Serafeimidis and Smithson (1999), Farbey et al. (1999) and Galliers and Leidner (2003) identified the need for the organisational context to be incorporated into the evaluation of IT/IS investment and to provide a holistic project management approach. This chapter examined the context (purpose, life cycle stages and stakeholders) of evaluation in three Irish organisations and found the following theoretical implications.

The literature categorises the purposes of evaluation into ex ante (before implementation) and ex post (after implementation) or formative and summative (Remenyi 2000; Walsham 1993). This study found that evaluations in all organisations were both summative and formative. The summative evaluations only occurred at proposal and business case stages, where high-level management made the decision. Formative evaluations occurred more often and in a more formalised approach when the methodology was defined and managed where they occurred continuously throughout the life cycle and used to promote a culture of stakeholder participation, change management, benefit realisation learning and decision making.

Researchers have stressed that evaluation should not be considered an isolated activity, but an organisational activity (Huang and Trevisan 2003; Willcocks 1996). This study found that evaluation tends to be more an organisational activity when it is decentralised and where a formal methodology (life cycle, templates, standards and guidelines) exists that supports decision making, stakeholder governance, change management, benefit realisation and organisational learning.

Previous research indicated that organisations that do evaluate concentrate on life cycle models that are only suitable for the development of the system and not evaluation, which lack elements of control and monitoring of benefits and do not facilitate organisational learning and feedback (Ashurst and Doherty 2003). During the research it was uncovered that the size and resources of the organisations impacted whether they either researched good practice in evaluation or developed their own life cycle models, to overcome the difficulties of using traditional models. The two largest organisations (VHI and BOI) had the resources, both financial and personnel, to develop such models and research best practice, whereas Celtic, as a family-run organisation, did not.

Many authors have noted a need for a continuous evaluation approach (Byrd et al. 2005; Gregory and Jackson 1991; Small and Chen 1995; Willcocks 1996).Whereas all organisations defined continuous stages of evaluation in this study, the degree to which they continuously evaluated related to the project/programme management. The two largest organisations (VHI and BOI) had specific project management levels for monitoring the evaluation methodology, whereas Celtics projects are managed at a centralised management level that oversee all business processes and may not implement all stages due to constraints.

Previous research indicates that more subjective evaluations are conducted at the proposal stage, where decisions are made on 'gut' (Farbey et al. 1999; Nijland 2004). This study found that the degree of subjectivity varies with the data the decisions are based on and the level of authority needed to make decision. The least subjective decisions were made where objective quantitative and qualitative data were used and when the executive management committee made the decision.

Research has shown that ex ante evaluations are most common, especially the business case (Serafeimidis and Smithson 1999). This study found that business case evaluations were common with decisions made at a centralised management level on the requirements, strategic alignment, benefits, risks, costs and technology options.

Research has shown that evaluation is rarely implemented during the development stage (Serafeimidis and Smithson 1999; Nijland 2004; Beyon-Davies et al. 2004). The findings of the study indicate, however, that evaluation did take place at the development stage and was used to monitor and control the project progress and manage change. More advanced practices also evaluate the 'readiness' of the organisation to accept the system at this stage.

Usability testing has increased over the last decade (Pressman 2000; Hughes and Cottrell 2002). The findings in this research support previous research, as usability testing was common to all three case studies, matching the business objectives against the functionality of the system.

Research indicates that ex post evaluations are not carried out as much as they should be (Nijland 2004; Willcocks 1996). This study found that evaluation at this stage relates to the governance of the project review process, where evaluation is more likely to occur when there is clear responsibility for the process. Activities include lesson-learnt exercises, benefit realisation and a project closure process. When evaluations did not occur, time constraints were cited as the reason.

Costs and change management should be evaluated at the maintenance stage as the majority of costs incur here (Pressman 2000; Hughes and Cotterell 1999; Fitzgerald 1998). The findings of the research suggest that no specific practices were defined in the evaluation methodology for maintenance, as once the project was closed, maintenance becomes a business function with the IT department implementing minor changes with any major changes resulting in a new project/programme.

Numerous authors (Farbey et al., 1999; Deschoolmeester et al. 2004; Frisk and Planten 2004; Serafeimidis and Smithson 1999; Ballentine and Stray 1999) have called for the need to develop holistic IS evaluation guidelines. Farbey et al. (1999) noted that although much literature has focused on IS evaluation, little has provided guidelines for managers who wish to address this problem. Serafeimidis and Smithson (1999) suggest that guidelines and models for management must address organisational issues through a holistic project management approach. This chapter addressed the need to develop IS evaluation guidelines that focused on the organisational context in a holistic project management approach. The three case studies presented in this study along with existing evaluation models were used to collect expertise on IS evaluation.

The Evaluation Life Cycle Model for Project Management proposed aims to provide an understandable and holistic approach to the evaluation of IS investments. The model defines eight stages of evaluation and indicates the stakeholders involved at each stage. Flow arrows also indicate the progression of evaluation along the project life cycle, which includes feedback loops based on the evaluation results. A detailed description of each stage is provided and includes an explanation of the purpose of evaluation, stakeholders involved and the benefits and measures.

It is hoped that these guidelines provide project managers with an effective methodology to evaluate IS investments. An analysis of current good practice and an evaluation of life cycle models were used to formulate these guidelines and to include all elements required for a holistic methodology. Current models provide consistency across all stages and do not provide the same level of detail, with regard to stakeholders' governance as the proposed Evaluation Life Cycle Model for Project Management in this chapter.

Further research should test and validate the management guidelines proposed in this chapter. More conclusive selections of benefits and measures could also be applied to these guidelines pending testing. Furthermore, research into the relationship between different investment types (infrastructure, transactional, informational and strategic) and the need for evaluation could contribute valuable observations on IS portfolio management.

References

Abma, T.A. (2000) 'Dynamic Inquiry Relationships: ways of creating, sustaining and improving the inquiry process through recognition and management of conflicts', *Journal of Qualitative Inquiry*, 6(1): 133–151.

Al-Shehab, A.J., Hughes, R. and Winstanley, G. (2004) 'Using Causal mapping methods to identify and analyse risk in information system projects as a post-evaluation process', in D. Remenyi (ed.) *Proceedings of the 11th European Conference on IT Evaluation*, Amsterdam, The Netherlands, pp. 9–16.

Ashurst, C. and Doherty, N. (2003) 'Towards the Formulation of a 'Best Practice' Framework for Benefits Realisation in IT Projects' [Online] Available from: http://www.ejise.com/volume6-issue2/issue2-art1.htm [Accessed 5 June 2004].

Ballentine, J. and Stray, S.J. (1999) 'Information Systems and other capital investment: evaluation practices compared', *Journal of Logistics Information Management*, 12(1): 78–93.

Bank of Ireland (2005) *Company Information* [Online] http://www.bankofireland.ie/html/gws/about_us/about_the_group/company_overview/index.html [Accessed 16 June 2005].

Bannister, F (2001) 'Citizen Centricity: A Model of IS Value in Public Administration', *Electronic Journal of Information systems Evaluation*, 5(2).

Beyon-Davies, P., Owens, P. and Williams, M. (2004) 'Information Systems evaluation and the information systems development process'. *Journal of Enterprise Information Management*, 17(4): 276–282.

Byrd, T.A., Thrasher, E., Lang, T. and Davidson, N.W. (2005) 'A process orientated perspective of IS success: examining the impact of IS on operational cost', *The International Journal of Management Science*, 34(5): 448–460.

Celtic Linen (2005) *Market Analysis Report* 2005.

Denzin, N. and Lincoln, Y. (2005) *The SAGE Handbook of Qualitative Research* (3rd ed.). New York: Sage.

Deschoolmeester, D., Braet, O. and Willaert, P. (2004) 'On a balanced methodology to evaluate a portfolio of IT investments' in D. Remenyi (ed.) *Proceedings of 11th European Conference on IT evaluation proceedings*, pp. 115–126.

Doherty, N. King, M. and Al-Mushayt, O. (2003) 'The Impact of inadequacies in the treatment of organisational issues on Information Systems Development projects', *Journal of Information and Management*, 41: 49–62.

Drummond, H. (1999) 'Are we any closer to the end? Escalation and the case of Taurus', *Journal of Project Management*, 17(1): 11–16.

Eason, L. (1998) *Information Technology and Organisational Change*. London: Taylor & Francis.

Farbey, B., Land, F. and Targett, D. (1993) How *to Assess Your IT Investment: A Study of Methods and Practice*. Oxford: Butterworth-Heinemann.

Fitzgerald, B. (1998) 'Executive Information Systems without Executives', in D. Avison and D. Edgar-Nevill (eds.) Matching Technology with Organisational Needs, *Proceedings of Third Conference of the UK Academy for Information System*s, Lincoln University, UK, McGraw-Hill, pp. 298.

Frisk, E. and Planten, A. (2004) 'IT Investment Evaluation – A survey amongst managers in Sweden', in D. Remenyi (ed.) *Proceedings of the 11th European Conference on IT Evaluation*, Amsterdam, The Netherlands, pp.145–154.

Galliers, R. and Leidner, D.E. (2003) *Strategic Information Management: Challenges and Strategies in managing Information Systems*. Boston, MA: Butterworth-Heinemann.

Goulielmos, M. (2003) 'Outlining organisational failure in information systems development', *Disaster Prevention and Management: An International Journal*, 12(4): 319–327.

Gregory, A.J. and Jackson, M.C. (1991) 'Evaluating organizations: a systems and contingency approach', *Systems Practice*, 5(1): 37–60.

Hogbin, G. and Thomas, D. (1994) *Investing in Information Technology – Managing the Decision Making Process.*, London: McGraw-Hill.

Huang, Y.M. and Trevisan, M.S. (2003) 'Evaluability assessment: a primer', *Practical Assessment, Research & Evaluation*, 8(20).

Hughes, B and Cotterell, M. (2002) *Software Project Management* (3rd ed.). London: McGraw-Hill.

Irani, Z., Sharif, A.M., Love, P.E.D. and Kahrarman, C. (2002) 'Applying Concepts of Fuzzy Cognitive Mapping to Model the IT/IS Investment Evaluation Process', *International Journal of Production Economics*, 75(1): 199–211.

Mangan, A. and Stahl, B.C. (2002) 'Who is responsible for ISIS? The Irish Credit Unions Problem of Introducing a Standardised Information System' in R. Hackney (ed.) *Business Information Technology Management: Semantic Futures*. Manchester: Manchester Metropolitan University Business School, Manchester, UK.

Naughton, E. (2004) 'Room for better project management' [Online] Available from: http://www.projectmanagement.ie [Accessed 21 January 2005].

Nijland, M. (2004) '*Understanding the use of IT evaluation methods in organisations'*, Ph.D. thesis, University of London.

Patton, M.Q. (2001) *Qualitative Evaluation and Research Methods* (3rd ed.). Newbury Park, CA: Sage.

Pressman, R. (2000) *Software Engineering: A Practioners Approach*. London: McGraw-Hill.

Remenyi, D. (1999) *IT Investment Making a Business Case*. Oxford: Butterworth-Heineman.

Remenyi, D., Money, A. and Sherwood-Smith, M. (2000) *The Effective Measurement and Management of IT Costs and Benefits* (2nd ed.). Oxford: Butterworth-Heinemann.

Serafeimidis, V. and Smithson, S. (1999) 'Rethinking the approaches to information systems investment evaluation', *Logistics Information Management*, 12: 94–107.

Silvius, A.J. (2004) 'ROI Doesn't Matter: Insights in the True Business Value of IT' in D. Remenyi (ed.) *Proceedings of the 11th Conference on IT Evaluation*, Amsterdam, The Netherlands.

Small, M.H. and Chen, J. (1995)'Investment justification of advanced manufacturing technologies: an empirical analysis', *Journal of Engineering and Technology Management*, 12(1): 27–55.

Walsham (1993) *Interpreting Information Systems in Organisations.* Chichester: Wiley.

Willcocks, L.P. and Lester, S. (1997) 'In search of information technology productivity. Assessment issues', *Journal of the Operational Research Society*, 48(11): 1082–1094.

VHI (2005) http://www.vhi.ie/about/index.jsp [Accessed 24 June 2005] About page.

ORE: A Framework to Measure Organizational Risk During Information Systems Evolution

Aditya Agrawal, Gavin Finnie and Padmanabhan Krishnan

Bond University, School of Information Technology, {gfinnie,pkrishna}@bond.edu.au

Abstract Information systems (IS) change initiatives often represent the single largest investment (and therefore risk) for large corporations, yet there exist few management frameworks in the literature to help decision makers measure organizational risk in a balanced manner during this organization-wide change process. The ORE framework has been developed as a design science artifact based on the Leavitt diamond paradigm as a multi-criteria, relative risk, condition consequence, management decision framework enabling decision makers to calculate and compare risk evolution at fixed points of the change cycle and make structured and balanced risk mitigation decisions. In this chapter the principles, architecture and elements of ORE are described.

1 Introduction

Information systems are a vital part of corporate operations, tactics, and strategy, and are often critical to business competitive advantage (Klaus et al. 2000). With any change in process or systems there are always associated risks and information system evolution projects are often the largest corporate-wide change projects. Hence their failure can seriously impact the continued survival of the corporation (Sumner 2000). Sixty-seven percent of enterprise application initiatives can be considered negative or unsuccessful (Davenport 1998). However, software process change is inevitable and should ideally be based on quantitative software measurement programs (Offen and Jeffery 1997). Yet most organizations do not have formal risk assessment methodologies and metrics to help management measure the change in risk as the organization evolves (Dedolph 2003). One of the reasons for lack of management use of formal methods is that few models directly address the ultimate purpose of metrics, which is to provide managers causal support for improved decision making (Fenton et al. 2007).

There are two approaches to addressing this shortcoming. The first is to develop a framework where absolute risk and its impact are measured. It is easy to use a framework where absolute risk is measured qualitatively (e.g., three levels such as high, moderate, and low). However, such a framework has limited applicability as the qualitative risk is always high. One can also measure absolute risk

C. Barry et al. (eds.), *Information Systems Development: Challenges in Practice, Theory, and Education, Vol.2*, doi: 10.1007/978-0-387-78578-3_7,
© Springer Science+Business Media, LLC 2009

and impact in financial terms, but developing accurate absolute risk measures is a time-consuming and difficult process. This is because one needs to estimate the events that are risky, the probability of each event actually occurring and the impact (cost) of the event when it eventuates. From a change management or system evolution point of view an early quantitative indicator of potential risk and its evolution is useful (Nogueira 2000). Nair (2006) identifies the three main estimation methodologies as Analogy, Top-Down and Bottom-Up. Analogy uses historical date to estimate current measurements; Bottom-Up combines individual component estimations to compute overall estimations, while Top-Down emphasizes overall estimations and ignores low-level individual components estimations.

The Project Management Institute's (PMI) Guide to the Project Management Body of Knowledge (Project Management Institute 2000) defines risk management as "the systematic process of identifying, analyzing, and responding to project risk with the aim of minimizing the probability and consequences of adverse events to project objectives." Curtis (1989) explains how software systems needed to be analyzed in their broader organizational context. Technical metrics such as Function Points, Halstead's measures, and McCabe metrics for cyclomatic complexity etc. were developed to measure and analyze different artifacts in the software development process. However, risk management of individual software development/ evolution projects are only a small part of the overall risk in enterprise-wide systems evolution (Keene 1981). Chang (2004) uses an open-ended Delphi-type survey to capture two main categories of information system implementation issues as lack of incorporation of organizational context and reluctance to accept dissenting views. Enterprise-wide risk evaluation therefore requires both individual project-specific and organizational-wide factors to avoid change, which is a technical success but an organizational failure. The Leavitt diamond (Leavitt 1965) provides a balanced organizing paradigm for consideration of all major organizational aspects during corporate change. It identifies the main dimensions as Task, Technology, Structure, and People. For technology-based organizational change Sawy (2001) proposes a translation of these dimensions as business processes, organizational form, information technology usage, and human resources.

For technical risk Higuera and Haimes (1996) describe a taxonomy-based approach to risk identification. Possible risks are categorized into Product Engineering, Development Environment, and Program Constraints. Each category contains a list of factors and an associated questionnaire as guidance for risk elicitation. The taxonomy-based approach provides an empirical referential structure enabling the risk assessment team to quickly and comprehensively survey and choose the risks (and weight them) most relevant to their organizational domain. The software development, evolution, and deployment phenomenon itself is considered as an n-dimensional space where each dimension is a relevant risk-causing element to the successful completion of the project (Gluch 1994). At any point in time the state of the system is thus expressed as a point in space with values relating to each risk dimension. This enables management to assess whether the state is desirable/undesirable and how the state might change and take corrective measures as necessary. This methodology emphasizes a relative risk, condition consequence approach to risk identification and measurement (away from root cause analysis) enabling decision making-oriented measurement.

The approaches described provide important guidance in developing a risk measurement framework. The Organization Risk Evaluation (ORE) framework has been developed to provide a quantitative measure of risk and support development of a risk scale calibrated to the organizational specifics which allows management to compare risk evolution versus system evolution and make strategic risk mitigation decisions. Based on PMI guidelines, ORE has been designed to support a structured approach to risk measurement that helps to manage change complexity and can be used throughout the evolution life cycle. All three estimation methodologies have been reflected in the ORE architecture. It supports an organizational condition consequence approach by viewing the organizational system risk at a point in time due to contributions by metrics that are part of all four Leavitt organizational dimensions and by emphasizing cause and effect relationships in assessing risk evolution. Balance and measurement of all organizational dimensions are considered within the metrics and architecture of ORE, combining judgment and measurement.

Two paradigms characterize much of IS research, behavioral science, and design science. In design science, knowledge and understanding of the problem domain and its solution are achieved in the building and application of the designed artifact. IS research is therefore concerned with the development of behavioral theories and design artifacts to add to the knowledge base, and application studies to the environment to test and refine the knowledge base (Hevner et al. 2004). A new information system is a complex political and social game (Keene 1981) where the context is critical and it is difficult to isolate the impact of a small number of variables due to highly complex interactions. Hence interpretative research methods (Skok and Legge 2001) are relevant. They need to be combined with traditional software engineering risk identification and measurement techniques to enable measurement of organizational risk.

ORE has been developed as a design science model whose purpose is to enable risk measurement during information systems evolution. It is a multi-criteria, relative risk, condition consequence framework that can be applied at comparable times in various aspects of information system development, deployment, and change. The time granularity of framework application is user-definable, allowing multiple applications of ORE during the same system evolutionary phase, which is flexibility missing in most risk assessment methodologies.

This chapter is organized as follows. Section 2 provides an overview of the ORE architecture and its organizational decision-making model. ORE is formally defined in Section 3 and the constituent elements are described in Section 4. Section 5 concludes the chapter and describes further avenues of work.

2 ORE Framework Overview

The ORE framework has a multilevel architectural design based on a set of core principles and a hierarchical organizational decision-making model that enables effective use in management decision making. ORE supports both buy and build approaches to information systems evolution. Figure 1 illustrates the framework architecture.

The typical levels of decision making in an organization can be divided as operations, tactics, and strategy (Emery and Trist 1965). ORE provides support for all three levels of decision making. Based on the principle of divide and conquer, a corporate-wide evolution project would be broken into management wrappers named technical subprojects. Using the principle of separation of concerns (Torsten and Guido 1997) three levels of management would look after the operational, tactical, and strategic dimensions of the evolution respectively.

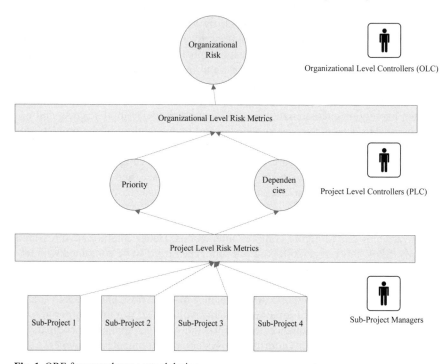

Fig. 1. ORE framework conceptual design

The technical subproject managers would use ORE subproject factors (and associated metrics) to measure operational concerns across all organizational dimensions using a balanced Leavitt diamond-based approach. At the tactical level, the Project Level Controllers (PLCs) would use the risk assessments from all subprojects to assess the progress of the corporate project. In a typical organization, the PLC would be the business heads of all the functional departments affected by the change. The PLC would make tactical resource allocations decisions and smooth communication flows between and within project teams. Their judgment of progress would flow to the Organizational Level Controller (OLC) who typically would be a team of executives. Based on their understanding of business objectives the OLC would set and revise project dependencies and priorities and establish the strategic direction of the systems change.

The ORE methodology is based on the paradigm of fixed time sampling in a cyclic process as illustrated in Fig. 2. ORE is designed to support the constant change (Volker and Rohde 1995) by allowing organizational decision makers to measure risk at certain comparable points in time such as the inception phase of each change cycle (this aspect is defined formally in Section 3). More importantly, ORE allows application multiple times within the same evolutionary phase. Hence the time granularity of ORE application is flexible. ORE timestamps each risk assessment and uses them to build a self-referential risk scale that is fully customized to the organizational specifics and can be credibly used to measure and compare organizational risk at later comparable times. The results of the analysis can be used to make risk mitigation decisions thus providing structure to an evolving and changing world.

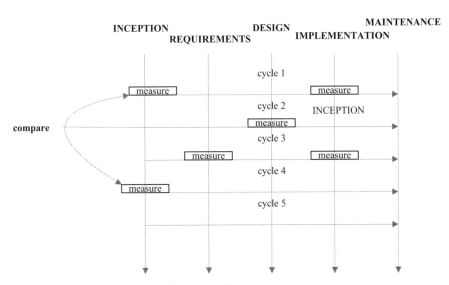

Fig. 2. ORE allows fixed time sampling in a cyclic process

3 Formal Definitions of ORE

The design science framework defined in Hevner et al. (2004) and the representational theory of measurement (Roberts 1979) is used to define the ORE framework as a design science artifact and facilitate real-world comprehension of the measures developed.

This work produces a viable model (ORE) which provides utility in understanding and measuring organizational risk during information systems evolution. The process described in the chapter essentially involves building a framework (the artifact) based on past research using a measurement theoretic definition and providing heuristic guidance for its application and validation.

The ORE methodology of risk computation involves identifying a set of factors F with members $F_1 \ldots F_n$, assuming fixed weights $\omega_1 \ldots \omega_n$ for each factor. For each factor F_i identify a set of metrics M_i consisting of metrics $M_{i_1} \ldots M_{i_n}$. At any given time t, only a subset of F may be relevant, say F^t. Further, the contribution to a factor $F_i \in F^t$ at time t may only be a subset of M_i, say M_i^t. The risk value due to factor F_i at time t can be denoted as $\sum_{M_i \in M_i'} M_i(t)$. Thus organizational risk value at time t is $\sum_{F_i \in F'} \omega_i * F_i(t)$. Two organizational risk measures at times t_1 and t_2 are comparable if $F^{t_1} = F^{t_2}$, and for every $F_i \in F^{t_1}$, $M_i^{t_1} = M_i^{t_2}$, that is the set of factors and metrics are the same.

Complete measurement-theoretical and design science formal definitions of ORE as well as proposed framework validations are described in the ORE Technical Report which is available at http://shakti.it.bond.edu.au/~sand/csa0702.pdf. They are omitted from here due to space limitations. Design, however, is both a process and a product. It describes the world as acted upon (artifact) and as sensed (process). Hence we have included the formal methodology definition to enable essential comprehension of the ORE design.

4 ORE Components: Subproject Risk Assessment

A subproject is a management wrapper with specific technical objectives. ORE defines a balanced set of factors to measure technical, process, organizational form, and people issues during subproject evolution which are described in Sections4.1–4.10. Different subsets of these factors or metrics may be chosen for specific subprojects based on whether a buy or build approach to information systems has been undertaken, organizational specifics, etc. In the following subsections each factor is described using the notation: Factor $= \sum_{i \in I} f_i * w_i$

The contribution of each factor is calculated as a weighted sum of the various metrics for that factor indicated by an index set I. Only the elements of I, viz. the set of metrics is stated.

4.1 Technology Change

The use of new technologies in a company has been observed to be an important and recurring problem in the industry (Tatikonda and Rosenthal 2000). Measuring the effect of technology change requires consideration of the amount of technological change in the product (or service), the amount of process change this entails, and the interdependence and integration of the new technologies with existing technical infrastructures. All these factors are weighted and combined in an appropriate manner based on the domain to provide a holistic measure of the risk due to technological change. Technology change metrics are: Product Technology Novelty, Process Technology Novelty, and Technology Interdependence.

4.2 Size Change

Incorrectly sized projects (with respect to implications on cost, effort, and time projections) add risk to the change process (Ropponen and Lyytinen 2000). Size is measured by using the Function Points metric (Albrecht 1979) which is suitable for management information system projects (Nair 2006).

4.3 Requirements Change

Requirements change metrics are the birth rate (BR) and the death rate (DR). Studies have shown that the early parts of the system development cycle such as requirements and design specifications are especially prone to error due to changing business requirements. The birth rate and death rate metrics provide a way to calculate the effect of new requirements during evolution (BR) and the changes in previous requirements (DR). A typical function can be $INT\left(\dfrac{BR+DR}{10}\right)$ (Nogueira 2000), where INT( ) takes a numeric argument and converts it to the nearest integer.

4.4 Personnel Change

Loss of key personnel during software evolution often triggers loss of key knowledge and experience (Bennett and Rajlich 2000). Staff turnover and productivity trends during a project are important indicators of change management success and indicate new staffing requirements, training, and learning requirements on the new system etc. all of which importantly affect project risk. The first metric is $\dfrac{Direct}{Idle}$ which represents the productivity ratio and stands for the direct time spent on the project by all the personnel involved divided by the idle time they spent. This ratio has been found useful in differentiating high productivity scenarios from lower productivity ones (Nogueira 2000). Values between 2 and 6 represent high productivity scenarios, while values less than 2 represent low productivity scenarios. The second metric is ΔPersonnel which represents the personnel turnover during the last evolution cycle.

4.5 Parallelism

Software evolution with a high degree of parallelism might allow several tasks to be carried out concurrently. However, it also represents a greater management overhead. On the other hand less parallelism leads to the weakest link issue due to sequential dependencies (Capital Broadleaf International Pty. Ltd. 2005). A balanced approach to scheduling activities based on the specifics of the environment is the middle path towards risk mitigation. Therefore, parallelism is measured using the ratio $\omega_{EC} \dfrac{\text{Concurrent phases}}{\text{Sequential phases}}$ where ω_{EC} is the environment constant.

ω_{EC} is based on the suitability of the environment for concurrent/sequential work. The ratio will have a value of 1.0 if the environment does not impose any advantage for either scheduling mechanisms. For example, it will seek to increase risk if the environment is better suited for sequential work and there are more concurrent phases.

4.6 Ranked Metrics

The following project sub-metrics are designed to elicit subjective expert assessments regarding people and political-based risk criteria for IS projects based on the recommendations of the Information Systems Audit and Control Association (2002).

Development Platform: The subproject manager makes a judgment about the risk due to development platform ranked on a five-point scale based on whether the development platform is proprietary or open source, the length and quality of the platform's track record, scalability of the development platform (Fenton 1998) and support and constant improvement provided for the platform.

This metric is expected to be of utility in build-based information system evolution projects where modules or the entire system are being custom designed and coded on single or multiple development platforms.

Manpower Outsourcing: Manpower outsourcing is an important part of modern corporate strategy and this metric incorporates this business reality into the risk assessment and decision-making process. It is expected to be of utility in build-based information systems evolution projects. The subproject manager makes a judgment on a five-point scale based on the percentage of manpower outsourcing relative to the total manpower required for the project, overseas or local outsourcing, and the number of manpower suppliers and their track record.

Project Team: The importance of team cohesion and leadership is difficult to overestimate in a project and the criteria are designed to elicit the project manager's assessment of project team leadership and inter-team communication and cohesion. Each team is ranked on a scale of 10 based on size, organization, and experience of team, and the project management experience of team leader.

4.7 Default Subproject Factor Weights

ORE assigns a default set of weights to all subproject factors based on empirical results collected and organized by the software risk program at Carnegie Mellon University (CMU SRP) (Higuera et al. 1996) described in Section 1. The CMU SRP organizes risk-causing dimensions into three main classes (with associated subclasses): Product Engineering, Development Environment, and Program Constraints. All the main classes have approximately equal weighting. Subproject factors are assigned to appropriate classes. Therefore, Technology Change and Size Change are assigned to Product Engineering (subclass Design). Requirements Change to Product Engineering (subclass Product Engineering). Personnel Change to Program Constraints (Resources). Parallelism has been assigned to Development Environment (Management Process). Development Platform is assigned to Development Environment (Development System), Manpower Outsourcing to Program Constraints (Resources), and Project Team to Development Environment (Work Environment).

Factors from all main classes are represented in ORE; however, some subclasses are not used. Subclasses in use are scaled to ensure that they equal total risk for their class while maintaining their weightings between each other within each main class. The overall subproject risk equation may be expressed as,

ρ (Subproject) = 0.1(Technology Change) + 0.1(Size Change) + 0.2(Requirements Change) + 0.37(Personnel Change) + 0.18(Parallelism) + 0.09(Development Platform) + 0.37(Manpower Outsourcing) + 0.06(Project Team)   (1)

4.8 Project Priority and Dependency

Project priorities (0–10) are set by the Organizational Level Controller (OLC) based on considerations of subproject scope, budget, and political issues. Priorities are used to weight the subprojects risk contribution to organizational risk and enable structured consideration of what-if scenarios and resource allocations.

The dependency measure helps describe cause and effect relationships between subprojects. ORE looks at project dependency relationships as graphs and by default propagates the entire parent project risk (weighted by priority) to the children. For example, if projects B, C, and D are dependent on A, then each of their risks equals the sum of their own risks and their dependency risks (i.e., A's risk). Once a project is complete, its risk becomes zero; hence the graph self-adjusts the risk values as evolution progresses. Additionally, not all projects may be related to one another in this simple way. These dependency relationships and the effect of dependency can be modified as per the organizational specifics.

4.9 Overall Organizational Risk Equation

Drawing from Eq. 1 and priority and dependency models the default organizational risk equation may be mathematically expressed as

$$\rho(\text{Organizational}) = \sum_{i=1}^{n} (\rho_i * \sigma_i + \delta_i) \tag{2}$$

where ρ_i stands for subproject risk of project i, σ_i stands for priority for subproject i, and δ_i stands for $\sum_{j \in \{\rho_{i_1} \cdots \rho_{i_n}\}} \rho_j * \sigma_j$ where ρ_{i_x} represents the xth project on which ρ_i depends and σ_j represents the priority of ρ_j. There are n subprojects in the organizational information systems evolution.

4.10 Tool Support and Case Study

As per design science guideline 5, Research Communication (Hevner et al. 2004), to demonstrate framework application for a management audience we have developed a detailed hypothetical case study application of ORE. A preliminary version of the ORE framework-based tool also has been developed for testing and development purposes. A copy of the case study and the tool is available at http://shakti.it.bond.edu.au/~sand/projects.htm. Due to space limitations they have not been further described in this chapter. Please address any comments to {gfinnie,pkrishna}@bond.edu.au.

5 Conclusions and Directions for Further Work

The ORE framework is a design science artifact to measure organizational risk during information systems evolution. Organizational risk is considered a composite of the risk caused by different organizational elements based on the Leavitt's diamond paradigm. The framework develops its own scale of reference by time-stamping the organizational risk assessments conducted. ORE enables fixed time sampling of risk during cyclic organizational change and maintenance processes and is based on the paradigms of balance, cycle, and time. Balance between prescription and generality is part of design by providing default functional configurations and weightings to all framework metrics and models with the flexibility to modify them to fit domain specifics. ORE generates subproject risk measures for project managers, collated subproject risk for Project Level Controllers, and a composite organizational risk measure including subproject risk, priority, and dependencies for the Organizational Level Controller. ORE therefore provides a scalable and sufficiently abstract structure to measure and manage the complexity and risk of organizational change during information systems evolution. ORE also attempts to enforce decision-making discipline by incorporating numbers and judgment within the methodology.

There are several avenues for further work on ORE. The framework is generic and needs refinement for different application domains. ORE is currently being applied in various corporate projects and we plan to document usage experience in forthcoming application papers. Application and documentation in a variety of business scenarios will allow the framework to mature and guidelines for the framework elements to develop aiding in its application in different domains. Communication flows are an important indicator of organizational success of the information systems change process and can be measured through artifacts such as number of emails and chat messages in a given period of time. These can be visualized as a Kiviat graph and ratio of balance can be scaled and included into the organizational risk calculation (Bruegge and Dutoit 1998). The organizational risk could be broken up into front office and back office components to allow decision making to focus on lessening front office risk at the cost of increasing back office risk and deploying resources as necessary (Evangelidis 2003). The Analytic Hierarchy process (Saaty 1980) or Multi-Attribute Utility theory (Keeney and Raiffa 1993) can be used to enhance the effectiveness and structuredness of the weighting process. The framework could be integrated into standards such as the IEEE Standard for Quality Assurance Plans (IEEE Standards Board 1998) used to help in building and assessing secure systems.

References

Albrecht, A.J. (1979) Measuring Application Development Productivity. Proc IBM Application Development Joint SHARE/GUIDE Symposium, pp. 83–92, Monterey, CA.

Bennett, K. and Rajlich, V. (2000) Software Maintenance and Evolution: A Roadmap. Paper presented to Conf on Future of Software Engineering, ACM, pp. 75–87, Limerick, Ireland.

Bruegge, B. and Dutoit, H.A. (1998) Communications Metrics for Software Development. IEEE Transactions on Software Engineering, 24(8): 615–628.

Capital Broadleaf International Pty. Ltd. (2005) @Risk 4.0 Tutorial Notes: Quantitative Risk Modeling. http://www.broadleaf.com.au/tutorials/Tut%20Starting.pdf (15 Sept. 2005).

Chang, S.I. (2004) ERP Lifecycle Implementation, Management and Support: Implications for Practice and Research. Proc 37th HICSS, Hawai'i.

Curtis, B. (1989) Three Problems Overcome with Behavioral Models of the Software Development Process. Paper presented to Proceedings of the Eleventh International Conference on Software Engineering, IEEE, pp. 389–399, Pittsburgh, USA.

Davenport, T.H. (1998) Putting the Enterprise into the Enterprise System. Harvard Business Review, pp. 121–131.

Dedolph, F.M. (2003) The Neglected Management Activity: Software Risk Management. Bell Laboratories Technical Journal, 8(3): 91–95.

Emery, F.E. and Trist, T.L. (1965) The Causal Texture of Organizational Elements. Human Relations, 18(1): 21–32.

Evangelidis, A. (2003) FRAMES-A Risk Assessment Framework for E-Services. Electronic Journal of E-Government, 2(1): 21–30.

Fenton, N.E. (1998) Software Metrics, A Rigorous and Practical Approach. Course Technology. International Thomson Computer Press, Boston, MA.

Fenton, N.E., Radlinkski, L., Neil, M. and Marquez, D. (2007) Improved Decision-Making for Software Managers Using Bayesian Networks. Submitted to The 6th Joint Meeting of the

European Software Engineering Conference and the ACM SIGSOFT Symposium on the Foundations of Software Engineering, Drubovnik, Croatia, September 3–7.

Gluch, D.P. (1994) A Construct for Describing Software Development Risks. Technical Report CMU/SEI-94-TR-14, Software Engineering Institute, Carnegie Mellon University.

Hevner, A.R., March, S.T., Park, J. and Ram, S. (2004) Design Science in Information Systems Research. *MIS Quarterly*, 28(1): 75–105.

Higuera, R.P. and Haimes, Y.Y. (1996) Software Risk Management. Technical Report CMU/SEI-96-TR-012, Software Engineering Institute, Carnegie Mellon University.

IEEE Standards Board (1998) IEEE Standard for Software Quality Assurance Plans. Standard published by the Software Engineering Standards Committee of the IEEE Computer Society.

Keene, P.G.W. (1981) Information Systems and Organizational Change. Communications of the ACM, 24(1): 24–33.

Keeney, R. and Raiffa, H. (1993) Decisions with Multiple Objectives: Preferences and Value Tradeoffs. Revised Edition. Cambridge University Press, Cambridge.

Klaus, H., Rosemann, M. and Gable, G.G. (2000) What is ERP? Information Systems Frontiers, 2(2): 141–62.

Leavitt H.J. (1965) Applied Organizational Change in Industry: Structural, Technological and Humanistic Approaches. In James G. March, editor, Handbook of Organizations, pp. 1144–1170, Rand McNally and Company, Chicago, IL.

Nair, M. (2006) A Survey of Software Estimation Techniques and Project Planning Practices. Proc 7th ACIS International Conference on Software Engineering, Artificial Intelligence, Networking and Parallel/Distributed Computing, IEEE, Las Vegas, NV.

Nogueira, J. (2000) A Risk Assessment Model for Evolutionary Software Projects, Ph.D. thesis submitted to the Naval Postgraduate School USA.

Offen, R.J. and Jeffery, R. (1997) Establishing Software Measurement Programs. IEEE Software, 14(2): 45–53.

Project Management Institute (2000) A Guide to the Project Management Body of Knowledge (PMBOK Guide). Technical Report, Project Management Institute of USA Inc.

Roberts, F.S. (1979) Measurement Theory with Applications to Decision Making, Utility, and the Social Sciences. Addison-Wesley, Reading, MA.

Ropponen, J. and Lyytinen, K. (2000) Components of Software Development Risk: How to Address Them? IEEE Transactions on Software Engineering, 26(2): 98–111.

Saaty, T.L. (1980) The Analytic Hierarchy Process. McGraw-Hill, New York.

Sawy, O.A.E. (2001) Redesigning Enterprise Processes for E-Business. McGraw-Hill Irwin, Singapore.

Skok, W. and Legge, M. (2001) Evaluating Enterprise Resource Planning Systems Using an Interpretive Approach. Paper presented to ACM SIGPCR, San Diego, CA.

Information Systems Audit and Control Association (2002) IS Auditing Procedure P1: IS Risk Assessment Measurement.

Sumner, M. (2000) Risk Factors in Enterprise Wide Information Management System Projects. Proc ACM SIGCPR Conf on Computer Personnel Research, pp. 180–187, Chicago, IL.

Tatikonda, M. and Rosenthal, S. (2000) Technology Novelty, Project Complexity and Product Development Project Execution Success. A Deeper Look at Task Uncertainty in Product Innovation. IEEE Transactions on Engineering Management, 47(1): 74–87.

Torsten P.G.R., Guido T. (1997) Separation of Powers and Public Accountability. The Quarterly Journal of Economics, 112(4): 1163–1202.

Volker W. and Rohde M. (1995) Towards an Integrated Organization and Technology Development. Proc Conf on Designing Interactive Systems, Processes, Practices, Methods, and Techniques. Ann Arbor, USA.

Evaluating the Driving Factors and the Suppressing Factors Related to IS Outsourcing in Four Finnish Information Systems Organizations

Pasi Juvonen

South Carelia Polytechnic, Faculty of Technology, pasi.juvonen@scp.fi

Abstract This chapter presents the results of a research project, in which the current situation related to the information systems (IS) outsourcing practices in four Finnish information systems development organizations was evaluated. The evaluation was based on employees' own perceptions, and it consisted of analyzing the current IS outsourcing practices in the case companies, driving factors related to IS outsourcing, suppressing factors related to IS outsourcing and an evaluation of the company's readiness to utilize IS outsourcing. This qualitative study used grounded theory as the research method. The analysis elicited that the IS outsourcing decisions in these case companies have been mostly based on cost-related factors. The cost pressures are coming both from the shareholders and the customers. Cost reduction seemed to be the major single driver for outsourcing information system development (ISD) work. Besides, even if most of the case companies have already outsourced parts of their ISD projects, based on the interviewees' expressions the cost savings in these projects have not been remarkable. In some cases the total costs of the project have been estimated to be even higher. However, the case companies seem not to be familiar with the cost structure of the outsourced projects. The interviewees also felt that their company's ISD practices were not ready for the use of outsourcing. The level of English skills and the lack of domain knowledge among subcontractors were the other mentioned suppressing factors related to IS outsourcing.

1 Introduction

Globalization of industries has naturally affected also the ICT industry. Several trends are going on in the ICT field right now. ICT service providers have been consolidated into large multinational enterprises. New ways of developing software, i.e., distributed or virtual software teams and participation in open source software projects, have also come up. Since Eastman Kodak made its decision to outsource its IT operations to IBM Corporation in 1989 (Senn and Gefen 1999),

C. Barry et al. (eds.), *Information Systems Development: Challenges in Practice, Theory, and Education, Vol.2*, doi: 10.1007/978-0-387-78578-3_8,
© Springer Science+Business Media, LLC 2009

information systems and software development outsourcing have become a trend in the ICT field. The changes that IS outsourcing will cause have a significant impact on economics of software business worldwide.

One of the recent trends mentioned in the field of ICT has been the outsourcing of information technology work and concentrating it to larger organizations (Dibbern et al. 2004). This trend has in recent years focused on offshore software development. The main drivers behind the offshore software development are the needs to reduce software development costs (Kakabadse and Kakabadse 2002) and to gain access to a huge resource pool and latest technologies (Marcus 2004). Countries such as India, Russia and China have in recent years become significant players in this market.

Software companies in high labour cost countries encounter a totally new challenge in this situation. Their development methods, processes, practices, business models and business networks require reorganization. They must either somehow utilize IS outsourcing and make profit out of it, or find other solutions to be efficient and profitable in this new situation.

This chapter introduces the current situation related to IS outsourcing in four Finnish ISD organizations. It presents their current cooperation practices and discusses the driving factors and the suppressing factors that affect the company's decision to outsource or not to outsource parts of its ISD projects.

2 Literature Review

The outsourcing in the ICT industry is not a new phenomenon. It originated from the professional and the facility management services in the financial and operation support areas during the 1960s and 1970s (Lee). The outsourcing has little by little become a serious strategic choice for ICT companies. In recent years IT outsourcing has also been a subject of numerous studies in several different disciplines. This literature study was first made in October 2006, and it was updated in the beginning of April 2007. Generally, outsourcing has been defined as a management approach that allows delegating operational responsibility for processes or services previously delivered by an enterprise to an external agent (Swink 1999; Elmuti and Kathawala 2000). IT outsourcing has been defined as a practice, where its assets and resources are transferred to a third party (Willcocks and Kern 1998; Gilley and Rasheed 2000).

Literature related to information technology outsourcing is plentiful. Several terms are used in the literature interchangeably addressing the same issue, i.e., information technology (IT) outsourcing and information systems (IS) outsourcing. Furthermore, the term offshoring is also commonly used interchangeably with outsourcing. Offshoring has been defined as a practice where domestically supplied services are replaced by imported services (Bedzarnik 2005). To make the terms clear, the term IS outsourcing is used in this chapter to address both IT and IS outsourcing concepts. Besides, terms such as a supplier, a vendor and a subcontractor are used to some extent interchangeably in the literature. In this chapter, a subcontractor is used as a synonym for a vendor or a supplier.

Several studies have addressed the driving factors that seem to support out-sourcing decisions in the companies. Another popular subject of studies has been undesirable consequences of IS outsourcing. A cross section of relevant literature and some common concepts related to IS outsourcing are presented in Table 1.

Table 1. A cross section of relevant literature related to IS outsourcing

Focus	Concept(s)	Author(s)
Driving factors related to IS outsourcing	Cost reduction, access to latest technologies and skills	Carmel (1999), Ketler and Willems (1999), Goo et al. (2000), Hersleb and Moitra (2001), Khan et al. (2003), Rottman (2006)
	Improved quality	Laplante et al. (2004)
	Solution to the IT skills shortage	Ketler and Willems (1999), Lacity and Willcocks (2001), Nicholson (2001), Khan et al. (2003), Amberg et al. (2005)
	Pressure to cut down costs	Matloff (2004)
	Reduction of debt	Smith et al. (1998)
Suppressing factors and undesirable consequences related to IS outsourcing	Difficulties in coordi-nation and control	Carmel (1999), Ovaska et al. (2003)
	Hidden costs, transac-tion costs	Duncan (1998), Aubert et al. (1998), Khan et al. (2003), Overby (2003), Barthelemy (2003), Kobayashi-Hillary (2005)
	Cost savings are far from expected	Lacity and Hirschheim (1993), Smith et al. (1998), Senn and Gefen (1999), Barthelemy (2001), Lindholm and Suomala (2004), Matloff (2005)
	Quality problems	Matloff (2005)
	Language, cultural issues, trust, threat of vendor opportunism	Sabherwal (1999), Khan et al. (2003), Narayanaswamy and Henry (2005), Nguyen et al. (2006)
	Risks and risk mitigation	Lacity and Willcocks (2001), Taylor (2005), Gonzalez et al. (2005), Aubert et al. (2005), Erickson and Evaristo (2006), Sakthivel (2007)

Several theoretical lenses have also been used to describe and interpret pheno-mena related to IS outsourcing. The Transaction Cost Economics (TCE) approach has been used to provide a view on risk management. The Resource-Based View (RBV) concentrates on value, accessibility and control of valuable resources – those resources that may affect the competitive advantage of the firm. Based on the literature study, these two approaches seem to be the most popular theories to explain how to avoid hazards in the IS outsourcing decision making. Also the Life Cycle Costing (LCC) and Total Cost of Ownership (TCO) theories have been used in several studies to evaluate the costs of IS outsourcing. The outsourcing research has been directed in recent years from the strategic and the economics views to a social view (Lee et al. 2000).

An extensive review of IS outsourcing literature and also the research approaches and theories used in IS outsourcing studies has also been presented by Dibbern et al. (2004). They report that the maturity of the IS outsourcing research is growing. Furthermore, when IS outsourcing as a research issue matures there will also be new subjects for research. The study addresses, for example, partnerships, equity deals, offshoring and backsourcing as the upcoming research issues. So, it seems that the IS outsourcing research might shift from analyzing the outsourcing decision process to analyzing relationship management and learning from experiences. The work of Dibbern et al. has been complemented by Sargent (2006). Sargent's analysis of the literature points out that the outsourcing relationship, as well as its attributes and processes, should be studied more carefully to be able to understand complex challenges related to it.

To summarize, numerous studies have been made on IS outsourcing. Some of them present its benefits and some of them present its drawbacks. Several studies also address the best practices and pitfalls of IS outsourcing supported with empirical evidence. The most recent research trend concentrates on the social aspects of IS outsourcing. Some relevant literature and common research topics addressed by them were presented in this short literature review.

3 Research Process

This research is done in cooperation with Lappeenranta University of Technology. Five researchers participated in the data collection and analysis phases of the study. The study was conducted among six Finnish information systems development organizations starting in August 2006. Four of them were analyzed for this article. The research will last till the end of December 2007. In the beginning of the study, a framework of the contexts where information systems development organizations nowadays operate was created. In the beginning, also a few representatives of the case companies were interviewed to gather some basic information about the employees' own views on their company's targets of improvement related to their ISD practices. After these preliminary discussions with the companies the targets of improvement were gathered, analyzed and reflected to our framework. The targets of improvement that the interviewees mentioned were taken into account when the interview questions were designed.

The ultimate target of this research project is to provide more understanding about the linkage between organizational context and information systems development work. Fitzgerald et al. 2002 define context as 'both the place where the information system will be implemented and the environment within which the development process will take place'. Based on these research objectives I focused on IS outsourcing. The objectives of this study were twofold. The first goal was to study the current state of the cooperation and IS outsourcing experiences in the case companies. The second was to evaluate the readiness to utilize IS outsourcing in the case companies. To be able to fulfil these objectives, I formulated my personal research question as follows:

Q1: What are the driving factors and the suppressing factors related to information systems outsourcing in the case companies?

The data for this qualitative study was collected using theme-based interviews. A total of 29 interviews were made in six Finnish information systems development companies between October and December 2006. The interviews lasted from 30 minutes to 3 hours, depending on the interviewee's role in the company. Employees acting in different roles, i.e., software analysts, project managers and line managers, were interviewed to provide a richer insight into the company's current ISD practices. The interviews were transcribed as text and analyzed with the grounded theory method (Strauss and Corbin 1990). Qualitative research requires the researcher's ability to interpret the interviewee's actions and verbal expressions. Furthermore, these interpretations have to be validated from the data and the experiences of other researchers and practitioners (Klein and Myers 1999).

The analysis of the data was made in close cooperation with another researcher, so the interpretations were constantly validated and the investigator triangulation was utilized (Denzin 1978).

The analysis started with an open coding phase, where each researcher had his own viewpoint on the data. My personal viewpoint was 'The driving factors and the suppressing factors related to IS outsourcing'. The open coding phase (Strauss and Corbin 1990) was based on certain seed categories that in other words meant an interesting phenomenon related to the viewpoint I had selected. The original seed categories for my analysis were: change, collaboration competences and context.

The open coding phase was followed by an axial coding phase, which in practice proceeded almost in parallel with the open coding phase. During the axial coding phase the observations were grouped into three different categories: cooperation and IS outsourcing experiences, driving factors related to IS outsourcing and suppressing factors related to IS outsourcing. During the open and axial coding phases, theoretical sampling (Strauss and Corbin 1990) was utilized to guide further data collection. Two specific interviews were made to be able to build a better picture of the situation in the case companies.

The analysis was closed with a selective coding phase. In the selective coding phase the core of the results was formed, the analysis of the current situation related to IS outsourcing in the case companies was evaluated and research reports were written.

4 Findings

In this section the results of this study are presented. In Section 4.1, the four case companies analyzed for this chapter are briefly introduced. Section 4.2 reports the driving and the suppressing factors related to IS outsourcing in the case companies. In Section 4.3, the readiness to utilize IS outsourcing in the case companies is briefly evaluated based on the interview data. To avoid a loss of confidentiality among the companies the results are not presented in a case by case manner.

4.1 Introduction of the Cases

Company A is an internationally operating information systems development organization providing a number of products and services to its customers who come from several business domains. The forest industry division of this organization has participated in this study. This organization has several international cooperation partners worldwide, and it has also utilized several subcontractors in its ISD projects for many years. Besides, the organization has carried out several distributed ISD projects in cooperation with its foreign agency.

Company B operates in the agricultural sector, providing several services to its customer. It is currently owned by its customer. It has several technological partnerships with international enterprises. At the moment, the company has no subcontractors in ISD projects. It has experiences from utilizing both Finnish and foreign subcontractors in its ISD projects.

Company C is an internationally operating information systems development organization. It operates in the forest and saw industry sectors, providing a tailored product for enterprise resource planning. It also executes tailored projects and acts as a consultant for its forest industry customers. It has two remote offices in Finland with which they cooperate. It has also three foreign agencies placed in Central Europe. Furthermore, it has a lot of cooperation experience with its partners.

Company D provides information logistics services to its customer. It operates mainly in Finland, but it has also some ongoing projects in other European countries. At the moment the company is owned by its customer. It cooperates with numerous companies, and has utilized dozens of subcontractors. Some of the company's subcontractors have operated on-site in the company's premises.

4.2 The Driving Factors Related to IS Outsourcing

The main driving factor related to IS outsourcing in the case companies was a strong pressure to cut down costs in ISD projects. This demand is presented by either the shareholders or the customers. In some cases a customer had demanded a company to utilize IS outsourcing to cut down ISD costs. Some expressions from the interviews about the cost pressure are included here:

'...Well I think that cost pressure is quite high and it seems that they are more cost effective than for example in Finland...'

'...customer demanded us to use the XXXXXXX. Later on they demanded to expand that and to transfer the maintenance there...'

'...I would say that of course two of the most definitely important points are the ways that increase their competitiveness. I mean in that sense that what are the financial limitations or requirements and so on. I mean price...'

'...We replace our own work with the work of subcontractors because it is cheaper. This is usually done already when the project plan is made...'

'...When I started working in this company five years ago, IT costs were approximately 8 percent of turnover. Now they are approximately 4 percent. So we have to produce the same services with lower costs...'

Another strongly expressed driving factor was the company's need to utilize certain special technological competencies. The interviewees saw that these special competencies are more cost-effective to buy from a subcontractor than to produce them inside the company. Some comments from the interviews are included here:

'...they are based on some competence. We know that certain people are competent in some special area...'

'...When we get a new project and if we know that we don't have a certain competence in-house, we have a network of consults and subcontractors that will help us by providing their specialists...'

'...There might be some kind of technology or something that is not reasonable for us to learn or study...or put our effort on it...'

'...There are certain competencies that are not reasonable for us to produce by ourselves. We buy them from subcontractors...'

Both of these factors were strongly expressed in the interviews. In addition, the companies are interested in utilizing subcontractors as a resource pool. In some case companies, the former positive experiences from IS outsourcing were mentioned as a driving factor for expanding IS outsourcing in the future. Some of the interviewees also saw IS outsourcing as a possibility for the company to concentrate on their own core competencies.

4.3 The Suppressing Factors Related to IS Outsourcing

One of the main suppressing factors in utilizing IS outsourcing expressed by the interviewees was the language barrier. In most case companies the interviewees somehow expressed that their written and spoken English skills were not on the level required for operating with foreign subcontractors. They also expressed that at least in most and in some cases all of the documentation of the ISD projects is written in Finnish. Some expressions from the interviews were as follows:

'...We have the objective to use English as an official language in our organization, but it will take a long time. We have plenty of employees who are not able to communicate with the foreign language...'

'...If you were a representative of our management and you told me that we should use a subcontractor in a certain project... The first issue I would think of would be the language context. If I had XXXX pages of Finnish documentation and then ... would it be worthwhile to hire a foreign subcontractor...'

'...We had people here who couldn't speak English well and also the XXXXX staff had similar problems...'

The lack of domain knowledge among foreign subcontractors was also expressed in several interviews in different companies. Here are two comments describing the situation:

'...There are lots of offerers. There are probably also lots of competent employees, I suppose. Then, when we describe our business domain and tell about the domain knowledge requirements we have, the domain knowledge is not found...'

'There is not much domain knowledge. Then we should familiarize and educate them...'

The ISD practices in the case companies include a lot of hidden knowledge. Interviewees saw that the ISD practices in their company have been formed in the course of time, and their customer-oriented way of operating would be very difficult to document in such a way that it would be reasonable to outsource parts of it. In three of the companies, the interviewees expressed some dissatisfaction with the way how the ISD practices in their company were organized. They felt that their ISD practices should be somehow developed to a more formal model before they would be able to utilize IS outsourcing.

Table 2. The factors related to IS outsourcing in the case companies

Suppressing factors related to IS outsourcing	Driving factors related to IS outsourcing
Former contradictory experiences from IS outsourcing	Concentrating on core competencies
Documentation is done in Finnish	The access to a resource pool
Fear to outsource company's knowledge	Cost pressures
Language barrier	Former positive experiences from IS outsourcing
Subcontractors' lack of domain knowledge	Need for special competencies
Current state of the company's ISD practices	

There were also some other suppressing factors posed in the interviews. In one of the companies a rare technology is used, and the interviewees expressed that there have been no competent resources available for that technology. One of the companies has had contradictory experiences from its former IS outsourcing projects and the company is not interested in utilizing foreign subcontractors any more. Technically challenging environment was also mentioned in two of the case companies. They evaluated that an ISD project should last at least 6 months before it would be reasonable to utilize IS outsourcing. The summary of the finding in these four Finnish ISD organizations is presented in Table 2.

4.4 The Evaluation of the Readiness to Utilize IS Outsourcing

In most case companies the interviewees felt that their company's ISD practices are not formal enough for the use of IS outsourcing or, in some cases, for expanding it. The interviewees saw that before using foreign subcontractors, ISD practices inside their own company should be developed towards a more formal model.

Another topic that was mentioned in several interviews was the real benefit gained from IS outsourcing. Several interviewees in different companies felt that IS outsourcing produced a new group of different cost factors. Based on the interviews these cost factors have been identified, but they have not, however, been exactly calculated or analyzed. According to the interviews the total costs of the outsourced projects are not yet known. Some comments expressed in the interviews were as follows:

'...There were lots of problems and it wasn't cheaper at all. Lots of hours were spent and it was hard to even get any results...'
'...To summarize, it was good that programs worked, it could have been even worse if they had not worked at all. After all, it was probably not any cheaper, and the total cost of the maintenance has sure been bigger...'

Table 3 summarizes the four case companies and presents their current experiences related to IS outsourcing. The evaluation of the readiness to utilize IS outsourcing in the case companies based on the analysis is also presented.

Table 3. Summary of the case companies

	Context/-Customer domain	Type of current cooperation and IS outsourcing experiences	Evaluation of company's readiness to outsource
Company A	Forest industry	Special areas of technology, user interface of software project, partnering	Contradictory (somehow ready, somehow not ready)
Company B	Agriculture	Some software development projects	Not ready
Company C	Forest industry	Special areas of technology, cooperation in process interfaces	Not ready
Company D	Information logistics	Special areas of technology, software development outsourcing, partnering	Mostly ready

5 Discussion

The companies participating in this study came from three different customer domains. All of these case companies have some experiences from IS outsourcing or other types of relationships with other organizations in ISD. Based on the empirical evidence collected during this study, it is justified to argue that IS outsourcing is in practice much more complex to implement than a management of an organization presumes. Furthermore, it seems that IS outsourcing decisions have been mostly based on cost-related issues. However, there were no expressions in the interviews about evaluation of the costs that IS outsourcing causes.

There is naturally a number of limitations in this study. Only four ISD companies are analyzed for this study, so the results cannot be generalized to a wider context. Besides, a deep analysis about the IS outsourcing decision process and different cost factors related to it was not performed in this study. During the analysis, theoretical sampling was used to guide data collection, but timetables and resources forced to limit the number of detailed interviews. When you use theoretical sampling, you should have a lot of time and resources to make interviews, transcribe and analyze them, and may be able to take another round if it is necessary. Unfortunately, you probably do not have that much time and resources in a normal research project. In my opinion this is a significant weakness in the grounded theory method – it takes a lot of time and resources.

However, the results of this study support the previous studies made about IS outsourcing and reveals that the driving factors and the suppressing factors related to IS outsourcing reported in different contexts are mostly the same in this context as in the previously studied contexts. A deeper analysis of the total costs of certain outsourced ISD projects would be an interesting topic to explore in the future studies, and it certainly should be addressed.

Finland is an interesting case for this kind of study, because Finland has in recent years done extremely well in Global Competitiveness Reports. The results of this study implicate that although Finland is a highly competitive nation, there are still a number of challenges in utilizing outsourcing in ISD. It could be useful for other nations to benchmark how these challenges are dealt with in Finnish ISD organizations.

6 Summary

This study was a part of a larger, ongoing research project that investigates different contexts of information systems development organizations. This chapter focused on describing results of the current situation related to IS outsourcing practices in four Finnish ISD organizations. The analysis provided a group of driving and suppressing factors related to IS outsourcing in the case companies. Besides, the case companies' readiness to utilize IS outsourcing was briefly evaluated. The main driving factors were the demand for cost-effectiveness, the utilization of special technological competencies and the possibility to access a pool or resources. The main suppressing factors were the language barrier, the lack of domain knowledge among subcontractors and the challenging technological environment in the case companies.

Based on the results of this study, it was possible to answer the question 'what are the driving and the suppressing factors related to IS outsourcing in the case companies'. However, it was not possible to present how the outsourced ISD projects actually performed in the case companies. Therefore, more research is needed to analyze the situation more widely and on a more detailed level.

References

Amberg, M., Herold, G., Kodes, R., Kraus, R. & Wiener, M. (2005) IT offshoring – A cost-oriented analysis. *Manuscript for the CISTM, 2005.*

Aubert, B., Patry, M. & Rivard, S. (1998) Assessing the Risk of IT Outsourcing. *Proc HICSS-31.*

Aubert, B., Patry, M. & Rivard, S. (2005) A framework for information technology outsourcing risk management. *DATA BASE for Advances in Information Systems*, 36(4).

Bedzarnik, R. (2005) Restructuring Information Technology: its offshoring a concern? *Monthly Labor Review, August 2005.*

Barthelemy, J. (2001) The hidden costs of IT outsourcing. *Sloan Management Review*, Spring.

Barthelemy, J. (2003) The seven deadly sins of outsourcing. *Academy of Management Executive*, 17(2), 87–99.

Carmel, E. (1999) *Global Software Teams*. Prentice-Hall, Upper Saddle River, NJ. ISBN 0-13-924218-X.

Denzin, N. (1978) *The Research Act: A Theoretical Introduction to Sociological Methods*. McGraw-Hill, New York.

Dibbern, J., Goles, T., Hirschheim, R. & Jayatilaka, B. (2004) Information systems outsourcing: a survey and analysis of the literature. *DATABASE for Advances in Information Systems*, 35(4).

Duncan, N. (1998) Beyond Opportunism: A Resource Based View of Outsourcing Risk. *Proc HICSS-31.*

Elmuti, D. & Kathawala, Y. (2000) The effects of global outsourcing strategies on participants' attitudes and organizational effectiveness. *International Journal of Manpower*, 21(2), 112–128.

Erickson, J. & Evaristo, R. (2006) Risk factors in distributed projects. *Proc HICSS-39.*

Fitzgerald, B., Russo, N.L. & Stolterman, E. (2002) *Information Systems Development: Methods in Action*. McGraw-Hill, London. ISBN: 007709836 6.

Gilley, K.M. & Rasheed, A. (2000) Making more by doing less: an analysis of outsourcing and its effects on firm performance. *Journal of Management*, 26(4), 763–790.

Gonzalez, R., Gasco, J. & Llopis, J. (2005) Information systems outsourcing risks: a study of large firms. *Industrial management & Data systems*, 105(1).

Goo, J., Kishore, R. & Rao, H.R. (2000) A Content-Analytic Longitudinal Study of the Drivers for Information Technology and Systems Outsourcing. *Proc 21st Intl Conference IS (ICIS'00).*

Hersleb, J. & Moitra, D. (2001) Global software development. *IEEE Software* Mar/Apr.

Kakabadse, A. & Kakabadse, N. (2002) Trends in outsourcing: contrasting USA and Europe. *European Management Journal*, 20(2), 189–198.

Ketler, K. & Willems, J.R. (1999). A Study of the Outsourcing Decision: Preliminary Results. *SIGCPR'99, New Orleans, Louisiana, USA.*

Khan, N., Currie, W., Weerakkody, V. & Desai, B. (2003) Evaluating Offshore IT Outsourcing in India: Supplier and Customer Scenarios. *Proc HICSS-36.*

Klein, H.K. & Myers, M.D. (1999) A set of principles for conducting and evaluating interpretive field studies in information systems. *MIS Quarterly*, 23(1), 67–94.

Kobayashi-Hillary, M. (2005) A Passage to India. Pitfalls that the outsourcing vendor forgot to mention, *QUEUE*, Feb 2005.

Lacity, M.C. & Hirschheim, R. (1993) *Information Systems Outsourcing: Myths, Metaphors and Realities*. Wiley series in Information systems, New York.

Lacity, M. & Willcocks, L.P. (2001) *Global Information Technology Outsourcing: In Search of Business Advantage*. Wiley, Chichester.

Laplante, P., Costello, T., Singh, P. Bindiganavile, S. & Landon, M. (2004) The Who, What, Why, Where, and When of IT Outsourcing. *IEEE IT Professional, Jan–Feb.*

Lee, J., Huynh, M., Chi-Wai, K. & Pi, S. (2000) The evolution of outsourcing research: what is the next issue? *Proc HICSS-33.*

Lee, J. Outsourcing reference list. Available in html format in: http://www.is.cityu.edu.hk/staff/isjnlee/out_frame_tot.htm.

Lindholm, A. & Suomala, P. (2004) The possibilities of life cycle costing in outsourcing decision making. *Frontiers of e-business research 2004.*

Marcus, A. (2004) Insights on outsourcing – What's in It for Us? For Them? Where Are We Headed? *Interactions July + August 2004.*

Matloff, N. (2004) Globalization and the American IT worker. *Communications of the ACM,* 47(11).

Matloff, N. (2005) Offshoring: What Can Go Wrong? *IEEE IT Professional, July–Aug.*

Narayanaswamy, R. & Henry, R. (2005) Effects of Culture on Control Mechanisms in Offshore Outsourced IT Projects. *SIGMIS'05, April 14–16, 2005, Atlanta, Georgia, USA.*

Nguyen, P., Babar, M. & Verner, J. (2006) Critical Factors in Establishing and Maintaining Trust in Software Outsourcing Relationships. *ICSE'06 May 20–28, 2006, Shanghai, China.*

Nicholson, B. (2001) Global Software Outsourcing: The Solution to the IT Skills Gap. School of Accounting and Finance. *Workshop Report, 16 July 2001, University of Manchester, UK.*

Ovaska, P., Rossi, M. & Marttiin, P. (2003) Architecture as a coordination tool in multi-site software development. *Software Process* 8(4), 233–247.

Overby, S. (2003). *The Hidden Costs of Offshore Outsourcing – Offshore Outsourcing The Money.* Available in http format in http://www.cio.com/article/29654, September 1, 2003.

Rottman, J. (2006) Successfully Outsourcing Embedded Software Development. *IEEE Computer Society, January 2006.*

Sabherwal, R. (1999) The role of trust in outsourced IS development projects. *Communications of the ACM*, 42(2).

Sakthivel, S. (2007) Managing risk in offshore systems development. *Communications of the ACM*, 50(4)

Sargent, A. Jr. (2006) Outsourcing Relationship Literature: An Examination and Implications for Future Research. *SIGMIS-CPR'06, April 13–15, 2006, Claremont, California, USA.*

Senn, J.A. & Gefen, D. (1999). The Relation Between Outsourcing and the Return from Corporate IT Spending: Perceptions from Practitioners. *Proc HICSS-32.*

Smith, M.A., Mitra, S. & Narasimhan, S. Information systems outsourcing: a study of pre-event firm characteristics. *Journal of Information Systems*, 15(2), 61–93.

Strauss, A. & Corbin, J. (1990) *Basics of Qualitative Research, Techniques and Procedures for Developing Grounded Theory*, second edition. Sage, London.

Swink, M. (1999) Threats to new product manufacturability and the effects of development team integration processes. *Journal of Operations Management*, 17(6), 691–709.

Taylor, H. (2005) The Move to Outsourced IT Projects: Key Risks from the Provider Perspective, *SIGMIS-CPR'05 April 14–16, 2005, Atlanta, Georgia, USA.*

Willcocks, L.P. & Kern, T. (1998) IT outsourcing as strategic partnering: the case of the UK Inland Revenue. *European Journal of Information Systems*, 7(1), 29–45.

Strategic Dimensions of Software Development in a Supply Chain

G.H. Kruithof and T.D. Meijler

University of Groningen, Faculty of Management and Organization

{g.h.kruithof, t.d.meijler}@rug.nl

Abstract   This chapter explores the relationship between characteristics of a software market and strategic management of software development in a supply chain. The typical characteristics of software markets and software supply chains are described. A decision framework is developed which connects specific market characteristics to independent and dependent development approaches in a software supply chain. Key areas of a development strategy are the variability, the asset, the legacy integration and the change. The framework is preliminary validated by application to four typical reuse technologies.

1 Introduction

Software industry, as other industries, is forced to increase its efficiency continuously: developing larger, more complex systems with more functionality and better quality against lower prices and shorter time to market. Software industry has responded to such forces by using better tools and increasing reuse of existing software assets. Software reuse implies that that organizations can focus on the production of dedicated software assets such as commercial off the shelf (COTS) components that are incorporated as subassemblies in the software produced by other organizations. Hence, software reuse results in software production differentiation which leads to the emergence of software supply chains.

Software development in a supply chain is different from that in a single organization since it requires coordination of goals and business processes over multiple organizations. Therefore, more attention is required for strategic management, which can be defined as a process that is used to achieve mission and goals in the context of an external environment (Wright 1992). In the software industry, strategic decisions have to be made which are not encountered in other industries. They are, for instance, related to the choice of reuse technology, division of development over the supply chain and the selection of mechanisms that allow absorption of changes to software products. Understanding which strategic decisions

C. Barry et al. (eds.), *Information Systems Development: Challenges in Practice, Theory, and Education, Vol.2*, doi: 10.1007/978-0-387-78578-3_9,
© Springer Science+Business Media, LLC 2009

have to be made of software development in supply chains is therefore essential since it allows the increase of the performance of individual companies and the software industry as a whole.

In this chapter a framework is developed which relates the specific characteristics of a software market to the strategic decisions of software development in a supply chain. In Section 2 the specific characteristics of software markets are discussed. A short review of concepts of supply chain management adapted to software industry is provided in Section 3. The decision framework, which is derived in Section 4, links the characteristics of a market for software products to the strategic development decisions. The framework is applied in Section 5 on a generic level to four typical software reuse technologies. The chapter concludes with future research necessary for further validation of the decision framework.

2 Characteristics of Software Markets

A market for a software product has general properties that are common to any market and some properties that are a result from the specific nature of software. General properties are, for instance, its size, growth, profitability and heterogeneity with respect to customer needs. Another general property is overlap of customer needs in one specific software market with customer needs in other markets. For software development this implies that investments can be spread over a larger number of customers (Favaro et al. 1998). An example is a zip code component which is required in a logistics as well as marketing intelligence.

Markets are dynamic in the sense that needs of the customers change over time. For many traditional products, this implies that a product is depreciated after some time and replaced by another product that fulfils the new set of requirements best. However, for software markets new versions of a product have to be developed in such a way that they can be absorbed by customers of former versions. A well known example from the consumer market is the virus scanner which needs upgrading continuously. Furthermore, for some types of software products such as ERP products, customers accept a new version of the software product only if the data is migrated to the new version as well. Software markets differ in the frequency and predictability of change in customer needs. Upgrading software products also implies the risk of malfunctioning, and customers and markets differ with respect to the risk that is acceptable.

Another important characteristic of a software market may be the need to reuse a customer's existing applications or data sources in a new application. In a so-called green field situation this requirement is absent. Development of business applications in general requires incorporation of existing legacy systems of a customer. Legacy systems can be quite heterogeneous in a specific domain, due to different vendors and customizations. In some segments legacy may be encountered that can be characterized as homogeneous. One can therefore distinguish between the heterogeneity with respect to new functionality required and heterogeneity of existing legacy with which this new functionality has to be integrated.

3 Concepts of the Software Supply Chain

Software reuse enables the emergence of supply chains in the software industry. Hence, essential strategic decisions relate to the design of that supply chain. Postmus and Kruithof (2007) have reported on the coordination problems encountered in the supply chains of ERP manufacturers. They define a software supply chain as a network of firms that are engaged in the production, distribution, deployment and maintenance of a software product that is covered by a particular software license. Since software production is strongly focused on change, supply chain management in the software industry is primarily concerned with the management of the development, propagation and absorption of changes during the life cycle of that product.

Typical development roles in the software supply chain can be linked to development *for* reuse and development *with* reuse (Wegner 1987). The term reuse means incorporating assets in the development of new assets. It can be easily misunderstood, since it suggests 'using software again'. Development roles may or may not be separated by organizational boundaries, which leads to the distinction between *external* and *internal* reuse. For the emergence of a supply chain, external reuse is required. The software supply chain can be imagined as a chain of links in which development takes place. Links closer to the customer are referred to as downstream, whereas links further away from the customer are referred to as upstream in analogy with the flow of assets. Therefore, an organization that develops software with reuse requires an organization upstream that develops software assets for reuse. Reversely, an organization that develops assets for reuse requires another organization downstream that develops software assets with reuse. Organizations in the centre of longer supply chains combine development for and with reuse. As mentioned before, change is an essential attribute of software production. In a supply chain, any change to a software asset needs to be absorbed by the assets developed downstream and eventually by customers.

A development approach which can *in principle* be executed by a single manufacturing organization is defined here as an independent approach. A software manufacturer with an independent approach can choose to develop all assets in-house. This means that the independent approach determines the product architecture in the supply chain. When executed by a single organization, reuse is restricted to internal reuse. The definition of an independent approach implies that each software supply chain has exactly one manufacturer with an independent development approach. Independent approaches, however, do not exclude a combination with external reuse. Assets from other manufacturers can be reused in an independent development approach and some customer requirements can be left to be fulfilled by other manufacturers.

A dependent approach is defined as an approach which explicitly requires a complementary independent approach to be effective. Manufacturers with a dependent approach either develop software for reuse (upstream of an independent approach) or with reuse (downstream of an independent approach). A typical upstream dependent strategy is the production of a COTS component, intended to be used in other software products. Upstream-dependent approaches can often be combined with several independent approaches. Downstream-dependent approaches are often specific to the upstream-independent approach. Typical downstream-dependent approaches are production of a product family add-on (either domain-specific or customer-specific) or the specialization of generic models to a specific target market.

Generally, organizations upstream are directed towards the development of assets with functionality that is common to all customers. These assets offer (sometimes implicit) variability, such that organizations downstream can develop specific variants: the functionality which is adapted to match specific domain or customer requirements (Messerschmidt and Szyperski 2003). If the specificity of a product is defined as:

Specificity = variability/common functionality

then in a software supply chain the specificity of a product increases from upstream to downstream. Although the formula can be evaluated quantitatively, e.g. by function point analysis, it will be used here to indicate major differences between independent strategies only. The specificity can be evaluated for two dimensions: with respect to *the new functionality* that needs to be incorporated in a product, and also for *the integration capabilities* of a product with legacy of customers.

An example of software with a low specificity of new functionality is a virus scanner for the consumer market. In this product, only a few parameters can be adjusted to optimise performance, so that the variability of the product is low. Tailor-made software has a high specificity of new functionality per definition.

In a domain with homogeneous legacy, the required specificity for integration is low. Integration can, for instance, be achieved using a point-to-point integration. In a domain with heterogeneous legacy, the required variability in integration is much larger and a messaging-type of integration is required (Hohpe and Woolf 2007).

Combining an independent strategy with dependent strategy offers the possibility to achieve the desired specificity of a product with a lower time to market. However, the cost associated with coordination counterbalances the efficiency gain of specialization.

For any specific software market an optimum should be achieved with respect to five dimensions:

- Specificity of new functionality to be developed
- Specificity of legacy integration capabilities
- Cost of change absorption
- Efficiency in software development
- Time to market

In order to find the optimum for a specific situation, we need to understand the relation between strategic choices in software development and characteristics of a specific market situation.

4 Decision Framework

In this section a decision framework is developed. It is a normative framework that serves to convert market characteristics to the design and management of the supply chain.

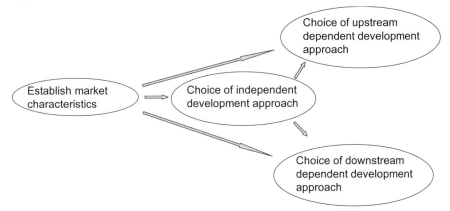

Fig. 1. Conceptual framework

Figure 1 shows the decision-making process which is used for the derivation of development approaches for a specific market. Arrows in Fig. 1 indicate the order in decision making. The evolution of the supply chain starts with an independent approach which is fully determined by the characteristics of the market. In a later stage, the supply chain length increases by incorporating upstream or downstream development.

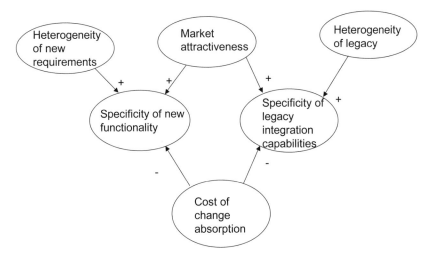

Fig. 2. Factors influencing the specificity of an independent strategy

Figure 2 provides an overview of the market characteristics, which determine the specificity that needs to be achieved by an independent development approach. Specificity with respect to both new functionality and legacy integration capabilities are indicated. A market with a high heterogeneity favours an approach with a high specificity (indicated by a + sign). However, the market attractiveness (size, profitability and growth) determines whether such a strategy results in a price which is acceptable. A high market attractiveness therefore enables a high specificity (also indicated by a + sign). In order to reduce the cost of change absorption, the specificity should be kept low (indicated by a – sign) since a high specificity increases the number of issues to be tested for absorption of a change.

As mentioned before, a company with an independent strategy can choose to include either upstream- or downstream-dependent production strategies in its supply chain. In Fig. 3 the market characteristics that influence this choice are given.

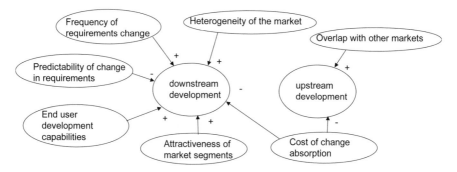

Fig. 3. Factors influencing the choice of dependent development strategies

In a market which is very heterogeneous, it is not always possible to realize sufficient variants of existing products with an acceptable time to market by a single company. The dynamic character of the market can be expressed in terms of the frequency with which requirements change as well as the predictability of the changing requirements. Downstream development can then be used to create a better balance in specificity, cost and time to market. However, since downstream development is often directed to dedicated segments of the entire market, the attractiveness of these segments determines whether downstream development is economically feasible.

Furthermore, introducing more developing entities in the supply chain raises the coordination cost. Therefore, downstream development is only feasible for markets which are sufficiently large. A special situation of downstream production is a market in which customers are capable of realizing part of the variability themselves. Downstream production may appear to be undesirable for software applications that are very critical and for which the risk of applying a change is large.

Allowing upstream-dependent strategies is interesting if overlap exists with other markets so that the cost of development can be spread over more markets. Also in the case of upstream development, the increase in cost of change absorption counterbalances the efficiency gains due to specialization and spreading investments over larger markets.

From Figs. 2 and 3 one can derive four strategic dimensions with respect to software development in a supply chain:

- The variability strategy determines to what extent the specificity of a software product matches the heterogeneity of the market and what mechanisms are used to achieve the required variability (Fig. 2).
- The legacy integration strategy determines to what extent and how the customers' existing software will be taken into account (Fig. 2).
- The asset strategy determines which assets will be developed in house, which assets will be developed upstream or downstream and how these assets will be integrated (Figs. 2 and –3).
- The main counterbalancing force in achieving specificity and specialization in the supply chain is related to the cost of change absorption. Therefore, a change strategy is required that determines how the dynamics of market requirements is translated in frequency and granularity of changes and how these changes will be absorbed by reusers and end-users (Figs. 2 and 3).

These four dimensions are shown in Fig. 4. The bidirectional arrows indicate that choices in one-dimension have influence on the choices in other dimensions.

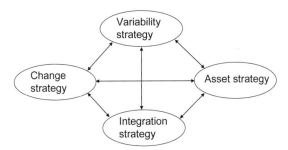

Fig. 4. Four dimensions of a software supply chain strategy

5 Discussion

Krueger (1992) has presented a review of software reuse mechanisms, among which are high-level languages, design and code scavenging and software architectures. Modern software development approaches (both dependent as well as independent) often incorporate more than one of the reuse mechanisms originally mentioned by Krueger. Four major software development approaches encountered in software industry today that can be characterized as an *independent* approach are:

- Packaged software (Sawyer 2000)
- Product family (Bosch 2001)
- Model-driven platform (Kleppe et al. 2003)
- Platform for legacy integration (Erl 2004)

Table 1. Strategic dimensions for typical independent development strategies

	Packaged software	Product family	Model-driven platform	Platform for legacy integration
Variability strategy	Packaged software is not specific and intended for homogeneous markets. The variability consists of parameterization only.	Variability directed at developing a family of similar products, through so-called feature selection and parameterization (Bosch 2001). Production cost of one product can be low.	Applications for a specific organization are generated from business models. The variability that can be achieved is limited by the modeling languages of the platform.	Directed towards removal of any variability restrictions encountered in the legacy of a customer. The platforms allow definition of new business models and thus applications top of this legacy.
Integration strategy	In general isolated software does not require integration with other applications.	Focus is typically on Greenfield situations.	Certain platforms can enable integrating legacy systems through modeling.	Specifically directed towards reuse of existing components.
Asset strategy	Usage of a component framework (such as NET) for composition and usage of third-party components within this composition.	Reuse of COTS-components is possible. Some product families allow downstream development of product family add-ons.	Downstream specialization of generic business objects to branch models.	The asset strategy of a platform for legacy integration is directed towards the reuse of existing assets.
Change strategy	Changes from third-party component suppliers have to be absorbed by the application builder. Change at customer level only consists of patches and upgrades supplied by the application builder to the customers.	The producer of the product family is the main source of change. Change by the customer is usually restricted to feature selection and parameterization.	Sources of changes can be found in the platform, the branch models and the customer-specific models. Pluriform (2007) distributes many small changes with a high frequency and make sure these changes can be absorbed downstream.	The customer is the main source of change. The goal is to allow the customer to continuously change the applications.

The four independent approaches have been analysed with respect to these four strategic dimensions (see Table 1). This can be seen as a preliminary validation of the framework. Further case research is needed for validation of the framework and to assess differences between various areas of software development such as embedded software, tailor-made software, etc.

6 Conclusion

In this chapter a decision framework has been introduced that links characteristics of software markets to strategic management of software development in a supply chain. This framework is directed towards giving individual software manufacturers and the software industry in general better insight in their strategic decisions. The chapter shows that a strategy consists of the variability strategy, the legacy integration strategy, the change strategy and the asset strategy. The framework has been applied to four typical reuse approaches on a generic level to provide a preliminary validation. More research is needed for validation of the framework in specific cases.

References

Bosch, J. (2001) "Design and Use of Software Architectures." Addison-Wesley, Reading, MA, ISBN-10: 0201674947.

Erl, T. (2004) "Service-Oriented Architecture: A Field Guide to Integrating XML and Web Services." Prentice-Hall, Upper Saddle River, NJ, ISBN 0131858580.

Favaro, J.M., Favaro, K.R., and Favaro, P.R. (1998) "Value based software reuse investment." Annals of Software Engineering 5, 5–52.

Hohpe, G. and Woolf, B. (2007) "Enterprise Integration Patterns." Addison-Wesley, London, ISBN 0321200683.

Kleppe, A., Warmer, J., and Bast, W. (2003) "MDA explained, the model driven architecture, practice and promise." Addison-Wesley, Reading, MA, ISBN 032119442X.

Krueger, C. (1992) "Software Reuse." ACM Computing Surveys, 24(2), 131–183.

Messerschmidt, D.G. and Szyperski, C. (2003) "Software Ecosystem." MIT, Cambridge, MA, ISBN 0262134322.

Pluriform (2007): www.pluriform.nl

Postmus, D. and Kruithof, G.H. (2007) "Supply chain coordination in the ERP industry." Submitted to the Supply Chain Management: International Journal.

Sawyer, S. (2000): "Packaged software: implications of the differences from custom approaches to software development." European Journal of Information Systems, 9(1) 47–58.

Wegner, P. (1987) "The Object-oriented classification paradigm." In P. Wegner and B.D. Shriver, eds, Research directions in object oriented programming, pp. 479–560. MIT, Cambridge, MA.

Wright, P., Pringle, C.D. and Kroll, M.J. (1992) "Strategic management, text and cases." Allyn & Bacon, Boston, MA, ISBN 0205134211.

Assessment Tools as Drivers for SPI: Short-Term Benefits and Long-Term Challenges

Sune Dueholm Müller[1], Jacob Nørbjerg[2] and Hiu Ngan Cho[3]

[1] University of Aarhus, Aarhus School of Business, Department of Business Studies, sdm@asb.dk

[2] Copenhagen Business School, Department of Informatics, jan.inf@cbs.dk

[3] IBM Denmark, Financial Services Sector, hiucho@dk.ibm.com

Abstract Full-scale software process maturity assessments are costly, can have large organizational impact and are carried out at long (12–24 months) intervals. Consequently, there is a need for techniques and tools to monitor and help manage an SPI project through inexpensive, ongoing progress assessments. In this chapter we present findings from two cases of using such a tool. We have found that the tool does provide useful snapshots of the status of SPI projects, but that long-term use of the tool introduces costs and challenges related to modifying and tailoring the tool to both the organizational context and the SPI implementation approach. Also, persistent use of an assessment tool may jeopardize assessment reliability due to wear-out and routinization.

1 Introduction

Software process assessments produce insight into the current state of an organization's software development practices, help prioritize improvement initiatives and are used to periodically evaluate and replan ongoing SPI initiatives (Humphrey 1990; McFeeley 1996; CMMI Product Team 2002). The dominating approaches to SPI evaluate software processes against a normative model of 'best practice' such as CMMI-SE/SW (CMMI Product Team 2002), Bootstrap (Haase et al. 1994), and most recently CMMI for Development (CMMI Product Team 2006).

Norm-based assessments are, however, relatively rare events due to their cost and high organizational impact. Thus, 12–24 months are typical intervals between assessments (SEI 2005). Assessments are, furthermore, primarily used to identify software process problems and set goals for improvement initiatives at the organizational level, but are not suitable for evaluating local (project level) software processes and software process improvements (Daskalantonakis 1994).

There is, therefore, a need for techniques and tools to monitor SPI projects and help software practitioners assess their own practices and document improvements between regular full-scale assessments (Daskalantonakis 1994; Arent et al. 2000). To this end, the tools and techniques should be relatively easy to use, require little outside help or support, and have low cost of use (time spent on an assessment). The tools and techniques should, furthermore, be consistent with the framework used in full-blown appraisals in order to be able to document improvements in terms of the overall organizational SPI project.

Previous experiences show that regular tool-based assessments at the local level are low in cost and low in impact, but help disseminate knowledge about good software practices, facilitate reflection about own practices, and create commitment to the implementation of new and improved practices (Daskalantonakis 1994; Arent et al. 2000).

These results are encouraging, but there is a need for more research into the long-term role and effect of assessment tools in SPI. In this chapter we therefore set out to explore the use of tool-based assessments to drive and support SPI projects over long periods of time. The research is based on the use of a Web-based assessment tool to support SPI projects in two different organizations (CMMI Product Team 2002).

In one of the organizations, the use of the tool was studied over a period of 2 years and in the other over 6 months. The study shows that (a) the tool can be a useful driver in SPI projects but not without proper management support and pressure; (b) although the tool allows for quick and low-cost maturity assessments in projects, the long-term costs of maintaining and using the tool are non-trivial; (c) long-term use of the tool carries a risk of reduced reliability of answers due to routinization of respondents.

In the next section we briefly introduce software process maturity and assessment methods, and discuss previous research on tool support for software process assessments. Section 3 describes the tool, and section 4 outlines the research method. The two cases in which the tool has been used are presented in section 5, and the results are summarized and discussed in section 6. Section 7 concludes the chapter.

2 Software Capability Models and Assessments

The dominating approaches to SPI are based on a norm or model that specifies 'good' or mature software processes against which an organization can compare its own practices. Well-known models include CMMI (CMMI Product Team 2002) and Bootstrap (Haase et al. 1994). The models describe increasing levels of maturity from the lowest level characterized by frequent budget and time overruns, quality problems, low efficiency, to the highest level at which processes are well-defined (and followed), there is careful and detailed monitoring of projects, and ongoing planned and controlled fine-tuning of processes. The assumption is that as an organization increases its maturity level, it will also improve its performance, i.e. the accuracy of estimates, the quality of products and the efficiency of its processes.

The maturity models have been criticized for being too large and complex for small- to medium-sized companies to use and for their lack of support for tailoring to different business and application domains (Bollinger and McGowan 1991; Bach 1995; Aaen 2002; Aaen and Pries-Heje 2004). Critics have also argued that the maturity models may lead organizations to focus on the requirements of the model instead of the problems the organization actually faces (Iversen et al. 1999). The maturity models have, nevertheless, gained wide recognition in spite of criticism, thus underlining the need for research into their basis and application.

Assessments provide a basis for benchmarking and comparing organizations which is useful when, for example, selecting a software supplier. Thus, a dominant player like the U.S. Department of Defense requires potential software suppliers, i.e. sub-contractors, to be certified at CMMI level 3 (Hansen and Nørbjerg 2005). Additionally, the models give firms undertaking SPI a tested and well-known framework for assessing their processes and prioritizing improvement initiatives.

The models are very complex, however, and describe each maturity level in great detail. The specification of the CMMI-SE/SW, for example, comprises 573 pages (CMMI Product Team 2002). Consequently, a full-scale appraisal against a maturity model is a time-consuming and costly affair that involves a team of trained appraisers and may take as long as several weeks. Therefore, companies undertaking model-based SPI typically repeat such appraisals only at 12–24 month intervals (SEI 2005).

2.1 Assessment Methods and Tools

Based on a literature survey, we divide methods, tools and techniques for software process assessments into three main groups. First, there are the assessment methods, questionnaires and other tools, and assessor training programmes that accompany the major maturity models (Dunaway and Masters 1996). Some research has produced additional computer-based tools for results visualization (Hunter et al. 1997) and support for prioritization of improvement initiatives (Gorschek and Wohlin 2004).

A second group of research addresses assessment techniques and tools with lower organizational impact and cost, often adapted to smaller organizations. The RAPID assessment method based on the SPICE model (ISO 1999) provides for one-day assessments and has been used successfully in small- to medium-sized organizations (Cater-Steel et al. 2006). Also based on the SPICE framework, the SPINI and MARES assessment methods facilitate adaptation of an assessment to the needs and resources of small enterprises (Gresse von Wangenheim et al. 2006). Iversen et al. describe the use of a questionnaire-based survey to assess an organization according to level 2 of the now retired SW-CMM (Iversen et al. 1998), and Kautz et al. outline an approach inspired by GQM to select a few improvement areas in very small organizations (Kautz 1998, 1999). Finally, the

Problem Diagnosis approach proposes to focus on software process issues and problems experienced by key organizational players in order to build support and commitment for improvement initiatives (Iversen et al. 1999).

All of the above methods and tools focus on the assessments used to initialize an improvement programme and evaluate results. Such assessments are, however, disjoint from day-to-day development activities and are not designed for ongoing monitoring of improvement projects. They are, therefore, less suited for practitioners and local managers who need to verify that improvement projects progress according to plan (Daskalantonakis 1994; Arent et al. 2000). Consequently, a third group of research focuses on tools and techniques aiming to provide rapid, low-cost, low-impact assessments and feedback to SPI projects. Daskalantonakis reports how Motorola used a 'progress assessment' technique to assess software projects according to the SW-CMM (Paulk et al. 1993) thereby providing useful information about the overall SPI project's progress (Daskalantonakis 1994). The technique used (internal) facilitators to support the assessment and was used quarterly over a period of 2 years in one of Motorola's divisions. A similar approach was used in the Danish subsidiary of L.M. Ericsson, but supplemented with so-called Ultra Light Assessments (ULA) performed monthly in individual projects. The ULA uses an Excel spreadsheet with questions pertaining to the key practices of CMM level 2. A ULA can be completed by a project manager and his team in 0.5–1 day. Lessons from both L.M. Ericsson and Motorola show that such frequent progress monitoring and reporting support commitment, participation and learning among practitioners in SPI projects, Furthermore, management receives frequent reports and feedback about the overall SPI status and progress (Daskalantonakis 1994; Arent et al. 2000).

The EBAT tool described in this article can, similarly to the ULA, be used for regular and project-level assessments of practices against a maturity model (CMMI) and thus help monitor and guide SPI projects. In this chapter we present results from its use in two different organizations and (in one case) over a prolonged period of time. This article extends previous research through a longitudinal study and an inter-organizational comparison of the effects of using the tool.

3 The EBAT Tool

EBAT (Electronic-Based Assessment Tool) is a semi-automated self-assessment tool that can be used to measure a systems development unit's degree of CMMI level 2 compliance with minimal tailoring of the tool. Basically, EBAT consists of a Web-based questionnaire and a calculation module to produce a maturity profile of the systems development unit being investigated.

CMMI level 2 addresses project management related concerns and issues. In keeping with this, EBAT was developed for use in projects with project managers and project participants as the target group. The tool can, however, be used to assess other organizational units against the CMMI level 2 requirements. Thus,

EBAT has on occasion been used to produce a 'temperature' reading of an entire department's state of health in terms of process maturity across projects.

3.1 History

EBAT was originally developed in Systems Inc. (see section 5.1) because of a need for swift data collection and data processing when assessing the maturity of software engineering practices (as defined by the SW-CMM) through question-naires. The basic idea was to obtain a detailed and valid picture of the degree of CMM compliance with as little manual data processing as possible. The first step was therefore to make an electronic equivalent to existing questionnaires like the Questionnaire-Based Assessment method (Arent and Iversen 1996) and the Flexi-ble Assessment Questionnaire Tool (Vestergaard and Kristensen 1998) supple-mented with automated maturity rating generation and compilation of maturity profiles for the unit of analysis in question (an entire development department, a single project group, or some other unit). Later it was decided to revise and update the tool to include not only software engineering but also systems development practices mirroring the SEI move from CMM to CMMI. EBAT has undergone a number of other changes and modifications since its original inception, including tailoring the questionnaire to different roles in a project, e.g. project manager and systems developer.

3.2 Types of Questions

The questionnaire includes more than 200 questions covering both the specific and generic practices of the CMMI. The questions take the form of scenarios. The questions are grouped according to the process areas of the maturity model, e.g. project planning, requirements management and configuration management. Each question contains two scenarios, one describes best practice according to the CMMI, whereas the other describes 'poor' practice. The respondent is asked to judge which of the two scenarios best corresponds to the practices of the unit be-ing assessed. A comment field is attached to each question inviting respondents to elaborate and justify their answers.

The question in Fig. 1 is one of many within the process area of Project Plan-ning (PP) that covers one of the specific practices at CMMI level 2.

By computing and comparing the answers for each project group (or the like) to the process requirements specified by the CMMI it is possible to not only iden-tify strengths and weaknesses of existing practices but also to calculate a CMMI level 2 maturity rating for the project in question. An example of the overall ma-turity profiles of a project is illustrated in Fig. 2.

4 Research Method

This article is the result of a longitudinal study of the long-term use of EBAT in two organizations. One organization has used the tool regularly from the fall of 2004 through the fall of 2006 as part of ongoing SPI efforts. During this time period an estimated 100 assessments have been performed with the tool. One of the authors participated in the company's Software Engineering Process Group (SEPG) and was responsible for the maintenance and deployment of the tool.

In the second organization, assessments were performed over a shorter time period to determine the overall maturity of a development department.

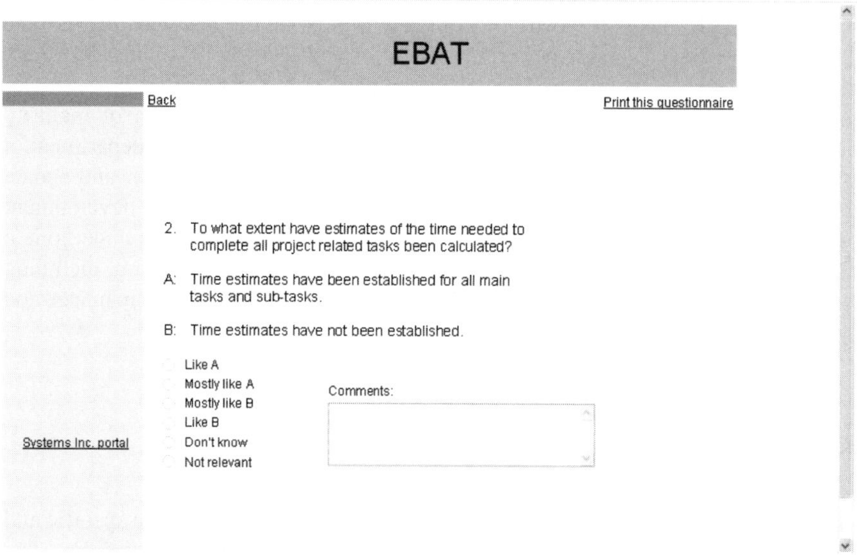

Fig. 1. Example question

Several data sources have been used to calibrate the tool and evaluate its usability and accuracy as an assessment tool; i.e. questionnaire comments provided by respondents, interviews, minutes and audio recordings of meetings, audits to ensure the validity of assessment results, introductory meetings to familiarize respondents with the questionnaire and presentations of assessment results. Project managers, project participants and managers have had the opportunity to voice concerns, reservations, criticism, suggestions for improvement and praise. Their comments and feedback have subsequently been used in analyses of the assessment results and contribute to confirm their reliability and validity as well as the findings reported here.

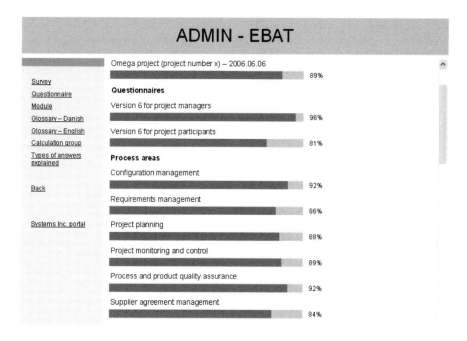

Fig. 2. Example maturity profile

5 Using the Tool

EBAT has been used at Systems Inc., an independent company, and Software Consultants, a subsidiary of a larger engineering and construction consultancy firm.

5.1 Systems Inc.

Systems Inc. is a large Danish systems development company that offers mission critical solutions (i.e. space and defense systems) on a global scale. In 2004 Systems Inc. initiated a company-wide process improvement project labeled Business Process Improvement Project (BPIP). The CMMI was the chosen model, and CMMI level 2 process compliance was the immediate project goal.

Systems Inc. management decided to rely on measurements as a key driver in implementing new and improved processes. Measurements have been used regularly and systematically to ensure that implementation targets are met and non-compliance issues are reported. EBAT has been an integral part of the measurement strategy, and the tool is still used for determining whether systems development practices at the project level are compliant with both required and expected CMMI model components. Since project kick-off EBAT has been used in more than 30 new and ongoing projects. Measurements have been performed on average every 3–4 months to evaluate the progress of putting new processes into practice. During this period EBAT has provided a longitudinal view of the evolution of process maturity at the project level. The tool has rendered improvements readily visible, and when expected changes have failed to occur, EBAT has been used to identify weak spots and areas for improvement in the projects' practices. Today, having reached the project's goals, EBAT is primarily being used to ensure that practices do not degenerate, but that processes are being institutionalized as the 'way we do business around here.'

Management values EBAT as a catalyst and driver in BPIP. EBAT is viewed as a process 'temperature gauge,' i.e. as a means of getting a snapshot of the development practices of each project that can be used as a basis for corrective actions whenever results fall short of expectations. Some other qualities that have been attributed to EBAT include its educational properties in terms of illustrating best practices through the scenarios in each question. On the other hand EBAT has received mixed reviews among project managers and participants. Some people have been put off by the time needed to fill out the questionnaires, and others have found several of the questions too abstract or difficult to understand. Still others, typically project managers, have welcomed the regular 'health check' of projects.

Some challenges have emerged through the process of using and adapting EBAT to suit the needs of Systems Inc. Repeated measurements have on occasion led to mindless and superficial answers to the questions on the questionnaire. Also, total costs of using the tool have been higher than expected due to continuous updates to accommodate suggested enhancements as well as analyses of results and feedback.

5.2 Software Consultants

Software Consultants began as the IT department of a construction and engineering consultancy group, but is now an independent subsidiary. The company supports and develops information systems for some of the biggest Danish companies as well as central and local government institutions and authorities.

In May 2005 an outside consultant carried out a CMMI light assessment at Software Consultants which placed the company at level 1. In the fall of that year Software Consultants formulated a vision and a strategy plan for 2005–2008 in which increased software process maturity was made an explicit goal. In February 2006 two of the authors performed a preliminary investigation into one department at Software Consultants using EBAT and interviews with project managers and developers. As many as 28 employees from four different projects were asked to complete the online survey and 22 completed it. The results from the survey showed that Software Consultants was still a level 1 (CMMI) organization in spite of a year's SPI effort. The survey itself was carried out with little organizational impact and cost, although respondents were unfamiliar with several terms in the questionnaire and therefore needed further instruction and guidance.

Comments from the interviews following the EBAT measurement indicate that developers and project managers saw the survey itself as a vehicle for learning about software processes and maturity and as an opportunity for reflecting on their current practices. They did not, however, initiate improvements themselves, but expected management to take responsibility for improvements based on the survey findings.

6 Discussion

The two cases show that an online tool like EBAT can provide valid and helpful insights and reflections about an organization's software practices for developers, project managers, and management. The relatively short time needed to fill out the questionnaire (1–2 h) and the immediate feedback makes the tool a useful instrument for repeated assessments in an ongoing SPI initiative.

We observed that the assessment tool was not in itself an independent driver in the SPI projects. At Software Consultants respondents accepted the assessment results, but relied on management initiative to start improvements. At Systems Inc. project-by-project assessment reports and other forms of status reporting have ensured management attention and pressure that has pushed the SPI efforts forward. These findings correspond to results from previous studies of project level tool based assessments (Daskalantonakis 1994; Arent et al. 2000).

Our longitudinal study revealed, however, other costs and challenges that must be considered if an assessment tool is to be used repeatedly over a long period of time. These costs and challenges pertain to tool tailorization, training of respondents and communication of results. Also, the initial learning and reflection over own practices resulting from using the tool may be substituted by wear-out and routine responses which leads to less reliable results in the long run.

6.1 Tailorization

EBAT can be used in its generic form to obtain results that are recognized as valid by the people being investigated, but richer results are obtained when the wording of questions are adapted to the jargon and terminology used by the employees.

The word 'review' provides an example of this. Many employees at Systems Inc. associate the word 'review' with a technical inspection of some sort. However, many practices in the CMMI, on which the phrasing of the questions in the questionnaire is based, use this term in other contexts; e.g. GP 2.10: 'Review Status with Higher Level Management' (CMMI Product Team 2002). Consequently, other words had to be used depending on the underlying meaning of the question. To avoid questions being misunderstood, pilot assessments were performed to identify key words and concepts that were interpreted differently than intended. Also, several project managers and project participants were interviewed and asked to interpret each question in the questionnaire in order to identify unintelligible and ambiguous questions. Lastly, questionnaire comments have been collected continuously and used to rephrase questions as needed. The need to tailor assessment questionnaires to local culture and terminology has also been reported elsewhere (Iversen et al. 1998).

In addition to tweaking the wording of the questions, the need to adapt the questionnaire to different groups presented itself. Based on an examination and interpretation of the CMMI, this group tailored the questionnaire to different project roles, e.g. project managers and project participants by removing, for example, questions regarding a project manager's responsibilities from the version of the questionnaire used by systems developers. This adaptation has reduced annoyance and aversion among respondents but have taxed a lot of internal development resources.

Thus, it appears that when EBAT or a similar tool is used not only to create snapshots that highlight strong and weak points of current practices, but is used proactively through longer periods, it proves beneficial to adapt the generic questionnaire to the jargon of the particular organization and context.

6.2 Total Costs of Using the Tool

Calculating the direct costs of using an assessment tool like EBAT, e.g. the man-hours needed by respondents to fill out the questionnaires, is pretty straightforward. The long-term use of the tool revealed, however, other partly hidden costs.

First, the tailorization discussed above adds to total costs. Second, it was necessary to instruct the respondents in how to answer the questions due to the complexity of the questionnaire. Consequently, at Systems Inc. a number of introductory meetings were held prior to sending out questionnaires. Judging from the questions raised at those meetings and misunderstandings that have been corrected, it is safe to say that such meetings increase the reliability of the collected data. Similarly, at Software Consultants it was necessary to instruct and help respondents understand unfamiliar terms used in the questionnaire. This training increases the cost of using the tool, but also helped strengthen the reliability of the results.

Third, while EBAT provided quick and, on the face of it, relatively inexpensive snapshots of process maturity, long-term use added costs related to analysis and dissemination of results. In order to provide as much valuable information as possible to projects, the need arose to supplement the standardized reports produced by EBAT with project specific analyses of responses. The standard reports show maturity level ratings and degrees of goal compliance, but do not pinpoint the reasons for non-compliance with defined processes. Specific goal 2 (a required model component) reads, for example, 'A project plan is established and maintained as the basis for managing the project' (CMMI Product Team 2002). However, knowing that a particular project does not completely satisfy this requirement does not tell us why. Perhaps project risks have not been adequately identified (specific practice 2.2-1), or maybe a data management plan has not been prepared (specific practice 2.3-1). Thus, to be able to provide constructive feedback to the projects measurements of these so-called specific practices have been implemented at Systems Inc. The unforeseen need for implementing these measurements and for preparing customized assessment reports has substantially increased the cost of using EBAT at the company.

A final source of increased costs was the need to adapt the form and content of assessments to the process implementation strategy. At Systems Inc. individual implementation plans for each project spelled out when compliance was expected for which processes. Due to the variation in these implementation plans, questionnaires with different subsets of questions were needed at different times, e.g. if a project opted not to comply with certain requirements management processes at the time of an assessment, questions addressing those practices would be removed to reduce the time needed to complete the questionnaire. Needless to say, this kind of tailoring increases the time needed to prepare a questionnaire as part of an assessment and thereby the costs.

Thus, it appears that long-term use of assessment tools in SPI to provide insight into and feedback about improvement progress incurs costs over and above the immediate effort of an assessment.

6.3 Short-Term Learning – Long-Term Wear Out

Assessments are a useful learning vehicle in SPI, but repeated assessments over long time periods created routinization and wear out among respondents. Reactions from Systems Inc. employees suggest that if respondents recognize and remember questions from a previous assessment, they become less attentive and less motivated to answer questions faithfully. Several respondents have admitted to switching on 'the autopilot' when filling out the questionnaire, because they could recall the questions and had formed opinions beforehand regarding the answers. Analysis of surprising assessment results substantiated the claim of routinization. Respondents having submitted identical answers to consecutive questions (e.g. a respondent answering 'not applicable' to numerous questions in a row) were asked to clarify the rationale behind their answers. Failure to provide convincing arguments gave the impression of taking a short cut to finish the questionnaire as quickly as possible. Others hinted that they had answered 'don't know' (with unfortunate consequences for maturity ratings) in sheer irritation of seeing the same questions again. This long-term effect of repeated assessments may be offset by using facilitators (Daskalantonakis 1994), but this will add to the overall costs of assessments.

7 Conclusion

Tools such as EBAT are a means to low-cost and low-impact assessments of software/systems development processes. Thus, these tools provide a useful way to repeatedly gauge the state of an ongoing SPI project and hence support the SPI effort.

Our findings suggest, similar to other research, that a single tool-based assessment is cheap and can be performed in a short time. Our longitudinal study of tool use suggests, however, that tool-based project assessments induce costs and challenges in the long run. The tool must be tailored to the organization's needs and continuously adjusted as the SPI project progresses, and time must be set aside for sending out questionnaires and reminders, analyzing and interpreting the results, and providing feedback based on the answers. Also, repeated assessments may reduce the reliability of answers due to routinization and wear out. This problem may be countered with the use of facilitators which, however, adds to overall costs. Therefore, assessment tools like the one reported here may be an inexpensive way of getting a feel for the strengths and weaknesses of an organization's development practices, but it is far more demanding to use the tool as a lever in SPI.

References

Aaen, I. (2002). Challenging Software Process Improvement by Design. Proceedings of Xth European Conference on Information Systems, Gdansk, Poland.

Aaen, I. and Pries-Heje, J. (2004). Standardising Software Processes - An Obstacle for Innovation? Proceedings of the sixth IFIP 8.6 working conference, Leixlip, Ireland.

Arent, J., Andersen, C. V., Iversen, J. H. and Bang, S. (2000). Project Assessments: Supporting Commitment, Participation, and Learning in Software Process Improvement. Proceedings of the 33rd Hawaii International Conference on System Sciences, Maui, Hawaii.

Arent, J. and Iversen, J. H. (1996). *Udvikling af metode til modenhedsmålinger i software-organisationer baseret på the Capability Maturity Model*. Aalborg University, Denmark.

Bach, J. (1995). Enough about Process: What We need are Heroes. IEEE Software, vol. 12, no. 2, pp. 96–98.

Bollinger, T. B. and McGowan, C. (1991). A Critical Look at Software Capability Evaluations. IEEE Software, vol. 8, no. 4, pp. 25–41.

Cater-Steel, A., Toleman, M. and Rout, T. (2006). Process improvement for small firms: An evaluation of the RAPID assessment-based method. Information and Software Technology, vol. 48, no. 5, pp. 323–334.

CMMI Product Team (2006). *CMMI for Development, Version 1.2*. SEI, Pittsburgh, PA.

CMMI Product Team (2002). *Capability Maturity Model Integration (CMMI), Version 1.1, Staged Representation (CMMI-SE/SW/IPPD/SS, V1.1, Staged)*. SEI, Pittsburgh, PA.

Daskalantonakis, M. K. (1994). Achieving Higher SEI Levels. IEEE Software, vol. 11, no. 4, pp. 17–24.

Dunaway, D. K. and Masters, S. (1996). *CMM-Based Appraisal for Internal Process Improvement (CBA IPI): Method Description*. SEI, Pittsburgh, PA.

Gorschek, T. and Wohlin, C. (2004). Packaging software improvement issues: a method and a case study. Software: Practice and Experience, vol. 34, no. 14, pp. 1311–1344.

Gresse von Wangenheim, C., Varkoi, T. and Salviano, C. F. (2006). Standard Based Software Process Assessments in Small Companies. Software Process: Improvement and Practice, vol. 11, no 3, pp. 329–335.

Haase, V., Messnarz, R., Koch, G., Kugler, H. J. and Decrinis, P. (1994). Bootstrap: Fine-Tuning Process Assessment. IEEE Software, vol. 11, no. 4, pp. 25–35.

Hansen, B. and Nørbjerg, J. (2005). Codification or Personalisation - a simple choice? Proceedings of the 28th Information systems Research seminar In Scandinavia, Kristiansand, Norway.

Humphrey, W. S. (1990). *Managing the Software Process*. Addison-Wesley, Reading, MA.

Hunter, R., Robinson, G. and Woodman, I. (1997). Tool Support for Software Process Assessment and Improvement. Software Process: Improvement and Practice, vol. 3, no. 4, pp. 213–223.

ISO (1999). *Information Technology - Software Process Assessment - Part 5: An Assessment model and Indicator Guidance*. ISO, Geneva, Switzerland.

Iversen, J., Johansen, J., Nielsen, P. A. and Pries-Heje, J. (1998). Combining Quantitative and Qualitative Assessment Methods in Software Process Improvement. Proceedings of the 6th European Conference on Information Systems, Aix-en-Provence, France.

Iversen, J., Nielsen, P. A. and Nørbjerg, J. (1999). Situated Assessments of Problems in Software Development. Database for Advances in Information Systems, vol. 30, no. 2, pp. 66–81.

Kautz, K. (1999). Making Sense of Measurement for Small Organizations. IEEE Software, vol. 16, no. 2, pp. 14–20.

Kautz, K. (1998). Software Process Improvement In Very Small Enterprises: Does It Pay Off? Software Process: Improvement and Practice, vol. 4, no. 4, pp. 209–226.

McFeeley, B. (1996). *IDEAL: A User's Guide for Software Process Improvement*. SEI, Pittsburgh, PA.

Paulk, M., Curtis, B., Chrissis, M. and Weber, C. (1993). *Capability Maturity Model for Software (Version 1.1)*. SEI, Pittsburgh, PA.

SEI (2005). *Process Maturity Profile. Software CMM. 2005 Mid-Year Update*. SEI, Pittsburgh, PA.

Vestergaard, C. A. and Kristensen, L. (1998). Diagnosticering i forbindelse med softwaregrocesforbedring: Udvikling af en spørgeskemabaseret metode baseret på CMM niveau 2 til diagnosticering af softwareprocessen. Aalborg University, Denmark.

Improving Organizational Performance by Raising the Level of Business Process Orientation Maturity: Empirical Test and Case Study

Rok Škrinjar and Mojca Indihar Štemberger

University of Ljubljana, Faculty of Economics
rok.skrinjar@ef.uni-lj.si, mojca.stemberger@ef.uni-lj.si

Abstract   The extensive literature on business process management suggests that organizations can enhance their overall performance by adopting a process view of business. It has been shown in previous studies that the companies which have reached higher business process maturity level consistently outperform those that have not reached them. This chapter presents the results of the empirical research that confirms the impact of business process orientation on organizational performance in transition economy by using structural equation modelling. The link is even stronger than in the original investigation. Besides that more detailed specification of organizational performance that includes non-financial performance measures has been used. The results show that business process orientation leads to better non-financial performance and indirectly to better financial performance. Because of this important finding, this chapter also presents the methodology for assessing, analyzing and enhancing process orientation using two case studies.

1 Introduction

Organizations are continually under competitive pressures and are forced to re-evaluate their business models and underlying business processes. Business processes represent a core of the functioning of an organization because the company primarily consists of processes, not products or services. In other words, managing a business means managing its processes (McCormack and Johnson 2001). The extensive literature on business process management (e.g. Davenport 1993; Hammer and Champy 1993; McCormack and Johnson 2001; Burlton 2001; Harmon 2003) suggests that organizations can enhance their overall performance by adopting a process view of business. Most of the literature on business process management lacks research or an empirical focus (McCormack 1999). However,

C. Barry et al. (eds.), *Information Systems Development: Challenges in Practice, Theory, and Education, Vol.2*, doi: 10.1007/978-0-387-78578-3_11,
© Springer Science+Business Media, LLC 2009

McCormack and Johnson (2001) showed that business process orientation has a positive impact on business performance.

Based on the original study a joint empirical research by Faculty of Economics in Ljubljana and Zagreb was carried out in Slovenia. The aim was to test the impact of process orientation maturity level on organizational performance. This chapter presents the results of the empirical research that confirms the impact of business process orientation on organizational performance. While a similar research has been carried out by McCormack and Johnson (2001) our contribution is the verification of the link in transition economy and more detailed specification of organizational performance that includes non-financial performance measures. Because of the impact of process orientation on organizational performance we used the business process orientation maturity measurement instrument to asses the current state of BPO in two companies and based on the problems identified present guidelines for managers to improve BPO maturity.

This chapter is structured as follows. Section 2 reviews the relevant literature about business process orientation, organizational performance and the link between the two concepts. In section 3 the research model is conceptualized and suitable hypotheses are developed. Section 4 aims to present a methodological framework for the study and provides results of data analysis. Section 5 presents the methodology for assessing, analyzing and enhancing BPO on two case studies. Section 6 concludes with a summary of the main findings, discusses them from theoretical and practical standpoints, and outlines directions for future research together with the limitations of the study.

2 Literature Review

2.1 Business Process Orientation

The competitive global market climate of the new millennium has raised awareness of business processes as the most important management paradigm. The process 'option' is now becoming a mandatory requirement (Levi 2002). In other words, in conformity with new business philosophy, the organization should be designed to provide both vertical and horizontal information flow as necessary to accomplish the organization's overall goals (Daft 2004). Looking beyond functional boundaries, business processes emerge – the way business actually works becomes clear. Moreover, a firm's performance reflects the efficiency of its processes and that demands a process orientation.

Process orientation still isn't recognized as an independent discipline, it rather represents a generic concept of numerous management philosophies which use process perspective to improve business performance (Lindfors 2003). Although empirical evidence is lacking, several models have emerged during the last few years that have been presented as the high-performance, process-oriented organization needed in today's and tomorrow's world. Deming, Porter, Davenport,

Short, Hammer, Byrne, Imai, Drucker, Rummler-Brache and Melan have all defined what they view as the new model of the organization. This 'new way of thinking' or 'viewing' the organization has been generally described as business process orientation or BPO (McCormack and Johnson 2001).

Although definitions of the business process orientation vary, we adopt the McCormack's and Johnson's (2001) definition of process orientation: An organization that, in all its thinking, emphasizes process as opposed to hierarchies with a special emphasis on outcomes and customer satisfaction.

It is evident that all organizations are compounds of business processes, although they do not necessarily have a process view. However, a process approach can be applied on each organization and a level of process orientation can be determined. Levels of process orientation are often presented by process maturity concept. In the current business environment, there is no scarcity of process maturity models. For the purpose of this research the BPO maturity model was readjusted from McCormack and Johnson (2001). The BPO construct describes a four-step pathway for systematically advancing business processes along the maturity continuum (Ad Hoc, Defined, Linked and Integrated level). Each step builds on the work of the previous steps to apply improvement strategies that are appropriate to the current maturity level. The following definitions for the stages that an organization goes through when becoming business process oriented are provided:

- Ad Hoc: The processes are unstructured and ill-defined. Process measures are not in place and the jobs and organizational structures are based upon the traditional functions, not horizontal processes.
- Defined: The basic processes are defined and documented and are available in flow charts. Changes to these processes must now go through a formal procedure. Jobs and organizational structures include a process aspect, but remain basically functional. Representatives from functional areas (sales, manufacturing, etc.) meet regularly to coordinate with each other, but only as representatives of their traditional functions.
- Linked: The breakthrough level. Managers employ process management with strategic intent and results. Broad process jobs and structures are put in place outside of traditional functions.
- Integrated: The company, its vendors and suppliers, take cooperation to the process level. Organizational structures and jobs are based on processes, and traditional functions begin to be equal or sometimes subordinate to process. Process measures and management systems are deeply imbedded in the organization (McCormack and Johnson 2001; McCormack 2003).

BPO construct is built on the following individual dimensions: process view, process jobs, process management and measurement. Process view involves a focus on the workflows and processes across the organization. The goal is to get as much as possible out of the process and not of the individual person (Häggström and Oscarsson 2001). It is instructive because it follows work as it proceeds across the organization. Perhaps even more important, functional roles and titles reflecting the traditional hierarchical structure are replaced by process owners – leaders who are responsible and accountable for the operation and improvement of the core business (Tenner and DeToro 1996). Along with process owners, process teams become the main building element of organization which emphasizes the process job category. Finally, process management, supplemented with process measures, has as much to do with changing the culture and the way of thinking, as it is to do with changing the organizational structure. It is this most fundamental aspect of the transition that the majority of organizations have failed to appreciate (O'Hanlon 2003). Neumann et al. see the main task of process management in accompanying the process implementation, and ensuring the continuous, incremental improvement of the organization's processes (zur Muehlen 2002).

2.2 Organizational Performance

One cannot evaluate organizational performance without taking organizational goals into consideration. The modern business environment demands a multi-goal orientation. Profit theory (Cyert and March 1963) is no longer a valid measure of organizational performance and neither are other approaches that only take the interests of shareholders (owners) of a company into account. Today's business environment is characterized by the increasing importance and strength of various stakeholder groups.

It has become quite obvious that all stakeholders need to be taken into account when assessing a modern company's performance. This is the main idea of Freeman's Stakeholder theory (Freeman 1984, 1994). The stakeholder view maintains that firms have stakeholders rather than just shareholders to account for. The view that the corporation has obligations only to its stockholders is replaced by the notion that there are other groups to whom the firm is also responsible. Groups with a 'stake' in the firm include shareholders, employees, customers, suppliers, lenders, the government and society (Atkinson et al. 1997; Berman et al. 1999; Harrison and Freeman 1999; Hillman and Keim 2001; Riahi-Belkaoui 2003; Tangem 2004).

One important notion revealed in many studies is that building better relations with primary stakeholders like employees, customers and suppliers could lead to increased shareholder wealth. A sustainable organizational advantage may be built with tacit assets that derive from developing relationships with key stakeholders (Hillman and Keim 2001). When studying the relationship between stakeholder management and a firm's financial performance, Berman et al. (1999) found that fostering positive connections with key stakeholders (customers and employees) can help a firm's profitability.

Due to the significance of various stakeholders, organizational performance should not solely be assessed by financial indicators. There are several approaches (Tangem 2004) to organizational performance measurement that encompass different stakeholders' perspectives. The Balanced Scorecard (BSC) (Kaplan and

Norton 1992, 1993, 1996) is the most established and most commonly used (Neely 2005), but by far not the only one.

2.3 Link between BPO and Organizational Performance

Most organizations that have made an attempt to move toward process orientation agree that it does indeed provide numerous benefits, including cost savings through a more efficient execution of work, improved customer focus, better integration across the organization, etc. Main advantages of process-based organizational structure, in comparison to functional one, are in economical design of business processes, as well as in reducing cycle time (Sikavica and Novak 1999), in increased flexibility of the firm along with improved customer satisfaction. Namely, even though processes don't appear on the balance sheet as such, managers intuitively recognize that they are assets, not expenses (Keen 1997). A key source of process benefit is improving hand-offs between functions, which can occur only when processes are broadly defined (Oden 1999). A process orientation leads to cycle time reduction by doing a good job of coordinating work across functions. The faster time cycles mean reduced inventories and faster receipt of cash. The reduced working capital translates into reduced costs of carrying inventory and cash. Other costs are reduced because duplication of work across functions is eliminated. A process orientation eliminates such redundant activities, verifying input once for all functions (Galbraith 2002).

Implementing BPO as a way of organizing and operating in an organization will improve internal coordination and break down the functional silos that exist in most companies. Research has shown that this increase in cooperation and decrease in conflict improve both short- and long-term performance of an organization (McCormack et al. 2003). Furthermore, the more business process oriented an organization is, the better it performs both from an overall perspective as well as from the perspective of the employees. Satisfied employees perform better and execute their tasks more effectively and efficiently. They are less inclined to change jobs (Karatepe et al. 2006) and are less frequently absent.

There are rare authors who have empirically investigated the impact of BPO on organizational performance. Two of them are McCormack and Johnson (2001), who conducted an empirical study to explore the relationship between BPO and enhanced business performance. The research results showed that BPO is critical in reducing conflict and encouraging greater connectedness within an organization, while improving business performance. Their results indicate a surprisingly strong relationship between BPO and overall performance. Process orientation also changes the interaction between a firm and its business partners (suppliers and customers) – by integrating processes beyond the boundaries of a firm. Transaction-based cooperation is transformed into long-term partnership that results in increased performance for all links in a supply chain (Hendricks et al. 2007; Cousins and Menguc 2006).

3 Research Hypotheses and Model Conceptualization

The main purpose of the following sections of this chapter is to test if higher levels of business process orientation lead to better organizational performance. While a similar research has been carried out by McCormack and Johnson our contribution is the application of the link in transition economy and detailed specification of organizational performance. Since the theoretical background of the BPO and OP constructs has been presented in the first part here only the hypothesized relationships between them is presented. To thoroughly test the link between BPO and OP we formulated three hypotheses:

H1: The higher the level of business process orientation a firm achieves the better it performs financially.

H2: The higher the level of business process orientation a firm achieves the better it performs non-financially in terms of more satisfied employees, customers and suppliers.

H3: Better non-financial performance leads to better financial performance.

In Fig. 1 the conceptualized model along with the hypothesized relationships is shown.

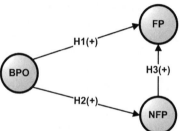

Fig. 1. Conceptual model and direction of impact between constructs

4 Research Methods and Data Analysis

In order to test the proposed hypotheses our instrument was composed of two parts. The first part measuring BPO was adopted from the original study conducted by McCormack and Johnson (2001). This part of the instrument was amended in two sections: (1) One question was added to the Process view section; (2) two questions were added to the process management and measurement section. Altogether BPO construct was measured using 15 items. Even though the original instrument from McCormack and Johnson included an overall organizational performance construct, it was only measured with two items. As our goal was to tap deeper into the problem we choose not to use this operationalization of organizational performance construct. Therefore we devised our own instrument for organizational performance measurement. This represents the second part of our research instrument. Theoretically it is based on the balanced scorecard (Kaplan and Norton 1992, 1993, 1996) and its main goal is to measure different facets of organizational performance, namely the financial and the non-financial. We used 19 items to measure the organizational performance. In autumn 2005, empirical data were collected through a survey of 1,267 Slovenian companies that had more than 50 employees. Questionnaires were addressed to CEOs or senior managers estimated as having adequate knowledge of the BPO and performance within their companies. A total of 203 managers responded.

To test the hypothesized relationships we employed the combined exploratory-confirmatory approach. In the first phase we analyzed the questionnaire items using the exploratory factor analysis in order to test if the item in fact measure pre-specified constructs. The main concern in this part is 'Do items really measure the specified constructs?.' We used the statistical package SPSS 13.0 to run a series of data reduction tests. Data were subjected to Factor Analysis technique using principal axis factoring extraction method combined with Varimax rotation. Using .50 loading cut-off value, which according to Comrey and Lee (1992) is a good score, we removed several items for further data analysis since they did not load appropriately on their factors.

After subjecting the data to factor analysis the purified data was used to operationalize the measurement of BPO and OP constructs. The constructs consisted of the following scales:

1. **BPO construct**:
- Process view (PROCV)
- Process jobs (PROCJ)
- Process management and measurement (PROCMM)

2. **Financial performance construct**:
- FINA1 (measuring ROA)
- FINA2 (value added per employee)

3. **Non-financial performance construct**:
- NFSUP (measuring the relationship with suppliers)
- NFEMP1 and NFEMP2 (measuring the satisfaction of employees)
- NFCUST (measuring the relationship with customers)

In the second phase of our analysis following the approach proposed by Diamantopoulos and Siguaw (2000) we tested the relationships between constructs using the structural equation modeling using Lisrel. First step in our analysis was the assessment of model fit whereby we were interested whether the hypothesized model is consistent with the data. First we examined the measurement part of the model. Our aim was to determine the validity and reliability of the measures used to represent the constructs of interest. Validity reflects the extent to which an indicator actually measures what is suppose to measure. The validity can be assessed by examining the magnitude and significance of the loading paths λ that represents direct relationship between the indicator and the construct. All λ's should be significant (t-values should exceed 1.96) and exceed .50 threshold (Hair et al. 1998; Prajogo and McDermot 2005). In our case all indicator loading values were significant (at $p < 0.01$ or better – t-values exceed 2.64) and exceed .50 which provides validity evidence in favor of the indicators used to represent the constructs at interest.

To test the composite (construct) reliability the composite reliability index (CRI) and average variance extracted (AVE) were calculated. Composite reliability assumes that a set of latent construct indicators is consistent in the measurement (Škerlavaj et al. 2006). There is no generally acceptable standard for adequate values of CRI. Koufteros (1999) suggested values above .80, while Diamantopoulos and Siguaw (2000) were satisfied with .60. AVE is similar to CRI with the one exception that standardized loadings are squared before summing them (Hair et al. 1998; Koufteros 1999). The cut-off value most often used for AVE is .50 (Bagozzi and Yi 1988; Hair et al. 1998), while there are also cases where a milder restriction of .40 was employed (Diamantopoulos and Siguaw 2000). As it can be seen from the Table 1 all values for CRI and AVE surpass the prescribed values, therefore the reliability of indicators is acceptable.

Table 1. Composite reliability index and average variance extracted

	CRI	AVE
BPO	.76	.52
FP	.86	.75
NFP	.80	.51

Before examining the hypothesized relationships the global fit of the model needs to be assessed. There is a plethora of goodness-of-fit indices that can be used as summary measures of a model's overall fit (Diamantopoulos and Siguaw 2000). Research evidence supports the need to use more than one index (Breckler 1990; Bollen and Long 1993; Tanaka 1993; Coenders et al. 2003). $\chi 2$ per degrees of freedom, comparative fit index (CFI) and nonnormed fit index (NNFI; also named the Tucker – Lewis fit index: TLI) are used most often to assess model fit (Koufteros 1999). The ratio $\chi 2$ per degrees of freedom should not exceed 2, while models exhibiting CFI and NNFI indices greater than .90 have an adequate fit. Some researchers (Coenders et al. 2003) even suggest a cut-off value of .95.

Results of fitting the model to the data show that the model had a good fit as values for all of the most frequently used indices fall within the acceptable range: $\chi 2/2 = 2$; NNFI $= .94$, CFI $= .96$. In Fig. 2 the path diagram of our model is presented.

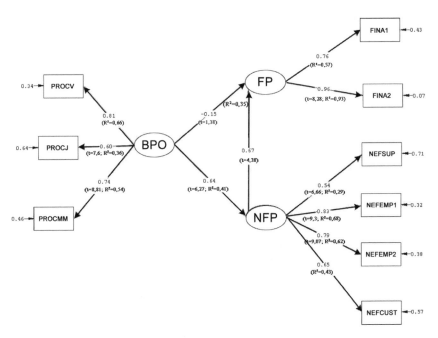

Fig. 2. Path diagram of conceptualized model

As the overall model exhibited good fit the structural part can be examined. The aim is to determine whether the theoretical relationships specified by our hypotheses are indeed supported by the data. Three issues are of relevance here. First, we look if the signs of the parameters representing the paths between the constructs indicate the same direction as hypothesized. In that regard only hypotheses 2 and 3 are supported by the data as there is a positive sign between BPO and NFP and between NFP and FP. Hypotheses 1 is not supported as the direction of relationship in not as stated. Second, we examine the statistical significance of parameters. Again only paths representing second and third hypotheses were found to be statistically significant (t values: 6.27 and 4.83, respectively). The relationship between BPO and FP was not found to be statistically significant. Third, the squared multiple correlations (R^2) for the structural equations are inspected as they indicate the amount of variance of endogenous constructs that is accounted for by independent constructs. For the hypotheses 2 and 3 the R^2's are high (.41 and .35, respectively) indicating strong relationship. Again the lack of the direct relationship as stated in hypothesis 1 was reconfirmed in very low R^2 (.079) for the path representing that link.

Considering all three aspects of the structural relationship we accept the second and the third hypothesis but reject the first one. Hence the impact of BPO on organizational performance has been confirmed.

5 Methodology to Assess, Analyze and Enhance Process Orientation – Example With Two Companies

Since higher levels of BPO lead to better organizational performance we present the methodology for assessing, analyzing and enhancing business process orientation within a single company. The methodology will be presented on two case studies of two companies. The assessment of company's BPO is done by using a BPO measurement instrument. While it is preferable that several key employees fill in the questionnaire and the average scores are analyzed, we have used single set of data for each company from our existing data and have not conducted additional interviews to gather more data from different employees. After data are gathered they are plotted on several diagrams that serve as an input for analysis. Each diagram shows the scores of the company being analyzed and average scores for a larger group of companies that present a benchmark, a reference point. This group can be defined in different ways depending on the goals of the analysis. In our case our reference point is the entire sample and represents the average process orientation of all companies included in the survey. Alternatively, the group could be formed based on the industry (for instance, if a manufacturing company was analyzed it might be more informative to compare its scores only with the subset of manufacturing companies) or the best in class, etc.

Analysis is carried out on three levels: overall BPO level, BPO component level and the detailed inspection of each component (process view, process jobs and process management and measurement). As gaps and insufficiencies are identified guidelines and initiatives are developed to close these gaps and enhance the business process orientation.

5.1 The Companies – A Brief Introduction

Our case study includes two companies very different in nature. Company A manufactures female and male garments. They provide complex production and fashion engineering services for its own and global fashion brands. They have five specialized production units. In 2005 they have generated about 76 million euro revenues. In last few years they have manufactured over 2 million pieces of clothing per year. Currently they employ 4,580 employees. Faced with fierce competition in textile manufacturing industry they have been struggling to stay competitive and profitable for many years and have gone through numerous restructurings in order to survive. Company B is a local affiliate of an international banking corporation. They offer wide range of financial products in retail and corporate market and with its connections with international headquarters they offer a unique selling proposition in the local market. Currently they employ over 200 employees.

5.2 The Analysis – Overall BPO and BPO Components

Data gathered with BPO measurement instrument is initially plotted on the diagram that shows the overall BPO score and the scores for individual components. Additionally, the scores of organizational performance are also included. The diagram for overall BPO and BPO components is shown in Fig. 3. The diagram is horizontally divided into four lanes each representing a particular maturity level. Vertical lanes represent overall BPO score, individual component scores and organizational performance scores. In each vertical segment there are three colored rectangles: yellow (middle) represents the average scores of all the companies included in the sample; blue represents the scores of Company A; pink represents the scores of Company B. Our analysis starts at the overall BPO score.

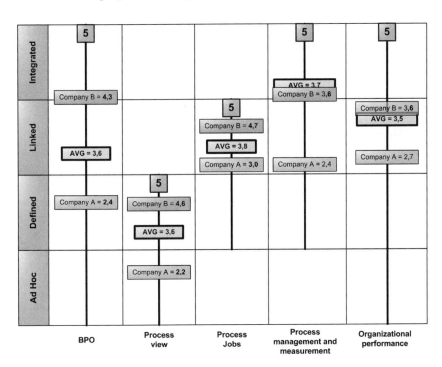

Fig. 3. Overall BPO and BPO components

As it can clearly be seen the composite BPO score of Company A is well below average at 2,4. This places our Company A in the middle of the Defined level of process orientation maturity. Their processes are defined and documented to a certain degree and changes to them must go through formal procedure. Some aspects of process orientation are beginning to emerge yet functional organization with all its rigidities is still predominant. Company A is lagging behind the majority of companies in terms of process orientation maturity and will have to undergo many organizational changes and implement various practices in order to achieve higher levels of BPO maturity. Current low level of BPO maturity prevents this company to be responsive to market needs and pressures and hinders the optimization of their processes which all leads to below average performance. While all aspects of BPO are deficient, the main problems can be identified in the process view component and in the process management and measurement component where the scores are far below average. The particular problematic areas and their potential remedies will surface in the next section where the detailed component analysis is presented.

Company B has reached the frontier of the Integrated maturity level thereby significantly surpassing the average company. This company has a well-defined and documented process and the organizational culture that supports the process way of thinking and functioning. Functional structure has been scaled down and transformed in a way that the processes are clearly visible and fluidly pass different departments. One area of improvement potential is the process management and measurement component of BPO where Company B slightly lags behind the average. Implementation of integral process management and measurement would lead to truly optimized processes that would culminate in increased productivity, efficiency and overall performance.

5.3   Detailed BPO Components Analysis

What lies behind the low level of maturity in Company A and ligh level in Company B can further be identified by carefully inspecting individual items for each component. Process view component is about the process definition and documentation, process centric culture and mindsets and process-oriented information system design and is the foundation for business process orientation. Higher levels of BPO maturity cannot be reached if an organization has not established a strong process view. On the other hand solely focusing on and institutionalizing the process view practices and neglecting the other two components hinders the advancements on higher maturity levels.

The reasons for below average score for the process view component of Company A can be seen in Fig. 4 as the individual item scores all lag behind the average. First and second item capture the perception and the mindsets of employees in an organization. In case of Company A employees do not see the business as a series of linked processes and do not think in terms of processes. Even though some processes are defined and documented (item 3), we speculate that these process definitions and documentations were carried out due to requirements of ISO 9001:2000 certificate acquisition which they hold. Such definitions and documentation are not sufficient and only scratch the surface of true functioning of the organization. This is confirmed by item 4 that shows that processes are not transparent and employees do not know how processes flow and only understand small portions of them, those pertaining to their tasks. To implement a process view, the foundation of BPO, Company A should put effort in true process definition and documentation. While such projects are cumbersome, the results outweigh the effort. Only thorough process modeling can unveil how work is done and make processes transparent. Additional benefit is that employees included in modeling project quickly adopt process way of thinking and since usually many people participate in such project the perception is broadly spread.

Company B has firmly adopted the process view which can be seen from high scores on all items. Interesting notion is that while all the processes are well documented and even information system development is process oriented, employees still do not see the linkages of processes nor do they have complete understanding of how processes work. Even though this is not a severe problem there is still room for improvement in that regard. Company B should disseminate the knowledge about their processes among employees through internal workshops and seminars which would result in broader understanding of processes.

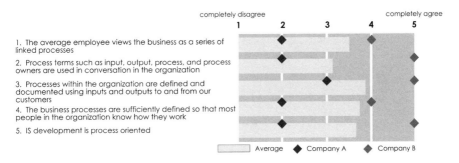

Fig. 4. Detailed analysis of process view component

Below average scores for process jobs component for Company A further confirms that work is organized in a traditional – hierarchal fashion (see Fig. 5). While jobs are not just simple tasks employees rarely have to solve problems and are not learning new things frequently, which is not a surprise since jobs cannot really be process oriented if the processes are not defined. On the other hand Company B has empowered its employees to execute multidimensional tasks and supports the ongoing learning process.

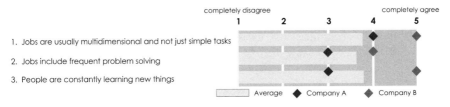

Fig. 5. Detailed analysis of process jobs component

Process management and measurement practices are what takes the company to the highest level of business process orientation maturity. It enables the continuous improvement of business processes, which keeps an organization competitive. As in process jobs component Company A scores for process management and measurement component were all below average. The same reason applies here: what is not defined can't be measured and this is the case for Company A.

Interestingly, Company B that in overall BPO score significantly surpasses the average company, in Process management and measurement component scored slightly below average. This is the main area that the company has to work on in the future if they would like to yield the benefits of mature BPO in terms organizational performance. Particularly, more effort should be put in the development of performance measures that would quantify the performance goals. In order to measure them appropriate information technology should be implemented or their existing information system customized in a way that would enable these measurements. Once they capture the performance measurements and analyze the gaps between the current values and target values further process improvements can be made.

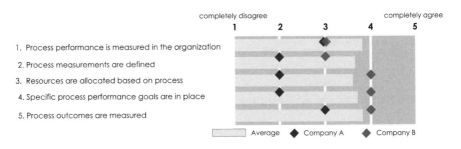

Fig. 6. Detailed analysis of process management and measurement component

With the BPO maturity measurement instrument (see Fig. 6) we assessed two companies' BPO levels and identified the areas that are either problematic or that have potential for further advancements. In Company A it was clear that the foundation for process orientation has not been laid and their efforts should therefore be concentrated in the definition, documentation and modelling of their processes and disseminating this knowledge to their employees. Company B, while already quite mature in BPO, still has potential in process management and measurement area. Defining process measures, measuring them and improving processes based on those measures will enable them to improve their overall performance.

6 Discussion and Implications

The main goal of our study was to determine whether higher levels of business process orientation lead to better organizational performance. The data from the empirical study that has been subjected to rigorous statistical techniques has shown support for that. Therefore, based on our hypotheses we conclude that higher levels of business process orientation lead to better financial and non-financial performance. Furthermore, it had been shown that there is a strong direct impact of BPO on non-financial performance. On the other hand no such impact has been found between BPO and financial performance. This does not mean that there is no connection whatsoever. It has been shown that BPO has strong indirect impact on financial performance through non-financial performance.

The contribution of our study is twofold: first the extension of the original study (McCormack and Johnson 2001) whereby we have scrutinized the effects of BPO on OP in much more detail by capturing and analyzing performance in coherence with the stakeholder theory (Freeman 1986) and balanced scorecard approach (Kaplan and Norton 1992, 1993, 1996). We did that by inclusion of key stakeholders (customers, employees and suppliers) in assessment of non-financial performance in addition to financial performance. Our conceptualization of the model therefore included two distinct yet related constructs of organizational performance. The extension of the organizational performance was made by significantly expanded measurement instrument for capturing organizational performance. This approach has proved to be useful as we were able to decompose the impact of BPO on OP and reveal the deeper structure of the relationship. Second we carried out the study in the transition economy and found that the original findings are also applicable in this socio-economic environment.

The results of our study also have many practical implications for managers. As companies renovate themselves and adopt new practices striving to attain higher levels of process orientation it enables them to improve their relationship with its key stakeholders employees, customers, and suppliers by creating a fertile environment for conducting business. Clearly such environment is also a catalyst for better financial performance. Therefore, as business environment gets more competitive business process orientation offers a way to adapt to new conditions and circumstances. Since higher business process orientation maturity levels leads to better organizational performance managers need to familiarize themselves with this concept and practical implementation issues. They need to examine their current practices, structures and management and measurement processes and assess the current state. BPO maturity model then serves as a road map for their improvement and renovation efforts as we have shown on our two case studies.

Though we rejected the first hypotheses postulating the positive effect of BPO on financial performance this of course is not conclusive. The lack of significant effect might be due to time lag in the effects. Clearly organizational renovation and process improvement practices cannot and do not happen instantaneously but take a lot of time. Financial results of such efforts might not arise immediately. This points to one limitation of our research, namely the study has not been devised in a longitudinal nature. Therefore, time lag in effects cannot be detected. This dimension is left for future research. Another limitation of our study relates to the questionnaires and surveys in general as they are subjective in their nature. Data gathered in this manner might be biased (companies might think they are better that they actually are or would like to present themselves better) and that has to be considered when interpreting results. Also for comprehensive analysis of BPO maturity of any given company, several key employees should answer the questionnaire and analysis should be carried out on the averaged data which was not the case in our case study as we have only used the answers of one employee. Inclusion of additional datasets is left for future work. On the agenda for future work is also the inclusion of Croatian companies in the model in order to extend the applicability of the findings. For analyzing time lag in effects and for gaining wider generalization ability the study will be repeated in Slovenia and Croatia and extended to new countries.

References

Atkinson, A.A., Waterhouse, J.H. and Wells, R.B. (1997) A stakeholder approach to strategic performance measurement, Sloan Management Review 38, pp. 25–37.

Bagozzi, R.P. and Yi, Y. (1988) On the evaluation of structural equation models. Academy of Marketing Science 16(1), 74–94.

Berman, S.L., Wicks, A.C., Kotha, S. and Jones, T.M. (1999) Does stakeholder orientation matter? The relationship between stakeholder management models and a firm financial performance, Academy of Management Journal 42(5), 488–506.

Bollen, K.A. and Long, J.S. (1993) Testing Structural Equation Models. Sage, Newbury Park, CA.

Breckler, S.J. (1990) Applications of covariance structural modeling in psychology: cause for concern? Psychological Bulletin 107(23), 260–273.

Burlton, R.T. (2001) Business Process Management: Profiting from Process. Indianapolis, Sams.

Coenders, G., Casa, F., Figuer, C. and Gonzalez, M. (2003) Relationship between parents' and children's values and children's overall life satisfaction—a comparison across countries. Frankfurt am Main: 5th Conference of the International Society for Quality-of-Life Studies, Johan Wolfgang Goethe-University.

Comrey, A.L. and Lee, H.B. (1992) A First Course in Factor Analysis. (2nd ed.), Lawrence Erlbaum, Hillsdale, NJ.

Cousins, P.D. and Menguc, B. (2006) The implications of socialization and integration in supply chain management, Journal of Operations Management 24, 604–620.

Cyert, R.M. and March, J.G. (1963) A behavioral theory of the firm. Englewood cliffs, NJ: Prentice-Hall.

Daft, R.L. (2004). Organization Theory and Design, Thompson, Mason, Ohio.

Davenport, T.H. (1993) Process Innovation: Reengineering Work through Information Technology. Harvard Business School Press, Boston.

Diamantopoulos, A. and Siguaw, J.A. (2000) Introducing LISREL. SAGE Publications, London.

Freeman, E.R. (1984) Strategic Management – A Stakeholder Approach, Pitman, London.

Freeman, E.R. (1994) Politics of stakeholder theory: some future directions, Business Ethics Quarterly 4, 409–422.

Galbraith, J.R. (2002) Designing Organizations: An Executive Guide to Strategy, Structure, and Process, Jossey-Bass, San Francisco.

Häggström, C. and Oscarsson, K. (2001) Making Companies More Efficient by Process Orientation – Describing and Mapping Business Processes, Master Thesis, Chalmers University of Technology & Royal Institute of Technology, Göteborg/Stockholm.

Hair, J.F., Anderson, R.E., Tatham, R.L. and Black, W.C. (1998) Multivariate Data Analysis, 5th ed. Prentice-Hall, London.

Hammer, M.H. and Champy, J. (1993) Reengineering the Corporation: A Manifesto for Business Evolution. Harper Business, New York.

Harmon, P. (2003). Business Process Change: A Manager's Guide to Improving, Redesigning, and Automating Processes, Morgan Kaufmann, San Francisco.

Harrison, J.S. and Freeman, J.S. (1999) Stakeholders, social responsibility, and performance: empirical evidence and theoretical perspectives, Academy of Management Journal 42, 479–485.

Hendricks, K.B., Singhal, V.R. and Stratman, J.K. (2007) The impact of enterprise systems on corporate performance: A study of ERP, SCM, and CRM system implementations, Journal of Operations Management 25, 65–82.

Hillman, A.J. and Keim, G.D. (2001) Shareholder value, stakeholder management, and social issues: What's the bottom line?, Strategic Management Journal 22(2), 125.

Kaplan, R.S. and Norton, D.P. (1992) The Balanced Scorecard – Measures that Drive Performance, Harvard Business Review 70(1), 71–79.

Kaplan, R.S. and Norton, D.P. (1993) Putting the balanced scorecard to work. Harvard Business review 9/10, 134–147.

Kaplan, R.S. and Norton, D.P. (1996) Using the balanced scorecard as strategic management system. Harvard Business Review 1/2, 75–85.

Karatepe, O.M., Uludag, O., Menevis, I., Hadzimehmedagic, L. and Baddar, L. (2006). The effects of selected individual characteristics on frontline employee performance and job satisfaction, Tourism Management 27, 547–560.

Keen, P.G.W. (1997) The Process Edge – Creating Value Where It Counts, Harvard Business School Press, Boston.

Koufteros, X.A. (1999) Testing a model of pull production: a paradigm for manufacturing research using structural equation modeling. Journal of Operations Management 17, 467–488.

Kueng, P. (2000) Process performance measurement system: a tool to support process-based organizations, Total Quality Management 11(1), 67–85.

Levi, M.H. (2002) The Business Process (Quiet) Revolution: Transformation to Process Organization, Interfacing Technologies Corporation, http://www.interfacing.com/rtecontent/document/CreatingProcessOrganization03.pdf

Lindfors, C. (2003) Process orientation: An approach for organizations to function effectively, http://cic.vtt.fi/lean/singapore/LindforsFinal.pdf

McCormack, K. (2003) Benchmarking using the BPO Maturity Model, BPM Opinions Series, http://www.bpmresources.com

McCormack, K.P. and Johnson, W.C. (2001) Business Process Orientation – Gaining the E-Business Competitive Advantage, St. Lucie Press, Florida

McCormack, K.P., Johnson, W.C. and Walker, W.T. (2003) Supply Chain Networks and Business Process Orientation, St. Lucie Press, Florida

Oden, H.W. (1999) Transforming the Organization: A Social-Technical Approach, Quorum books, Westport.

O'Hanlon, T. (2003) Process Landscapes, http://saferpak.com/process_manage_articles/-Process%20Landscapes.pdf

Prajogo, D.I. and McDermott, C.M., (2005) The relationship between total quality management practices and organizational culture. International Journal of Operations and Production Management 25, 1101–1122.

Riahi-Belkaoui, A. (2003) Intellectual capital and firm performance of US multinational firms – a study of the resource-based and stakeholder views, Journal of Intellectual Capital 4(2), 215–226.

Sikavica, P. and Novak, M. (1999) Poslovna organizacija, Informator, Zagreb.

Sirgy, J.M. (2002) Measuring corporate performance by building on the stakeholder model of business ethics, Journal of Business Ethics 35(3), 143–162.

Škerlavaj, M., Indihar Štemberger, M., Škrinjar, R. and Dimovski, V. (2006). Organizational learning culture—the missing link between business process change and organizational performance, Int. J. Production Economics, doi:10.1016/j.ijpe.2006.07.009.

Tanaka, J.S. (1993) Multifaceted Conception of Fit in Structural Equation Models. Sage, Newbury Park, CA.

Tangem, S. (2004) Performance measurement: from philosophy to practice, International Journal of Productivity and Performance Management 53(8), 726–737.

Tenner, A.R. and DeToro, I.J. (1996) Process Redesign: The Implementation Guide For Managers, Prentice Hall, New Jersey.

zur Muehlen, M. (2002) Workflow-based Process Controlling, Logos Verlag, Berlin.

The Information Systems Security Process: Through an Anthropological Lens

Amanda Freeman[1], Larry Stapleton[2] and Gabriel Byrne[3]

[1]Waterford Institute of Technology, Department of Computing, Maths and Physics, afreeman@wit.ie

[2] Waterford Institute of Technology, Department of Computing, Maths and Physics, lstapleton@wit.ie

[3] University College of Dublin, Graduate School of Business, gabriel.byrne@ucd.ie

Abstract Developing and designing security systems and subsystems is a vital component of the ISD process, yet often is not considered until after the software has been developed. This reflects the low value that ISD places upon security. Some researchers argue that the type of development methodology used by developers is a reflection of their values. In this chapter we investigate five of the most common ISD methodologies described in the ISD literature, and also examine to what extent each of these methodologies incorporates security as part of the development process. This chapter will also show findings of a study that measured the values of potential developers from Ireland and various other countries around the world, to see if they value security. The study showed that current ISD methodologies are out-of-step with developers' attitudes in terms of information systems security (ISS).

1 The Importance of Values in Human Activity

There has been a growing interest in recent years in the analysis of human values (Kluckhohn 1951; Rokeach 1973; Schwartz and Bilsky 1987, 1990). Schwartz (1990, 878) defines values as 'concepts or beliefs, that pertain to desirable end states or behaviours, they transcend specific situations, guide selection or evaluation of behaviour and events, and are ordered by relative importance'. Values play a key role in human activity as they provide strong explanations of behaviour. Knowing persons values enables us to predict how he/she will behave in various experimental and real-life situations (Rokeach 1973). Research into values has provided valuable insights into individual, group and organisational levels of analysis. Sarros and Santora (2001) believe that organisations with strong cultures and clear values increase their chance of success and longevity. Barrett (1998)

C. Barry et al. (eds.), *Information Systems Development: Challenges in Practice, Theory, and Education, Vol.2*, doi: 10.1007/978-0-387-78578-3_12,
© Springer Science+Business Media, LLC 2009

attributes a strong organisational culture to be one where values are shared amongst staff and management. Values are also said to play a key role in individual and managerial decision making. Major decisions are generally referred to individuals' values for approval (Hall 2001).

Whilst many researchers have mentioned the role of values in ISD (Hedberg and Mumford 1975; Kling 1978; Dagwell and Weber 1983; Kumar and Welke 1984; Mumford 2000; McGuire et al. 2006) there is a paucity of academic research that examines values in terms of information systems security (ISS) development. The objective of this chapter is to demonstrate, how ISD research is out-of-step with the security values of potential developers from different cultures. In order to achieve this objective, we explore some of the most common ISD methodologies described in the literature and examine the role of security in each of these methodologies. This chapter will also show findings of a study that was conducted in which we analysed the values of potential developers using the Short Schwartz's Value Survey (SSVS). In this study we measured the values of Irish computer students and computer students from various countries around the world. In particular, the following research question will be addressed and explored through the study: Do current ISD methodologies reflect developers' values in terms of ISS?

2 Systems Security Development

The protection of information has been a major challenge since the beginning of the computer age. Given the widespread adoption of computer technology for business operations, the problem of information protection has become more urgent than ever. Surveys indicate that companies are suffering severe financial losses due to security breaches (PricewaterhouseCoopers 2005; CSI/FBI 2005). Many researchers argue that a significant amount of these breaches are caused by poor software design (McGraw and Wyk 2005; Villarroel et al. 2004). One of the reasons given for this is that security is generally only considered in the software engineering process after the software has been developed (Moutatidis et al. 2004; Villarroel et al., 2004). In order for software to be secure it is vital that security plays a major role in all aspects of the software development process. Ideally, security should be designed into the development process upfront and revisited throughout the development process (Villarroel et al., 2004). However, McGraw and Wyk (2005) argue that software development efforts in large organisations are often far removed from security concerns.

There are many definitions of ISS. However, in terms of this research we use the definition of Tryfonas et al. (2001, 183) in which they describe ISS as 'the principles, regulations, methodologies, techniques and tools we establish to protect an information system, or any of its parts, from potential threats'. The act of aligning ISS and software development is a serious undertaking for any organisation. McGraw and Wyk (2005, 79) state that 'software security appears to be in the earliest stages of development, much as ISS itself was 10 years ago'. One reason given for this is the fact that most software developers lack security expertise (Moutatidis et al., 2004). McGraw and Wyk (2005) assert that most software developers lack the required security knowledge to develop secure systems. Dhillon (1995) and Ghosh et al. (2002) believe that it is vital that developers work with security specialists.

They argue that people are a critical component of the software security equation. They feel that any software that makes unrealistic or unreasonable security-related demands on users is software that is destined to be breached. According to Baskerville (1993, 377) 'what is missing in many instances is the involvement of concerned users, enlightened developers, experienced security specialists or other parties who understand how to incorporate controls into systems while the systems are still in development'. Therefore, it is vital that ISS development involves all the stakeholders within the business.

3 Systems Security as a Values Problem in ISD

One novel way of analysing the role of stakeholders in software security development is to look at the values of each group involved. By making value stances explicit it helps us to interpret the meanings various groups have assigned to particular issues relating to security software development (Kling 1978). For example, it is widely accepted that both management and staff play a key role in the implementation and success of ISS (Dhillon and Backhouse 2000; Dhillon 2001; Freeman and Doyle 2006). Research shows that the type of methodology chosen by a developer tends to be based on their values (Kumar and Welke 1984; Dhillon 1995; Orvik et al. 1998). Kling (1978) believes that focusing on value orientation illustrates an important aspect of computings' social impact. Knowing persons' values should enable to predict how he/she will behave in various situations.

Hedberg and Mumford (1975) conducted a values study where they were concerned with whether or not developers held a view of users, which was different to the users' view of themselves. They measured the developer's values in terms of Theory X versus Theory Y view of system users. They found that developers tended to have a Theory X view of users (users who like order and do not want personal control over their activities). In contrast they found that the users themselves believed that job designs should be based on Theory Y (e.g. jobs should be flexible allowing self-determination by responsible self-achieving individuals). They believe that this difference in values would ultimately lead to conflict and could result in user resistance in terms of the technology produced. Kumar and Welke (1984) measured the values of developers using England's (1967) value methodology. They looked at the behaviour relevance of values by classifying them as operative (most likely to govern behaviour) versus non-relevant (values having no impact on behaviour). They argued that developers in ISD subscribe to technical and economic values and consider social, political and psychological design ideals as non-relevant to the system design process. Kumar and Welke (1984) believe that, due to lack of time and money, developers tend to focus their attention on high-priority work, i.e. their values will focus on getting the systems built. If that is the case, the fact that security is not brought into design from the very start would suggest that developers may not value security. To date no research has been carried out that looks at the values of the developers in ISS development. This chapter addresses this gap.

In order to understand how values can be explored, Section 4 reviews the literature on measuring personal values.

4 Measuring Personal Values in ISD

Based on the work of Rokeach (1973), Schwartz and Bilsky (1987) devised a theory of universal types of values as criteria by viewing values as cognitive representations of three universal requirements which are, biologically based needs of the organism, social interaction requirements for interpersonal coordination and social institutional demands for group welfare and survival.

In order to measure values of individuals Schwartz (1992) developed the Schwartz's Value Survey (SVS). In the SVS, 57 values are used to represent ten motivationally distinct value domains that are theoretically derived from universal requirements of human life, which are, Power (social power, authority, wealth), Achievement (success, capability, ambition, influence on people and events), Hedonism (gratification of desires, enjoyment in life, self-indulgence), Stimulation (daring, a varied and challenging life, an exciting life), Self-direction (privacy, creativity, freedom, curiosity, independence, choosing one's own goals), Universalism (broad mindedness, beauty of nature and arts, social justice, a world at peace, equality, wisdom, unity with nature, environmental protection), Benevolence (helpfulness, honesty, forgiveness, loyalty, responsibility), Tradition (respect for tradition, humbleness, accepting one's portion in life, devotion, modesty), Conformity (obedience, honouring parents and elders, self-discipline, politeness) and Security (national security, family security, social order, cleanliness, reciprocation of favours (Lindeman and Versasalo 2005). Results of these 10 domains have shown to load two bipolar dimensions; Conservation (whether people resist change and emphasise self-restriction and order) versus Openness to Change (whether people are ready for new experiences and emphasise independent action and thought) and Self Transcendence (whether people are willing to transcend selfish concerns and promote the welfare of others) versus Self Enhancement (whether people are more motivated to enhance their own personal interests even at the expense of others). These two dimensions reflect the different motivational goals of the 10 basic values and the two major conflicts that organise the whole value system (Lindeman and Verasalo 2005, 177).

One could argue that high-achieving information systems developers would score high on Openness to Change (self-direction, stimulation, etc.) versus Conservation (tradition, conformity, security [not to be confused with computer security]). The personal values of Openness to Change include those values valued by all stakeholders of ISD namely: creativity, curious, choosing ones own goals, freedom, daring, varied life and exciting life.

The personal value of privacy is also included in the value type 'Self-direction' suggesting that a high score on the bipolar value of Openness to Change and Self-direction would indicate information systems developers to be visionary types of people with a sense of self-respect for the personal value of privacy.

This research will be focusing on the personal value of privacy in terms of measuring security beliefs. When people talk about security, they often mean data confidentiality. Clearly, there is some relationship between security and privacy. In order to have privacy we must have security. If we want to protect information we have to ensure that the appropriate security measures are in place.

Lindeman and Verasalo (2005, 171) argue that, 'in many studies, a scale with 57 items may be too time consuming to fill in, and may take up too much space on a questionnaire'. With that in mind they developed a shorter version of the SVS, which they called the Short Schwartz's Value Survey (SSVS). In the SSVS, Lindeman and Verasalo (2005) set out to see if, by asking respondents to rate the importance of the ten values directly, Conservation and Self-Transcendence could be reliably and validly examined with a shortened version of the Schwartz's Value Survey. As regards ISD many researchers believe that the type of methodology used is based on the values of the developer (Kumar and Welke 1984; Dhillon 1995; Orvik et al. 1998). However, according to Baskerville (1993) advances in security methodologies lag behind advances in general system development methodologies. It is possible that a reason for this could be that security is not valued in the ISD community. In Section 4 we will give a brief account of some of the most widely reviewed ISD methodologies in the literature and we will look at to what extent each of these methodologies incorporate security as part of the development process.

5 Overview of ISD Methodologies and the Extent to Which They Address Security Issues

5.1 SSADM

SSADM (Structured Systems Analysis & Design Methodology) is one of the most widely used 'hard' structured methodologies, and it is for this reason that it was chosen for review in this chapter. It is said to be a data-driven methodology as it places a large emphasis on data modeling and the database. It is a highly structured methodology that provides very detailed rules and guidelines to project developers. Version 4 of SSADM consists of five stages and each stage is made up of a series of steps which use appropriate techniques for the tasks involved. Each of the stages and steps has defined inputs and outputs (Avison and Fitzgerald 1995). Goodland and Slater (1997) define the steps as feasibility study, requirement analysis, requirements specification, logical systems specification and physical design. After each stage users are involved in formal quality assurance reviews, and informal walkthroughs where each stage is signed off before developers move on to the next stage. A weakness in SSADM as a methodology is that it does not provide any support for the planning, construction and implementation stages of development. The only emphasis placed on security in the SSADM methodology is in the requirements specification stage. However, security is only mentioned briefly in terms of access privileges and unauthorised access (Goodland and Slater 1997).

5.2 Object-Orientated (OO) Methodology – (UML/UP)

The essence of object-orientated analysis and design is to emphasise the problem domain and logical solution from the perspective of objects (things, concepts, or entities) (Larman 1998, 6). According to Dennis et al. (2006) any object-orientated approach to developing information systems must be, use case-driven, architecture-centric, and iterative and incremental. The OO methodology focused on in this chapter is the Unified Modelling Language (UML) Unified Process (UP). Carew and Stapleton (2004, 85), describes UML as 'a graphical modelling language for specifying systems from an object-orientated perspective'. UML itself is not a methodology; it is a modelling notation that provides a variety of modelling diagrams, but it does not stipulate underlying process for developers to follow. Nonetheless, the authors of UML have provided the Unified Process (UP) as a suitable methodology. Bruegge and Dutoit (2000) describe the five types of notation used in UML as, use case diagrams which are used at the requirements elicitation stage to represent the functionality of the system, class diagrams which are used to describe the structure of the systems, sequence diagrams which are used to formalise the behaviour of the system, state diagrams which are used to describe the behaviour of an individual object as a number of states and transition between these states and finally, activity diagrams which describe the system in terms of activities. Unlike the other methodologies mentioned in this chapter UML does take security into account in the systems design phase and also in the testing phase. However, it only focuses on security in terms of authentication, access controls and encryption.

5.3 Soft Systems Methodology

The Soft System Methodology was developed by Peter Checkland as a way to deal with problem situations in development where there is a high social, political and human component involved. It is a seven-stage/four-activities systems thinking approach for unstructured problems in the real world (Checkland 1999). What makes the Soft System Methodology different from most other methodologies is that it focuses on 'soft' problems in ISD as opposed to 'hard' problems that are more technically orientated. Checkland (1999) argues that it is easy to model data and processes, but to understand the real world it is essential to include people in the model. In 1990, Checkland revised the SSM 7 Stage Model and presented the four-activities model of SSM. Essentially, both models are similar in that they both focus on the 'soft' aspects of ISD. This methodology focuses on the 'soft' side of ISD and there is no specific reference to security.

5.4 Multiview

Multiview is described by Iivari (2000, 199) as a 'methodology that explicitly attempts to reconcile ideas from several information systems development approaches, most notable the Soft System Methodology (SSM)'. As a methodology it looks at both the human and the technical aspects of ISD.

There are five stages in the Multiview methodology and according to Avison and Wood-Harper (1990) these stages aid in answering all the vital questions of users. The stages in Multiview are as follows: analysis of human activity, analysis of information, analysis and design of socio-technical aspects, design of the human–computer interface and design of technical aspects. The first stage looks at the organisation itself, the second stage analyses the entities and functions of the system. Stage three includes user participation, to identify how the system can be fitted into the users' working environment. The fourth stage is concerned with the implementation of the computer interface. Avison and Wood-Harper (1990) believe that this is a vital step as the way in which users interact with a system plays an important role in whether users' accept a system. Finally, in the fifth stage the developer focuses on the efficient design and the production of a full system specification. Whilst security is mentioned in Multiview it is only briefly discussed and this discussion takes place as part of a case study.

5.5 ETHICS

Effective Technical and Human Implementation of Computer-based System (ETHICS) is a methodology developed by Enid Mumford. ETHICS takes the view that in order for technology to be successful it should fit closely with organisational and social factors (Avison and Fitzgerald 1995). Mumford (2000) believes that an improved quality of working life and enhanced job satisfaction of the users must be a major objective of the systems design process. ETHICS is a seven-stage methodology based on the participatory approach to information systems development. The seven stages are: diagnosis of user needs, setting efficiency and job satisfaction objectives, developing alternative design strategies, strategy selection to achieve objectives, hardware and software selection, implementation and systems evaluation (Mumford 1990). Participation plays a role in many methodologies, but it plays a vital role in ETHICS. The role of the developer in ETHICS is very different to the role of the developer in the previously mentioned methodologies, in that the developer together with the user develops the systems. Security is not mentioned in the ETHICS methodology.

This section gives a broad overview of some of the most widely used ISD methodologies that are covered in the literature. Looking at these methodologies we can see that with the exception of SSADM and the Object-Orientated methodology security is not considered. Form this we can see that if developers tend to value the less-structured methodologies there is a greater chance that security will not feature in the development process. This may help to explain why security is often only considered in the software development process after the software has been developed.

Our research question is: Do current ISD methodologies reflect developers' values in terms of ISS?

Based on the little attention paid to ISS in the ISD literature we propose the following hypothesis:

H1: Security will be poorly valued by potential ISD developers.

A survey was conducted to explore this question. The following sections present and interpret the findings of this study.

6 Research Method – Participants and Procedures

The sample consists of Irish computing students (78.9%) and foreign students (21.1%) from the following countries, China, Pakistan, Nigeria, England, Italy, France, Sudan, Poland, Ukraine, Russia, Spain, Malawi, and South Africa. The sample consists of 161 participants representing a convenient sample, which is appropriate for a preliminary study of this nature. The respondents ranged from first year computing students up to computing master's students. The participants were told that the study concerned values and that participation was voluntary and all information would be treated confidentially. Using the Short Schwartz's Value Survey participants were presented with the name of a value along with its value items. Participants were asked to rate the importance of each value as a guiding principle in their life. The ten values were rated on a nine-point scale ranging from –1 (opposed to my principles), 0 (not important), 3 (important) to 7 (of extreme importance).

7 Results

Table 1 compares the mean scores for each of the ten values in terms of Irish and Non-Irish students. From this table we can see that the top four values that Irish students value as guiding principles in their life are: Self-direction (5.21), Benevolence (4.87), Achievement (4.74) and Security (4.17). In terms of foreign students the top four values they value as guiding principles in their life are: Self-direction

(5.39), Security (4.82), Benevolence (4.79) and Universalism (4.50). These findings show us that participants do in fact value privacy, with Self-direction scoring highest with both Irish (5.21) and Non-Irish (5.39) participants.

Table 1. Mean value scores for Irish and Non-Irish students

Values	Irish			Non-Irish		
	N	Mean	Std. Dev	N	Mean	Std. Dev
Power	124	2.87	2.453	32	2.81	2.278
Achievement	125	4.74	1.660	33	4.33	2.160
Hedonism	123	3.44	2.423	32	3.22	2.181
Stimulation	124	4.09	1.913	32	3.94	2.094
Self-direction	126	5.21	1.641	33	5.39	1.519
Universalism	126	3.98	2.261	34	4.50	2.352
Benevolence	126	4.87	2.009	34	4.79	2.086
Tradition	125	2.43	2.315	33	3.06	2.738
Conformity	125	2.84	2.305	34	3.29	2.368
Security	125	4.17	2.003	33	4.82	1.722

−1 = opposed to my principles, 0 = not important, 3 = important, 7 = of supreme importance

Table 2 illustrates that the Irish participants score quite high on Openness to Change (32.97%) and Conservation (24.43%) as do their Non-Irish counterparts. In terms of Self-Enhancement the Non-Irish participants score slightly lower (17.78%) than the Irish participants (19.69%). In terms of Self-Enhancement there is very little difference between the Irish participants (22.9%) and the Non-Irish participants (23.13%). The fact that both groups scored highly on Openness to Change and Conservation shows that the potential developers in both groups are independent thinkers who embrace new challenges, but they also have a certain amount of order in what they do. In terms of Self-Enhancement both groups scored quite low, with the Non-Irish students valuing it even less than the Irish students. This would indicate that while these students do to some extent want to enhance their own personal interests it is not a huge motivating factor in what they do.

Table 2. Comparison of bipolar domains

	Openness to Change	Conservation	Self-Enhancement	Self-Transcendence
Irish	32.97%	24.43%	19.69%	22.9%
Non-Irish	31.26%	27.82%	17.78%	23.13%

8 Synthesis of Findings

In Section 4.5 we asked the research question; do current ISD methodologies reflect developers' values in terms of ISS? We then hypothesised that security would be poorly valued by potential ISD developers, on the basis of the treatment of security in the ISD literature.

We see that this is not in fact the case as privacy is highly valued by both groups of participants. Hence this hypothesis is rejected. In terms of whether current ISD methodologies reflect developers' values of ISS, we can see from the literature and the findings that this is not the case. The literature shows that with the exception of SSADM and the Object-Orientated methodology security is not considered in any of the other methodologies discussed. This clearly shows that current ISD research is out-of-step with developers' attitudes to security.

9 Limitations of the Study

A major limitation of this study is that we define all the students who took part in this study as potential developers when they may in fact not chose software development as their chosen career. We only examined five methodologies that are most commonly referred to in the literature. We acknowledge that in practice quite often organisations use a combination of different methodologies and we also acknowledge that in other cases some organisations may use no methodology or may use a methodology not mentioned in this chapter. It is also important to highlight that there are many standalone security methodologies that have been developed regularly.

10 Conclusion

Security is a vital component of ISD, yet often is not considered until after the software has been developed. We have shown that some of the most common ISD methodologies do not even consider security as part of the software development process. We postulated that the lack of security integration into the software development process may be attributed to developers not valuing security. Our findings show that the participants in this study place high value on the value of Self-direction. A personal value attributed to Self-direction is privacy. We believe that if a person places a high value on privacy this means that they place high value on security as you cannot have any form of privacy without some form of security. We argue that the participants in this study do value security and hence we believe that, common ISD methodologies do not reflect developers' values in terms of ISS. It is likely that ISD practices present, at some level, moral dilemmas for ISD professionals. The future direction of this research involves a field study using the Schwartz Value survey to measure the values of developers and end-users. The ultimate goal of this work will be to measure, what is the impact on the ISS development process if the developers, end-users and management have different values? This ongoing research aims to address this major gap in the ISD literature.

Acknowledgments   This research has been funded by the Irish Research Council for Science, Engineering and Technology (IRCSET).

References

Avison, D. E. & Fitzgerald, G. (1995) Information Systems Development: Methodologies, Techniques and Tools. McGraw-Hill, New York.

Avison, D. E. & Wood-Harper, A. T. (1990) *Multiview: An Exploration in Information Systems Development*. McGraw-Hill, London.

Barrett, R. (1998) *Liberating the Corporate Soul*. Butterworth-Heinemann, Woburn, MA.

Baskerville, R. (1993) Information Systems Security Design Methods: Implications for Information Systems Development. *ACM Computing Surveys*, **25** (4), 376–414.

Bruegge, B. & Dutoit, A. (2000) Object-Orientated Software Engineering: Conquering Complex and Changing Systems, Prentice-Hall, New Jersey.

Carew, P. & Stapleton, L. (2004) Towards a Privacy Framework for Information Systems Development. In Caplinskas, A. et al. (Eds.) *Information Systems Development: Advances in Theory, Practice, and Education*. Springer, Lithuania.

Checkland, P. (1999) *Systems Thinking, Systems Practice*. Wiley, New York.

CSI/FBI (2005) Computer Crime and Security Survey 2005. Computer Security Institute.

Dagwell, R. & Weber, R. (1983) System Designers' User Models: A Comparative Study and Methodological Critique. *Communications of the ACM*, **26** (11), 978–995.

Dennis, A., Wixom, B. & Roth, R. (2006) *Systems Analysis Design*. Wiley, New Jersey.

Dhillon, G. (1995) Interpreting the Management of Information System Security. *School of Economics and Political Science.* University of London, London.

Dhillon, G. (2001) Violations of Safeguards by Trusted Personnel and Understanding Related Information Security Concerns. *Computers and Security*, **20** (2), 165–172.

Dhillon, G. & Backhouse, J. (2000) Information System Security Management in the New Millennium. *Communications of the ACM*, **43** (7), 125–128.

England, G. W. (1967) Personal Value Systems of American Managers. *The Academy of Management Journal*, 10, 53–68.

Freeman, A. & Doyle, L (2006) An Exploratory Study Investigating the Role of Information Systems Security in SMEs in the South East of Ireland. *EUTIC06 Colloquium*, University of Brussels, Belgium.

Ghosh, A., Howell, C. & Whittiaker, J. (2002) Building Software Securely from the Ground Up. *IEEE Software*, Feb 2002, 14–16.

Goodland, M. & Slater, C. (1997) *SSADM: A Practical Approach*, McGraw-Hill, London.

Hall, B. P. (2001) Values Development and Learning Organizations. *Journal of Knowledge Management*, **5** (1), 19–32.

Hedberg, B. & Mumford, E. (1975) The Design of Computer Systems: Man's Vision of Man as an Integral Part of the Systems Design Process. *Human Choices and Computers*. North-Holland, Amsterdam.

Iivari, J., Hirschheim, R. & Klein, H. K. (2001) A Dynamic Framework for Classifying Information Systems Development Methodologies and Approaches. *Journal of Information Systems*, **17** (3), 179–219.

Kling, R. (1978) Value Conflicts and Social Choice in Electronic Funds Transfer System Developments. *Communications of the ACM*, **21** (8), 642–657.

Kluckhohn, C. (1951) Values and Value-Orientation in the Theory of Action. In Parsons, T. & Shils, E. (Ed.) *Toward a General Theory of Action*. Harvard Business Press, Cambridge, MA.

Kumar, K. & Welke, R. J. (1984) Implementation Failure and System Developer Values: Assumptions Truisms and Empirical Evidence. The Fifth International Conference of Information Systems, Tuscon, Arizona.

Larman, C. (1998) Applying UML and Patterns: An Introduction to Object-Orientated Analysis and Design. Prentice-Hall, New Jersey.

Lindeman, M. & Versasalo, M. (2005) Measuring Values With the Short Schwartz's Value Survey. *Journal of Personality Assessment*, **85** (2), 170–178.

McGraw, G. & Wyk, K. (2005) Bridging the Gap Between Software Development and Information Security. *IEEE Security & Privacy*, **3** (5), 75–79.

McGuire, D., Garavan, T., Saha, S. & Donnell, D. O. (2006) The Impact of Individual Values on Human Resource Decision-Making by Line Managers. *International Journal of Manpower*, **27** (3), 251–273.

Moutatidis, H., Giorgini, P. & Manson, G. (2004) When Security Meets Software Engineering: A Case of Modelling Secure Information Systems, *Information Systems Journal*, 2005 (30), 609–629.

Mumford, E. (1990) *Designing Human Systems for New Technology*. Manchester Business School Press, Manchester.

Mumford, E. (2000) A Socio-Technical Approach to Systems Design, *Requirements Engineering*, **2** (5), 125–133.

Orvik, T. U., Olsen, D. H. & Ssin, M. (1998) Deployment of System Development Methods. In Zupancic, J., Wojtkowski, W., Wojtkowski, W. G. & Wrycza, S. (Eds.) *Evolution and Challenges in System Development*. Bled, Slovenia.

PricewaterhouseCoopers (2005) Information Security Breaches Survey 2005.

Rokeach, M. (1973) *The Nature of Human Values*. Collier Macmillan, London.

Sarros, J. & Santroa, J. (2001) Leaders and Values: A Cross-Cultural Study. *Leadership and Organization Development Journal*, **22** (5), 243–248.

Schwartz, S. H. (1992) Universals in the Content and Structure of Values: Theoretical Advances and Empirical Tests in 20 Countries. *Advances in Experimental Social Psychology*, 25, 1–65.

Schwartz, S. H. & Bilsky, W. (1987) Toward a Universal Psychological Structure of Human Values. *Journal of Personality and Social Psychology*, **53** (3), 550–562.

Schwartz, S. H. & Bilsky, W. (1990) Toward a Theory of the Universal Content and Structure of Values: Extensions and Cross-Cultural Replication. *Journal of Personality and Social Psychology*, **58** (5), 878–891.

Tryfonas, T., Kiountouzis, B. & Poulymenakou, A. (2001) Embedding Security Practices in Contemporary Information Systems Development Approaches. *Information Management & Computer Security*, **9** (4), 183–197.

Villarroel, R., Medina, E. & Piattini, M. (2004) Incorporating Security Issues in the Information Systems Design. *Fifth Mexican International Conference in Computer Science (ENC'04)*. IEEE Computer Security.

Securing Systems Intelligently: The Logical Approach

Brian Shields and Owen Molloy

National University of Ireland Galway, Department of Information Technology,
brian.shields@geminga.it.nuigalway.ie, owen.molloy@nuigalway.ie

Abstract The quantity of generated information we store and need to access is colossal. Security of this information is becoming an issue of greater importance as the techniques and granularity with which it can be accessed become more advanced. Availability of information is a key component of any security system, although the information must be protected, it must also be available to the people who need it as and when they request it. However, increasing the methods by which it is accessible automatically increases the chance it may be compromised. Security systems are now using advanced levels of encryption, digital signatures containing biometric data and highly complex access control policies. We are proposing a security framework with an access control system which reduces the complexity involved in defining authorisation permissions, particularly in structured documents such as XML where the user may be granted restricted access. Our solution employs techniques usually reserved for intelligent systems and the semantic web.

1 Introduction

An organisation often has a need to share information securely with members of that organisation, or indeed members of another organisation. The definition of what 'securely' means can cause some consternation among certain groups of people.

Access control is the area of security in which our work lies. Access control has been a large area of study for years, with more effort being applied to it recently inline the growth of online information systems, the increase in data which is protected and the increase in the number of users, authorized or otherwise.

RBAC has become the most widely used method of defining and enforcing access control in information systems since its inception in 1995 (Sandhu et al., 1996). RBAC works on the premise that role groups exist in the system; it then controls access of information with respect to these groups. To access information a user must be a member of a role and assume the authorisation privileges of that role.

C. Barry et al. (eds.), *Information Systems Development: Challenges in Practice, Theory, and Education, Vol.2*, doi: 10.1007/978-0-387-78578-3_13,
© Springer Science+Business Media, LLC 2009

In a typical RBAC system, the individual roles are granted access to resources. Resources can be processes or information. Each relevant file must be accounted for in the role permissions, if it is not then it is usually assumed that role lacks the appropriate permissions to access the file. With the development and now widespread adoption of XML as an information representation, particularly in Web environments, the task of permission assigning has become extensively more difficult. There is a large body of research investigating XML access control, which will be discussed in Section 6. All of this work proposes different ways of granting and restricting access to individual attributes and element of the XML file. In a large system this can increase the security workload exponentially.

This chapter proposes another solution to this problem. A solution we regard as reducing a lot of the time-intensive activities of assigning role permissions to the elements and attributes of an XML file. We present a way of writing rules which will determine the permissions for each role. This activity is carried out at a schema level, yet different permissions may be assigned to alternative documents, or document elements, of the same schema. Most XML access control systems require the user to specify permissions at both a schema and instance level as, after all, a role may have permissions to access one document and not another, yet both are instances of the same schema. For example, a doctor may access one patient record and not another, while both patient records have the same schema.

We propose an intelligent authorisation system that can decide the permissions for an individual at the time they request information. We use description logic and decidable rules to provide the necessary intelligence for this. In this chapter we apply this system to the Electronic Patient Record (EPR) from the area of Health Informatics.

This chapter is organised as follows. Section 2 provides an overview of the two main technologies: description logics and rules. Section 3 is an overview of our security framework including a detailed description of our system architecture. Section 4 presents our access control system, the main components involved and how they interact with one another. Section 5 explores some related research in XML access control. We conclude the chapter and detail some potential future avenues for our research in Section 6.

2 Overview of Technologies

In this chapter we propose the use of some less well-known technologies as part of our authorisation system. In this section we attempt to introduce two research areas: description logic and rules or rule-based systems. We then present the application of these research areas which we apply to our work, the Web Ontology Language (OWL) (McGuinness & van Harmelen, 2004) and the Semantic Web Rule Language (SWRL) (Horrocks et al., 2004), respectively.

2.1 Description Logic

Description logic is a family of logic-based knowledge representation (KR) formalisms. Description logic is a descendant of semantic networks and KL-ONE and describe a domain in terms of concepts, roles and individuals. Concepts have also been referred to as classes, roles as relationships and individuals as instances. Description logic has two key characteristics:

- Formal Semantics – which are decidable fragments of First Order Logic (FOL)
- Inference Services – which in turn provide decision procedures

The architecture of a typical DL system is composed of two principal components: a knowledge base and an inference or reasoning engine. The knowledge base consists of two types of knowledge:

- Tbox – or terminology box is the schema or description of the knowledge. It contains the hierarchical structure of the data and relationships between its concepts
- Abox – or assertion box is actual data. It is instance information of the concepts described in the TBox

OWL, or the Web Ontology Language, is a web standard as specified in the World Wide Web Consortium (W3C) Recommendation of February 2004. OWL is built on top of Resource Description Framework (RDF) and is written in XML. It is based on description logic and has three sub languages:

- OWL Full – is the union of OWL Syntax and RDF
- OWL DL – is restricted to the FOL fragment. OWL DL is fully decidable
- OWL Lite – is the "easier to implement" subset of OWL DL

OWL DL benefits from the years of research into description logic. It has well defined semantics. Its formal properties, such as complexity and decidability, are well understood by the DL community. There are many known DL reasoning algorithms and highly optimised implemented systems that can be easily applied to OWL DL.

2.2 Rules

Rules are becoming an increasingly important part of business information systems. They abstract some of the business logic from the core software components of the system and therefore make it easier to develop the system, but more importantly they allow the relatively straightforward update or modification of the business logic. This can now become the task of an analyst familiar with the rule language, rather than that of the developer who wrote the system. This is one of the reasons we have decided to represent our access control logic in the form of rules.

There are four main types of rules used in rule systems:

- Derivation or deduction
- Transformation rules
- Integrity constraints
- Reaction or Event-Condition-Action (ECA)

For the purpose of our system, and most logic systems, we will be exclusively using derivation or deduction rules. The nature of this type of rule is to examine certain information and assert new information based on its findings.

The number of rule languages available today is getting larger. According to Tim Berners-Lee's semantic technology stack (Berners-Lee, 2000), rules are the next step in knowledge engineering systems. We have chosen Semantic Web Rule Language (SWRL) as the language in which to represent our rules. SWRL is a combination of the OWL and the work done by the RuleML community. It extends OWL by adding simple Horn style rules. A rule of this nature states that if the antecedent, or 'if part,' of the rule is true then the consequent, or 'then part,' of the rule must also hold true. SWRL is a W3C proposed standard.

3 Framework Architecture

Although a security solution such as this is almost completely composed of or related to access control, there are a number of other services which must be in place to offer a complete security framework. These services include a Key Management Service, an Encryption and Decryption Service and a Framework Management Service.

Figure 1 shows the proposed architecture of the proposed security framework which will be discussed in the remaining part of this section.

3.1 Key Management Service

The security framework will provide a service which will create, manage and store X.509 digital certificates. These certificates will be used as security tokens in requesting SOAP message headers to provide a non-repudiative user identity.

The Key Management Service will be designed and implemented using the XKMS (XML Key Management Specification) Standard from OASIS (Ford et al., 2001). This provides two principle services:

- XML Key Information Service Specification (XKISS) – This service locates a public key in order to encrypt information for an individual or to verify signed information.

- XML Key Registration Service Specification (XKRSS) – This provides a number of services to register, recover, reissue and revoke keys.

In addition to implementing the services specified in XKMS, the security framework will store keys locally in order to reduce the interruption time between users requesting a service and when that service is called. Keys for new users will be registered or created through the Framework Management Service.

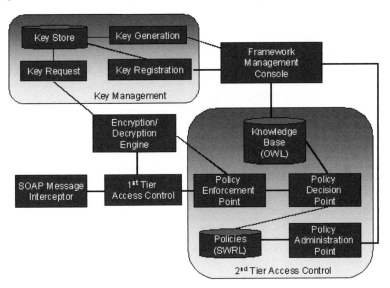

Fig. 1. Proposed Security Framework Architecture

3.2 Encryption and Decryption Service

In addition to protecting information while in storage, the Security Framework must enforce a strict security policy on the confidentiality of information while 'on the wire.' All communication between remote clients and the Security Framework will be encrypted by the sender; be that the client or the framework. The designers of the Web Service endpoints may specify additional encryption policies.

The Encryption and Decryption services will be exposed services from the encryption/decryption engine. This engine will encrypt and decrypt information according to a public key. If User$_A$ makes a Web Service request to a Web Service managed by the Security Framework, the SOAP request is, at the very least, encrypted using our public key. The request will be subject to first tier authorisation (detailed in section 4); upon successful authorisation, the message will be fully decrypted by the encryption/decryption engine, using our private key, and passed to second tier authorisation. The response returned to the requester is encrypted using their public key which is located using the Key Management Service.

3.3 Framework Management Service

The Framework Management Service will be a HTTP and SOAP management centre used by the administrators of the Security Framework. It is essentially a front-end management of the different components of the framework. It will have five principal responsibilities:

- Uploading and registering or creating new keys
- Register valid Web Service endpoints
- Create/edit/remove access control policies
- Add/remove/edit users and semantic user descriptions
- Add/remove/edit semantic resource descriptions.

4 Access Control Model

Figure 2 is an architecture diagram of our proposed access control solution. This architecture has two fundamental areas: design-time components and runtime components. Both of these areas have access to our reasoning engine. We are using Hoolet as our reasoning engine.

The design time components include all the modules which are involved in preparing and customising the solution for a particular domain or problem. It has three components: an Ontology Loader, a Schema Mappings Engine and a Rule Parsing Engine. The Ontology Loader accepts an OWL-DL ontology as an XML file, verifies if it is consistent and loads it into the reasoning engine. The Schema Mappings Engine parses an XML mappings file which provides our authorisation system with knowledge of the structure of XML files. The Rule Parsing Engine receives and parses an XML file containing access control rules written in SWRL. These rules are made available to the reasoning engine at runtime.

The runtime components of our authorisation system include all the modules involved in making an access control decision on a client request for information and enforcing this decision. The system will use these components to decide what parts of the requested XML file will be made available to the requesting client, and then prune the file appropriately. There are three components in this section of our system: an Instance Mapping Engine, and Instance Query Engine and an XML Pruning Engine. The Instance Mapping Engine uses the previously defined schema mappings to map each element and attribute to their counterparts in the ontology. The Instance Query Engine takes each element and attribute of the XML file and queries the reasoning engine about the access control levels for it, as possessed by the requesting client. The XML Pruning Engine uses the results of these queries to prune any element or attribute to which the requesting client lacks the appropriate access.

4.1 Design Time

From Figure 2 we can see that the architecture of our system is composed of two distinct areas. This section attempts to explain the first of these sections, design time. The section has three parts, each one dealing with one of the components of the design time area; ontology design, access control rules specification and XML Schema to OWL DL mappings.

Before we can begin reasoning about access to the information system, we must first develop an ontology representing the information stored. There are six steps which we use to create the ontology:

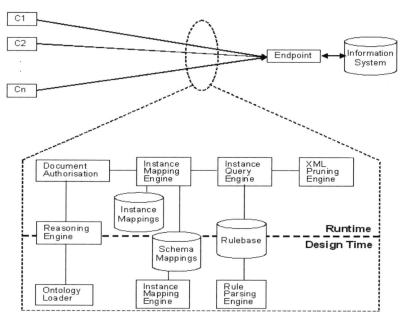

Fig. 2. Access Control Module Architecture

1. **Determine the scope** – The ontology for our system must include any information which can be shared with users.

2. **Reuse existing ontologies** – If any of the information in the scope has been previously defined in an ontology then this can be imported and re-used.

3. **Define the classes and class hierarchy** – The concepts of the domain are specified. In our example we have the classes Medic, Surgeon, Nurse, ClinicalInformation, etc. These are then organised into a hierarchical structure by specifying relationships between them. We use three general relationships for creating the ontology hierarchy: subsumtion, disjoint and equivalent.

4. **Define the properties of the classes** – Classes alone will not provide enough information. Once the main concepts are represented by classes we must define the internal structure of these concepts. Two types of properties may be defined: ObjectProperties which relate two classes to each other and DatatypeProperties which are common simple types such as integer and string.

5. **Define the facets of the properties** – The property facets refer to the property type, cardinality and possible legal values it may store.

6. **Create instances** – Once the ontology is designed, instances of each class must be created. Each of these instances is referred to as an object of its class.

One of the most important functions of an access control system, second only to their enforcement, is the design and deployment of the access control rules. There is a module in our system architecture called the 'Rule Parsing Engine.' This module accepts rules, written in SWRL, parses them for correctness and completeness, and loads them into the reasoning engine for later assertion. We use deduction rules (also called derivation or 'if-then' rules) in our access control system. Deduction rules, as described in section 3, present a number of assertions (antecedent), all of which must be true for the resulting assertion (consequent) to be true. All rules in our system currently have a consequent 'hasAccessToInformation(p, o)' where p is some defined user of the system and o is the object they have access to. 'hasAccessToInformation' is an OWL Object Property. It is defined in our ontology as having a domain of 'Person' and a range of 'Information.' This is read 'Person hasAccessToInformation Information.' This can be explained further by example. The following rule says that a doctor may access the details of a patient if he/she is the treating physician of that patient.

```
Doctor(?p) ^ Patient(?o) ^ treats(?p, ?o) →
        hasAccessToInformation(?p,?o)
```

Doctor and Patient are OWL classes as defined in our ontology. 'Doctor(?p)' asserts that the variable p is an instance of Doctor. 'treats' is an OWL Object Property and is defined in our ontology as having the Doctor class as its domain and a range Patient. 'treats(?p, ?o)' asserts that the instance p and the instance o are a legal domain and range of the object property. In keeping with the nature of deduction rules, if the three assertions on the antecedent, or left side, of the rule are true, then our reasoning engine will verify that the assertion on the consequent, or right side, of the rule will also hold true. In reality, rules in a health care system would be far more complex, and therefore we have developed some more multifarious examples. One such example is:

```
Medic(?x) ^ Medic(?y) ^ TestRequest(?a) ^
TestResult(?b) ^ supervises(?y, ?x) ^
requestedBy(?a, ?x) ^ hasResult(?a, ?b) →
      hasAccessToInformation(?x, ?b)
```

which reads: A medic has access to results of all tests requested by anyone they supervise.

The ontology or ontologies defining the elements of the system do just that, define the elements of the system and their relationships to one another. This must now be linked in some way to the data structures that pass in and out of the system so the access control rules can be applied to it. For example, using our EPR, we must take each individual element from it and tell the security engine what that element means in terms of our ontological description of our system. Naming conventions can be an issue as one hospital system may call junior doctor medics where another hospital may call them interns. These differences become irrelevant as long as they are mapped to the appropriate item in the ontology. The mappings take place from the schema of the XML file in question. Schema to ontology mappings or XSD to OWL mappings have received a lot of interest recently. One can create a mapping from the schema to the ontology which will hold true for all XML instances of that schema which may be created. Three types of mappings exist: Class Mappings, Object Property Mappings and Datatype Property Mappings.

Class Mappings are mappings between elements or attributes of the XML file and OWL DL Classes from the ontology. The snippet of XML in Listing 1 is an example of a simple Class Mapping. We noticed when designing the mapping module of our security engine that OWL classes often mapped to parent elements in the XML schema, i.e. 'class elements' contained only child elements, they did not contain any text element or attributes. Therefore in order to uniquely identify an object of this class mapping when an XML file is presented, we allow the user to specify data from somewhere else in the XML file to act as the identifier. The unique identifier must be an ancestor of the class element in question and is identified using an XPath expression.

Object Property Mappings are mappings between elements or attributes of the XML file and OWL DL Object Properties from the ontology. Listing 2 contains an example of a simple object property mapping. As with the class mappings, object property mappings must specify the element of the XML Schema which is being mapped and the object property in the ontology it is being mapped to. We must also specify the appropriate domain and range of the object property, this is necessary for some complex assertions about an individuals access rights. Listing 2 shows that the XML item in question is being mapped to 'madeBy' object property of the ontology. It is important to specify that we mean the 'madeBy' property from the statement that 'ClinicalObservation madeBy Medic' as the object property 'madeBy' can exist with other domains such as 'ClinicalDirection.'

Datatype Property Mappings are the mappings between elements or attributes of the XML file and OWL-DL Datatype Properties of the ontology. Listing 3 contains an example of a simple datatype property mapping. Datatype property mappings are the least complex of the three mappings. They contain three elements, the element of the XML Schema which is being mapped, the datatype property from the ontology it is being mapped to and the type of the property, i.e. string, int, etc. Datatype properties will be leaf elements or attributes in the XML file. They are used when providing temporal access control for the data.

4.2 Runtime

This section explains the processes involved in the runtime area of the system architecture of our system as seen in Figure 2. There are three areas which we cover in this section: the compilation of XML Mappings from our Schema mappings in the previous subsection, formatting and executing queries on our access control system and pruning the XML document before it is sent to the requesting client.

We explained in the previous subsection how the XML Schema to OWL Mappings are created and used. This alone would have been sufficient to provide the access control of a basic RBAC system. We can restrict access according to the group or role a person belongs to. However, in this section we describe how to further specify this access control. To achieve this we must be able to reason on the instance information and not on general concepts. When an XML file is requested and is awaiting return, its appropriate schema mapping configurations are loaded. The XML file is then parsed and the instance information added to the mappings. Care is needed when parsing instance information. The XML file is accessed for the information according to XPath information supplied in the mappings configuration.

```
<ClassMapping>
    <xmlItem>PatientRecord/PatientInformation</xmlItem>
    <owlItem>PatientInformation</owlItem>
    <identifiedBy>PatientRecord/PatientInformation/idNum</identifiedBy>
</ClassMapping>
```

Listing 1 – Class Mapping

```
<ObjectPropertyMapping>

<xmlItem>PatientRecord/ClinicalInformation/ClinicalObservation/madeBy</xmlItem>
    <owlItem>madeBy</owlItem>
    <domain>ClinicalObservation</domain>
    <range>Medic</range>
```

Listing 2 – Object Property Mapping

```
<DatatypePropertyMapping>
    <xmlItem>PatientRecord/PatientInformation/idNum</xmlItem>
    <owlItem>ID_num</owlItem>
    <type>string</type>
</DatatypePropertyMapping>
```

Listing 3 – Datatype Property Mapping

In our example, we have the XPath expression '/patientRecord/clinicalInformation/observation/idNum.' According to the schema of our EPR, we can have multiple 'observation' elements and therefore we need to ensure we are parsing the correct 'idNum.' This is important as the requesting client may have access to some 'observation' elements and not others. Using instance information in our reasoning engine will allow us specify tighter access control rules such as 'A doctor may only access the information of a patient in his direct care.' Usually, to achieve this level of control, it is necessary to provide instance information in the access control rules.

Once the instance mapping is complete we have our own object structure representing the XML file. Each element and attribute is represented by one object. This object contains information on the element such as name, value, type (which comes from the schema) and a mapping to its counterpart in the ontology. From these objects we can create individual queries which we send to the reasoning engine. A Semantic Access Control Query is a triple *(individual₁, property, individual₂)*, where: *individual₁* is the user trying to access information; *property₁* is always the OWL Object Property *hasAccessToInformation*; *individual₂* is the instance information the user is trying to access. For example, 'surg123 hasAccessTo p12345.obs123)' is querying the reasoning engine whether the surgeon surg123 has access to the information of the observation obs123 of patient p12345. The reasoning engine will return 'yes' or 'no.' This result is stored in out XML item representative object and will be used when pruning the XML file.

Any alterations made to an XML file at runtime can prove troublesome, especially when the file must satisfy a schema. The first action of the pruning engine is the alteration of the XML Schema file. The level of restriction of the schema must be addressed. All cardinality of elements and attributes within complex element structures are changed to '0 or more.' This will ensure that, after pruning, an XML file is still of valid structure, according to its schema. The root node of the XML file is retrieved. In a depth first traversal of the tree, each XML node is examined for pruning. On selection of an element or attribute, the pruning engine finds the corresponding object representation in our system and gets the result from the query execution. If the result was 'yes,' the node is passed over and the next in the tree is selected. If the result was 'no' the XML item is removed from the XML file. If the item is an element, all children are also removed. Once all elements and attributes have been examined and removed if necessary, the authorisation system returns the document to the Web service response and lets it continue as normal.

5 Related Work

There has been much work done in the area of fine-grained access control of XML documents. Bertino et al. (1999), Damiani et al. (2000) and Kudo et al. (Kudo & Hada, 2000) all present ways of securely accessing XML documents at an element level.

Damiani et al. (2004) describe a means of providing access control, enriched with semantics, of resources by extending existing policy languages. They present an extension to XACML (XACML Technical Committee, 2005) which enables the specification of users and resources in terms of 'rich ontology-based meta-data.' This approach successfully achieves access control to resources in the traditional sense, i.e. files and processes.

Qu et al. (2004) propose OREL, an ontology based Rights Expression Language (REL) to control a users rights to access digital content. They essentially add reasoning capabilities to existing RELs such as XrML.

Qin et al. (Qin & Atluri, 2003) define a model for access control for the semantic Web based on concept definitions. Access control decisions are at a concept level as defined in an OWL ontology. They describe the benefits of a semantically rich access control model in terms of the reduction of administration efforts in updating the authorisation policies. Although they do present an intelligent, rich access control model, they apply it to semantic concepts as defined on a Web page. It is not applied to XML documents.

Xiaopeng et al. (2005) present an access control model for grid computing which uses semantic descriptions. They describe the entities of the system and the access control policies in the Semantic Policy Language and then use semantic reasoning to determine access rights and resolve potential conflicts. This application of semantic access control is exclusively applied to grid resources.

Agarwal and Sprick (2004) (Agarwal et al., 2004) and Yague et al. (Yague & Troya, 2002; Yague et al., 2003) provide us with examples of how they ensure access control for semantic Web services.

Our work is trying to achieve a lot of what has been discussed in this section, although we are trying to merge it all together. We provide semantic access control of XML documents, and we provide it to an element level of granularity.

6 Conclusions and Future Work

We have proposed an intelligent solution to XML access control which we believe will dramatically reduce the workload involved in authorisation administration. As each new schema is added to the system a mapping file is also added. No authorisation details have to be added for either schema or instance as access control is enforced on the underlying information rather than the document itself.

Work has already started in creating an ontology, including some sample instance information, for the Health Level 7 (HL7) information standard. HL7 is the standard for information transfer in the health domain. Other work we have committed to completing in our system include temporal- and geographical-based access control using SWRL builtins; the addition of a secure update facility for the XML documents; testing alternative reasoning engines for increased reasoning speed; and a more intelligent querying system which will use knowledge of the document structure to reduce the number of queries executed.

References

Agarwal, S. & Sprick, B. (2004) Access Control for Semantic Web Services. *IEEE International Conference on Web Services.* San Diego, CA.

Agarwal, S., Sprick, B. & Wortman, S. (2004) Credential Based Access Control for Semantic Web Services. In *2004 AAAI Spring Symposium Series,* Stanford, CA.

Berners-Lee, T. (2000) Keynote Address. *XML 2000.* http://www.w3.org/2000/Talks/1206-xml2k-tbl/slide10-0.html.

Bertino, E., Castano, S., Ferrari, E. & Mesiti, M. (1999) Controlled Access and Dissemination of XML Documents. *2nd ACM Workshop on Web Information and Data Management.* Kansas City, MO.

Damiani, E., Capatini di Vimercati, S., Fugazzo, C. & Samarati, P. (2004) Extending Policy Languages to the Semantic Web. *International Conference on Web Engineering.* Munich Germany.

Damiani E., Capatini di Vimercati, S., Paraboschi, S. & Samarati, P. (2000) Securing XML Documents. *7th International Conference on Extending Database Technology.* Konstanz, Germany.

Ford, W., Hallam-Baker, P., Fox, B., Dillaway, B., LaMacchia, B., Epstein, J. & Lapp, J. (2001) XML Key Management Specification (XKMS). http://www.w3.org/TR/2001/NOTE-xkms-20010330/.

Horrocks, I., Patel-Schneider, P. F., Boley, H., Tabet, S., Grosof, B. & Dean, M. (2004) SWRL: A Semantic Web Rule Language Combining OWL and RuleML. http://www.daml.org/2003/11/swrl/.

Kudo, M. & Hada, S. (2000) XML Document Security Based on Provisional Authorization. *7th ACM Conference on Computer and Communication Security.* Athens, Greece.

McGuinness, D. L. & van Harmelen, F. (2004) OWL Web Ontology Language. http://www.w3.org/TR/owl-features/.

Sandhu, R. S., Coyne, E. J., Feinstein, H. L. & Youman, C. E., (1996) Role-Based Access Control Models. *IEEE Computer.* 29(2):38-47.

The Rule Markup Initiative. http://www.ruleml.org/.

Qin, L. & Atluri, V. (2003) Concept-Level Access Control for the Semantic Web. *2003 ACM Workshop on XML Security.* Fairfax, VA.

Qu, Y., Zhang, X. & Li, H. (2004) OREL: An Ontology-Based Rights Expression Language. *13th World Wide Web Conference.* New York.

XACML Technical Committee (2005) XACML 2.0 Specification Set. http://docs.oasis-open.org/xacml/2.0/access_control-xacml-2.0-core-spec-os.pdf.

Xiaopeng, W., Junzhou, L., Aibo, S. & Teng, M (2005) Semantic Access Control in Grid Computing. *11th International Conference on Parallel and Distributed Systems.* Fukuoka, Japan.

Yague, M. I. & Troya, J. M. (2002) A Semantic Approach to Access Control in Web Services. *EuroWeb 2002. The Web and the GRID: From E-Science to E-Business.* Oxford.

Yague, M. I., Mana, A., Lopez, J. & Troya, J. M. (2003) Applying the Semantic Web Layers to Access Control. *14th International Workshop on Database and Expert Systems Applications.* Prague. Czech Republic.

Trust Ontology for Information Systems Development

Kamaljit Kaur Bimrah, Haralambos Mouratidis and David Preston

University of East London, School of Computing and Technology
bimrah@uel.ac.uk, haris@uel.ac.uk, david17@uel.ac.uk

Abstract   In this chapter we review a number of works related to trust modelling and we identify some important limitations. In particular, we first argue that an ontology for trust modelling should include a number of concepts related to trust such as reputation, privacy and security. Then we discuss the current state of the art and illustrate that these works fail to consider all these concepts in a unified conceptual framework. We then describe the development of an ontology that considers trusts and its related concepts and we briefly illustrate how such ontology can be used to assist information systems developers in analysing trust-related issues of information systems. In doing so, we use a case study from the health care domain.

1 Introduction

Information systems play a colossal and equally imperative part in today's modern world. The grounds on why individuals are moving towards such systems are because they see optimistic results. Jøsang et al. (2005) argue that individuals are willing to trust information systems, as they trust other humans, knowing that there are potential risks. Once they trust, if they have a good experience, then trust is gained, hence the fabrication of trust, building reputation, which proves beneficial for potential users. On the other hand, if the individuals have a bad experience, then there is no trust for the future, causing a bad reputation for a particular information system.

Therefore, it is important that trust issues are considered during information systems development process. As argued by Yu (Yu and Liu 2001) 'Trust is becoming an increasingly important issue in the design of many kinds of information systems.' Recent research by Sutcliffe (2006) and Chopra and Wallace. (2003) has shown that trust should be considered from the early stages of the information systems development process. Chopra and Wallace (2003) argue that one of the reasons for this need comes from the necessity to identify early in the development process any conflicts or inconsistencies between the requirements introduced to

C. Barry et al. (eds.), *Information Systems Development: Challenges in Practice, Theory, and Education, Vol.2*, doi: 10.1007/978-0-387-78578-3_14,
© Springer Science+Business Media, LLC 2009

the system by trust and security considerations and the system's functional requirements. Sutcliffe (2006) highlights that 'design and trust intersect in two ways.' He argues that information system users will have a positive experience only if the systems are designed so the users trust them. This role is to be fulfilled by good design (Sutcliffe 2006). Some form of 'ownership' should also be allowed in such systems, which allows the user to customise them and adapt according to his/her needs; this in turn actually *facilitates trust*. The second way that Sutcliffe (2006) mentions that design and trust are intersected is by having 'technology acting as a mediator of trust between people, organizations or products.' In essence, Sutcliffe means that the uncertainty that is present in relationships should be reduced by technology, this in return will make information more accessible; enhancing trust.

However, Kethers (2005) and Li et al. (2004) conclude that in information systems development, trust is either not considered by the software system developers or if it is considered, it is usually considered as a sole concept isolated from the rest of the development process. The main problem is that there is a lack of ontological and methodological support to model and reason about trust with its related concepts in one allied framework. This situation provides the foremost motivation for our research. In particular, our aim is to develop a reasoning and modelling framework that will enable information system developers to consider trust during the development of information systems.

In this chapter, we present work towards our aim. In particular, we describe an ontological foundation to support the modelling of trust and its related concepts. However, before coming onto the former, we discuss some trust definitions along with a number of concepts that are related to trust. Section 3 discusses limitations of related work while the penultimate section discusses the ontological foundation for trust and its related concepts. Section 5 concludes this chapter and indicates directions for future work.

2 Trust Definitions and Concepts

What is trust? On what basis would you trust somebody or something? Would you try a new shampoo on instinct or would you need someone else's recommendation? According to the literature, trust is difficult to define, convey, measure or specify. Michael et al. (2002) say that '...Trust is a term with many meanings,' and this is justified by a large number of definitions proposed in the literature. Almenarez et al. (1994) define trust as the belief that an entity has about another entity, from past experiences, knowledge about the entity's nature and/or recommendations from trusted entities. Similarly Robinson (1996) indicates that trust is one's expectations, assumptions or beliefs about the likelihood that another's future actions will be beneficial, favourable or at least not detrimental to one's interests. A more 'common sense' form of trust is derived from Alford (2004); he says that to trust someone is to be confident that in a situation where you are vulnerable, one will be disposed to act benignly towards you. In the same way Maarof and Krishna (2002) say that trust is the firm belief in the competence of an entity to act dependably, securely and reliably within a specified context. Although these definitions use different terms and define trust differently, they all agree that trust is related to a number of other concepts and it should not be considered in isolation. The following section provides a discussion on trust-related concepts.

From the above definitions it is clear that trust is frequently defined and described in terms of *confidence, expectation, belief* and *faith*. All of these concepts capture the common theme that the trustor (a particular trusting) anticipates that the trust will be upheld by the trustee (a particular other in which the trust is placed) (Chopra and Wallace 2003). Consider for instance, an Internet-based information system. If the system is believed not to have strong security, then potential users might be reluctant to trust that the system is safe to use. On the other hand, if someone believes the system will be secure, more likely they will have faith in using it. These situations are related with the concept of *initial trust*. Li et al. (2004) defines initial trust as trust in an unfamiliar object, dealing with a relationship in which the trustor does not have meaningful experience, knowledge or affecting bonds with the trustee. Jøsang and Patton (2004) say that since trust is based on experience over time, establishing initial trust can be a major challenge to new users of information systems.

Closely tied to initial trust is also an important concept, *reputation*. Jøsang et al. argue that if the trusting subject does not have a good reputation, then it may be discarded and distrusted. In later work (Jøsang et al. 2007) the same authors have stated that reputation is what is generally said or believed about a person's or thing's character or standing. Although reputation can be used in many contexts, in our case we are interested in Information Systems reputation. Consider for instance the case where a user can select from a selection of information systems. Given the choice users are more likely to select an information system with good reputation (on a number of features such as security, reliability and so on) rather than an information system with a low reputation. Even if the latter supports more features than the former.

Another important concept is *risk*. Risk emerges when the value at stake in a transaction is high, or when this transaction has a critical role in the security or the safety of a system (Jøsang and Lo Presti 2004). However, the potential for risk is distinguished. A number of individuals do trust when they know that risk could be a potential, however, some individuals may decide not to trust due to this risk element. Individuals are aware of the potential risk(s), yet they still wish to trust, however if this risk materialises, then how would this affect the trust aspect? This may cause the user never to use and/or trust the system again, or it may not. It is said by (Numan 1998) that a situation is experienced as being full of risk when a person expects that in the future he/she might eventually experience negative results that they can't control because of a direct result of this situation.

Analogous conclusions have been reached by a large number of works associated to trust from the security modelling community (Mouratidis and Giorgini 2006). If an information system user is aware of the security aspects being adequately covered then they may feel more confident in using the system; in other words they are keener to trust. However, if the user is not sure of the security aspects, then they may decide against using the system. Although *'few works have tried to directly link trust with security'* (Lo Presti et al. 2003), it is argued by Yu (Yu and Cysneiros 2002) *that 'privacy, security and trust are increasingly demanding attention in today's networked based systems, they are frequently demanding tradeoffs to be considered and requirements to be negotiated there, they have to be taken into account at the earliest stages of the software development process.'* Mayer et al. (2005) similarly state that *'security engineering should begin at early stages of IT system development, including the use of risk analysis'.* This will allow us to identify potential risks that might affect the amount of trust that users are willing to place in an information system, and therefore analyse the potential trade-offs.

From the above discussion we conclude that concepts related to trust are risk, initial trust, reputation, security and privacy. Although we do not claim that this is a complete list, we consider these concepts as the minimum set of concepts related to trust, which were derived from a number of existing ontologies (Viljanen 2005), (Kim et al. 2005), (Cuske et al. 2005), Simmonds et al. 2004), (Casare and Sichman 2005), (Martimianno) and (Mouratidis et al. 2003). All these shall be introduced in the subsequent segment.

3 Related Work

The literature describes a number of research works related to trust models (Li 2004; Abdul-Rahman and Hailes 2000; Maarof and Krishna 2002; Purser 2001; Carbone et al. 2003) and methodologies for considering some trust aspects (Yu and Liu 2001; Mouratidis et al. 2002; Kethers et al. 2005; CAMS and the Department of Commerce and Trade 2003; Alberts et al. 2003; Mayer et al. 2007; Stolen 2002). Such works, although important they are not directly related to our efforts to provide an ontological foundation for trust. Closer to our work, is an effort to define trust related ontology. Such efforts have concluded in a number of ontologies focused on security (Kim 2005; Simmonds 2004; Mouratidis et al. 2003; Martimiano 2005), trust (Viljanen 2005), and risk (Cuske et al. 2005), reputation (Casare 2004). Other trust related concepts, such as privacy, although might have been considered partially in some ontological efforts (Golbeck and Hendler 2004; Chang et al. 2005), they have no corresponding ontologies. However, an important limitation of these ontologies is the fact that they are independent. In other words, they do not consider trust and its related concepts but they are focused on some of the concepts. For example, as declared in (Viljanen 2005) there are problems in the trust ontology '...the sharing of the trust relationship data may be restricted because of privacy or security reasons'. The latter have not been taken into consideration into the building of the ontology. It has been established that privacy and security are trust related concepts, and even though security has its own ontology, this and privacy have not been incorporated, therefore causing the sharing constraint of the trust related data. On the other hand, there are seven different security ontologies which have been accumulated to form the NRL Security Ontology (Kim 2005). Saying this, even though seven separate ontologies are combined together to form the NRL Security Ontology, the authors argue for the need for further ontologies to address issues which have not been addressed before such as 'privacy policies, access control and survivability'. It is mentioned in (Cuske et al. 2005) that 'an extension of the technology risk ontology's scope is feasible, e.g. by including risk measurement'. It is has been concluded that even though there are ontologies available, we are lacking an ontology that will consider trust and its related concepts in a unified ontological framework. In the next section we describe such ontology.

4 An Ontological Foundation for Trust and its Related Concepts

4.1 The Methodology Selection

The first challenge during the development of our ontology was the choice of the methodology for the ontological development. To help the selection, a number of requirements were identified including the following: (i) It should be clear and concise. We wanted a methodology that was straightforward to follow, and where the development steps are well defined, and well explained to the new ontology developer; (ii) It should be flexible enough to be adapted to your purpose if needed; (iii) It should have been employed previously in a number of projects, and preferable by novice (with respect to their knowledge of the methodology) developers.

After reviewing a large number of ontology methodologies (Fernandez-Lopez and Gomez-Perez 2002; Gomez-Perez et al. 2004; Jomes et al. 1998; Lau and Sure 2002; Noy et al. 2001; Pinto and Martins 2004) and taking into consideration the above requirements, it was decided that the METHONTOLOGY methodology be used for our ontology development. Out of all the methodologies we reviewed, the METHODOLOGY is the most popular choice for ontological development and one of the few methodologies that is accepted by external organizations (Gomez-Perez et al. 2004). Other pulling factors towards the METHONTOLOGY methodology was that it has been employed widely even by inexperienced users (Pinto, and Martins 2004). It is also worth mentioning that the METHONTOLOGY methodology is recommended by FIPA for ontology development (Gomez-Perez et al. 2004). The following figure shows the ontology life cycle which is proposed in the METHONTOLOGY methodology.

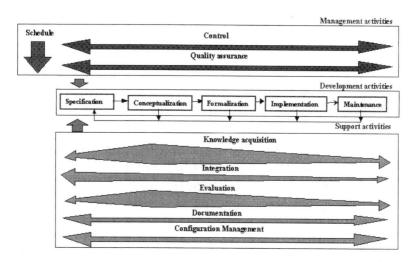

Fig. 1. Development process and life cycle of METHONTOLOGY (Gomez-Perez et al. 2004)

4.2 Ontology Requirements Specification Document

An important issue on specifying an ontology is to understand its exact requirements. This includes understanding the domain of the methodologies, potential uses and potential users. As mentioned above, our work draws concepts from a number of domains related to trust and its related concepts (risk, security, reputation, privacy). The presented ontology is about trust and its related concepts, which are most important, and which should be taken into consideration during the information systems development. Our long-term aim is to employ the ontology as a basis for a reasoning and modelling methodology for the development of trusted information systems. Nevertheless, the ontology itself has a number of possible end-users. These are stated along with the possible scenarios for the ontology use: (a) Methodology designers – the ontology could be employed with the aid of a methodology which takes into contemplation trust or any of its related concepts. (b) Researchers wanting to know about trust related concepts and the relationships – the ontology could be employed by individuals wanting to find out the main trust-related concepts. (c) Current ontology researchers/developers – the ontology could be utilised by other ontology developers who are enhancing their current ontology. (d) New ontology researchers/developers – the ontology could also be exploited by ontology developers who are attempting to design their own ontology and need some direction. (e) Developers of information systems – the ontology could also be used by developers of information systems who are researching into trust-related issues with regards to security for their system.

4.3 Ontology Acquisition

Acquiring knowledge for the ontology was deemed of high importance, as it would form the base of the ontology. If not all avenues were researched in regards to acquiring knowledge then the ontology may not be regarded as complete. Uschold and Gruninger (1996) have mentioned that in order to get a complete scope of the ontology, brainstorming and grouping activities need to be carried out. Brainstorming is important as it 'produces all the potentially relevant terms and phrases.' After brainstorming, the next step would be to group the relevant terms together. The aim of this is to 'structure the terms loosely into work areas corresponding to naturally arising sub-groups' (Uschold and Gruninger 1996). However before all this, initial forms of knowledge acquisition were required, such that of informal text analysis, this was to study the main concepts which were given in books and handbooks. This study enables one to fill in the set of intermediate representations of the conceptualization. Next, would be the requirements for formal text analysis; this precedes the formal text analysis. For this the first thing to do is to identify the structures which are to be detected and the kind of knowledge contributed by each one; this would be concepts, attributes, values and relationships. Sources of knowledge acquisition were books, handbooks, figures, tables and other ontologies.

After delving into the different sources of knowledge acquisition, it came to light that there were many ontologies which looked at the concepts that we regarded as being related to trust. Such ontologies were extracted and the sub-concepts, attributes and the instances of them were highlighted and examined. From this examination we acquired the knowledge for our ontology, modifying as per our needs and requirements. In regards to our ontology, by acquiring all this knowledge, via the numerous sources available, we were able to declare the sub-concepts of our main concepts, their respective instances, attributes as well as relationships.

4.4 Ontology Development

Following knowledge acquisition, the main development process took place. According to the METHONTOLOGY, the main development takes place in the conceptualisation activity. During that activity, many different tasks are identified.

Therefore, in demonstrating the development of our ontology we refer to these tasks. It is worth mentioning that due to lack of space, in this chapter we demonstrate the development of our ontology focusing only on the concept of initial trust, and for the same reason of space restriction; the ontology is displayed in textual format in this chapter; however, the ontology has been graphically defined with the aid of the Protégé tool.

The first task in the development of the ontology involves the building of the glossary of terms that identifies the set of terms to be included on the ontology, their natural language definition (description), their type and their synonyms and acronyms. Considering the concept if Initial Trust, a number of terms can be identified that contribute towards the ontological analysis of the concept. These are illustrated in Table 1. For instance, trusting belief is of type concept and it is described as the trusting subject's perception that the trusting object has attributes that are beneficial to the trusting subject.

Table 1. Glossary of terms related to initial trust

Name	Synonyms	Acronyms	Description	Type
Initial trust	-	-	Trust in an unfamiliar object, dealing with a relationship in which the trusting subject does not have credible, meaningful experience, knowledge, or affective bonds with, the trusting object	Concept
Experience	-	-	The past experience (if any) that the trustor has of the trustee	Attribute
Personal Judgement	-	-	If the trustor has no experience of the trustee, they can use their personal judgement	Attribute
Trusting belief	-	-	The trusting subject's perception that the trusting object has attributes that are beneficial to the trusting subject	Concept
Competence	-	-	Trusting object's ability to do what the subject needs	Instance Attribute
Benevolence	-	-	Trusting object's caring and motivation to act in the subject's interests	Instance Attribute
Integrity	-	-	Trusting object's honesty and promise keeping	Instance Attribute

When the glossary of terms has been finalised, the next task involves building the concept taxonomies to classify the various concepts. The output of this task is one or more taxonomies where concepts are classified. Following our example of initial trust, Fig. 2 illustrates part of the taxonomy related to that concept.

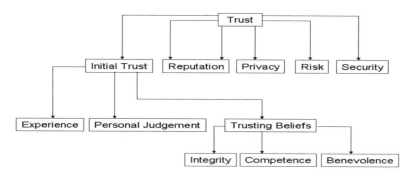

Fig. 2. Partial taxonomy of initial trust

The following task involves building an ad hoc binary relation diagram to specifically identify the relationships between concepts of a particular taxonomy and concepts of other taxonomies.

For instance, a high-level binary relation can be identified between the main concepts of the initial trust taxonomy, the trust taxonomy and the reputation taxonomy as illustrated in Fig. 3. Identifying the relationships between the various taxonomies of the ontology, allows us to build the concept dictionary, which mainly includes the concept instances for each concept, their instance and class attributes, and their ad hoc relations. A partial representation of the concept dictionary for our trust ontology, focused on the initial trust taxonomy is illustrated in Table 2.

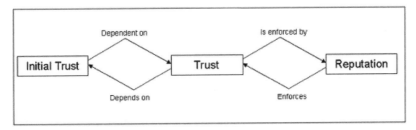

Fig. 3. Partial ad hoc binary relation diagram

An important issue is the exact definition of the various relations as they appear in the binary relation diagram, and on the concept dictionary. It is important to precisely identify the source concept, the source cardinality, the target concept and the inverse relation.

Table 2. Partial concept diagram

Concept name	Class attributes	Instance attributes	Relations
Experience	Present?	-	-
Personal Judgement	-	-	
Trusting beliefs	What are the trusting beliefs?	Competence	Belief present
		Benevolence	
		Integrity	
Trusting intention	What are the trusting intentions?	Willingness to depend	
		Subjective probability of depending	
Disposition to trust	-	Faith in humanity	Is dependant on
		Trusting stance	Depends on
Institution based trust	-	Structural assurance	
		Situational normality	

An illustration of some of the relations of our ontology is shown in Table 3.

Table 3. Binary relations definition

Relation name	Source concept	Source cardinality (max)	Target concept	Inverse relation
Dependent on	Initial trust	N	Trust	Depends on
Depends on	Trust	N	Initial trust	Dependant on
Is enforced by	Trust	N	Reputation	Enforces
Enforced	Reputation	N	Trust	Is enforced by

It is also important to describe in detail each instance attribute that appears on the concept dictionary. The output of this task is in the form of a table where instance attributes are defined in terms of their concept name, value types, value range and cardinality. For example, an instance attribute name is competence, with the concept name as trusting beliefs, and value type as a string. The same will be done for all the other instance attributes.

The next step involves the detailed description of each class attribute that appears on the concept dictionary. For example, the output of this step is the description of the class attribute (what are the trusting beliefs?) in terms of its defined concept (trusting beliefs), its value type (string), its cardinality and its values. The same will be done for all the remaining class attributes.

4.5 Case Study

To validate our ontology, we have used a case study from a domain where trust and its related concepts play an important role, the health care domain. Consider the scenario where a patient is seeing a GP for the first time. The reason for this is because the patient has moved house and has had to change to a nearer practice closer to their new home. Travelling to the previous practice, where the patient has been going for years, was not practical due to the distance. To illustrate our ontology, we illustrate the instantiation of some of the concepts of our ontology in relation to the above case study. Consider for instance the questions related to trust that might be running through the patients head for example; can they trust the GPs information system? For example, how does one know that the information system used by the GP has been developed with security in mind? The patients may be apprehensive that so much of their personal information is at effortless access on the information system, hence the patient may be averse to providing information because of such simple access and they are not convinced of the level of security of the information system. They also may be sceptical about the reliability of the system and how their personal details are stored. They may worry that if the information that is held on them is inaccurate, then wrong decisions might be taken by the GP. In order to develop a usable information system is it important to fully understand the environment in which the system will be placed, and most importantly understand all the various implications that might affect the trust not only on the information system but also on its users. Therefore, it is important that an ontological analysis takes place to assist information system developers in understanding the answers to the above questions. Our ontology is able to capture all these issues. For example, for the above simple example, a number of concepts could be employed from our ontology to enable information system developers to introduce a number of features on the system that will that will help to balance the trust related issues that are imposed by the environment of the system.

5 Future Work and Conclusions

In this chapter we have argued for the need to produce a trust ontology that will include a number of trust-related concepts. Our argument is consistent with a number of arguments presented in the literature. We have reviewed a number of related works and we have identified a number of important limitations. To overcome these limitations we have concentrated our efforts in developing a novel ontology that considers trust and its related concepts in one ontological framework. We have also illustrated the development of such ontology by focusing, due to page limitations, to the development of one of the ontology's concept, initial trust. We have also illustrated with the aid of a case study from the health sector how our ontology can assist information systems developers to analyse a number of trust issues related to the environment of a potential information system. However, our work is not complete. We are aiming to formalise our ontological framework and apply it in full to a complex case study that will help to evaluate the formalisation.

Acknowledgments Firstly, we would like to show gratitude to EPSRC for their funding with regards to this project and secondly we would like to express thanks to the staff at St Patrick's College, (London) for their support in our research.

References

Abdul-Rahman, A., Hailes, S (2000) Supporting Trust in Virtual Communities. *In Proceedings of the Hawaii International Conference on System Sciences 33.* Maui, Hawaii.
Alberts, C., Dorofee, A., Stevens, J., Woody, C. (2003) Introduction to the OCTAVE Approach. *Software Engineering Institute.* Carnegie Mellon University, Pittsburgh, PA.
Alford, J. (2004) Building Trust in Partnerships Between Community Orgnization and Government. *Changing the Way Government Works Seminar.* Melbourne.
Almenarez, F., Marin, A., Campo, C., Garcia, C. (2004) PTM: A Pervasive Trust Management Model for Dynamic Open Environments. *First Workshop on Pervasive Security, Privacy and Trust, PSPT'04 in conjunction with Mobiquitous.* Boston.

Cams and the Department of Commerce and Trade (2003) A Security Management Framework for Online Services.

Carbone, M., Nielsen, M., Sassone, V. (2003) A Formal Model for Trust in Dynamic Networks. *BRICS Report RS-03-4.*

Casare, S., Sichman, J. (2005) Towards a Functional Ontology of Reputation, *Proceedings of the Fourth International Joint Conference on Autonomous Agents and Multiagent Systems.* The Netherlands.

Chang, E., Hussain, F.K., Dillon, T. (2005) Reputation Ontology for Reputation Systems. *International Workshop on Web Semantics (SWWS)*, pp. 957–966.

Chopra, K., Wallace, W.A. (2003) Trust in Electronic Environments. *Proceedings of the 36th Hawaii Conference on System Sciences (HICSS'03).* Hawaii.

Cuske, C., Korthaus, A., Seedorf, S., Tomczyk, P. (2005) Towards Formal Ontologies for Technology Risk Measurement in the Banking Industry. *Proceedings of the 1st Workshop Formal Ontologies Meet Industry.* Verona, Italy.

Fernandez-Lopez, M., Gomez-Perez, A. (2002) Deliverable 1.4: A Survey on Methodologies for Developing, Maintaining, Integrating, Evaluating and Reengineering Ontologies.

Golbeck, J., Hendler, J. (2004) Accuracy of Metrics for Inferring Trust and Reputation in Semantic Web-Based Social Networks. *Engineering Knowledge in the Age of the SemanticWeb: 14th International Conference, EKAW 2004, Proceedings Whittlebury Hall, UK.* Springer, Berlin/ Heidelberg.

Gomez-Perez, A., Fernandez-Lopez, Corcho, O. (2004) *Ontological Engineering*, Springer-Verlag, London.

Jomes, D., Bench-Capon, T., Visser, P. (1998) Methodologies for Ontology Development. *In Proceedings of IT&KNOWS - Information Technology and Knowledge Systems - Conference of the 15th IFIP World Computer Congress.* Vienna/Austria/Budapest, Bulgaria.

Jøsang, A., Patton, M.A. (2004) Technologies for Trust in Electronic Commerce. *Electronic Commerce Research Journal,* 4, 9–21.

Jøsang, A., Kesar, C., Dimitrakos, T. (2005) Can We Manage Trust? *3rd International Conference on Trust Management (iTrust).* Paris.

Jøsang, A., Ismail, R., and Boyd, C. (2007) A Survey of Trust and Reputation Systems for Online Service Provision. *Decision Support Systems*, 43(2), 618–644.

Jøsang, A., Lo Presti, S. (2004) Analysing the Relationship Between Risk and Trust. IN DIMITRAKOS, T. (Ed.) *Proceedings of the Second International Conference on Trust Management.* Oxford.

Kethers, S.E.A. (2005) Modelling Trust Relationships in a Healthcare Network: Experiences with the TCD Framework. *In Proceedings of the Thirteenth European Conference on Information Systems.* Regensburg, Germany.

Kim, A., Luo, J., Kang, M. (2005) Security Ontology for Annotating Resources. In Meersman, R.T.Z. (Ed.) *Lecture Notes in Computer Science.* Agai Napa, Cyprus, Springer-Verlag Berlin/ Heidelberg.

Lau, T.S., Sure, Y. (2002) Introducing Ontology-based Skills Management at a Large Insurance Company. pp. 123–134.

Li, X., Valachich, J.S., Hess, T.J. (2004) Predicting User Trust in Information Systems: A Comparison of Competing Trust Models. *The Proceedings of the 37th Hawaii International Conference on Systems Sciences.* Hawaii.

Lo Presti, S., Cusack, M., Booth, C. (2003) Deliverable WP2-01 - Trust Issues in Pervasive Environments. QinetiQ & the University of Southampton.

Maarof, M.A., Krishna, K. (2002) A Hybrid Trust Management Model For MAS Based. Information Security Group, Faculty of Computer Science and Information System University of Technology Malaysia. 81310 Skudai, Johor.

Martimiano, A.F.M., Moreira, E.S. (2005) An OWL-based Security Incident Ontology. *In:Proceedings of the Eighth International Protege Conference.* pp. 43–44 Poster.

Mayer, N., Rifaut, A., Dubois, E. (2005) Towards a Risk-Based Security Requirements Engineering Framework. *11th International Workshop on Requirements Engineering: Foundation for Software Quality (REFSQ'05), in conjunction with CAiSE'05*. Porto, Portugal.

Mayer, N., Heymans, P., Matulevicius, R. (2007) Design of a Modelling Language for Information System Security Risk Managemen. *1st International Conference on Research Challenges in Information Science (RCIS 2007)*. Ouarzazate, Morocco.

Michael, J. B., Hestad, D.R., Pedersen, C.M., Gaines L.T. (2002) Incorporating the Human Element of Trust into Information Systems. *IAnewsletter*, 5, 4–8.

Mouratidis, H., Giorgini, P., Manson, G., Philip, I. (2002) Using Tropos Methodology to Model an Integrated Health Assessment System. *Proceedings of the 4th International Bi-Conference Workshop on Agent-Oriented Information Systems (AOIS-2002)*. Toronto-Ontario.

Mouratidis, H., Giorgini, P., Manson, G. (2003) An Ontology for Modelling Security: The Tropos Approach. In Palade, V., Howlett, R. (Ed.) *Proceedings of the 7th International Conference on Knowledge-Based Intelligent Information and Engineering Systems*. Oxford, England.

Mouratidis, H., Giorgini, P (2006) Integrating Security and Software Engineering: Advances and Future Vision. Idea Group.

Noy, N.F., McGuinness, D.L. (2001) Ontology Development 101: A Guide to Creating Your First Ontology. *Technical Report KSL-01-05*. Stanford Knowledge Systems Laboratory.

Numan, J. (1998) Knowledge-Based Systems as Companions: Trust, Human Computer Interaction and Complex Systems. University of Groningen.

Pinto, H.S., Martins, J.P. (2004) Ontologies: How Can They Be Built? *Knowledge and Information Systems*, 6, 441–464.

Purser, S. (2001) A Simple Graphical Tool for Modelling Trust. *Computers and Security*, 20, 479–484.

Robinson, S.L. (1996) Trust and Breach of the Psychological Contract. *Administrative Science Quarterly*, 41, 574–579.

Simmonds, A., Sandilands, P., Ekert, L.V. (2004) An Ontology for Network Security Attacks. In Manandharm, S., A., J., Desai, U., Oyangi, Y., Talukder, A. (Ed.) *Lecture Notes in Computer Science*. Kathmandu, Nepal, Springer Berlin/Heidelberg

Stolen, K. (2002) Model-Based Risk Assessment - the CORAS Approach, *In Proceedings of the First iTrust Workshop*.

Sutcliffe, A. (2006) Trust: From Cognition to Conceptual Models and Design. In Dubois, E., Pohl, K (Ed.) *18th International Conference, CAiSE 2006, June 5–9, 2006 Proceedings*. Luxembourg, Luxembourg, Springer-Verlag, Berlin/Heidelberg.

Uschold, M., Gruninger, M (1996) Ontologies: Principles, Methods and Applications. *Knowledge Engineering Review*, 11, 69.

Viljanen, L. (2005) Towards an Ontology of Trust. Lecture Notes in Computer Science. Copenhagen, Denmark. Springer, Berlin/Heidelberg.

Yu, E., Liu, L (2001) Modelling Trust for System Design Using the i* Strategic Actors Framework. In Verlag, S. (Ed.) Proceedings of the workshop on Deception, Fraud, and Trust in Agent Societies held during the Autonomous Agents Conference: Trust in Cyber-societies, Integrating the Human and Artificial Perspectives.

Yu, E., Cysneiros, LM (2002) Designing for Privacy and Other Computing Requirements. *2nd Symposium on Requirements Engineering for Information Security*. Raleigh, North Carolina.

Model Curriculum for a Bachelor of Science Program in Business Information Systems Design (BISD 2007): Organisational Impacts

Sven Carlsson[1], Jonas Hedman[2] and Odd Steen[3]

[1] University of Lund, Department of Informatics, sven.carlsson@ics.lu.se

[2] University College of Borås, School of Business and Informatics, jonas.hedman@hb.se

[3] University of Lund, Department of Informatics, odd.steen@ics.lu.se

Abstract In the light of technological changes, changes in business contexts, decreased number of IS students, changes in educational systems, etc., IS education commentators have urged the IS community to develop new and alternative IS curricula. In response to this, we present a model curriculum for a Bachelor of Science program in business information systems design (BISD 2007). The curriculum has a strong design focus. Students should after completing the program have specified business information systems design capabilities; hence, the program is capabilities-driven. This chapter presents the general rationales for the program as well as the specific program design rationales. The program is presented with expected learning outcomes and how the students should be able to fulfil the outcomes. In addition, we discuss the organizational impacts of a new and innovative program.

1 Introduction

Information Systems (IS) model curricula have a long and important history for the IS community. An IS model curriculum has a number of intended user groups and roles. For instance, academic executives can gain insights into the unique resource requirements of an IS program, academic heads can be inspired to maintain and develop their own programs, accreditation boards need a widely accepted definition of the IS discipline, IS faculty can obtain support in curriculum development, non-IS faculty can get ideas on what general IS skills are required, practitioners and academics can use it for interaction, and students can gain better understanding of the discipline and the content of a program (Gorgone et al. 2002).

IS model curricula are continuously revised due to rapid developments in Internet and Web technology, improved computer skills of incoming students, increased interest in accreditation and new and increasingly critical IS applications, such as e-commerce and ERP-systems. The IS 2002 model curricula (Gorgone et al. 2002) is widely accepted and used in North America and is developed through a collaborative effort between the following organisations: ACM, AIS and AITP. It builds upon the previous IS model curricula, IS' 97, and new inputs from practitioners and academics.

Over the past 5 years or so the IT industry and the IS discipline have seen their best and worst days: the crash of dot.com and telecom companies on several stock markets, the boom and fall of the job market, the major decrease in students' education applications, the questioning of IT's role in business and society, the outsourcing and offshoring of IT functions and the questioning of the academic IS discipline (Davis et al. 2005). There are also a number of events that are positive for the IS discipline, such as increased importance of the IS function and increasing IT investments, and convergence between IS and business. These events have a clear impact on curricula (Davis et al. 2005; Aspray et al. 2006), leading to the requirements for new skills and capabilities of the IT workforce (Gartner 2006a, b). In a study (Abraham et al. 2006) sponsored by the Society for Information Management (SIM) it was found that business domain understanding, functional area industry knowledge and social skills will be more critical for in-house IT personnel in the future. Project planning, budgeting and scheduling are important skills in the near term as are knowledge of ERP, integration, wireless technology and security. Programming, operations and help-desk skill requirements will decline in demand.

In response to these events and requirements for new skills and capabilities there have been several requests for new and innovative IS curricula. The ACM Job migration task force Aspray et al. (2006) and Hirschheim et al. (2005) discuss educational responses in relation to offshoring. Davis et al. (2005) propose five proactive steps in order to secure the future of the IS discipline. Two out of the five recommendations address IS education: 'Be Aggressive in Research and Teaching at the Fuzzy Boundaries of Applications with Shared Responsibilities' and 'Add Real Value to Students in IS Courses for Nonmajors'. Zwieg et al. (2006) make a similar recommendation. Abraham et al. (2006) suggest, based on the analysis of 104 senior IT executives in Europe and the USA, that 'IS programs must offer a functionally integrated curriculum and deliver it in an experiential business context'. In the DESRIST 2006 panel 'Design Leaders Perspective on the Future of Design Science in IS' education and curricula issues were raised and the development of new curricula and in particular how to incorporate IS design science research knowledge and IS design knowledge into these were discussed and asked for. In his December AIS President's Message, Michael Myers reported from the AIS Council Strategic Planning Meeting held in December in conjunction with ICIS 2006. One of the issues discussed and decided on was the development of multiple curricula that apply worldwide. Said Myers: 'We realize that it is not feasible for just one IS curriculum to meet the needs of all IS programs around the world. ... Therefore we agreed that multiple curricula need to be developed'. Besides these proactive responses, the Bologna process in Europe forces academic institutions to change their curricula.

Summarizing, to address the above identified problems and issues and as a response to calls for actions, the Board and Dean at Lund University School of Economics and Management (LUSEM) decided that it was time to develop a new attractive and innovative IS bachelor program (curriculum).

In the process of developing a new IS curriculum, we examined and evaluated the IS 2002 model curricula. The IS 2002 model was not suitable for the following reasons: (1) although, there is a greater emphasis on skills and capabilities in IS 2002 than in IS 1997, IS 2002 is still to a large extent course-oriented and not capabilities-driven, (2) the IS 2002 has a structure based on program structure conditions in the USA and Canada and these do not fit the European structure, and (3) IS 2002 lacks a clear design focus. This chapter presents an Information Systems (IS) undergraduate model curriculum based on a IS design perspective: Business IS Design (BISD 2007).

This chapter is structured according to the following logic. The next section describes briefly the local design context, constraints and affordances. This is followed by a presentation of the curricula. Finally we discuss the organizational consequences of BISD 2007s.

2 Design Setting, Process, Constraints and Affordances

LUSEM's Board appointed a task group for the development of the new curriculum. The primary group consisted of three people (one professor and two senior lecturers). A working reference group representing the students' future employers and IS professionals and a second working reference group of students representatives were established. In June 2006 the Swedish Parliament (Riksdagen) decided to amend the Higher Education Act (1992:1434) and the Higher Education Ordinance (1993:100) to incorporate parts of the Bologna process (Regeringskansliet 2006). Besides this, a number of events triggered the development of the new IS program (BISD 2007) and also in part constrained and afforded the basis for the curriculum:

1. The requirements for new skills and capabilities, identified by Abraham et al. (2006), Aspray et al. (2006) and Gartner (2006a, b), such as understanding of business domains, functional area industry knowledge, social skills, project management, commercially of the shelf products, integration of IS and wireless technology, were taken into account.
2. A vision of creating a design science inspired IS curriculum focusing on educating business information systems designers instead of system developers or computer engineers.
3. The Bologna Declaration (CRE 2006), the Swedish adaptation of the declaration (Regeringskansliet 2006) as well as the local (university and school) adaptation of the declaration meant that new programs had to be developed or descriptions of current programs had to be adapted to the declaration and the Dublin descriptors.

4. All IS programs and IS departments in Sweden were evaluated a couple of years ago. The evaluation report suggested three activities to be implemented: (1) programs should be focused (few departments can deliver high-quality programs without having a focus), (2) increase cooperation with other departments and universities, and (3) reduce the number of available study places in IS programs. LUSEM's Board and Dean decided to reduce the number of students in the IS programs and required the new program to be more focused and stronger aligned with the school's vision and strengths.

In essence, we adapted to constraints and affordances of the Bologna declaration based on both the national and local regulations by focusing on the skills and capabilities. For this to be functional, a new pedagogical design was needed that focused on the capabilities instead of content. Through this the curriculum render integrated and deep learning essential for IS design possible. The next section describes the result of the process.

3 The Business Information Systems Design Curriculum

In this section, we describe the curriculum, i.e. BIDS 2007. Initially, the underpinning values are presented in short. Then we describe the expected learning outcomes followed by the specific knowledge areas. We also provide the outlines, the structure of the program and finally some examples of examination tasks.

3.1 The Underpinning Values

The assumed work role, Business IS designer, is not yet well-established within the practice or education. However there is a growing demand for people with the skills and abilities to develop business and IS in concert rather than for technical equilibrists, who has an in-depth knowledge in programming and algorithmics.

IS-designers design IS for purposeful human business activities. Thus, a central concept is business activity, which is central in the design and use of information systems. Business activities, including the design of information systems, are organised in a formal way with regard to structure, processes, rules and power relationships and emerge in an informal way with regard to cultural and cognitive structure, such as norms, values and informal power relationships, as well as other social arrangements within the organisation.

Individuals, i.e. people, reside within and outside of the formal organisation and constitute the most important part of the business – no people no business. In that sense, people represent an actor that fulfils personal goals as well as the contextual goals. The link that glues people and business activities together is information. Therefore, IS has to be designed with regard to all these aspects independently whether it is a business organisation or a governmental agency.

Since the curriculum for the IS Design education programme is built on the notion of designing artificial systems and artefacts for business contexts the training of design ability and capability is central. We have thus put emphases on those qualifications and learning outcomes that connect to skills and capabilities. Therefore, we started by asking us the questions 'What should the students be able to do? What should their skills be?' and phrased the answers as 'applying knowledge and understanding' descriptors. On a general level, these descriptors say that the students should have the skill and capability to design IT-supported business solutions and improvements in the form of artificial systems and artefacts. Based on this we went on to elaborate the other qualifications and devise the descriptors such that they would provide support to, and be necessary contributions to, the "applying knowledge and understanding" descriptors.

3.2 Pedagogical Stance

One very important constraint was that the curriculum should be built on first cycle, Dublin Descriptor qualifications and the expected learning outcomes be clearly expressed. However, these constraints can also be viewed as affordances, since they 'afford' us to think of and elaborate on what students are expected to know and be able to do after completing the education. Hence, they also functioned as 'driving principles' and had us focus on the most important aspects first. We connected those constraints and affordances to Bowden's (2004) pedagogical model for curriculum design (see Fig. 1).

Bowden's (2004) contrast content and capability focused on curriculum design. The content focused is the common design, which takes its point of departure in a given content, e.g. modelling of entity types using UML, and centres a course on this. All the problems and examples of the course thus deal with UML for modelling entity types. In another course, the content could be to model business processes also using UML and in a third course the content could be Business Rules and modelling of these using OCL (object constraint language – a part of UML) or another relevant 'language'. All the examples and problems in the courses would be targeted at respectively entity types, business processes and business rules without any attempts to view these as different perspectives of business modelling. The content of UML is the primary goal of the courses, not the capability to model business problems and solutions using relevant techniques and knowledge. Therefore, the students would likely only reach surface learning (Marton and Säljö 2000) of three isolated aspects of business modelling. They would probably not be able to transfer knowledge from one content-focused course to another or develop the capability to meet similar, but not exactly the same problem situations. The needed integration of knowledge across contexts and contents would be left for the students to achieve by themselves without support from the content-focused curriculum.

Using van Aken's (2004) classification we can distinguish three different types of designs an Business IS design professional makes when designing and implementing an IS-solution: (1) an object-design, which is the design of the IS solution, (2) a realization-design, which is the plan for the implementation of the IS solution, and (3) a process-design, which is the professional's own plan for the problem-solving cycle and includes the methods and techniques to be used in object- and realization-design. The program should give the students the possibility to develop capabilities for all three types of designs.

Based on the underlying view of the design of information systems, the role in business activities, and human beings a number of learning outcomes crystallised.

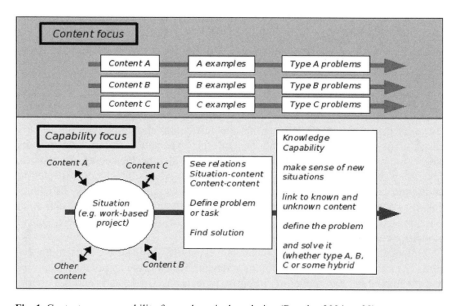

Fig. 1. Content versus capability focused curriculum design (Bowden 2004, p. 39)

3.3 Expected Learning Outcomes

The learning outcomes are presented in five categories, based on the Dublin descriptors:

Applying knowledge and understanding: The student, individually and as a member of a group, is expected to demonstrate the skills and ability to:

1. Design IS in order to achieve improvements and innovative change in organisations and business activities
2. Apply theories, design methods and tools for the development of IS

3. Participate in and manage IS-related change and innovation projects in national and international settings
4. Deploy IS and ICT in organisations and business activities
5. Plan, carry out and report design and natural science investigations

Making Judgements: The student should be able to:

1. Analyse and evaluate theories, processes, models, methods and tools for IS-related design work from different perspectives
2. Critically examine, analyse and evaluate IS design and change proposals from different perspectives
3. Analyse and evaluate IS, organisations, business activities, competencies and resources for IS, and evaluate project work and group dynamics
4. Critically examine scientific studies and other reports
5. Evaluate the individual's own knowledge and need for other knowledge
6. Appraisal of outlooks and general tendencies in society in relation to IS and automatic data processing with regard to relevant scientific, societal, human and ethical aspects

Knowledge and Understanding: The student should demonstrate the knowledge and understanding for:

1. The foundation, the history, the theories, the concepts and the contemporary research issues within the scientific field and knowledge area
2. Relevant IS design processes, models, methods and tools
3. How IS and its use affects or may affect organizations, business activities, society and individuals
4. How requirements, wishes, needs by organizations, businesses, society and individuals may be fulfilled by IS and its use
5. Different organisational structures and business activities and their relationship to IS
6. How data, information and knowledge may cooperate, be applied and used in organisations and businesses activities
7. Different ways of organizing IS-related work, in general, and project work, in particular
8. Important perspectives, theories, models, frameworks for the design and use of IS and ICT
9. Perspectives on and approaches for the deployment of IS in organisations and business

Communication skills: The student should be able to:

1. Independently and in group plan and present good presentations in speech, writing, symbol language and pictures of ideas, plans, solutions in dialog with varying stakeholders
2. Use computer-based support systems for collaboration in IS design work

Learning skills: The student should:

1. Demonstrate the ability to learn new relevant theories, models, methods and techniques as well as critically examine these for professional work and further studies

3.4 Knowledge Areas and Content Based on Expected Learning Outcomes

Based on the defined learning outcomes we outlined a number of knowledge areas with content. The knowledge areas with its content are central, since these are the ground for a student's possibility to reach the outlined learning outcomes. Knowledge areas with content are the basis for individual courses.

Design of IS and business

1. The history, theories and concepts of the scientific and knowledge area
2. Design as problem-solving process
3. Design of artefacts and artificial systems
4. Modern paradigms, models, methods, techniques and tools for integrating the design of IS, organisation and business, and for evaluating the IS design process and its artefacts in the form of ideas, plans and solutions
5. Requirements and change management of integrated design of IS, organisation and business as well as systems maintenance, and test management
6. Ethical, legal, power and security issues in the design of IS
7. The field of profession for IS-designers (including competences, roles, tasks, lifelong learning, professional ethics, genus and gender issues as well as sustainable development)

Business, organizational and IS knowledge

1. The history, theories and concepts of the scientific field and knowledge area
2. Private, public and non-profit organisations
3. Organization theory and business knowledge (including structure, business processes, communication, functions, co-work, coordination, innovation systems, entrepreneurship, standards and quality models, change management, strategy, goals, decision and action)
4. Information management (data, information and knowledge)
5. IS classes and instantiations
6. Modern paradigms, models, methods, techniques and tools for implementing IS in different contexts
7. Stakeholder and power perspectives in the diffusion and adaptation of IS

8. Evaluation of IS use
9. Outlooks, perspectives and general tendencies in society in relation to IS

Information and communication technology knowledge

1. The history, theories, and concepts of the scientific field and knowledge area
2. ICT classes and instantiations, computer and ICT-architecture, and ICT quality models and standards
3. Software engineering
4. Outlooks, perspectives and general tendencies in society in relation to ICT

Project work for IS and ICT

1. Management and planning, organisation, group dynamics, standards/ techniques/tools and project work in national and international environments

Systematic investigations

1. Basic scientific paradigms, approaches, methods and techniques within design science and natural/behavioural sciences
2. Presentation, critic, defend and evaluation of investigations

3.5 Structure, Training Skills and Examination Tasks

The objective was to design a curriculum that focused on important IS design capabilities as a focus for course content. The capabilities should be important for the whole education and not be constrained to delimited courses. The capabilities are thus structured as flows stretching over several semesters and courses to provide the opportunity for the students to reach integrated, deep learning of IS design (cf. Section 3.3 for details). In each flow, the particular capability is intended to accommodate progressively higher levels of problem complexity. Thus, the structure of the program is not based on content. It is based and structured along the learning outcomes. The course names are based on the main knowledge areas to be covered during the course; this is depicted in Table 1 along with some of the training skills and examination tasks. We believe that this is a key component in an IS program. In order to stimulate deep learning, the student is expected to save all examinations tasks and other assignments in a learning portfolio, which the student can show to potential employees after completion of the program. In addition, the idea is to use the leaning portfolio for both program and course evaluations. In that way, the evaluation will be of a continuous and formative nature.

Table 1. Training skills, and examination tasks

Courses	Training skills	Examination task
Introduction	Read and position oneself within the scientific field	Plan and present an exhibition and write a report of an Internet-based IS
Business design basic	Design and development of a simple prototype of an e-shop using contemporary development tools	Design and develop an e-shop solution and prototype
Design of business systems	Design and configuration of ERP system	Configured ERP system, e.g. accounting module with documentation
Business design cont.	Design of a innovative mobile application that interacts with an ERP system	Requirements specification with models
The computer and technology, deployment and use of systems	Realization of previous course's mobile application	A functional application
Integration project	Design of an artificial system using contemporary approaches, methods, techniques and tools	Documentation, presentation, and defence of design process and artificial system
Degree project	Based on design science or natural/behavioural sciences	Degree work, opposition and defence

4 Consequences and Potential Implications of the Curriculum

The curriculum has implication not only for the didactic and pedagogic of the education, but for the educational system at LUSEM. At present, most programs at LUSEM are organised in a traditional way and built up of courses offered by different departments such as Informatics and Business Administration.

The Board of LUSEM is the owner. To help the Board in its work of managing the programs, each program has a steering committee, which is supposed to supervise the program and its development. A steering committee has representatives (members) from the different departments involved in a program.

The steering committee has limited power and limited possibility to influence the programs. The department's that develop and give the courses that make up the programs have major power and possibility to influence the programs. The department, which subject area is the major in the program, has naturally the greatest possibility to influence a program's content. In addition, the curriculum for a program often does not specify what content should be covered or what learning outcomes should be fulfilled, which leaves much judgment and great influence over the programs to the individual departments.

In the case of the present IS program the curriculum does not specify the *what* (content of a finer granularity than subject area), *how* (pedagogy) or *why* (learning outcomes) of the education, but leaves that to the different departments to specify. This means that the education (program) is a patchwork of what the individual departments see as possible and interesting to teach based on the interest in each own subject area (in many cases driven by professors' focus), more or less regardless of how this will combine into a preferable whole as an education. Also, since the specification of the electives, non-Informatics single-subject courses (which is a degree prerequisite) says no more than the amounts of credits and faculty, there is no way to ensure that these courses contribute to the what, how and why of the education in a good way.

Based on the discussion it seems clear that the subject areas and their respective departments exercise too much influence over the current IS program rather than providing education with suitable pedagogy and content. The education and program is formed of subject areas and not of learning outcomes.

The proposed curriculum discussed in this chapter requires a completely different educational organization and structure. The curriculum is built on the notion that learning outcomes are the determinants of the what, how and why as well as drivers of learning. Based on this notion, the curriculum is laid out as capabilities-oriented and parallel tracks of progression towards learning outcomes. Since capabilities are focused the necessary content provided by the different, involved departments must be targeted towards the intended capability and learning outcomes.

Through this layout the departments lose control over the program and can no longer provide what they deem is interesting or what they find is most favourable (from a variety of perspectives) to teach. Instead, they must cooperate to provide the right content at the right moment to support a certain capability and, thus, learning outcome. As an example, it would not be sufficient for the Business Administration department to provide the education programme with a 15 ECTS credits course in Organisation Theory to their own liking and as one interrupted unit. Instead, these 15 credits would be specified to the what and how based on the education programme, and certainly be distributed in time and order as content linked to specific tracks and capabilities.

To make this work education has to be organised as Undergraduate and Graduate Schools with clear responsibilities and power to develop, control and manage the programs. Each program would be coordinated by a group of selected researchers and teachers with the power to negotiate with and 'purchase' content from different departments. Each, steering group should be responsible to develop and alter the programs to preserve their actuality and foundation in research as well as technological and business development. In this way, the influence and power over the program is moved from the departments to the Undergraduate and Graduate Schools, which more or less buys education (knowledge areas with content) from the departments. Through this, there is a possibility that a program can become an integrated whole which provide students with deep learning possibilities targeted at learning outcomes and capabilities.

The effect in the end, if this layout would be put in place, could be that educations can form their own subject areas. Instead of just, e.g. Informatics and Business Administration maybe "IS Development" would become a subject area on its own merit. This would lessen the subject areas' and departments' independence in relation to an education program. However, single-subject courses and research would still be the responsibility of departments and traditional subject areas.

5 Conclusions

In response to calls for new curricula, technological changes, changes in business contexts, etc. we have developed a new IS curriculum, Business Information Systems Design (BISD 2007).

The curriculum meets the goals and restrictions in the Bologna Declaration and Dublin Descriptors as well meets the requirements of new skills and capabilities outlined (Abraham et al. 2006; Gartner 2006a, b). This is critical for European curricula and for the student's employability.

We also think that BISD 2007 is based on a better alignment between pedagogical for example model than the traditional. Based on our experiences it is tempting to suggest that BISD 2007 will prepare students better for working life. However, there are some organizational issues in the current process of delivering courses to students, due to a strong departmental structure.

References

Abraham, T., Beath, C., Bullen, C., Gallagher, K., Goles, T. Kaiser, K. and Simon, J. (2006) IT Workforce Trends: Implications for IS Programs. Communications of the Association for Information Systems 17, 1147–1170.

Aspray, W., Mayadas, F. and Vardi, M. (2006) Globalization and Offshoring of Software: A Report of the ACM Job Migration Task Force. The Association for Computing Machinery.

Bowden, J. A. (2004): Capabilities-driven curriculum design. In Moore, I. (Ed.) Effective learning and teaching in engineering. Routledge, New York.

CRE Confederation of EU Rectors* Conferences and the Association of European Universities (2006) The Bologna Declaration on the European space for Higher Education: An Explanation. http://ec.europa.eu/education/policies/educ/bologna/bologna.

Davis, G., Massey, A. and Bjorn-Andersen, N. (2005) Securing the Future of Information Systems as an Academic Discipline. The Twenty-Sixth International Conference on Information Systems.

Gartner (2006a, 22 June) How to Lead and Manage the IT-Literate Workforce. Number: G00138404, Gartner.

Gartner (2006b, 23 January) Evolving Roles in the IT Organization: The Application Manager. Number: G00132784, Gartner.

Gorgone, J. T., Davis, G. B., Valacich, J. S., Topi, H., Feinstein, D.L. and Longenecker Jr, H. E. (2002) Model Curriculum and Guidelines for Undergraduate Degree Programs in Information Systems, Association for Information Systems.

Hirschheim, R., Loebbecke, C., Newman, M., and Valor, J. (2005) Offshoring and its Implications for the Information Systems Discipline. The Twenty-Sixth International Conference on Information Systems.

Marton, F. and Säljö, R. (2000) Kognitiv inriktning vid inlärning. In Entwistle, N. (Ed.) Hur vi lär. Prisma, Stockholm.

Regeringskansliet (2006) The 2007 Higher Education Reform, http://www.sweden.gov.se/sb/d/7580

van Aken, J. (2004) Management Research Based on the Paradigm of the Design Sciences: The Quest for Field-Tested and Grounded Technological Rules, Journal of Management Studies 41(2).

Zwieg, P. et al. (2006) The Information Technology Workforce: Trends and Implications 2005-008, MIS Quarterly Executive 5(2).

Project Managers – Do They Need to Be Certified?

Orla McHugh and Mairéad Hogan

Department of Accountancy & Finance, National University of Ireland, Galway,
orla.mchugh@nuigalway.ie, mairead.hogan@nuigalway.ie

Abstract   The purpose of this study is to examine the drivers behind the certification of project managers in Irish organisations, to identify the benefits and drawbacks of project management certification and to determine whether it is really necessary for project managers to be certified. Five organisations in Ireland participated in the study and one project manager from each organisation was interviewed. The size of the organisations, the level of experience of the project managers interviewed and the certification programmes completed varied. Differences as well as similarities across the organisations were identified. The results of the study put forward that the selection of an appropriate certification programme can depend on factors such as the availability of certification providers for training and support; the ease with which the certification programme can be adapted to suit the business; and the requirement to renew certification. While the findings show that project management certification does have several benefits these benefits do not require certification and could be realised by simply having good project management practices in place.

1 Introduction

In recent years there has been a dramatic increase in the amount of project-based work, which has been instigated by factors such as developments in information technology, changes in environmental regulations, increasing customer involvement, increased productivity, the drive towards shorter product life cycles and the complexity of inter-organisational relationships [6, 12]. As a result, the growth in project management has come about more through necessity than through desire [17, p. 36]. To date, the failure rate of Information Systems (IS) projects is very high, with the ineffective monitoring of tasks and risks, user resistance, project politics, lack of communication, ineffective management of changes and inadequate hand-over procedures contributing to failure [20, 45]. These IS project failures can have serious consequences for the competitiveness and survival of an organisation [45], particularly as organisations are using IS projects for competitive advantage [5]. However, project performance can improve by project managers meeting their responsibilities within an organisation that supports professional project management practice [46].

Although a simple definition of project management is not possible, project management can be defined as a combination of management, planning and the management of change [3], while another definition states that project management is the art and science of planning, designing and managing work throughout all phases of the project's life cycle and attempting to achieve planned objectives within specific time and cost limits, through the optimum use of resources, using an integrated planning and control system [1].

2 Project Management in Organisations

The growth of project management in organisations has come about since the 1960s when organisations began searching for new management techniques and organisational structures that could support a changing environment [16, p. 48]. The traditional, functionally structured organisation did not permit the cross-functional cooperation essential to successful project performance [28]. Project management was often ad hoc, with informal procedures established for particular projects [23]. The use of project management has become more prominent in recent years due to the demand for better quality software projects delivered on time and within budget. Research has shown that projects that do not have a project manager or do not follow a methodology or a defined process are more likely to fail as ultimately, the project manager is responsible for the delivery of a project and is fundamental to ensuring that the project is a success [27, 44].

2.1 Difficulties Facing Project Managers

Project managers can face many difficulties when managing software projects, which relate to poorly defined specifications, lack of a project plan, unrealistic deadlines and budgets, and lack of user involvement [15, 44]. It is not uncommon for users to frequently change requirements during a project and, as a result, software projects often fall short of what was required [15]. In addition, project managers may not have the support of senior management resulting in inadequate resources to complete the project or difficulty dealing with any political issues that may arise [16, 30, 38].

Another issue project managers face is that they often find themselves in the role with little or no formal training [8, 33]. Even though organisations are increasingly aware of the value of project management, and of the training and development required to deliver that value [4, 26], it is rare for project managers to have formal training [35]. Project managers are rarely selected because they have been developed for the role. They may be promoted on the basis of their technical skills, but they often lack the necessary team management skills [24], which can leave them ill-prepared to take on the responsibility of managing a project and a team [33]. Few organisations offer project management training programmes and even fewer are requiring an internal or external project management certification [8], which is of concern to the authors as organisations are not seeing the benefit of having a focused and comprehensive approach to training. If organisations commit to educating and training project managers, the knowledge gained will improve their performance and skills, resulting in additional benefits through the better management of projects, and an increased chance of project success [22, 41, 44].

3 Project Management Certification

Recognition of the power of project management has resulted in many training organisations offering courses in this field, varying from in-house training to external courses to internationally recognised certification programmes [18]. Certification is a way of improving a discipline by promoting the practical implementation of standards, the awareness of a body of knowledge, the recognition of a code of ethics, and the need for professional development, resulting in the establishment of a comprehensive competency benchmark for the profession [31, 40]. As businesses become increasingly global there is a growing need to accredit professional certification of individuals on an international basis [2]. It is important for project managers to continue their training to keep up to date with advances in the profession as 'project skills don't stop with certification' [26]. Up until now, formal education in project management has essentially been post-experience [41].

3.1 Project Management Certification Organisations

There are an increasingly large number of organisations engaged in corporate project management training [36, 43], which is also reflected in the increase in membership of project management organisations such as the Project Management Institute (PMI), International Project Management Association (IPMA), various Projects IN Controlled Environment (PRINCE2) accredited organisations in the UK and the Institute of Project Management in Ireland [43, 26, 21, p 36]. This growth in training providers has both positive and negative implications [43]. The positive are: the project management discipline is beginning to be recognised as a profession; more training means a better educated workforce; and more training is available, accessible and at competitive prices. On the negative side, how can we be certain that the content and quality of the course is of a certain standard?

Outside of the accredited project management organisations there are certificates of various descriptions offered by training firms, academic institutions and other agencies where the meaning of certification can vary [2]. Because of this lack of certainty regarding many programmes, employers prefer certification from professional associations, such as the PMI and the IPMA [2]. These use a Project Management Body of Knowledge (PMBoK), which is an essential element of achieving full professional status for project managers and project management [42, p. 2]. In the UK, an alternative to the certification programmes that focuses on the PMBoK process groups is PRINCE2 certification. There are a wide range of accredited organisations in the UK and worldwide that provide certification in PRINCE2 [25]. The PMI have a continuing certification requirements programme that supports the ongoing educational and professional development of certified Project Management Professionals [32]. In contrast to this, practitioners that are certified in PRINCE2 do not have to renew their certification on a recurring basis.

3.2 Benefits to Obtaining Project Management Certification

Certification can benefit an industry by supporting minimum competency standards; encouraging use of disciplined practices; and building awareness of best practices [40]. It can provide project managers with an internationally acknowledged certificate of their qualification and competence, ensuring that they have the necessary skill set and experience to manage a project successfully [2, 13, 14]. Certification can also ensure that project management standards are understandable and comparable across an organisation [11, 38, p. 30]. It can help project managers to define the levels of skill and types of experience they need to achieve to advance in their careers. As a job seeker they can hold a distinct advantage if they have a marketable certification [11, 38, p. 30]. It can also provide improved process efficiency; improved quality and quality awareness; improved communications; improved documentation and improved customer satisfaction within an organisation [39]. By developing qualified project managers and using the right tools and methods, the progress of projects can be monitored, results can be predicted and risks can be evaluated, all of which lead to project success [11]. Without best practices becoming the standard and a documented project management methodology to provide continuous improvement, companies will not complete projects within budget and they will also fail to measure up to rising customer expectations for on-time delivery and quality [37].

3.3 Challenges to Obtaining Project Management Certification

Achieving a professional certification requires a commitment of time and money as well as several years of practice in the field [2]. It can be costly in terms of the amount of employee time required to achieve certification, the training of additional staff in the use of the associated project management methodology, and the maintenance of the methodology [39]. It can increase the amount of documentation required for a project and can add so much structure to a project that some believe it can interfere with new and better ways of operating [39]. Also, some certification programmes, for example the PMP certification from the PMI, require individuals to renew their certification every four years to remain certified [32], which can add an additional cost to an organisation.

3.4 Motivation for the Research

In recent years many organisations in Ireland are certifying their project managers. This is based on the increase in the number of individuals that have been certified in the past number of years by organisations such as the IPMA [13]. There is little evidence in the literature to demonstrate why organisations want their project managers to be certified, why they want their project managers certified with an industry-recognised certification, or why a specific project management certification programme is selected. There is some information in the literature relating to the benefits of obtaining project management certification. However, details on the challenges and difficulties to organisations of obtaining and maintaining that certification are scant. This research aims to address these gaps and obtain an in-depth look at project management certification in Ireland, with the hope that it might provide some insight into current practices in organisations in Ireland.

4 Research Methodology

The completion of an internationally recognised project management certification programme is relatively recent to organisations in Ireland. As there was little existing research on the subject under investigation, the objectives of this research highlighted the need for exploratory research. It was deemed more appropriate to use an inductive approach for this study, resulting in the selection of case study for this research. It was decided to conduct multiple case studies, as opposed to a single case study, to obtain a broader view of practices in several organisations, which would allow for the comparison and analysis of practices across organisations. For the purposes of this research five case studies were employed, as it was thought that this number would allow a certain amount of comparison and may be representative of current practices in organisations in Ireland.

As the researchers wished to gather detailed opinions and perspectives on the subject of project management certification, the primary method of data collection was a semi-structured personal interview. This allowed open-ended questions to be asked, which provided the depth of information required by the researchers.

4.1 Target Profile of the Organisations

The target profile of participant organisations for this research was:
(a) Organisations that are service providers were the primary focus of this research. (b) Organisations in Ireland that employ more than 50 individuals, on the assumption that organisations smaller then these would not have dedicated project managers. Large multinational organisations such as Microsoft were excluded as it was felt that organisations such as these would have had project management certification programmes in use for quite a number of years and that they would be more representative of the programmes employed in their country of origin. (c) Organisations were required to have at least one project manager that had completed a recognised project management certification programme or an adapted version of a recognised certification in the past one to three years. This time period was selected because organisations where project managers completed the project management certification programme more than three years ago would possibly not be able to recall the benefits/drawbacks of completing a certification programme.

5 Findings and Analysis

Research interviews were conducted in April and May 2006 with one project manager in each organisation. The level of experience of the project managers interviewed varied across the organisations. It must be noted that the responses of each interviewee to the questions were based on their own experiences and knowledge of completing a project management certification programme within the context of their organisation. These views do not necessarily represent the overall view of each organisation. Five organisations participated in the research and a high-level profile of each participating organisation is presented in Table 1.

Table 1. High-level profile of organisations

	Case One	Case Two	Case Three	Case Four	Case Five
Industry	Financial Services	Building Society	Technology Services	Financial Services	Insurance Services
Total Employees	65	1,000	4,000	2,500	2,000
IT staff	14	80	50	200	170
Location of offices	Ireland and UK	Ireland	Worldwide	Ireland, Europe, USA	Ireland
Certification programme	PMI/IPMA	PRINCE2 Adaptation	PMI/IPMA	Adapted from PMI	PRINCE2 Adaptation
Year certified	2005	2003	2004	2003	2005

Some of the organisations have several office locations within Ireland or have offices in multiple locations around the world. As practices can vary across locations within the same organisation for the purposes of this research the findings relate to the location in which the interview was conducted.

5.1 Selection and Completion of a Certification Programme

All of the organisations that participated in the research made a decision in the last number of years to certify their project managers. The certification programmes chosen were reasonably consistent across the organisations as shown in Table 1, and consisted of PMI, IPMA, or PRINCE2 certification. Only two of the project managers interviewed (cases one and two) had any involvement in the decision as to which certification programme was selected. Both of these project managers highlighted the need for certification to management, who in turn requested that the project managers identify a suitable course. In both cases the project managers selected a certification programme that was recommended to them by colleagues.

Four of the project managers interviewed (cases one, two, three and five) were aware of the reasons for selecting a particular certification programme and the associated project management methodology while the fifth project manager interviewed (case four) was not aware of the reasons as to why the particular certification programme was selected. The reasons varied across the organisations depending on their specific requirements. There was a general requirement for a certification programme that used a project management methodology that is widely recognised by other organisations. In one organisation (case three) where CMMI was being implemented, CMMI recommended the implementation of the project management methodology from the PMI certification programme. This organisation was partly influenced by this requirement and partly influenced by its parent organisation in the United States where the value of PMI certification was seen in other US-based organisations. Case five is also implementing CMMI, but this organisation does not seem to have been influenced by the recommendation of CMMI. The main focus in this organisation related to having a methodology where certification, training, assistance and support can be provided by more than one supplier. As a result, PRINCE2 certification was selected because of the availability of numerous training providers.

5.2 Drivers of Project Management Certification

The main driver, which was consistent across the large organisations (cases two, three, four and five) was a decision by senior management to implement a uniform approach to project management within the organisation as a whole. Another organisation (case two) believed that by certifying their project managers and implementing a project management methodology as a result, they would save money in the long term by helping to bring projects in on time and within budget.

However, in two organisations (cases three and five) there were additional factors that influenced management's decision to obtain certification. Both of these organisations were driven by a desire to obtain CMMI certification, of which a requirement is to have a project management methodology in place. Case three, whose customers are external to the organisation, also wanted to have certified project managers as a potential differentiating factor when competing with other vendors for business. The project manager in this case was of the opinion that their customers would see the value in having certified project managers and the project manager interviewed believes that the organisation was pursuing certification to ensure they were winning new projects, which may be due to the industry in which this organisation operates.

In the smallest organisation (case one) the project managers were able to directly influence management and to set out a business case for obtaining certification, which would progress their own careers yet at the same time have a positive impact on the organisation. The decision to complete a certification programme was made within a very short timeframe, which contrasted with the longer timeframe required for the larger organisations, which may be due to the small size of this organisation.

5.3 Benefits of Completing a Certification Programme

Regardless of the size of an organisation or its industry type, the completion of a certification programme by project managers can benefit both individuals and organisations [13]. The benefits identified in this study are shown in Table 2.

Table 2. Benefits of project management certification

Benefits of project management certification	No. of respondents
Defines standard project management practices through the implementation of a standard project management methodology	5
Defines the role and the skills required to become a project manager	3
Project management positions held by qualified individuals	3
Helps to establish the project management credentials of an individual	2
Assists with external recruitment	1

All of the project managers identified the implementation of a standard project management practices as a benefit to the organisation. In particular, cases four and five also found that having a standard project management methodology in place: facilitates the movement of team members from one project to another project; can reduce the overhead required for training of new staff members; and makes it is easier for new staff to become aware of the processes that must be followed when working on a project. However, a third project manager (case three) believed that there were no major additional benefits following the implementation of their new industry-recognised methodology after the completion of the certification programme, as they had a good methodology in place prior to certification.

Three of the larger organisations (cases two, four and five) stated that certification helps to: define the role of the project manager; define career paths; and define competency profiles for each role in a way that staff can understand. These organisations all have a hierarchical organisation structure with a vertical chain of command and the definition of roles and career paths is of particular importance to staff within these types of organisations. These organisations also found that project management positions are now held by individuals that are suitably qualified to be in the role and have completed a certification programme. Prior to the certification the project managers selected were not always the most suitable for the position. By having a certification programme in place and making certain that all project managers in these organisations complete the certification programme ensures that only individuals that are suitably qualified can hold the role of project manager. However, one project manager (case two) did state that in some instances projects were still run by project managers that were not yet certified. This was due to the fact that all project managers are not yet certified as a result of training budget restrictions or time constraints in relation to their existing workload. While the remaining two organisations (cases one and three) also have a vertical reporting structure, the organisation structure is flatter than the larger organisation as the number of employees in each office is small and there are a reduced number of layers within the chain of command.

Two project managers (cases two and five) stated that certification can help to establish the project management credentials of an individual. Once certified individuals retain the qualification if they leave an organisation, unless there is a requirement to renew the certification, after which period the certification will be no longer be valid. Certification can also help with external recruitment according to one organisation (case five). An organisation can advertise for project managers with a specific certification, which can result in reduced overhead in training and getting a new staff member up to speed with the project management practices that are in place. While this was identified as a benefit to certification, none of the project managers interviewed stated whether they had recruited individuals that were already certified.

5.4 Challenges to Obtaining and Maintaining Certification

The findings also identified some challenges to obtaining and maintaining certification as is shown in Table 3.

.

Table 3. Challenges to obtaining and maintaining project management certification

Challenges to obtaining and maintaining certification	No. of respondents
Training budget restrictions, thus lengthening the time required to certify all project managers	3
Time and effort required to complete certification	2
Lack of re-certification (relates to PRINCE2)	2
Cost of re-certification (relates to PMI)	1

The main difficulty for certifying project managers in three of the larger organisations (cases two, three and five) was in relation to training budgets, which has lengthened the time required for all project managers to become certified. The project manager in the other large organisation (case four) was not aware of any issues in relation to the training budget. In contrast, this was not an issue in the smallest organisation (case one) as both project managers completed the certification programme at the same time.

Project managers (cases one and three) that participated in the six-month long PMI/IPMA training course, rather than an internally adapted certification course, stated that obtaining certification was very time-consuming. The certification had to be completed within a certain timeframe, and required the project managers to spend one day a week attending classes. None of the remaining three project managers (cases two, four and five), who completed certification programmes that were customised for the organisation, detailed any issues with workloads or time commitments when completing their certification programme. This may suggest that there may be issues with completing an out-of-the-box certification programme as opposed to a customised certification programme. There were no downsides identified in relation to the provision of time for staff to complete the programme or the cost of the certification programme, which was borne by the organisations in all cases.

There may be some difficulties in the future in relation to renewing the PMI/IPMA certification. Even though the organisations that selected these certification programmes (cases one, three, and four) welcome the continuing certification programme, one project manager interviewed (case three) expressed a view that the budget may not be available within their organisation to complete all the tasks that are required to renew certification. None of these three project managers were entirely sure what had to be done to renew their certification. This may be due to the fact that there is still a substantial amount of time before their certification has to be renewed. However, one of these project managers (case three) felt that the time period between certification and the renewal of certification is quite short as the first two years of the four year certification period could be spent implementing and rolling out the associated methodology, which does not allow much time to complete all the other requirements for recertification, in addition to their daily workload. In contrast, certification renewal is not required in the organisations that implemented an adapted version of PRINCE2 (cases two and five) as there is no renewal programme in place. However, both of these project managers were of the opinion that maybe there should be a recertification programme for PRINCE2.

6 Conclusion

Certification can encourage the use of disciplined practices and build awareness of best practices [40]. This study agrees with these and also finds that the main driver in larger organisations for the completion of a project management certification programme was a desire by senior management to have a uniform approach to project management across the organisation. In contrast, the main driver in the smallest organisation was the personal desire of the project manager to enhance her career prospects and her knowledge of project management, which was not identified as a driving factor in the existing literature. This may suggest that project managers in a small organisation can directly influence management to obtain their support. The main driver for the organisation that provided technology services was the expectation of external customers that their suppliers would have certified project managers. This may suggest that organisations could require certification in order to maintain a competitive advantage, which adds to the existing literature.

While obtaining professional certification does cost time and money [2, 39], the findings of this research show that organisations were willing to pay for the cost of the certification and to allow their staff the time to complete the certification programme. However, this study found that project managers that participated in the PMI or IPMA certification programme found it very time-consuming. This would suggest that individuals who wish to complete the PMI or IPMA certification programme should take this into account when making their decision. This was not the case with the standard PRINCE2 certification as this certification programme can be completed within a week. It was also found that if an organisation decides to develop a customised certification programme, this can take a substantial amount of time and money, which also needs to be taken into consideration.

Project management certification can provide several benefits to project managers and to an organisation [11, 38]. The results of this research concur with these and also add to them by finding that certification helps to: define the role of the project manager; define career paths; and define competency profiles for each role. These findings were more prevalent in the larger organisations where they wanted a clear definition of the competency requirements for project managers and only wanted individuals who were suitably qualified to hold the position to manage projects. In addition, the larger organisations also stated that certification can help with external recruitment, resulting in a reduction in the overhead of training of new staff members, which was not identified as a benefit within the existing literature.

Three of the four large organisations in this study tailored the certification programmed to meet their needs. The large organisations that did adapt the certification programme were well-established and have been in existence for many years while the large organisation that did not adapt had expanded through the acquisition of other organisations. This may suggest that large, well-established organisations require a certification programme that can be modified to fit with their existing business processes. This agrees with existing findings, which states that many organisations adapt an industry-recognised certification programme to their own specific requirements, as project life cycles are different in every organisation [47].

The literature did not identify any issues in relation to the renewal of project management certification or the lack of recertification programmes. Yet, the findings of this research identified the lack of a recertification programme with PRINCE2 as a possible drawback to this certification programme. The findings also showed that while individuals who completed the PMI and IPMA certification programmes welcomed the recertification programme, they were of the opinion that the cost of recertification and the time required to complete all the required tasks for recertification may be an issue in the future.

In conclusion, organisations considering project management certification need to think about their reasons for doing so. It is possible that if there are good project management practices already in place that are used consistently across an organisation that there may not be a requirement to certify project managers. Prior to certification one organisation had implemented an internally developed methodology and had recognised the benefits of using a standard methodology that are presented in the existing literature [1, 9, 10, 19, 29]. As a result, in this organisation there was no evidence to suggest that the completion of a certification program was of any additional benefit to the organisation in terms of project management practice. What was evident from this research was that there exists a desire for certification in order to have internal and external recognition that certain quality standards were in place in relation to project management. There was also an aspiration that project managers should be suitability qualified to be in the role. However, certification can be costly and organisations must be willing to spend the necessary time and money if they wish to pursue certification, which may also include additional costs for the renewal of certification or for the customisation of the certification programme to suit the needs of the business.

6.1 Limitations of the Research

There are a number of limitations to this research. Firstly, the findings are only representative of five organisations studied at a particular point in time in a specific office location in Ireland and cannot be generalised to all organisations. Secondly, the findings were based on the opinion of one project manager in each of the participating organisations. Thirdly, four of the five cases studied were large organisations whereas the remaining organisation was small. The findings relating to the small organisation cannot be directly compared or contrasted with any of the other organisations studied. Finally, this research focused on PMI, IPMA and PRINCE2 certification as these certification programmes are internationally recognised.

Other certification programs could have been considered in order to examine project management certification more broadly. Caution should be exercised in relating the findings of this research to contexts other than similar organisations that have obtained PMI, IPMA or PRINCE2 certification.

References

[1]   Abbasi, G. Y. and Al-Mharmah, H. (2000) Project management practice by the public sector in a developing country, International Journal of Project Management, 18(2), 105–109

[2]   Adams, P. S., Brauer, R. L., Karas, B., Bresnahan, T. F. and Murphy, H. (2004) Professional Certification: its value to SH&E Practitioners and the Profession, 49(12), 26–31

[3]   Atkinson, R. (1999) Project management: cost, time and quality, two best guesses and a phenomenon, its time to accept other success criteria, International Journal of Project Management, 17(6), 337–342

[4]   Bernstein, S. (2000) Project offices in practice, Project Management Journal, 31(4), 4–7

[5]   Brancheaum, J. C. and Wetherbe, J. C. (1987) Key issues in Information Systems management, MIS Quarterly, 11(1), 23–45

[6]   Bredillet, C. N. (2005) Reconciling uncertainty and responsibility in the management of projects, Project Management Journal, 36(3), 3

[7]   Carbone, T. A. and Gholston, S. (2004) Project manager skill development: A survey of programs and practitioners, Engineering Management Journal, 16(3), 10–16

[8]   Dicks, R. S. (2000) The paradox of information: Control versus chaos in managing documentation projects with multiple audiences Proceedings of the 18th ACM International Conference on Computer Documentation: Cambridge, MA, pp. 253–259

[9]   Elonen, S. and Artto, K. A. (2003) Problems in managing internal development projects in multi-project environments, International Journal of Project Management, 21(6), 395–402

[10] Guthrie, S. (1998) IBM's commitment to project management, Project Management Journal, 29(1), 5–6

[11] Hartman, F. and Ashrafi, R. A. (2002) Project management in the information systems and information technologies industries, Project Management Journal, 33(3), 5–16

[12] IPMA (2005) International Project Management Association [Online] [Accessed 16 January 2006] Available from the World Wide: www.ipma.ch/asp/default.asp?p=90

[13] IPMI (2005) Institute of Project Management of Ireland [Online] [Accessed 16 January 2006] Available from the World Wide Web: www.projectmanagement.ie/

[14] Jurison, J. (1999) Software project management: the manager's view Communications of the ACM, 2(3), Article 17

[15] Kerzner, H. (2001) Project management: A systems approach to planning, scheduling and controlling , 7th edn, Wiley, New York

[16] Kerzner, H. (2006) Project management: A systems approach to planning, scheduling and controlling, 9th edn, Wiley, New York

[17] Loo, R. (1996) Training in project management: a powerful tool for improving individual and team performance Team Performance Management 2(3), 6–14

[18] Loo, R. (2002) Working towards best practices in project management: a Canadian study, International Journal of Project Management, 20(2), 9398

[19] Mahaney, R. C. and Lederer, A. L. (2003) Information systems project management: an agency theory interpretation, Journal of Systems and Software, 68(1), 1–9

[20] Mantel, S. J., Meredith, J. R. and Shafer, S. M. (2001) Project management in practice, Wiley, New York

[21] McCreery, J. K. (2003) Assessing the value of a project management simulation training exercise, International Journal of Project Management, 21(4), 233–242

[22] Milosevic, D. Z. (1996) Standardizing unstandardized project management, NorthCon 1996 Conference Proceedings, Seattle, WA, p. 12

[23] Nellore, R. and Balachandra, R. (2001) Factors influencing success in integrated product development (IPD) projects, IEEE Transactions, 48(2), 164–174

[24] OGC (2003) PRINCE2, [Online] [Accessed 13 January, 2006] Available from the World Wide Web: www.ogc.gov.co.uk

[25] Pappas, L. (2005) The state of Project Management Training, PM Network, 19(8), 59

[26] Parker, S. K. and Skitmore, M. (2005) Project management turnover: causes and effects on project performance, International Journal of Project Management, 23(3), 205

[27] Payne, J. H. (1993) Introducing formal project management into a traditional, functionally structured organization, International Journal of Project Management, 11(4), 239

[28] Payne, J. H. and Turner, J. R. (1999) Company-wide project management: the planning and control of programmes of projects of different type, International Journal of Project Management, 17(1), 55–59

[29] Pitagorsky, G. (1998) The project manager/functional manager partnership, Project Management Journal, 29(4), 7–16

[30] Pierson, L., Frolick, M. N. and Chen, L. (2001) Emerging issues in IT certification, Journal of Computer Information Systems, 42(1), 17–21

[31] PMI (2005) Project Management Institute [Online] [Accessed 16 January 2006] Available from the World Wide Web: www.pmi.org/info/PDC_CertificationsOverview.asp?

[32] Pressman, R. (1998) Fear of trying: the plight of rookie project managers, IEEE Software, 15(1), 50–54

[33] Sauer, C., Liu, L. and Johnston, K. (2001) Where Project Managers are Kings, Project Management Journal, 32(4), 39–51

[34] Sawaya, N. and Trapanese, P. (2004) Security Distributing & Marketing, 34(3), 73

[35] Scanlin, J. (1998) The Internet as an enabler of the Bell Atlantic Project Office, Project Management Journal, 29(2), 6–7

[36] Schwalbe, K. (2006) Information technology project management, 4th edn, Thomson Course Technology, Boston, MA

[37] Stevenson, T. H. and Barnes, F. C. (2002) What industrial marketers need to know now about ISO 9000 certification: A review, update, and integration with marketing, Industrial Marketing Management, 31(8), 695–703

[38] Tripp, L. L. (2002) Benefits of certification, Computer, 35(6), 31–33

[39] Turner, J. R. and Huemann, M. M. (2000) Current and Future Trends in the Education of Project Managers, [Online] [Accessed 15 January 2006] www.pmforum.org/library/papers/2000/TurneronCompetence.pdf

[40] Turner, J. R. and Simister, S. J. (2000) Gower Handbook of Project Management, 3rd edn, Gower Publishing Ltd., Aldershot, England

[41] Ward, J. L. (1999) What does the growth in project management training organizations mean for our profession?, Project Management Journal, 30(4), 6–7

[42] Wateridge, J. (1997) Training for IS/IT project managers: A way forward, International Journal of Project Management, 15(5), 283–288

[43] Winklhofer, H. (2002) Information systems project management during organizational change, Engineering Management Journal, 14(2), 33–37

[44] Yetton, P., Martin, A., Sharma, R. and Johnston, K. (2000) A model of information systems development project performance, Information Systems Journal, 10(4), 263

[45] Zielinski, D. (2005) In Training, 42, 18–23

SArt: Towards Innovation at the Intersection of Software Engineering and Art

Anna Trifonova, Salah U. Ahmed and Letizia Jaccheri

Department of Computer Science, Norwegian University of Science and Technology (NTNU), {trifonova, salah, letizia}@ idi.ntnu.no

Abstract   Computer science and art have been in contact since the 1960s. Our hypothesis is that software engineering can benefit from multidisciplinary research at the intersection with art for the purpose of increasing innovation and creativity. To do so, we have designed and planned a literature review in order to identify the existing knowledge base in this interdisciplinary field. A preliminary analysis of both results of our review and observations of software development projects with artist participation, reveals four main issues. These are software development issues, which include requirement management, tools, development and business models; educational issues, with focus on multidisciplinary education; aesthetics of both code and user interface, and social and cultural implications of software and art. The identified issues and associated literature should help researchers design research projects at the intersection of software engineering and art. Moreover, they should help artists to increase awareness about software engineering methods and tools when conceiving and implementing their software-based artworks.

1 Introduction

Art finds expression in numerous products in society, where the development of products is complex, competitive, global and intercultural in scope. Art and computer science are in contact from the 1960s (Sedelow 1970). The advent of multimedia technology has changed art production processes and the way both music, video, and figurative is fruited by consumers. Our assumption is that the interaction between software technology and art is also beneficial for the software technologists.

In this context at the Norwegian University of Science and Technology (NTNU) we have initiated the SArt project that will explore the intersection between software engineering (SE) and art. Our first task is to answer the following questions: How do software engineering and art intersect? How do software engineering and

C. Barry et al. (eds.), *Information Systems Development: Challenges in Practice, Theory, and Education, Vol.2*, doi: 10.1007/978-0-387-78578-3_17,
© Springer Science+Business Media, LLC 2009

art influence and can involve each other? What has been done until now in this area by other researchers in computer science?

According to our knowledge, this is the first attempt to answer these questions, although there has been a proposal to extend the Information Systems (IS) research onto the art domain (Oates 2006a). There is no established knowledge base in this interdisciplinary field and finding what research has been done previously appears not to be a trivial task. We have initiated a literature review, the preliminary outcomes of which had confirmed that both software engineers and artists might profit by further research in this interdisciplinary field.

This chapter has three main goals. Firstly, we aim at promoting interest and discussion in the interdisciplinary field between art and software engineering. Secondly, we present our understanding of how the two areas influence on each other and stress on the potential benefits for software engineering – innovation and creativity (Glass and DeMarco 2006). Last but not least, we discuss the process of making a survey of the state-of-the-art, aiming at completeness of the literature review. We show the preliminary outcomes of it which might be a starting point for other researchers and practitioners in the area.

Section 2 gives some more details on our project – SArt – with its objectives and current involvements. In Section 3 we discuss research methodology issues. A subsection is dedicated to the procedure of making the literature review in a systematic way. Section 4 shows the preliminary results of it. Section 5 is dedicated to a discussion and Section 6 – conclusions – is followed by references.

2 The SArt Project: Goals, Background, and Motivation

2.1 About the Project

The SArt project (http://prosjekt.idi.ntnu.no/sart/) is conducted inside the Software Engineering group at the Department of Computer Science at the NTNU. The focus of the project is the exploration of research issues in the intersection between software engineering and art. Our final objective is to propose, assess, and improve methods, models, and tools for innovation and creativity in software development. Our activities are mainly oriented at academic research. However, we also take part in different artistic projects.

This project confronts the interdisciplinary problem of integrating software designs originating from different academic genre into better products for society. The research methods will be based on empirical software engineering (Kitchenham 2004; Hevner et al. 2004; Wohlin et al. 2000) and will benefit from the interaction with experts from different disciplines, e.g., artists.

2.2 Objectives

The principal objective of the SArt project is to propose, and assess, and improve methods, models, and tools for innovation and creativity in software development. Particular attention will be paid to art influenced software development. Subgoals are:

G1. Develop knowledge on the interdisciplinary nature of software production in which the software engineering process interacts with the artistic process.

G2. Develop empirically based theories, models, and tools to support creativity and innovation in software technology development.

G3. Educate competent practitioners and researchers in the interdisciplinary field of software innovation and transfer of knowledge to the software industry and artist communities.

2.3 Projects

As part of SArt we are involved in three projects including both artists and software developers. Here we give a short description of those projects, showing the problems and the challenges the participants have encountered.

Flyndre (www.flyndresang.no) is a sculpture located in Inderøy, Norway. It has an interactive sound system that reflects the nature around the sculpture and changes depending on parameters like the local time, light level, temperature, water level, etc. The first version of the software was written by the sound composer and was a single CSound (http://csounds.com/) script file that was hard to modify, maintain and upgrade. However, the author discovered that it created a lot of interest among other composers and music technology enthusiasts. In order to improve the architecture of the software and publish it as open source software (OSS) with appropriate licenses, a multidisciplinary team, including software developers and NTNU students (as part of the "Experts in Team" course, see Jaccheri and Sindre 2007), was necessary. In this way (as OSS) the software attracts more developers and composers to utilize it and further improve and/or upgrade it.

Sonic Onyx (http://prosjekt.idi.ntnu.no/sart/school.php) is an installation project initiated by the Trondheim municipality in 2007. The goal is to decorate a junior high school with an interactive sculpture with which the people will be able to interact. The users will be allowed to send messages, images, or sound files from mobile phones, laptops, and hand-held devices through Bluetooth technology. The received files will be converted into sound and played by the sculpture. For the development of the hardware and the software sound subsystems a team of students from Hist (www.hist.no) is created and is working in collaboration with the artist (i.e. the sculpture designer). The members of the project use open source technology, like PureData (http://puredata.org/), Apache (http://www.apache.org/), Python (http://www.python.org/), due to availability of free software that allows development of low-cost software and community support for maintenance and upgrade.

Open Digital Canvas (http://veggidi.opentheweb.org/) is a project which aims to embellish a white wall at NTNU with a number of main boards with LEDs on them, creating a big matrix of light pixels. We wish to push the concept of openness a step further by keeping the hardware, software, and behavior as open as possible. In the project the artist, the student, and members of the computer science department work together to create a platform that will allow freedom of artistic expression and be a source of inspiration and reflection around interdisciplinary education and research.

Our experience in the described projects shows that software engineering theories and tools can play an important role for the improvement of the development process and the design of the software architecture. We have observed functional requirements, software usage, development trends, and challenges that are common or very similar for these projects. For example, the artists want to use some of the latest technologies in their artworks (e.g., different sensors in Flyndre or Bluetooth file interchange in Sonic Onyx sculpture), thus software developers are often not experienced and have to learn on the fly. The developing time and budget are limited. This might lead to neglecting the design of the software or the planning of the development process and might have many negative consequences (e.g., the software is created without proper architecture, thus it is difficult for modification and upgrade; the documentation is poor or missing, thus reuse is hard). Software evaluation, testing, and maintenance might also be problematic, as the funding is generally limited to the artwork creation. The software engineering perspective helps increasing the awareness in these issues. The artists seek for a cheap way to create their artwork and the software development is performed by students that are even less experienced. The software requirements are often not well defined and might change frequently. The artists would like to have a Web site in addition to the main software that will present details about the artwork itself and provide a user-friendly interface to observe and/or control the system. Common interest of using Open Source software is also visible from all three projects. Interestingly, there is also a desire to provide the created software as an open source. However, we observe difficulties in the choice of proper OSS licenses.

3 Methodological Issues

The following section explains our research approach. We use the Information System Research framework developed by Hevner et al. (2004) to reflect about the SArt research framework (Fig. 1).

- *Knowledge base*: There is an established knowledge base of foundations and methodologies in software engineering (e.g., SWEBOK; Bourque and Dupuis 2004). For the field of software engineering and art there is no established knowledge base. The first step to establish such knowledge base is to perform a literature review (Oates 2006b).

- *Environment*: Our experience in collaborating with local artists, observing artistic projects available on the Web, participation to art festivals, tell us that artistic projects that involve both software engineers and artist exist and pose needs to our research. Moreover, we observe that the game industry (e.g., funcom.com in Norway) employs artists as part of their developing teams.
- *Research*: Our task as researchers in this multidisciplinary field is that of contributing to establishing the knowledge base at the intersection of art and software engineering. In this phase of our research process we focus on literature review and projects observation. The next step will be that of developing new theories and artifacts that we will evaluate by means of empirical studies, having in mind our goals as introduced in Section 2.

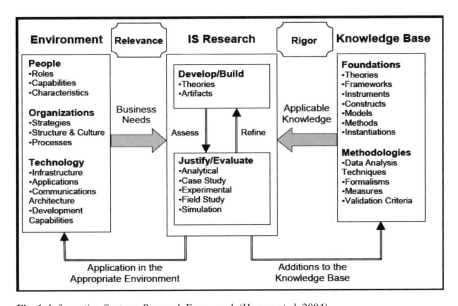

Fig. 1. Information Systems Research Framework (Hevner et al. 2004)

3.1 Literature Review

A review of the available literature at the intersection between software engineering and art is necessary to answer the question posed above: *What has been done until now in this area by other researchers in computer science?* The goal of the review is to establish our knowledge base, as discussed above. It will, hopefully, reveal research gaps and open questions in the field.

Performing an interdisciplinary review poses a set of challenges. One of them is to find the proper keywords to search for relevant articles. The keyword "art" is problematic to use as part of a search in the computer science world as the combination "state of the art" is used in almost all papers. This made the keyword search difficult. Another challenge is to define the criteria according to which to treat the article as relevant or irrelevant.

We have defined a process (Fig. 2) according to which to perform this literature review in a systematic way, following the advices, guidelines, and suggestions of Hart (1998) and Kitchenham (2004). The procedure includes a three steps process: (1) planning the review; (2) conducting the review; and (3) reporting the review. We have adopted this procedure in the following way.

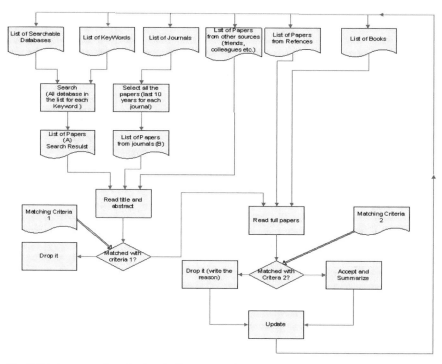

Fig. 2. SArt process of conducting the literature review

3.2 Planning the Review

During the planning phase we have set in advance and agreed on common relevance criteria for inclusion/exclusion of articles in the literature review. We have also identified the search strategies, including a list of searchable electronic databases of scientific publications and a starting list of keywords.

The selection criteria based on which to consider an article relevant or not were cleared and polished in several iterations at the beginning of the literature review. Relevant articles are those that address one or more of the following issues:

- Artists' requirements for software and/or habits in utilizing it.
- Software development processes and/or methodologies used for the software developed with artist's participation. This might include software created for artistic purposes (e.g., digital art, art installations, etc.), artists programming/producing software (e.g., software art), or participation in the development of software by other means.
- Collaboration between artists and software developers or computer scientists
- Research questions at the intersection between art and software (pose and/or answer).
- The influence of software and digital culture on art and/or the influence of art on software development.

During the planning phase we have identified the following search strategies for finding relevant articles, to aim at completeness of our literature review:

- *Keyword search in electronic databases:* We have identified a starting list of searchable electronic databases (e.g., IEEE Xplorer, ACM Digital Library, Google Scholar) and an initial list of keywords (see Table 1). Searches with each keyword (from the art-related terms) and combination of keywords should be performed in each of the electronic databases. In most of the cases no limitation on the published year was applied. In those cases when the search resulted to over 100 entries the search was limited to the last 10 years of publication. Both initial lists (i.e., the search engines used and the keywords) are being continuously extended with new entries that appeared relevant during the literature review.

Table 1. Initial list of keywords

Software Engineering-related terms	Art-related terms
Software engineering; software development; requirements; collaboration	Art; software art; media art; digital art; blog art; net art; generative art; art installation; artist; artwork; aesthetics; creativity

- *Thoroughly search the papers published in selected relevant journals and conferences*: We have identified a list of relevant journals and conferences (see Table 2) that, according to our previous experience or to their Web site description have a high probability of containing a large number of relevant articles. These journals and conferences are mainly focused to interdisciplinary research in software and art. We have planned to thoroughly examine/read the titles and abstracts of the papers from each of these journals and conferences for the past 10 years. New entries are continuously being appended to this list during the review process.

Table 2. Initial list of journals and conferences

Journal/Conference
MIT Press Leonardo – Online Journal on Art, Science and Technology, 40 years of publications (http://www.leonardo.info/)
IEEE Computer Graphics and Applications – A journal on theory and practice of computer graphics (www.computer.org/cga)
Read_Me conference – The proceedings from years 2002-2004 are published in "READ_ME: Software Art & Cultures", by Olga Goriunova and Alexei Shulgin (eds.), Aarhus University Press (December 2004)
Convergence - The International Journal of Research into New Media Technologies, since 1995 (http://convergence.beds.ac.uk/)
ACM Siggraph - publications in Computer Graphics and Interactive Techniques (http://www.siggraph.org/publications)
Proceeding books of ARS Electronica – festival for art, technology and society (http://www.aec.at/en/global/publications.asp)

- *Finding articles from the references of papers that are reviewed*: On the initial step this list of papers from reference is empty and is filled on a later stage of the process. It is when we are reviewing, i.e., reading fully the relevant articles selected from search strategies described above, that we can find some referenced papers that appeared to be relevant (from the citation and title). In this case we include them directly into the list of related papers to be reviewed/read in full, in order to gain deeper understanding of the field.
- *Other resources*: We have included in the review process the possibility of getting relevant articles from other sources. Some papers might be referred to us by colleagues and friends. Other articles we might find by looking at the publication lists of well-known researchers in the field and/or from institutions working in this area. The list of these papers is being continuously updated. Here we also include the articles and books that we knew from before and that have motivated our work, like Glass (1995), Greene (2004), Harris (1999) and Sedelow (1970).

3.3 Conducting the Review

Articles Selection: The inclusion/exclusion of the articles is made in two steps. Initially, the selection criteria (i.e., the first list given above) are interpreted liberally, so that unless the articles identified by the electronic and manual searches could be clearly excluded based on titles and abstracts, full copies were obtained. The selected articles were independently reviewed (i.e., read fully) by two or more of the authors of this paper.

Data extraction: When fully reading the articles the authors analyze its content and summarize it in a table. The inclusion/exclusion in the review was discussed until agreement is reached. The authors also produced annotations about the content.

Statistics generation and synthesis: The produced table with articles' annotations and summaries allows easy generation of certain statistical data (years of publication; conferences in which relevant articles occur more regularly; authors actively working in the area, etc.).

The conducting of the review is an iterative process in which the initial lists of keywords, relevant journals, and books is being updated with new entries found in other/previous articles.

3.4 Reporting the Review

We have conducted the first phase of the review. We have performed trial searches with most of the initial keywords defined and selected a number of papers (maximum ten from each search). In total about 50 articles have been reviewed so far. In this first iteration we have clarified the process steps and our relevance criteria which will allow us to decide the focus of our further study. In this chapter we discuss the preliminary outcomes of the review. Additionally, relevant books and the observation of a number of Web sites have contributed to our understanding of the field.

4 Research Issues Found in the Literature

In this section we present some of the research work/papers we have reviewed in our first phase of literature review and found relevant according to the selection criteria described in Section 3. The issues presented here are neither complete nor exhaustive; rather it is aimed to make a further contribution to the review result by grouping the articles according to the issues that have been discussed (Oates 2006b). As certain papers discuss more than one of the issues they are referenced more than once. This is a preliminary trial to create some classification/taxonomy of the research in the field. We also shortly propose hints for further software engineering research in each category.

4.1 Software Development Issues

- *Requirements/needs for software and software functionality within the artist community*. Artist Jen Grey (2002) discusses her experimentation with an alternative input mode (3D) – Surface Drawing© by Steven Schkolne – that she evaluates as very good for producing her artworks. The author has used the software in "a unique way to draw live models, a purpose for which it was not intended". Though it is not discussed by the author, this article points us the need for further research on the artists needs for software functionality of the general-purpose software. Such research might include studies on how the commercial and OSS available software match the artists needs. Meanwhile, a separate study might be needed on how to best discover the software requirements in projects that involve software development for art systems, like art installations reported by Marchese (2006) and the projects we described in Section 2.

-   *Evaluation in art projects.* Marchese (2006) describes the software developer's perspective on the creation of an interactive art installation. The author reports that the understanding of the system requirements is "the most important part of the process". This is consistent with the software engineering body of knowledge. Software systems are developed according to customer requirements (in art as in other fields). The customer (the artist in this domain) will differ from the user of the product. The artist might want certain interactions to be triggered when a spectator approaches the artwork. For creating the software in the proper way, however, it is needed to understand how the artwork as a whole will be perceived by the spectator and a special attention should be paid on the fact that user's evaluation or acceptance testing might appear only after the product is released (i.e., the artwork is in the museum and the exhibition is opened).

-   *Software tools.* Edmonds et al. (2004) have presented their approach to building interactive systems. Based on the collaborative work between artists and computer scientists (the authors themselves) report that there is a need (for the artists) for "a bridge between the use of an environment that requires programming knowledge and the 'closed' application, which does not provide sufficient flexibility". They suggest that further research is needed in this direction. An example of bridging such a gap is shown by Machin (2002) where a simulator and an application specific language has been developed for the artist's experimentation in the creation of an art installation. Machin reports that the offered solution was accepted very well by the artist and is a viable approach for augmenting the artists' freedom. Similarly, Biswas et al. (2006) also point out the need of an intermediate tool to support the designers (i.e., artists) when, together with software developers, are creating mobile context-aware applications. Such tool might also facilitate collaboration in multidisciplinary projects by minimizing the "semantic gap between the designer/artist's content design artifacts and technologist's system implementation" (Biswas et al. 2006). Many artists discuss their desire for more control over the software creation and experimentation (require to put their hands on the code), as currently available software and tools limit their creativity. However, they are not always very experienced in software development and programming. An additional software level between the artists and the low-level software development might be the way to solve the problem. Shoniregun et al. (2004) discuss issues like watermarking, streaming, encryption, and conditional access for protecting the artworks. The authors propose a smaller granularity technique as appropriate to deal with this problem. A software engineering study on different possibilities, provision of guidelines, and if necessary, development of proper tools will be beneficial for the artists.

- *Software development methods.* A case study discussed by Marchese (2006) shows that agile methods of software development, and more specifically the Adaptive Software Development, was suitable for the specific needs of a project in which a multimedia art installation was created. Meanwhile, Jaimes et al. (2006) suggest that human-centered computing is appropriate in many cases when multimedia is used, including digital art and in museums to augment exhibitions. A further study is needed in order to understand and provide guidelines on what software development methods are appropriate when developing software within art and in what particular cases (e.g., one method might be appropriate for art installations, another for generative music; different methods might be appropriate according to the artists programming experience or programmers' specific knowledge).

- *Collaboration issues.* Biswas et al. (2006),as mentioned above, point out that the tool they have provided (Mobile Experience Engine) is expected to also facilitate the design transfer from artists to technologies that use it. A necessity to understand the collaboration between artists and software developers in projects of common interest is also discussed in Harris (1999). For example, Harris mentions that some artists might be accustomed in working in studios instead of offices as the software developers. Different expression habits might be foreseen (e.g., artists sketching storyboards, while developers drawing software architectures); establishment of common language and understanding might be problematic. In the panel discussion of ACM Symposium on User Interface Software and Technology '98, panelists from both art and science background discussed the pitfalls, and issues of collaboration (Meyer and Glassner 1998). They pointed out that miscommunications occur frequently and due to the varying culture, collaboration is not always smooth. The strengthening of the collaboration between these two communities is also an aim in more recent events (e.g. ACM SIGCHI Conference 2006). The organizers mention (Jennings et al. 2006) that one of the gaps between the HCI community and media artists is that the first one (HCI) is a formalized discipline, while artists prefer research-in-practice (experimentalism). Marchese (2006), also mentioned earlier, claims that the Adaptive Software Development method is useful in artist–scientist collaboration as it minimizes the management infrastructure and focuses on communication to foster collaborative problem solving. Candy and Edmonds (2002) have identified a number of factors underlying successful collaborations. These factors were evaluated against seven collaboration case studies which were conducted by the COSTART project (www.creativityandcognition.com/costart). They have also derived three models of cocreativity in the collaboration. A possible outcome of software engineering study over collaboration issues is to provide guidelines on how to ensure successful collaboration. Further outcome might include even the design of tools for fostering it.

- *Business model.* In the recent years more artists are exploring the Internet as a medium to reach their audience/spectators. Nalder (2003) mentions that with the Internet as a way to transmit art the focus falls on the individual spectator, rather then museum type of art presentation. The OSS tools, developed in cooperative spirit and distributed via the Internet, enable artists to experiment and create low-cost artworks. However, not all artworks are supposed to be free of charge – there are entities, like software{ART}space (www.softwareartspace.com) that are providing commercially digital artworks. The proposed by Shoniregun et al. (2004) small granularity technique for artwork protection is an example to deal with this problem. Other approaches might be proposed by the software engineering field to face this new business model of the digital/software art.

4.2 Educational Issues

- *Artists' mastery of computer skills.* The need of interaction between artists and technology/technologists is discussed often in educational context. Garvey (1997) discusses the importance of the inclusion of computer graphics courses in the fine arts syllabus. However, keeping the balance between the traditional file arts skills (e.g., drawing, painting, sculpture) and digital skill mastery is of a great importance. According to the author, most of the largest companies in computer animation, film, and game industry have growing requirement for personnel skilled in computer 2D and 3D modeling and animation, but give preference on strong traditional art education, stating that it is easier to teach an artist to use a computer, than a programmer to create art.

- *Multidisciplinary collaboration between art and computer science students.* Multidisciplinary courses and common projects between art and science students are gaining importance. In fact, an essential part of the publications in between art and science report experiences of such initiatives. Ebert and Bailey (2000) discuss a 3D animation course with clear and well-defined educational goals of such course. The authors also report very positive outcomes: both types of students (artists and informatics) have interacted and produced not only interesting and nice looking animations and characters, but in some cases plug-ins for one of the commercial products for 3D animation (i.e., Maya). Morlan and Nerheim-Wolfe (1993) also discuss the educational goals of a course including collaboration between art and science students. These differ slightly for the two groups and apart from mastering certain skills in their own domain the course had to foster "the strengthening of interpersonal communication skills and the development of project management abilities in both art and computer science students". Parberry et al. (2006) describe their mainly positive experiences from a course and projects in game programming also offered to the two groups of students. The authors mention, however, that "there is a significant barrier to communication between the artists and the programmers". They also discuss practical issues that were found problematic, like the choice of game engine and incompatible file format (commercial vs. free tools). Different approaches are taken by the educators in different courses – combining lectures with hands-on work (Ebert and Bailey 2000), allowing the students to choose their project colleagues (Morlan and Nerheim-Wolfe 1993) or not. A further study might provide guidelines for optimizing the process of art and technology students working together in courses or educational projects.

- *Art in computer science curricula.* Zimmerman and Eber (2001) describe a course on Virtual Reality and its "implications for computer science education". The authors state that "for the majority of the computer science students, the whole concept of artistic expression was not something they dealt with on a regular basis; simply raising their awareness and increasing their tolerance of this very different area was considered a successful outcome". Fishwick, however, shows bigger expectations about the influence of art on computer science. In his paper (Fishwick 2003) he describes the Digital Art and Science (DAS) curricula provided at the University of Florida. The author discusses the importance of combining computer science and art in the educational phase and the positive experiences obtained. The author suggests that such practices will stimulate creativity in computer science students – "A human-centered focus on experience, presence, interaction, and representation forms the core of the arts. Perhaps, then, the arts can lead computer science in new directions". The author discusses the need of interaction between art and science not only at College, but also in Master and PhD educational levels. Fishwick (2007) suggests that experiments and experience of the students in the aesthetic computing (see below) will "encourage students to design entirely new human-computer interfaces for formal structures".

4.3 Aesthetics Issues

- *Aesthetic of the code.* Bond (2005) discusses several different aspects of the beauty of the software and the software as art. Firstly, he talks about Knuth's perfectionist's view of code and programming practices (Knuth 2001). With time it sometimes evolves into programs that do not have any utility value, like the one-line programs, but are still showing the mastery of programming. Artists, however, take a different direction (the example given is a poem written in Perl) – the programming language is used to create a syntactically correct program to convey human sentiments to humans. More recently, the programs themselves are appreciated as artworks (at Transmediale - www.transmediale.de, Read_Me - http://readme.runme.org/ and other art festivals). Cramer and Gabriel (2001) state that the software "is inevitably at work in all art that is digitally produced and reproduced" and discuss its part in the aesthetics of the whole artwork. This need has led to the formation of the "software art" movement in the artistic community.

- *Aesthetic in software art.* Although in Software Art the software is considered artwork, it is not always about the beauty of the code, as in the previous section. Cramer (2002) writes "As a contemporary art, the aesthetics of software art includes ugliness and monstrosity just as much as beauty, not to mention plain dysfunctionality, pretension and political incorrectness". Manovich (2002), on the other hand, discusses the new aesthetics in the artworks created by software artists using Flash (see http://www.macromedia.com/software/flash/about/) and similar programs – "Flash generation invites us to undergo a visual cleansing". Such new aesthetics influences on the whole production of digital artifacts for the Internet.

- *Aesthetics in user interfaces.* Aesthetic is addressed in the area of human–computer interaction considering interface design. Bertelsen and Pold (2004) propose aesthetics interface criticism as an alternative to the traditional assessment methods within human–computer interaction. The authors state that the interface criticism is to be done by someone with "at least some basic knowledge in aesthetics, and ideally some experience with art and literary criticism", and that the average systems engineer would not be able to perform the needed task without prior training. This shows the importance of incorporating art community in the user interface design, which is expected to lead to production of better interfaces to the developed software, but also to an expansion of the body of knowledge in user interface design.

4.4 Social and Cultural Implications of Software/Technology on Art

- Software art, mentioned above, is concerned also with the cultural and social implications of the technology, and software as part of it, on the society and art. For example, Broegger (2003) discusses that one of the implications of the use of commercial software when creating an artwork is the de facto coauthorship with the software developers (he exemplifies Macromedia). Manovich (2002) states that "Programming liberates art from being secondary to commercial media". Nalder (2003) provides a reflection on the way technology changes the society and how this affects on art. For example, with the wide use of Internet people have become afraid for their privacy and artists explore such implications and show them in their artworks. According to the author, NetArt treats the new information and communications technologies and systems "not merely as the tool of communication, but as the subject of their art".

5 Discussion

In this section we will try to summarize what we have learnt from the first iteration of the literature review in its early stage. As we have mentioned in the beginning we are looking at the intersection between art and software engineering and based on the above discussed articles we answer the following question:

How do software engineering and art intersect, i.e. how do software engineering and art influence and can involve each other?

The model we depict in Fig. 3 stems from our prior understanding of the field of software engineering and art, the knowledge that had motivated us and pushed us into this field. It has been refined by the knowledge we have developed during our literature review. In addition, it has been supported by our observations on artistic projects and web sites and participation in conferences and festivals.

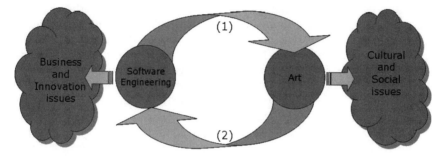

Fig. 3. Relations between the fields of software engineering and art

The field between software engineering and art is interesting for theorists and practitioners from both areas. The review shows that both computer science researchers and contemporary artists discuss issues, experiences, and problems encountered in this interdisciplinary field. The relationship is bidirectional, but the points of interest might differ according to from whose perspective we look at it.

On Fig. 3 the influences of software engineering on art is shown with the arrow (1). Contemporary artists often use digital technology in their artwork in a wide range of ways. Computer graphics, music, and animation were already popular in 1980s (see PRIXARS - http://prixars.aec.at/). Artists follow closely the changes and upgrades of the technology, moving from simple digital image creation to the production of interactive installations. With the expansion of the Internet artists start to explore also the WWW technologies. There is a continuously growing need for them to be familiar with the computer tools provided by software engineers and developers to produce their artworks. This need is being incorporated in the art education (see "Educational issues" in Section 4), providing more and more courses for mastering skills in production of digital art (e.g., 2D and 3D modeling, computer animation, etc.). More recently interdisciplinary courses and projects are also offered, thus often putting informatics students and art students to work side-by-side. The depth in which the artists submerge into technology depends on the required functionality for the production of the artwork and on the availability of tools that would satisfy artists' needs. In some cases when such tools do not exist or impose undesired limitations, the artists learn even to program and write their own programs (e.g., some cases in "software art"). In other cases they turn to computer professionals for development of the specific hardware and/or software (most of the papers described in "software development issues" section above). This points to the need of particular attention of software engineering research towards the specific needs of artists.

Looking from the perspective of software engineer, artists might be seen as customers that need especially designed software. In order to support and satisfy their requirements theories, methods and tools from software engineering might be used.

Interestingly, there is a trend in artistic community of returning to the roots of software, i.e., a return to programming. The "software art" movement incorporates the idea that the artist digs into the software code for producing the artwork. Artist community acknowledges the importance of software in art and in the community in general. In fact, in 1999 one of the biggest Festivals on Digital Arts – Ars Electronica (www.aec.at) gave one of its prizes to Linux. The returning of artists to programming, however, is not always due to appreciation of the software and with the goal to raise it as an artwork. It is sometimes due to the limitations it poses on artwork creation, as discussed in Section 4.4. This gives us an indication that there is a serious gap in the software support of the art production. There is a need of research in order to understand the artists' needs and provide them the appropriate tools for the artwork creation, without limiting their creative processes (see "software tools" subsection above). The research might also be directed on the processes of software development when artists and programmers work together for creating an artwork (like interactive installations). There is a need to understand what the most appropriate methods are and how to foster the collaboration between such multidisciplinary groups.

Arrow (2) on Fig. 3 shows the influences of art on software engineering. This relation is not as obvious as (1), but from the point of view of software engineers we are interested in it. The question is how can/is art influence on software development and what changes in the area of software engineering are brought by the intersection with art? This means to find out how art, artists, the collaboration with them and/or the study over existing artistic practices might help to enrich the theories, models and tools in software engineering.

One such possibility is suggested by Harris (1999) and was one of the main ideas behind the Xerox PARC Artists-in-Residence Program:

PAIR is an opening into using some of the methodologies of art in scientific research, which is a creative activity itself and therefore is always on the lookout for new techniques to be borrowed from other professionals.

In other words, the creativity of computer scientists or software developers might be triggered by the close interaction with artists in such a manner that to propose innovative solution to specific problems, build novel tools, discover new approaches to processes, original methodologies, etc. Similar expectations might be seen in some cases presented in "art in computer science curricula" above (i.e., Fishwick 2007).

Another possibility is suggested by Briony Oates (2006a) – to explore the artists' understanding of visual aesthetics, developed over hundreds and thousands of years and apply it on computer artifacts. What is meant here is that when digital visualization is involved artists might be the best judges. They might also be the best source of practical ideas for solving concrete visualization problems and/or propose innovative solutions. These issues are discussed in "aesthetics in user interfaces" subsection above. Meanwhile, there are many cases that computer scientists do not involve artists in such situations. For example, a paper presented at IEEE/WIC International Conference on Web Intelligence 2003 (Yazhong et al. 2003) proposes an approach for music retrieval based on mood detection, together with an innovative 3D visualization of the music in which the user should browse and select. The authors suggest that the visual representation of the songs should be related to some of the parameters that identify the mood of the song (e.g., the tempo). However, their study is not related with any study on how colors and moods are related. An inclusion of the artists' opinion and knowledge in such study would probably lead to much better results than the somehow confusing ones shown in the article.

6 Conclusions

Art and software engineering intersect in a variety of ways. However, there is no established knowledge base for this interdisciplinary domain. This field is young and there are not established journals like in other interdisciplinary fields (e.g., medical informatics). Based on our projects (shortly presented in Section 2) and our prior knowledge in this domain we have identified the need for deeper understanding of how software engineering and art intersect and how they influence and can help each other. To the best of our knowledge, this is the first attempt to make a systematic review of the state-of-the-art research in between software engineering and art.

Here we have presented the preliminary results of the literature review, showing in which directions research is being done. We have discussed our understanding of the intersection between art and software engineers and stressed on the possible benefits of such interaction for the software engineering. Creativity and innovation might be expected, together with improvements in the aesthetics direction.

We have discussed in details the process of making a systematic review of this interdisciplinary field. Our experience is that it is not a trivial task, but it is a necessary starting step for establishing the knowledge base. Some of the benefits of it are to reveal the gaps that need further research, create a collection of relevant papers and show previous positive or negative experiences and lessons learned.

Throughout the SArt project at NTNU we aim at gaining better understanding of how software engineering and art are connected by completing the systematic literature review described here. In our future work we will develop empirically based theories, models, and tools to support creativity and innovation in software technology development, fostered by the intersection with art.

Acknowledgments   Part of this work was carried out by Anna Trifonova during the tenure of an ERCIM "Alain Bensoussan" Fellowship Programme.

References

Bertelsen, O. W. and Pold, S. (2004) Criticism as an Approach to Interface Aesthetics. Nordic conference on human-computer interaction (NordiCHI '04), Tampere, Finland, October 23–27, ACM International Conference Proceeding Series; Vol. 82.

Biswas, A., Donaldson, T., Singh, J., Diamond, S., Gauthier, D. and Longford, M. (2006) Assessment of Mobile Experience Engine, the development toolkit for context aware mobile applications. ACM SIGCHI international conference on Advances in computer entertainment technology (ACE '06), Hollywood, USA, June 14–16.

Bond, G. W. (2005) Software as Art. Communications of the ACM. 48(8) August, pp. 118–124.

Bourque, P. and Dupuis, R. (eds.) (2004) Guide to the Software Engineering Body of Knowledge. IEEE CS Press. ISBN 0-7695-2330-7.

Broegger, A. (2003) Software Art - an introduction. The online magazine Artificial, September 24, available online at http://www.artificial.dk/articles/software.htm, last visited on 21/03/07.

Candy, L. and Edmonds, E. (2002) Modeling Co-Creativity in Art and Technology. The fourth Conference on Creativity & Cognition (C&C'02), Loughborough, UK, October 14–16.

Cramer, F. (2002) Concepts, Notations, Software, Art. read_me 1.2 catalogue, available online at http://cramer.plaintext.cc:70/all/software_art_and_writing, last visited 13/04/2007.

Cramer, F. and Gabriel U. (2001) Software Art. American Book Review, issue "Codeworks" (Alan Sondheim, ed.), Sept. 2001, available online at http://cramer.plaintext.cc:70/all/software_art_and_writing, last visited 13/04/2007.

Ebert, D. S. and Bailey, D. (2000) A Collaborative and Interdisciplinary Computer Animation Course. ACM SIGGRAPH Computer Graphics 34(3), 22–26.

Edmonds, E., Turner, G. and Candy, L. (2004) Approaches to Interactive Art Systems. In Yong Tsui Lee, Stephen N. Spencer, Alan Chalmers, Seah Hock Soon (eds.), Proceedings of the 2nd International Conference on Computer Graphics and Interactive Techniques in Australasia and Southeast Asia 2004, Singapore, June 15–18, 2004. ACM 2004, ISBN 1-58113-883-0.

Fishwick, P. (2003) Nurturing next-generation computer scientists. IEEE Computer Magazine 36(12) Dec., pp. 132–134.

Fishwick, P. (2007) Aesthetic Computing: A Brief Tutorial. Book Chapter to appear in Fernando Ferri (eds.) Visual Languages for Interactive Computing: Definitions and Formalizations. Idea Group Inc.

Garvey, G. R. (1997) Retrofitting Fine Art and Design Education in the Age of Computer Technology. ACM SIGGRAPH Computer Graphics 31(3), 29–32.

Glass, R. L. (1995) Software Creativity. Prentice Hall. ISBN 0131473646.

Glass, R. L. and DeMarco, T. (2006) Software Creativity 2.0. developer.* Books. ISBN 0977213315.

Greene, R. (2004) Internet Art. Thames & Hudson. ISBN 0500203768.

Grey, J. (2002) Human-Computer Interaction in Life Drawing, a Fine Artist's Perspective. Sixth International Conference on Information Visualisation (IV'02).

Harris, C. (eds.) (1999) Art and Innovation: The Xerox PARC Artists-in-Residence Program. MIT Press. ISBN 0262082756.

Hart, C. (1998) Doing a Literature Review: Releasing the Social Science Research Imagination, SAGE. ISBN 0761959742.

Hevner, A. R., March, S. T., Park, J. and Ram S. (2004) Design Science in Information Systems Research. MIS Quarterly 28(1), 75–105.

Jaccheri, L. and Sindre, G. (2007) Software Engineering Students meet Interdisciplinary Project work and Art. To appear in proceedings of 11th International Conference on Information Visualisation, Zurich, Switzerland, 2–6 July.

Jaimes, A., Sebe, N. and Gatica-Perez D. (2006) Human-Centered Computing: A Multimedia Perspective. 14th International Annual Conference on Multimedia, Santa Barbara, CA, October 23–27.

Jennings, P., Giaccardi, E. and Wesolkowska M. (2006) About Face Interface: Creative Engagement in the New Media Artis and HCI. CHI workshop 2006, Montreal, Canada, April 22–23.

Kitchenham, B. (2004) Procedures for Performing Systematic Reviews. Keele University Technical Report TR/SE-0401. ISSN:1353-7776, available online at http://www.elsevier.com/framework_products/promis_misc/inf-systrev.pdf, last visited 13/04/2007.

Knuth, D. E. (2001) Things a computer scientist rarely talks about. In CSLI Lecture Notes. Number 136. Center for the Study of Language and Information, Stanford, CA, 2001.

Machin, C. H. C. (2002) Digital Artworks: Bridging the Technology Gap. The 20th Eurographics UK Conference, Leicester, UK, June 11–13.

Manovich, L. (2002) Generation Flash. International workshop Multimedia and the Interactive Spectator. University of Maastricht, May 16-18, available online at http://www.fdcw.unimaas.nl/is/generationflash.htm, last visited 13/04/2007.

Marchese, F. T. (2006) The Making of Trigger and the Agile Engineering of Artist-Scientist Collaboration. Tenth International Conference on Information Visualisation (IV'06).

Meyer, J. and Glassner, A. (1998) Artists and Technologists working together. The 11th annual ACM symposium on User interface software and technology (UIST '98), San Francisco, CA, Nov. 1–4.

Morlan, J. and Nerheim-Wolfe, R., (1993) Photographic Rendering of Environmental Graphics in Context: A Collaboration Between Art and Science Made Simple. ACM SIGGRAPH Computer Graphics Journal 27(1), 10–12.

Nalder, G. (2003) Art in the Informational Mode. Seventh International Conference on Information Visualization (IV'03).

Oates, B. (2006a) New frontiers for information systems research: computer art as an information system. European Journal of Information Systems 15, 617–626.

Oates B. (2006b) Researching Information Systems and Computing. SAGE. ISBN 978141290224.

Parberry, I., Kazemzadeh, M. B. and Roden, T. (2006) The Art and Science of Game Programming. ACM SIGCSE Bulletin, Proceedings of the 37th SIGCSE technical symposium on Computer science education SIGCSE '06. 38(1).

Sedelow, S. Y. (1970) The Computer in the Humanities and Fine Arts. ACM Computing Surveys 2(2): 89–110.

Shoniregun, C. A., Logvynovskiy, O., Duan, Z. and Bose, S. (2004) Streaming and Security of Art Works on the Web. Sixth IEEE International Symposium on Multimedia Software Engineering (ISMSE'04).

Wohlin, C., Runeson, P., Høst, M., Ohlsson, M. C., Regnell, B. and Wesslen, A. (2000) Experimentation in Software Engineering: An Introduction. Kluwer. ISBN 0792386825.

Yazhong, F., Yueting, Z. and Yunhe P. (2003) Music Information Retrieval by Detecting Mood via Computational Media Aesthetics, IEEE/WIC International Conference on Web Intelligence (WI), Oct. 13–17, pp. 235–241.

Zimmerman, G. W. and Eber, D. E. (2001) When Worlds Collide! An Interdisciplinary Course In Virtual-Reality Art", ACM SIGCSE Bulletin, Proceedings of the thirty-second SIGCSE technical symposium on Computer Science Education (SIGCSE '01) 33(1).

Effects of Natural Language Complexity on Student Performance in Object-Oriented Domain Analysis

Ke Li, Jenny Coady, Rob Pooley and Rick Dewar

MACS, Heriot-Watt University, Edinburgh, UK
kl21@macs.hw.ac.uk, jenny@macs.hw.ac.uk, rjp@macs.hw.ac.uk, rick@hw.ac.uk

Abstract   This chapter examines whether there is more to teaching students how to identify object-oriented (OO) concepts in domain analysis than has perhaps previously been appreciated. Understanding domain descriptions, expressed in natural language, in the early stages of software development is crucial to the success of a project.   A study is presented which measured the performance of senior undergraduate computing students in terms of the types of errors they make as they tried to understand and identify important domain concepts. It concludes that the form of natural language used has an influence on the accuracy of a person's interpretation. In particular, students have a tendency to be confused by complex sentences and domain irrelevant information. In addition, students fail to notice important concepts indicated by infrequently appearing words.

1 Introduction

In modern software development, systems being developed are becoming larger, more complex, more likely to change and, arguably, less familiar to developers. It is generally accepted that understanding the problem to be solved is more difficult and important than building the software system itself (Brooks 1987). In this chapter we are concerned with the understanding how such understanding is hampered for students learning to apply object-oriented approaches. This research hopes to find more effective means to teach such techniques.

The activity of understanding the problem to be solved is called *domain analysis* in information systems development. Since object-orientation was popularized for software engineers by Booch (1994) and Rumbaugh et al. (1991), OO domain analysis has become widely applied in practice. Increasingly the broader concerns of information systems as a whole have been addressed from this standpoint. One of the suggested strengths of object orientation, in contrast with earlier structured approaches, is indeed the belief that objects can bridge the communication gap

C. Barry et al. (eds.), *Information Systems Development: Challenges in Practice, Theory, and Education, Vol.2*, doi: 10.1007/978-0-387-78578-3_18,
© Springer Science+Business Media, LLC 2009

between domain concepts and software system elements (Korthaus 1998, Loos & Fettke 2001, Mentzas 1999) and, therefore, between end-users, analysts and designers. The aim is to understand the information system in the context of an organization as a whole along with the purely technical aspects. To perform OO domain analysis requires a good knowledge and thorough understanding of object orientation. However, teaching and learning OO domain analysis has proven to be very difficult. In particular, distinguishing the *domain-relevant* concepts can be problematic for students.

Understanding the problem is also vital for successful development in the real world. A number of approaches have been applied to help technical experts understand the problem of OO domain analysis, e.g., use case analysis (Jacobson et al. 1992), scenarios, and the "what vs. how" problem approach (Jackson 1994). Most of these techniques suggest ways to communicate with non-technical stakeholders efficiently, thereby obtaining and organizing valuable information that forms a basis for both the requirements for the system being developed (use case models) and the structuring of its design (class diagrams). Modeling is perhaps the commonest technique that students are taught for domain analysis, frequently using the Unified Modeling Language, UML (Pooley & Wilcox 2004). Issues related to teaching and learning UML have been discussed in previous studies in software education (Hadjerrouit 2005, Cybulski & Linden 2000), but the results presented here focus on how natural language might effect the outcome of object-oriented analysis using UML.

The techniques of object-oriented design starting from textual analysis may address the problem of interpreting stakeholder requirements when used by experienced professionals, however, they are less effective in teaching and learning contexts. UML is not easy to learn and the problem needs to be understood before the UML model can be constructed. Students often do not have a chance to communicate with stakeholders, to clarify and develop their understanding. Generally, students are given a textual domain description on which to practise. Such descriptions are usually small, but even a problem domain that includes a limited number of domain concepts is typically represented using complex natural language structures. What is more, case studies by Svetinovic et al. (2005) show that the difficulty of developing domain concepts is independent of the size of the domain description.

There is no doubt that natural language is inescapable in domain analysis, no matter what methodology is applied and what techniques are used. Hence, analyzing such natural language-based data to develop domain relevant concepts is crucial in both practice and teaching. Many attempts have been made to address this issue, including the development of automated natural language processing systems, which apply linguistic techniques to discover domain relevant concepts, and then to observe mappings between OO concepts and natural language elements (Li et al. 2005).

Motivated by the findings of previous studies, it can be seen that the difficulties in teaching and practicing UML may be affected by the complexity and ambiguity of natural language, as well as its own complexity. The focus of this chapter is to investigate how to support students working with natural language descriptions of problem domains, and thereby to encourage better understanding of systems, leading ultimately to better designs. The research questions concerning students in this task are:

- What typical errors occur when translating domain descriptions to system designs?
- Can the form of natural language in domain descriptions influence such translations?
- How can such considerations be applied to improve information systems education?

Section 1 is a brief review of related work, focusing on natural language. Section 3 describes the experimental methodology and design, where the selection of participants, notations and scenarios is explained. The results from the three scenarios chosen are presented in Section 4. In section 5, these results are discussed and, in section 6, conclusions are drawn.

2 Review of the Related Work

Efforts at exploring mappings between the concepts of information systems and natural language elements have resulted in different strategies that provide clues for extracting important domain concepts (Chen 1983, Halliday 2003, Juristo & Moreno 2000), including analysis of parts of speech, use of special words, structures in the language used and fundamental semantic relationships between words. However, there are no agreed simple rules to guide the identification of domain relevant concepts.

Based on the mappings selected by each researcher, natural language processing techniques have been used in a number of systems that automatically, or semi-automatically, identify domain relevant concepts. Some even output OO diagrams (Mich 1996, Delisle et al. 1999). This kind of approach is typically based on the assumption that the importance of a concept is strongly correlated with the frequency of its appearance in the text (Goldin & Berry 1997). Lecoeuche's (2000) approach does not rely on this assumption and can be used to complement approaches that do. His approach is capable of capturing important concepts that appear both frequently and infrequently in the text. This approach is based on information extraction techniques which allow requirements engineers to set up a "baseline text" as a searching base from which to extract domain relevant concepts. The performance of this approach, therefore, relies on the selection of the baseline text. Important domain concepts cannot be elicited if they are not defined in the baseline text.

3 Experimental Methodologies and Design

This study is based on an experiment looking at how natural language may affect models produced by applying object oriented modeling approaches. The motivation is to understand the obstacles faced in identifying OO concepts from text.

3.1 The Choice of Participants

It was deemed important that each participant possess equivalent, if limited, experience and knowledge of OO domain analysis. In order to find a group with the number of suitably experienced students required for significant results, the decision was made to use a penultimate (third) year class of undergraduates in the Computer Science Department of Heriot Watt University. All of the participants had studied UML and been involved in exercises using it with textual, parts-of-speech-based analysis.

3.2 The Choice of Notation

UML remains the most commonly used OO notation both in practice and education. Among the various types of diagram in UML, use case diagrams and class diagrams are generally considered to be the most relevant for domain modeling. Use case diagrams are often used for communication between different stakeholders, while class diagrams represent static relationships among the important concepts of a specific domain. Given that the focus of this study is domain analysis, rather than domain information gathering, UML class diagrams were chosen. These were also useful, since the students had been exposed to UML in earlier teaching, minimizing the overhead in preparing them for participation.

3.3 The Choice of Scenarios

In choosing the scenarios for this experiment, the following criteria were defined. The scenarios must:

- Consist of a domain description (in English) and corresponding UML class diagram
- Be relatively simple, so that they can be tackled in around 10 min
- Be independent of prior, specialized domain knowledge, so that they can be understood easily and quickly by all participants

- Be published elsewhere previously; it is assumed that the authors of these scenarios are experts, and their artifacts are of a high quality

The chosen three scenarios are Bank System (BS) (Pooley & Wilcox 2004), Elevator Problem (EP; 2006) and Film Management (FM; (2006).

3.4 Method

The experiment compared how students understand information given in natural language with how they respond to an OO model. The inputs were Domain Descriptions (DDs) and corresponding Domain Models (DMs). The outputs were: a First Derivative Domain Model (1stDDM), a Second Derivative Domain Model (2ndDDM) and a Derivative Domain Description (DDD) (see Fig. 1).

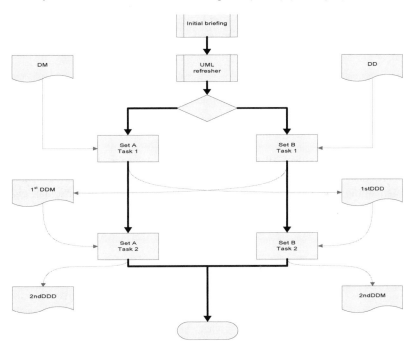

Fig. 1. Scenario of experimental design

As many as 63 students participated in this study. As there were three scenarios, participants were asked to form teams of three, with each person in a team working on a different scenario. Each scenario had a DD (in English) and a DM (a class diagram).

- Before the experiment began, the participants were given a 5-min refresher course by a lecturer on UML Class diagram notation.

- Half of the teams (set A) started from the DD of their scenario and produced a DDM; the other half (set B) started from the DM and produced a DDD.
- Students then worked on a second scenario; those who had worked from a DM worked on a DDD generated by another team member and vice versa.

For each part, students had about 10 min. It was vital that participants only saw one part of a scenario during the experiment to prevent undue bias.

3.5 Analysis

For each scenario, the following OO concepts were compared with their counterparts in the original class diagram:

- C, classes identified by the participants, including methods and attributes
- A, association relationships identified by the participants
- G, generalization relationships identified by the participants

4 Results

4.1 Scenario One: Bank System

Class *Account* is equally well-identified in both 1stDDM and 2ndDDM and class *Customer* has a slightly higher percentage in 1stDDM than 2ndDDM (see Table 1). The remaining concepts are identified better in the 2ndDDM. In particular, classes *Branch* and *Transfer* are not identified in the 1stDDM, but by 86% and 71% in the 2ndDDM. Irrelevant class *Employee* is added by 40% in 1stDDM, and by 0% in 2ndDDM.

Table 1. Domain concepts identified in Bank System

Domain classes	1stDDM	2ndDDM	Domain relationships	1stDDM	2ndDDM
Account (C)	100%	100%	Account – Savings Account (G)	60%	86%
Customer (C)	60%	57%	Account – Current (G)	40%	86%
Savings Account (C)	60%	86%	Account – Customer (A)	20%	57%
Current Account (C)	60%	86%	Account – Statement (A)	20%	100%
Statement (C)	40%	71%	Account – Branch (A)	0	86%
+Employee	40%	100%	Account – Transfer (A)	0	71%
Branch (C)	0	86%			
Transfer (C)	0	71%			

4.2 Scenario Two: Elevator Problem

The lowest percentage of 1stDDM is 17% for class ElevatorButton, which has a much higher percentage in 2ndDDM (see Table 2).

Table 2. Delivered domain concepts of Elevator Problem

Domain concepts	1stDDM	2ndDDM	Domain concepts	1stDDM	2ndDDM
Elevator (C)	83%	100%	ElevatorController – Button (A)	33%	86%
Button (C)	67%	86%	ElevatorController – Door (A)	17%	29%
FloorButton (C)	33%	71%	Button – ElevatorButton (G)	17%	57%
ElevatorController (C)	33%	100%	Button – FloorButton (G)	17%	57%
Door (C)	33%	43%	Elevator – ElevatorController (A)	0%	86%
ElevatorButton (C)	17%	71%			

4.3 Scenario Three: Film Management

The data also shows that two concepts are identified by 100% of students in 2ndDDM but only 83% and 33% in 1stDDM. Overall, the results for 1stDDM are worse than for 2ndDDM (see Table 3).

Table 3. Delivered domain concepts of Film Management

Domain concepts	1stDDM	2ndDDM	Domain concepts	1stDDM	2ndDDM
Scene (C)	100%	100%	Scene – Setup (A)	75%	83%
Setup (C)	100%	100%	Setup – Take (A)	50%	83%
Take (C)	75%	100%	Scene – Internals (G)	50%	83%
Internals (C)	75%	83%	Scene – Externals (G)	50%	83%
Externals (C)	75%	83%	Location –External (A)	0%	50%
Location (C)	75%	83%			
+Reel	17%	100%			

4.4 Overall Results

The case studies highlight an interesting result. In all three scenarios, the classes that students seem to have difficulty discovering in the 1stDDM were identified by most students in their 2ndDDM. It can perhaps be reflected that the 1stDDM was based on a natural natural language description, while the 2ndDDM was based on something closer to a *controlled* natural language description (Kuhn et al. 2006), which only includes information on domain relevant concepts represented in simple English structures (the DDDs shown in Fig. 1). In a typical DDD written by a student, compared to the original DD, it only includes key concepts; the irrelevant information is filtered out. The relationships between these key concepts are made with simple sentence structures.

5 Discussions

The results obtained from this experiment give us some idea of how far students' understanding of a problem in OO analysis is influenced by the simplicity of natural language used in the domain description. This section describes what went wrong and why in cases where students got things "wrong". The data used in this discussion are the results of 1stDDM, as that is based on the original DD.

The errors made by the students are classified into four types represented by a taxonomy given in Fig. 2. Based on the analysis in the previous section, the main mistakes can be categorized into two kinds: the added extra concept – refers to irrelevant concepts that are identified, and the missing concept – refers to important concepts ignored by the students.

Errors	Understanding problem domain	Added unimportant concepts	Nonexistent concept
			Existing concept
		Missing important concepts	Incorrect interpretation
			Not interpreted

Fig. 2. Taxonomy of Error Types

5.1 Added Unimportant Concepts

5.1.1 Nonexistent Concepts

Collected class diagrams show that many students added extra attributes to classes. For instance, 60% of the 1stDDMs of BS contain class *Customer* and 40% of these contain extra attributes that not appear in the original DD (such as *customer name, customer id*, etc.). This might be caused by: (i) the use of personal knowledge relevant to the problem; or (ii) expectation that classes often have such attributes and methods, perhaps mimicking previous text book examples. For the latter point, it is thought that although the domain description is clear and detailed enough for people to understand the problem, students may feel that the information given is incomplete and the added attributes are required for later activities (i.e., system design).

5.1.2 Existing Concepts: Personal Nouns

The results show that students may consider an actor to be an instance of a class. Students can be divided into three groups, according to how they interpreted nouns referring to an actor: (i) all the actors are classes; (ii) actors are not classes; (iii) an actor may or may not be a class. The 40% of students who considered Employee as a candidate class, also all considered Customer as a candidate class. Conversely, the majority who did not consider Employee as a candidate class, did not take Customer as a candidate class either. Furthermore the collected outputs show just 20% of the class diagrams contain class Customer alone. The sentence that *"employee"* is involved in, is *"Bank employees may check any account that is held at their branch. They are responsible for invoking the addition of interest and for issuing statements at the correct times."* Clearly, it says that employees communicate with the system. However, it does not specify any static relationship between employee and any other concepts. This should have been seen as a sign that employee should not be identified as a class, but a potential actor.

The results may indicate that, relating to the first example, students need better guidance on (i) under which circumstances actors should be identified as a class; in particularly, the classification of personal nouns, (ii) understanding natural language structures in terms of transforming domain concepts to OO concepts.

5.2 Missing Concepts

5.2.1 Not Interpreted

It was found that a Low Appearance Frequency (LAF) in the domain description does not necessarily result in missing interpretation of domain relevant concepts. For instance, scenario BS has class *Branch*, missing in all the 1st DDMs and, class *Statement* is only identified by 40% of students. In the original DD, *Branch* appears three times and *Statement* only appears once in the text. The results reveal that the importance of a concept to a domain may be independent of its frequency of occurrence in the text, questioning the findings of (Lecoeuche 2000). Yet, students may have missed the concept, or its importance, as a function of its prevalence in the text. The question remains of how to distinguish the important concepts from all the others.

5.2.2 Incorrect Interpretation

With the same frequency as class *Branch*, class *Transfer* is also missed out in all the 1stDDMs. In the scenario BS, Transfer appears as a method in 60% DDMs. Specifically, 40% of the students interpreted Transfer Money as a method of class *Customer* and, 20% of students considered *Transfer* as a method of class *Account*.

Unlike branch, transfer can be used in this context as a verb as well as a noun, which may give rise to confusion. Based upon the results collected from this experiment, one cause of incorrect interpretation might be related to activity nouns that can refer to behaviors of concrete things, as well as to the concrete things themselves, and also LAF in the text. This prompts the question, "Under what circumstances should such activity nouns should be interpreted as a domain relevant class?"

Another example of incorrect interpretation classes involved in generalization relationships. All students identified class *Account*, but most of them did not identify both classes *Savings Account* and *Current Account*, recognizing only one of them. Furthermore, 20% identified class *Account*, but had both specializations as attributes. From a linguistic perspective, this indicates that two compound nouns that share a common part may both have a generalization relationship with this shared part.

Nevertheless, the appearance frequency of a particular noun remains an important aspect in class identification. In particular, the results demonstrate that students do not have a problem in identifying the key concepts with Highest Appearance Frequency (HAF). In the scenario BS, the HAF concept is *Account* (appears seven times); in the scenario FM the HAF concept is *Scene* (appears seven times); and in the scenario EP the HAF is *Elevator* (appears eight times). However, at least in this experiment, it is possible that domain relevant concepts appear infrequently. Therefore, the question is how to capture important concepts with LAF. Tentatively, this study suggests the following aspects to be considered as indicators of important concepts which have LAF in the text.

- There appears to be a relationship between LAF nouns that are important domain concepts and the scenarios' HAF nouns. Looking at the BS scenario, *Branch* and *Transfer* both occur three times and were both denoted VD. However, the latter occurs in the same sentence as the HAF, *Account*, twice and the former only occurs once.
- For nouns associated with roles, and again looking at BS, where there is customer and employee, it can perhaps draw on the sentence structure "Subject-Verb-Object" for insight.

Juxtaposing "*Accounts are assigned to one or more customers*" and "*Bank employees may check any account...* ". However, only *Customer* is a qualified class since the verb *assign* implies a persistent relationship between the subject noun *Accounts* and object noun *Customers*. On the contrary, the verb *check* indicates a behavior of *Employees* to *Account*, rather than associating *Employees* and *Account*. Hence, *Employees* seem to be external users acting on the system. Students should be taught that special verbs (e.g., assign, belong to) or compound prepositions (e.g., is part of) can help to avoid this type of incorrect identification.

6 Conclusions

The results of this study indicate that there are four typical errors students make which form two categories: added extra concept and missing concept. Although these results need further investigation to study the role of student bias, and prior learning, they offer a view of the issue from a new angle and suggest possible improvements in teaching object oriented analysis using UML. Due to the crucial role of natural language in early stages of software development, students will benefit in analyzing problem domains if they are taught how to interpret natural language as OO concepts. For instance, how to deal with important nouns which refer to concrete things but appear infrequently in the text, and also how to find important concepts indicated by infrequent action nouns or roles.

It appears that generic rules offered in academic textbooks are inadequate to prevent mistakes by inexperienced analysts. While simplified syntax might appear to remove some of these difficulties, stakeholders may well be unhappy with the restrictions this imposes. It is unlikely that all real-life domain descriptions will ever be controlled natural language descriptions. Instead, students need to be prepared for the variety of natural language that customers inevitably produce; this is where new teaching methods involving peer assessment and role playing can be brought to bear.

In conclusion, it is suggested that merely teaching students how to use OO techniques superficially in domain analysis is not enough. Underpinning language usage is subtle, requiring deep understanding, to avoid crucial mistakes.

References

Booch, G. (1994). Object-Oriented Analysis and Design With Applications, Second Edition. Benjamin/Cummings, Redwood City, CA.

Brooks, J.F.P. (1987). No silver bullet – essence and accidents of software engineering. *IEEE Computer*, 20(4): 10–19.

Chen, P.P.-S. (1983). English sentence structure and entity relationship diagrams.. Information Sciences, 29: 127–149.

Cybulski, J.L. and Linden, T. (2000). Learning systems design with UML and patterns, IEEE Trans. Educ., 43(4), 372–376, Nov.

Delisle, S. Barker, K. Biskri, I. (1999). Object-Oriented Analysis: Getting Help from Robust Computational Linguistic Tools. 4th International Conference on Applications of Natural Language to Information Systems (OCG Schriftenreihe 129), Klagenfurt, Austria, pp. 167–171.

Elevator Problem, (2006). http://www.geocities.com/SiliconValley/Network/1582/uml-example. htm. Accessed 12 December.

Film Management, (2006). http://www.inf.unibz.it/~calvanese/teaching/03-ESSLLI/ESSLLI-03-slides-1.pdf, accessed 12 December.

Goldin, L. and Berry, D.M. (1997). AbstFinder, A Prototype Natural Language Text Abstraction Finder for Use in Requirements Elicitation. Automated Software Engineering, 4(4):375–412, October.

Hadjerrouit, S. (2005). Learner-centered web-based instruction in software engineering, IEEE Trans. Educ., 48(1): 99–104, February.

Halliday, M.A.K. (2003). On Language and Linguistics, edited by J.J. Webster, Continuum, London/New York.

Jackson, M.A. (1994). The role of architecture in requirements engineering. Proc. IEEE International Conference on Requirements Engineering, p. 241, IEEE Computer Society.

Jacobson, I. Christerson, M. Jonsson, P. Overgaard, G. (1992). Object-Oriented Software Engineering: A Use Case Driven Approach. Addison-Wesley/ACM, Reading, MA.

Juristo, N. and Moreno, A.M. (2000). How to Use Linguistic Instruments for Object-Oriented Analysis, IEEE Software, May/June, pp. 80–89.

Korthaus, A. (1998). Using UML for business object based systems modeling. In M. Schader, and A. Korthaus (eds), The Unified Modeling Language – Technical Aspects and Applications, pp. 795–825, Heidelberg, Germany.

Kuhn, T. Royer, L. Fuchs, N.E. Schroeder, M. (2006). Improving Text Mining with Controlled Natural Language: A Case Study for Protein Interactions. In Ulf Leser, Barbara Eckman, and Felix Naumann, editors, Proceedings of the 3rd International Workshop on Data Integration in the Life Sciences (DILS'06), Lecture Notes in Bioinformatics, Springer, 2006.

Lecoeuche, R. (2000). Finding comparatively important concepts between texts. Proc. 15th IEEE International Conference on Automated Software Engineering, 11–15 September, pp. 55–60.

Li, K. Dewar, R.G. Pooley, R.J. (2005). Towards Semi-automation in Requirements Elicitation: mapping natural language and object-oriented concepts, Proc. of the Doctoral Consortium at the 13th IEEE International Requirements Engineering Conference, Nancy A. Day (ed.), Paris, France, 29 August–2 September.

Loos, P. and Fettke, P. (2001). Towards an integration of business process modeling and object-oriented software development. Technical Report, Chemnitz University of Technology, Chemnitz, Germany.

Mentzas, G. (1999). Coupling object-oriented and workflow modeling in business and information reengineering. Information Knowledge and Systems Management, 1(1): 63–87.

Mich, L. (1996). NL-OOPs: From Natural Language to Object Oriented Using the Natural Language Processing System LOLITA. Natural Language Engineering, 2(2): 161–187.

Pooley, R.J. and Wilcox, P. (2004). Applying UML Advanced Application, Elsevier.

Rumbaugh, J. Blaha, M. Premerlani, W. Eddy, F. Lorensen, W. (1991). Object-Oriented Modeling and Design. Prentice Hall, Eaglewood Cliffs, NJ.

Svetinovic, D. Berry, D.M. Godfrey, M. (2005). Concept Identification in Object-Oriented Domain Analysis: Why Some Students Just Don't Get It, Proc. 13th IEEE International Conference on Requirements Engineering, Paris, France, 29 August–2 September.

Facilitating Experience and Re-experience: The Role of 'Virtualisation' in Information Systems Development Education

Sean Duignan[1] and Tony Hall[2]

[1] Galway-Mayo Institute of Technology, School of Science, sean.duignan@gmit.ie

[2] National University of Ireland Galway, Education Department, tony.hall@nuigalway.ie

Abstract This chapter describes the use of virtualisation technologies to facilitate teaching and learning on educational programmes in Information Systems (IS). Platform virtualisation is particularly beneficial to learning in this area as it allows for core system components to be visualised by the learner rather than abstracted from her, which, in the experience of the authors is a characteristic of a deeper learning and understanding in the context of learning about information systems. The authors contend that there may be a tendency to abstract *physical* system design considerations in IS education, largely because teaching/classroom/laboratory infrastructures make it difficult to accommodate meaningful teaching and learning in the area of physical system design. The result may lead to an unbalanced programme offering, skewed toward the application of formal analytical techniques and tools to develop the logical information system, and devoid of meaningful experience of the physical system designs used to host these information systems. The authors are motivated to address this imbalance through the application of platform virtualisation technologies in the support of IS learning. An orienting theoretical framework is presented that highlights the significance and relevance of constructionist thinking, sociality, collaborative learning, the notion of a 'spiral curriculum', and the development of 'habits of the mind' in learners (in particular; developing and asking questions of 'connection' and 'conjecture'). Experiences of teaching and learning with virtualisation technologies are presented, the future research objectives of the authors are presented and the case for virtualised appliances as a new type of electronic portfolio is posited.

1 Introduction

At its core, Information Systems Development (ISD) is about contextualised problem solving. Typically, this problem solving is an iterative process involving (problem) analysis and (solution) design. This approach to problem solving is well evidenced in most higher education programmes in Information Systems (IS),

C. Barry et al. (eds.), *Information Systems Development: Challenges in Practice, Theory, and Education, Vol.2*, doi: 10.1007/978-0-387-78578-3_19,
© Springer Science+Business Media, LLC 2009

where subjects such as *Systems Analysis & Design* and *Software Engineering* play a central role.

With regard to analysis for instance, *divide-and-conquer* and *functional decomposition* of the problem, along with the application of formalised rules and techniques, are core learning objectives, focusing on the development of analytical thinking skills in the learner. Design and engineering typically tend to focus on the *logical design* of the system (in terms of process and data modelling, system inputs and outputs, system interface design and error handling). On the other hand, *physical* system design tends to be simplified or abstracted at best, or is dismissed as not directly relevant to the subject matter in hand. Abstraction of non-intuitive concepts must be considered carefully though – how, when and where will learning of these concepts take place then? Frequently, the intention (or hope!) is that physical system design and related concepts will be 'picked up' elsewhere in the programme.   Depending on the nature and objectives of the educational programme, such an approach may be acceptable. We suspect in some instances however, that the 'avoidance' of the physical aspects of information systems design and development is not pedagogically motivated, but is instead due to the unstructured, poorly supported, potentially volatile and increasingly complex nature of the physical aspects of information systems. Ironically, the more complex the physical aspects of information systems become (e.g. distributed, scalable, secure, tiered architectures), the greater is the need for meaningful educational experiences for students of ISD, but the more difficult it becomes to facilitate and scaffold such learning experiences. This difficultly is primarily *logistical* in nature, rather than for example, intellectually prohibitive or pedagogically unsound.

Notwithstanding the merits of *analysis* and the development of analytical thinking skills in students, without an (at least) equal focus on contextually meaningful design and development activity, learning and the construction of new knowledge is more difficult to achieve. This has certainly been the case in other educational domains, where it has been shown that even university students have great difficulty in grasping non-intuitive abstract concepts (Furió & Guisasola 1998). As others have found (Resnick & Ocko 1991), our experience as education researchers and practitioners, is also that design activities have greater educational value when students are given the freedom to create something that is meaningful to themselves and/or to their community of peers. '*Greater educational value*' in the sense that such work tends to be of a higher quality, results in the construction of new knowledge or skills in the learner and is approached with a (perceived) higher level of motivation than for example, 'recipe-based' design/practical activity. It is for these reasons that the authors have looked to emergent *virtualisation technologies* and to their potential application in educational settings relating to information systems development. In particular, we feel that virtualisation has an important role to play in supporting teaching and learning of the sometimes-neglected aspects of *physical* system design.

Platform virtualisation software products allow for the creation and execution of multiple *virtual machines* (also referred to as *virtual appliances)*, running side-by-side, on the same physical machine. Each virtual machine has its own set of (virtual) hardware (CPU, RAM, DVD-ROM, Network Interface, etc.) upon which an operating system and application base can be loaded. Within each virtual machine, the operating system sees a consistent collection of hardware, independent of the actual physical hardware components. As these virtual machines are 'contained' within the virtualisation software, virtual machines can be created, destroyed, modified, interconnected and cloned without affecting software applications or hardware resources outside of the virtualisation container. This is particularly beneficial to *learning through experience* in ISD educational settings.

2 A Case for Platform Virtualisation in ISD Education

The concept of 'virtualisation' in computer science is not new; it is almost 50 years since Strachey argued the case for processor virtualisation through a term he coined as *time-sharing* (Strachey 1959). In its broadest sense, virtualisation refers to the *abstraction* of computer resources. The Java Virtual Machine (JVM) for instance, is a core component of the popular Java platform. The JVM is implemented in software, is available for most hardware platforms, and sits between the user/system developer and the actual hardware as an essential middleware component. The result is that the code developed, because it has been developed for the *virtual* machine, can be compiled and executed (without any changes) on any hardware platform that can implement a JVM. This 'write once/run anywhere' open portability feature is a compelling feature of Java. Indeed, this feature may contribute to the popularity of Java as a teaching language in IS programs in higher education. When teaching Java programming, the focus, rightly, is on learning the programming language – not on the peculiarities of the underlying operating system(s) and hardware platform(s).

The fact that the machine has been abstracted however is not so useful when the focus is on the teaching and learning of other aspects of the IS curriculum – the physical design of information systems for instance, and related concepts in the fields of data networking, operating systems and information system architectures. In such subject areas, the ability to interact with the *actual* machine, in order to visualise and configure its core components is a most useful aid to understanding and to learning. Not only does such interaction balance and enrich the direct learning experiences, it also has the potential to reinforce learning elsewhere – design decisions resulting from earlier analytical activity for instance, can be tested *in the wild*, and verified or rejected, as appropriate.

A difficulty posed in the classroom and laboratory however is that such activity can be quite 'destructive,' resource intensive, and time-consuming. Constructing an *n-tiered* architecture to physically host an information system, installing operating system and database platforms, partitioning fixed disks, implementing a cluster of machines, etc… are all somewhat destructive in their nature. In a college laboratory environment, a further mitigating factor is the (typical) requirement to leave the machine(s) in a specific and useable state for the next users of the laboratory. Furthermore, subject-specific dedicated hardware and laboratory space can be difficult to come by, particularly as there will be a limited use of such resources. It is for these reasons that physical system design may not always get the attention it requires on educational IS programmes.

Acknowledging the issues identified above with respect to the direct teaching and learning of the physical aspects of information systems design, and motivated by the desire to enrich learning on analytical-centric programmes (through verifiable substantiation or rejection of design decisions taken), we investigated the potential of hardware (platform) virtualisation as a possible useful and usable approach. Although not specifically designed or intended for an educational setting, we have found that platform/hardware virtualisation is particularly beneficial to this context nonetheless, and particularly to physical information system design activity where abstraction, as a concept, is not so useful, and where the provision of dedicated computer hardware and laboratory space is not feasible. In summary, we suggest that *learning by experiencing and doing*, in a reflective social setting is conducive to a deeper level of learning in students and that virtualisation technologies are highly accommodating of such learning and experiential activity.

3 Theoretical Framework

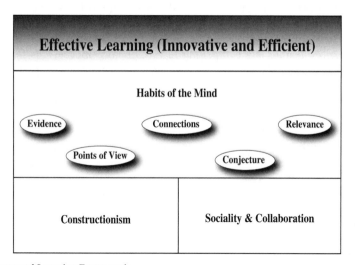

Fig. 1. Proposed Learning Framework

Fundamentally, the authors are interested in a meaningful application and use of Information and Communication Technologies (ICT) in the teaching and learning of Information Systems Development (ISD) in higher education. '*Meaningful application and use*' must support, and be supported by, established theories of learning and pedagogy. With regard to the research described in this chapter, the theoretical framework underpinning our work is influenced by a number of themes including constructivism and constructionism, activity theory and active learning, communities of practice, sociality, collaborative learning, diversity of learning context, the notion of a spiral curriculum and the development of 'habits of the mind' in learners. We suggest that aspects of these philosophies and practices can be combined to provide a framework for effective learning. Figure 1 below depicts what we theorise as an educational framework within which 'effective learning' in an ISD context can take place.

With respect to learning transfer (i.e. the degree to which a behaviour will be repeated in a new situation) we propose 'effective learning' to mean an appropriate balance between efficiency and innovation as per the *optimum adaptability corridor* proposed by (Schwartz 2005), in which learning is seen as a trajectory along the two axes of innovation and efficiency. Directly underpinning this type of learning is the ability for learners to ask questions; questions which develop 'habits of the mind' (Meier, 1995). The 'habits' aspect of this pedagogy is itself underpinned by the fundamentals of constructionism, social and collaborative learning environments. These influences are contextually considered and described in the sections that follow.

3.1 Social Constructionism

Piaget's theory of constructivism suggests that through a process of accommodation and assimilation, individuals construct new knowledge from their *experiences* (Piaget 1995). This assimilation occurs when the individual's experiences are aligned with their internal representation of the world. Similarly, the physicist and educator Andrea diSessa describes learning as a *re-experiencing* process (diSessa, 1986). In particular, he contends that learners do not learn a new concept when they are taught the definition. Rather, *experiencing* and *re-experiencing* the concept in different contexts is central to learning. Through such experiences, initial intuitions are gradually reorganised into more complete models. Indeed, this idea of learning through experience and re-experience is at the heart of Bruner's notion of a 'spiral curriculum': "*A curriculum as it develops should revisit these basic ideas repeatedly, building upon them until the student has grasped the full formal apparatus that goes with them*" (Bruner, 1960). Bruner further argues that a practical approach to teaching and learning should be taken that emphasises the importance of *structure*, rather than simply the mastery of facts and techniques: "*If earlier learning is to render later learning easier, it must do so by providing a general picture in terms of which the relations between things encountered earlier and later are made as clear as possible*" (Bruner, 1960). Based on our experiences, we suggest that virtualisation technologies present a practical and structured platform upon which pedagogically sound spiral curricula can be built for teaching and learning in Information Systems.

Based on constructivist learning theory, *constructionism* is an educational method principally associated with the work and writings of Seymour Papert, and in essence proposes that people learn most effectively through making things. Constructionism suggests that students will be more deeply involved in their learning if they are constructing something that others will see, critique and perhaps use. It is further suggested that learning happens "*especially felicitously in a context where the learner is consciously engaged in constructing a public entity, whether it's a sand castle on the beach or a theory of the universe*" (Harel and

Papert 1991). Through the process of construction, learners face complex issues that they are motivated to address because of the underlying motivation associated with the construction of the artefact. 'Meaningfulness' to the learners (experience) is critical then. As a case in point, Papert suggests that part of the trouble of learning mathematics at school for instance, is that it is not like mathematics in the real world (Papert 2005). If these theories of *knowledge construction through experience* hold true, we must ensure that education programmes in the field of information systems development (ISD) are fully embracing of them. Similar to Papert's observation with regard to mathematics at school, we contend that ISD in education needs to be like ISD in the real world and that virtualisation is an enabling technology in that regard.

Lev Vygotsky has been a major influence on both activity theory and modern constructivist thinking. A central contribution of Vygotsky is that all higher mental functions originate in the social environment, and that consequently socially meaningful activity is an important influence on human consciousness. Vygotsky furthers his argument through his concept of the '*Zone of Proximal Development*' – the distance between the actual developmental level in a learner as determined by independent problem-solving ability, and the level of potential development as determined through problem solving under adult guidance, or in collaboration with more capable peers (Vygotsky 1978). The zone of proximal development represents then, the amount of learning possible by a learner given the proper instructional conditions. We suggest that the nature of platform virtualisation makes it a suitable candidate for collaborative technology-based 'scaffolding' within information systems development education. Notably too, virtualisation technology is not only useful for disseminating knowledge, but more importantly, it exists as a support tool to help learners to *experience* and build knowledge. Finally, and as is the case with platform virtualisation, instructional settings that provide a diversity of context that can be controlled by the learner tend to increase motivation in her by increasing challenge, control and curiosity (Squire et al. 2004).

3.2 Collaborative Learning

With regard to the themes of collaborative learning and sociality, the authors perceive an emerging role for communities of practice (CoP) in ISD education. A CoP is a group of individuals who share a concern, a set of problems, or a passion about a topic and who deepen their knowledge and expertise in the area through regular interaction with each other (Wenger et al. 2002). In our experience, this is how our students frequently go about their business (of learning) anyway – on individual projects as well as on group projects. Furthermore, this type of social, co-operative learning is evident now within the world of virtualisation – we have found numerous instances of pre-configured virtual appliances available for download and immediate productive use (VMWare 2007, Mindtouch 2007, Microsoft 2006). We posit that such facilities along with their related *blogs* and *discussion forums* are the initial seeds of emerging electronic communities of practice that will bloom in time. Collaborative virtualisation is emerging in the real world because there is a need for it (VMWare 2007); these developments will be most beneficial to students of information systems design and development going forward. In particular, such developments will allow for the meaningful construction (and experience) of a physical information system upon which a logical system can be deployed.

3.3 Habits of the Mind

A progressivist and a learning theorist, Deborah Meier's philosophy of education encourages the development of five 'habits of the mind' in learners (Meier 1995, Kohn 2004). These habits are crucial for exercising judgment on complicated matters and involve raising questions about: *Evidence, Points of View, Connections, Conjecture,* and *Relevance.* It is habits such as these that lead us to ask good questions and seek solid answers, a principal goal of any educational programme? According to Kohn, it is not only the ability to raise and answer these questions that is important, but also the disposition to do so (Kohn 2004). None of these five habits stand separately; and the way in which we use these habits will vary with context (e.g. a mathematical proof, developing a computer-based information system, assessing a scientific hypothesis, critiquing a journal article). To what extent these habits have been developed (and used) by learners can be evidenced in the course of their work. The authors suggest that, within the realm of ISD education in particular, platform virtualisation is conducive to such habits of the mind – not only in seeking answers, but also in asking good questions.

4 Experiences of Teaching and Learning with Virtualisation

As the purpose of our study was to gain some qualitative insights in to student learning using virtualisation technologies in a specific (local) context, we employed a research methodology drawing on the tools and techniques of *action research* (Somekh 2006) and *design-based research* (Barab & Squire 2004, Baumgartner & Bell 2003); both of which have origins in the social and learning sciences. Accordingly, observation, field notes, semi-structured interviews and learner reflection were some of the research and recording methods used.

Working with two groups of students – third year and fourth year IS undergraduates (36 students in total), we employed *VMWare*, a platform virtualisation software product, as a core tool in the teaching of '*Operating Systems*' and '*E-Commerce Infrastructure Technologies*' to these students. Like similar virtualisation products, the *VMWare workstation* product allows multiple virtual machines to run in isolation, side-by-side, on the same physical machine. Each virtual machine has its own set of virtual hardware (CPU, RAM, DVD-ROM, Network Interface, etc.) upon which an operating system (various) and applications are loaded. Within each virtual machine, the operating system sees a consistent collection of hardware, independent of the actual physical hardware components.

4.1 Configuration and Systems Management Considerations

At a purely operational/logistical level, the immediate benefits of using this approach are flexibility and mobility, i.e. virtual machines can be created anywhere – the only requirement is that the physical host machine has the 'container' software installed, i.e. *VMWare* or a similar virtualisation solution. In our situation, we were able to run (and continue to do so) complex configuration laboratories without worrying about affecting the standard configuration of the physical machine that would be required later by other laboratory users. Virtual devices are also easily cloned and copied across physical hosts and can be stored centrally for reuse over and over again. An added bonus is the generous educational licensing agreements that appear to prevail presently. Virtual machine *players* in general tend to be free, and in many cases licensing of the virtual machine *maker* software is free for validated academic use (subject to registration etc.) or is available for purchase at a substantially discounted price. Furthermore, virtual machines created in one virtualisation environment tend to be useable in other virtualised environments (another benefit of hardware virtualisation!).

4.2 Classroom Experiences

With regard to the teaching of *Operating Systems*, elementary tasks such as allowing students access to and modification of the machines Basic Input Output System (BIOS), something previously approached with extreme caution, if at all, can now be fully facilitated and actively encouraged. Additionally, tasks such as fixed disk partitioning and formatting, which were typically taught 'in theory,' and at best cautiously demonstrated in a controlled environment, can also be actively facilitated and encouraged. Full and customised installations of popular commercial and open source operating systems have been tried first hand by students. Aspects of system security and maintenance, likewise approached with a degree of caution in the past, can now be fully embraced. We suspect that the students have learned from these experiences. Furthermore, we have observed a significant increase in students 'hands-on' skills and an emerging confidence in their practical ability with respect to some of the complex 'internal' aspects of operating system configuration. Many students have noted that, as the machines they are working on are virtual machines, at worst they will only 'mess up' the virtual environment within which they are working. The actual physical machine is never affected – the *VMWare* software presents the virtual machine(s) in a secure sandbox. We feel that this feature, a safety net of sorts, is key in getting students to actively engage with the subject area, to participate and to experiment, and ultimately to experience. Importantly too, as virtual machines in *VMWare* are stored as files on the physical host machine, it is very easy to migrate/deploy previously configured virtual machines to another physical host (simply copy the appropriate files to the new location!).

In addition to the teaching and supervised laboratory activity the students were assigned a group-based project (2–3 students per group) involving the construction, configuration and interoperation of a series of virtual machines to a defined specification and with the aim of providing a suitable physical platform for an enterprise information system. Within the various groups, members agreed on and then assumed responsibility for specific tasks, worked on them independently, and saved their 'work-in-progress' to shared locations for others to work on later. The authors suggest that such activity is a tangible example of computer-supported collaborative learning in practice. Encouragingly also, student engagement with the subject area (and the lecturer) increased – more time on task was observed in the lab, more email activity was exchanged between lecturer and students, and more questions were asked, particularly ones that could be categorised as questions of *connections* (how is this related to that?) and *conjecture* (how might things be otherwise? what if...?) within Meier's 'habits' framework referred to earlier.

The virtual machine paradigm and associated technology has also been used by the authors for teaching and learning in the subject area of *E-commerce Infrastructure Technologies*. This is a final year (year 4) subject that aims to foster an understanding of advanced technical infrastructures and their impact on information system performance including scalability, reliability, and security. The ability to build multiple virtual machines, with different operating systems and installed application base, has significantly helped in more accurately demonstrating, experiencing and understanding Internet-based enterprise architectures from *client-server* to *n-tier architectures* for distributed applications, as well as interoperability infrastructures incorporating *XML*, *SOAP* and *web services*. In the past, such architectures have typically been referred to in the abstract, as part of classroom lecture material, rather than in the actual, as part of laboratories utilising virtualisation technologies. Acknowledging diSessa's insight with respect to the importance of *experiencing* and *re-experiencing* a concept in different contexts (rather than being provided with a mere definition) (diSessa, 1986), we are excited by this contextual shift in our programmes from instructionist learning based in parts on memorisation, to a learning based on constructionist principles. In addition, we have found it most useful that many pre-configured virtual machines have already been 'built' and are available for download free of charge. The *VMWare* Web site for instance, includes a 'Virtual Appliance Marketplace' where many purpose-built virtual machines can be freely downloaded for use and modification as appropriate (VMWare 2007). Others in the virtualisation space provide similar offerings. This has been particularly useful to aspects of our curriculum that deal with the evaluation and comparison of competing architectures. Referring to Meier's 'habits of the mind' framework again, the existence of pre-configured virtual appliances facilitates a timely answering (or attempt at answering!) contextually relevant questions in this subject area (e.g. *what if....?* scenarios are easily *experienced, tested* and *verified*). Furthermore, the ability to introduce high-level 'macro' concepts (e.g. the concept of a file system) in the early stages of a module (and build meaningful artefacts using this concept), and then to revisit the concept much later in the module, at a more granular or 'micro' level (e.g. file system security/performance considerations) whilst still keeping and using the artefacts previously built, introduces a continuity of thinking and learning that is very much in the vein of Bruner's notion of a 'spiral curriculum' (Bruner, 1960).

4.3 Student Feedback/Experiences

Feedback received from students on their experiences with virtualisation has been positive. In addition to the sense of security that appears to prevail (*"It's just a virtual machine, and its my virtual machine to work on as I wish"*), it has also been noted by students that the ability to *visualise* physical aspects of a system, aspects frequently abstracted in the past, has helped their understanding significantly. We were surprised for instance that in a class of almost 20 fourth year students, all of whom had previously studied elementary system architectures and operating system principles, and now taking an advanced course in e-commerce system infrastructures, that only one of them had ever actually installed and configured an operating system. It might be for this reason that students appear to enjoy 'trying out for themselves' destructive tasks for instance; almost as if to verify that what they have been alerted to as dangerous, is in fact dangerous (deleting disk partitions, altering system BIOS settings, etc.). As teachers we acknowledge the importance of visualisation in learning (particularly in learning abstract concepts), in this instance facilitated through virtualisation. A number of students have investigated virtualisation and virtualised appliances (virtual devices) beyond the scope and requirements of their college courses. Some have investigated using virtualisation to implement a required platform for a favoured legacy computer game, not supported by their current operating environment. Others are investigating the use of virtualisation to provide a 'known good' operating platform for their development work (frequently the actual operating environment in a college laboratory is missing essential components through accidental or intentional deletion). These activities have become popular since students learned how to mobilise and migrate virtual devices (the virtual device is simply stored as a (sometimes quite large!) file on the physical host). Questions with regard to software licensing on virtual devices, the use of virtualisation for information hiding, virtual software-testing frameworks, and virtual device cloning have been raised by students and discussed in class, led largely by the student population, even though, according to the curriculum, such material is not 'examinable.' It is activities such as these that prompt the authors to suggest that virtualisation software in particular represents a new revolution in educational technology, akin to that imagined for computer= supported learning environments that would "…. [S]ee students learning in modes that provide them wide flexibility and freedom for creativity in understanding tasks they feel are personally meaningful, while at the same time learning important subject matter" (diSessa 1999).

5 Future Work (Virtual Device as Electronic Portfolio?)

The authors intend to extend their use of virtualisation technologies further in their teaching activity in future academic years, and to extend their research and analysis of this practice with a view to developing a qualitative understanding of the potential for virtualisation in scaffolding student learning of abstract concepts in information systems development and related disciplines. We are particularly interested in deepening our understanding of what it means to learn by experience and re-experience and the possible role that virtualisation has to play in that regard. We are also interested in researching the role, if any, that virtual appliances may have to play as electronic portfolio solutions for students of IS/Computing. Virtual appliance/device, as electronic portfolio, in our opinion has potential. This potential is briefly discussed here and, going forward, it is intended to further research the issues raised.

An electronic portfolio is a collection of electronic learning evidence or artefacts, assembled and managed by a user, usually in an online environment. The electronic nature allows for dynamic management of the portfolio in real time, and depending on the software environment, different 'views' to different audiences (peers, lecturers, potential employers, the general public, etc.) may be permitted thus increasing the useable purposes of the portfolio. An e-portfolio can also serve as a learning record that provides actual evidence of achievement. Typical ePortfolio solutions, e.g. *ePortfolio.org* (CTDLC 2007) are provided through customisable web-portals that allow portfolio 'owners' to record personal and career details and to store supporting digital evidence, whilst also supporting various views of the portfolio depending on viewer 'status.' In our opinion, such portfolios are not unlike virtual appliances – both technologies have the potential to have a measurable impact on educational culture and practice, both technologies are student centred and emphasise a student's autonomy over the technology, both technologies promote constructionist educational philosophies. We wonder then to what extent can an appropriately configured virtual appliance serve as an assessable portfolio of work within the educational domain of information systems? We envisage executable virtual devices being submitted by students, which implement appropriate physical and logical infrastructures upon which their, e.g. software projects execute. The need for compatible environments between submitter and assessor is removed, and the rich canvas that is a virtual appliance is there to be exploited to its fullest. Furthermore, with ever-increasing storage and network bandwidth capacity, storing and sharing virtual appliances in an online environment is entirely possible.

Portfolios are particularly useful when the assessment focus is on the achievement and maintenance of competencies – specifically where evaluation involves measuring progress against a competency threshold, rather than measuring performance relative to other people. This type of assessment is becoming increasingly popular within information systems and related disciplines – do virtual appliances, embodied as portfolio 'containers' have an enabling role to play? The portfolio centric pedagogy encourages important activities such as reflection, supposition, establishment of connections, reuse, re-examination and the development of quality personal practices to emerge through a process of construction, collaboration and feedback (Lynch and Purnawarman 2004).

6 Concluding Comments

In 'Computers, Networks and Education,' Kay intuitively notes that a concept of 'knowledge ownership' exists in modern cultures, and that educators need to realise that learners have a psychological need for a personal franchise in the culture's knowledge base (Kay 1991). The author goes on to cite the potential for technology to facilitate learning through its great potential for interactivity, multimedia capabilities, simulation capabilities, universal library capabilities and the ability to present information from many perspectives – *"you don't understand anything, until you understand it in more than one way"* (Kay 1991). In our opinion, virtualisation technology builds on these characteristics further by providing a learner-centred virtual repository for the construction and showcasing of knowledge and learning; a deeper learning formed through experience and re-experience.

References

Barab, S. & Squire, K. (2004) Design-Based Research: Putting a Stake in the Ground. Journal of the Learning Sciences, 13(1), 1–14.

Baumgartner, E. & Bell, P. (2003) Design-Based Research: An Emerging Paradigm for Educational Enquiry. Educational Researcher, 32, 5– 8.

Bruner, J. S. (1960) The Process of Education. Cambridge, MA, Harvard University Press.

Ctdlc (2007) Connecticut Distance Learning Consortium - ePortfolio.org.

Disessa, A. (1986) Artificial Worlds and Real Experience. Instructional Science, 14, 207– 227.

Disessa, A. A. (1999) How Should Students Learn? Journal of Computer Documentation, 23, 14–18.

Furió, C. & Guisasola, J. (1998) Difficulties in learning the concept of electric field. Science Education, 82, 511–526.

Harel, I. & Papert, S. (1991) Constructionism. New Jersey, Ablex Publishing.

Kay, A. (1991) Computers, Networks & Education. Scientific American, Sept 1991.

Kohn, A. (2004) What Does it Mean to be Well Educated?, Boston, Beacon Press.

Lynch, L. L. & Purnawarman, P. (2004) Electronic Portfolio Assessments: Are They Supporting Teacher Education? Tech Trends, 48, 50–57.

Meier, D. W. (1995) The Power of Their Ideas: Lessons for America from a Small School in Harlem. Boston, Beacon Press.

Microsoft (2006) Virtual Hard Disk (VHD): www.microsoft.com/vhd.

Mindtouch (2007) Free Virtual Appliance Download: www.mindtouch.com/deki

Papert, S. (2005) Constructionism vs. Instructionism. Text of speech delivered by Seymour Papert to conference of educators, Japan, mid-1980s.

Piaget, J. (1995) The Child's Construction of Reality. London, Routledge.

Resnick, M. & OCKO, S. (1991) LEGO/Logo: Learning Through and About Design. Epistemology and Learning Memo No. 8, MIT Media Laboratory.

Schwartz, D. L., BRANSFORD, J. D. & SEARS, D E. (2005) Efficiency and innovation in transfer: Transfer of Learning from a modern multidisciplinary perspective. J. Mestre (Ed). Greenwich, CT, Information Age Publishing, pp. 1–51.

Somekh, B. (2006) Action Research: A Methodology for Change and Development. Maidenhead/New York, Open University Press.

Squire, K., Barnett, M., Grant, J. M. & Higginbotham, T. (2004) Electromagnetism supercharged!: learning physics with digital simulation games. Proceedings of the 6th International Conference on Learning Sciences, Santa Monica, CA.

Strachey, C. (1959) Time Sharing in Large Fast Computers. Proceedings of the International Conference on Information Processing, UNESCO, Paris.

Vmware (2007) Virtual Appliance Marketplace: http://www.vmware.com

Wenger, E., Mcdermott, R. & Snyder, W. M. (2002) Cultivating Communities of Practice. Boston, Harvard Business School Press.

The Concept Map-Based Knowledge Assessment System with Reduction of Task Difficulty

Alla Anohina, Egons Lavendelis and Janis Grundspenkis

Department of Systems Theory and Design, Riga Technical University, Latvia
{alla.anohina@cs.rtu.lv, egons.lavendelis@cs.rtu.lv, janis.grundspenkis@cs.rtu.lv}

Abstract   The chapter presents the concept map-based knowledge assessment system which provides the learner a possibility to change the degree of task difficulty by asking the system to insert additional concepts in the offered structure of the concept map. The scoring systems both for learners who solve the original task and who use reduction of the degree of task difficulty are described in details. The difficulty reduction mechanism is explained. Evaluation results of the developed system in four learning courses are discussed.

1 Introduction

Knowledge assessment is one of the significant components of the teaching and learning process which simultaneously carries out several functions: provides information on learning progress both to the teacher and the learner, allows the learner to master and to improve certain skills in parallel to knowledge control, habituates the learner to study regularly, makes the learner responsible for his/her education, allows to make corrections in the learning process. One of the common didactic principles postulates, that it is necessary to make knowledge control and assessment systematically in all stages of the learning process (Albrehta 2001). The advantages of systematic assessment are twofold. The learner can keep track of his/her progress and receive help timely in order to correct misconceptions and fill gaps in his/her knowledge. The teacher can analyze suitability and quality of learning content and teaching methods, and change them timely in order to promote the more effective and qualitative learning process. However, knowledge assessment in the traditional learning process demands additional time and workload from the teacher as it is necessary to prepare tasks or questions, to organize assessment activities, to check and to analyze learners' works and to deliver feedback. This is a reason why computer-based solutions for knowledge assessment have been investigated already for a long time. Computer-assisted knowledge

C. Barry et al. (eds.), *Information Systems Development: Challenges in Practice, Theory, and Education, Vol.2*, doi: 10.1007/978-0-387-78578-3_20,
© Springer Science+Business Media, LLC 2009

assessment systems provides the following advantages (Lambert 2004; Mogey and Watt 1996; Oliver 2000): they are less subjective than a human-teacher, allow to make knowledge control for large number of learners efficiently, do not demand exhausting work from the teacher related with checking of learners' works, allow to provide a fast feedback both to the teacher and to learners, provide greater flexibility regarding time and place of knowledge assessment and potential for more frequent knowledge control.

Computer-assisted assessment systems are classified in systems of objective testing and systems of subjective testing (Seale 2002). Systems of objective testing offer a learner a set of questions, which answers are pre-defined. Systems of subjective testing can assess learners' submitted works for content, style, originality. In spite of the fact that both kinds of systems have some definite advantages, important drawbacks have been identified as a result of the analysis. Firstly, objective testing does not allow to offer original answers and thus there are some restrictions on learner's knowledge and skills which can be assessed. According to (Mogey et al. 1996; Bull 2003), systems based on objective tests can assess no more than first four levels in the well-known Bloom's taxonomy (Bloom 1956), which includes three levels of lower-order skills (Knowledge, Comprehension and Application), and three levels of higher order skills (Analysis, Synthesis and Evaluation). Secondly, objective testing assesses only factual, often fragmentary knowledge instead of the learner's understanding of interrelations and significance of knowledge units within the learning course. Thus, after assessment it is difficult to determine, whether the learner has a certain structure of knowledge. Systems of subjective testing typically are based on essays or free-text responses and thus allow the learner to offer original answers and judgments, so they can assess higher order skills. Systems of such kind use methods of artificial intelligence, especially natural language processing that simultaneously causes drawbacks of these systems: strong dependence on the learning course and natural language, as well as complex structure and functional mechanisms. Moreover, usage of essays and free-text responses for systematic knowledge assessment is a questionable thing due to high cognitive load for learners.

The performed analysis allows to conclude that there is a necessity for knowledge assessment systems which would allow to assess higher order skills and learners' understanding of structure of knowledge within the learning course, would not be dependent on the learning course and natural language, would provide less complex structure and functional mechanisms, could be used for systematic knowledge assessment. The chapter offers to use concept maps as a basis for such a system.

The remainder of the chapter is organized as follows. Section 2 briefly describes concept maps. The developed knowledge assessment system is presented in section 3. Section 4 gives attention to the results of experimental evaluation of the developed system in four different learning courses and discusses learners' answers to the offered questionnaire. The last section presents conclusions.

2 Concept Maps as a Knowledge Assessment Tool

Concept maps were developed by Novak in 70th of the last century. According to (Cañas 2003) concept maps can foster the learning of well-integrated structural knowledge as opposed to the memorization of fragmentary, unintegrated facts and allow to externalize and make explicit the conceptual knowledge (both correct and erroneous) that learners have in a problem domain. For knowledge assessment concept maps are usable in any stage of the learning course: at the beginning of teaching in order to determine knowledge which the learner already has, during the teaching to identify changes in learner's knowledge, and at the end of the learning course in order to determine the achieved knowledge level. Regular usage of concept maps in the learning course provides valuable information both to the learner and to the teacher. The learner can make sure that the learning material and relationships between studied concepts are correctly understood, and reveal problems timely. The teacher can keep track of learners' understanding of the learning material and their misconceptions, and to make corrections when they are necessary.

A concept map is represented as a graph (Fig. 1) with labeled nodes that correspond to concepts in a domain and with arcs that indicate relationships between pairs of concepts. Arcs can be directed or undirected and with or without linking phrases on them. A linking phrase specifies the kind of the relationship between concepts. Semantic units in concept maps are propositions stated by concept-link-concept triples (Cañas 2003). They are meaningful statements about some object or event in the domain. Concept maps can display both hierarchical and non-hierarchical relationships. The former are referred as segments which represent a particular hierarchical group of concepts. The latter are displayed by cross-links between concepts in different segments. According to (Cañas 2003) in practice concepts are arranged in a semi-hierarchical manner, not in a strict hierarchy.

Concept maps allow to offer tasks of various degrees of difficulty. These tasks vary in a range from "fill-in tasks" to "construct-a-map tasks" (Ruiz-Primo 2004). In "fill-in tasks" learners are provided with a blank structure of a concept map and lists of concepts and/or linking phrases which they should insert into the structure. "Construct-a-map tasks" allow the learner to choose which concepts and how many of them should be included and how they will be related in their concept maps. The variety of tasks and their scoring systems is described in (Ruiz-Primo 2004).

Thus, the following conclusions can be made about usage of concept maps in knowledge assessment. Concept maps allow to assess knowledge corresponding to higher levels of Bloom's taxonomy (Bloom 1956), especially when learners need to identify the most suitable linking phrases or most prominent and most useful cross-links in a concept map (Novak and Cañas 2006). Concept maps allow to assess learners' understanding of knowledge structure within the learning course, instead of the degree of memorization of separate facts (Cañas 2003). Concept maps are universal enough because a certain set of concepts and relationships among them are an integral part of the majority of learning courses. Concept maps allow to develop computer-assisted knowledge assessment systems which are based on manipulation of graphical objects. In this case natural language processing that provides less complex structure and functional mechanisms of the system, as well as its independence from natural language, is not necessary. Concept maps can be used in any stage of the learning course and for any knowledge assessment form, inter alia for systematic knowledge assessment. So, concept maps are a good alternative for objective and subjective testing systems.

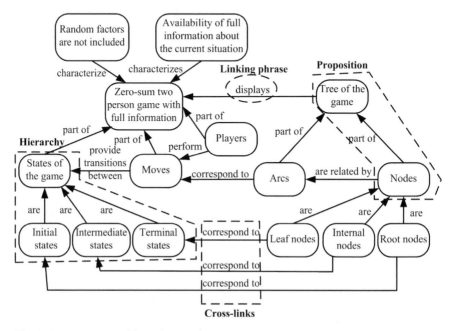

Fig. 1. A concept map and its major constituent parts

A number of commercial and non-commercial concept map-based graphical software packages and tools already exist, for example, AXON Idea Processor (web.singnet.com.sg/~axon2000/), Inspiration (www.inspiration.com), IHMC CmapTools (cmap.ihmc.us), which provide such functions as concept map construction, navigation and sharing, and can be used as a useful learning tool. However, these products do not assess created concept maps. Only several systems provide assessment of concept map-based tasks (Gouli et al. 2004; Chang et al. 2001; Tsai et al. 2001). In spite of the fact that the mentioned systems support knowledge assessment, they consider assessment as a discrete event, and thus ignore the necessity for systematic knowledge assessment. The proposed system solves this problem. Moreover, the system provides a possibility to vary the degree of task difficulty and, as a consequence, enables more accurate assessment of the knowledge level.

3 The Developed System

The developed system supports systematic knowledge assessment allowing the teacher to assess the learners' knowledge level at each stage of the learning course by using concept maps. It is based on assumption that the teacher divides the learning course into several stages. A stage can be any logical part of the learning course chosen by the teacher, for example, a topic or a chapter. At the end of each stage learners receive a concept map-based task for knowledge assessment.

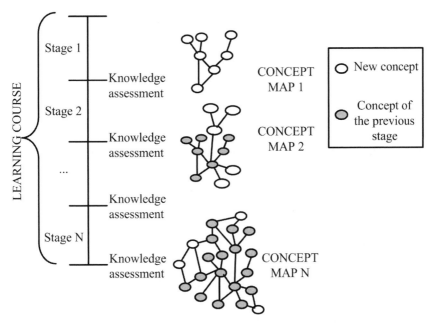

Fig. 2. The usage of concept maps for systematic knowledge assessment

A method for concept map construction by the teacher has been developed and is described in (Anohina and Grundspenkis 2007). Concepts which are taught in the initial stage of the learning course and relationships among them are included into the first concept map. At the next stage, learners acquire new concepts and the teacher adds them to the concept map of the initial stage but does not change relationships among concepts that already are in the concept map. It means that a concept map of each stage is nothing else than an extension of the previous one. The concept map of the last stage includes all concepts and all relationships among them. Figure 2 illustrates the usage of concept maps for systematic knowledge assessment.

As already mentioned there are several types of concept map-based tasks that can be used for knowledge assessment. In our approach only one of them is provided: a filling of a teacher-prepared concept map structure by a given list of concepts.

Linking phrases are not used. Two types of relationships are included: important conceptual relationships and less important conceptual relationships (Anohina et al. 2006). Important conceptual relationships are those which the teacher considers as important knowledge in the learning course. Less important conceptual relationships specify desirable knowledge.

It is necessary to discuss appearance of a concept map structure in different assessment stages. At the first stage only initial concepts pre-defined by the teacher are already inserted in the concept map structure. At all other stages the concept map structure is extended by new concepts and relationships and contains concepts pre-defined by the teacher, as well as concepts which the learner has correctly inserted in previous stages or the system has inserted performing reduction of task difficulty.

3.1 Scoring System

In the proposed system a learner's concept map is compared with a teacher's concept map. An algorithm for concept map comparison has been developed. The algorithm is sensitive to the arrangement and coherence of concepts. It is based on assumption that learner's understanding of the presence of the relationship between two concepts has the primary value, while the type of the relationship and places of concepts within the structure of a concept map are secondary things. The algorithm is capable to recognize five patterns of learner's solutions which are described in details in (Anohina and Grundspenkis 2006). Briefly they can be characterized as follows:

Pattern 1: The learner has related concepts exactly as the teacher. In this case the learner receives 5 points regarding every important relationship and 2 points regarding every less important relationship.

Pattern 2: The learner has defined a relationship which does not exist in the teacher's concept map. The learner receives no points in this case.

Pattern 3: The learner has defined a relationship which exists in the teacher's concept map. The type of the relationship is correct, but at least one of the concepts is placed in an incorrect place. The learner receives 80% from maximum score for the correct relationship.

Pattern 4: The learner has defined a relationship which exists in the teacher's map, the type of the relationship is wrong, and at least one of the concepts is placed in an incorrect place. The score received by the learner is 50% from maximum score for the correct relationship.

Pattern 5: A concept is placed in a wrong place, but its place is not important. The learner receives maximum score for the corresponding relationship.

So, taking into account the described patterns, the learner's concept map is evaluated using the following equation:

$$P = \sum_{i=1}^{n} p_i {}^* c_i \qquad (1)$$

where P- learner's score after the completion of the task; p_i- maximal score according to the type of ith relationship (5 points for each important relationship and 2 for less important relationship); c_i-coefficient which corresponds to the degree of ith relationship's correctness (based on the previously described patterns, for example, for pattern 3 the value of c_i is 0.8); n number of relationships in the concept map structure.

3.2 Difficulty Reduction

During the task performance the learner can ask to reduce the degree of task difficulty. This possibility allows the learner to find a task which is most suitable for his/her knowledge level and therefore to assess a knowledge level of a particular learner more accurately. Difficulty reduction consists of two steps. Firstly, the analysis of the learner's concept map is done and incorrectly inserted concepts are removed from the concept map structure and added to a general list of concepts. Concepts are considered as incorrectly inserted if they have no correct relationships or they are in the incorrect place and the place is important. Correct relationships of removed concepts are saved and shown to the learner in explanatory hints when he/she moves cursor on the concept. Secondly, after removing incorrectly inserted concepts the learner chooses the number of concepts which he/she wishes the system would insert into the concept map structure. Concept insertion is no more possible in three cases. First, the learner has completed the task. Second, the remaining list of concepts to be inserted contains only the minimal number of concepts (pre-defined by the teacher) that the learner should insert by him/herself. Third, by inserting the next concept the learner would loose the possibility to complete the task successfully (to receive 50% of the maximal possible score).

In case of difficulty reduction the system fills free nodes (nodes without labels of concept names) of the concept map structure according to their degrees. The degree of the node is the number of incident arcs (incoming and outgoing) for this node (Harary 1969). Nodes with average degrees are inserted first of all. An average degree is chosen because concepts with the smallest degree give very little help to the learner, but concepts with the highest degree are key ones which the learner must know. To fill blanks in the concept map structure, nodes are sorted on the basis of their degrees. A concept which corresponds to the node which has an average index in the sorted list is inserted and the process repeats. The algorithm for concept insertion is shown in Fig. 3.

3.3 Scoring System for Learners Who Used Difficulty Reduction

Coming back to the evaluation of the learner's concept map it is necessary to note that the Eq. 1 is used in case when the learner has filled a concept map structure by himself/herself without asking to reduce the degree of task difficulty. However,

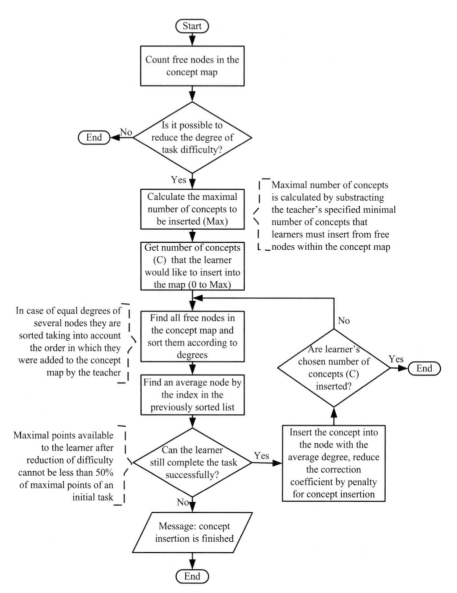

Fig. 3. An algorithm for concepts insertion into the structure of the concept map in case of reduction of the degree of task difficulty

mechanisms are needed to compare those learners' results that completed an original task and those who used reduction of the degree of task difficulty. A correction mechanism which takes into account two types of help that the learner receives during the reduction of task difficulty has been developed. Firstly, concepts inserted by the system facilitate the further solving of the task. Secondly, each time when the learner asks to reduce the degree of task difficulty his/her solution is checked and incorrectly inserted concepts are removed from the concept map structure. In fact, the learner receives additional information that can help him/her to complete the task. Therefore, a correction coefficient which depends on the number of reduction times and the number of concepts inserted by the system has been introduced. Additionally the learner does not receive points for relationships between concepts which are pre-defined by the teacher or inserted by the system.

An initial value of the correction coefficient is 1 because if the learner has not reduced the degree of task difficulty, it is not necessary to change his/her result. In case of difficulty reduction this coefficient should be smaller and is calculated using the following equation:

$$k = 1 - f(s) - g(j,m), \qquad (2)$$

where k is the correction coefficient; s is the number of difficulty reduction times; j is the number of concepts inserted by the system and m the total number of concepts in the structure of a concept map.

Function $f(s)$ is linear because for each time when the learner checks his/her solution the punishment should be the same. Function $g(j, m)$, in its turn, is nonlinear and depends on the number of inserted concepts. It is convex because punishment for the first time when the learner asks to reduce the degree of task difficulty should be less than for each next time. It is assumed that such policy can stimulate the learner to complete the task by him/herself and to use difficulty reduction as seldom as possible. So, the equation for the correction coefficient is acquired by substituting functions $f(s)$ and $g(j, m)$ with the appropriate expressions. In the developed knowledge assessment system the following equation is used:

$$k = 1 - c_s * s - \frac{\sum_{i=1}^{j}(a + \Delta * \frac{(i-1)}{m})}{m} \qquad (3)$$

where c_s – penalty for each difficulty reduction time; s – number of difficulty reduction times; a – penalty for the first insertion of concepts by the system; j – total number of concepts inserted by the system; m – total number of concepts in the concept map; Δ – penalty increase for each concept insertion.

Thus the learner's concept map is evaluated by using an equation acquired by combining Eqs. 1 and 3:

$$P = (\sum_{i=1}^{n} p_i * c_i) * (1 - c_s * s - \frac{\sum_{i=1}^{j}(a + \Delta * \frac{(i-1)}{m})}{m}) \qquad (4)$$

The following values of the coefficients were obtained by examining concept maps of different courses: $c_s = 0.01$, $a = 0.07$ and $\Delta = 1.5$. This choice of coefficients for implementation purposes is based on the assumption that the learner is allowed to ask the system to insert approximately 35% of all concepts and still be able to complete the task successfully in case he/she inserts all other concepts in correct places.

3.4 Feedback

After the completion of the task the learner receives feedback which consists of: maximal score that the learner could receive by completely correctly filling the concept map structure of the current stage; actual score received by the learner; number of points additionally acquired by him/her comparing with the previous stage; the learner's concept map with labels representing his/her received points for every relationship. The labels are in form of "x of y" where x stands for points acquired by the learner and y for maximal possible points for this relationship. Relationships are also colored in different tones according to their correctness.

Feedback for the teacher is the following: points acquired by learners in each stage; learners' concept maps with errors marked in red; statistical information about learners' concept maps. Statistical information contains: list of relationships that learners typically define in their concept maps, but which do not exist in the teacher's concept map; list of relationships that are in the teacher's map but rarely appear in learners' concept maps; list of relationships which are important in the teacher's concept map, but learners define them as less important relationships.

4 Evaluation Results of the Developed System

The developed system was evaluated in four learning courses at Riga Technical University and Vidzeme University College in Latvia. As many as 44 students were involved in evaluation process, 35 of them filled a questionnaire after using the system. The goal of the questionnaire was to acquire students' opinion on three main topics: chosen approach to knowledge assessment, usage and usefulness of task difficulty reduction, and work with the system.

Questions asked in the first topic showed that 86% of learners liked to use concept maps for knowledge assessment, 8% of students did not like this and 6% were indifferent (Fig. 4). Seventy-four percent of the learners also admitted that concept map filling helped them to understand the learning course and 26% of students had opposite opinion (Fig. 5).

Figure 6 illustrates that it was difficult for students to fill-in the concept map structure (60% of students answered that is was difficult and ≈11% that it was very difficult). However, only one third of students (10 learners) used the difficulty reduction. Other students mentioned in their answers that they did not want to reduce their results. However, 80% of the learners who used difficulty reduction rated it as useful because it facilitated the further performance of the task (Fig. 7).

The most important part of the third topic was feedback evaluation. Feedback provided by the system was admitted as useful and showing learners' misunderstandings (77% of learners). The form of feedback representation (received points for each relationship) was also rated as demonstrative: 54% of learners rated it as demonstrative and 40% as partly demonstrative.

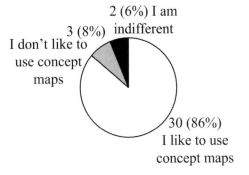

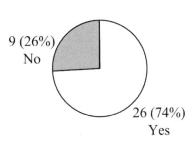

Fig. 4. Students' answers on the question "Do you like to use concept maps for knowledge assessment?"

Fig. 5. Students' answers on the question "Whether the concept maps helped you to understand the learning course?"

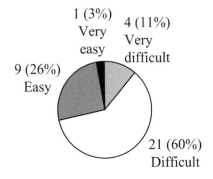

Fig. 6. Students' answers on the question "Was it difficult for you to fill concept maps?"

Fig. 7. Students' answers on the question "Whether the reduction of the degree of task difficulty facilitated the solving of the task?"

5 Conclusions

This chapter describes the concept map-based knowledge assessment system in which learners can reduce the degree of task difficulty. This possibility allows to assess a knowledge level of a particular learner more accurately.

The developed system has three discriminative features in comparison with other concept map based and computer-assisted assessment systems. First, the system supports systematic knowledge assessment and allows the teacher to extend the initially created concept map for the new stage of assessment. The second unique feature is an algorithm that compares the teacher's and learner's concept maps and is sensitive to the arrangement and coherence of concepts. The third feature is an opportunity to reduce the degree of task difficulty. Moreover, the developed system are a Web-based application that allows to use it from any remote location with Internet connection, as well as it provides the convenient and clear graphical user interface both for learners and teachers.

The system has been evaluated in four learning courses. Experiments have shown the effectiveness of the developed system for systematic assessment of learners' knowledge. The learners who used difficulty reduction rated it as a useful feature of the system.

Acknowledgments   This work has been partly supported by the European Social Fund within the National Programme "Support for the carrying out doctoral study program's and post-doctoral researches" project "Support for the development of doctoral studies at Riga Technical University".

References

Albrehta, D. (2001) *Didaktika.* RaKa, Riga.

Anohina, A. and Grundspenkis, J. (2007) A Concept Map Based Intelligent System for Adaptive Knowledge Assessment. In: O. Vasilecas, J. Eder and A. Caplinskas (Eds.), *Frontiers in Artificial Intelligence and Applications*, Vol. 155, Databases and Information Systems IV. IOS Press, Amsterdam, The Netherlands, pp. 263–276.

Anohina, A. and Grundspenkis, J. (2006) Prototype of Multiagent Knowledge Assessment System for Support of Process Oriented Learning. In: *Proceedings of the 7th International Baltic Conference on Databases and Information Systems* (Baltic DB&IS 2006), July 3–6, Vilnius, Lithuania, pp. 211–219.

Anohina, A., Stale, G. and Pozdnakovs, D. (2006) Intelligent System for Student Knowledge Assessment. In: *Scientific Proceedings of Riga Technical University*, Computer science, 5th series, Vol. 26. RTU, Riga, pp. 132–143.

Bloom, B.S. (1956) *Taxonomy of Educational Objectives.* Handbook I: The cognitive domain. David McKay Co Inc, New York.

Bull, J. (2003) *Introduction to computer-assisted assessment* [online]. University of Wolverhampton, retrieved May 8, 2006 from http://asp2.wlv.ac.uk/celt/download.asp?fileid=44&detailsid=200008

Cañas, A.J. (2003) *A Summary of Literature Pertaining to the Use of Concept Mapping techniques and technologies for education and performance Support.* Technical Report submitted to the Chief of Naval Education and Training, Pensacola, FL.

Chang, K.E., Sung, Y.T. and Chen, S.F. (2001) Learning Through Computer-Based Concept Mapping with Scaffolding Aid. *Journal of Computer Assisted Learning*, No.17, pp. 21–33.

Gouli, E., Gogoulou, A., Papanikolaou, K. and Grigoriadou, M. (2004) COMPASS: An Adaptive Web-based Concept Map Assessment Tool. In: *Proceedings of the 1st International Conference on Concept Mapping*, September 14–17, Pamplona, Spain.

Harary, F. (1969) *Graph Theory*. Addison-Wesley, Massachusetts.

Lambert, G. (2004) *What is Computer Aided Assessment and How Can I Use it in My Teaching?* (Briefing paper) Canterbury Christ Church University College, Canterbury.

Mogey, N. and Watt, H. (1996) The Use of Computers in the Assessment of Student Learning [online]. In: G. Stoner, *Implementing Learning Technology*. Learning Technology Dissemination Initiative, retrieved May 8, 2006 from http://www.icbl.hw.ac.uk/ltdi/implementing-it/cont.htm

Novak, J.D. and Cañas, A.J. (2006). *The Theory Underlying Concept Maps and How to Construct Them*. Technical Report IHMC CmapTools 2006-01, Florida Institute for Human and Machine Cognition, Florida.

Oliver, A. (2000) *Computer Aided Assessment-the Pros and Cons* [online], retrieved December 8, 2005 from http://www.herts.ac.uk/ltdu/learning/caa_procon.htm

Ruiz-Primo, M.A. (2004) Examining Concept Maps as an Assessment Tool. In: *Proceedings of the 1st International Conference on Concept Mapping*, September 14-17, Pamplona, Spain.

Seale, J. (2002) *Using CAA to Support Student Learning* [online]. Learning Technology and Support Network, retrieved May 8, 2006 from http://www.alt.ac.uk/docs/eln004.pdf

Tsai, C.C., Lin, S.S.J. and Yuan, S.M. (2001) *Students' Use of Web-based Concept Map Testing and Strategies for Learning*. Journal of Computer Assisted Learning, 17(1), pp. 72–84.

The Complexity of an E-Learning System: A Paradigm for the Human Factor

Adriana Schiopoiu Burlea

Department of Management & Marketing, University of Craiova, Romania
aburlea@central.ucv.ro

Abstract   The purpose of this chapter is to investigate how an e-learning platform – TESYS – contributes to learning development activities. This chapter is aimed at contributing to the increase of the understanding of the influence of the information systems on building new learning perspectives for different categories of users. The results reveal that there are statistically significant differences regarding the ages of the persons considered in the research, but their expectations and needs referring to the e-learning platform seem to be the same. The real differences come from the difficulties of the individual use of the facilities offered by the information systems and from the human factor's level of involvement in the improvement of this system. Consequently, there are visible discrepancies in the use of the e-learning platform and these disparities are not only age - and sex - related but also related to the person's knowledge in the field.

1 Introduction

Specialists have been more preoccupied about the development of the information systems from the perspective of the technological informatics infrastructure, research devoted to the technology infrastructures embedded in the information systems lacking to some extent in literature. The advantages of e-learning are presented both according to the relation between price and results - as a force for "profit and efficiency" and a source for competitive advantage (Swanson 2001), and according to the flexibility in delivery and in the pace and distribution of learning (Galagan 2000). The academic literature is wanting, particularly in the area of human resources involved in e-learning and in the area of technological needs, learner support, and evaluation. In this context specialists have to pay attention both to the social and human aspects that accompany the introduction of an information system into an organisation. The author hopes to have two significant contributions to the field. First, we introduce some key ideas from the literature as well as the chapter's theoretical framework regarding the relationship between IS–HR and e-learning system. This section argues for a humanistic system development approach to e-learning in order to translate human resources requirements into a system that supports effective learning. Second, we illustrate the difficulty of developing an e-learning platform for diverse student base. The purpose of this study is to examine the impact of e-learning system on human system for the use of a Tesys platform that incorporates both technical and learning features.

2 Information Systems versus Human System

Time pressure has become so powerful that neither the organisations nor the persons themselves pay attention to the human factor even if this factor can be a sine qua non of the information system development (ISD). Specialists are mainly preoccupied with explaining how social phenomena shape both the development and use of technologies (MacKenzie and Wajcman 1999) or to analyzing and interpreting the effects of information technology over the human factor in cultural or organisational contexts (Slaton and Abbate 2001). The lack of dialogue between the specialists in the IT field and human resources (HR) generates severe dysfunctions within the two systems (technical and human). Thus the human system bears the stress – it does not have skills for self-directed learning and technology management, it is not self-motivated, and is not prepared for isolation, while the technical system "suffers" from its partial and inefficient use. When the stage/limit of reciprocal exploring is over, the user passing on to "friendly collaboration", the interaction between IS and HS (Figure 1) leads:

- To continual perfection and improvement of the IS quality
- To the building up of further knowledge on the basis of others' contributions, thus HS achieving new competences

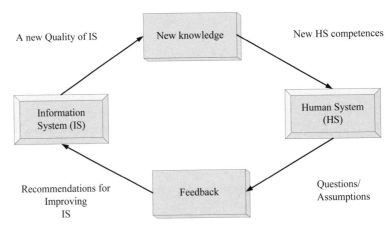

Fig. 1. Interaction model between IS and HS

This model represents two key actors of the e-learning process (the IS and the HS) and, whether aware or not of the fact, the human actor needs to make decisions and incorporate their questions and assumptions into the IS with the purpose of improving the latter's quality (Orlikowski and Iacono 2001). The results indicate that the HS's acquisition of competencies depends on the quality of the information system. Furthermore, if HS is a prior step in the feedback process, then the process is influenced more by the competencies of the HS. Thus, the design and implementation of the IS must be concerned not only with narrow technical activities, but also with organizational and social structures, and with the analysis of the necessities and expectations of the human factor. As a result, e-learning could represent the mechanism by which the organization transforms the individual's knowledge into intellectual capital at different levels (individual and group levels, dependent or independent learners who study) and brings forth the opportunity that knowledge should to be achieved and shared (Burlea Schiopoiu 2003).

Furthermore, e-learning becomes an important engine for the development of the human factor and a technological solution to the economic, social, and cultural problems of an organization. For example, the use of e-learning system, through its potential of transforming implicit knowledge into explicit knowledge, has furthered instructional methods to improve student interaction, commitment, and motivation (Varlamis et al. 2005).

E-learning environment provides the student with a relevant feature for acquiring and sharing knowledge (Pukkhem and Vatanawood 2005). Furthermore, advanced technological solutions may provide structural support and guidance for the learning process through the implementation of active learning strategies.

3 Methodology

The method used in this study has been a mixture of qualitative methods and data analysis.

The semi-structured face-to-face interviews were carried on with the aim to examine the perceptions of the students regarding the information and knowledge that they can acquire by using the e-learning platform, and the factors that contribute to their finalizing or quitting the courses.

Our research is an empirical inquiry that investigates the e-learning phenomenon within its real-life context (Yin 2003) and in connexion with the limits of the human factor.

In the research we employed a wide range of qualitative methods, which included direct and participative observation of the learners' implication in the process of acquiring new knowledge by using the e-learning platform.

The interview protocol consisted of two sections: on the one hand, the level at which the e-learning platform corresponds to the needs and expectations of the attendants, taking into consideration the diverse age categories, and, on the other hand, their involvement in the improvement of the e-learning platform.

Because of the semi-structured nature of the research, the quantity and quality of data varied greatly between respondents.

The method of data analysis is a cyclic process that involves collecting data, analysis, and theory generation until the grounded theory becomes formally related to the existing knowledge.

Because the interviews were taken at the end of the project, we needed to use two groups of persons for our research:

1. Persons that have enrolled in the course and graduated from it – 42 persons (31 women and 11 men)
2. Persons that have enrolled in the course and did not graduate from it – 31 persons (20 women and 11 men)

Ethical issues were observed, by inviting participants to take part in the two groups, and by giving them the option to withdraw if they felt uncomfortable and by making the results available for their further scrutiny to agree accuracy.

Content analysis was used to process the original texts of team project reports and the transcripts of interviews conducted. The participants were interviewed for a period of approximately 1 hour and they were encouraged to express their experience related to the use of the Tesys platform. Post-analysis follow-up interviews with participants were used in order to confirm the validity of the results.

The SPSS was used to organize and categorize the large amount of qualitative data collected from documents and interviews.

The following questions guided the process of data collection (see Table 1):

Table 1. Questions that guided data collection

QA. Questions referring to the information system (IS)	QB. Questions referring to the human system (HS)
QA1. What is the relationship between the architecture of the e-learning platform and the types of knowledge that you need?	QB1. What were your expectations when joining this course and to what extent were they satisfied?
QA2. How did the using of the e-learning platform contribute to the improvement of the individual process of learning and acquiring new competences?	QB2. Do you think that acquiring new knowledge by means of the e-learning system is beneficial to you?
QA3. How did you evaluate the efficiency of using the e-learning platform?	QB3. How was your knowledge acquired in the e-learning system evaluated?

4 Study Design

This section assesses the use and implementation of e-learning application through case study.

The implementation of the approach used a platform for e-learning – Tesys. This platform was funded in 2005 by the European Union project named "Training program via e-learning in the fields of economics and informatics for developing the labour force from the Oltenia region" (Burdescu and Mihaescu 2006). At present, the application is available and can be visited at http://stat257.central.ucv.ro.

The main goal of the Tesys is to offer guidance in the learning process and to give possible solutions to several of their instructional needs, into both formal and non-formal learning process. The Tesys application has the following structure: three sections, each consisting of four disciplines – contents range from technical knowledge to soft skills. Each discipline is assigned to a section and has as attributes a name, a short name, the year of study, and the semester when it is studied and the list of maximum three professors who teach the discipline. A course participant may be enrolled to one or more sections. All the course content was selected to reflect the needs of the students.

The information system is very complex and contains the following elements:

- Support applications for the communication between students and their professors
- Support applications for on-line and off-line training
- Applications for the course participants' evaluation at exams
- Applications for creating, updating, and using databases, with questions and problems
- Applications for statistic analysis: of the candidates' results and of the test construction (difficulty, structure)

The platform itself is a web application used by administrator – sysadmin, secretary, professor in a collaborative manner in order to accomplish a learning process. Each of these four roles has been assigned a set of modules. The e-learning platform needs to provide and support several categories of the "expectations".

From the analysis of the e-learning architecture we can notice the accessibility to information of the students, irrespective of their status — novice, intermediate, and advanced up to experienced – because, the platform provides and supports several categories of the "expectations".

Course attendants have access to personal data and can modify them as needed. A feedback form is also available. It is composed of questions that check aspects regarding the usability, efficiency, and productivity of the application with respect to the student's needs. After successful course completion, the students received a diploma by the providing academic institution – the University of Craiova.

5 Data Analysis

In order to emphasise the factors that influence the relation between the e-learning system and the students involved in the project we have studied the following variables: age and sex.

At first, in order to take part in the course, 722 candidates aged between 21 and 64 years old have enrolled (see Table 2). Data analysis shows that there is statistically significant age differences between persons considered in the research. Thus, 499 women (69.11%) showed interest for the online course and only 223 men (30.89%).

Table 2. Structure of student groupings

Age categories	Gender		Total	Percent
	Female	Male		
21– 22 years	15	6	21	2.9
23–30 years	171	105	276	38.2
31–35 years	130	35	165	22.9
36–45 years	66	20	86	11.9
46–50 years	64	21	85	11.8
51–61 years	53	35	88	12.2
61–64 years	0	1	1	0.1
Total	499	223	722	100.0

The structure according to age categories is not homogeneous; the groups between 21 and 45 years of age represent the main part (75.9%). These first statistics made us look into the causes that might lead to these discrepancies and we have catalogued them into:

1. **Human causes** – lack of interest for the course subject
2. **Technological causes** – course performance system by using the e-learning platform

The activity of the course participants varied widely and only some of them completed the whole period of the project. In order for our study to be valid we followed the statistical evolution of the learners till the end of the project and we noticed that only 412 persons (57.06%) aged between 23 and 61 (see Table 3) graduated eventually.

Table 3. Structure of graduating student (GD) and of non-graduating student (NG) groupings

Age categories	Gender				Percent	
	Female		Male			
	GD	NG	GD	NG	GD	NG
23–30 years	92	94	49	62	34.22	50.32
31–35 years	74	56	17	18	22.09	23.87
36–45 years	39	27	9	11	11.65	12.26
46–50 years	55	9	18	3	17.72	3.87
51–64 years	46	7	13	23	14.32	9.68
Total	306	193	106	117	100	100

The results indicate that there are statistically significant differences between the ages of the persons considered in the research, but their expectations and needs related to the e-learning platform seem to be the same. Despite the fact that many course participants failed to gain the required new competencies, most of them welcomed the insights and new ideas they acquired through the online discussions.

The final results made us think more about the fact that responsible for the learners having quitted the course might be the information system (IS) – the e-learning platform. However, these results made us think about the fact that the information system (IS) – the e-learning platform could be "responsible" for the giving up of the course, because the participants felt they should have direct access to resources that support active, independent, and self-reflective learning.

At this point, it is impossible to draw any general conclusions from this preliminary evaluation, because it is only a statistical approach. New analysis is necessary in order to gain practical insight and, to generate some evidence-based claims about the e-learning platform possibility and limitations (e.g., lack of personalisation or lack of collaboration and interactivity).

6 Results

The course participants' satisfaction is the perception of the distance between the created needs and expectations, and what they have received through the e-learning

Table 4. Motivations referring to the information system (IS) and to the human system (HS)

Mis. Motivations referring to the information system (IS)	Percent	
	Persons that have graduated	Persons that have quit the course
Mis1. They have considered that at the end of the course they would have more knowledge than at the beginning of it, as well as more practical competences in using an information system, a fact that might open up new professional perspectives for them.	100	100
Mis2. The newness of the online way of acquiring knowledge independent of time and place	95.24	95.55
Mis3. The perception of the utility of the e-learning system	90.48	87.10
MHs. Motivations referring to the human system (HS)		
Mhs1. The ample curricula of the courses and possibility to attend a desired number of sections at the same time – new competencies	100	100
Mhs2. The fact that the course was free of charge - the cost advantages were also considered in relation with the costs saved on traveling and time away from the job	57.12	38.71
Mhs3. The possibility of obtaining a certificate that might give a certain professional stability to the course participants	11.90	25.80

system. The students' motivations for attending the course are different, whether they graduated or not. In Table 4 it is presented a hierarchy of these motivations after having analyzed the interviews.

Participants' response analysis elicited the main reasons that motivated them to attend the course as being related to those referring to the information system, a fact that leads to the conclusion that the e-learning system proved very attractive (see Table 5).

Table 5. Answers referring to the information system (IS) and to the human system (HS)

AnA. Answers referring to the information system (IS)	AnB. Answers referring to the human system (HS)
AnA1. All activities are related to student outcomes and objectives Navigation may cause confusion	**AnB1.** Course materials are easily to locate, accessible
AnA2. Technology requirements are well explained Objectives and questions are given and written in such a way that they are clear and measurable	**AnB2.** All the interviewed people agreed that it is beneficent for them to achieve new knowledge through the e-learning system, the novice from the 51–64 age group considered that the classical learning system is more "comfortable" for them, because during the program they often felt lost and frustrated.
AnA3. Assessment measures student progress towards course material The relationship between cost/knowledge/time is efficient The platform provides frequent and timely feedback Interaction between student-professor is facilitated by the use of communication tools	**AnB3.** The course participants considered that, through the e-learning system, their knowledge is valued in a superior way, and at the same time it offers them the possibility to manage time efficiently. Consequently, there is a close connection between the period of time allotted to the course and personal time available

However, some course participants quit the course for varied reasons:

- All the persons that have been interviewed no matter the age class, indicated as main cause of giving up – the insufficient time to finalize the chosen course type.
- Persons between 51 and 64 years old said they had given up the course because it was no longer useful for the development of their professional career.
- Persons between 46 and 51 years old said they had given up the course because they did not have enough knowledge to use the platform and that is why they could not finish tests in time.
- As many as 80.65% of the persons that were interviewed said they had enough knowledge in order to use the information system and especially because it is attractive and motivating to acquire new knowledge, but the main shortcoming consists in the fact they did not have access to computers in the time interval they wanted to assign to studying. Consequently, for this category of course participants' technology was one of the main barriers to the development of the e-learning strategy.

From the analysis of the interviews we conclude that the e-learning system will become an important means of acquiring knowledge, for all categories of course attendants, irrespective of age, sex, and level of knowledge in the informatics field. The perception of course attendants' needs and expectations varied from group A – GD (at group A level the e –learning is perceived as a system that limits the level of interactivity) to group B – NG (at group B level the e-learning is the most popular form of learning), due to the diversity of the age categories and to the different levels of knowledge in the field of using the information systems.

From the analysis of the interviews we have noticed that we were confronted with a lack of clear goals and a lack of prioritization of course attendants' needs. Further, because e-learning was relatively new as learning system there was a lack of direct interaction with the course attendants. Consequently, the team project did not meet the course attendants' different needs stemming from professional differences in expectations and practices:

Through Tesys platform the difference of perception between the needs and the expectations of the course attendants is eliminated because those who have created the platform are in permanent contact with the former.

7 The Scenario of the TESYS Platform Perfecting

In our survey, general satisfaction regarding both the content and interface of the Tesys was reported, but review of the interview data revealed the importance of improving the e-learning platform. In order to meet the needs and expectations of the different categories of users, the Tesys platform should have certain characteristics:

1. **It has to be rapid** – on the one hand to prevent the user from abandoning the e-learning activity if the computer does not respond very quickly – Horwath (1999) recorded anxiety in novice users when the technology failed to respond within 15 seconds, and on the other hand, in order not to make out of the lack of free time for studying the main reason of abandon.

2. **It has to be simple** – so that the user, irrespective of the level of knowledge of informatics, should be able to manage the system and stimulate the growth of the user's responsibility for their own learning in the release of personal potential.

3. **To allow the development of the users' creativity** – by a strategic use of the connection between personal experience and technological performance of the Tesys platform.

4. **To have a high motivational level** in order to attract people of the age categories between 21 and 35 years old who had abandoned the course in a high proportion – 74.19% of the total number of people who abandoned the course (see Table 3).

The process of perfecting the platform has followed, on the one hand, the growth of the platform accessibility level for those who had minimal knowledge of using the information systems, and on the other hand, the increase of the platform complexity level for those who had multiple competences in using the information systems. Moreover, it is essential to improve students' satisfaction by means of increasing the quality of the platform. Consequently, technological capability and interactivity of the e-learning platform are fundamental.

The team charged with the improvement of Tesys platform consists of specialists in the fields of informatics, management of human resources, and in the management of business affairs. This diversified structure of the team favors the elimination of barriers that were identified during the interviews. For the Tesys to satisfy the different needs and expectations of the users, team project considered using the "computer-game" method to reconfigure the e-learning platform, so as to encourage attendance, enhance attention, increase interest, and promote interaction between course attendants.

By defining each level the exigencies of the course attendants can be expressed through close levels. For example if "informatics knowledge" is minimal, these pieces of knowledge are levels 0 or 1. Consequently, passing from level 0 to level 1 can be done only after the course attendants have obtained the minimal score for level 0. The iterative process repeats itself for each level and it reaches the next stage – e-learning modules are created, taking into account the clients' demands and resource management, planning, and capitalization constraints. Thus, the course attendants are helped to identify the relevant course from the level available to them.

First, because time constraints were indicated, especially by the course attendants who had abandoned the course, as being a significant barrier, the working out of a three-dimensional correlation strategy between the initial knowledge level of the participants, time constraints, technical and cultural background of the students was pursued – this shortcoming can be transformed into a competitive advantage. Through Sysadmin – the course attendants are assisted in order to manage their time and reduce anxiety levels and the negative perception about a course perceived as difficult. It is also possible to use the platform to conduct multiple choice examinations, eliminating, thus, time constraints.

Second, the students' degree of accepting the e-learning material was improved, a barrier which was mentioned especially by the students who had abandoned the course, as being a powerful de-motivating factor. Another difficulty faced by the students was the fact that they had to work hard when they were supposed to answer different questions which had scarce explanation in the course.

The collecting and processing of the students' requests led to the elaboration of courses structured on levels of competences, the platform monitoring user activity through a log file which records each executed action. The new courses deal with technology, billing and computer applications, soft skills, management, and strategy covering a lot of topics. Consequently, these courses are more accessible, include more information and are more logical.

Third, course attendants' autonomy has increased and also the assessment of their experience. Individual learning processes are conducted by emotions and feelings and every individual student creates his/her own interpretation of perceived information. As a consequence, by perfecting the Tesys platform individualized feedback was supplied to each student, reducing the degree of uncertainty and enhancing motivation. From the moment in which a course attendant is registered to a course, a personal profile will be elaborated depending on various variables like: age, sex, competencies, skills, initial knowledge level, learning style, personality, motivation, goals, and expectations. Consequently, course attendants may download only course materials for the disciplines that belong to the sections to which they are enrolled. They can take tests and exams with constraints that were set up by the administration through the year structure facility.

Fourth, the technological barriers have been eliminated by implementing some technological solutions that reduced the level of sophistication of the Tesys platform, a fact that lead to reducing the course attendants' frustration and the growth of their degree of satisfaction and their reliance on self-instruction and self-motivation. The solutions for reducing the level of sophistication of the platform had the following consequences:

- The increase of interactivity and integration
- Better formative assessment of students
- Reducing students' frustration
- Increasing levels of satisfaction
- Improving attendance

In this way, the e-learning platform can no longer be considered a barrier to the full realization of course attendants' potential, and the continual furthering of the e-learning platform has become very important for the improvement of the learning process quality.

8 Conclusions

The themes that emerged from this research show how course attendants value their relationship with the e-learning system and that their educational experience is influenced by the learning platform. Although statistically speaking, we had a diversified population from the point of view of age, sex, and level of knowledge in informatics, the main barrier in accepting e-learning was represented by the complexity of the Tesys platform. The difficulties of individually using the facilities offered by the information system were signaled more frequently by the categories of age from 46 to 64 years old and mainly by women.

The structure of the e-learning platform has to encourage participation and insure the fidelity of all course attendants irrespective of age. This will be possible only by means of a technology that promotes collaboration and provides mixed solutions. Most importantly, the use of the e-learning platform depends on several learning contexts and students' age levels. The degree of the human factor involvement in improving this system was greater in the age segment of 21–35 years old. Irrespective of sex people were interested in improving the Tesys platform. The role of the team project is that to incorporate course attendants' both technological and pedagogical preference perspectives into their use of the e-learning platform in order to valorise the training e-learning experience.

The advantages of an e-learning pedagogy are not fully exploited because of the limitations in technology and other strategic human priorities. Further research is needed to understand how the course attendants engage in the e-learning system, and whether a relationship between students' commitment and e-learning system is possible. This is essentially due to the role of course attendants' commitment in predicting success of the e-learning system, because the course attendants' commitment may be a more important factor than student satisfaction in the link to knowledge. The relationship between the human factor and technological complexity could represent emerging issues that warrant further research, because e-learning has become an important source of organizational learning with a significant impact on employee performance.

References

Burdescu, D.D. and Mihaescu, C. (2006) TESYS: E-Learning Application Built on a Web Platform, International Conference on E-Business, Setubal, Portugal, pp. 315–319.

Burlea Schiopoiu A. (2003) *The Role of Strategic Intellectual Capital in the Management of Organizational Change*, The Sixth International Symposium on Economic Informatics, Bucharest, pp.1088–1093.

Horwath, A. (1999) *Novice Users' Reaction to a Web-Enriched Classroom.* Virtual University Journal, 2, 49–57.

Galagan, P.A. (2000) *E-Learning Revolution, Training and Development*, 54(12), 25–30.

Latour, B. (1987) *Science in Action*, Harvard University Press, Cambridge, MA.

MacKenzie, D. and Wajcman, J. (1999) *The Social Shaping of Technology*, Open University Press, Buckingham, pp. 3–27.

Orlikowski, W.J. and Iacono, C.S. (2001) Research commentary: desperately seeking the 'IT' in IT research - a call to theorizing the IT artifact, Information Systems Research, 12(2), 121–134.

Pukkhem, N. and Vatanawood, W. (2005) *Instructional Design Using Component-Based Development and Learning Object Classification.* Fifth IEEE International Conference on Advanced Learning Technologies (ICALT'05), pp. 492–494.

Slaton, A. and Abbate, J. (2001) *The Hidden Lives of Standards:Technical Prescriptions and the Transformation of Work in America*, in Allen, M.T. et al. (Eds), Technologies of Power, MIT Press, Cambridge, MA, pp. 95–144.

Swanson, S. (2001) *E-Learning Branches Out*, Information Week, February, pp. 42–60.

Varlamis, I. Apostolakis, I. and Karatza, M. (2005) A framework for monitoring the unsupervised educational process and adapting the content and activities to students' needs. WISE Workshops 2005, pp. 124–133.

Yin, R.K. (2003) *Case Study Research Design and Methods*, 3rd ed., Sage, Thousand Oaks, CA.

Specification for Designing Web-Based Training Courses and an Application Model Based on IT

Michal Kuciapski

University of Gdansk, Department of Information Systems, m.kuciapski@univ.gda.pl

Abstract   The aim of the article is to propose a specification for designing web-based training courses and a general application model created on the basis of the design system drawn up. The application will be able to create prototypes of modules and courses based on their design. It will also generate multimedia design documentation for development. The starting point of the article is an analysis of the problems associated with the lack of standards and applications for the design and production of web-based training courses. The concept of a specification system for designing web-based training courses is described in the second part. The last part of the article presents guidelines and a general model of the application for the process of instructional design. The application functions are modelled on the basis of the specification for instructional design and the aim is to accelerate the development of courses. The article is based on the author's three-year experience of instructional design linked to e-learning project work and on individual research into the specifications of other instructional designers for e-learning module projects.

1 The Current State of Instructional Design and the Associated Problems

Many multimedia and e-learning specialists worldwide took part in a European Commission workshop titled "eLearning Content: Access Rights, Creation, Sharing and Reuse" that took place in Brussels in October 2004. These included representatives of such organisations as the BBC, Giunti Interactive Labs, RAI Educational, SAP and Cisco. Criticism was voiced of the current state of e-learning material and the use of information and communication technologies (ICT) in education. Two of the critics, Adam Horvath (Horvath 2005) and Professor Peter Baumgartner (Baumgartner 2005), pointed out the need for the creation of universal standards for designing e-learning materials and courses. Such standards would support and increase the efficiency of the work of instructional designers.

Many of the problems alluded to arose during the author's participation in the Baltic Sea Virtual Campus project, which involved a network of universities from

C. Barry et al. (eds.), *Information Systems Development: Challenges in Practice, Theory, and Education, Vol.2*, doi: 10.1007/978-0-387-78578-3_22,
© Springer Science+Business Media, LLC 2009

all ten countries in the Baltic Sea region. The aim of this project was the creation of a virtual campus and the preparation of online study programmes. In the course of the author's work on the project as Instructional Designer and ITC Coordinator and in researching many instructional design systems, it was noticeable that a number of problems were associated with a lack of standards and applications for the design and production of WBT courses. These may be summarised as follows:

- Imprecise course design
- Lack of important functionalities
- Incompatibility between course design and implementation and, linked with this, the consumption of additional time and resources in making modifications
- The need for additional time to understand the designs of other instructional designers
- Inefficiency arising from a lack of IT support during the design process
- Inefficiency arising from inadequate integration of course design and the development processes

2 The Concept of a Specification System for Designing Web-based Training Courses

To prevent main problems regarding course development process a detailed specification of such process that is obligatory during course development curriculum. It assures high quality of created courses and minimises the risk of development delays. Conception of developed process model on the general level of circumstantial is presented on Fig. 1.

The process was developed iteraly based on experience got during courses preparation for Baltic Sea Virtual Campus online studies and especially resolving connected problems. Later separate analysis was made for further course preparation process model modernisation and more general adaptation. It assumes sequential development of each of the modules with some analogy to the cascading software engineering. Separate modules build the whole course. This makes that the course is developed successively and the whole process is very similar to spiral software engineering process, where the course is continually updated and revised as new modules are prepared. Problems that occurred during project Baltic Sea Virtual Campus that changed the course development process were:

- Time delays in getting parts of module materials from authors
- Designing multimedia objects that changed the author conception
- Getting additional information from authors for multimedia objects preparation
- Proper understanding of instructional design by multimedia production team
- Creation of reusable objects, learning units, and modules

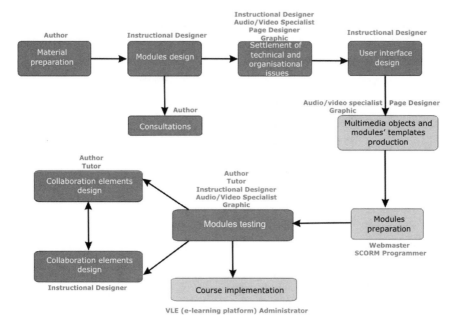

Fig. 1. E-learning course preparation process

The whole process documentation contains much more detailed description with templates, review points, and umbrella activities. Also very precise communication standards were developed to insure a proper style o informing in multipartner environment: free university faculties, administration, and private multimedia company.

The course is understood as a final product that can be directly offered to students (customers). It consists of modules. Modules are the biggest logical component that could be used in other courses after proper adaptation. For example, prepared course Economical Environment for setting up new business consisted of two big modules: Macro-economical environment for setting up new business and Micro-economical environment for setting up new business. Those modules may be used in other courses after removing learning units and objects specific for Baltic Sea region.

The e-learning course components (Fig. 2) design process should start with the choice of concept for the educational learning sequences. A learning sequence is a strict schema of combining learning objects and other type components. Choice of learning sequence is strictly connected with the aim of the course: self-training, customised self-training, blended learning, tutorial, practical workshop, and reference. A number of types of essential learning sequence may be distinguished (Horton 2000): classical tutorials, activity-centred lessons, learner-customised tutorials, knowledge-paced tutorials, exploratory tutorials, and generated lessons.

OBJECT 1:
Object TITLE: The different types of decisions in the management process
identification: GI LU2-1-3_1-1

Picture 1
Compatible with the following one.

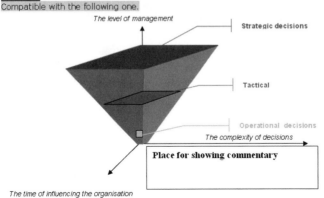

Fig. 2. Component design example

Interakcja 1
Entering on the ellipsis area causes showing proper commentary:
Strategic decisions
*Strategic decisions are characterized with a long time of bringing to light themselves results
(often irreversible), with the muchness of the complexity and this that are undertaken on
the highest level of the organizational hierarchy.*
Tactical decisions
*Tactical decisions embrace segments of strategic decisions, are less complicated and compound, more
quickly influence on the organization and are undertaken on the middle-level management.*

A detailed choice of learning sequencing type has a direct impact on the design components and is also related to the style of learning, teaching, and course organisation (Clark and Mayer 2003). The instructional designer should therefore have an unconstrained choice of learning components (Ryder 2007), depending on the type used. Learning component is a learning object or another item type used in building learning units.

Types of used components is strictly connected with chosen learning sequence. The different components that can be distinguished include the introduction to a learning unit, the learning object, the learning path, activity preparation, activity, summary, tests (pre-test, post-test, remediation, adaptation), the multimedia object list and retrieval. Main element is learning unit that groups components into a main logical and physical element of module. Its role is very similar to chapters in books. Leading part of learning units are learning objects. Learning object is the smallest modular and digital entity for educational e-learning content. Learning objects due to its modularity are reusable and can be used in different learning units, modules and courses. For all these components design templates are needed that facilitate and accelerate the design process and ensure a high standard of course or module specification.

Figure 2 presents a part of example design based on one of the design templates drawn up. Each specification starts with the name of a component (not on the figure), usually learning object. It is similar to the name of a learning object

(Fig. 3) but without the last element - id of learning object on Web page. The number of Web pages is contained in the name for final production support and helps in the management of bigger components. Later specifications consist of two possible sequentially put elements: text and multimedia objects. The main part in template is reserved for multimedia objects design (Fig. 2) as they are key elements of specification of whole component. Each multimedia object has its identification, title, and sequences of design described later in the article.

An important design element is the proper naming of components on the basis of the learning sequence (Fig. 3). There are often hundreds of these with a large number of multimedia and interactive elements. The specification drawn up then consists of an extremely large number of files and pages. It is very difficult for such a quantity of material to be handled by, amongst others, instructional designers, graphic designers, and web masters, who inevitably have to trawl through it when searching for a particular object design for further use or modification. This makes it extremely important to have a naming standard for components, component sub–pages, and objects within components. An example of an appropriate name using the numbering system researched is TDD LU1-4-4-1_3-1 (Fig. 3).

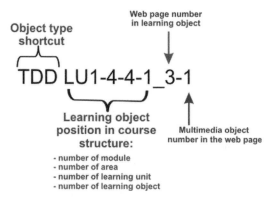

Fig. 3. Naming system

Any high-quality WBT (e-learning) course needs attractive multimedia and interactive material, in keeping with the dictum that "sleeping learners do not learn" (Thalheimer 2002). Well-designed and imaginatively created multimedia objects not only increase the visual attractiveness of didactic modules but also present the material more effectively. A high degree of interactivity ensures greater commitment from students participating in the course over the whole syllabus. Proper design templates must be created for a wide spectrum of classified multimedia objects according to the object types established during research (Fig. 4).

Part of a multimedia object design and the multimedia object created on the basis of it is presented in Fig. 5. As there are many types of learning sequences, components and, in particular, multimedia objects, the most time-consuming elements of designing an e-learning course, the number of design templates that form a specification is quite large.

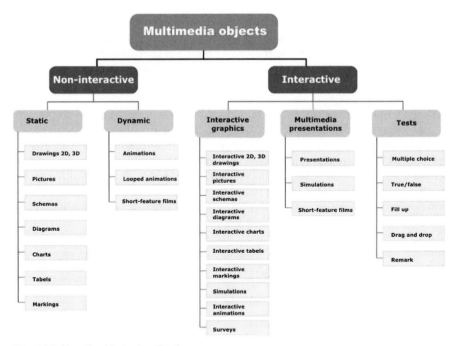

Fig. 4. Multimedia objects classification

The example presents a design of the object type 'animation with commentary.' The object has in the begging its object number on the Web page ('Object1'). Next is the title of the learning object for use during Web page containing the learning object creation. Third design element is id of multimedia object which identifies its type and localisation in module. The example (Fig. 5) presents project for animation with commentary, one of more advanced types. Proper design has a character of scenario. It starts with a begging picture (section 'Picture 1'), if appropriate, and later a number of sequences of animations (sections 'Animation n,' where n is the number of animation section). Each sequence contains a text spoken by a lector and written in italics and a number of synchronised actions written to a strict schema and marked out in grey. All the actions described are executed with a structural script sequence similar to programming languages but with no similar to programming language keywords and control statements syntactic. It has only global guidelines. Each control statement must have exactly defined start time, description of elementary animation activities and finish time. Times are given relationally to earlier animation sequence and given in seconds. Additionally number of iterations may be given.

OBJECT 1:
OBJECT TITLE: Elements important in decision process
identification: ANTC LU1-3-1-1_1-1

Picture 1
In the begging of animation there is **no starting picture**. The lectors speach is shown also in the form of text in the buttom right part of animation player strictly synchronized with the speach.

Animation 1
In decision process two things are particularly important. These are **information** *and* **information channels***, through which the information and decisions get to interested people.*
Apears the folowing picture.

Animation 2
3 seconds break. Highlight of **Information** field.
Information must be concrete (from **this moment** until the **end of sentence** in sequence synchronized with lector speech under the field **Information** is showing the following text in proper points: concrete, clear, understandable, delivered in written form, minimizes the possibilities of over interpretation, minimizes lack of interpretation of decision) *clear, understandable and delivered in written form, which minimizes the possibilities of over interpretation or lack of interpretation of decision.*

Animation 3
3 seconds break. The **following example diagram** of company organization structure shows on the right side. I could take nearly all free space.

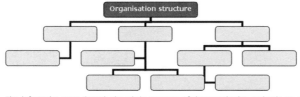

The information goes through the whole structure of the organization and only on the importance of decision taken, depends how detailed it is (starts and takes approx. **10 sec.** animation of moving documents with the name **Information** on them from the bottom of diagram to upper parts throw the lines).

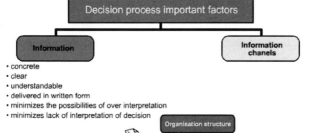

· concrete
· clear
· understandable
· delivered in written form
· minimizes the possibilities of over interpretation
· minimizes lack of interpretation of decision

Fig. 5. Fragment of design project and created based on it multimedia object

3 General Application Model Based on a Specification System for Designing Web-based Training Courses

The general specification presented should finally be implemented as a software application that will enable e-learning multimedia objects, modules, and courses or their prototypes to be designed (Fig. 6). Everything needs to be compatible with SCORM (Sharable Content Object Reference Model), so that the application will also allow modules created earlier on design projects to be reused.

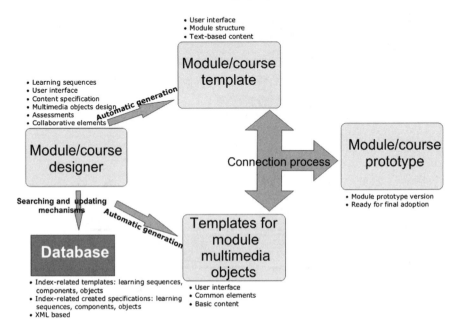

Fig. 6. General model of an application to support instructional designers

The model shows how the general structure of the application should be developed. It also presents the flow of the module creation process and the elements taken in during this. This kind of application should prove an important tool for instructional designers and will enable the process of course development to be accelerated. Currently, the course or module design process is carried out as shown using word processing applications supported by graphics programmes. The production of multimedia objects rarely exploits the similarities between most of these objects, which often differ only in their didactic content. Their prototypes are not generated on the design foundation and are constructed from scratch or on the basis of previously created multimedia objects. The same applies to course or module Web page production. The educational content has to be entered manually, even when an authoring tool is used. Like multimedia objects these are not generated on the design foundation. The lack of integration between the processes described increases the time and costs needed for course or module creation. An application developed on the basis of the model constructed will strengthen the framework of course preparation.

4 Summary and Conclusions

In the present study the general concept of a specification and the application model based on it for designing Web-based training courses has been shown. As the starting point the current state of instructional design and its associated problems were analysed. The successive elements that should be taken into consideration during the development of the instructional design specification have been described and a solution proposed. The specification presented contains a proposed numbering system, multimedia object classification, and an example of one of the researched design templates used. On the basis of the specification put forward a general application model has been described which would give great support to instructional designers.

The proposed specification for Web-based training courses was used in practice during the Baltic Sea Virtual Campus project in the development of two large e-learning courses for the Transregional Management master's course 'The Economic Environment for Setting up New Business and Transregional Organisations and Networks.' During the first stages of development the errors in learning objects linked to the translation of the module design to the final version reached nearly 45%, 53 errors of various kinds in slightly over 120 learning objects. The errors were mainly associated with multimedia objects and a large number arose because of imprecise design. This meant that additional time was needed to make modifications and more expense was incurred as a result. After the templates had been developed to a consistent design specification, the number of errors decreased significantly, to below 20 percent, 87 in approximately 450 learning objects. Most of them were standard errors such as a missing element or a misspelling. Further enhancements were made to the design templates in the course of research.

References

Baumgartner P. (2005) DG for Education and Culture, European Commission, 1–3
Clark R. & Mayer R.(2003) E-learning and the Science of Instruction, Wiley, 51–138
Horton W. (2000) Web-Based Training: How to Teach Anyone Anything Anywhere Anytime, Wiley, 136–148
Horvath H.(2005) Sharing and Reusing e-Learning Content, European Commission, 2005, 1–5
http://www.europa.eu.int/comm/education/programmes/elearning/workshops/index_en.html (2005)
Ryder M. (2007) http://carbon.cudenver.edu/~mryder/itc_data/idmodels.html
Thalheimer W. (2002) Stop Aiming for Interactivity!, http://www.elearningmag.com/ltimagazine/article/articleDetail.jsp?id=21297

Enhancing Efficiency and Effectiveness of Online Asynchronous Support Using Case-Based Reasoning Within an Online Learning Environment

Noel Carroll

Galway-Mayo Institute of Technology, School of Business, noel.carroll@gmit.ie

Abstract   This chapter is generally concerned with the current nature of online learning asynchronous support within third-level colleges. It is specifically concerned with evaluating the current use or lack of use of asynchronous online learning support tools and evaluating methods of enhancing asynchronous online support, by employing Case-Based Reasoning (CBR). This chapter constitutes a contribution to the issues of pedagogical quality, with reference to effectiveness and efficiency of online learning support technologies. It argues that students must assume greater control of monitoring and managing the cognitive and contextual aspects of their learning. The significance of this chapter is that it emphasises the need for lecturers to take more responsibility to provide structure and guidance that will encourage and support students assuming increased control of their learning. The fundamental challenge presented within this chapter, is to create and sustain a quality online learning environment of increased value for lecturers and students, using Artificial Intelligence (AI) techniques to explore the economic value of reusable online support, thus enhancing the overall effectiveness and efficiency of online asynchronous support.

1 Introduction

This chapter is based on a work-in-progress, for a Masters in business, with the aim to evaluate whether online asynchronous support tools and technologies can be enhanced for student learning within third-level colleges.

Berge (2003) stated that in recent years there has been a growing interest in developing methods to enhance education through the exploitation of Information and Communication Technology (ICT). Within the third-level college sector there is appreciation that pedagogical objectives may be enhanced through the use of ICT (DiPaolo 2004). Students have increased interaction with other peers, experts, or sources of information, regardless of their physical location. Online systems have increasingly more tools available in encouraging students' participation and motivating students' interaction (Mabrito 2006). Devedzic (2004) stated that there have been new developments in Web technologies using Artificial Intelligence (AI) techniques to support methods in making the Web more intelligent and provide higher-level services to its users. AI is an ongoing attempt to replicate the behaviours associated with observed human intelligence (Walsham 2003).

There is an agreement among the Higher Education (HE) institutions that there is need to change in order to meet the challenges of the knowledge society (Sánchez et al. 2004). There is a growing emphasis on developing new ICT-related pedagogy (Israel and Aiken 2007). Knowledge management (KM) is a tool for the creation, archiving and sharing of information, expertise and insight within and across communities of people so it would be possible to use unstructured information to help people learn and improve their performance (Elial et al. 2006). The benefits of developing artificial intelligence structures and strategies within an online learning environment are to enhance a students learning experience (Vedder 1990).

Nichols (2003) explains that a theory can be described as a set of hypotheses that apply to all instances of a particular phenomenon, assisting in decision-making, philosophy of practice and effective implementation through practice. The process of learning is not too defined – hypotheses were developed to give explanation to this process (McCormick et al. 1998). These include behaviourism, cognitivism and constructivism, which are briefly outlined below.

McCormick and Paechter (1998), examines behaviourism, as an approach to psychology which implies that learning is the result of operant conditioning. Operant conditioning is a process both named and investigated by B. F. Skinner. The word 'operant' refers to the way in which behaviour 'operates on the environment.' Cognitivism (psychology), also known as Cognitive Information Processing (CIP), claims that learning involves the use of memory, motivation and thinking, and that reflection plays an important part in learning (Ally 2004). Constructivism views learning as a process in which the learner actively constructs or builds new ideas or concepts based upon current and past knowledge (www.Moodle.org).

2 Asynchronous Communication

Asynchronous communication allows people time to consider the discussion and time for reflection on their contribution. Asynchronous communication does not require that all parties involved in the communication need to be present and available at the same time. The application of asynchronous communication breaks the traditional concept of time and space, generating new educational possibilities and opportunities. Examples of this include e-mail, discussion boards, and mobile phone text messaging. In essence, online learning is concerned with improving the quality of learning through using interactive technologies, online communications and information systems in ways that other teaching methods cannot compete with

(Clarke 2003). Asynchronous online learning has the potential to support higher-order learning in an effective and unprecedented manner (Garrison et al. 2000).

Asynchronous online learning has the potential to significantly enhance the intellectual quality of learning environments (Garrison et al. 2000). In order to exploit this to its full potential, online learning must be embedded as part of the standard teaching methods. It must be perceived by students as a resource for facilitating effective learning for delivering of education (Donnelly and O'Rourke 2007). Online asynchronous communication can be an excellent method of providing higher-order thinking amongst students (Sloffer et al. 1999). Within the HE sector, colleges are starting to implement online learning into students learning activities (Skilbeck 2003). The tools encourage students to take more responsibility for their education and to develop greater interaction and improve learning activities. Using asynchronous tools allow students learn best not only by collecting information, but also by testing it, interpreting it and learning through discovery while also adding flexibility to their own learning.

3 Expert Systems

The term expert system refers to computer programs that apply considerable knowledge of specific areas of expertise to the problem-solving process (Bobrow et al. 1989). The term expert is intended to imply both narrow specialisation and competence, where success of the system is often due to this narrow focus. Just as human experts have varying levels of expertise, so too do computer systems (Bobrow et al. 1989). Although, in general, expert systems have less breadth of scope and flexibility than human experts, and for this reason are sometimes criticised for creating unrealistic expectations, according to Luger et al. (1998), it is more productive to ask about the level and range of expertise of a given program (i.e. how well does it do on a specific set of tasks), rather than struggling with the imprecise boundary of what constitutes 'expert.'

According to Luger et al. (1998) the response to inefficiency has continued interest in automatic theorem provers in the realisation that a system does not have to be capable of independently solving extremely complex problems without human assistance. In response to inefficiency, according to Luger et al. (1998), many argue that purely formal, syntactic methods of guiding searches are inherently incapable of such a huge space and that the only alternative is to reply in on the informal, ad hoc strategies that humans seem to use in solving problems. This is the approach underlying the development of expert systems, and has proved to be a successful one. Case-Based Reasoning (CBR) is a subset of expert systems. This is a very useful technique within domain-specific knowledge, for example, medicine. This reliance on the knowledge of the lecturer for the systems problem-solving strategies is a major feature of expert systems (Luger et al. 1998). Educational data can be centrally stored, to create an expert system, which can offer huge promise within an online learning environment.

4 Online Learning

There is a growing appreciation on the importance of online learning within the tertiary educational sector, for education and for the possibilities in providing pedagogical value to the function of learning (DiPaolo 2004). It is stated in the Joint Information Systems Committee (JISC), whatever technology is chosen, support is the fundamental element. It was also defined by Clarke (2003) that online learning:

...[E]xploits interactive technologies and communication systems to improve the learning experience. It has the potential to transform the way we teach and learn across the board. It can raise standards, and widen participation in lifelong learning. It cannot replace teachers and lecturers, but alongside existing methods it can enhance the quality and reach of their teaching.

4.1 Efficiency

Monitoring student's problems may become challenging and calculating the effectiveness and efficiency of the level of online support may be very difficult to put a value on (Vedder 1990). A powerful strategy expert's use is reasoning with 'cases,' or examples of past problems and their solutions (Luger et al. 1998). CBR is a method used within the field of artificial intelligence, which exposes cognitive actions, including learning and problem solving. This allows for efficient gathering of knowledge as solutions are recorded from past cases and learn from past experiences (successful or failed solutions).

Measuring efficiency in online learning is problematic (Tattersall et al. 2006). Efficiency refers to productivity calculation of quality and amount of output against the standard resources input. If the delivery of the online support requires additional hours of the lecturers' time, there is clearly an efficiency problem (Han 1999). From a student's perspective, efficiency encourages and promotes a 'just-in-time' learning environment, as queries can be dealt with in a relatively rapid period of time (minutes, rather than days). This continual time commitment is the prime resource that makes online support staff feel uncomfortable. An efficient course model must be developed to achieve the economic utilisation of a rational amount of department time to offer its students support. This model should also cater for the efficient consumption of student time, to seek this support.

As quoted from Cooze (1991):

Due to the obvious difficulties inherent in the measurements of efficiency with regard to the myriad of factors that impinge upon student achievement, one may conclude that we face a pervasive ignorance about the production function of education; that is, the relationship between school inputs and outputs.

Spector (2001) also states that:

Learning outcomes and generalisable results are seldom studied with the rigor associated with more established solutions; if we apply the WYMIWYG principle (what you measure is what you get), then we really do not know what we are getting.

Any permanent, successful, online management model must identify the legitimacy of efficiency that is based on realistic input and output ratios (Han 1999). For most courses the most precious resource is faculty time. The lack of efficiency will eventually risk the maintainability of effectiveness (Han 1999). Automation encourages efficiency within an online environment (i.e. the non-requirement of time resources), for example:

It frees up lecturers time, and allows additional time to improve or enhance the learning content It allows students to pose ad hoc questions in relation to course content, therefore promoting self development, reflection on material covered within class and higher order thinking within a 'just-in-time' learning environment.

Institutions use data on the educational inputs and outputs as factors in quality assessment systems (Tattersall et al. 2006). Efficiency data may help to provide evidence for success or failure of new educational technologies (Tattersall et al. 2006). The efficiency rate of education can be measured by dividing the total students participating in a course (input) against the number of students that successfully complete the course (output) and multiplying the sum by 100 to calculate an efficiency percentage rate, i.e.

$$Educational\ Efficiency = ((Output\ /\ Input)\ *\ 100)$$

4.2 Effectiveness

The term affordance is used to describe a potential for action, offered by an environment to actors in that environment and the perceived capacity of an object to enable the self-assurance of a learner. The term was introduced by psychologist James Gibson (Greeno 1994). Action transforms affordance into effectivities which extend human capacity (Ryder and Wilson 1996).

Table 1. Variables of online effectiveness (Adapted from Strother 2002)

Level	Variable of effectiveness	What the variable of effectiveness measures
1	Response	Was the student satisfied with the online learning and did they complete it?
2	Learning	What did the student learn from the online experience?
3	Performance	How did the online learning program affect their performance?
4	Support	Was support available and did the students benefit from the support, i.e. increased exam results?
5	Result	Were improvements in student performance attributable to online learning?

Online learning should be effective in providing 'quality' feedback and support in relation to skills a student possesses or to students in need of additional assistance to maintain or advance their educational skills (Kolodner et al. 2005). Table 1 outlines the effectiveness of online learning that can be evaluated using five variables: response, learning, performance, support and result.

In this Knowledge Economy era, a just-in-time access to learning content and an efficient way to access increasingly distributed knowledge sources is necessary, in order to solve the problem of knowledge obsolescence (Elial et al. 2006). According to Luger et al. (1998), expert systems were built to solve a range of problems in domains such as medicine, mathematics, engineering, computer science, law and business. CBR is a subset of expert systems, as outlined above. These methods involve new learning approaches characterised by the right knowledge, delivered to the right person, at just the right time, in the right way and just enough content (Elial, et al. 2006).

5 Increasing Asynchronous Support

The requirements for delivery of support have shifted in recent years, and some services require a faster turnover and problem resolution (Davenport 2005). The iterative cycle of learning consists of applying knowledge, interpreting feedback, explaining results and revising memory provides a model for promoting learning, through the use of CBR. This implies that feedback given by simulations needs to be specific enough about outcomes for learners to be able to clearly identify their misconceptions and logical errors.

The following asynchronous tools can be identified as having a clear outcome. These tools may be used to enhance asynchronous support, which is illustrated in Table 2:

5.1 CBR Versus Instructor-Enhanced Asynchronous Support

Table 2 briefly outlines asynchronous tools that can expand into online asynchronous support, to develop a 'just-in-time' learning environment, to allow rapid responses for the students. This in turn will increase efficiency by requiring fewer resources, for example, time from the lecturer.

Third level educational data should be reusable to aid the development of support, and possibly, sharable on a national, or an international basis. CBR uses an explicit database of problem solutions to address new problem-solving situations (Luger et al. 1998). These may be collected from human experts through the knowledge engineering process or may reflect the results of previous search-based successes or failures (Luger et al. 1998).

Table 2. Asynchronous tools and the application of CBR

Tool	Input	Output	CBR
Assessments, Online Quizzes, Surveys or Polls	Students effort to display what they have learned about a particular topic(s)	Grade on the percentage of how much of a particular topic they are knowledgeable with, feedback to student	**Nearest-Neighbour Indexing Techniques (NIT).** Build cases on the level of satisfactory progress, for example, 0–25% is very poor, 25-40% is poor, 40–55% satisfactory, 55%+ very satisfactory
Discussion Boards	Threaded discussion, reflection on a topic, higher reflection on debate, discussion or providing help on a topic	Ability to track student progress, relevance of discussion, participation, time logs, guidance and monitoring of students, group projects.	**Goal-based scenarios (GBS).** Students must achieve some valuable goal that requires them to learn targeted knowledge and skills, mapped through CBR. Case libraries as a resource allow students to learn from others' experiences. CBR can build cases to set certain criterion that needs to be addressed, to prevent irrelevant discussion, track interaction times, and progression within material, i.e. once a discussion has reached a high standard of reflection, and discussion, GBS sends a link to allow students to progress to another level.
Databases	Query	Answer or Response	**Case Storage, Retrieval and Adaptation**. Allow cases to be retrieved based on a Nearest Neighbour Techniques or build a confidence level to allow certain responses to be suitable or acceptable.
Email	Question, query or advice sought of the lecturer, submission of assignments.	Answer, feedback, suggestion sent onto the student. Queries can be addressed in a classroom environment or course content can be modified to clarify the issue for future students	**Inductive Indexing Techniques (IIT).** Build a form to allow students to send queries and allow cases to be retrieved that best match the key terms of the question.

Enhancing efficiency and effectiveness of student support and lecturers resources (mainly time) allows for richer interactivity and engagement of the learner and lecturer experience. Online asynchronous support can be enhanced through the use of CBR as outlined in the table above. The tools allows students to learn not only by collecting knowledge, but also by testing it, interpreting it and learning through discovery while also adding flexibility to their own learning. The advantages of applying CBR to asynchronous tools, instead of instructor support are outlined as follows:

1. ***Nearest-Neighbour Indexing Techniques (NIT)*** is a method that is highly effective, as there is only one path to be tried. The NIT is fallible as it does not require finding the shortest path, but it is a possible compromise when the time required makes exhaustive searches impractical (Luger et al. 1998). According to Valenti et al. (2003), using computers to increase our understanding of the textual features and cognitive skills involved in the creation and in the comprehension of written texts, for example, essays and reports, within an online exam environment. This will provide a number of benefits to the educational community. Valenti et al. (2003), highlights several standard text categorisation techniques are used to fulfil this goal: first, independent Bayesian classifiers allow assigning probabilities to documents estimating the likelihood that they belong to specific classes; then, an analysis of the occurrence of certain words in the documents is carried out and a k-nearest neighbour technique is used to find those essays closest to a sample of human graded assignments (or lecturers sample answer). Asynchronous support is applied to this method as it allows assignments to be submitted and rapid response may be given to the student, thus allowing them to correct any errors within their original submission. This allows students to take greater control of their own learning. A growing number of statistical learning methods have been applied to solve the problem of automated text categorization in the last few years, including regression models, nearest neighbour classifiers, Bayes belief networks, decision trees, rule learning algorithms, neural networks and inductive learning systems.

2. A ***goal-based scenario (GBS)*** is a method that will allow students to achieve some valuable goal that requires them to learn targeted knowledge and skills, mapped through CBR. Case libraries as a resource allow students to learn from others' experiences. CBR can build cases to set certain criterion that needs to be addressed, to prevent irrelevant discussion, track interaction times, and progression within material, i.e. once a discussion has reached a high standard of reflection, and discussion, GBS sends a link to allow students to progress to another level. According to Kaplan (2006), online asynchronous distributed authoring and problem solving systems are focusing attention toward particular authoring and problem-solving topics using a threaded discussion group and reward matrix. Kaplan (2006) also discusses how this mechanism can be used for directing the attention and focus of large numbers of people who are solving problems using a tree-based problem space, where the tree-based problem space may be a virtual problem space. Algorithms and procedures can be used for evaluating nodes in the virtual problem space and assigning values via a pay-off matrix that serves to focus the attention of large numbers of students and to create useful system for solving multilevel problems leveraging human expertise (Kaplan 2006). Students access the problem tree and the reward matrix over a network communication medium.

3. ***Case Storage, Retrieval and Adaptation*** allows cases to be retrieved from a database of predetermined solutions. Characteristics of cases are extracted and adapted to match the criteria of new problems by experts, and logged into the database for future student queries. Databases are a very central asynchronous tool for this activity.

4. ***Inductive Indexing Techniques (IIT)*** allows building a form to permit students to send queries and retrieves cases to be retrieved that best match the key terms of the question. Students now interact with others to exchange, arrange, manage and interact with their peers and lecturers. Interactive activities include communication, data gathering and collaborative problem solving. Email can be exploited by building a form-like interface to allow students to send queries and allow cases to be retrieved that best match the key terms of the question, through semantic networks and natural language modelling.

Engaging students in class activities is a critical matter. Today, online education has more tools to encourage students' participation and engagement (Han 1999). Online platforms such as Moodle, provides learners with a collection of tools such as threaded discussions, messaging, shared whiteboards, quizzes, tests, surveys and other forms of assessment (Elial et al. 2006). The advantages of this include the availability of authoring tools for developing online courseware, cheap and efficient storage and distribution of course materials, hyperlinks to suggested readings and digital libraries (Devedzic 2004).

The field of reasoning is very important for the development of AI-based educational software. As outlined in Figure 1, CBR implies reasoning from experience or 'old cases' in an attempt to solve problems. It attempts to analyse the outcomes to provide an account of why the proposed type of solution succeeded or failed (Salem 2000).

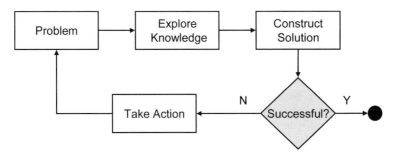

Fig. 1. The process of CBR

Maintaining a Knowledge Base (KB) where students' queries or answers are stored and the use of a CBR diagnosis process to detect and derive a relevant case (a possible answer) is an efficient solution to the difficulty of online education support (Tsinakos 2003). A further advantage to providing solutions is that the lecturer can query the system concerning the questions asked by students, identifying details such as student grade or topic of the question. This allows the lecturer to obtain valuable information, for example, the topics students had the most questions on (indicating what material is not clear enough), which questions were asked by highly or lowly graded students (providing insight on the weaknesses of those students as a group) (Tsinakos 2003).

Intelligence of an online educational system provides for some form of knowledge-based reasoning in the analysis of query resolutions, and in providing interactive problem-solving support (Devedzic 2004). According to Luger et al. (1998), all case-based reasoners share a common structure, in addressing a new problem:

1. Retrieve appropriate cases from its memory
2. Modify a retrieved case so that it will apply to the current situation
3. Apply the transformed case to the new problem
4. Save the solution, with a record of its success or failure, for future use

Student queries can be quite varied. Some cases can be recorded as relational data where subsets of arguments are matched with other arguments (Kolodner et al. 2005). Kolodner et al. also outline that others can be a more complex structure, for example, decision trees. The more complexity that is built into rules the more probable it is that a course is created that does not fully cater to the learners requirements (Funk 2002).

6 Conclusion and Future of the Research

There are many benefits of online asynchronous support to students. As outlined, these include accessibility at unscheduled times for both the student and the lecturer. This chapter outlines the need for further investment in the development of automated online asynchronous support, to develop a 'just-in-time' learning environment, and allow rapid response for the students, thus requiring fewer resources, for example, time of the student and lecturer.

Online asynchronous communication can be an excellent method of providing higher order thinking amongst students. However it can be enhanced through the use of CBR and the development of a KM cycle, which will integrate asynchronous online learning technologies and applying KM to our HE sector. The tools mentioned above that may adopt CBR methods allows students to learn not only by collecting knowledge, but also by testing it, interpreting it and learning through discovery while also adding flexibility to their own learning. This allows students to be more involved, and take greater responsibility for their own education – but through guidance and support of lecturers. Students should be more involved in the cycle by acquiring new pieces of knowledge and developing new skills. We live in a 'Renewable Resources Age.'

This chapter proposes the need for a 'Renewable Knowledge' system within our third-level colleges, which offers greater flexibility and personalisation of online learning. Third-level education is much more than accessing information. Education is about the collection, study and execution of ideas to solve problems or to generate new questions. This chapter highlights the importance of KM as it deals with methods, models and strategies to capture reuse and maintain knowledge. KM is highly relevant for online asynchronous support tools and technologies and especially later developments in KM where different methods and techniques from artificial intelligence, more specifically, case-based reasoning are used to enhance online asynchronous support for students and lecturers.

The central activity within my research is to evaluate how effective and efficient are the online asynchronous support tools and technologies for students learning within third-level colleges. Knowledge combined with support is a richer form of learning that we should take advantage of. In the future, I will continue my research of online asynchronous support tools and their application to both educational quality and supportive information tasks. This research will allow me to evaluate whether new information types and embedded techniques may be necessary to create a tighter coupling between education and technologies. The primary objective therefore is to quantify and qualify the use of asynchronous support technology and tools in enhancing the support of students within third-level colleges. I will measure the breath of diffusion of online asynchronous support already in operation within Irish Universities and Institutes of Technology.

According to my literature review, the design and creation of online asynchronous support activities is difficult to accomplish. However, if we use the capabilities and affordances of technology, we may introduce a method to improve online asynchronous support. The use of reusable data and AI to produce online support is one possibility to affect such change and enhance the quality of email, discussion boards and online assessments, within an online learning environment.

References

Ally, M. (2004) 'Theory and Practice of Online Learning', Chapter 1 - Foundations of Educational Theory for Online Learning, retrieved from website: http://cde.athabascau.ca/online_book/pdf/TPOL_book.pdf

Berge, Z.L. (2003), 'Barriers to eLearning', Fourth Annual Irish Educational Technology Users Conference Waterford, Ireland, 22 and 23 May

Bobrow, D.G., Mittal S., Stefik Mark J. (1989), 'Expert Systems: Perils and Promises', Communications of the ACM, 29(9)

Clarke, C. (2003), 'Towards a Unified e-Learning Strategy', Department for Education and Skills, UK, Consultation Document, http://www.dfes.gov. uk/elearningstrategy/strategy.stm

Cooze, J. (1991) 'The Elusive Concept of Efficiency in Education' Faculty of Education, Autumn, retrieved from website: http://www.mun.ca/educ/faculty/mwatch/vol1/cooze.html

Davenport, D. (2005) 'Developing an e-Learning Support Model', November

Devedzic, V. (2004), 'Education and the Semantic Web', 'International Journal of Artificial Intelligence in Education', 165–191

Dipaolo, A. (2004), 'A Symposium eLearning as a Strategic Imperative for universities in Ireland' conference, DCU, 4 November, retrieved from website: http://www.crossborder.ie/pubs/e-learningreport.pdf

Donnelly, R. O'Rourke, K. (2007), 'What now? Evaluating eLearning CPD practice in Irish third-level education' in Journal of Further and Higher Education, 31(1), 31–40.

Elial, G., Secundo, G., Taurino, C., (2006), 'Towards unstructured and just-in-time learning: the "Virtual eBMS" e-Learning system', Current Developments in Technology-Assisted Education (2006), retrieved from website: http://www.formatex.org/micte2006/pdf/1067-1072.pdf

Funk, P. (2002), 'Case-Based Reasoning and Knowledge Management to Improved Adaptability of Intelligent tutoring Systems', Workshop on Case-Based Reasoning for Education and Training at 6th European Conference on Case Based Reasoning, pp 15–23.

Garrison, A., Randy, D., Anderson, T. Archer W. (2000) , 'Critical Thinking, Cognitive Presence, and Computer Conferencing in Distance Education' American Journal of Distance Education, April

Greeno, J.G. (1994) 'Gibson's Affordances', Psychologists Review, 101(2), 336–342

Han, Xiaoxing, P. (1999), Exploring an Effective and Efficient Online Course Management Model, Newsletter: 5(2), November 15

Israel, J. Aiken, R. (2007), 'Supporting Collaborative Learning with an Intelligent Online System', International Journal of Artificial Intelligence in Education, 17, 3–40

Kaplan, C.A., (2006) 'Method and system for asynchronous online distributed problem solving including problems in education, business, finance, and technology', retrieved from http://www.freepatentsonline.com/7155157.html

Kolodner, J.L., Cox M.T., Gonzalez P.A. (2005), 'Case-Based Reasoning-inspired approached to education', The Knowledge Engineering Review, 20(3), 299–303

Luger, G.F., Stubblefield, W.A., (1998), Artificial Intelligence – Structures and Strategies for Complex Problem Solving, Third Edition, 'Artificial Intelligence: Its roots and scope', pp 235–240

Mabrito, M. (2006), 'A study of Synchronous Versus Asynchronous Collaboration in an Online Writing Class', The American Journal of Distance Education, 20(2), 93–107

McCormick, R. Paechter, C. (1998), Learning and Knowledge', Paul Chapman Publishing

Nichols, M. (2003), 'A theory for eLearning', Educational Technology & Society, March, pp. 1–10

Ryder, M., Wilson, B. (1996), 'Affordance and Constraints of the Internet for Learning and Instruction'. Retrieved from website: http://www.cudenver.edu/~mryder/aect_96.html

Sánchez, I.A., Savage T., Tangney B. (2004) 'Higher Education (HE), Information Communication Technology (ICT) and Learning: ICT for replication OR innovation?'

Skilbeck, M. (2003), 'Towards an Integrated System of Tertiary Education - A Discussion Paper', http://www.dit.ie/DIT/news/2003/Skilbeckdiscussionpaper_march2003.pdf

Sloffer, S.J., Dueber, B., Duffy, T.M. (1999), 'Using Asynchronous Conferencing to Promote Critical Thinking: Two Implementations in Higher Education', Proc 32nd HICSS

Strother, J.B. (2002), 'An Assessment of the Effectiveness of e-learning in Corporate Training Programs', The International Review of Research in Open and Distance Learning, 3(1)

Spector, M.J. (2001), 'An Overview of Progress and Problems in Educational Technology', Interactive Educational Multimedia, 3, 27–37

Tattersall, C., Waterink, W., Höpperener, K.R. (2006), 'A Case in the Measurement of Educational Efficiency in Open and Distance Learning', Distance Education, 27(3), 391–404.

Tsinakos, A. (2003), 'Asynchronous distance Education: Teaching using Case Based Reasoning', Turkish Online Journal of Distance Education – TOJDE, 4, July

Valenti, S., Neri, F., Cucchiarelli, A., (2003), 'An Overview of Current Research on Automated Essay Grading', Journal of Information Technology Education, 2, 2003

Vedder, P. (1990), 'Measuring the quality of Education', Swets and Zeitlinger, pp 1–22

Walsham, B., (2003), 'Simplified and Optimised Ant Sort for Complex Problems: Document Classification', http://www.csse.monash.edu.au/hons/se-projects/2003/Walsham/Benjamin_Walsham_Thesis_Main.pdf

Effort Estimation Using Social Choice

Stefan Koch and Johann Mitloehner

Vienna University of Economics and Business Administration, Institute for Information Business, stefan.koch@wu-wien.ac.at, mitloehn@wu-wien.ac.at

Abstract In this chapter, we argue for adopting mechanisms from the field of social choice for effort estimation. Social choice deals with aggregating the preferences of a number of individuals into a single ranking. We will use this idea, substituting these voters by different project attributes. Therefore a new project only needs to be placed into rankings per attribute, necessitating only ordinal values. Using the resulting aggregate ranking, the new project is again placed between other projects, whose actual expended effort can be used to derive an estimation. In this chapter, we will present this method together with a sample application and validation based on the well-known COCOMO 81 data set.

1 Introduction

The estimation of effort and costs for developing information systems has been a topic of research for a long time (Jorgensen and Shepperd 2007). This has led to the development of several methods for effort estimation (Boehm et al. 2000a), including the well-known COCOMO (Boehm 1981), its update COCOMO II (Boehm et al. 2000b), Putnam's model (Putnam 1978), approaches based on the function point metric (Albrecht and Gaffney 1983; Matson et al. 1994), and also proprietary versions like SLIM or ESTIMACS. Nevertheless, the predictive quality has still been limited, as exemplified by many software projects running over budget or alloted time frame. The reasons for these problems are manifold, including the inherent uncertainty of software development, and the huge diversity in projects and adopted processes, which necessitate careful adoption and calibration of models.

Besides these mostly algorithmic approaches, a class of models has been developed based on machine-learning concepts (Srinivasan and Fisher 1995). The proposed methods have used, among others, neural nets (MacDonnel and Gray 1996; Srinivasan and Fisher 1995), regression trees (Selby and Porter 1988) or case-based reasoning, respectively analogy-based estimation (Shepperd et al. 1996; Shepperd and Schofield 1997; Myrtveit and Stensrud 1999).

Advantages are among others that a wide range of metrics can be employed to characterize a software project, in comparison to algorithmic approaches, which most often and basically use a single metric like lines-of-code or function points. Also Kitchenham and Mendes (2004) have argued that multidimensional output

C. Barry et al. (eds.), *Information Systems Development: Challenges in Practice, Theory, and Education, Vol.2*, doi: 10.1007/978-0-387-78578-3_24,

metrics are necessary to capture the full richness of software development. Problems of some of these approaches are on the one hand the necessary data base of appropriate projects, and that the exact computation is sometimes difficult to grasp, which might lead to a decrease in acceptance, especially at management level.

In this chapter, we will argue to adopt techniques from the area of social choice for effort estimation. The advantage is that while arbitrary metrics can be used in arriving at an estimation, the process is fully transparent and easily understood. This approach is most akin to analogy-based estimation, with some differences as will be described here. We will also provide a discussion of the paired comparisons proposed by Miranda (2001) for estimation, inspired by the analytic hierarchy process (Saaty 1990).

The structure of the chapter is as follows: In the next section, an introduction to the topic and the techniques of social choice will be presented. Then, we will apply these ideas to effort estimation, for illustration using an available open and well-known dataset, the COCOMO data. We will shortly describe the dataset and the available metrics, then apply the effort estimation procedure and provide an analysis of the results and the method overall. The chapter will end with conclusions and directions for future research.

2 Social Choice

In social choice individuals express preferences over a set of candidates, and some aggregation algorithm (a voting rule) is used to find a corresponding winner or set of winners. We define such a problem by a set of n voters providing rankings for m alternatives, resulting in a "profile", e.g. for alternatives a, b, c and rankings a > b > c, b > c > a, c > a > b, b > c > a, the problem of rank aggregation consists of finding an aggregate ranking x >= y >= z such that the preferences stated by the voters are expressed in the aggregate ranking; e.g. a suitable aggregation from the example above is b > c > a, where alternative b is the only element in the winner set. An aggregation resulting from the application of a voting rule may contain indifferences, and the winner set may contain more than one alternative. In social choice problems we are interested in the winner set only, while the problem of finding a ranking of all candidates is referred to as a social welfare problem in the literature. Profiles are typically assumed to consist of strict orderings only; in this work we allow for indifferences in the input rankings, such as x > y = z which means that in this ranking the alternatives y and z are considered equal, while x is better than both y and z. As will be shown, allowing for indifferences gives more flexibility and possibilities in the effort estimation.

There are several demands that are usually placed on aggregation rules. One of the most important is the Condorcet criterion: if an alternative x exists that beats all other alternatives in pairwise comparisons, x is a Condorcet winner (Fishburn 1977), and an obvious demand on an aggregation rule is that it select x as a winner. Another demand on aggregation rules is that the aggregate relation should not contain any cycles and represent a complete weak order of the alternatives. Voting rules fulfill these demands to differing degrees.

Not all social choice voting rules support the existence of weak rankings, as we will employ in this application. The following description gives a short overview of voting rules from social choice theory that are based on margins; these margin-based rules allow for resolving indifferences in an easy and intuitive way. The margin of x versus y is $M(x,y) = |x > y|-|y > x|$ i.e. the number of rankings where x is preferred to y minus the number of rankings where y is preferred to x. We extend this definition for profiles with indifferences by excluding the indifferent voters from the count: rankings with indifference of x and y do not contribute to the margin of x versus y.

Simple Majority (SM): The simple majority rule is a well-known procedure based on margins: a positive margin means that x wins against y in pairwise comparison and results in $x > y$ in the aggregate relation, a negative margins leads to $y > x$, and a zero margin means indifference $x = y$. This rule can easily result in cycles, such as $x > y$, $y > z$, $z > x$ (drop the fourth voter from the example given above to arrive at a cycle). This limits the use of the simple majority rule in practical applications.

Maximin (MM): The Maximin rule scores the alternatives with the worst margin they each achieve and ranks them according to those scores.

Copeland (CO): The Copeland rule scores the alternatives with the sum over the signs of the margins they achieve and ranks them according to those scores.

Borda (BO): The Borda rule assigns decreasing points to consecutive positions, such as 2 points for first place, 1 point for second and zero for third. The alternatives are then ranked according to their total scores.

Note that all rules including the Borda relation can be computed from the margins alone; see, e.g., Klamler (2005). Since those rules are based on the same data they will generally produce similar results; however, e.g., for the profile $((a>d>c>b),(b>a>d>c),(b>a>c>d))$ the margins are $((0,-1,3,3),(1,0,1,1),(-3,-1,0,-1),(-3,-1,1,0))$, and the rankings resulting from the margin-based rules are SM and CO: $(b>a>d>c)$, MM: $(b>a>c=d)$, and BO: $(a>b>d>c)$, i.e., SM and CO produce exactly the same aggregate ranking, MM still selects the same winner but introduces an indifference with c and d, while BO selects candidate a instead of b as the winner. More details on these and other commonly used voting rules and their properties can be found, e.g., in Fishburn (1977) and Saari (2001). Some observations on the proximity of the results the rules mentioned deliver can be found in Eckert et al. (2006).

3 Application and Analysis

3.1 Main Idea

For using social choice in effort estimation, we will employ a basic analogy: Voting rules can be used for effort estimation by replacing voters with project attributes. This means that each attribute considered provides a ranking of all projects available in the database. Since indifferences are allowed it is straightforward to obtain a weak ranking from numeric project attributes; this is the method we will apply in our ex-post study. However, note that an ordinal scale is sufficient for the application of these methods: experts need only supply rankings for past projects in terms of the various attributes, which simplifies the gathering of input data. Each ranking therefore gives the impression of "size" or "complexity" of the projects according to one attribute. The aggregated ranking of all attributes will then represent an overall picture of the projects' "complexity", and thus a ranking of the efforts necessary to implement them.

For estimating a new project, the process is straightforward: According to each attribute, the project is put into the respective ranking. Therefore, no quantification is necessary, the project is simply classified to be either between two existing projects in the ranking, or equivalent. After this has been accomplished for all attributes, a social choice voting rule is employed to arrive at an aggregate ranking. In this aggregate ranking, the new project again is ranked somewhere between two other projects (or equivalent to one or more projects). As for all the other projects the expended efforts are known, we have a ranking that gives the information between which efforts the new project will be located. We can than either use both values to arrive at a upper and lower bound, or compute the mean to arrive at a single value.

We will discuss this with a small example first, before moving to the validation using a large data set. In this example, we know three projects (A, B, and C) with their actual effort, their size in function points (Albrecht and Gaffney 1983) and their programmer capability. Project A has 1,500 function points, medium programmer capability and actual effort of 150 person-months, B has 1,200 function points, high capability and 80 person-months, and C 900, low capability and 72 person-months. This results in the ranking A > B > C for the "voter" function points, and C > A > B for capability. If we want to derive an effort estimation for a new project D, we need to place it into these ranking. First, we determine that the function point count will be smaller than A, but larger than B, resulting in the new ranking A > D > B > C. The programmer capability is equivalent to A, resulting in the second ranking C > A = D > B. Using a social choice voting rule, for example the Borda rule, results in an aggregated ranking of A > D > C > B. We see that D is ranked between A and C, so the effort is estimated to be between their values of 1,500 and 1,200, or 1,350 if a single value is needed.

3.2 Data Set

The COCOMO Project Data Base contains project attributes and actual effort data for 63 software projects; since its publication in the classic volume by Boehm (1981) it has been used as a database for many software project effort estimation methods because of its ready availability and the possibility of comparison with other approaches. For the same reasons the COCOMO data set is used in this work.

The attributes used in this work are RELY (required software reliability), DATA (data base size), CPLX (process complexity), TIME (time constraint for cpu), STOR (main memory constraint), VIRT (machine volatility), TURN (turn-around time), ACAP (analysts capability), AEXP (application experience), PCAP (programmers capability), VEXP (virtual machine experience), LEXP (language experience), MODP (modern programming practices), TOOL (use of software tools), and SCED (schedule constraint). We explicitly do not include the lines-of-code, respectively KDSI (kilo delivered source instructions) of the projects, as this metric is difficult to estimate at the beginning of a project.

3.3 Application of Social Choice Voting Rules

In order to apply the social choice aggregation rules to the COCOMO data set the transition from rational values to ordinal values has to be made. This results in 15 rankings for the 63 projects, corresponding to the 15 project attributes. The project attributes in the data set are available in numeric format with values ranging from 0.70 to 1.66; however, in the evaluation of the projects there are only a limited number of different values actually used, e.g., only five levels for RELY are attributed to the projects. Therefore, many indifferences are contained in the rankings that form the base for the aggregation by the social choice rules. Fortunately, the use of margin-based aggregation rules allows for easy treatment of these indifferences, since indifferent voters simply do not contribute to the corresponding margins. The transformation from COCOMO values to rankings is therefore straightforward.

The voting rules are applied with the individual attribute rankings as input; the corresponding aggregate project rankings regularly contain indifferences, i.e., some ranks are shared by several projects; therefore, to derive an estimate for a project x whose actual effort is not known we distinguish the following cases: (1) Project x shares its rank with other projects; in this case we use the mean of the other projects' efforts as the estimate. (2) Project x is the only occupant of rank r with ranks r–1 and r+1 occupied by other projects; in this case we use the mean of the minimum effort at rank r-1 and the maximum effort at rank r+1 as the estimate. (3) Project x is ranked as new top or bottom; in this case we use the current maximum or minimum effort as an estimate.

We use this method to arrive at estimates for each of the 63 projects in the COCOMO 81 data set, effectively treating each project as if it were not part of the data set and its actual effort were to be estimated from its attributes and the remaining 62 projects. This jackknifing approach provides us with a performance evaluation of the estimation method.

3.4. Analysis of Estimation Accuracy

In order to study the performance of effort estimation we did not use standard measures such as average deviation since a few widely inaccurate estimates influence the overall measure in a way that is not representative of the quality of the whole approach. Other measures such as the PRED30 more closely capture the perceived estimation quality. In this type of measure the percentage of estimates that lie within a certain range of the actual values is stated, such as the number of estimates that lie within 30% of the actual values. In our work we use the PRED30 measure to evaluate the accurateness of the estimation.

Aggregating the rankings derived from the COCOMO project attributes in a straightforward manner results in rather poor performance; however, by eliminating some project attributes from the rank aggregation a PRED30 value of 0.30 can be reached with the Copeland and Simple Majority voting rules, i.e., 30% of the projects were estimated within a 30% range of their actual efforts. The Borda rule fares a little worse with PRED30 values of 0.28, and the Maximin rule achieves a PRED30 value of 0.25. Table 1 shows the corresponding project attributes used for the rank aggregation. Since the aggregation rules use the margin data in different ways the combinations of attributes that result in maximum prediction accuracy are not identical for all rules (see Table 1). These optimal combinations for each rule were found by trying all 2^{15} combinations of the 15 project attributes.

Table 1. Project attributes used in aggregate rankings, and the correlation r of each attribute with the actual project effort; the acap and aexp rankings have been inverted for aggregation.

	rely	data	cplx	time	stor	virt	turn	acap	aexp	pcap	vexp	lexp	modp	tool	sced
SM	x			x	x		x			x					
CO	x				x	x	x			x					
BO		x		x	x					x	x				
MM	x	x	x	x	x		x			x	x	x		x	
r	0.21	0.45	0.01	0.15	0.10	0.02	0.21	-0.15	-0.04	0.16	0.07	0.09	0.27	0.00	0.02

The accuracy of the resulting estimates is similar to the initial Basic COCOMO model estimates of 29% for PRED30 (Boehm 1981, p. 84); however, any comparison of estimation accurateness has to take into account the fact that the estimation approach described in this work does not rely on rational values for the project attributes; rankings are sufficient. In practical applications this translates into a significant advantage for this approach since experts do not have to provide numeric values for the project attributes; it is sufficient to provide rankings, which are usually much easier to derive from past experience and expertise. We also did not include the lines-of-code (KDSI) available for each project, which is difficult to estimate at project start, although using the social choice approach, only a ranking of existing projects would be necessary. It is to be expected that including this project attribute, which COCOMO uses as main cost driver, would significantly enhance the predictive quality.

4 Conclusions and Future Research

It has been shown that using social choice voting rules for rank aggregation a software project effort estimation method can be constructed that achieves an estimation accurateness comparable to traditional regression-based approaches, especially when taking into account the fact that only ordinal values are needed. While in this ex-post study rational values were used to derive project rankings for each attribute, the practical application of the approach only calls for ranking projects according to attributes, which is usually a much easier task than specifying rationally scaled values.

The approaches in effort estimation showing the most semblance to the method presented here are analogy-based estimation (Shepperd et al. 1996; Shepperd and Schofield 1997; Myrtveit and Stensrud 1999) and paired comparisons (Miranda 2001). Both social choice and analogy-based approaches can deal with any number of variables, and search for the most similar projects. On the other hand, analogy-based estimation necessitates that the values of the different variables are expressed for the project to be estimated on a rational scale, and similarity is computed based on the Euclidean distance in the resulting n-dimensional space. In the social choice approach, projects only need to be ranked according to each attribute, then the different rankings are aggregated to determine similar projects. The estimation approach presented by Miranda (2001) based on AHP (Saaty 1990) is detailed for the case of size estimations. Using comparisons between each of the entities with a given limited verbal scale ("equal" "slightly/much/extremely", "smaller/bigger") results in a vector of weights which can be used to arrive at estimates for the size of all entities, if at least one reference point out of them is known. The semblance to social choice lies mostly in the fact that no quantification is needed from the user, only comparisons. In fact, the resulting vector is a form of ranking. The difference lies mostly in the fact that this approach is geared towards estimating a single attribute for several entities based on a single reference point, while social choice as described uses an arbitrary list of variables and aggregates the resulting ranking, thus leading to an overall picture and an effort estimate, but only for a single new project at a time; and since there are only weak preference assertions there is no need for a translation of verbal scales into numeric values as in AHP and similar methods.

Using a well-known data set, we have demonstrated the accuracy and applicability of the social choice method. On the other hand, there is still room for improvement in the estimation accuracy of the approach as presented by applying some extensions. Currently, each project attribute is either included in the ranking, or it is discarded. As some attributes clearly have a stronger relationship to resulting effort than others, the next step would be to have more voters than attributes, with several voters giving their ranking according to a single attribute. For example, we might include ten voters using a ranking based on function points, while only two use the programmer capability. This would result in different weights assigned to the attributes, which currently is only binary. Using the ranking of known projects according to their actual expended efforts as "target" aggregated ranking, these weights, i.e., number of voters, could be optimized using appropriate techniques.

References

Albrecht, A.J. and J.E. Gaffney (1983) "Software Function, Source Lines of Code, and Development Effort Prediction: A Software Science Validation", *IEEE Trans Software Eng*, 9(6), 639–648.

Boehm, B.W. (1981) *Software Engineering Economics*, Prentice Hall, Englewood Cliffs, NJ.

Boehm, B.W., Abts, C., and S. Chulani (2000a) "Software development cost estimation approaches – A survey", *Annals of Software Engineering*, 10, 177–205.

Boehm, B.W., Abts, C., Brown, A.W., Chulani, S., Clark, B.K., Horowitz, E., Madachy, R., Reifer, D.J., and B. Steece (2000b) *Software Cost Estimation with COCOMO II*,Prentice Hall PTR, Upper Saddle River, NJ.

Eckert, D., Klamler, C., Mitlöhner, J., and C. Schlötterer (2006) "A Distance-based Comparison of Basic Voting Rules", *Central European Journal of Operations Research*, 14(4), 377–386.

Fishburn, P. C. (1977) "Condorcet Social Choice Functions", *SIAM Journal of Applied Mathematics*, 33, 469–489.

Jorgensen, M. and M. Shepperd (2007) "A Systematic Review of Software Development Cost Estimation Studies", *IEEE Trans Software Eng*, 33(1), 33–53.

Kitchenham, B. and E. Mendes (2004) "Software Productivity Measurement Using Multiple Size Measures", *IEEE Trans Software Eng*, 30(12), 1023–1035.

Klamler, C. (2005) "On the Closeness Aspect of Three Voting Rules: Borda – Copeland – Maximin", *Group Decision and Negotiation*, 14(3), 233–240.

MacDonnel, S.G., and A.R. Gray (1996) "Alternatives to Regression models for estimating Software Projects", *Proc IFPUG Fall Conference*, Dallas, Texas, pp. 279.1–279.15.

Matson, J.E., Barrett, B.E., and J.M. Mellichamp (1994) "Software Development Cost Estimation Using Function Points", *IEEE Trans Software Engineering*, 20(4), 275–287.

Miranda, E. (2001) "Improving Subjective Estimates Using Paired Comparisons", *IEEE Software*, 18(1), 87–91.

Myrtveit, I., and E. Stensrud (1999) "A Controlled Experiment to Assess the Benefits of Estimating with Analogy and Regression Models", *IEEE Trans Software Eng*, 25(4), 510–525.

Putnam, L.H. (1978) "A General Empirical Solution to the Macro Software Sizing and Estimating Problem", *IEEE Trans Software Eng*, 4(4), 345–361.

Saari, D. (2001) *Decisions and Elections – Explaining the Unexpected*, Cambridge University Press.

Saaty T.L. (1990) *Multicriteria Decision Making: The Analytic Hierarchy Process*, RWS Publications, Pittsburgh.

Selby, R.W., and A.A. Porter (1988) "Learning from Examples: Generation and Evaluation of Decision Trees for Software Resource Analysis", *IEEE Trans Software Eng*, 14(12), 1743–1756.

Shepperd, M., and C. Schofield (1997) "Estimating Software Project Effort Using Analogies", *I IEEE Trans Software Eng*, 23(12), 736–743.

Shepperd, M., Schofield, C., and B. Kitchenham (1996) "Effort Estimation Using Analogy", *Proc ICSE 1996*, Berlin, Germany, pp. 170–178.

Srinivasan, K., and D. Fisher (1995) "Machine Learning Approaches to Estimating Software Development Effort", *IEEE Trans Software Eng*, 21(2), 126–137.

Work Progress Estimation from Structured Requirements Specifications

Christian Kop

Alpen-Adria-Universität Klagenfurt, Applied Informatics, chris@ifit.uni-klu.ac.at

Abstract   In practice the system analyst is confronted with a bulk of requirements. He has to structure and to decompose them until he can start to model the structure, functionality, and behavior of the information system. In such a situation it is hard to find out the progress of his work. A proposal on how to estimate this work progress is presented here.

1 Introduction

In practice the system analyst is confronted with a bulk of requirements. He has to classify and decompose them until he can start to model the structure, functionality, and behavior of the information system. In such a situation it is hard to find out the progress of his work. A good indicator of the work progress is the completeness of the already collected requirements. In Costello and Liu (1995) completeness of requirements depends on the amounts of "*to be completed*" statements or equivalent possibilities such as the degree of decomposition. However, a low degree of composition does not always mean that a requirement is incomplete. It might also mean that a requirement is already simple and there is no need to further decompose it. Thus such a metric strongly depends on the level of abstraction of a certain requirement. If this level is not given, no quantitative evidence of completeness can be given. Furthermore annotations like "*to be completed*", "*to be supplied*", or something equivalent only work if they are really inserted as placeholders. If this is not done, the requirements might be treated as complete since the analyst simply forgets the fact that a certain requirement is incomplete. Furthermore if natural language requirements are given, it is hard to decide which kind of information is missing. If the system analyst does not know if some requirements are incomplete, it will be hard for him to estimate the progress of his work. To overcome the disadvantages that it is not clear at which step a requirement should be further decomposed, the solution would be to set a definite end. That means there must be a lowest level of requirements specification which cannot be further decomposed. This solves the decomposition problem and each requirement which is not at the lowest level is by default incomplete. However this does not

C. Barry et al. (eds.), *Information Systems Development: Challenges in Practice, Theory, and Education, Vol.2*, doi: 10.1007/978-0-387-78578-3_25,
© Springer Science+Business Media, LLC 2009

also solve the problem to decide the completeness and thus the work progress of the low-level requirements.

The more the requirements are structured, the more it is possible to determine which kind of information is missing and thus to decide if a requirement is incomplete or not. Furthermore it is much easier for structured requirement specification that a computer-supported way will work to estimate the (in)completeness and thus work progress. Hence, low-level requirements must be structured in order to support the estimation of completeness. As a solution, in this chapter glossaries will be introduced to structure requirements and to support this estimation. During requirements elicitation the requirements should be decomposed until glossary columns can be filled out.

Therefore, the chapter is structured as follows. Firstly an overview of the related work is given. In Section 3 the glossary approach called KCPM (Klagenfurt Conceptual Predesign Model) for structuring requirements specifications is introduced. It is a model that can be understood as an interlingua between natural language requirements and conceptual models. It uses glossaries for representing requirements in a structured way. In Sections 4–6, the several possibilities to estimate the work progress from glossaries are described. Section 7 summarizes this chapter.

2 Related Work

There are many methodologies which help to communicate with the stakeholders. Such approaches use goal modelling, scenarios, and story boarding (Mylopoulos et al. 1999; Rolland et al. 1998; Sutcliffe et al. 1998; Schewe et al. 2004). An end-user manual style for requirement specification documents is used in Berry et al. (2004). In Koch and Escalona et al. (2004) other approaches like interviewing, brain storming, joint application development, questionnaires, and checklists are mentioned. Most often end users themselves still prefer natural language. However, natural language has a big disadvantage. It is ambiguous and even for already collected requirements it is hard to determine if they are complete or if something is missing. For natural language requirements, in Costello and Liu (1995), an approach to estimate the completeness was discussed. However, this approach mainly depends on the decomposition of requirements and the number of statements like "to be completed". As it was already mentioned in the introduction this could lead to some problems (e.g., when to end with the decomposition and forgotten "to be completed" statements). Researchers also propose controlled natural language for requirements specifications (Hoppenbrouwers et al. 2005; Rupp 2002), (Fuchs et al. 1999). For the requirements pattern defined in Rupp (2002), in Pikalek (2006) also some measures are given to check the quality according to the IEEE quality standards for requirements (e.g., completeness, traceability, unambiguous, etc.). Although a controlled language helps to disambiguate requirements, the problem might arise that requirements that belong together are scattered in a text. Glossaries can be seen as a continuation of controlled languages. Information that belongs together is collected together (for details see

Section 3). Thus, among the other mentioned methodologies glossaries represent one way to communicate with the end users. Tabular representation for the specification of input and output behavior of functions was already used in the 1970s (Hoffmann and Weiss 2001). In the 1980s, the DATAID approach used glossaries as a central concept of their methodology. This approach was extended by the KCPM approach (Mayr and Kop 2002). Similar techniques, namely forms and templates nowadays are used for use cases (Cockburn 2000) and in the NDT approach (Escalona et al. 2004). For requirements specifications, glossaries can be seen as the "final point". On one hand it is still a mean for communication with the end user on the other hand the structured and classified information is a good starting point for the transformation of the requirements to the conceptual model.

3 Glossaries to Structure Requirements Specifications

In practice, it is the task of a system analyst to extract the right information out of the bulk of information. Doing this task a system analyst is more like a doctor who has to find out what the problem of the patient is. If the system analyst has some pattern in mind for what he should search or what he should ask the end user, he will do his task better and the quality will rise. In such a situation glossaries can support the business analyst. A glossary is structured as follows. Each row in the glossary represents a notion of the domain or the feature of a system. Each column represents information that should be considered during requirements elicitation. Glossaries can not only be used for the elicitation of structured requirements, they are also useful to document requirements sources and additional information. Figure 1 shows the relationship between different kinds of structured requirements (requirements modelling objects), requirements sources, and additional information. All these will be described in detail in the following sections.

3.1 Modelling Requirements

The most important modelling notions of the static part of the approach are: thing-type and connection-type. **Thing-type** is a generalization of the notions class and attribute used, e.g., in UML diagrams. Thus, typical thing-types are, e.g., *author*, *book*, *contract* as well as characteristics like *customer name*, *product number*, *product description*. In KCPM the question whether the notion is a class or an attribute is not very important since it is possible to derive these notions in a subsequent transformation step automatically (Mayr and Kop 2002; Kop et al. 2006). This supports the elicitation process since the business analyst can concentrate to find the right notions. Figure 2 shows some information that can be collected for thing-types.

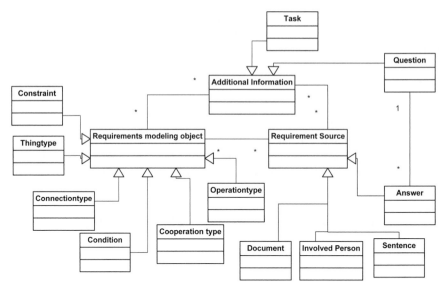

Fig. 1. Relationship between the most important concepts

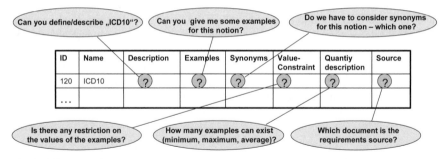

Fig. 2. Thing-type glossary

Things are related within the real world. To capture this, the KCPM model introduces the notion of **connection-type**. Two or more thing-types can be involved in a connection-type. This is based on the NIAM (ORM) object/role model (Nijssen and Halpin 1989). A Sentence (business rule) leading to a connection type could be the following: *Authors write books.*

The model is open for specific semantic connection-types (possession, composition, generalization, identification, etc.), e.g., *An ISBN number identifies a book.*

Operation types are used to model services as described in (Hesse and Mayr 1998). Therefore they can be seen as a generalization of the conceptual notions such as use case, activity, action, method, service. Each operation type is characterized by references to so-called thing-types, which model the actors (executing actors and calling actors of the operation type) and service parameters. For instance an ATM could be the executing actor which provides a service *give* *money*. A customer is the calling actor of that service. The thing-type *money* could be an outgoing service parameter. Thing-type *customer-code* could be the ingoing service parameter. Beside these notions represented as columns in a glossary, operation types are specified in detail also by other columns. These columns are: **description of the operation type, duration, frequency of usage, execution description**.

Other KCPM concepts for modelling behavior are **cooperation type** and **condition**. For details on these notions the reader is referred to (Kop and Mayr 2002). Nonfunctional requirements are collected currently with the concept **constraint**.

3.2 Requirements Sources

A modelling language for requirements modelling must also have an aspect for modelling the requirements sources. Currently sentences, documents, and involved persons (inv. persons) are the main requirements sources.

The **sentence** is the smallest unit of requirements source. It can be generated manually but mainly it is generated if KCPM notions are derived automatically from a requirements specification text (Fliedl et al. 2007). In this case for each notion the sentences are listed, in which the notion was mentioned and could be derived from.

The whole **document** is used for the requirements source, if there is no need to relate KCPM notions to a sentence. If a notion is related to a document, then it means that the notion appears in that document. It is a common practice to manage documents according to some features. In KCPM, documents are managed according to the following characteristics: **title of the document, owner, creator, received from person, last update, priority, purpose of the document, format, and document abstract**.

The source "**involved person**" deals with the fact that often requirements are given without any document, they are just said. Similar to (Rupp 2002), involved persons can be classified according to the following characteristics: **title, first name, last name** of the person, **telephone number, email, preferred communication media, preferred communication style, reachability, reason of involvement, organizational function**, and **first meeting at**.

3.3 Additional Information

If the system analyst has still some detailed question to a certain concept (a thing-type, an operation type, or a concrete requirements document) which he cannot answer by himself, then he can note this as a **question**. Such a question is treated as an **open question** until it is answered (**answer**). Since such an answer can be a source for new requirements the answer can also be seen as a special source.

In practice a system analyst cannot always complete a certain requirement modelling object at once. Therefore he can also define **tasks** which specify what he has to do in the future. An example for a task might be: *"don't forget to go to the library and look, if notion 'Z' is better explained in the document XY!"*. He can also define tasks for requirement sources like a document. If the task is not finished, then it is treated as an **open task**. A flag "**finished**" and the date at which it was finished, specifies that the task has been finished. For each task also a **deadline** can be defined.

4 Underlying Idea for Analyzing the Elicitation Progress

The relationships between requirements modelling objects, requirements sources open questions, and open tasks, as well as the glossary structure of requirements modelling objects and requirements sources can be now used for analyzing the requirements elicitation progress.

4.1 Requirements Decomposition and Completeness

In Costello and Liu (1995) it was stated, that requirements with a low decomposition might be a hint for incompleteness. But it also might be possible that this requirement is already a low-level requirement which does not need any further decomposition. Such a statement is very ambiguous. In fact it tells nothing about completeness of a requirement. If a low-level requirement is expressed in glossaries, then requirements which do not match with such a pattern can be treated as incomplete. The empty glossary columns can be counted. In that way completeness can be determined. This will be described in the next section.

4.2 Number of Filled Columns Per Requirements Modelling Object

If a requirement is classified and structured, using a requirement modelling object and its columns, then the progress of the work can be better determined. It can be analyzed to which extend a certain requirements modelling object is filled. In this section this is demonstrated for thing-types but it can be applied to other requirements modelling notions.

If glossary columns are used to structure and classify the requirements then counting the number of filled columns for a certain concept (e.g., a certain thing-type-like "customer") and divide this by the total amount of glossary columns is a simple way to determine to which extend the glossaries are filled. With this result, the analyst will get an overview to which extend information is collected for a certain concept. The columns ID and name of thing-type can be ignored, since a system analyst cannot store a thing-type without given it a name. The ID will be generated automatically. All other fields might be empty, since the system analyst might not have all information at the moment. Hence, for the counting of filled and empty columns, the following thing-type glossary columns must be considered: thing-type description, quantity description, synonym, example, format description, and value constraint.

The total amount of columns for a thing-type is 5. Now the number of filled columns might be counted and divided by 5 in order to get the percentage of filled columns. However, there is one problem which must be considered. Not for all columns information must be collected. There are mandatory columns and optional columns. One way to solve this problem would be to count only the mandatory columns. Another solution would be to include a weighting factor W_c to each of the columns. The weighting factor depends on the experience and knowledge of the analyst. The weighting factor is a number between 0 and 1 and expresses how important a certain column is for a certain requirements modelling object (e.g., for all the thing-types). The weighting factor must be defined individually for each column. Let's take the value constraint column in the thing-type glossary. If the analyst thinks that at the end there will be a percentage of 80% of thing-types for which the column must be filled, then the column for value constraints will get the weighting factor 0.8. Of course, the weighting factor also depends on the subsequent steps of the information system development. If a column entry is needed during conceptual modelling, design, or implementation then the weighting factor must be higher. If such a factor W_c is taken into consideration when counting the total amount of columns for a concept i, then the total amount of columns that can be filled is not simply n but:

$$T_i = \sum_{c=1}^{n} W_c$$

This means that instead of just counting the columns 1...n, the importance of the column (e.g., 0.5 for the first column, 0.8 for the second column, etc.) are summarized (see also the given example below). However, T_i has one restriction. The value for T_i must be >0. In other words, at least one of the W_c values must have a value >0. The reason is the following: If T_i is 0 then this means that all information for a requirements modelling object is optional. Normally such a situation must not appear!

To determine the fill factor of a certain concept i, now, it has to be counted how many of the columns are really filled. Therefore $F_{c,i}$ is introduced. $F_{c,i}$ indicates whether a certain column c for a certain concept i is filled or not. It has the value 1 if it is filled and 0 if it is not filled. For the estimation of the fill factor P_i of a concept i the values of $F_{c,i}$ for all the columns must be counted and weighted. This result is then divided by the weighted total amount of columns for i (T_i). The result P_i has a value between 0 and 1. A value near 0 means the concrete concept is totally incomplete and has to be completed. A value near 1 means, that every important column is completed. The whole formula for the fill factor estimation is given below:

$$P_i = \frac{\sum\limits_{c=1}^{n} (F_{c,i} * W_c)}{T_i}$$

Following the formula only filled columns are counted now in the dividend since $F_{c,i}$ is 0 if they are empty. Furthermore the importance of the column for counting is taken into consideration. If a column is completely optional that means it does not matter if it is empty or filled, then the weighting factor is 0 and it is neither counted in the dividend nor in the divisor. For the better understanding, let's suppose the following simple example according to Table 1. The table can be interpreted as follows. There are three thing-types (*customer, product, customer name*) which are already collected. For simplicity it is assumed, that each thing-type has only the following columns (*description, quantity description, example, and synonym*). Furthermore the necessity or importance to fill the columns is weighted (see W in the brackets after the column names). This columns weights are valid for all the thing-types (description = 1, quantity description = 0.1, value constrain = 0.1, synonym = 0.1).

Table 1. Example for work progress determination

	Typical thing-type columns			
	Description (W =1)	Quantity description (W = 0.1)	Example (W = 0.1)	Synonym (W = 0.1)
$P_{customer}$	1	0	1	1
$P_{product}$	0	0	1	1
$P_{customer\ name}$	1	0	1	1

The value 1 in different cells $F_{c,i}$ (for i = {customer, product or customer name} and c= {description, quantity description, example, synonym}) of the rows $P_{customer}$, $P_{product}$ and $P_{customer\_name}$ means that the cell is already filled with information. The value 0 in these cells means that this cell for the row/column is still empty for a certain thing-type *customer, product* or *customer name*.

Let's now look at *customer* ($P_{customer}$). Three of the columns are treated as filled with information (see value 1 in the row $P_{customer}$). Usually, the fill factor would be 0.75 %. However, in this special example, the first column "*description*" is mandatory (W = 1) but it is not really necessary that the other three columns ("*quantity description*", "*example*" and "*synonym*") must be filled out. The three other ones only have the value 0.1 for the weighting factor W. In this case, the fill factor $P_{customer}$ is approximately 0.92. This reflects the situation that a mandatory column is filled. Let's now look at *product* (row $P_{product}$). Here the mandatory column "*description*" is not filled (since the value for F in the cell "*product*"/"*description*" is 0), then the fill factor $P_{product}$ will fall to approximately 0.15 completed although two (less important) columns (in our example: example and synonym) are filled. Following this approach the work progress for customer name ($P_{customer\_name}$) is also 92 % completed.

With the above formula the analyst has the work progress status of one concept (e.g., *customer*) if the progress overview for all concepts of a certain requirements modelling object (e.g., all thing-types) must be determined then the sum of all progress values P_i is divided by the total number k of all collected concepts of a certain requirements modelling object (e.g., all thing-types).

$$S = \frac{\sum_{i=1}^{k} P_i}{k}$$

5 Further Measures for Requirements Modelling Objects

Beside the measure given in the previous section further progress indicators can be determined based on:

- Relationship between a certain requirements modelling object and the requirements sources from which it was derived.
- Relationship between a certain requirements modelling object and the open open questions and open tasks

5.1 Relationship to the Requirements Sources

For a business analyst it is always important to know which requirements modelling objects can be traced back to it's sources (e.g., documents, sentences). Thus it is necessary to provide him with an overview measure to which percentage his already collected requirements are related to sources. Once again this is described using the notion thing-type. A certain thing-type can be traced back to a requirements source if it has a relation to such a source (e.g., "*customer*" ←→ "*document X* "). Thus, firstly the number of thing-types which has at least one relation to a certain requirements source must be counted. Let's name this number of thing-types as R. Then R must be divided by the total number of thing-types N (= R / N). The result is the percentage of thing-types which can be traced back to a source.

5.2 Relationship to Open Questions and Open Tasks

Beside the concepts itself and their requirements sources, there is a third possibility for measuring. Each concept and also each requirements source are related to open questions and a list of open tasks. These two notions are used in the measurement with the following assumption:

- If a concept (e.g., customer) has at least one open question, then it is more likely that a certain concept is not well understood.
- If a concept has at least one open task, then it is more likely that it is incomplete since something must still be done.

Therefore a certain concept (e.g., customer) in general is treated as incomplete independent of its value P_i if it is related to at least one open question or one open task. An overview percentage of concepts of a certain requirements model object (e.g., a thing-type) that have no open question and no open tasks can be computed similar to 5.1. The number of concepts of a certain requirements model object which have neither an open task nor an open question (= U) is divided by the total number of concepts collected within this requirements model object N (= U/N).

6 Progress Indicators for Requirements Sources

The measures given in the previous sections can also be applied to requirements sources. From the point of view of a certain requirement source the following measures can be estimated:

- Number of filled columns per requirements source
- Relationship between a certain requirements source and derived requirements modelling objects
- Relationship between a certain requirements source and open questions about this source.

6.1 Number of Filled Columns

This measurement says something about the state of documentation of the requirements source. With the weighting factor the system analyst can influence how important it is to collect a certain kind of information about a requirements source. The formula for P_i and S as described in Section 4.2 can be reused.

6.2 Relationship to Derived Requirements Modelling Objects

Especially during the early phase of requirements elicitation, the system analyst has to speak with many end users. It is a common practice that most of the end users give the systems analyst many documents and materials to read. Even if the analyst is an expert in a domain he cannot simply ignore these materials since there may be some important information that might explain some details he does not know. If there is a requirements source (e.g., a document) that is not connected to a requirements modelling object, then this means that this document has not been analyzed so far or the document is not so important for the project. If the requirements source still has no connection to a requirements modelling object also in a later stage of the requirements engineering process, then the analyst must reconsider the importance of a document, sentence or a person for the project.

6.3 Relationship to Open Questions and Open Tasks

The idea is that an open question or task can be formulated also if the content of a requirements source is not understood. (e.g., an open question could be "*I do not understand section 2 of Document X* "). This works similar to the measure given in Section 5.3.

7 Conclusion

In this chapter an approach was introduced which allows the determination of the work progress during requirements elicitation. In different requirements engineering projects it was always a successful strategy to use glossaries during the elicitation process. From the empty columns it could be easily determined which kind of information is still missing. This chapter is an attempt to generalize this strategy in order to automate it. It should help the business analyst to determine to which extend he has completed the elicitation of already gathered requirements. Particularly, if a column is empty or is related with an open question/task, then this is a hint that something is missing and of poor quality, but if the column is filled with some information this cannot be taken as a hint that the collected information is of good quality. This is still an unsolved problem in requirements engineering since it mainly depends on the experience of the business analyst which no computer supported system can solve at the moment.

The results of the work progress determination can be visualized in different ways. (e.g., graphically). For the interpretation of the results thresholds should be used which describe the state of completion (e.g., >80% = fully, >50% = largely, >15% partly, <= 15% incomplete). This is similar to a rating technique used in SPiCE (van Loon, 2004).

Using glossaries for structuring requirements also supports the transformation of the glossary contents to conceptual models. Thus it is also a good starting point for model driven software development. Using the OLIVANOVA (a trademark of CARE-T Spain) modelling approach (Pastor et al. 2004) as the target model, good mapping results from KCPM have been achieved already (Kop et al. 2006).

Acknowledgments   I would like to thank Prof. Mayr who has influenced my way of thinking about requirements and conceptual models.

References

Berry, D.M, Daudjee, K., Dong., J., Fainchtein, I.,. Nelson, M.A., Nelson, T., Ou, L. (2004) User's manual as a requirements specification: case studies. Requirements Engineering Journal, 9, 67–82.

Cockburn, A. (2000).Writing Effective Use Cases. Addison Wesley, Boston.

Costello, R.J., Liu, D.-B (1995) Metrics for Requirements Engineering. Journal of Systems and Software, 29(1), 39–63.

Escalona, M.J., Reina, A.M., Torres, J., Mejías M. (2004) NDT: a methodology to deal with the navigation aspect at the requirements phase. OOPSLA Workshop: Aspect-Oriented Requirements Engineering and Architecture Design.

Fliedl, G. Kop, Ch., Mayr, H.C. Salbrechter A., Vöhringer J., Weber G., Winkler, Ch. (2007) Deriving static and dynamic concepts from sophisticated tagging. DKE Journal, 61(3), 403–578.

Fuchs, N.E., Schwertel, U., Torge, S (1999) Controlled Natural Language Can Replace First-Order Logic, Proceedings ASE '99, 14th IEEE International Conference on Automated Software Engineering, ASE'99, Cocoa Beach, FL, October 1999.

Hesse, W, Mayr, H.C. (1998) Highlights of the SAMMOA Framework for Object Oriented Application Modelling, Proceedings of the 9th International Conference of Database and Expert Systems Applications (DEXA'98), Lecture Notes in Computer Science, Springer Verlag, 1998, pp. 353–373.

Hoffman D., Weiss D.M. (eds.) (2001) Software Fundamentals – Collected Papers by David Parnas, Addison Wesley, Boston.

Hoppenbrouwers, S.J.B.A, Proper, H.A, van der Weide T.P (2005) A fundamental View on the Process of Conceptual Modeling. In.: Delcambre L et. al.: (eds.), 24th International Conference on Conceptual Modeling (ER2005), LNCS 3716, pp. 128–143.

Koch N., Escalona M. J. (2004). Requirements Engineering for WebApplications: A Comparative Study. Journal of Web Engineering, 2(3), 192–212.

Kop, C. Mayr, H.C. (2002). Mapping Functional Requirements: From natural language to Conceptual Schemata, Proceedings of the 6th International Conference Software Engineering and Applications, Acta Press, pp. 82–87.

Kop, C., Mayr, H.C., Yevdoshenko N. (2006) Requirements Modeling and MDA, Proposal for a combined approach. In Proceedings of the 15th International Conference on Information Systems Development (ISD 2006), Budapest, August 2006, Springer Verlag.

Mayr, H.C, Kop, Ch. (2002) A User Centered Approach to Requirements Modeling, Proc. Modellierung 2002, Lecture Notes in Informatics LNI p-12, GI-Edition, pp. 75–86.

Mylopoulos, J., Chung, L., Yu, E. (1999) From object oriented to goal oriented Requirements Analysis.Communications of the ACM, 42(1), 31–37.

Nijssen, G.M., Halpin, T.A., (1989) Conceptual Schema and Relational Database Design – A Fact Oriented Approach. Prentice Hall, Upper Saddle River, NJ.

Pastor, O., Molina, J.C., Iborra, E. (2004) Automated Production of Fully Functional Applications with OlivaNova Model Execution., ERCIM News, No. 57, 62–64.

Pikalek, Ch. (2006) Messbare Qualität von Anforderungsdokument, Javamagazin, No. 1, pp. 75–81.

Rolland, C., Souveyet, C., Ben Achour, C. (1998) Guiding Goal Modeling Using Scenarios, IEEE Transaction on Software Engineering, 24(12), 1055–1071.

Rupp, C. (2002) Requirements-Engineering und –Management, Professionelle, iterative Anforderungsanalyse für IT-System, Carl Hanser Verlag, 2nd edition.

Sutcliffe, A., Maiden, N.A., Minocha, S., Manuel, D. (1998) Supporting Scenario-Based Requirements Engineering. IEEE Transactions on Software Engineering, (24)12, 1072–1088.

Schewe, K.D., Thalheim, B., Zlatkin, S. (2004) Modelling Actors and Stories in Web Information Systems, 3rd International Conference on Information Systems Technology and its Applications, LNI p-48, 2004, pp. 13–23.

Van Loon, H. (2004) Process Assessment and ISO/IEC 15504 – A Reference Book. Springer, New York.

Towards Ontology-Based MAS Methodologies: Ontology-Based Early Requirements

G. Beydoun[1], A. K. Krishna[2], A. Ghose[2] and G. C. Low[3]

[1] University of Wollongong, School of Information Systems and Technology, beydoun@uow.edu.au

[2] University of Wollongong, School of Computer Science and Software Engineering, aneesh@uow.edu.au

[3] University of New South Wales, School of Information Systems, Technology and Management, g.low@unsw.edu.au

Abstract   An ontology-based MAS methodology can offer support for software extensibility, interoperability and reuse which are critical concerns for long-term commercial viability of any MAS. These concerns underpin the eventual adoption of agent technology by industry. Existing AOSE methodologies lack adequate support for these concerns. This research is part of an ongoing effort to produce a methodology that uses ontologies as a central modeling artifact. In this chapter we propose an early requirement phase which is ontology centric. We integrate this requirement phase into an ontology-based methodological framework. Further, we identify ontology-related interdependencies between requirement, analysis, and design phases. Our early requirement is a novel approach that integrates i* with ontological analysis.

1 Introduction

Ontologies are an explicit formal specification of a domain model agreed by many people from a domain of practice (Gruber, 1993). They can be used to mediate communication within an IT system, between people themselves, or between people and an IT system. In recent years, they have become an essential tool to structure and share collections of related Web pages, in order to transform WWW into a semantic web (Davies et al., 2003). Currently, there are many freely available domain ontology repositories (e.g., DAML repository [http://www.cse.dmu.ac.uk]).

Few Agent-Oriented Software Engineering (AOSE) methodologies include ontologies in their models and processes (e.g., Dileo et al., 2002, Girardi and Serra, 2004). The inclusion of ontologies in such works is confined to the analysis phase of the development life cycle. For instance, the authors of Girardi et al. (2004)

distinguish between an initial ontology and a domain model geared towards designing a MAS and specify how a *domain model* that includes goal and role analyses is developed from an initial ontology. Similarly, in Dileo et al. (2002), the MaSE methodology is extended to incorporate the use of an ontology to mediate the transition between goal and the task analyses within the analysis phase. Beydoun et al. (2006) suggest using ontologies as a central software engineering construct, throughout the whole development life cycle and to address software interoperability, reusability, and verification concerns for MAS.

This research continues by integrating an ontology-based early requirements phase that integrates i* with ontological analysis. This early requirement phase is supported by a domain ontology which underpins the development of the whole system. In addition, a degree of structure is added to this informal consultation process via the use of Requirements Capture Templates (RCTs). We argue for the use of elicitation templates that reflect the information requirements of the underlying modeling notation and the domain enterprise ontologies to ease the elicitation process.

The chapter is organized as follows: Section 2 presents the background and related work. In particular, it highlights how ontologies originated in the process of developing knowledge-based systems (KBS) to address reuse concerns. Section 3 views a MAS as a distributed collection of knowledge-based systems and accordingly highlights how ontologies can be accommodated during and throughout the development life cycle of a MAS. Section 4 discusses how the domain ontology can assist in completing a set of Requirements Capture Templates (RCT) while the completed templates can similarly suggest gaps in the ontology. Section 5 uses the analysis of Sections 3 and 4 to sketch an actual MAS ontology-based methodology that supports early requirements engineering activities and reuse. Section 6 concludes with a summary and future work.

2 Ontologies and Knowledge-Based Systems

In KBS development, ontologies have been successfully used to enhance reusability and interoperability and to verify various products of software development (e.g., Uschold and Grueninger, 1996). Categorization of knowledge into domain knowledge, problem-solving knowledge, and an investigation of techniques necessary to use the provided knowledge and to turn it into a working system resulted in the realization that specific techniques for different kinds of problems are necessary in order to build relatively complete and competent systems. This resulted in collections of reusable problem-solving methods (PSMs) that are used in conjunction with reusable domain-dependent ontologies forming the structural basis of the knowledge area of the problem to be solved (e.g. Puppe, 1993; Benjamins, 1995; Motta and Zdrahal, 1996). This impetus for the ontology-based view of a KBS as comprising a PSM and a suitable ontology is central to many KBS methodologies (e.g., Wielinga et al., 1992; Benjamins et al., 1998; Cairo, 1998; Shreiber et al.,

2001) and reduced KBS analysis and design to ontology engineering coupled with a suitable choice of a PSM from an existing PSM library (Benjamins, 1995).

3 Ontologies for MAS Development

In this section, we consider a MAS as a "distributed knowledge" system. This allows us to incorporate domain-independent ontological analysis in a MAS methodology by considering differences in the way knowledge is used for a single agent system versus a multiagent system (i.e. a distributed knowledge system).

In a MAS, each agent has a localized knowledge base. Agent knowledge bases may overlap. Shared knowledge is usually of some concern, but certainly each agent will have its own private knowledge component. In a MAS, two or more agents interact or work together to achieve a set of goals. The coordination between agents possessing diverse knowledge and problem-solving capabilities usually enables the achievement of global goals that cannot be otherwise achieved by a single agent working in isolation. MAS are thought to be an answer to a number of well-known shortcomings of general PSM (Russell and Norvig, 2003): incomplete knowledge requirement specification, incomplete PSM requirement, and limited computational resources. Given a single agent within a MAS and single independent agent in a KBS, we observe the following differences: some agent ontologies may be incomplete in a MAS, individual PSM for agents may be insufficient for their own goals in a MAS, and agents within a MAS may have limited execution resources. We also note that not all agents in a MAS have the same PSM. We now overview how each of these differences characterize the way agents may interact within a MAS, highlighting six additional requirements resulting from these differences.

Using ontologies in developing a MAS is complicated by having to simultaneously provide knowledge requirements to different PSMs that are still required to share results using a common terminology. This is even complicated further because individual PSM may operate at different levels of abstraction of the domain, they may be complementary, and they may have varying degrees of prescription to the domain requiring various degrees of adjustment to suit the domain. In other words, how much specificity they exhibit to a given domain may vary. In the Belief-Desire-Intention (BDI) (Padgham and Lambrix, 2000) architecture of agents, a PSM essentially specifies how plans are generated and dumped and how beliefs are updated and maintained/shared [in the BDI architecture a PSM is represented by a plan]. Within a single agent KBS, ontologies were conceived and used to strengthen a single PSM for a given domain. Their use for KBS was never intended to *simultaneously* strengthen different PSMs for the same domain. Therefore, in developing MASs, we may additionally need the following requirements:

- Requirement 1: Ontology mappings are required to allow individual problem solvers (of individual agents) to interact and to use a common domain conceptualization (belonging to the same ontology).

- Requirement 2: Verification of individual PSM knowledge requirements against allocated ontologies is required at design time. This verification would be to ensure that the PSM of individual agents has sufficient domain knowledge to undertake its roles within the system.

A domain ontology underlying knowledge requirements of all agents is available. However, the version available to an individual agent, matching its PSM, is not necessarily complete (as is assumed to be the case for single-agent systems). In addition to 1 and 2, we add:

- Requirement 3: Knowledge extensibility is required at the agent level at least to accommodate any new ontological units added to the system about the domain. This can often create inconsistencies (Beydoun et al., 2005b).
- Requirement 4: Associated with 3, a structured and understood knowledge representation is required to resolve inconsistencies. This would be a common knowledge representation language into which distinct agent knowledge bases, possibly represented in different languages, are mapped to detect and resolve inconsistencies.

An agent PSM is not assumed to be sufficiently powerful to respond to all events it encounters during its lifetime within a MAS. It usually negotiates cooperation from other agents. Current practices often assume that functional goal analysis is sufficient to specify the knowledge requirement for agents (Giunchiglia et al., 2003), and any deficiencies in its later problem-solving capacity are assumed to be offset by that cooperation. However, in our view, without consideration of its actual PSM (or other available PSM within the system), there is no guarantee that this cooperation would ultimately work. This suggests:

- Requirement 5: Iteration between the PSM design and the goal analysis is required to ensure that the chosen problem solver for a given agent is capable of meeting its specified goals.
- Requirement 6: A consideration of the total PSMs of all agents is required to ensure that system goals are achievable.

In Section 5 we develop the above analysis into an ontology-based methodology model which accommodates these six ontology-related design considerations. However, we first outline the first phase of this methodology, an ontology driven early-phase requirement phase in Section 4.

4 Towards Ontologies-Driven Early-Phase Requirement

Early-phase requirements engineering activities have usually been performed informally (Yu, 1997), beginning with stakeholder interviews and discussions about the existing system(s) and rationale for the new system. Initial requirements are often considered to be ambiguous, incomplete, inconsistent, and usually expressed informally. A key well-known challenge is that of eliciting meaningful requirements in unstructured settings such as interviews and discussions.

Unni et al. (2003) added structure to this informal consultation process via the use of Requirements Capture Templates (RCTs). An RCT represents one means of eliciting, in a targeted fashion, the information required to populate models in an underlying conceptual modeling language. These templates are generated via a principled transformation process from the meta-model of the underlying conceptual modeling language, which we briefly outline here. Without loss of generality, it is assumed that a meta-model is represented, UML-style, as a collection of classes and associations. A RCT is generated for each class, with a slot for each attribute of the class, labeled by the attribute name. For each association in which the class participates, an additional slot is created in the template, labeled by the ID of the associated class. Consider the following example of an abstract meta-model and a collection of RCTs corresponding to this meta-model.

In Unni et al. (2003), a collection of RCTs for populating i* Strategic Dependency (SD) and Strategic Rationale (SR) diagrams were devised (Tables 1–3). To obtain these RCTs from the i* meta-model, a given high-level task in an i* SR diagram may participate in multiple dependencies with other actors and this is reflected directly in the RCT in Table 2 with possibly many slots associated with each activity that requires that the source and target actors as well as the name of the dependency be listed. In effect, these are forms that the modeler seeks to fill out in the course of a stakeholder consultation session and that must eventually be signed off by both the modeler and the stakeholder. The process of filling out these forms provides structure to stakeholder interview sessions. These forms have also been designed to seek information specific to the needs of the underlying agent-oriented conceptual model that the modeler seeks to build. In other words, they share the same underlying meta-model with i*. Stakeholders are thus able to provide focused input to the conceptual modeling task, while being shielded from the complexity of understanding and using the conceptual modeling language. In this context, the role of the domain ontology is twofold: the ontology validates the meta-model used by RCT and i*. In addition it may provide part of the information required to complete the model captured by them. Conversely, the process of completing the RCT and i* offers an opportunity to check the available domain ontology for completeness. When incompleteness is detected, domain experts' advice is sought (see Fig. 1). These methodological guidelines are based on our experiences with early-phase requirements modeling of the emergency services organization using the i* framework (Yu, 1997, 2001) and are further detailed in the rest of this section.

The semantic web initiative has led to a large number of Web-based ontologies being developed. These may be viewed as a large distributed collaborative knowledge engineering exercise. It is therefore not unreasonable to assume that analysts and application developers would have access to reusable enterprise ontologies as well as reusable function/activity-specific ontologies. A simple approach to conceptualize an ontology is to view it as a concept vocabulary coupled with a set of rules. The rules may be structural that may, for instance, organize concepts in a class hierarchy, or they may be semantic constraints or business rules. An example is a rule in a banking application that requires interest rates for loan accounts to be always higher than those for savings accounts.

Table 1. Organizational unit template for department details

Organisational Unit Template	
Department Details	
Department Name	
Name of the Department head	
Designation of Department head	
Department Rationale	
High-Level Functions of the Department	
Modeler Signature	Stakeholder Signature

Table 2. Function elaboration template for function elaboration

Function Elaboration Template			
Function Elaboration for the Department			
Department Name			
Function Name	(Use separate sheet for each function)		
Function Rationales	(Use separate sheet for each function)		
Activity Details for the Function			
Activity Name and Description	(Use separate sheet for each activity under the function)		
Activity Rationales			
Actor(s) involved in the activity	(Unique list of Actor(s))		
Relationship / dependencies actor(s) to achieve / satisfy the above activity			
Source Actor	Relationship/ Dependency	Target Actor	Additional information / elaboration on the relationship
Modeler Signature		Stakeholder Signature	

Table 3. Activity elaboration template for internal intentional characteristics of actor(s) to achieve the activity

Activity Elaboration Template		
Internal Intentional Characteristics of individual actor(s) to achieve the activity (Use multiple rows to describe multiple internal tasks for each actor)		
Department Name		
Function Name		
Activity Name		
Actor(s) involved	(Unique list of Actor(s))	
Actor	Internal Task / Means to achieve the activity by individual Actor	Additional information on task or means to achieve the activity or Actor Rationales
Modeler Signature		Stakeholder Signature

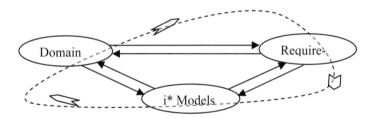

Fig. 1. Ontology-model-template coevolution: the ontology validates the meta-model underlying early requirements and provides part of the information required to complete models captured. Early requirements also offer an opportunity to check the available domain ontology for completeness.

The availability of such reusable ontologies is a motivation for our ontology-based methodological development of MAS in general and is translated in this chapter to early-phase requirements engineering via agent-oriented conceptual modeling. The use of a preexisting ontology can significantly ease the early-phase requirements modeling task by providing some modicum of guidance to a modeler who might be venturing into the task with no prior knowledge or understanding of the application domain. A preexisting domain ontology can thus help provide focus to a modeler's early interactions with stakeholders. However, we propose to formalize the process by which ontology-driven elicitation might take place. This is then generalized into a full ontology life cycle in the requirements elicitation context. We are interested in two distinct scopes of the domain ontology: enterprise ontologies and function/task-specific ontologies. Enterprise ontologies can provide guidance in identifying actors while constructing high-level SD and SR models, by making available certain default organizational structures. These can also provide a vocabulary for more refined (lower-level) SD and SR models. Function/task-specific ontologies (often included within enterprise ontologies) provide detailed concept vocabularies for specific tasks, which can serve as elicitation triggers.

Ontologies can also provide a benchmark for completeness that serve to drive the elicitation process. Informally, a conceptual model is deemed to be complete with respect to an ontology if it makes reference to every concept in the concept vocabulary of the ontology. This is in many ways analogous to the notion of completeness of formal theories. A theory is considered complete with respect to a language L if it commits to the truth or falsity of every proposition in L. When completed, our requirement phase will use this notion of completeness of a conceptual model relative to an ontology to generate elicitation triggers. In effect, every instance of incompleteness, i.e., every concept in the concept vocabulary that is not referred to by the conceptual model, serves as a trigger for further questions/probes from the modeler.

Ontologies can also support consistency testing of conceptual models. A conceptual model would be deemed inconsistent relative to an ontology if it violated any of the rules associated with the ontology. These could be violations of the structural rules (for instance if a subclass–superclass relationship is reversed in a model) or violations of semantic constraints (for instance, an activity that involves an actor making his/her appointments schedule publicly available may violate security constraints). Again each instance of inconsistency can serve as an elicitation trigger, obliging the modeler to seek out additional information in the process of resolving the inconsistency (usually by appropriately modifying the conceptual model).

Much of our prior discussion assumes that a domain ontology is made available to the modeler at the start of the elicitation phase. Problems may arise if pre-existing ontologies, where available, are incomplete. Key concepts from the domain may not be included in the concept vocabulary, while key relationships may not be represented in the rule-set. The challenge (and perhaps the opportunity), is to then devise early-phase requirements modeling methodologies that as well as maintain and update ontologies (as shown in Fig. 1). In other words, not only can ontologies help build conceptual models for early requirements, but the reverse is also true. The process of building a conceptual model can reveal gaps in an ontology – most obviously in its concept vocabulary, but conceivably also in its set of rules. An ontology can help design a requirements capture template, but completed templates can similarly suggest gaps in ontologies. A requirements capture template can serve as a basis for conceptual model building (described in Section 4), but a conceptual model can suggest alternative ways of structuring requirements capture templates (RCTs).

5 Ontology-Based Methodology Outline

In our methodology, we assume that the choice of PSM may be made independently of domain analysis and that a domain ontology describing domain concepts and their relationships is available (even if not complete). Such an ontology may be available from an existing repository (e.g., DARPA, 2007) or a domain analysis may be considered the first stage of developing the system to identify concepts and their relationships (e.g., as proposed in Cordi et al., 2004) . Given such a domain ontology and the six software engineering requirements from Section 3, we sketch features of the analysis and design phases for an ontology-based MAS methodology including the ontology-based early requirement phase described in Section 4. We assume that the domain ontology that includes, amongst others, the meta-model of conceptual modeling language (e.g., i*) being used for this early-phase requirements engineering phase. Note that ontologies and meta-models are indistinguishable in abstract terms.

A general comment about using ontologies as a basis for developing MAS is that there is interplay between the role of reuse and other roles of ontologies in a MAS. Various reuse roles cannot be smoothly accommodated (e.g., interoperability at run-time) without careful consideration of run-time temporal requirements. For example, an ontology's role in reasoning at run-time is based on fulfilling PSM knowledge requirements at design time. This requires scoping domain analysis for each individual agent at design time towards requirement 2 in Section 3. As discussed, this requirement recognizes that the key to ontology-based design of a MAS is the appropriate allocation of a PSM to individual agents in order to match system requirements. Goal models are usual ways to express requirements (e.g., Wooldridge, 2002; Giunchiglia et al., 2003).

Supported by the domain ontology, our early requirement phase generates a high-level description of system goals and roles expressed in the i* model. In this, we generate RCTs from the meta-model of the underlying conceptual modeling language. Note that other than i* (Yu, 2001), other goal-oriented languages such as KAOS (Lamsweerde et al., 1991) and AOR (Wagner, 2000) are all good candidates for this purpose. We incorporate support for the i* model template coevolution via the iterative nature of the early requirements identification and validation between the domain ontology model and the requirements templates and i* models (Fig. 1). There will be an iterative process in deriving the system goals and roles from the requirements templates and i* models. These models provide for further validation of the domain ontology. Any inconsistencies noted should cause another round of requirements identification and incompletness of domain ontology detected triggers further domain expert advice by the requirement engineers. The role and goal models are further refined to provide a clear association between agent roles and lower-level goals to enable associating PSMs (using PSM libraries) and system goals in the early stages of a MAS design.

The remainder of the system can then be developed with appropriate ontological mappings (Fig. 2). Chosen problem-solving capabilities for different agents in a given MAS do not necessarily have the required degree of domain dependence.

Hence, for a PSM chosen for some agents, the ontology required may need to be adapted. For this, the domain ontology is again the most convenient reference point. Ontology mapping (between portions of the domain ontology and the local agent's knowledge) is required to ensure that all PSMs have their knowledge requirement available to their reasoning format (e.g., as described in Fensel, 1997). The ontology mapping from the domain ontology and the knowledge requirements are the raw material to develop the knowledge bases for individual agents. Agents need to communicate their results and instigate cooperation using a common language. For this purpose, we recommend a global communication ontology (as in Esteva et al., 2002), rather than many-to-many individual mappings between agents. Such a communication ontology is most conveniently based on the available domain ontology, and it depends on the individual ontology of each agent. In some cases, an ontology mapping may be required between PSM ontologies and the communication ontology. The same adaptation between the reasoning and domain ontology can be used to map the result of reasoning back to a common communication ontology (based on the domain ontology).

Towards requirements 3 and 4, hierarchical ontologies are one way to have flexible domain ontology refinement for agents according to their PSMs, and to

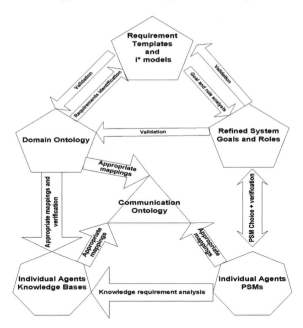

Fig. 2. Ontology-based MAS development methodological sketch supporting early phase requirements modeling: (1) Development starts with a domain ontology to identify goals and roles via the early requirements identification stage. (2) These are used to index an appropriate set of PSMs. (3) Individual ontologies for each PSM are extracted from the initial ontology for reasoning. (4) Verify against the knowledge requirement of chosen PSM. (5) Develop a common communication ontology out of ontologies of Step 4 and appropriate mappings with individual local ontologies. (6) Verify further against communication ontology.

accommodate differences in the strength of the PSM of agents. A common hierarchical domain ontology can be used as a starting point for verification during development and for multiple access at multiple abstraction levels depending on the individual knowledge requirement of each agent PSM. For this purpose, Multiple Hierarchical Restricted Domain (MHRD) ontologies, employed by many authors (e.g., Eschenbach and Heydrich, 1995), are well understood and expressive for most domains. MHRD models are sets of interrelated concepts that are defined through a set of attributes, so the presence of axioms between these attributes is not considered. There can be *part-of* and taxonomic relations among the concepts so that attribute (multiple) inheritance is permitted.

6 Conclusion and Future Work

Long-term reuse of software engineering knowledge and effort involved in developing MASs is a concern that is largely ignored in current MAS methodologies. Our ongoing effort (Tran et al., 2006) to address this, is centered on using an ontology-founded MAS methodology to produce reusable MAS components and designs. Our effort is quite unique in that current use of ontologies in MAS methodologies is limited to the early analysis phases or to express the communication languages for agents within the system. We have a current methodology (Tran et al., 2006) which propagates the use of ontologies throughout the whole MAS development. In this chapter, we elaborated the activities and the models used in the early requirement phase of such a methodology. We highlighted how this phase can be used to lead into an ontology-based analysis phase to produce the goal and role models of a multi agent system. This early requirement phase is underpinned by an i* model which is generated using early requirement templates and a domain and an enterprise ontologies. These ontologies are used as a verification tool as well in developing the role and goal models. Our work is geared towards "extendable closed" systems. In the case of "open systems", introducing new agents may require at *runtime* extending the communication ontology or some local ontologies to allow cooperation with new agents. This is beyond our current scope. However, we note that we never assume that local ontologies for agents are complete from the agent perspective (see Section 3). This is a step along the way to implementing completely "open systems".

As for the later phases of our methodology, there are a number of existing agent-oriented methods with differing concerns and assumptions that can be combined to produce a largely domain-independent unified approach. The result would be a comprehensive framework that addresses the ontology concerns elucidated here and combines all domain-dependent techniques. This would produce the equivalent of PSM banks, but for the MAS software development process itself. We are currently examining different ways to unify all domain-dependent concerns of existing methodologies and interleave the domain-independent ontological software engineering guidelines as outlined in this chapter. Meta-modelling-based method engineering as we outlined in Beydoun et al. (2005a) is particularly promising as are the very recently published foundational ontological ideas of Guizzardi and Wagner (2005).

References

Benjamins, R. (1995) Problem solving methods for diagnosis and their role in knowledge acquisition. International Journal of Expert Systems: Research and Applications 2, 93–120.

Benjamins, V. R., Plaza, E., Motta, E., Fensel, D., Studer, R., Wielinga, B., Schreiber, G. & Zdrahal, Z. (1998) IBROW3 - An Intelligent Brokering Service for Knowledge-Component Reuse on the World Wide Web. *Banff Knowledge Acquisition Workshop (KAW98)*. Canada.

Beydoun, G., Gongalez-Perez, C., Low, G. C. & Henderson-Sellers, B. (2005a) Synthesis of a Generic MAS Metamodel. *International Conference on Software Engineering Workshops (SELMAS2005)*. St Louis, USA, pp. 27–31.

Beydoun, G., Hoffmann, A., Breis, J. T. F., Martinez-Béjar, R., Valencia-Garcia, R. & Aurum, A. (2005b) Cooperative Modeling Evaluated. International Journal of Cooperative Information Systems, World Scientific 14, 45–71.

Beydoun, G., Tran, N., Low, G. & Henderson-Sellers, B. (2006) Foundations of Ontology-Based Methodologies for Multi-agent Systems. Springer LNCS, pp. 111–123.

Cairo, O. (1998) The KAMET Methodology: Content, Usage and Knowledge Modeling. In Gaines, B. & Musen, M. (Eds.) *11th Banff Knowledge Acquisition for Knowledge-Based Systems Workshop (KAW98)*. Canada.

Cordi, V., Mascardi, V., Martelli, M. & Sterling, L. (2004) Developing an Ontology for the Retrieval of XML Documents: A Comparative Evaluation of Existing Methodologies. *AOIS2004 @CaiSE04*.

Darpa, (2007) DAML Ontology Library, http://www.daml.org/ontologies/, accessed 28 June 2007.

Davies, J., Fensel, D. & Harmelen, F. V. (Eds.) (2003) *Towards The Semantic Web: Ontology-driven Knowledge Management*, Wiley, London.

Dileo, J., Jacobs, T. & Deloach, S. (2002), Integrating Ontologies into Multi-Agent Systems Engineering, paper given at 4th International Bi-Conference Workshop on Agent Oriented Information Systems (AOIS2002), Italy.

Eschenbach, C. & Heydrich, W. (1995) Classical mereology and restricted domains. International Journal of Human-Computer Studies 43, 723–740.

Esteva, M., Cruz, D. D. L. & Sierra, C. (2002) ISLANDER: an electronic institutions editor. *International Conference on Autonomous Agents & Multiagent Systems (AAMAS02)*. Italy.

Fensel, D. (1997) The tower-of-adaptor method for developing and reusing problem-solving methods. In Plaza, E. & Benjamins, R. (Eds.) *European Knowledge Acquisition Workshop*. Spain, pp. 97–112.

Girardi, R., Faria, C. G. D. & Balby, L. (2004) Ontology-Based Domain Modeling of Multi-Agent Systems. *OOPLSA Workshop*. pp. 295–308.

Girardi, R. & Serra, I. (2004) Using ontologies for the specification of domain-specific languages in multi-agent domain engineering. *CAiSE Workshops (2) 2004*. pp. 295–308.

Giunchiglia, F., Mylopoulos, J. & Perini, A. (2003) The Tropos Software Development Methodology: Processes, Models and Diagrams. IN Giunchiglia, F., Odell, J. & Weiß, G. (Eds.) *Agent-Oriented Software Engineering III: Third International Workshop, AOSE 2002*. Springer, pp. 162–173.

Gruber, T. R. (1993) A Translation Approach to Portable Ontology Specifications. Knowledge Acquisition 5, 199–220.

Guizzardi, G. & Wagner, G. (2005) On the ontological foundations of agent concepts. In Bresciani, P., Giorgini, P., Henderson-Sellers, B., Low, G. & Winikoff, M. (Eds.) *Agent-Oriented Information Systems II.* Springer, pp. 113–128.

Lamsweerde, A., Dardenne, A. & Dubisy, F. (1991) The KAOS Project: Knowledge acquisition in automated specification of software. *Proceedings of the AAAI Spring Symposium Series.* Stanford University.

Motta, E. & Zdrahal, Z. (1996) Parametric design problem solving. *10th Banff Knowledge Acquisition for Knowledge Based System Workshop.* Canada.

Padgham, L. & Lambrix, P. (2000) Agent Capabilities: Extending BDI Theory. *17th National Conference on Artificial Intelligence (AAAI-2000).* Austin, Texas, USA, pp. 68–73.

Puppe, F. (1993) *Systematic Introduction to Expert Systems: Knowledge Representation and Problem-Solving Methods,* Springer-Verlag, Berlin.

Russell, S. & Norvig, P. (2003) *Artificial Intelligence, A Modern Approach, the Intelligent Agent Book,* Prentice Hall, Upper Saddle River, NJ.

Shreiber, G., Akkermans, H., Anjewierden, A., Hoog, R., Shadbolt, N., De Velde, W. V. & Wielinga, B. (2001) *Knowledge Engineering And Management: The CommonKADS Methodology,* MIT Press, London.

Tran, Q. N. N., Beydoun, G. & Low, G. C. (2006), Design of a Peer-to-Peer Information Sharing MAS Using MOBMAS (Ontology-Centric Agent Oriented Methodology), paper given at ISD, Budapest, 31 Aug–2 Sept.

Unni, A., Krishna, A. K., Ghose, A. K. & Hyland, P. (2003), Practical Early Phase Requirements Engineering via Agent-oriented Conceptual Modelling, paper given at 14th Austral-Asian Conference on Information Systems (ACIS-2003), Perth, Nov.

Uschold, M. & Grueninger, M. (1996) Ontologies: Principles, Methods and Application. Knowledge Engineering Review 11, 93–195.

Wagner, G. (2000) Agent-Object-Relationship Modeling. *Proc. of Second International Symposium - from Agent Theory to Agent Implementation together with EMCRS 2000.*

Wielinga, B., Schreiber, G. & Breuker, J. (1992) KADS: a modelling approach to knowledge engineering. Knowledge Acquisition 4, 5–53.

Wooldridge, M. (2002) *Multi Agent Systems,* Wiley, Chichester.

Yu, E. (1997) Towards Modelling and Reasoning Support for Early-Phase Requirements Engineering. *3rd IEEE Int. Symp. on Requirements Engineering.* Washington D.C., pp. 226–235.

Yu, E. (2001) Agent Orientation as a Modelling Paradigm. Wirtschaftsinformatik 43, 123–132.

An Information System Quality Framework Based on Information System Architectures

Thanh Thoa Pham Thi and Markus Helfert

School of Computing, Dublin City University, Ireland
thoa.pham@computing.dcu.ie, markus.helfert@computing.dcu.ie

Abstract   Recent approaches view the Quality of Information Systems (IS) as the result of an IS development process and the quality of IS products. As quality is regarded as a multidimensional concept and its meaning depends on the context and the perspectives, many different IS quality frameworks and models are proposed. Typically, these frameworks include a set of characteristics, so-called quality factors, contributing to the quality of IS. Some approaches are based on the IS delivery process for the selection of quality factors; while some other approaches do not clearly explain the rationale for their selection. Moreover, often relations or impacts among selected quality factors are not taken into account. Quality aspects of information are frequently considered isolated from IS quality. The impact of IS quality on information quality seems to be neglected in most approaches. A systematic analysis of objective quality factors impacting on the overall quality of IS is necessary. This would provide a systematic view on IS quality as well as the rationale for selected quality factors. By identifying the root causes of defects, it would help to improve IS quality. Our research aims to propose such a quality framework based on Information System Architecture, as it allows understanding the elements and relations of IS. Focusing on IS architecture, we can identify the rationale of each quality factor that impacts on IS quality. Quality factors are identified for various abstraction levels of IS architecture. Besides, we also present impacts among different quality factors that help to analyze the root causes of IS defects.

1 Introduction

Foremost research related to quality of information systems can be categorized in two stream of research:

1. Data quality (e.g., Ballou and Pazer, 1995; Pipino et al., 2002; Wang and Strong, 1996) which refers to the quality of data in databases and data warehouses.

C. Barry et al. (eds.), *Information Systems Development: Challenges in Practice, Theory,*
and Education, Vol.2, doi: 10.1007/978-0-387-78578-3_27,
© Springer Science+Business Media, LLC 2009

2. Information system quality (Duggan and Reichgelt, 2006; Perry et al., 1994) and software quality (Wong, 2006; Vidgen et al., 1993; Gordon et al., 1998) which are related to the quality of IS products and software products.

Due to the heterogeneous perspectives of multiple IS stakeholders, research on IS quality produced a large number of criteria lists with a diversity on criteria definitions (Duggan and Reichgelt, 2006). For instance, in some approaches, the selection of quality factors is based on key factors of the IS delivery process (Duggan and Reichgelt, 2006), while other approaches seem to select quality factors and criteria arbitrarily (Kitchenham and Pfleeger, 1996). This shows that there is no common rationale for selecting quality criteria. Finally, to our best knowledge, there is no commonly accepted model or framework on IS quality. Besides, most research approaches on data quality, typically study data quality at the database and data warehouse level, isolated from IS quality.

However, data are stored in databases according to a predefined structure and rules specified during the IS development process. Therefore, data quality is also impacted by specifications and quality of specifications in the IS development process. In the IS context, the user and IS developer (i.e., those who contribute to the production of IS product) are the principal stakeholders, and thus – in our view – the study of IS quality cannot be isolated from the structure of IS or IS architecture.

In this chapter, we propose an IS quality framework based on IS architecture. This takes into account the perspectives of user and IS developer. IS architecture present a generic and logical framework that describes IS structures including its elements and relation among them. Following the approach, we introduce a set of quality factors that contributes to IS quality. We present impacts and relations among quality factors including impacts on data quality. Our quality framework allows to contribute to manage the quality in IS and identify root causes of defects.

The chapter is organized as follows. Section 2 presents an overview of existing frameworks of information system quality. Section 3 presents an overview of information system architectures. Section 4 introduces our quality framework that is based on IS architecture followed by a comparison of our framework and other approaches. Finally the conclusion of our research is presented in Section 5.

2 Related Concepts of Quality in Information Systems

In this section, we review the concepts of information system quality and software quality.

2.1 Information Systems Quality

An overview of current literature reveals a large diversity of perspectives of IS quality. They may be subjective based on the interests of stakeholders, or they aim to address objective properties of systems. Duggan and Reichgelt (2006) summarized different quality factors of selected approaches. They analyzed the literature concerning several dimensions of IS quality such as timely delivery and relevance beyond deployment, benefits outstrip life-cycle cost, ease of access and use of delivered features, acceptable response times, provision of required functionality and features, reliability of features and high probability of correct and consistent response, maintainability easily identify sources of defects, scalability to incorporate unforeseen functionality and accommodate growth in user base and finally usage of the system.

Duggan and Reichgelt (2006) propose an IS quality model. The model is based on key concepts of the IS delivery process such as IS delivery paradigm, IS deployment, software engineering, software production method, and systems development methodology. IS quality concerns the whole process from the methodology used for IS development to the process of transferring a completed system. The IS quality model of Duggan and Reichgelt (2006) describe various dimensions that influence IS quality such as People, Perceptions, Process, Practices, Products, and Success. This model also presents relations between different dimensions such as the IS quality, which is impacted by the process management practices employed and by the people. Similarly, Perry et al. (1994) stated that the competence and experience of an IS specialist are central of the high-quality IS product.

Another popular model, the Information System success (or effectiveness) model proposed by DeLone and McLean (1992) presents various factors measuring different dimensions; "system quality" measures technical success; "information quality" measures semantic success; and "use, user satisfaction, individual impacts" and "organizational impacts" measure effectiveness success. An updated version of this model (DeLone and McLean, 2003) introduced a new dimension of "service quality".

For us, the model proposed by Duggan and Reichgelt (2006) is interesting because it assumes an objective analysis. The model also presents relations among different dimensions. However, the presentation of the model is generic and it is not obvious how different criteria contribute to IS quality.

2.2 Software Quality

Software quality is another important aspect of quality considerations for IS, as it is ultimately associated with the extent to which software satisfies its users" (Yilmaz and Chatterjee, 1997). According to Vidgen et al. (1993), the quality of software emphasizes the quality of the production of artifacts (including the production process and the product), whereas the quality of an information system stresses the use of this artifact in an organizational context. Therefore, in our opinion, IS quality includes software quality.

There are numerous models and frameworks for evaluating software quality (Wong, 2006). For instance, Gordon et al. (1998) defines the software quality with quality factors as follows:

- *Quality of Design* includes criteria as Correctness, Maintainability, and Verifiability
- *Quality of Performance* includes Efficiency, Integrity, Reliability, Usability, and Testability
- *Quality of Adaptation* includes Expandability, Flexibility, Portability, Interoperability, and Intra-operability

In addition, the standard ISO 9126 defines a set of characteristics for software quality evaluation:

- *Functionality* is a set of attributes that bear on the existence of a set of functions and their specified properties. The functions are those that satisfy stated or implied needs.
- *Usability* is a set of attributes that bear on the effort needed for use, and on the individual assessment of such use, by a stated or implied set of users.
- *Reliability* is a set of attributes that bear on the capability of software to maintain its level of performance under stated conditions for a stated period of time.
- *Efficiency* is the set of attributes that bear on the relationship between the level of performance of the software and the amount of resources used, under stated conditions.
- *Maintainability* is the set of attributes that bear on the effort needed to make specified modifications.
- *Portability* is the set of attributes that bear on the ability of software to be transferred from one environment.

While these and similar models help to manage the quality of software (and thus the quality of IS), most models do not consider the impacts among various quality factors or provide indications of causes of defects. In this regard, these models have to be extended.

3 Information System Architecture

This section presents an overview of IS architectures as well as some selected approaches. IS architecture describes an integrated structural design of a system, its elements and their relationships depending on given system requirements (Bernus and Schmidt, 1998). IS architecture is also defined as "a logical structure for classifying and organizing the descriptive representations of an Enterprise that are significant to the management of the Enterprise as well as to the development of the Enterprise's Systems" (Zachman, 1987). Most often an IS is considered under various views such as information, function, organization, resource, and different level abstractions that depend on the IS stakeholders' perspectives.

For instance, Zachman (1987) as one of the most popular frameworks, defines IS architecture as a matrix in which the rows represent different abstraction levels, each of which is said to represent the perspective of a named role in the organization such as Scope (contextual level), Owner (conceptual level), Logical Designer (logical level), and Builder (Physical level); the columns represent different views/aspects of IS such as Data, Function, Network, Organization, Time and Motivation. Each cell of this matrix describes relevant models or diagrams used for depicting the correspondent view in the correspondent abstraction level.

Another more general framework is the GERA modeling framework (Bernus and Schmidt, 1998). The GERA framework describes what models of enterprises are needed and maintained during the "enterprise life". This framework structures IS at three dimensions, such as:

1. Life-cycle Dimension provides the controlled modeling process of enterprise entities according to the life-cycle activities. This dimension is similar to different abstract levels in relation to different IS stakeholder's perspectives in the Zachman framework.
2. Genericity Dimension that provides the controlled instantiation process from generic and partial to particular.
3. View Dimension that provides the controlled visualization of specific views of the enterprise entity. Some among them are information, function, organization, and resource views.

Each cell in the framework presents models of a correspondent view, a correspondent stage in the life-cycle and an appropriate degree of generality.

TOGAF, The Open Group Architecture Framework (cf. http://www.opengroup. org/architecture/wp/), is an industry standard architecture framework. It allows designing, evaluating, and constructing appropriate architecture for an organization. The key to TOGAF is the TOGAF Architecture Development Method (ADM) – a proven approach for developing enterprise architecture descriptions that meets the needs of the specific business (Leist et al., 2006). TOGAF mainly consists of three parts: (1) The TOGAF ADM, (2) Enterprise Continuum, and (3) Resource Base. The architecture development cycle of IS consists of eight phases within the description of different inputs and outputs of each phase (i) architecture vision, (ii) business architecture, (iii) information system architectures, (iv) technology architecture, (v) opportunities and solutions, (vi) migration planning, (vii) implementation governance, and (viii) architecture change management.

In summary, IS architectures help to understand the IS structure, decrease the complexity of the IS development through different views and levels and it is independent with IS development process.

4 A Quality Framework in Information System

We developed a quality framework based on the IS architecture (Fig. 1). For our work we followed initially the framework proposed by Zachman because of its simplicity and flexibility; it is independent of specific methodology, any appropriate technique may be placed in the framework to produce specification documents in each abstract level (Leist et al., 2006). In our framework, the quality factors are selected from the perspectives of user and IS developer regarding different abstraction levels in the IS architecture. Main interesting aspects are data, function, process, and organization units.

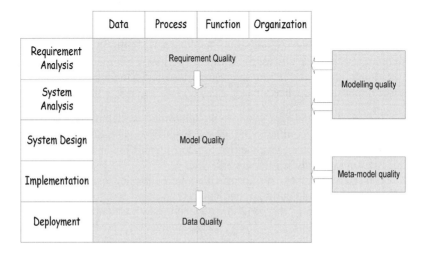

Fig. 1. Quality framework in IS based on IS architecture

The perspective of user concerns the evaluation of the final product, the requirement satisfaction, and the fitness for use. Meanwhile, the perspective of IS developer concerns the quality of different models specified at different abstract levels and the quality of the system implemented. We illustrate our framework with a very simple example based on the development of an IS for the library management. According to the Zachman's IS architecture, the concerned abstract levels (rows) are requirement analysis, system analysis, system design, implementation, and deployment. In this example, we are interested in data and process views (column). An appropriate model is represented in each cell. Along with this architecture, different descriptions at cell level will be presented in the following sections.

4.1 Quality Factors in the Framework

For our framework we selected quality factors such as requirement quality, model quality, meta-model quality, modeling quality, and data quality. The requirement quality and data quality factors belong to the user's perspective, meanwhile the model quality, meta-model quality, and modeling quality factors belong to an IS builder's perspective.

4.1.1 Requirement Quality

User requirements are analyzed in the early stage of the IS development process. The requirement determination is made by collecting information from conversations with users, collecting existing documents and files or computer-based information (Valacich et al., 2006). The requirement determination allows to at least understand the issues such as the business objectives; the information needed; when, how, and by whom or what data are moved; the rules governing how data are handled and processed (Valacich et al., 2006). Requirements may be functional, nonfunctional, and interface requirements. Defects of requirements may meet one of the following criteria (Davis, 1988):

- The requirements may be incomplete, inconsistent, and/or contain redundancy.
- They may not accurately convey the intent of the stakeholders.
- In transitioning from the original requirements to the design, the original intention might not be accurately preserved.
- Over the course of the development of the system, the requirements may change.
- The system requirements may not be adequate to meet the needs of the intended application domain.
- The number and complexity of the set of requirements may tax people's short-term memory beyond its limits.
- The alignment between the requirements for a system, its design, and the implementation may be not preserved.

   In order to evaluate such defects, the following criteria of the requirement quality are proposed (following common approaches for defining these criteria).

- *Completeness*: there is enough information to proceed to the next stage or phase of work without risking a serious amount of rework.
- *Consistency*: the lack of conflict or contradiction among requirements.
- *Accuracy*: that accurately conveys the intent of the User.

   For our example of a library IS, the user requirements of this system are analyzed as follows:

- Business objectives: Management of Reader, Book, Borrowing, and Reservation.
- The processes description: An available book can be borrowed by readers, if the book is unavailable, the reader can make a reservation. The borrowing time is generally 3 days; however, if the reader is staff then the borrowing time is 30 days. The reader can renew her/his borrowing.
- The system shall run on the Internet, readers can access any time the status of books, consult their borrowing. Only the librarian can make borrowing and reservation.

Certainly, the requirements captured above are not complete. There is not enough information for the borrowing process. For instance, what are the different states of a book? Is a book blocked for a reservation after it is returned? If it is not blocked, it becomes available then can it be borrowed by others? So how a reservation can be fulfilled? etc. The missing information will impact the succeeded stages of IS development.

4.1.2 Meta-Model Quality

In this chapter we use the terminologies *meta-model* and *model* according to the OMG four-layer meta-models (OMG, 2002). A *meta-model* owns constructs and rules that allow specifying or describing a *model*. A model is an instance of its meta-model. In the context of IS architectures, at the analysis and design levels, different *meta-models* are used to describe different aspects/views of IS such as data view, functional view, organizational view, etc. The result of this description is various *models*.

A "good" meta-model should allow analysts and designers to describe completely, precisely, and faithfully what they intend to describe. In the other words, the quality of a meta-model depends on its expressive power and on how it supports designers in the modeling process to obtain a sound specification. Criteria concerning subjective evaluation or social method evaluation (i.e., interview) such as the simplicity and the understandability of a meta-model are out of the scope of this chapter. Next, we define quality criteria for meta-models as follows:

Completeness: The meta-model allows describing different information that cannot be described (or limited) by other meta-models, this criteria concerns the expressive power of the meta-model. For instance, the class diagram of UML owns constructs allowing describing the object behavior (method), the instantiation relationship, and the aggregation relationship. Meanwhile, the Entity-Relationship model (Chen, 1976) (or meta-model) does not; or the class diagram of UML does not describe dynamic specialization and keep track of objects, but the IASDO model does (Pham-Thi et al., 2006; Pham-Thi and Helfert, 2007).

Consistency: The meta-model is consistent itself and helps designers to obtain a consistent model. Rules defined on a meta-model should ensure the meta-model is consistent and its instances (model) are also consistent. For instance, any process has its input and output information. If the input information does not exist then the output information does not exist either. The IASDO meta-model allows its instance to satisfy this rule.

Accuracy: The meta-model is accurate itself and helps designers to obtain an accurate model. Rules defined on a meta-model should ensure the meta-model is accurate and its instances (model) are also accurate. For instance, the Data Flow Diagram has a set of rules (Celko, 1987) to ensure the accuracy of its instance, one of them is "no process can have only input data flows, no process can have only output data flows".

Based on specified requirements, different conceptual models or specifications concerning different IS views are modeled using different meta-models. The user interface, functionalities, and logical models are also specified. Therefore the meta-model quality is considered at the *system analysis* and *system design levels*. The experience of analyst and designer impacts the modeling process. The *meta-model quality*, *model quality*, and *modeling quality* are considered at these levels.

4.1.3 Model Quality

Model quality includes conceptual model quality and logical model quality. Conceptual model quality is defined as "the total quality of features and characteristics of a conceptual model that bears on its ability to satisfy stated or implied needs" (Moody, 2005). The logical model is a transformation of the conceptual model into the design level in IS architecture. In the literature, several works are realized on evaluating the conceptual model quality. Based on this definition and in order to develop a framework for conceptual model quality, Moody (2005) synthesized eight different approaches (deductive, codification, inductive, social, analytical, reverse inference, Goal-Question-Metric model, and Dromey's methodology). In conclusion they stated that there is no common standard for conceptual model quality.

Moody and Shanks (1994) have proposed a quality framework for quality evaluation of data models. This framework is composed of six quality factors: completeness, integrity, understandability, simplicity, integration, and implementability. Each factor is associated with a weight, which indicates the importance of the factor. Completeness is defined by Moody and Shanks (1994) as the ability of the data model to meet all user information and functional requirements. Furthermore, Lindland et al. (1994) and Krogstie et al. (1995) proposed a quality framework that is focusing on three main criteria: syntax, semantic and pragmatics. Syntactical quality of a model relates to the syntactical correctness of the model compared to the meta-model. Semantic quality depends on the relevance of models for the modeling domain (i.e. modeling subject).

According to Krogstie et al. (1995) there are two characteristics in the semantic quality: *validity* means there are no statements in the model that are not correct and relevant about the domain, and *completeness* means the model does not miss statements that are correct and relevant about the domain. The pragmatic quality of a model depends on the easy comprehension of this model and the feasibility concepts.

In summary, we define the quality criteria of the conceptual model with adaptation from research mentioned above as follows:

Completeness: The completeness of a conceptual model means the model does not miss statements that are correct and relevant about the domain. Certainly, the completeness of a conceptual model depends on the completeness criteria of requirements quality. For instance, the class diagram obtained in the example of library management above will be not complete in relation to the defined requirements if it misses the reader status information (i.e., if a reader is a staff). The activities diagrams are not complete in relation to the user need if these diagrams do not describe *block a book* activity.

Accuracy: The accuracy of a conceptual model means there is no statements in the model that are not correct and relevant about the domain.

Consistency: The model is consistent with the meta-model in the syntax, the model satisfies validation rules of the meta-model (if exist) and there is no contradiction of statements in the model.

These quality factors are evaluated with the application domain (or the user need) rather than with the requirements captured. Returning to our example, if a class diagram of library management system does not describe the *reader status*, then this model is incomplete. If an activity diagram concerning borrowing process does not include the activity *renew*, then this model is incomplete. Various models are produced at the *system analysis* and *system design levels*, therefore the model quality is considered at these levels.

4.1.4 Modeling Quality

The modeling quality depends on the experience, skill, and objectiveness of modelers. In our framework, the modeling quality can also be understood as the experience and the skill of programmers. Schuette and Rotthowe (1998) stated that the subjective position of the modeler is the characterizing issue for the result of the modeling process and proposed a Guidelines of information Modeling (GoM) including six principles which are Construction adequacy, Economic efficiency, Language adequacy, Systematic design, Clarity, and Comparability. The GoM allows the modeler to follow principals in order to reduce the subjectivism in the information modeling process and to improve the quality of information/data models. The experience and skill of analysts impact the requirement-capturing process as well as the modeling process in the system analysis and the system design level. Therefore, the modeling quality is considered at the requirement analysis level, the system analysis level, and the system design level.

Furthermore, based on specifications made in the design level, the IS is developed and implemented. The developer skill impacts the implementation. So the modeling quality is also considered at the implementation level. The result of modeling process is models, specifications or implemented system. The quality of modeling can be evaluated through the quality of these products. Therefore, we do not define quality criteria of modeling quality in our framework.

4.1.5 Data Quality

Data quality is multidimensional within 15 dimensions (Wang and Strong, 1996), which can be grouped in four categories: intrinsic data quality, contextual data quality, representational data quality, and accessibility data quality. Frequently, data quality is evaluated by widely accepted dimensions such as completeness, accuracy, consistency, and timeliness (Ballou and Pazer, 1995; Kovac et al., 1997).

Completeness: No data is missing and is sufficient breadth and depth for the task at hand. Completeness can be measure on a database level or an application domain level. For example on a database level, if data is filled in all attributes of a table in a relational database then this occurrence is complete. In contrast on an application domain level, the existence of an attribute or entity in the data model represents completeness.

Consistency: If different data represent the same thing then they have the same format and value. For instance, a book (logical book) has several copies (physical book). In the case a reservation is fulfilled; then data in the related database must represent that the borrowed copy belong to the same book reserved.

Accuracy: Data is correct in its value and data is correct regarding integrity rules.

Timeliness: Data is sufficiently up-to-date for the task at hand.

The implemented systems produce and transform data for serving the user needs. Thus, data quality is considered at the *deployment level* in IS architecture.

4.2 Impacts and Relations of Quality Factors

There are effectively two quality levels of model quality. The first level is that the obtained models are relevant to described requirements. In other words, these models are complete, accurate, and consistent with defined requirements. The second level concerns the satisfaction of the models to user needs. If the requirement is not complete, accurate or consistent with the user need then we cannot obtain models having quality in relation to the user needs even though they can be qualitative in relation to defined requirements. In other words, the requirement quality impacts the model quality (cf. the arrow in Fig. 1).

Data is described by a conceptual data model. The completeness and consistency of data in database may be dependent on the conceptual model. Consequently, the conceptual model may impact the quality of data (cf. the arrow in Fig. 1). For instance, if integrity rules on data consistency are specified with data models and the system implementation respects the specification then the data consistency can be managed. In other words, if the requirements are not well-captured or defined, then the system cannot satisfy the users.

The meta-model also impacts the model quality (cf. the arrow in Fig. 1), especially the expressive power property. If the meta-model does not allow describing a certain situation of the application domain then the model cannot present that situation. For example, most meta-model for process modeling does not support to describe the responsibility of an organizational role for process execution as well as the privilege on data access. Thus, it may occur that the inconsistency at the model level such as a role R is responsible for the process execution P that produces information I, but the role R does not have the privilege of creating I. In this case, the modeler must control it by adding rules. Thus the expressive power of the meta-model impacts on the expressive power of the conceptual model; whether the meta-model includes explicit rules for validating the conceptual model or validating the model implicitly by the experience of its designers. A meta-model of high quality may help to improve or ensure the quality of the conceptual model.

Modeling quality also impacts the model quality (cf. the arrow in Fig. 1). The case above shows that if the meta-model does not support constructs to model that situation and the rule concerning that situation is not specified by the modeler then the model is inconsistent.

The requirement quality and data quality belong to the end user perspective because the end user can evaluate them. Meanwhile the model quality, the modeling quality and the meta-model quality belong to IS developer perspective (i.e., analyst, designer, IS programmer, database administrator, etc.).

4.3 Comparison of our Framework and other Frameworks of IS Quality

We have presented a framework of IS quality as well as other approaches of IS quality and software quality. Different quality factors are defined in different frameworks. We build on concepts defined in literature such as requirement quality, model quality, modeling quality, and data quality. These concepts were extended by the concept of meta-model quality. However, there is a lack of research on integrating the concepts to an overall IS quality model. Based on IS architecture, along with different abstraction levels, we incorporated quality factors in IS Architecture frameworks, which provides the rationale for our selection of quality factors. For the reason of simplicity and ease of measurement, we define a homogeneous set of quality criteria concerning each quality factor such as completeness, accuracy, and consistency. Besides, in our opinion, the requirement quality is the most important factor that contribute to the "fitness of use" of the IS product. However, the requirement quality is not mentioned in most other approaches.

Our framework also presents the relation of data quality with IS quality; the data quality is impacted by the IS development process and data quality is a factor that contributes to the IS quality. This relation also lacks in other approaches.

Most approaches do not present the impacts of quality factor, while the model of Duggan and Reichgelt (2006) present the impact of different dimensions at a generic level so it is not easy to apply. The presentation of impacts and relations among quality factors in our framework shows a systematic view on IS quality and it helps to manage the IS quality.

5 Conclusion

In this chapter, we present a quality framework of IS that is based on IS architecture. The IS framework proposed by Zachman was selected because of its popularity, simplicity, and independence. Quality factors included in our framework are requirement quality, model quality, meta-model quality, modeling quality, and data quality. These factors are mentioned in literature, but foremost approaches fail to propose a coherent and consistent framework. Our contribution of this research is to clarify the relationship between various factors in the context of IS architecture. Our approach helps to obtain a systematic view on quality in IS and assists to identify defects in IS. Our framework shows that the requirement quality is the most important aspect, as it affects the quality of deliverables in the lower levels. With this framework, studying data quality does not only focus on the database level but it also requires focusing on model quality, modeling quality, meta-model quality, and requirement quality. This helps to find out the root cause of defects. The selection of quality factors in our framework is based on IS architecture. Indeed, they are concrete and impacted by the user and IS Developer's perspective. Our quality framework allows managing the quality of data and IS. Our future works aim to develop this IS quality framework by studying the measurement of each quality factor.

References

Ballou, D.P.; Pazer, H.L.: Designing Information Systems to Optimize the Accuracy-Timeliness Trade off, *Information Systems Research*, 6, pp. 51–72, 1995.

Bernus, P.; Schmidt, G.: Architectures of Information Systems, in Handbook on Architectures of Information Systems, Springer Verlag, Berlin, 1998.

Celko, J.: I.Data Flow Diagrams, Computer Language 4, January 1987.

Chen, Pin-Shan P.: The Entity-Relationship Model - Toward a Unified View of Data. *ACM Transactions on Database Systems*, 1(1), March 1976.

Davis, A.: A Comparison of Techniques for the Specification of External System Behavior, *Comm. ACM*, 31(9), 1988.

DeLone, W.H.; McLean, E.R.: Information Systems Success: The Quest for the Dependent Variable. *Information Systems Research*, 3(1), 60–95, 1992.

DeLone, W.H.; McLean, E.R.: The DeLone an McLean Model of Information Systems Success: A Ten-Year Update. *Journal of Management Information Systems*, 19 (4), 9–30, 2003.

Duggan, E.W.; Reichgelt, H: The Panorama of Information Systems Quality, in Duggan, E.W. and Reichgelt H. (eds), Measuring Information Systems Delivery Quality, Idea Group, 2006, ISBN: 1-59140-857-1.

Gordon Schulmeyer, G.; McManus J.I.: Handbook of Software Quality Assurance, Prentice Hall, New Jersey, 1998

Krogstie, J.; Lindland, O.I.; Sindre, G: Defining Quality Aspects for Conceptual Models. In Proceedings of the International Conference on Information System Concepts (ISCO3). Towards a Consolidation of Views. Marburg, 1995.

Kovac, R.; Lee, Y.W.; Pipino., L.L: Total Data Quality Management: The case of IRI. The 2nd ICIQ 1997, MIT Press, Massachusetts.

Kitchenham, B.; Pfleeger, S.: Software Quality: The Elusive Target. IEEE Software, 1996.

Leist Susanne; Zellner Gregor: Evaluation of Current Frameworks, The 21st Annual ACM Symposium on Applied Computing, SAC'06, Dijon, France, April 2006.

Lindland, O.I.; Sindre, G.; Solvberg, A: Understanding Quality in Conceptual Modeling. IEEE SOFTWARE 2/1994, pp.42-49, 1994.

Moody, D.L.; Theoretical and practical issues in evaluating the quality of conceptual models: current state and future directions. *Data and Knowledge Engineering Journal* 55, 243–276, 2005.

Moody, D.L.; Shanks., G: What Makes a Good Data Model? Evaluating the Quality of Entity Relationship Models. The 13th International Conference on entity Relationship Approach, LNCS 881, pp. 94–111, 1994.

OMG – Object Management Group. Meta Object Facility (MOF) specification. Technical report, OMG, Version 1.4, April 2002.

Opengroup: http://www.opengroup.org/architecture/wp/

Pham Thi, T.T.; Helfert, M.: Modelling information manufacturing systems, *Internatinal Journal of Information Quality*, 1 (1), pp. 5–21, 2007.

Pham Thi, T.T.; Dong Thi, B.T; Bui, M.T.D; Léonard, M.: Spécification de workflow avec le modèle IASDO (Workflow specification with the IASDO model) , IEEE the 4th RIVF, Ho-ChiMinh city, February 2006.

Pipino, L.; Lee, Y.W.; Wang, R.Y: Data quality Assessment. *Communication of ACM*, 45(4), 211–218, 2002.

Perry, D.E.; Staudenmayer, N.A.; Votta, L.G.: People, Organizations and Process Improvement. *IEEE Software*, 11, 36–45, 1994.

Schuette, R.; Rotthowe, T: The Guidelines of Modelling- An approach to Enhance the Quality in Information Models. In International Conference on Conceptual Modelling, ER'1998, LNCS 1507, pp. 240–254, 1998.

Valacich, J.S.; George, J.F.; Hoffer, J.A.: Essential of Systems Analysis and Design, 3rd Edition, Prentice Hall, Upper Saddle River, NJ, 2006.

Vidgen, R.; Wood-Harper, T.; Wood R.: A soft systems approach to information systems quality. *Scandinavian Journal of Information Systems*, 5, 97–112, August 1993.

Wong, B.: Different Views of Software Quality, in Duggan, E.W. and Reichgelt H. (eds), Measuring Information Systems Delivery Quality, Idea Group, 2006, ISBN: 1-59140-857-1.

Wang, R.Y., and Strong, D.M. : Beyond Accuracy: What Data Quality Means to Data Consumers". Journal of Management Information Systems 12(4), 3–53, 1996.

Yilmaz M. R., Chatterjee S., Deming and the Quality of Software Development, Business Horizon, Nov–Dec, 1997

Zachman, J.A.: A Framework for Information Systems Architecture. *IBM systems Journal*, 20, 3, 1987.

On Finding Suitable Designs for Whole-Part Relationships in Object-Relational Databases

Erki Eessaar

Tallinn University of Technology, Department of Informatics, eessaar@staff.ttu.ee

Abstract Whole-part relationships have secondary characteristics, the values of which determine the nature of a relationship. This chapter presents an approach that allows database designers to find a set of suitable designs for implementing a whole–part relationship in a database. This approach takes into account values of the secondary characteristics of relationships. These values determine a set of structural and behavioral constraints that must be implemented in a database. Different designs use different means for implementing these constraints. The proposed approach can be used in the context of any data model or database system. However, in this chapter we consider the underlying object-relational data model of SQL:2003.

1 Introduction

The concept "data model" is semantically overloaded. It has the following meaning in this work, if not explicitly stated otherwise: an abstract, self-contained, implementation-independent definition of elements of a 4-tuple of unordered sets {T, S, O, C} that together make up the abstract machine with which database users interact. In this case: T is a set of data types and types of data types; S is a set of data structure types; O is a set of operator types; C is a set of integrity constraint types. This definition is an improved version of the definition that is provided by Date (2003). Examples of data models are network, relational and object-relational.

In this work, we are interested in the object-relational (OR) data model. Currently there is no common OR data model. In this chapter, we consider the underlying data model of SQL:2003 standard ("OR_{SQL}") (Melton 2003), which is a well-known OR data model approach. We call a database system (DBMS) that uses this data model as $ORDBMS_{SQL}$. OR_{SQL} combines a relational data model (as specified by SQL:1992 or earlier standard versions) with the features of object-oriented programming, "including complex data structures, collections, encapsulation, inheritance and Object IDentity (OID)" (Soutou 2001).

Conceptual, logical, and physical data models can be used in order to describe a database of an enterprise. These models can be created by using UML (Muller 1999). UML allows us to express a whole-part relationship as either an aggregation or a composition. Barbier et al. (2003) and Guizzardi (2005) have analyzed

UML 1.4 and UML 2.0, respectively. They have found that the UML approach of defining whole-part relationships is too imprecise. Their research about properties of whole-part relationships deals mostly with conceptual modeling. On the other hand, studies about implementing whole-part relationships in an OR_{SQL} database (e.g., Pardede et al. 2004) use the UML classification of whole-part relationships as a basis. In this chapter, we use the results of research about whole-part relationships in order to improve the results of database design process. Barbier et al. (2003) list and explain primary and secondary characteristics of whole-part relationships. We assume that the readers are familiar with the basic principles of these characteristics. In this chapter, we propose that database designers should use the secondary characteristics in order to differentiate between different sorts of relationships and find suitable designs.

Lindland et al. (1994) propose semiotic quality improvement framework of conceptual modeling that distinguishes syntactic, semantic, and pragmatic quality. We can apply its principles during the database development as well. A data model is an abstract language (Date 2003). A logical data model that is designed according to a data model D or a physical data model that takes into account a database language DL of a DBMS are models that are created based on languages D and DL, respectively. We use these languages in addition to a set of languages that allow us to represent the designs (e.g., UML). Validity and completeness are the goals of semantic quality (Lindland et al. 1994). "Validity means that all statements made by the model are correct and relevant to the problem. /.../ Completeness means that the model contains all the statements about the domain that are correct and relevant" (Lindland et al. 1994). If we want to achieve these goals in a database design, then among other things, we have to preserve semantics of relationships in a database as much as possible by using the means of a data model and a database language. We can do it by enforcing structural and operational properties of the relationships and objects, which participate in these relationships.

The *first goal* of this chapter is to propose an approach that allows database designers to find *a set of designs* that describe how to implement a whole-part relationship in a database. The participation of each design in this set must be well-founded. We achieve this by using values of secondary characteristics of whole-part relationships as a basis of the selection process. This approach does not use the classification of whole-part relationships that is provided by UML. This approach can be used in order to create software systems that guide database design process. The *second goal* is to present an example of the use of this approach based on OR_{SQL} data model.

The rest of the chapter is organized as follows. Firstly, we analyze the existing state of the art about implementing whole-part relationships in an OR_{SQL} database. Secondly, we present an approach that allows us to find a set of suitable database designs. Thirdly, we use this approach in order to find a set of OR_{SQL} database designs. We also compare the proposed approach with the results of other studies. Finally, we draw some conclusions.

2 The State of the Art of OR$_{SQL}$ Database Design

Studies about implementing whole-part relationships in an OR$_{SQL}$ database consider aggregations (Pardede et al. 2004), compositions (Muller 1999; Pardede et al. 2005) or both (Marcos et al. 2001). The current approaches of representing whole-part relationships in an OR$_{SQL}$ database are sometimes not *methodical enough*. Next, we explain the problems.

Some studies propose to use the same design in case of relationships that have different properties. For example, an aggregation design, which is proposed by Marcos et al. (2001), is the same as one of the designs of a general one-to-many relationship that is proposed by Soutou (2001). Another example is that Mok (2002) proposes an algorithm that allows us to generate specifications of nested tables that are in a nested formal form, based on a database schema specification. This algorithm considers functional dependencies but do not treat aggregations and compositions differently than associations that do not have these properties.

Some studies provide limited explanations why to use a particular design if there is a particular kind of relationship. For example, Pardede et al. (2004) propose to create a base table (let us call it BT) based on an entity type that has role *Whole* in an aggregation. This table has a column with a multiset or an array type in order to record data about parts. A value in these types is a collection of values that have a user-defined type (let us call this user-defined type as T). Type T is created based on a specification of an entity type that has role *Part*. However, the authors do not explain how the use of user-defined types helps us to implement "shareability" and "existence independent" properties of an aggregation. In addition, this design proposal is incomplete. A type is a named finite set of values (Date 2003). For example, the structured type T is a set of all possible part representatives and it is not possible to insert new parts into that set or delete existing ones (Date and Darwen 2006). In this case, we could use an additional base table, which has a column with the type T in order to preserve data about parts after data about a whole is deleted from BT. Pardede et al. (2004) do not describe this or other means to preserve data about parts.

Some studies suggest designs that lead to data redundancy and cause update anomalies. A property of an aggregation is that a part may simultaneously belong to more than one whole. If we use the design that was described in the previous paragraph in case of an aggregation (like Pardede et al. [2004] propose to do), then data about the same part can be duplicated in different rows of a base table.

Some studies suggest designs that could increase the complexity without providing additional value to a database user. Date (2003) points to the problems of using pointers at the *logical* database level. Smith and Smith (1977) write about implementation of aggregations: "Pointers are objects which have no real-world analog and serve to dramatically increase the complexity of database interactions." Nevertheless, Marcos et al. (2001) propose the use of reference types (which are sets of pointers) in order to implement whole-part relationships.

Some studies do not take into account all the important features of OR$_{SQL}$. An example of this kind of feature is a viewed table that is a mandatory feature of OR$_{SQL}$ (Melton 2003). Viewed tables could have columns that have a collection type. In addition, the wording of proposals is sometimes not precise enough. For example, Marcos et al. (2001) and Pardede et al. (2004) write that designers of an OR$_{SQL}$ database have to create a set of tables. However, OR$_{SQL}$ distinguishes between base tables and viewed tables (Melton 2003). A reader can find out that the authors do not consider viewed tables only by studying fragments of source code.

Some studies propose too asymmetrical database designs. It is true that instance-asymmetry and type-antisymmetry are examples of *primary* characteristics of whole-part relationships and therefore all whole-part relationships must possess these characteristics (Barbier et al. 2003). However, symmetry is an important property of good language design (Date 1984). Blaha et al. (1988) think that a symmetrical representation of an association relationship in a database simplifies search and update. However, Marcos et al. (2001) and Pardede et al. (2004) propose the use of columns with array types in order to record data about parts. A table is a multiset of rows. An array is an *ordered* collection (we can refer to its elements by using ordinal position), but a multiset is an *unordered* collection. Therefore, we cannot use arrays in order to implement relationships in an OR$_{SQL}$ database if we want to treat participants of a relationship in a uniform way. If we record data about parts by using columns of base tables that have a multiset type, then it is also deviation from the symmetry property. In this case, parts and wholes require the use of different principles of retrieval of data and enforcing constraints. Halpin (2000) thinks that collections make it harder to conceive and express constraints in conceptual models as well as in implementation models. Soutou (2001) also finds that collections make it harder to enforce integrity constraints and express some queries.

3 An Approach of Finding a Set of Suitable Database Designs of a Whole-Part Relationship

Specific types of whole-part relationships can be defined in terms of secondary characteristics (Barbier et al. 2003). Examples of the secondary characteristics are lifetime dependency, existential dependency, separability, and shareability (Barbier et al. 2003). Values of the secondary characteristics determine *structural* (minimum and maximum cardinality) and *behavioral* constraints of a relationship. Therefore, these values can guide the selection of a set of suitable database designs.

Figure 1 presents a domain model of the proposed approach. The *general principle* of the approach is that a designer has to determine values of the secondary characteristics of a relationship and select a platform. The values determine a set of constraints that must be enforced in a database. The platform determines a set of design templates that could be used as a basis in order to find a set of suitable designs. Each design template consists of a set of mandatory elements and a set of elements, the creation of which depends on constraints. The result of the selection process is a set of suitable designs that are found based on templates. Each design in this set is the *union* of mandatory elements of a template and constraint-dependent elements of the template that must be created due to constraints of a particular relationship.

A platform is either a DBMS or a data model. Why should we differentiate them? Each DBMS has an underlying data model. In this work, we are interested in OR_{SQL}. However, the approach is not limited with this data model.

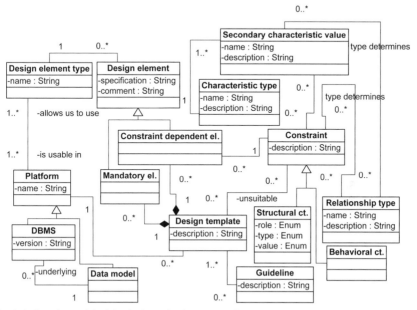

Fig. 1. A domain model of the design selection approach

A database language that is provided by a DBMS allows us to create elements that are proposed by the underlying data model of the DBMS. Generally, there *is not* one-to-one correspondence (bijection) between elements of a data model (they belong to sets T, S, O, and C – see Introduction) and elements that are provided by a database language that is created based on this data model. For example, the database language of $ORDBMS_{SQL}$ Oracle (Oracle 2007) allows us create materialized views and instead-of triggers. These kinds of elements are not specified in OR_{SQL} (Melton 2003). On the other hand, Türker and Gertz (2001) write that currently no DBMS allows us to create assertions (general constraints), although OR_{SQL} specifies them.

A database designer can find a set of suitable designs based on design templates. Each design template consists of a set of design elements (base tables, triggers, primary key constraints, etc.). Specification of an element could be recorded and presented as a free-form text or as a set of statements in a database programming language. Some of these elements are mandatory. It means that they *have* to be created if this template is used. On the other hand, some design elements must be created due to the constraints of a particular relationship (see class *Constraint dependent el.* in   Fig. 1). Table 1 gives an overview of these constraints. Entity types B and A that participate in a relationship (see Table 1) have roles Whole and

Part, respectively. Sign "*" means "unlimited", whereas "p", "m", and "n" mean that there is a finite value that is bigger than one. For instance, the following notation states that each part can be associated with at most one whole "[B]◇-..1------..-[A]".

Table 1. Mapping between values of some secondary characteristics of whole-part relationships and structural constraints of a relationship

Type of secondary characteristic	Value of a characteristic	Structural constraints – min. and max. cardinality
Shareability	Locally exclusive part	[B]◇-..1------------..-[A]
	Locally shareable part	[B]◇-..n-------------..-[A] [B]◇-..*-------------..-[A]
Lifetime dependency (For example, the work of Barbier et al. (2003) contains an illustration of cases 1–9.)	Lifetime dependency 1, 2, 4	[B]◇-1..------------0..-[A] [B]◇-m..-----------0..-[A]
	Lifetime dependency 3, 7	[B]◇-0..------------0..-[A]
	Lifetime dependency 5	[B]◇-1..------------1..-[A] [B]◇-1..-----------m..-[A] [B]◇-m..-----------1..-[A] [B]◇-m..---------p..-[A]
	Lifetime dependency 6, 8, 9	[B]◇-0..------------1..-[A] [B]◇-0..-----------m..-[A]
Existential dependency	Essential part	[B]◇-..-------------1..-[A]
	Inseparable part	[B]◇-1..-------------..-[A]
Separability	Optional whole	[B]◇-0..-------------..-[A]
	Mandatory whole	[B]◇-1..-------------..-[A] [B]◇-m..------------..-[A]
	Optional part	[B]◇-..-------------0..-[A]
	Mandatory part	[B]◇-..-----------1..-[A] [B]◇-..----------m..-[A]

We differentiate between cardinality values one and more than one, because they could cause the selection of different database designs. For example, if the *maximum* cardinality in the association end connected to the part is one ([B]◇-..------..1-[A]), then a design that uses a base table column with a row type in order to record data about parts already enforces this cardinality constraint. However, if we use a base table column with a multiset type for the same purpose, then we have to enforce this constraint by using triggers or declarative database constraints. For the same purpose, we differentiate between finite values that are bigger than one (m, n, and p) and unlimited (*). In addition, some values of the secondary characteristics have associated *behavioral* constraints. Essential part has a behavioral constraint "B instance is existentially dependent on A instance". Inseparable part has a behavioral constraint "A instance is existentially dependent on B instance".

It is possible that we cannot use some design templates if a constraint is present because it leads us to the selection of an unsuitable design. A design that is created based on a template is *suitable* if it satisfies all the following conditions: it does not cause uncontrolled (Date 2006) data redundancy, it specifies how to implement all the selected constraints based on the selected platform and there are no contradictions between the elements of the design.

Let us assume that we have to find a suitable design in the presence of the constraint "[B]◇-..n------..-[A]". If we create a base table based on the entity type B and create a column of this table that has a collection type based on the entity type A, then we may have to repeat data about the same entity (with type A) in more than one row. If we create two separate base tables based on A and B, then the constraint "[B]◇-..-------1..-[A]" can be implemented in OR$_{SQL}$ by using an assertion. On the other hand, we cannot implement this constraint by using a declarative constraint in an ORDBMS$_{SQL}$ that does not support subqueries in a table CHECK constraint or assertions. We also cannot use triggers (as specified in SQL:2003) in this case because it is not possible to defer execution of a trigger procedure until the end of a transaction. An example of contradicting design elements is a pair of uniqueness constraints C1 and C2, which are associated with the same base table, where the set of unique columns of C1 is a proper subset of the set of unique columns of C2.

Next, we explain how to find constraints that characterize a relationship. A database designer can do that by selecting values of secondary characteristics, by selecting relationship types or by selecting individual constraints.

Values of the secondary characteristics determine a set of constraints that must be implemented in a database. Some of the values of the secondary characteristics are incompatible. For instance, only the lifetime dependencies 5, 6, 8, and 9 (from the set of all lifetime dependencies) are compatible with the characteristic value "essential part" (Guizzardi 2005). Information about incompatibility of characteristic values is important in the proposed approach, because it allows us to evaluate sets of characteristic values. In addition, if a designer determines characteristic values of a relationship, then the selected values determine the set of values that the designer *cannot* use in order to characterize this relationship.

How can we find incompatible values of the secondary characteristics? Two characteristic values v1 and v2 are incompatible, if a relationship cannot be characterized by both of these values because they cause the selection of incompatible constraints. We have found that some structural constraints that determine properties of *the same association end* are incompatible for the following reasons:

1. v1 and v2 determine minimum cardinality constraint values a1 and a2, respectively so that a1◇a2. For example, optional whole and mandatory whole are incompatible for this reason.
2. v1 and v2 determine maximum cardinality constraint values b1 and b2, respectively so that b1◇b2. For example, locally exclusive part and locally shareable part are incompatible for this reason.
3. v1 and v2 determine minimum and maximum cardinality constraint values a1 and b2, respectively so that a1>b2. For example, locally exclusive part and lifetime dependency 1 *may* be incompatible for this reason.

Sometimes a value of a secondary characteristic has more than one associated constraint (see Table 1). If these constraints are incompatible, then a database designer has to select one constraint from this set of incompatible constraints.

Guizzardi (2005) proposes an extension to the UML 2.0 metamodel that would allow us to specify four types of conceptual whole-part relations based on the entities they relate – *componentOf, subQuantityOf, subCollectionOf, memberOf*. Some of these relationship types are characterized by specific values of the secondary characteristics. In addition, some of these relationship types have additional constraints. For example, the properties of relationship type *subQuantityOf* determine the following values of cardinality constraints: "[B]<>-..1-------1..1-[A]" (Guizzardi 2005). Therefore, we can treat these relationship types as macros, the selection of which determines a set of constraints of a relationship.

It is also possible that some constraints are not associated with any secondary characteristic value. For instance, values of the secondary characteristics, which are considered in this chapter, do not determine the constraint "[B]<>-..-----..n-[A]".

4 On Implementation of Whole-Part Relationship in an OR$_{SQL}$ Database

In this section, we present an example of the proposed approach based on OR$_{SQL}$ data model. We assume that design templates are OR$_{SQL}$-specific and do not use any not-standardized feature. We use a conceptual data model with entity types A and B. These entity types are associated with a generic binary whole-part relationship: [B]<>------[A] where B has role Whole and A has role Part. B has attributes a and b and A has attributes c and d. Values of attributes a and c are unique identifiers of entities with type B and A, respectively. We also assume that attributes a, b, c, and d have type INTEGER (INT).

Next, we present an *incomplete* set of possible OR$_{SQL}$ database design templates. Each design template consists of a set of mandatory elements and a set of constraint-dependent elements (see Fig. 1). Table 2 specifies mandatory elements. "All rows of a table are of the same row type and this is called the row type of that table" (Melton 2003). Therefore, we specify OR$_{SQL}$ tables in terms of their row types. In addition, we show primary and foreign keys, if they belong to the set of mandatory elements. Declarations of the row types (see Table 2) consist of the pairs of attribute and type identifiers. Fields of a row are ordered in OR$_{SQL}$. However, order of fields has no significance in our example. The phrase "part MULTISET {ROW (c INT, d INT)}" means that a table has column *part* with a constructed multiset type. We assume that all the columns in the base tables are mandatory (they prohibit NULLs), if not explicitly stated otherwise.

Table 2. Mandatory elements of a set of design templates for implementing a whole-part relationship in an OR$_{SQL}$ database

ID	Specification of elements
1	Base table: *B*: ROW (a INT, b INT, part MULTISET {ROW (c INT, d INT)}) PRIMARY KEY (a)
2	Base table: *B_*: ROW (a INT, b INT) PRIMARY KEY (a) Base table: *A*: ROW (c INT, d INT) PRIMARY KEY (c) Base table: *AB*: ROW (a INT, c INT) FOREIGN KEY (a) REFERENCES B_(a), FOREIGN KEY (c) REFERENCES A(c) Viewed table: B: ROW (a INT, b INT, part MULTISET {ROW (c INT, d INT)})

Table 3. Constraint-dependent elements of the set of design templates {1, 2} and constraints that prevent the use of these templates

Constraint/ Template	1	2
[B]◇-0..--------..-[A]	There must be a row in B that represents the missing whole. Column $B.b$ is optional.	-
[B]◇-1..--------..-[A]	-	A set of assertions.
[B]◇-m..--------..-[A]	X	A set of assertions.
[B]◇-..1--------..-[A]	A set of triggers or assertions.	Column $AB.c$ has uniqueness constraint.
[B]◇-..n--------..-[A]	X	A set of triggers or assertions.
[B]◇-..*--------..-[A]	X	-
[B]◇-..--------0..-[A]	Column $B.part$ is optional.	-
[B]◇-..--------1..-[A]	-	A set of assertions.
[B]◇-..------m..-[A]	A set of triggers or assertions.	A set of assertions.
[B]◇-..--------..1-[A]	A set of triggers or assertions.	Column $AB.a$ has uniqueness constraint.
[B]◇-..--------..n-[A]	A set of triggers or assertions.	A set of triggers or assertions.
[B]◇-..--------..*-[A]	-	-
B inst. is existentially dependent on A inst.	A set of triggers.	A set of triggers.
A inst. is existentially dependent on B inst.	-	A set of triggers.

Table 3 presents constraint-dependent elements of design templates 1 and 2 (see Table 2). Sign "-" means that we *can* use the template if the constraint is present and there is no need to use constraint-dependent elements due to this constraint. Sign "X" means that the design template *cannot* be used if the constraint is present due to the resulting data redundancy. For example, characteristic value "locally shareable part" prevents the use of design template 1 because it leads to data redundancy.

4.1 An Example Scenario of Finding a Set of Suitable Designs

The proposed approach can be used as a basis of an expert system that assists a database designer. It can be integrated into a CASE environment or could be a separate tool. We have created a prototype of this system by using MS Access DBMS. We created its logical data model based on the domain model that is presented in Fig. 1. A designer who uses this prototype has to select a platform and determine values of the secondary characteristics of a whole-part relationship. Based on this information, the system presents a set of suitable designs for this relationship. If a system records selections of a designer, then this information can be used in order to generate documentation of the relationship and design decisions.

Next, we present a scenario. We assume that the platform is OR_{SQL}. We denote the set of characteristic values from which a designer can select values and the set of selected values as PV and SV, respectively. If a designer selects a characteristic value, then the system removes it from PV and adds to SV. In addition, the system removes a value v from PV if v has one or more associated structural constraints (where *the only* difference of these constraints is in the cardinality value) and *all* these constraints are *incompatible* with at least one constraint that is already selected by the designer. We mention the latter removals explicitly in the next scenario:

1. *Designer*: Locally shareable part, more precisely "[B]◇-..*--------..-[A]".
2. *System*: Selected structural constraints: "[B]◇-..*--------..-[A]". Removes "locally exclusive" from PV.
3. *Designer*: Optional whole.
4. *System*: Selected structural constraints: "[B]◇-0..*--------..-[A]". Removes "lifetime dependencies 1, 2, 4, 5", "mandatory whole" and "inseparable part" from PV.
5. *Designer*: Essential part.
6. *System*: Selected structural constraints: "[B]◇-0..*--------1..-[A]". Selected behavioral constraint: "B inst. is existentially dependent on A inst.". Removes "lifetime dependencies 3, 7" and "optional part" from PV.
7. *Designer*: Constraint "[B]◇-..--------..*-[A]".
8. *System*: Selected structural constraints: "[B]◇-0..*-----1..*-[A]".

Values of the secondary characteristics determine structural and behavioral constraints of a relationship. The system can find a set of designs based on information about constraints. If at least one of the selected constraints causes the creation of an unsuitable design based on a design template, then this template cannot be used in that case. In the current example, we cannot use template 1 because its use will cause data redundancy due to "locally shareable part" property (see Table 3).

A suitable design that is created based on template 2 has the following *constraint-dependent elements*: (1) a set of assertions that implement the constraint "[B]◇-..---1..-[A]", (2) a set of triggers that implement the behavioral constraint: "B inst. is existentially dependent on A inst.". In addition, the system can present design guidelines (see class *Guideline* in Fig. 1). For example, it could present guidelines about how to find the primary key of a base table if it is not specified in a design.

4.2 Discussion

Zhang et al. (2001) describe how to preserve relationship semantics in an OR_{SQL} database. A similarity with our work is that they also do not limit their work with the classification of relationships that is provided by UML. Instead, they consider structural and operational properties of relationships. One difference with our work is that they *do not* limit their work with whole-part relationships. They do not consider the secondary characteristics of whole-part relationships. Instead of using UML, which is widely used by software engineering professionals, they propose that database designers should learn and use a new language, in order to create Entity/Semantic Relationship diagrams.

On the other hand, Guizzardi (2005) proposes an extension to UML, which would allow database designers to specify values of the secondary characteristics in conceptual models that are presented as UML class diagrams. Therefore, if we base our work on these characteristics, then we contribute to the creation of a kind of bridge between conceptual and logical database designs that allows database designers to generate more expressive logical and physical data models (than is possible today) based on a conceptual data model and at the same time still use UML.

Another difference between our work and the work of Zhang et al. (2001) is that they propose an extension of the underlying data model of a DBMS. They present extension module ORIENT that extends Informix ORDBMS$_{SQL}$ by providing CREATE RELATIONSHIP statement. On the other hand, we use only the means that are already provided by data models or DBMSs that implement these models. Our approach is not limited by one particular data model or DBMS.

An advantage of our proposed approach is that it allows us to justify the creation of each design element and to prevent the creation of unnecessary design elements. It also helps us to avoid selection of designs that lead to data redundancy. If an expert system is created based on this approach, then it is possible to gradually extend it: by adding support to new data models and DBMSs or by improving design templates if a corresponding data model or a DBMS is improved.

A disadvantage of our proposed approach is that it allows database designers to find *a set of* suitable designs, instead of *exactly one* design that is the best in the given circumstances. It is possible that this set is empty. If this set contains more than one design, then selection of the *most suitable* design from this set is still a task of a human user. Values of database design metrics, which are calculated based on the proposed designs, could assist this decision-making process. A problem is that current OR$_{SQL}$ database design metrics (Piattini et al. 2001) are quite limited. For instance, they do not take into account CHECK constraints and viewed tables. Therefore, the future work must include the identification of suitable database design metrics and possibly development of new metrics. In addition, in this work we do not consider all the secondary characteristics of whole-part relationships (for instance, transitivity). The future work must take into account all the secondary characteristics.

5 Conclusions

In this chapter, we proposed a novel approach, the use of which allows database designers to find a set of suitable designs for implementing a whole-part relationship in a database. The search process is based on the values of secondary characteristics of whole-part relationships. We presented a domain model of the approach and used this model in order to create a prototype of an expert system. We presented an example of the use of this approach based on the underlying data model of SQL:2003, which is a well-known object-relational data model approach. The results show that this approach can be used as a basis of an expert system that allows us to make well-founded design decisions.

References

Barbier, F., Henderson-Sellers, B., Le Parc-Lacayrelle, A. and Bruel, J. (2003) Formalization of the Whole-Part Relationship in the Unified Modeling Language. IEEE Trans. Software Eng. 29(5), 459–470.

Blaha, M.R., Premerlani, W.J. and Rumbaugh, J.E. (1988) Relational database design using an object-oriented methodology. Comm. of the ACM. 31(4), Apr., 414–427.

Date, C.J. (1984) Some principles of good language design: with especial reference to the design of database languages. SIGMOD Rec. 14(3), Nov, 1–7.

Date, C. J. (2003) An Introduction to Database Systems. 8th ed. Pearson/Addison-Wesley, Boston.

Date, C. J. (2006) Date on Database: Writings 2000-2006. Apress, Berkeley, CA.

Date, C. J. and Darwen, H. (2006) Databases, Types and the Relational Model. 3rd edn. Addison-Wesley, Reading, MA.

Guizzardi, G. (2005) Ontological Foundations for Structural Conceptual Models. Telematica Instituut Fundamental Research Series No. 15. Ph.D. thesis, University of Twente.

Halpin, T. (2000) Modeling Collection in UML and ORM. In Proc. 5'h IFIP WG8.1 Int. Workshop on Evaluation of Modeling Method in System Analysis and Design, Kista, Sweden (June).

Lindland, O.I., Sindre, G. and Solvberg, A. (1994) Understanding quality in conceptual modeling. IEEE Software 11(2), 42–49.

Marcos, E., Vela, B., Cavero, J. M. and Caceres, P. (2001) Aggregation and composition in object-relational database design. In: Caplinskas A., Eder J. (eds) Research Communications of ADBIS'01(1). pp. 195–209.

Melton, J. (2003) ISO/IEC 9075-2:2003 (E) Information technology — Database languages — SQL — Part 2: Foundation (SQL/Foundation), http://www.wiscorp.com/SQLStandards.html

Mok, W. Y. (2002) A comparative study of various nested normal forms. IEEE Trans. Knowledge Data Eng. 14(2), 369–385.

Muller, R. J. (1999) Database Design for Smarties: Using UML for Data Modeling. Morgan Kaufmann Publishers, San Francisco.

Oracle® Database SQL (2007) Reference 10g Release 1 (10.1) Part Number B10759-01. Oracle Corp., http://download-west.oracle.com/docs/cd/B14117_01/server.101/b10759/toc.htm

Pardede, E., Rahayu, J. W. and Taniar, D. (2004) Mapping Methods and Query for Aggregation and Association in Object-Relational Database using Collection. In Proc. of the ITCC(1)'2004. IEEE Computer Society, pp. 539–543.

Pardede, E., Rahayu, J. W. and Taniar, D. (2005) Composition in Object-Relational Database. Encyclopedia of Information Science and Technology. IDEA Publishing, pp. 488–494.

Piattini, M., Calero, C., Sahraoui, H. and Lounis, H. (2001) Object-Relational Database Metrics. L'Object, vol. March 2001.

Smith, J. and Smith, D. (1977) Database abstractions: aggregation. Comm. ACM. 20(6), 405–413.

Soutou, C. (2001) Modeling relationships in object-relational databases. Data Knowledge Eng. 36(1), 79–107.

Türker, C. and Gertz, M. (2001) Semantic integrity support in SQL:1999 and commercial (object-) relational database management systems. VLDB J. 10(4), 241–269.

Zhang, N., Ritter, N. and Härder, T. (2001) Enriched Relationship Processing in Object-Relational Database Management Systems. In Proc. of the Third International Symposium on Cooperative Database Systems for Advanced Applications, pp. 50–59.

On the Problem of Semantic Loss in View Integration

Peter Bellström

Karlstad University, Department of Information Systems, Peter.Bellstrom@kau.se

Abstract Integration is a key issue in conceptual database design. However, the integration process is very complex and error prone and may often cause semantic loss. Semantic loss, in this chapter, is described as a problem that occurs if one or several concept names and/or dependencies describing the meaning of a concept are lost during the view integration process. Semantic loss often occurs because of the way resolution methods are used today since not only similarities, but also differences between the views have to be identified, resolved, and simplified. The high focus on technical and implementation issues that most of the modeling languages adopt today may also cause semantic loss. In this chapter we argue that a modeling language that instead puts focus on concept names and dependencies should be applied. We also argue and propose alternative resolution and simplification techniques for name conflicts and inter-schema properties that instead of getting rid of concept names and dependencies keep these as long as possible in the integration process. Applying the proposed resolution and simplification techniques might counter an impoverishment of the language used in the views and/or schema and prevent semantic loss. The proposed resolution techniques might even contribute to a semantically richer global conceptual database schema.

1 Introduction

Schema integration, the origin of view integration, is defined as "[…] the activity of integrating the schemas of existing or proposed databases into a global, unified schema." [3]. View integration is a process divided into at least four phases: pre-integration, comparison of the views, conforming the views and merging, and re-structuring. Extension of the view integration process with an additional phase, pre-conforming the views, placed between comparison and conforming the views has also been suggested [7]. Nevertheless, during the view integration process the views and schema are modified since not only conflicts, such as *homonyms* and *synonyms*, but also inter-schema properties, such as *hypernyms–hyponyms* and *holonyms–meronyms*, need to be taken into account and resolved or simplified. Apart from conflict resolution and inter-schema simplification the global schema is, after merging, often restructured since it is highly possible that it contains redundant concepts and dependencies. During the view integration process the designers also have to consider several quality criteria [3, 4] of the final conceptual schema. One such quality criteria is minimality. A schema is minimal if "[…] no concept can be deleted from the schema without losing some information" [4]. Problems related to *information loss* in conceptual database design has been discussed in different contexts such as in structural conflict resolution (e.g., [23, 32]) and derived information (e.g., [14, 30]). Some work has also been conducted on *concept name compression* in connection with resolution of linguistic conflicts and inter-schema properties (e.g., [8, 9]), nevertheless work still needs to be conducted in this area.

In this chapter we therefore focus on both resolution techniques for linguistic conflicts and simplification techniques for inter-schema properties. We also focus on consequences for the language used in the views when choosing a specific resolution or simplification technique. Finally, we treat a view and a schema as a communication tool between the end users and designers (cf. [1, 12, 19]).

The research questions in this chapter are:

- What differentiates and relates information loss, concept name compression, and semantic loss?
- Does the strive for minimality, the use of different modeling constructs, or the use of noncomparable transformations cause semantic loss?

This chapter is structured as follows: first, we present an overview of the view integration process. Second, we describe and discuss the problem of semantic loss in view integration. Third, we show with an illustrating example a set of resolution techniques to linguistic conflicts and inter-schema properties. Fourth, we compare resolution and simplification techniques to illustrate how many of them may result in semantic loss. Fifth, we sum up the problem of semantic loss in view integration and end the chapter with a short discussion and conclusion.

2 The View Integration Process – View Integration in the Large

Conceptual database design is comprised of two phases where view design is the first and view integration the second. In *view design*, views for each end user or user group are defined and graphically illustrated using a modeling language such as the Entity-Relationship modeling language (ER) [13], the Unified Modeling Language (UML) [26], the Klagenfurt Conceptual Predesign Model (KCPM) [36] or the Karlstad Enterprise Modeling approach (EM) [18]. In *view integration*, the designed views are integrated into one global schema. There are several advantages with the two-phase conceptual database design approach, compared to defining a global schema at once. First, views preserve and highlight differences in how different end users view their organization, while a global schema may instead mask these [29]. Second, views may not only prevent premature design decisions, but also ensure that all views of the organization are taken into account [27]. Third, view integration is an effective technique for developing [16] and managing

[24] large database schemas. In the rest of this section we describe the view integration process as illustrated in Fig. 1.

Fig. 1. View integration process [7]

The first phase in the view integration process is *pre-integration*. It has been pointed out that this phase includes three main tasks: translate all views into a canonical modeling language, check for conflicts and inconsistencies in each view, and select integration strategies [31]. The second phase is *comparison of the views*. This phase also includes three main tasks: identification of name conflicts, identification of structural conflicts, and identification of inter-schema properties [21]. The third phase is *pre-conforming the views*. In this phase conflicts and inter-schema properties are simplified using inference rules to deduce new dependencies and/or concepts [7]. The fourth phase is *conforming the views*. This phase includes two tasks: resolution of conflicts and adding any new dependencies for identified inter-schema properties. The fifth phase is *merging and restructuring*. This phase also includes two main tasks: merging all views into one global schema and restructuring the global schema to improve the schema quality. This could mean introducing new dependencies identified earlier or during the merge of views. As also pointed out earlier, during the whole view integration process the graphical illustrations, the views, and the schema are changed and modified to facilitate the actual merge of views. It is important that the changes and modifications are carried out without any semantic loss, which otherwise could change the meaning of some part of the view or schema.

3 Semantic Loss in View Integration

Semantic loss is a major problem in view integration. During the view integration process, the views and schema are modified, which means that some part of one view or schema is changed. In other words, after the modification, we actually have a slightly different view or schema than before. During the modification, it is important that the meanings of a view or schema are not lost, thus keeping the view or schema intact at least when dealing with the semantic part. Although, this is rarely the case.

In this chapter we discuss semantic loss not only in connection with resolution and simplification of conflicts and inter-schema properties, but also in connection with schema restructuring. **Semantic loss** is therefore described as *a problem that occurs if one or several concept names and/or dependencies describing the meaning of a concept are lost during the view integration process*.

The related problem of ***information loss*** was mentioned in [23]. In [23] the authors described the problem in connection with view and schema transformations as follows "[…] a transformation is information preserving if any database instance structured according to the original schema can be losslessly converted into a database instance according to the transformed schema, and vice versa […]." The authors also point out an information difference between the user views and the global schema "[…] the original and transformed schemas will represent exactly the same real-world facts, although with a different modeling construct." [23].

In [4] the authors classify transformations into *information-preserving transformations*, not causing any problems and *information-changing transformations*, which may cause problems. The authors further classify an information-changing transformation as either *augmenting transformations* meaning the integrated schema contains ***more information*** than the input views, *reducing transformations* meaning the integrated schema contains ***less information*** than the input views, and finally *noncomparable transformations*, which is the case if the integrated schema neither contains ***more nor less information*** than the input views. Finally, the authors point out that conflict resolution techniques often apply noncomparable transformations and the task of adding inter-schema properties often apply augmenting transformations.

A slightly different approach to the problem of semantic loss is described in [8]. In [8] the authors criticize how view integration methods in general deal with similar concept names, such as synonyms, by compressing (merging) them into one concept name. ***Concept name compression*** is defined as: "a state which may occur if several concept names are merged (compressed) into one concept name, for example when choosing one of the concept names to represent a concept when trying to resolve a synonym conflict." [6]. Finally, in [9] the discussion on concept name compression was extended to include resolution and simplification techniques for concept names identified as homonyms or as an inter-schema hypernym–hyponym property.

4 Illustrating Example – View Integration in the Small

In this section we present an example showing how view integration could be conducted. This is done not only to illustrate the proposed and the emphasized resolution techniques, but also to give a reference point when discussing conflicts and inter-schema properties in the Section 5. Let us, therefore, first take a closer look at the example. The primitives used to define the views are illustrated in Fig. 2 and views to integrate are illustrated in Fig. 3. The example is a modified version of the one illustrated in [35].

Let us then briefly describe the idea behind EM and the adapted static primitives. In EM, we are dealing with implementation-independent descriptions of the future database. This means that we do not distinguish between classes and attributes and therefore draw each concept as a box. Between the boxes we draw different types of lines representing the in-between dependencies and finally at the end of each line we draw the cardinality.

Let us now return to Fig. 3. Both views have been translated from ER to EM in addition to replacing each many-to-many dependency with two one-to-many dependencies using a new concept in-between, e.g., *PUBLICATION-KEYWORD PAIRS*.

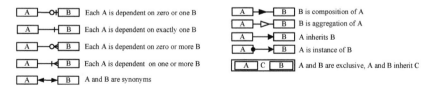

Fig. 2. Adapted and modified representation of static dependencies [18]

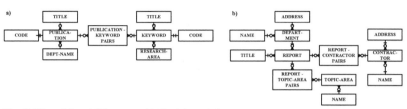

Fig. 3. View (a) and (b) prepared to be integrated

Before comparing the views we first have to check for conflicts and inconsistencies within each view. While doing so we may identify several problems that need to be resolved. In our example, we identified several homonyms in both views. In view (a) we identified *CODE* and *TITLE* and in view (b) *NAME* and *ADDRESS* as homonyms. These are resolved by introducing a combination of the dot-notation and the inheritance dependency [5, 7] according to the following inference rule: If *PUBLICATION* (0, m; 1, 1) *TITLE* then *PUBLICATION* (1, m; 1, 1) *PUBLICATION.TITLE*, *PUBLICATION.TITLE* inherits *TITLE*.

We now start to compare the views aiming to identify both similarities such as synonyms and inter-schema properties and differences such as homonyms. One homonym (*TITLE*) and two synonyms (*KEYWORD* (a) – *TOPIC-AREA* (b), *DEPT-NAME* (a) – *DEPARTMENT* (b)) are identified. The homonym is resolved in the same way as described earlier. The synonyms are resolved by introducing the mutual inheritance dependency between the two concepts [10, 20], e.g., *TOPIC-AREA* ◀—▶ *KEYWORD*.

We also identify a hypernym–hyponym inter-schema property between *PUBLICATION* and *REPORT*. Finally, we identify three holonym–meronym inter-schema properties: *PUBLICATION-KEYWORD PAIRS*, *REPORT-TOPIC-AREA PAIRS*, and *REPORT-CONTRACTOR PAIRS*. All inter-schema properties are documented because they are needed during merging and restructuring. The views are now superimposed into a first global schema. This is carried out by merging the concepts that are truly identical, including all synonyms and all remaining concepts into the global schema. We now have a first intermediate version of our conceptual database schema (Fig. 4).

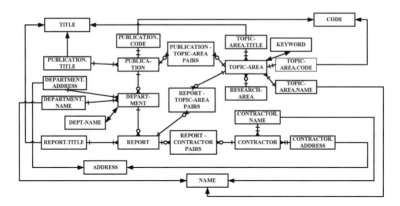

Fig. 4. First intermediate version of conceptual database schema

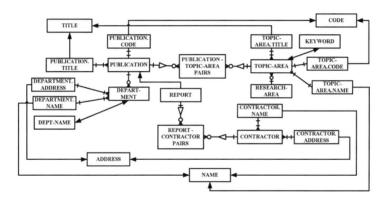

Fig. 5. Final integrated conceptual database schema

We now, once again, take a look at the documented inter-schema properties and introduce them into the schema. Between *PUBLICATION* and *REPORT* we introduce a hypernym–hyponym dependency [11] and the dependencies connected to *PUBLICATION-KEYWORD PAIRS*, *REPORT-TOPIC-AREA PAIRS* and *REPORT-CONTRACTOR PAIRS* are modified to meronym–holonym dependencies. This results in a second intermediate version of our schema. Finally, we have to improve the schema quality [3, 4] by removing redundant dependencies and concepts. In our case, we may remove dependencies and concepts that are truly redundant and that do not cause semantic loss. Nevertheless, when the designer and/or end user is slightly unsure, the concept and/or dependency should be kept in the schema. In our example, we remove *REPORT.TITLE* since *REPORT* inherits *PUBLICATION*, which is connected to the *PUBLICATION.TITLE* concept. We also remove the (1, 1; 0, m) dependency between *DEPARTMENT* and *REPORT* since this dependency is also inherited through *PUBLICATION*. Finally, we remove the *REPORT-TOPIC-AREA PAIRS* concept and the dependencies connecting it to other concepts. The final integrated global conceptual database schema is illustrated in Fig. 5.

5 Comparison of Resolution Techniques for Linguistic Conflicts

5.1 Comparison of Name Conflict Resolution Techniques

Name conflicts are mostly divided into homonyms and synonyms (e.g., [3, 23, 32]), however, other classifications (e.g., [31]) have been suggested. In [31] a name conflict is instead called a semantic conflict and extended with cyclic generalization a problem that occurs if there is a hypernym–hyponym dependency between *B and A* in one view and a hypernym–hyponym dependency between *A and B* in another view. The problem of synonyms and homonyms has also been described as a cause for headache and migraine [26].

The most ordinary resolution technique for name conflicts is simple renaming. This means that one or several concept names are changed – a concept is renamed. Renaming is an unclear and vague resolution technique and may most likely cause both concept name compression and semantic loss. Even so other more detailed and sophisticated resolution and supplement techniques have been proposed for both homonyms and synonyms.

For the *homonym* conflict it has been suggested to use resolution techniques such as prefixing the names [15, 28, 33] and standardization of names [22, 25]. In [4] the authors stress that one concept name should be kept and the other renamed, while in [24] the author propose that two homonyms should be resolved by renaming the concepts differently.

For the *synonym* conflict it has been suggested to use supplement techniques to renaming such as establishing an official list of synonyms [24] and to provide aliases [28]. Yet, the most ordinary resolution technique is still to rename synonyms the same, which means to select and keep one of the concept names and rename the other (e.g., [2, 4, 21, 23, 24]).

In [4] and [31] the authors describe a problem named *reverse subset relationship* or *cyclic generalization*. This problem occurs when we in one view have defined concept A as a specialization (hyponym) of concept B and in another view defined concept B as a specialization (hyponym) of concept A. In EM, this may instead indicate the occurrence of a synonym conflict. As described in Section 4 a synonym conflict is resolved by introducing the mutual inheritance dependency defined as "A ◀—▶ B if and only if A —▶ B, B —▶ A" [17], which also resolve the problem of reverse subset relationship and cyclic generalization.

Comparing the mentioned resolution techniques for homonyms and synonyms with the resolution techniques emphasized in Section 4 several benefits with the latter, if having a communication tool perspective, is identified. First, when using the proposed resolution technique for homonyms all concept names are retained and the semantic quality is improved. Second, when using the proposed resolution technique for synonyms, reverse subset relationship, and cyclic generalization, all concept names are retained.

5.2 Comparison of Inter-Schema Property Simplification Techniques

Inter-schema properties are not really conflicts; instead they express certain types of dependencies when two concept names are related to each other by certain constraints [4, 21]. In this section we describe and discuss simplification techniques for the inter-schema hypernym–hyponym property and the inter-schema holonym–meronym property. Although both these inter-schema properties are often mentioned it is important to notice that the type of inter-schema properties used in the views and/or schema depends on what primitives and dependencies the chosen modeling language has to offer.

For the *inter-schema hypernym–hyponym dependency* the most ordinary simplification technique is to introduce an is-a dependency (e.g., [23, 33]) between the concepts. Even so, applying EM we have two slightly different dependencies for this: generalization and subset hierarchy (Fig. 2). The ability for the concepts to overlap emphasizes the dependency to use.

For the *inter-schema holonym–meronym dependency* the most ordinary simplification technique is to introduce a part-of dependency (e.g., [33, 34]) between the concepts. However, applying EM we once again have two slightly different dependencies for this: aggregation and composition (Fig. 2). The cardinality between the concepts emphasizes the dependency to use.

Comparing the mentioned simplification techniques for the inter-schema hypernym–hyponym property we identify a difference between when and how specialization and subset-of should be used. In Fig. 6a, an example of generalization is given. While studying Fig. 6a, we identify three exclusive *PUBLICATION* types. This means that a *PUBLICATION* can only be specialized as one of the three at a given point in time. If we instead had drawn specialization arrows from each of the three *PUBLICATION* types to the *PUBLICATION* concept we should have a subset-of dependency. This dependency should be interpreted as *PUBLICATION* could be specialized as one or several types of *PUBLICATION* at a given point in time.

Comparing the mentioned simplification techniques for the inter-schema holonym–meronym property we again identify a difference between when and how aggregation and composition should be used. In the example given in Section 3 we introduced the aggregation dependency illustrating that both *PUBLICATION-TOPIC-AREA PAIRS* and *REPORT-CONTRACTOR PAIRS* are aggregated from their connecting concepts. Studying the cardinality we see that it is defined as (1, 1; 0, m) indicating that it is the aggregation dependency that should be introduced between the concepts. Composition is a stronger dependency compared to aggregation and the cardinality that indicates this type of dependency does not contain a zero. There are no examples of composition in Section 4. For the purpose of discussion, consider the *ORDER* (1, 1; 1, m) *ORDERLINE* example. It should be interpreted as one *ORDER* is composed of one or several *ORDERLINE* and that there is a strong ownership and coincidental lifetime between *ORDER* and *ORDERLINE*.

Before ending this section we again take a look at the views illustrated in Fig. 6. The problem illustrated in Fig. 6 has been described as follows: "The modification scenarios for the naming conflict involve renaming the concept; they can also involve adding some *inter-schema property*" [4].

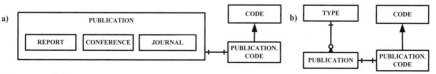

Fig. 6. Specialization (a) vs. regular concept (b)

The views in Fig. 6 illustrate two ways of defining a specific *TYPE* of *PUBLICATION* such as: (a) specialization and (b) regular concept. If the designer decides to adopt the regular concept (b) solution without documenting the actual *TYPE* of *PUBLICATION* given in view (a) (e.g., *TYPE {REPORT, CONFERENCE, JOURNAL}*) we end up with semantic loss. If the designer instead decides to adopt specialization without considering the *TYPE* concept we could end up with semantic loss. However, using one of the resolution and/or simplification techniques given in Fig. 7 all concept names are retained and therefore do not cause semantic loss.

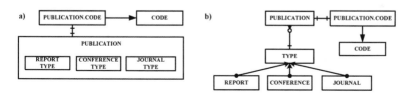

Fig. 7. Resolution of the specialization (a) vs. regular concept (b) problem

6 Summing up the Problem of Semantic Loss in View Integration

In this section we summarize the discussion about semantic loss in view integration by answering the two research questions asked in the introduction.

To answer the first research question we have to take a closer look at the definitions for each of the three problems. After studying them, it can be concluded that *information loss* is connected to implementation-dependent problems. This is the case, since information loss is used in connection with not only the capacity to *represent* a real-world fact, either as an entity, an attribute, or as a relationship, in a view or schema, but also the capacity to *store* a real-world fact in the future database.

Concerning *concept name compression* and *semantic loss*, these are instead both connected to implementation-independent problems. This is motivated by the fact that both are used in connection with the ability to *interpret* a concept and/or dependency in a view or schema. Furthermore, there is a difference between concept name compression and semantic loss. This means that they are not exactly the same, but overlap since concept name compression only deals with loss of concept names, while semantic loss is more generic, and also deals with loss of dependencies.

Moreover, information loss may cause both concept name compression and semantic loss, but the other way around is not necessary the truth. This is motivated by the fact that we might be able to store a real-world fact and at the same time have lost a concept name or dependency. In addition, concept name compression also means semantic loss, but semantic loss does not necessary mean that we have a state of concept name compression.

Studying the second research question we can see that it is divided into three parts where all can be answered with a truly yes. Let us shortly describe why this is the fact. First, *minimality* is used in connection with information loss, and information loss often causes semantic loss. Second, *the use of different modeling constructs* may cause both a state of concept name compression and semantic loss. Finally, *the use of noncomparable transformations* may cause concept name compression causing semantic loss. The problem has been described as follows: "[…] when we change a name into another name, to eliminate a homonym, we produce a new, noncomparable concept" [4]. In other words we do not know what the new concept contains since it contains neither more nor less information than before.

7 Conclusion and Short Discussion

In this chapter we argue that traditional resolution and simplification techniques for both name conflicts and inter-schema properties might cause a state of concept name compression and semantic loss. We also argue and illustrate alternative resolution techniques that do not cause these problems because all concept names are retained. Retaining all concept names do not only counter an impoverishment of the language used in the views, but also counter the occurrence of concept name compression and semantic loss. In addition, it could even contribute to a semantically richer global conceptual database schema.

Regarding the first research question it can be concluded that the concepts are used synonymously, but there are several differences between them. For instance, information and semantic losses are often treated as the same problem. However, semantic loss and concept name compression are problems that we have to deal with while defining the implementation-independent level of the future database such as the end user views and the conceptual database schema. On the other hand, information loss is a problem we have to deal with on an implementation-dependent level since it is used in connection with the ability to represent and store a real-world fact.

Regarding the second research question, it can be concluded that minimality, the use of different modeling constructs, and the use of noncomparable transformations cause semantic loss. This is the case since all three originate in the strive towards minimizing the number of concepts and/or dependencies in the global conceptual schema. While conducting conceptual database design, it is therefore important to choose and use a modeling language that focuses on the concepts, the dependencies, and what the end users actually want to illustrate and communicate with their views, lest we should end up in a state of concept name compression and semantic loss.

References

Ambrosio, A.P., Métais, E. and Meunier, J.-N. (1997) The Linguistic Level: Contribution for Conceptual Design, View Integration, Reuse and Documentation. Data & Knowledge Engineering. 21, 111–129.

Batini, C. and Lenzerini, M. (1984) A Methodology for Data Schema Integration in the Entity-Relationship Model, IEEE Transactions on Software Engineering. 10, 650–664.

Batini, C., Lenzerini, M. and Navathe, S.B. (1986) A Comparative Analysis of Methodologies for Database Schema Integration, ACM Computing Surveys. 18, 323–363.

Batini, C., Ceri, S. and Navathe, S.B. (1992) *Conceptual Database Design An Entity-Relationship Approach*. The Benjamin/Cummings Publishing Company, Inc., Redwood City, California.

Bellström, P. (2005) Using Enterprise Modeling for Identification and Resolution of Homonym Conflicts in View Integration. In: O. Vasilecas et al. (Eds.), *Information Systems Development Advances in Theory, Practice and Education*. Springer, New York, pp. 265–276.

Bellström, P. (2006a) View Integration in Conceptual Database Design – Problems, Approaches and Solutions. Licentiate thesis, Karlstad University Press, 2006:5.

Bellström, P. (2006b) Bridging the Gap between Comparison and Conforming the Views in View Integration. In: Y. Manolopoulos et al. (Eds.), *Local Proc of the 10th ADBIS Conf.*, pp. 184–199.

Bellström, P. and Carlsson, S. (2004) Towards an Understanding of the Meaning and the Contents of a Database through Design and Reconstruction. In: O. Vasilecas et al. (Eds.), *Proc of the 13th ISD Conf.*, pp. 283–293.

Bellström, P. and Carlsson, C. (2006) Language Aspects of Conceptual Database Design. In: M. Lind et al. (Eds.), *Proc of the 4th ALOIS Conf.*, pp. 211–223.

Bellström, P. and Jakobsson, L. (2006) Towards a Generic and Integrated Enterprise Modeling Approach to Designing Databases and Software Components. In: A.G. Nilsson et al. (Eds.), *Advances in Information Systems Development: Bridging the Gap between Academia and Industry*. Springer, New York, pp. 635–646.

Bellström, P., Vöhringer, J. and Salbrechter, A. (2007) Recognition and Resolution of Linguistic Conflicts: The Core to a Successful View and Schema Integration. In: W. Wojtkowski et al. (Eds.), *Information Systems Development New Methods and Practices for the Networked Society*. Springer, New York.

Boman, B., Bubenko, Jr, J.A., Johannesson, P. and Wangler, B. (1997) *Conceptual Modelling*. Prentice-Hall, Great Britain.

Chen, P. (1976) The Entity-Relationship Model – Toward a Unified View of Data. ACM Transactions on Database Systems. 1, 9–36.

Dey, D., Storey, V.C. and Barron, T.M. (1999) Improving Database Design through the Analysis of Relationships. ACM Transactions on Database Systems. 24, 453–486.

Engels, G., Gogolla, M., Hohenstein, U., Hulsmann, K., Lohr-Richter, P., Saake, G. and Ehrich, H.D. (1992) Concepual Modelling of Database Applications using an Extended ER Model. Data & Knowledge Engineering. 9, 157–204.

Frank, H. and Eder, J. (1998) Integration of Statecharts. In: *Proc of the 3rd COOPIS Conf.*, pp. 364–372.

Gustas, R. (1997) Semantic and Pragmatic Dependencies of Information Systems. Monograph, Technologija, Kaunas.

Gustas, R. and Gustiené, P. (2004) Towards the Enterprise Engineering Approach for Information System Modelling Across Organisational and Technical Boundaries. In: O. Camp et al. (Eds.), *Enterprise Information Systems V*. Kluwer, The Netherlands, pp. 204–215.

Hoppenbrouwers, S.J.B.A., Proper, H.A. and van der Weide, Th.P. (2005) A Fundamental View on the Process of Conceptual Modeling. In: L. Delcambre et al. (Eds.), *Proc of the 24th ER Conf.* Springer, pp. 128–143.

Jakobsson, L. and Bellström, P. (2007) Designing Software Components for Database Consistency – An Enterprise Modeling Approach. In: *Information Systems Development New Methods and Practices for the Networked Society*. Springer (in print).

Johannesson, P. (1993) *Schema Integration, Schema Translation, and Interoperability in Federated Information Systems*. Ph.D. thesis, Department of Computer & Systems Sciences, Stockholm University, Royal Institute of Technology, No. 93-010-DSV, Edsbruk.

Lawrence, R. and Barker, K. (2001) Integrating Relational Databases Using Standardized Dictionaries. In: *16th ACM Symposium on Applied Computing*. ACM Press, pp. 225–230.

Lee, M.L. and Ling, T.W. (2003) A Methodology for Structural Conflict Resolution in the Integration of Entity-Relationship Schemas. Knowledge and Information System. 5, 225–247.

Mannino, M.V. (2006) Database Design, Application Development & Administration. McGraw-Hill, New York.

Maier, D., Ullman, J.D. and Vardi, M.Y. (1984) On the Foundations of the Universal Relation Model, ACM Transactions on Database Systems. 9, 283–308.

Martin, J. and Odell, J.J. (1998) *Object Oriented Methods A Foundation*. Prentice-Hall, New Jersey.

Nuseibeh, B., Easterbrook, S. and Russo, A. (2001) Making Inconsistency Respectable in Software Development, The Journal of Systems and Software. 58, 171–180.

Parent, C. and Spaccapietra, S. (1998) Issues and Approaches of Database Integration. Communications of the ACM. 41, 166–178.

Parsons, J. (2002) Effects on Local Versus Global Schema Diagrams on Verification and Communication in Conceptual Data Modeling. Journal of Management Information Systems. 19, 155–183.

Rauh, O. and Stickel, E. (1993) Searching for Composition in ER Schemes. In: R.A. Elmasri et al. (Eds.), *Proc of the 12th ER Conf.* Springer, pp. 74–84.

Song, W. (1995) *Schema Integration – Principles, Methods, and Applications*. Ph.D. thesis, Department of Computer & Systems Sciences, Stockholm University, Royal Institute of Technology, No. 95-019, Edsbruk.

Spaccapietra, S. and Parent, C. (1994) View Integration: a Step Forward in Solving Structural Conflicts. IEEE Transactions on Knowledge and Data Engineering, 6, 258–274.

Storey, V.C. (1993) Understanding Semantic Relationships. VLDB Journal. 2, 455–488.

Storey, V.C. (2001) Understanding and Representing Relationship Semantics in Database Design. In: Z. Bouzeghoub et al. (Eds.), *Proc of the 5th NLDB Conf*, Springer, pp. 79–90.

Teorey, T.J. (1999) *Database Modeling & Design*. Morgan Kaufmann, San Francisco, CA.

Vöhringer, J. and Mayr, H.C. (2006) Integration of Schemas on the Pre-Design Level Using the KCPM-Approach. In: A.G. Nilsson et al. (Eds.), *Advances in Information Systems Development: Bridging the Gap between Academia and Industry*. Springer, New York, pp. 623–634.

Object-Relational Database Design: Can Your Application Benefit from SQL:2003?

George Feuerlicht[1], Jaroslav Pokorný[2] and Karel Richta[3]

[1]University of Technology, Sydney, Australia, jiri@it.uts.edu.au

[2]Charles University of Prague, Prague, Czech Republic, jaroslav.pokorny@mff.cuni.cz

[3]Czech Technical University of Prague, Czech Republic, richta@fel.cvut.cz

Abstract   Traditional database design methods based on information engineering principles and data normalization do not fully apply to SQL:2003 object-relational databases. New design methodologies and tools are needed to support complex data constructs used in today's software engineering practice. There are application domains such as spatial, geographical information systems (GISs) and multimedia applications where the use of object-relational features is mandatory. There are also many other application types that are good candidates for object-relational features, but are frequently implemented using purely relational design as designers hesitate to face the challenges of object-relational design. It can be argued that the use of object-relational features is limited in practice by the lack of design methodologies that can guide database designers in making informed decisions about design choices that involve comparisons of relational and object-relational solutions. In this chapter we discuss object-relational design guidelines and illustrate, using an example, that the object-relational implementation can provide significant benefits simplifying the resulting data structures and the implementation of database queries.

1 Introduction

The early research and development of object-oriented databases at the beginning of the 1990s was followed by the emergence of object-relational database approach that builds on the relational database model extending it with object-oriented features. An extensive effort by the database industry and researchers over a period of more than six years resulted in the specification of the SQL:1999 language standard (ISO/IEC 1999) that became the blueprint for the implementation of Object-Relational Database Management Systems (ORDBMSs). SQL:1999 and the more recent SQL:2003 (ISO/IEC 2003) provide support for a comprehensive range of features that enable the implementation of complex data types and relationships

C. Barry et al. (eds.), *Information Systems Development: Challenges in Practice, Theory, and Education, Vol.2*, doi: 10.1007/978-0-387-78578-3_30,
© Springer Science+Business Media, LLC 2009

that characterize modern database applications. However, the availability of such features does not automatically result in an improved design and a more efficient database implementation. Traditional database design methods based on data engineering principles that involve data normalization do not fully apply to object-relational databases. New design methodologies and tools are needed to support complex data constructs used in today's software engineering practice. ORDBMS must also address the problem of efficient storage and management of complex objects (Zhu et al. 2006) and XML data (Mlýnková and Pokorný 2005). The first attempts to propose methodologies for object-relational databases followed soon after the standardization of object-relational extensions in SQL:1999 (e.g. Marcos et al. 2001, 2004; Rahayu and Taniar 2002; Pardede et al. 2004).

Notwithstanding such efforts, there are still no widely accepted methodologies for ORDB (Object-Relational Database) design. In some cases, the design guidelines rely on proprietary extensions to the SQL standard available in specific ORDBMS products. Furthermore, enhancements included in SQL:2003 have not been systematically incorporated in such approaches. Currently available modelling and design tools vary in notation and constructs they support, but generally use entity types and their hierarchies and various forms of relationships, and have only limited support for SQL:2003. This holds true not only for entity-relational modelling tools, but also for UML-based tools that support object-oriented modelling. The richness of the object-relational data model (when compared to the relational model), and the repertoire of various constructs makes logical database design highly challenging as the number of design options for a given conceptual model dramatically increases. This makes it difficult to develop a methodology that designers can follow in order to map a conceptual schema (either object-oriented or entity-relationship) to an object-relational database, and at the same time maximizing the effectiveness and efficiency of the design.

Design of relational databases follows a structured methodology applying a set of well-defined transformations of the conceptual schema into normalized relations (3NF tables). Using the object-relational design, additional properties of the conceptual schema, such as its graph structure, need to be considered. Furthermore, object-relational design must take into account application requirements, as they impact on the choice of the most appropriate database structures. Consequently, the designer must understand how the data is going to be used by applications including the details of principal queries. In most standard business applications that use simple data structures (e.g. purchase order processing, customer relationship management, etc.) the use of object-relational features introduces unnecessary complexities into the design. In such cases purely relational design may represent the best solution. There are other application domains such as spatial, GIS (geographical information systems) and multimedia applications, where the use of object-relational extensions to represent application objects is mandatory. But, importantly, there are many other types of database applications that are good candidates for object-relational features, but are frequently implemented as relational databases because of the lack of suitable design methodologies that can assist with the evaluation of different design strategies. It can be argued that the use of object-relational features in SQL:2003 is limited in practice by the lack of design methodologies that can guide database designers in making informed decisions about design choices that involve comparisons of relational and object-relational solutions. In this chapter we show that object-relational features can provide significant benefits simplifying the resulting data structures and the implementation of database queries. In Section 2, we discuss the available literature dealing with the topic of object-relational database design. In Section 3, we overview the main conceptual constructs used in object-relational models and design tools, and in Section 4, we describe the corresponding SQL:2003 object-relational features. In Section 5, we introduce the transformation rules for mapping conceptual models to object-relational schemas and discuss their application using an illustrative example. In Section 6, we briefly summarize the main contributions of this chapter and identify the need for further research in this area.

2 Related Work

Approaches to object-relational design can be classified into two main categories: (1) general approaches based on the constructs of conceptual models and (2) domain-specific approaches based on data types used in specific domain applications, e.g. spatial data, XML data, and scientific data.

2.1 General Approaches

Marcos et al. (2001, 2004) consider a methodological approach for ORDB design using UML extensions. In the latter work Marcos et al. present guidelines for object-relational database design assuming that the conceptual schema is represented in UML and that the target language is SQL:1999. Paper by Urban and Dietrich (2003) illustrates how UML diagrams can be used to study mappings to different types of database systems, including ORDBSs based on the SQL:1999 standard. Some methodologies are specific to commercial products (e.g. Oracle), and incorporate vendor-specific features that are inconsistent with the SQL standards (see, for example, de Haan 2005). Another important area of research concerns the representation of complex objects. For example, Pardede et al. (2004) consider aggregation constructs and its representation in Oracle 9i. They propose two methods based on proprietary constructs, so called *index clustering* and *nested tables*.

2.2 Domain-Specific Approaches

Mapping spatial data models into object-relational database schemas has been the subject of extensive research interest. For example, the book by Parent et al.

(2006) is devoted to conceptual modelling of spatial and spatio-temporal databases based on the MADS (Modelling of Application Data with Spatio-temporal features) conceptual model. Authors discuss a structural dimension of MADS in the context of object-relational databases and SQL:2003. They developed a prototype that translates MADS conceptual models into corresponding database schemas for the Oracle and GIS-oriented systems ArcView, and MapInfo systems. The combination of XML and spatial features can be encoded in the Geography Markup Language (GML 2004). Zhu et al. (2006) propose an approach to map GML schema to object-relational database schema based on SQL:1999 and store non-spatial and spatial data from GML documents in object-relational spatial database. The mapping rules from GML schema to object-relational schema are established so that the structure and semantic constraints of the source GML schema can be preserved in the target object-relational schema. Cohen et al. (2006) consider object-relational representation of the Weather Research and Forecasting (WRF) Model. The main problem the authors attempt to address is how to represent multidimensional variables. ORDB approach offers a more effective solution than the Star or Snowflake schemas transformed into 1NF relations used in data warehousing applications. Authors use mainly ORACLE's built-in array types (collections) Variable Arrays (Varrays) and Nested Tables.

3 Conceptual Model Constructs

In this section we review the conceptual constructs used in database modelling and comment on their limitations in the context of ORDB design. Based on the traditional entity-relationship-attribute approaches, the constructs of conceptual models include: entity types (E), relationship types (R), attributes (A), weak entity types, and ISA hierarchies. The original Chen's approach to ERA (Entity-Relationship-Attribute) modelling includes n-ary relationships with arbitrary cardinalities, but the cardinality is typically restricted in commercial tools (e.g. Oracle Designer 2000) to binary relationships with cardinalities 1:N. ISA hierarchies are analogous to class hierarchies in UML. Perhaps, the most significant restriction in conceptual modelling concerns attribute structures. Although there is a natural use for multi-valued and composite attributes, most theoretical ERA approaches and practical tools support only simple (atomic) attributes, leading to direct transformation of conceptual structures to 1NF relations. Neglecting rather exotic conceptual constructs such as exclusive relationship types (ORACLE 2000), we further consider aggregation and composition. Aggregation and composition are not usually supported in ERA modelling tools, but in UML they are treated as *first-class* constructs. An *aggregation* is a part-of relationship, in which a composite object (a whole) consists of other component objects (parts). Shareable and existence-independent parts can be represented. We can differentiate between *simple aggregations* (Marcos et al. 2001), and aggregation hierarchies with several levels of aggregation. A *composition* is a special kind of aggregation in which parts are existentially dependent on the whole. Consequently, deletions result in removal of all dependent parts. More recently, conceptual models were extended to support XML data (e.g. Nečaský 2007). The notion of *hierarchy* is essential to modelling XML data. XML hierarchy can be based on general relationships between entities of two different entity types or modelled specifically using aggregation and composition. The root of the hierarchy can be identified using a graph analysis of the conceptual schema and the hierarchy and then transformed into XML Schema or directly into types and tables of the object-relational data model. Complex data types that can be represented using the object-relational model include *geometric complex types* (e.g. line, circle, and polygon) used in spatial databases (Zhu et al. 2006).

3.1 Illustrative Example

To illustrate some of the key features of the object-relational model, consider, for example, an Online Movie Database (OMDB) that maintains information about movies, actors, directors, and other movie-related information.

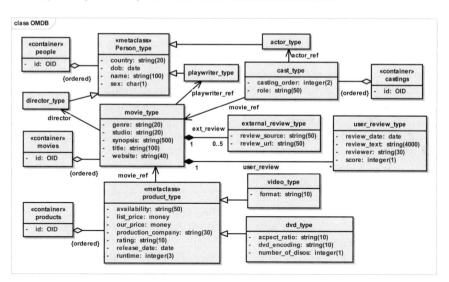

Fig. 1. Conceptual model of OMDB database

Users can browse this information on the OMDB website and purchase products (i.e. movie videos, DVDs, books, CDs and other movie-related merchandise). The movie information includes the movie title, director, the official movie website, genre, studio, short synopsis and the cast (i.e. actors and the roles they play in the movie). Each movie has up to five external editorial reviews, and unlimited number of user reviews entered by users online. OMDB website offers products for sale including movie videos and DVDs. Information about videos and DVDs includes title, rating, list price, release date and other relevant information.

This situation can be modelled using a UML Class Diagram shown in Fig. 1. We return to the OMDB model in Section 5 where we discuss the design options for transforming the conceptual model into SQL:2003 object-relational database implementation.

4 SQL:2003 Object-Relational Model

In this chapter we focus on object-relational databases whose type system is consistent with the SQL standard (i.e. SQL:2003 and its predecessor SQL:1999). The SQL:2003 model is a superset of the original relational model and a relation (table) remains the main data structure, potentially with a substructure that may involve complex objects. Objects in the SQL:2003 object-relational model are implemented using user-defined types (UDTs). UDTs are either *row types* or *structured types* that can include *methods* specifications and are *analogous* to Abstract Data Types (ADTs) in object-oriented databases. With a row type in a table column we can model composite attributes. Structured types can be used to type tables and columns. An *object* in SQL:2003 is a row of a typed table that includes an OID (Object Identifier). SQL:2003 includes constructors for two special user-defined *collection types*, ARRAY and MULTISET, that are used to implement multivalued attributes. Collection and row types allow the representation of multivalued and composite attributes, respectively, providing a mechanism for implementing de-normalized tables. The SQL:2003 standard further extends the data structures introduced in the standard SQL:1999 to provide more flexibility for implementation of multivalued attributes, changing array and multiset semantics in a number of significant ways. Arrays can be declared without specifying the cardinality, in which case the (maximum) cardinality is vendor-defined (potentially unbounded), and in SQL:2003 array nesting is unrestricted. Similarly, MULTISETs do not require specification of the maximum cardinality. The MULTISET construct in SQL:2003 allows differentiation between a NULL value and an empty set. Deleting the last element of a multivalued attribute in a table results in an empty set, as opposed to a NULL value. SQL:2003 defines advanced multiset support that includes comparison and set operators. There are three new aggregate functions: to create a multiset from the value of the argument in each row of a group (COLLECT), to create a multiset union of a multiset value in all rows of a group (FUSION), and to create the multiset intersection of a multiset value in all rows of a group (INTERSECTION).

5 Object-Relational Database Design

Following the description of the object-relational modelling constructs (in Section 3) and the SQL:2003 object-relational model in Section 4, we now consider object-relational database design describing the design choices available when transforming a conceptual model into a set of target SQL:2003 objects. SQL:2003 provides a rich environment for the implementation of database applications and presents the designer with a number of important decisions that include the choice between relational features and object-relational extensions. As the SQL:2003 model subsumes the relational model (i.e. SQL:1999 and SQL:2003 are supersets of SQL:1992), the designer can choose to implement the database as a purely relational database with untyped tables. Alternatively, the designer may decide to define all tables as typed tables and follow the object-relational approach. It is also possible to mix relational and object-relational features typing only selected tables. The designer needs to make decisions about using primary and foreign keys to implement relationships, or using OIDs and REFs (references) for typed tables. Implementation of relationship also presents a number of choices; for example, aggregation and composition can be implemented using separate tables, or alternatively using SQL:2003 multisets. Such design decisions are of key importance and must be based on clear design principles and guidelines, as once implemented the database cannot not be readily restructured to accommodate alternative design strategies.

In Section 5.1, we review the transformation rules for mapping conceptual constructs into SQL:2003 database structures. In Section 5.2, we discuss (using the OMDB example introduced in Section 3) the various design choices and the basis for making decisions about using object-relational features available in SQL:2003.

5.1 Transformation Rules for Mapping into SQL:2003

The transformation of a conceptual model into relational and object-relational database structures (i.e. typed or untyped tables) has been extensively investigated. Table 1 shows a typical set of mapping rules giving the correspondence between conceptual constructs and SQL:2003 database structures for both entity types and relationships.

A number of options exist for implementing aggregation and composition using SQL:2003 structures and these have been described in the literature. For example, the authors (Rahayu and Taniar 2002) present a classical relational solution with tables for the whole and the parts, and an additional aggregate table. The rows of the aggregate table are of the form (whole_id, part_id, part_type). In this approach referential integrity between aggregate and part tables is not expressible using the declarative SQL statements. The cardinality of the relationship between the whole and the aggregate is 1:N, and between the part and the aggregate tables is

1:1 or 1:N. The cardinality of the relationship between a part and the aggregate tables for a composition is 1:1. In addition to decisions about aggregate structures discussed earlier, the implementation of SQL:2003 style databases involves decisions about identifiers. Here, we differentiate between two basic approaches: object-oriented and value-based. The former uses identifiers implied by structured types with relationships represented via references (REF types) or via SQL:2003 multisets. Attributes of relationships can be added to multiset elements, so that, for example, arrays of rows, possibly with additional structures can be used into an arbitrary depth. A further design decision involves implementing relationships as bidirectional or unidirectional (the expressivity of both options is the same). Further options include representing relationships by a multiset of primary key values added to a row representing an entity. Ordering of arrays can be relevant for storing XML hierarchies, where ordering of child elements is of importance.

Table 1. SQL:2003 transformation mapping rules

Conceptual construct	SQL:2003	
	Type level	**Instance level**
Entity type	Structured type	Typed table
Attribute	Column type	
Multivalued	ARRAY/MULTISET	
Composed	ROW/structured type in column	
Calculated		Trigger/method
Relationship		
1:1	REF/REF	2 Typed tables
1:N	REF/[ARRAY∣MULTISET]	2 Typed tables
N:M	ARRAY/[ARRAY∣MULTISET]	2 Typed tables
Aggregation	REF/[ARRAY∣MULTISET]	2 Typed tables
Composition	REF/[ARRAY∣MULTISET]	2 Typed tables
Generalization	Type hierarchy	Table hierarchy
Hierarchy	Based on composition	

We have applied the transformation rules in Table 1 to the OMDB conceptual model shown in Fig. 1 and produced the following type definition:

```
create type external_review_type as object (...);
create type external_review_array
        as varray(5) of external_review_type;
create type user_review_type as object (...);
create type user_review_table as table of user_review_type;
create type person_type as object(...)not final;
create type director_type under person_type (...);
create type actor_type under person_type (...);
create type playwriter_type under person_type (...);
create type movie_type as object (...);
create type product_type as object(...)not final;
create type dvd_type under product_type (...);
```

```
create type video_type under product_type (...);
create type cast_type as object (...);
```

We show abbreviated versions of the type definitions and do not show the corresponding typed tables. In Section 5.2, we discuss the design guidelines used in transforming the OMDB conceptual model.

5.2 Design Guidelines

As noted earlier, implementation of the SQL:2003 style databases using the transformation rules in Table 1 involves design decisions about which object-relational feature to use and how it should be deployed. Similar to the design of relational databases, such design decisions must be based on solid guidelines and universal principles that include minimizing redundancy, maximizing reuse, and at the same time ensuring good query performance. Also importantly, the complexity of the design must be minimized as complex data structures lead to complexity of database applications and corresponding increase in the development and maintenance effort.

5.2.1 Data Normalization

The question of minimizing data redundancy when using composite and nested database structures deserves attention. Normal forms provide a set of guiding principles for relational database design that lead to the minimization of data redundancy. It can be argued that normalization is relevant to object-relational database design, although with some important caveats. For example, the use of non-atomic attributes (e.g. address type column that includes STREET, SUBURB and POSTCODE) violates 1NF, but in general does not lead to redundant data, but using a collection (e.g. VARRAY) to implement a repeated attribute such as phone numbers (e.g. HOME PHONE, WORK PHONE and MOBILE PHONE) leads to complex retrieval logic, and should be avoided altogether. The use of SQL:2003 collections should be reserved for the implementation of composition and aggregation; in such cases collections represent a separate data structure (although *embedded* in the parent table) and do not result in redundant data. Similarly, using OIDs avoids partial dependencies between key and non-key attributes (i.e. violation of 2NF), but attribute interdependencies between non-key attributes can still exist and lead to data redundancy, violating 3NF and causing update anomalies.

5.2.2 OIDs vs Keys

OIDs and REFs are generally used to implement complex relationships, and they are particularly useful for implementing multiple-level relationships, used for example in integrated circuit design, or component assemblies in manufacturing applications. The main advantage of using OIDs and REFs is the ability to navigate complex relationships without the need for relational joins, thus significantly reducing the number of database reads required to retrieve a composite object. OIDs and REFs typically incur additional storage and processing requirements that can be reduced by scoping references to a particular table. OIDs are also useful in situations where *natural* (attribute-based) identifiers are not available. We use OIDs throughout the OMDB database, for example, for the person, movie and product object types. This leads to simplification and improved clarity of queries. For example, the following query requirement:

List the cast for the movie 'The Godfather' (in order of importance) showing actors and the roles they play.

results in a relatively simple query:
```
SELECT C.ACTOR_REF.NAME, C.CAST_ROLE
FROM CASTINGS C
WHERE C.MOVIE_REF.TITLE = 'THE GODFATHER'
ORDER BY C.CASTING_ORDER;
```

5.2.3 Column vs Row Types

The SQL:2003 model allows the implementation of database objects as *column* or *row* types. Only row types have OIDs and should be used if referencing via REFs is required. Column objects (types) cannot be referenced directly and must be accessed via dot notation, e.g. employee.address.postcode (i.e. the corresponding row must be located first and then the column object accessed). Row types provide a comprehensive support for object features, including inheritance and method overriding. In the OMDB example we use typed tables throughout, and take advantage of subtyping and inheritance available for typed tables. The implementation of the PERSON type and all its subtypes (i.e. ACTOR_TYPE, DIRECTOR_TYPE and PLAYWRITER_TYPE) is a single typed table PEOPLE OF PERSON_TYPE. This design results in a simple solution for query requirements such as:

Are there any movies in which the director is also one of the actors/actresses?

The following query takes advantage of referencing and of the fact that both actors and directors have the same supertypes (i.e. PERSON_TYPE).

```
SELECT C.MOVIE_REF.TITLE, C.MOVIE_REF.DIRECTOR_REF.NAME,
C.ROLE
FROM CASTINGS C
WHERE C.ACTOR_REF = C.MOVIE_REF.DIRECTOR_REF;
```

5.2.4 Implementing Composition and Aggregation

As discussed earlier a number of distinct options exist for the implementation of composition and aggregation in SQL:2003. The general rule for using collections to implement compositions and aggregation is that each detail object must belong to a single master object, and that the detail objects have no meaning out of the context of the master object (e.g. book and book chapters). Additional decisions involve choosing the type of collection most suitable for a specific design scenario, e.g. a choice between VARRAYs and NESTED TABLEs using the Oracle implementation. VARRAYs are more efficient if the collection is manipulated as a single unit using special array functions. NESTED TABLES, on the other hand provide more options for access to individual records using SQL queries that take advantage of the database optimizer, but have increased storage requirements (nested tables include a 16bytes system generated NESTED_TABLE_ID that points to the parent row). OMDB uses VARRAYs to implement the external reviews and NESTED TABLEs to implement the user reviews. Both review types are a form of aggregation, as the individual review records have no meaning outside of the particular movie record. The decision to use VARRAYs for external reviews and NESTED TABLEs for user reviews is based on the consideration of the likely large number of user review records, and the benefits of using SQL queries rather than array processing methods. We have avoided using collections for the implementation of CASTINGS type as a separate table, which gives more flexibility and allows the use of the full power of SQL (including subqueries). The following example illustrates the point:

For all movies list the leading actress, i.e. the first billed actress (in the order of credits).

```
SELECT C.MOVIE_REF.TITLE, C.MOVIE_REF.GENRE,
C.MOVIE_REF.DIRECTOR_REF.NAME, C.ACTOR_REF.NAME
FROM CASTINGS C
WHERE C.CASTING_ORDER = (
SELECT MIN(CASTING_ORDER)
FROM CASTINGS
WHERE ACTOR_REF.SEX = 'F' AND MOVIE_REF = C.MOVIE_REF);
```

5.2.5 Generalization, Inheritance and Reuse

SQL:2003 supports the notion of subtypes and supertypes using user-defined types, including single inheritance and method overriding. This gives a number of design options for implementing supertype/subtype combinations. The *standard* relational transformation leads to separate (untyped) tables with each subtype transformed into a corresponding table; alternatively, the entire supertype/subtype combination is transformed into a single relational supertype table. Object-relational transformation follows the same pattern, but supports inheritance and method overriding. For example, the following function AGE is defined for the supertype PERSON and inherited by all its subtypes:

```
CREATE TYPE BODY PERSON_TYPE IS
  MEMBER FUNCTION AGE(DOB DATE) RETURN INTEGER IS
  ...
END;
```

The function can then be used to give the age of the director of the movie 'SUNSHINE'.

```
SELECT M.TITLE,M.DIRECTOR_REF.NAME,AGE(M.DIRECTOR_REF.DOB)
FROM MOVIES M
WHERE M.TITLE = 'SUNSHINE';
```

Method overriding can be used to set discount levels for different types of products:

```
CREATE TYPE BODY dvd_type AS
  OVERRIDING MEMBER FUNCTION SPECIAL_PRICE
  ...
END;
CREATE TYPE BODY video_type AS
  OVERRIDING MEMBER FUNCTION SPECIAL_PRICE
  ...
END;
```

6 Conclusions

The effective use of SQL:2003 object-relational features requires understanding of the design tradeoffs associated with alternative design strategies. In the absence of guidelines for object-relational database design practitioners tend to avoid using object-relational features altogether, missing out on the potential benefits that this approach provides. The main contribution of this chapter is to show that object-relational design can provide an elegant and an effective solution even for application types that are not normally regarded as candidates for object-relational implementation. We have illustrated using examples how object-relational features can be deployed in such database applications, discussing the design tradeoffs involved in adopting specific object-relational features such as collections, OIDs and REFs. Further work is needed to provide a fully comprehensive design methodology for object-relational databases that can serve as the basis for object-relational design tools. The inclusion of XML support in SQL:2003 creates another area of research interest and demand for design methodologies and tools. The availability of MULTISETs and ARRAY constructs in SQL:2003 makes ORDBMS systems suitable for the management of hierarchically structured XML data, but numerous design options exist that need to be evaluated in the context of specific application requirements. Detailed discussion of XML design issues is out of the scope of this chapter and will be the subject of further publications.

Acknowledgements   This research has been partially supported by the National Program of Research, Information Society Project No. 1ET100300419, and also by Ministry of Education of Czech Republic under research program MSM 6840770014 and also by the grant of GACR No. GA201/06/0756.

References

Cohen, S., Hurley, P., Schulz, K.W., Barth, W.L., Benton, B. (2006): ACM SIGMOD Record, Vol. 35, No 2, pp. 10–15.

de Haan, L. (2005): Mastering Oracle SQL and SQL*Plus. APress, Berkeley, CA.

Geography Markup Language (GML) Implementation Specification Version 3.0. (2004). Available at http://www.opengis.net/gml

ISO/IEC 9075:1999 (1999): Information Technology, Database Languages, SQL. Part 2: Foundations.

ISO/IEC 9075:2003 (2003): Information Technology, Database Languages, SQL. Part 2: Foundations.

Marcos, E., Vela, B., Cavero, M., Cáceras (2001): Aggregation and Composition in Object-Relational Database Design. In: Proc. of ADBIS 2001, Res. Communications, A. Caplinskas, J. Eder (Eds.), pp. 195–209.

Marcos, E., Vela, B., Cavero, M. (2004): A methodological approach for object-relational database design using UML. Informatik – Forschung und Entwicklung, Vol. 18, No. 3–4/April 2004, Springer, Berlin/Heidelberg, pp. 152–164.

Melton, J., Simon, A.R. (2003): SQL: 1999 – Understanding Relational Language Components, 2nd edition. Morgan Kaufmann, San Mateo, CA.

Mlýnková, I., Pokorný, J. (2005): XML in the World of (Object-)Relational Database Systems. In: Information Systems Development Advances in Theory, Practice, and Education 2004. Vasilecas, O., Caplinskas, A., Wojtkowski, G., Wojtkowski, W., Zupancic, J., Wrycza, S. (Eds.), Springer Science + Business Media, New York, pp. 63–76.

Nečaský, M. (2007): XSEM – A Conceptual Model for XML. In Proc. Fourth Asia-Pacific Conference on Conceptual Modelling (APCCM2007), Ballarat, Australia. CRPIT, 67. Roddick, J.F., Annika, H. (Eds.), ACS, pp. 37–48.

ORACLE (2000): Oracle Designer 6i: Systems Modeling. Volume 1 – Instructor Guide.

Pardede, E., Rahayu, W., Taniar, D. (2004): Mapping Methods and Query for Aggregation and Association in Object-Relational Database using Collection. In: Proc. of the International Conference on Information Technology: Coding and Computing (ITCC'04), IEEE, 2004, pp. 539–543.

Parent, Ch., Spaccapietra, S., Zimányi, E. (2006) Conceptual Modeling for Traditional and Spatio-Temporal Applications. The MADS Approach, Springer, Berlin/Heidelberg.

Rahayu, W., Taniar, D. (2002): Preserving Aggregation in Object-Relational DBMS. In: Proc. of ADVIS 2002, T. Yakho (Ed.), LNCS 2457, pp. 1–10.

Urban, S.D., Dietrich, S.W. (2003) Using UML Class Diagrams for a Comparative Analysis of Relational, Object-Oriented, and Object-Relational Database Mappings. In: Proc. of SIGCSE'03, February 19–23, 2003, Reno, Nevada, USA, pp. 21–25.

Zhu, F., Zhou, J., Guan, J., Zhou, S. (2006) Storing and Querying GML in Object-Relational Databases. In: Proc. of ACM-GIS'06, November 10–11, 2006, Arlington, Virginia, USA, ACM, pp. 107–114.

CellStore: Educational and Experimental XML-Native DBMS

Jaroslav Pokorný[1], Karel Richta[2] and Michal Valenta[3]

[1]Charles University of Prague, Czech Republic, jaroslav.pokorny@mff.cuni.cz

[2]Czech Technical University of Prague, Czech Republic, richta@fel.cvut.cz

[3]Czech Technical University of Prague, Czech Republic, valenta@fel.cvut.cz

Abstract This chapter presents the CellStore project, whose aim is to develop XML-native database engine for both educational and research purposes. In this chapter we discuss the basic concepts of the system and its top-level architecture. Then we discuss individual parts of the systems. The discussion is focused mainly on already finished and tested subsystems – low-level storage (we designed and implemented own binary storage model) naive XQuery implementation, and transaction manager. We plan to extend the system in a way to be used as an experimental back-end for web-based application of Semantic web and specialized XML storages. The whole project is managed with focus on clear object-oriented design and test-driven development.

1 Introduction

The main goal of the CellStore project (CellStore 2007) is to develop XML-native database engine for both educational and research purposes. We need such an engine because our students can look inside it and create new components for this engine, e.g., in-built XSLT engine, a query optimizer, and an index engine. We can experiment with the engine and try to develop active extensions, combined stream processors, and many other new ideas, as they are formulated, e.g., in work of Loupal (2006). Thus, XML-native database can look like an experimental and developmental platform.

There exist a lot of commercial and open XML database management systems (DBMS), see, e.g., a still updated overview by Bourret (2007), but none of them is sufficiently open for our purposes, or it contains some in-built errors or limits, which we are not able to overcome. For example, as it is mentioned by Bourret (2005), locking is often at the level of entire documents, rather than at the level of individual nodes, so multiuser concurrency can be relatively low. We decided to create a new engine, which can serve our purposes and which is focused on some

C. Barry et al. (eds.), *Information Systems Development: Challenges in Practice, Theory, and Education, Vol.2*, doi: 10.1007/978-0-387-78578-3_31,
© Springer Science+Business Media, LLC 2009

weak points of the exiting ones. We suppose to put up CellStore as an open source project. Consequently, such implementation can contribute to general trends in XML-native databases development.

This chapter presents some interesting points of the CellStore design and implementation. In Section 2, we state some issues related to XML database management systems. In Section 3, we discuss the basic concepts of the system CellStore and its top-level architecture. Then we talk about individual parts of the system. Section 4 contains some conclusions and suggestions for a future work.

2 What is an XML Database Management System?

Suppose we have a large and continually growing set of XML documents. Then the reasons for storing them in a database system are the same as, e.g., for relational data: *persistent storage, transactional consistency, recoverability, high availability, security, efficient search and update operations, and scalability.*

2.1 XML DBMS Definition

Any database management system (DBMS) is a set of programs which maintain the data and the data integrity and provide an interface for data definition and manipulation. By consensus in XML and database community, there is no official strict definition of XML DBMS, but any XML DBMS must fulfill the following:

1. It defines a (logical) model for an XML document. This model is used when XML documents are stored and retrieved from the database. As a minimum, the model must include elements, attributes, PCDATA, and document order.
2. The fundamental unit of (logical) storage is an XML document.
3. It does not require any particular underlying physical storage model. For example, it can be built on a relational, hierarchical, or object-oriented DBMS, or use a proprietary storage format such as indexed, compressed files.

2.2 XML DBMS Classification

We call DBMS *XML-enabled*, when its core storage and processing model is not the XML data model (e.g., DB2 and Oracle). On the other hand, we call DBMS *XML-native*, when it complies with the following conditions:

- The XML data model is the fundamental logical data model used both internally by the database and also exposed to database users when XML is the data type.

- The XML data model is the fundamental unit of physical storage of all XML data, without mapping to a different data model.

But let us mention also that Bourret (2005) said: "native XML database first gained prominence in the marketing campaign for Tamino ... it has never had a formal technical definition."

2.3 Issues of Building XML DBMS

To build a new XML DBMS, we have to make the following crucial decisions:

- Choose an appropriate XML data model
- Choose an appropriate storage model
- Select some query and manipulating language
- Select methods for optimization and indexing
- Solve support for transactions and multiuser access
- Decide a support for applications development – API

Based on the requirement (1) in Section 2.1 there is typically a common intuitive tree-like model supposed in the most of XML DBMSs. XML data model specifications include XPath 1.0 data model (the older one treats XML data as a set), XPath 2.0 and XQuery 1.0 data model by W3C (2007) (latterly, it treats XML data as a sequence), and, e.g., a type system-based model (XML-lambda introduced by Pokorný (2000) treats XML data as type instances).

A common view on mentioned issues concerns the DBMS architecture. Today's DBMS provide practically universal architecture applicable to many various types of tasks, i.e., by words of Stonebraker and Çetintemel (2005), *"one size fits all"*. In new DBMS architectures rather separated database servers *"made to measure"* are expected in accordance with requirements of particular applications. Besides traditional fields, as OLAP, data warehouses, and text retrieval, other candidates for separate engines are data stream processing, sensor networks, scientific databases, and, particularly, native XML databases.

Considering native XML databases, a solution with a separate engine is also our choice.

2.4 Storage Models

Storage models for XML data use a file system, a mapping XML data to relational or object-relational models, mappings XML data to object-oriented models, or a native XML storage. An attractive option is to store XML data in combination of two systems: structured portion of XML data in relational database and unstructured portion in native XML store.

File system approach is straightforward and popular, see, e.g., Xindice project by Apache (2007). It works effectively if we work with the whole documents. Problems are with effective querying. A lot of research had been done in mapping XML data to relational or object-relational model – for an overview; see Mlýnková and Pokorný (2005). This approach uses relatively sophisticated and effective techniques, typically appropriate for simple structures, but it is problematic with complex or cyclic DTDs – it leads to deep-nested SQL queries. Mapping to object-oriented models is typically based on DOM approach, where nodes (of XML document) are represented as unique objects. Relationships between nodes are represented by object's serialization. But this object-oriented approach seems to be unnecessary in general; it does not take advantage of simplifications in XML model with respect to object-oriented native storage. For example, Renner (2001) gives an overview of an efficient way to store XML data inside an object-oriented DBMS.

According to Wikipedia (2007), native storage for XML data maximally utilizes natural tree structure of XML documents and, on the other hand, it tries to adapt other well-done features of DBMS systems (user-rights model, transactions, etc.).

3 The CellStore Project

When we have formulated aims for CellStore (see Section 1), we have to decide requirements for development environment. It should be easy to change subsystem's functionality; it will be purely object-oriented for development and design. It must enable component reusing and be simple for use. We focus mainly on functionality not on GUI design. We require simple test-supported development, trace and log facilities for debugging and educational purposes, and rather "interpret" than "compilation", due to immediate change propagation. At the end we select Smalltalk/X as the first development environment.

A part of our project is inspired by XTC[1] (XML Transaction Coordinator) developed at University of Kaiserslautern. Similar to XTC we implemented XML engine in frame of five-layer data architecture as it was designed in (Härder and Router 1983) in the 1980s. The main difference is in the low-level storage – the XTC project uses B-trees as data storage.

3.1 The Top-Level Architecture of CellStore

The architecture of CellStore database management system is shown in Fig. 1. The system has two basic levels: CellStore database instance and low-level engine.

---

[1] http://wwwdvs.informatik.uni-kl.de/agdbis/projects/xtc/report/taDOM.html

The low-level engine serves as the data and text storage, the instance accesses data through this low-level engine. Figure 2 illustrates briefly, how the main components cooperate.

3.2 Storage Subsystem (Low-Level Storage)

We developed a new method for storing XML data. The method is based on the work of Toman (2004) and partially inspired by solutions used in DBMSs of Oracle and Gemstone. Structural and data parts of XML document are stored separately. Of course, it increases necessary time to store and reconstruct documents. But on the other hand, it provides a great benefit in disk space management, especially in the case of documents update and also in query processing and indexing-stored XML data.

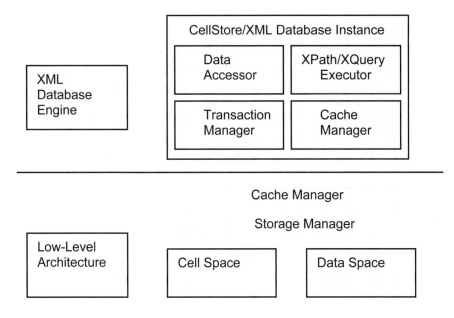

Fig. 1. The architecture of CellStore

Let us describe the storage model in more detail. The description is based on the first implementation version, because it is more illustrative. There exist improvements in the newer versions of CellStore, but they are not so important for this quick view.

XML data documents are parsed and placed in two different files during the storing process: the cell file and the data file. The structure of each of them is described in an individual subsection. We will illustrate the structure of files by an example of the following document:

```xml
<?xml version="1.0"?>
<!DOCTYPE simple PUBLIC
  "-//CVUT//Simple Example DTD 1.0//EN" SYSTEM simple.dtd">
<simple>
<!-- First comment -->
<?forsomeone process me?>
  <element xmlns="namespace1">
   First text
  <ns2:element xmlns:ns2="namespace2"
     attribute1="value1" ns2:attribute2="value2">
  </ns2:element>
  <empty/>
  </element>
</simple>
```

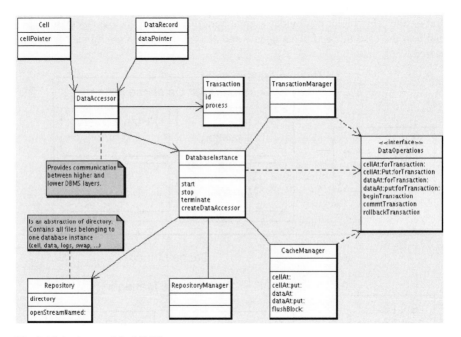

Fig. 2. Main class model of CellStore

Cell-File Structure. This file consists of fixed-length *cells*. Each cell represents one DOM object (document, element, attribute, character data, etc.) or XML:DB API object (collection or resource). Remind that this API is developed by XML:DB Initiative for XML Databases (XML:DB 2003). Cells are organized into fixed-length *block*.

Database block is the smallest I/O unit of transfer between disk and low-level storage cache. Only the cells from one document can be stored in one block. The set of blocks describing the structure of the whole document is called *segment*. Each block starts with header with a bitmap describing the density of the block. This storing strategy is effective also in the case of repeated changes of deleting stored documents.

Inside the cell structure internal pointers are used to represent parent–child and sibling relationships of nodes. Each cell consists of eight *fields*. The meaning of some fields can differ with different types of cells. The following cell types are in the system: character data, attribute, document, document type, processing instruction, comment, XML Resource, and collection.

The general structure of cell is described in Table 1.

Table 1. The general structure of cells

Name	Content	Reason
Head	1 byte	The type of cell
Parent	Cell pointer	Pointer to parent cell
Child	Cell pointer	Pointer to the first child
Sibling	Cell pointer	Pointer to the next cell brother (NIL if there is no one)
D1, D2, D3, D4	Depends on type	Contain either data or pointers (possibly to text file or tag file) depending to the type of cell

The example content of cell-file structure is shown in Fig 3.

Cell Block # 112233

	Head	Parent	Child	Sibling	D1	D2	D3	D4	
0x00	7F:F0:00:00	00:00:00:00	00:00:00:00	00:00:00:00	00:00:00:00	00:00:00:00	00:00:00:00	00:00:00:00	Free Cell Bitmap
0x01	09:00:00:00	010101:44	112233:03		112233:02				Document Cell
0x02	0A:00:00:00	112233:01			0000001	001122:01			<!DOCTYPE...
0x03	01:00:00:00	112233:01	112233:04		0000002				<simple>
0x04	08:00:00:00	112233:03		112233:05	001122:02				<!-- First comm
0x05	07:00:00:00	112233:03		112233:06	0000003	001122:03			<?forsomeone ...
0x06	01:00:00:00	112233:03	112233:07		0000004		0000005		<element ...
0x07	03:00:00:00	112233:06		112233:08	001122:04				First text
0x08	01:00:00:00	112233:06		112233:0B	0000004	0000007	0000006	112233:09	<ns2:element ...
0x09	02:00:00:00	112233:08		112233:0A	0000008		0000005	001122:05	attribute1="val...
0x0A	02:00:00:00	112233:08			0000009	0000007	0000006	001122:06	ns2:attribute2...
0x0B	01:00:00:00	112233:06			000000A		0000005		<empty />
0x0C									
0x0D									
0x0E									
0x0F									

Fig. 3. Cell-file structure

Text-File Structure. This file contains all text data (i.e. contents of DOM's text elements and attributes). The data is organized into blocks. One block belongs to only one document. The set of data blocks belonging to one document is called again a segment. Text pointer is a pointer to text file. It consists from the text block# and the record#.

Each text block contains a translation table which accepts the record number and returns the offset and the length of the data block. This is effective for storing data changes. The translation table grows from the end of block, while data grows from the beginning.

The translation table contains the number of actual records for these purposes. The header of a text block contains also the pointer to the root of its cell node. It is useful for fulltext searching – for the case we need documents containing some patterns. The example content of text-file structure is shown in Fig. 4.

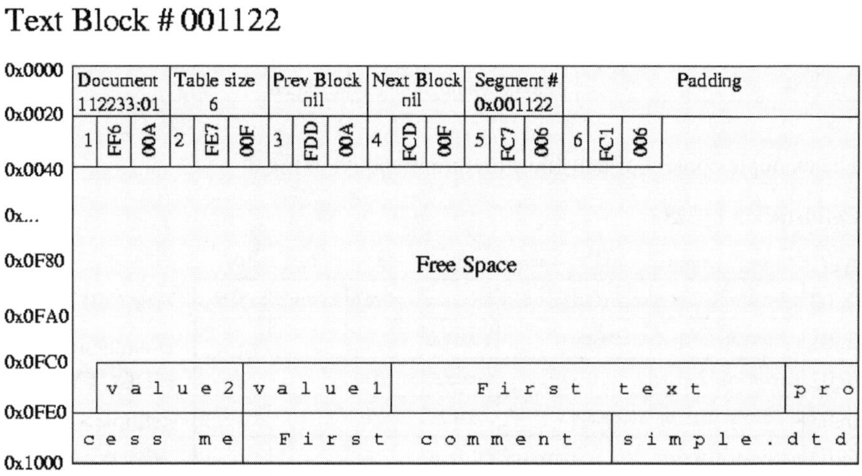

Text Block # 001122

| 0x0000 | Document | Table size | Prev Block | Next Block | Segment # | Padding |
| 0x0020 | 112233:01 | 6 | nil | nil | 0x001122 | |

| | 1 | FF6 | 00A | 2 | FE7 | 00F | 3 | FDD | 00A | 4 | FCD | 00F | 5 | FC7 | 006 | 6 | FC1 | 006 | |

Free Space (0x0F80 – 0x0FA0)

| 0x0FC0 | v a l u e 2 | v a l u e 1 | F i r s t   t e x t | p r o |
| 0x0FE0 | c e s s   m e | F i r s t   c o m m e n t | s i m p l e . d t d |

Fig. 4. Text-file structure

Tag-File Structure. This structure is used for storing the names of XML tags (elements, attributes, namespaces, etc.). It is supposed that this structure will fit all into memory. It is used often for reconstruction of document as well as storing the document. Each record of this structure also has its reference counter.

Low-level subsystem was fully implemented. Its stability had been tested on INEX data set. INEX is the set of articles from IEEE (see Gövert and Kazai 2002) for an overview. It contains approximately 12,000 individual XML documents (without figures); total size of the set is about 500 MB.

Current version of low-level subsystem allows individual setting of cell, cell-pointer, and block sizes. We did not do experiments with different values of these parameters yet.

3.3 Transaction Manager

Actual prototype implementation of transaction manager is based on taDOM model developed by Haustein and Härder (2003). The implementation provides a transaction manager GUI inspector, which presents actual transaction states and mutual dependencies. Figure 5 shows a simple simulation. There are two transactions in the system. The first one sequentially reads the paths (nodes) //a/b/c, //x/y/z and then modifies the path //a/b/c/d. The second transaction tries to read the path //x/y, which is locked for reading by the first transaction. Because the lock is for reading, the second transaction is successful, it obtains the data. Then the second transaction tries to write the path //a/b/c/d/e. At this moment the transaction is queued, because the parent node of the path node e is exclusively locked by the first transaction. We can also see all locked paths in the upper-middle window (the lock type is not depicted here).

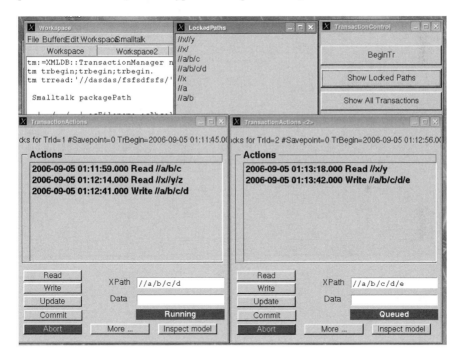

Fig. 5. Transaction manager GUI

3.4 XQuery Executor

Our actual (naive) XQuery implementation[2] is according to XQuery 1.0 specification by W3C, although it is not complete yet. Its design is strictly modular and ready for further development. The details are out of the scope of this chapter, but they were published in Vraný and Žák (2007).

Figure 6 shows XQuery console – a simple front end for XQuery executor. The query presented here uses two different data sources: CellStore storage and external data file. The query should return names of authors stored in the database and cited in the external article.

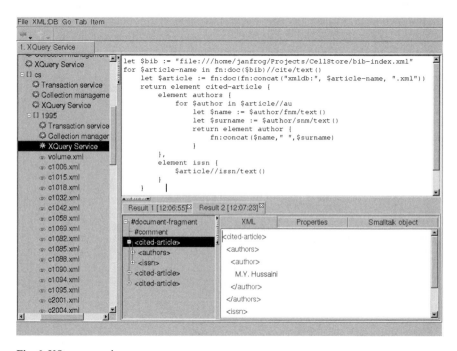

Fig. 6. XQuery console

4 Conclusions

This chapter describes basic concepts of the CellStore project, which we consider as a good starting point to many future works and experiments.

---

[2] Available on CellStore homepage (2007) for Linux and MS Windows actually.

Here are several topics which are actually in the stage of design or implementation:

- XQuery Update Facilities by W3C specification
- Database Cache Manager
- Another locking protocols implementation
- Index engine implementation
- GUI database management console with at least following tools:
  - XML initialization and data management (import, export, internal structure browser, etc.)
  - Improved XQuery console (including inner XQuery representation browser)
  - Improved transaction manager
  - Cache Manager browser
  - Light web-based database management console

Acknowledgments This research has been partially supported by the National Program of Research, Information Society Project No. 1ET100300419, Ministry of Education of Czech Republic under research program MSM 6840770014, grant of GACR No. GA201/06/0648 "Intelligent Web Technologies", and also by the grant of GACR No. GA201/06/0756 "Development of a Native Storage for XML Data".

References

Apache (2007) Xindice. http://xml.apache.org/xindice/

Bourret, R. (2005) XML and Databases.Available at
http://www.rpbourret.com/xml/XMLAndDatabases.htm

Bourret, R. (2007) XML Database Products. Available at
http://www.rpbourret.com/xml/XMLDatabaseProds.htm

CellStore Homepage (2007) http://cellstore.felk.cvut.cz/wiki

Gövert, N. and Kazai, G. (2002) Overview of the INitiative for the Evaluation of XML retrieval (INEX) 2002. In: Proc. of the first Workshop of the INitiative for the Evaluation of XML Retrieval (INEX), Dagstuhl, pp. 1–17.

Haustein, M. and Härder, T. (2003) taDOM: A Tailored Synchronization Concept with Tunable Lock Granularity for the DOM API. In: Proc. ADBIS'03 (Eds. L. Kalinichenko, R. Manthey, B. Thalheim, and U. Wloka), Springer-Verlag LNCS 2798, pp. 88–102.

Härder, T. and Reuter, A. (1983) Concepts for Implementing and Centralized Database Management System. In: Proc. Int. Computing Symposium on Application Systems Development, March 1983, Nürnberg, B.G. Teubner-Verlag, pp. 28–104.

Loupal, P. (2006) Querying XML by Lambda Calculi. In: Proceedings of the VLDB 2006 Ph.D. Workshop, Soul, Korea, CEUR Workshop Proceedings, Vol. 170.

Mlýnková, I. and Pokorný, J. (2005) XML in the World of (Object-)Relational Database Systems. In: Proc. of the 13th International Conference on Information Systems Development 2004, Vilnius, Lithuania, Springer Science + Business Media, Inc., pp. 63–76.

Pokorný, J. (2000) XML functionally. In: Proc. of IDEAS 2000 (Eds. B. Desai, Y. Kioki, and M. Toyama), IEEE Comp. Society, pp. 266–274.

Renner, A. (2001) XML Data and Object Databases: The Perfect Couple? In: Proceedings of the 17th International Conference on Data Engineering (ICDE.01).

Stonebraker, M. and Çetintemel, U. (2005) "One Size Fits All" An Idea Whose Time Has Come and Gone. In: Proc. Conference ICDE, Tokyo, Japan, pp. 2–11.

Toman, K. (2004) Storing XML Data in a Native Repository. In: Proc. of DATESO 2004, CEUR Workshop Proceedings, Vol. 98, pp. 51–62.

Vraný, J. and Žák, J. (2007) A modular XQuery implementation. In: Proc. of DATESO 2007, CEUR Workshop Proceedings, CEUR Workshop Proceedings, Vol. 235, pp. 47–54.

Wikipedia about XML. Avalable at http://en.wikipedia.org/wiki/XML

W3C XML sources. Avalable at http://www.w3.org

XML:DB (2003) Application Programming Interface for XML Databases. Avalable at http://xmldb-org.sourceforge.net/xapi/

An Integrated System for Querying Medical Digital Collections

Liana Stanescu, Dumitru Dan Burdescu, Marius Brezovan, Cosmin Stoica Spahiu and Eugen Ganea

Software Engineering Department, Faculty of Automation, Computers and Electronics, University of Craiova, Romania, stanescu@software.ucv.ro

Abstract This chapter presents an original dedicated integrated software system for managing and querying alphanumerical information and images from medical domain. The software system has a modularized architecture with the following functions: medical data acquisition from three primary sources, processing this information for extracting useful information, compacting data in a unitary format and storing the information in a database controlled by a multimedia relational database management system. The main and original function of the multimedia database management system (MMDBMS) is the possibility to execute content-based query, because the visual information is very important in the medical domain. The MMDBMS has a visual interface for building complex content-based visual query. This interface gives the possibility to choose the query image and the characteristics that will be used, i.e. colour, texture or their combination.

1 Introduction

One of the domains where a large quantity of alphanumerical and visual information is acquired daily is the medical one. This information is from the patient diagnosis and treatment process. Some of the medical data sources are:

- Electronic medical sheets; these files contain information as: patient name, birth date, medical antecedents, signs, main diagnosis, secondary diagnosis, values of the analysis and treatment.
- Medical images that are stored in digital format or images stocked on different media (x-ray film, paper, etc.).
- **D**igital **I**maging and **C**ommunications in **M**edicine (DICOM) files – these standard files are produced by the most part of medical devices (echograph, endoscope and magnetic resonance imaging) used in patient diagnosis. A DICOM file contains alphanumerical information (patient name, doctor name, consulting

C. Barry et al. (eds.), *Information Systems Development: Challenges in Practice, Theory, and Education, Vol.2,* doi: 10.1007/978-0-387-78578-3_32,
© Springer Science+Business Media, LLC 2009

date and diagnosis) and one or several images, in different formats, compressed or uncompressed.

That is why the problem of storing the medical image collections in digital format along with the associated information (patient name, diagnosis, consulting date and treatment), managing the database and executing efficient queries, it is intensely studied for finding new and more efficient solutions (Muller et al. 2004, 2005). A database is created and updated mainly to be used in the query process. One type of query process is the classical one (e.g. simple text-based query). It can be used in the following cases:

- The name of a patient is given and the database is used to find all the records referring to him/her including visual information (images).
- A diagnosis is given and all records with the same diagnosis (all the patients with the same diagnosis, over a period of time) are necessary.

The examples might go on. This kind of search might be an advanced search that contains several criteria connected by logical operators (and, or, not).

This type of digital multimedia collection can be used for a different type of query, i.e. content-based query. The content-based visual retrieval can be implemented at image level or region level (Del Bimbo 2001; Faloutsos 2005; Kalipsiz 2000; Khoshafian and Baker 1996). In the first case, the doctor selects a medical image (query image) and searches in the database all the images similar with it and the associated information (diagnosis and treatment). In the second case, the query needs selection of one or several regions in an image and searches in the database all the images that contain selected regions. This type of content-based query is built using visual characteristics (colour, texture or colour regions) that are automatically extracted from medical images when they are inserted in the database (Del Bimbo 2001; Smith 1997). Keywords or other alphanumerical information are not used. The content-based visual query can be very useful in:

- Diagnostic aid – the following situation appears frequently: the doctor visualizes a medical image, but he/she cannot establish the diagnosis exactly, he/she is aware of the fact that he/she has seen something similar before but does not have the means to search for it in the database; the problem can be solved by establishing that image as query image and the content-based image query will provide similar images from the database; it is very likely that among the retrieved images should be the searched image together with its diagnosis, observation and treatment; so the content-based image query can be directly used in the diagnosis process.
- Medical teaching – there is a series of applications for content-based visual query including other ways for access (text-based, hierarchical methods). Students can see the images in the database and the attached information in a simple and direct manner: they choose the query image and see similar images; this method stimulates learning by comparing similar cases and their particularities or comparing similar cases with different diagnosis.

- Medical research – using content-based visual query in this area brings up similar advantages for medical teaching. It can be used, for example, for finding certain types of images to be included in a study, for finding misclassified images, etc.

This chapter presents an integrated software system that can be used as an intelligent tool for creation, maintenance, simple text-based query and content-based visual query using colour and texture characteristics of the multimedia digital collections from medical domain. This dedicated software tool has the advantage of the following original functions presented in detail: data acquisition from three different medical sources, pre-processing and unifying data in a unitary format and storing the information in a database under the control of a multimedia relational database management system. MMDBMS permits database creation, table and constraints adding (primary key and foreign keys), inserting images and alphanumerical information, simple text-based query and content-based query using colour and texture characteristics. This software tool is easy to be used by medical personnel; it does not need advanced informatics knowledge and has the advantage of low cost. It is a good alternative for a classical database management system (MS Access, MS SQL Server, Oracle10g Server and Intermedia), which would need higher costs for database server and for designing applications for content-based retrieval (Chigrik 2007; Kratochvil 2005; Oracle 2005).

This chapter has the following structure: Section 2 presents the general architecture of the integrated medical system. Sections 3 and 4 present the techniques used for extracting data and images from DICOM files. There are also presented methods for extracting texture and colour information from images. Section 5 explains the method for representing the extracted data in a unitary format. Section 6 describes in details the MMDBMS that was implemented for managing and querying the multimedia databases. Section 7 presents the conclusions.

2 The General Architecture of the Integrated System

Figure 1 presents the general architecture of the medical system. In the first phase, the data acquisition from the three considered primary sources, electronic medical sheets, image files or DICOM files, must be executed. In the second phase, the processing of data obtained in the acquisition process is executed. Taking into consideration these three sources of data, the following tasks are performed:

- Processing DICOM files for extracting all the tags and images
- Processing image files for extracting the colour and textures features
- Processing electronic medical sheets for extracting all the tags and information

The third phase of system is medical data unification and designing a class hierarchy for the unified information.

In order to use different sources of medical data in a unitary way, and to allow new medical information to be integrated into the multimedia database medical system, a unified medical information format is proposed in this chapter. After a pre-processing action, all input information is collected into a repository. Each input file is decomposed into one or several header objects, which are linked to a large binary data file.

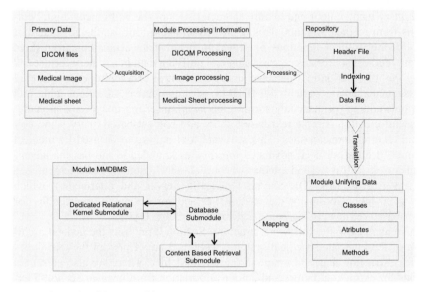

Fig. 1. General architecture of the system

The raw data contained into the binary file can be mainly numbers, strings or images, and the header file offers a simple and efficient way to access raw data. In order to use and process in a unitary way the medical information stored in the repository, an original method to unify this kind of information is proposed. As in a pure object-oriented language, a class hierarchy with a single and abstract root, called Object, is created. The instances of the leaf classes from this hierarchy represent objects that can be stored into the tables of the medical database. The module of unifying data extracts the information from the repository, creates the corresponding objects and populates the medical database.

So, the medical data that are now in a unitary format can be stored in a database having the structure designed by the user. The database is managed by a MMDBMS that has the main role to implement content-based visual query on colour and texture characteristics.

The most important modules of the integrated software system are described next.

3 DICOM File Processing

A DICOM file has the following structure (DICOM Homepage 2005):

- A preamble of 128 bytes
- Prefix (4 bytes) where are stored the letters 'D', 'I', 'C', 'M', which represent the signature of the DICOM file
- Data Set, which stores a set of information such as patient name, type of image and size of the image
- Pixels that compose the image (s) included into the DICOM file

Data Set is composed of a number of Data Elements. A Data Element is composed of several fields: data element tag, value representation, value length, value field and value multiplicity.

Taking into account every tag from the DICOM dictionary can make extracting the data from the DICOM file. This will be searched in the file and in case of finding it the corresponding value will be extracted.

The steps of extracting information from DICOM files are:

1. Verifying the existence of the characters: D, I, C and M.
2. Establishing the type of VR (ExplicitVR or ImplicitVR). This information is given by the UID (Unique Identifier), information stored in value field corresponding to the Transfer Syntax Tag.
3. Establishing the Byte Ordering (BigEndian or LittleEndian). The information is also given by UID, stored in value field of the same Transfer Syntax Tag. The DICOM standard contains all the values that UID can have.
4. Searching a tag in DICOM file according to the VR type and ByteOrdering.
5. Value extraction of the corresponding found tag.

DICOM Standard contains over 20 types of binary data or ASCII. The type of information stored in the value field is given by VR. In accordance with this type will be extracted strings, integer or byte-type information.

Next it describes the problem of image extracting from the standard DICOM files, taking into account the method of compression that was used, i.e. RLE and JPEG.

The images from DICOM files can be classified using several criteria:

1. The number of images stored in a file: single frame or multi-frame
2. Number of bits per pixel: 8, 12, 16 or 24 bits
3. Compression: without compression (raw) or with compression (RLE or JPEG)
4. Photometric interpretation: grey-scale images, colour images or palette colour images

In the images without compression, the extraction of pictures is made pixel by pixel, taking into account the number of bits stored for each pixel and the photometric interpretation (for monochrome images a pixel is stored using maximum 2 bytes and for colour images, a pixel is stored using 3 bytes). In the images that use compression it is necessary to have a decompression algorithm before saving.

4 Image Processing

On the images that were extracted from DICOM files or from the other sources two important processes are executed:

- Colour characteristics extraction
- Texture characteristics extraction

The two processes will be detailed below. In content-based visual query on colour feature (the colour is the visual feature immediately perceived on an image) the used colour space and the level of quantization, meaning the maximum number of colours are of great importance. The colour histograms represent the traditional method of describing the colour properties of the images. They have the advantages of easy computation and up to certain point are insensitive to camera rotating, zooming and changes in image resolution (Del Bimbo 2001; Smith 1997).

The solution of representing the colour information extracted from images using HSV colour space, quantized to 166 colours was chosen. It was proved that the HSV colour system has the following properties (Gevers 2004):

- It is close to the human perception of colours.
- It is intuitive.
- It is invariant to illumination intensity and camera direction.

The operation of colour quantization is needed in order to reduce the number of colours used in content-based visual query from millions to tens. The chosen solution was proposed by J.R. Smith, namely the quantization of the HSV space to 166 colours (Smith 1997). Because the hues represent the most important colour feature, a most refined quantization is necessary. In the circle that represents the colour, the primary colours, red, green and blue, are separated by 120 degrees. A circular quantization with a 20-degree step sufficiently separates the colours, such that the primary colours and yellow, magenta and cyan colours are each represented by three subdivisions. The saturation and the value are each quantized to three levels. This quantization produces 18 hues, 3 saturations, 3 values and 4 greys, and in total there are 166 distinct colours in the HSV colour space.

The experimental studies made both on images from nature and medical images have proven that choosing the HSV colour space, quantized to 166 colours, is one of the best choices in order to have a content-based visual query process of good quality (Stanescu et al. 2006a). The 166-colour histogram will be used in the content-based visual query process.

Together with colour, texture is a powerful characteristic of an image, existent in nature and medical images, where a disease can be indicated by changes in the colour and texture of a tissue.

There are many techniques used for texture extraction, but there is not a specific method that can be considered the most appropriate, depending on the application and the type of images taken into account (Del Bimbo 2001).

One of the most representative methods for texture detection is the method that uses co-occurrence matrices. For an image $f(x, y)$, the co-occurrence matrix $h_{d\phi}$ (i, j) is defined so that each entry (i, j) is equal to the number of times for that $f(x_1,y_1)$ = i and $f(x_2,y_2) = j$, where $(x_2,y_2) = (x_1,y_1) + (d \cos \phi, d \sin \phi)$ (Del Bimbo 2001).

In the case of colour images, one matrix is computed for each of the three channels (R, G and B). This leads to three quadratic matrices of dimension equal to the number of colour levels presented in an image (256 in our case) for each distance d and orientation ϕ. The classification of texture is based on the characteristics extracted from the co-occurrence matrix: energy, entropy, maximum probability, contrast, inverse difference moment and correlation (Del Bimbo 2001).

The three vectors of texture characteristics extracted from the three co-occurrence matrices are created using six characteristics computed for $d = 1$ and $\phi = 0$. It results 18 values, used next in the content-based visual query. The results of the content-based visual query process on medical imagery, using the colour histograms with 166 values in HSV colour space and co-occurrence matrices were presented in detail in Stanescu et al. (2006b).

5 Designing a Class Hierarchy for Unified Information

The information that is stored in the repository cannot be used directly. It has to be unified first. It has proposed a class hierarchy with a single and abstract root, called Object. The four subclasses of the Object class, Text, Number, Character and Image, represent predefined object types used in the proposed medical database. Whereas the first three are standard data types used as usual databases, the class Image allows to handle the queries concerning the medical images.

Associated to the class Image are four types of characteristics, extracted from images (Fig. 2):

- Colour histogram feature, having associated the class ColorHistogram
- Texture feature, with the associated Texture class
- Width feature, with the associated Width class
- Height feature, with the associated Height class

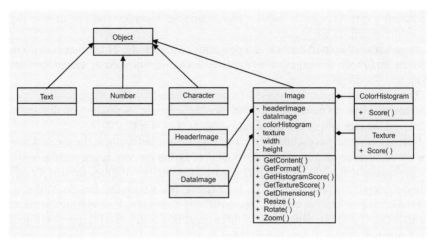

Fig. 2. Class hierarchy

The first two feature classes have a method called Score, which can be used in order to obtain numerical values measuring the similarity between images. All instances of class Image have four attributes: ColorHistogram, texture, width and height, which are instances of the ColorHistogram, Texture, Width and Height, respectively.

Because the query language used by the MMDBMS is a subset of the SQL-3 language, the methods of the Image class correspond to the similar SQL-invoked regular functions: Resize, Rotate, Zoom, HistogramScore, TextureScore, Content and Format (SQL/MM 2001).

6 The Dedicated Database Management System

6.1 Database and Table Management

To create a new database, the user must specify the name of the database in the dialog window. For each new database there will be made a new folder in the Databases folder, and all the information will be stored in this new folder. After creating a database, it will be listed in the tree on the left side of the application window. This tree is used to see all databases, including their tables.

To create a table, the user must select a database, where he/she wants it to be created. He must specify also the name of the table, the columns, primary and foreign keys, if any.

The names of the tables in a database are unique. When the user introduces a name that is identical with another table name in the database, he is notified. For each table it will be created a new file with a specific structure (a header area and a recording area). This file is created in the database folder having the name of the table and the .tbl extension. The user has to specify the structure of the table: the columns, data type, size and applicable constrains. The name of a column also has to be unique. This aspect is ensured by the database management system (DBMS). Three types of data are implemented: int, char and image. For the strings the user can specify the maximum size. A new type of data is introduced – Image. It permits storing in the database an image having one of the following formats: bmp, gif or jpg. In the same dialog window the user can specify the primary key. It can contain one or several columns. The user may specify a 1:m connection between two tables: a parent table (on the 1 side of the connection) and a son (on the m side of the connection). For this the foreign keys tag must be used, in the same window. The user easily chooses the parent and son table and the foreign key. The primary and the foreign keys must have the same type and the same size. If there is a connection between two primary keys, the connection will be 1:1. The structure of the table might be seen at any moment in the main window of the DBMS, using Components tag. Once the table is created, the user can add new records, modify or delete existing ones, using the record editor.

6.2 Data Organization

In the folder where the application is installed, there will be automatically created the 'Databases' folder. When creating a new database, a new folder is created in this folder, with the name of newly created database. All the files for the database will be created here.

Each table of the database is stored in a separate file having the '.tbl' extension. This file has two components: a header and a data area. The header is added when the user creates the structure of the table and data area, when the user inserts, updates or deletes records. The header will contain the following information regarding the structure of the table:

- Number of records for header.
- The header will contain a record for each column in the table. It will also contain a record for primary key of the table and a record for each foreign key.
- Size for each record in header (a header record contains data about a column in table: name, type and length in case of character string; or about primary key or about foreign key/keys).
- Header records.

In the data area an int type value is stored on 4 bytes. A character string has the following structure: it is written out and blank spaces are added until the maximum size is reached. If the string is bigger than the specified maximum size, then the string is truncated to the maximum size.

For an image, the following attributes are stored:

- Image type (bmp, jpg or gif)
- Image height and width
- Number of bytes needed to store the image
- The image in binary
- One hundred and sixty-six integer values representing the colour histogram
- Eighteen real values representing the texture vector

6.3 Content-Based Visual Query

The Multimedia Database Management System offers the possibility to build the content-based visual query using colour characteristic, texture characteristic or a combination of both, in an easy manner, at the image level, using the menus presented in the software window from Fig. 3. The elements of this window that permits content-based visual retrieval are:

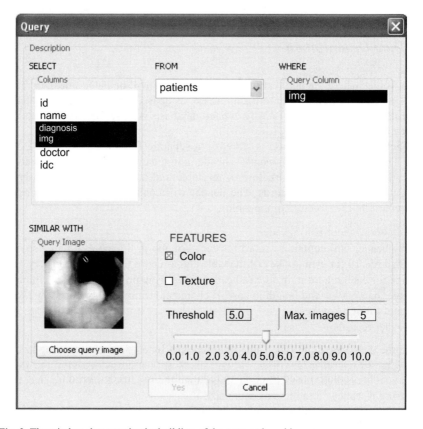

Fig. 3. The window that permits the building of the content-based image query

- Similar With – opens the window for choosing the query image.
- Select – permits to choose the field (or fields) that will be presented in the results of the query.
- From – it is one of the tables in database that will be used for the query.
- Where – the image type column used for content-based image query.
- Features – the characteristic used for content-based visual query is chosen – colour, texture or a combination of both.
- Threshold – a threshold of accepted similarity between query image and target image is chosen. An image with a similarity under this threshold will not be added into the resulted query images.
- Maximum images – specify the maximum number of images returned by the query.

The dissimilarity between images, taking into consideration the colour characteristic is calculated using histograms intersection method. For texture the Euclidian distance is used. If both distances are used in the query, the total distance is arithmetical average between the distances.

When building the query, a modified SQL Select command is actually performed, which is adapted for content-based image query. An example of such a modified command is:

Select patients.diagnosis, patients.img From Patients where Patients.img Similar with Query Image (method : color, max.images 5).

This modified Select command specifies that the results are obtained from Patients table, taking into consideration the values from diagnosis field, the images similar with the query image for colour characteristic, and there will be five resulting images. In the resulting set it is also presented the distance of the dissimilarity between the query image and the target image.

6.4 Experiments

The MMDBMS was tested using a system with the following characteristics: AMD Athlon 3000+ processor, 1 GB RAM Memory, 2x150Gb RAID HDD, Windows XP Professional operating system. Some of the preliminary results are presented in Table 1. In this phase, it was measured the time for displaying records (there is only one field of Image type in the records), and the execution time of the content-based visual query, taking into consideration the colour feature, the texture feature and their combination. The execution time for these three types of queries is good. The time necessary to display all the records is higher, because the kernel must display the binary image and all attached information. One of the solutions that could be used in order to reduce the time needed for displaying the images is to organize the display function in pages (e.g. 100 records on each page). The indexing solutions that will be implemented will improve significantly the presented values.

Table 1. The experimental results

Number of records	Display time (s)	Query time – colour (s)	Query time – texture(s)	Query time – both (s)
100	4.516	0.350	0.334	0.550
1,000	15.281	0.891	0.790	1.425
10,000	25.563	1.500	1.500	2.873
20,000	73.042	4.750	4.615	8.528

7 Conclusions

This chapter presents the modules of an integrated system designed for acquisitioning, processing, storing and querying numerical, textual and visual information from medical domain. There are also presented the relationships between these modules, along with the functions executed by each of them. The elements of originality of this integrated medical system are: the unified format for medical data that can be imported from different sources and the multimedia database management system kernel. This last module permits creating and deleting databases, creating and deleting tables in databases, updating data in tables and querying. The user can utilize three types of data: int, char and image. Storing the images in a binary format inside the database increases the data security, a major problem in the medical domain. There are also implemented the two constraints used in the relational model: primary key and referential integrity.

The MMDBMS can execute both simple text-based query using one or several criteria connected with logical operators (and, or, not) and content-based visual query at image level, taking into consideration the colour and texture characteristics. These characteristics are automatically extracted when the images are processed. The visual manner of building this type of query specific for multimedia data and the modified Select command that is sent for execution to the DBMS give originality to the software product. Persons that work in the medical domain might easily use all the functions of the software tool. For implementation the Java technology was used, which gives the platform more independence.

Creating a multimedia database designed to store alphanumeric data and medical images, along with a querying software system, is useful if looking from a technical point of view, by improving the administration of multimedia data, economically, by reducing the expenses regarding the medical logistics, and socially through the offer of a higher accessibility degree on territory, for doctors and for patients as well.

The unified medical information format and the modularized architecture allow in the future:

- To easy integrate new sources of medical input data
- To integrate into the multimedia database system a query system based on natural language
- To apply algorithms of image mining and image diagnosis

The final version of the presented integrated medical system will have a service-oriented architecture that will give a maximum attention to data security problem.

References

Chigrik, A. (2007) SQL Server 2000 vs. Oracle 9i, http://www.mssqlcity.com/Articles/Compare/sql_server_vs_oracle.htm

Del Bimbo, A. (2001) Visual Information Retrieval. Morgan Kaufmann, San Francisco, CA

DICOM Homepage (2005) http://medical.nema.org/

Faloutsos, C. (2005) Searching Multimedia Databases by Content. Springer, Berlin/Heidelberg

Gevers, T. (2004) Image Search Engines: An Overview. Emerging Topics in Computer Vision. Prentice-Hall, Englewood Cliffs, NJ

Kalipsiz, O. (2000) Multimedia databases. Proceedings of the IEEE International Conference on Information Visualization, London, England

Khoshafian, S. and Baker, A.B. (1996) Multimedia and Imaging Databases. Morgan Kaufmann, San Francisco, CA

Kratochvil, M. (2005) The Move to Store Images In the Database, http://www.oracle.com/technology/products/intermedia/pdf/why_images_in_database.pdf

Muller, H., Michoux, H., Bandon, N. and Geissbuhler, D. (2004) A Review of Content-Based Image Retrieval Systems in Medical Applications – Clinical Benefits and Future Directions. International Journal of Medical Informatics, 73, 1–23

Muller, H., Rosset, A., Garcia, A., Vallee, J.P. and Geissbuhler, A. (2005) Benefits of Content-based Visual Data Access in Radiology. Radio Graphics, 25, 849–858

Oracle (2005) Oracle InterMedia. Managing Multimedia Content, http://www.oracle.com/technology/products/intermedia/pdf/10gr2_collateral/imedia_twp_10gr2.pdf

Smith, J.R. (1997) Integrated Spatial and Feature Image SystemsRetrieval, Compression and Analysis. Ph.D. thesis, Graduate School of Arts and Sciences. Columbia University

SQL/MM Part 5 Still Image (2001) http://www.wiscorp.com/2CD1R1-05-stillimage-2001-12.pdf

Stanescu, L., Burdescu, D.D., Ion, A. and Brezovan, M. (2006a) Content-Based Image Query on Color Feature in the Image Databases Obtained from DICOM Files. International Multi-Conference on Computing in the Global Information Technology. Bucharest, Romania

Stanescu, L., Ion, A., Burdescu, D.D. and Brezovan, M. (2006b) Algorithms and Results in Content-based Visual Query of the Image Databases Resulting from DICOM Files. Synasc 2006. Bucharest, Romania

Information Management Between Academic and Internet Communities

Gábor Knapp and Tamás Rév

National Audiovisual Archive, Hungary, gabor.knapp@nava.hu, tamas.rev@nava.hu

Abstract The concept 'digital archive' can be approached either from the concept 'digital' (represented by the Internet) or from the concept 'archive' (represented by traditional collections as libraries). In our days these two approaches and the techniques used by them seem to be merged. This chapter describes the work-in-progress for a project of the National Audiovisual Archive (NAVA), Hungary. The project intents to use the software and social techniques developed for Internet applications to handle large number of very different kind of documents. The project also adopts and develops techniques to combine conventional content management systems using relational database and file-based systems. The primary collection of NAVA is the legal deposit of the programs of six television and three radio channels. However, several other valuable audiovisual contents are offered by content owners and embedded as special collections for long-term preservation. The applied research project was initiated by the data management problems that we met while integrating the special collections with very different quantity and quality of metadata, however, usability issues were also included. At the moment there are more questions than solutions, however, requirements of a new archive architecture using semantic web 2.0 techniques are outlined. Besides internal resources the work is also funded by the P2P Fusion FP6 EU project.

1 Introduction

The concept 'digital archive' can be approached either from the concept 'digital' (represented by the Internet) or from the concept 'archive' (represented by traditional collections as libraries). In our days these two approaches and the techniques used by them seem to be merged. This chapter describes the work-in-progress for a project of the National Audiovisual Archive (NAVA), Hungary. The project intents to use the software and social techniques developed for Internet applications to handle large number of very different documents. The project also adopts and develops techniques to combine conventional content management systems using relational database and file-based systems. The primary collection of NAVA is the legal deposit of programs of six television and three radio channels. However, several other valuable audiovisual contents are offered and embedded as special collections

C. Barry et al. (eds.), *Information Systems Development: Challenges in Practice, Theory, and Education, Vol.2,* doi: 10.1007/978-0-387-78578-3_33,

for long-term preservation. The applied research project was initiated by the data management problems that we met while integrating the special collections with very different quantity and quality of metadata, however, usability issues were also included. At the moment there are more questions than solutions, however, requirements of a new archive architecture using semantic web 2.0 techniques are outlined (Fig. 1). Besides internal resources the work is also funded by the P2P Fusion FP6 EU project.

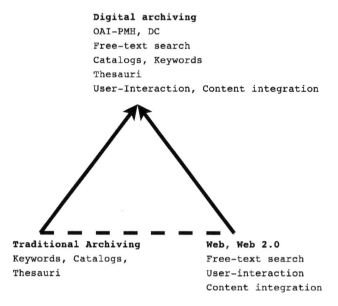

Fig. 1. Traditional archives and web 2.0

2 Setting the Stage

Traditional, academic archives collected, preserved and categorized physical objects, however, in the 1990s had to enter digital world due to the requirements of technology and the expectations of their audience. Traditional archives had qualified experts and had enough time to develop advanced semantic information management methods, databases for a large number of more or less homogenous objects. However, these methods were usually institute-specific, thus hardly can be applied for a different kind of collection or even for an archive of a different language.

On the other hand, as Internet became our everyday workplace, billions of documents (texts, pictures, videos and sounds) are created and uploaded that born, exist and live only in digital form. These documents are usually not categorized at all, and the best to be expected is a few uncontrolled keywords. However, there is a need to find relevant documents. For this reason the Internet community developed its own extremely efficient techniques for free text search and retrieval, the determination of relevancy using community-based techniques and tries to enhance semantics in documents by forcing users to use semantic tagging (Berners-Lee 1998).

First, we have to study all relevant aspects to outline and define the problem itself and find out what can be archived by what techniques, and what restrictions have to be applied. Topics of interest are the following:

1. The features of special collections versus the legal deposit collection
2. Relational database-based versus document-/file-based collection management
3. Document-/file-based search and retrieval, browsing and semantic support
4. Schema matching for different collections and clustering
5. User interaction, annotation, rating, authentication, authorization and access control
6. Alternative channels for content ingestion

2.1 Collections of NAVA

The primary object of NAVA is collecting Hungarian-made or Hungarian-related programs of the country-wide or public television and radio channels, however, the ingest and annotation of other segments of the audiovisual heritage becomes more and more important. These latter documents form the 'special collections' including a series of lectures on sciences, newsreels of the 1930s and World War II, Hungarian feature films, selected segments from the archive of the public television and films of the MediaWave festival. Each special collection has its own ingest process, metadata scheme and an own set of access control requirements. Table 1 summarizes the features and differences for the two cases.

Table 1. Conceptual differences between the primary collection and the special collections

Feature	Legal deposit archive	Special collections
Metadata scheme	Standardized, invariant	Multiple, variant and variable (!)
Process scheduling	Continuous task, 7 × 24	Occasionally, needs quick processing
Workflow	Well controlled	Unique solutions
Metadata source	Direct into database	Unique: doc, html, xls, xml, txt, paper
Media source	Automatic digitization	Unique: dvd, mpeg2, mpeg4, beta, vhs
Amount of data	About 100,000 records per year	Small: less than 1,000 record/collection
Access control	Determined by law	Unique agreements

As both the processing issues and the targeted audience, and also the system development process differ, it seems to be reasonable to handle special collections differently from the collection of legal deposits.

2.2 Relational Database Versus File-Based Data Management

The document/data processing techniques developed for the web are usually based on unstructured documents (may be structured, but the structure is unknown), the tool for search and retrieval is free text search using inverted indexes supported more or less by natural language or automatic clustering techniques. However, the databases of institutes are usually structured and organized into databases, and search and retrieval is based on SQL, which requires the knowledge of the database structure. Table 2 summarizes the main differences.

Table 2. Differences between database- and document-based search techniques

Feature	Database-based search	Document-based search
Requested knowledge	Database scheme	None
Query speed	Fast	Fast, when indexed properly
Flexibility of scheme	Hard to modify	Even single documents can be modified
Indexing	Continuous	As required (when new data arrives)

Semi-structured documents form a transition between the two extreme solutions. They are typically XML documents or documents that can be easily transformed to XML format. In the case of semi-structured documents, the semantics encoded in the structure usually cannot be utilized during indexing, however, can be very useful at the ordering of the hit list by clustering it, or at the calculation of some kind of relevancy.

2.3 Clustering the Tasks

The areas of development are divided into two groups. The first group contains the tasks that are related closely to the handling of special collections, especially to the multiple and variable metadata scheme handling. The second group stands for the exploitation of user interaction. Both groups are further divided into subtasks.

3 Alternate Handling of Special Collections

In this chapter the tasks are identified that have to complete while establishing a new collection, and at the same time, the alternative technology is given for the traditional archive. The functionality is expected to be more flexible, useful software tools are to be assembled or created. However, the usage remains basically the same: professional staff associates metadata and users are searching them. The introduction of user interaction, when users take an active part in metadata and content creation can be found in the following chapter.

3.1 Establishing a Special Collection – List of Requirements

The List of Requirements is a document that can be the starting point. At the beginning the use cases and basic requirements that can be deducted from previous experiences can be listed in this document. During development these data can be made more accurate and additional features can be added resulting the final User's Guide for Special Collections.

3.2 Know-How of Ingest and Transcoding

The Know-How of Ingest and Transcoding is a handbook of techniques and parameters that can be used at the media ingest phase. The objective is to summarize the resources that NAVA can use to record, store, encode or transcode the material to fit NAVA's requirements or possibilities. There are input devices (vhs, s-vhs, beta, dvd and digitization boards) in the beginning, recording and/or transcoder softwares/hardwares in the middle processing and media streaming capabilities at the end.

By the description and functional categorization a better utilization of our capacity is expected. Examining the capabilities and exploring the functional gaps, the investigations that have the most valuable effect by the less effort can be outlined. A specific object of this task to make formats open by establishing the MPEG-4 (Wikipedia 2007) AVC and SP processing capabilities on the whole production line to be prepared for mobile, Internet protocol-based or high-definition television. Now NAVA uses MPEG-2 for long-term preservation and RealMedia for online services). As ingested resources appear basically as files, and a suitable file structure and naming convention has to be elaborated.

3.3 How to Prepare a Metadata Scheme for a Special Collection?

This was the fist task that NAVA had to solve; these problems initiated the project itself. Metadata associated with special collections offered for archiving had extremely various format, syntax and semantics. To integrate a special collection, to provide access control and to categorize, the metadata structure should be studied and the relation between documents should be determined.

There are basic requirements that have to be fulfilled. The Dublin Core principles (Dublin Core Homepage 2003) should be used, that is, every field is optional and repeatable, and for unknown elements or attributes, the 'dumb down' technique is to be used. The Dublin Core base elements (Dublin Core Homepage 2006) should be used if possible, however, none of the elements are required (the filename itself can give the information for identification, but of course more metadata is suggested to support search and retrieval).

Usually, more or less metadata are associated with the media in several formats. In our practice xls, pdf, doc, xml, html, txt and paper are used. Forming the metadata scheme the studying of the associated metadata is necessary, but not enough. The investigation of the content can help to complete data, determine more relations, select characteristic images or clips or explore inner structure. According to the results more metadata elements can appear: administrative metadata for access control or change management, technical metadata for clips or keyframes, and more descriptive metadata to support search. At the end of this task the metadata schema for the special collection has to be appeared in XML schema form including elements and encoding schemes (i.e. controlled vocabularies and codepages) (Fig. 2).

As a metadata scheme is ready for a special collection, appropriate visualizing technique and design has to be made for displaying the entire record as well as the short hit list practically using XSLT technique or CSS.

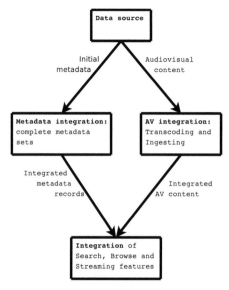

Fig. 2. Workflow of integrating special collections

3.4 Exploring Relations Among Special Collections

Up to this step, the special collections lived their own life. However, as simultaneous search capability is required, the schemas of different special collections have to be fitted. This is one of the most difficult tasks. As Dublin Core principles and element set was our guide. We always hoped that it is a relatively easy job, however, it proved to be extremely difficult in all cases. Some typical problems are listed below:

1. One element has to be parsed into two or more elements
2. More elements have to be mapped into one element
3. A free text field has to be mapped to a controlled vocabulary field
4. Two controlled vocabulary fields, with different vocabularies have to be matched

Besides the schema matching between each other, schemas have to be matched to Dublin core, or other extended, standardized schemas as DC.Culture, RSS or EBU/P-Meta for exporting and data exchange using the OAI-PMH 2.0 protocol (Lagoze et al. 2004).

3.5 Search, Retrieval and Browsing

Even metadata are harmonized semantically at a higher conceptual level and mapped to a common accepted scheme, the individual metadata schemes are expected to be very different. As metadata records appear as structured xml documents, free text indexing and search can easily implemented. During indexing and search, the semantic information cannot be utilized due to the large differences. However, at the ordering of the hit list, using the conceptual level matching, in the case of too many hits results can be clustered, or search term can be extended in the case of zero, or too little number of hits. Clustering categories and filters are to be selected by the project.

4 Supporting and Exploiting User Interaction

Adaptation of web techniques is proved to be a very useful practice in archive data management, and also expected to be an extremely useful practice in a web 2.0 environment. A large number of users with a wide range expertise can extend the limited annotating capability of a conventional archive. So several new data input channels can be opened. This experimental expansion of our archive is supported by the P2P-Fusion R&D project of EU 6th Framework Programme.

You can consider the new data input channels described below as a second mediaspace for the audiovisual material. The opportunity that users can choose content to be injected into the archives gives a chance to underground and subculture originators to be presented.

4.1 Community-Added Metadata: Folksonomy

Contrarily to taxonomy, folksonomy means that users are enabled and encouraged to assign metadata, and add new tags to the document description of the audiovisual material they can retrieve from the collections.

These tags are usually free words, but can be chosen from a controlled vocabulary or from the index of already assigned keywords as well. Users can also write recommendations, rate the documents and hence find some so-called taste buddies in the community and they can trust the recommendations and choices of each other. All the features and benefits of collaborative filtering could be listed here. Of course, certain fields or existing metadata added by the archivists is not allowed to edit by the users.

Technically, community-based data injection is based on users who add and edit metadata. Key features are tag-clouds, recommendations, community-based rankings and so forth. Content descriptions and reviews also play an important role. NAVA provides only the resources and the web user interface, and the rest must be done by the user community.

Data collected in a way described earlier shows new ways of document search and document browse interfaces. For example, clustering of the collaborative data space is a good way to build different views of the contents. Such a clustering can be done for instance following the community's taste buddy structure (Torrent-freak homepage 2006).

In this case the data input channel is the metadata posted by the user individuals. One could say, NAVA enables users to write its metadata. This is true, however, NAVA must give write access only to a subset of the metadata fields. Such a write access has to be granted to properly registered users, hence they are responsible for the meta content they post. Briefly, NAVA can take the advantages of the web 2.0 tools of user interfaces.

4.2 User Content Injection

The second type of user interaction refers to the creative reuse of audiovisual material. Users view, download, edit and annotate audiovisual material and possibly upload the changes. If a certain community decides (using rating, folksonomy, and/or simply by downloading it many times) that a piece of art is ready and good enough, it can be archived. The amount of injected content must somehow to be controlled, because NAVA has a finite storage capacity and it also has to comply with the intellectual property rights. In a technical point of view, the injection must be controlled too, so the content injectors can be traced back if needed (Fig. 3). This kind of user authentication is a key point of the community-based content reuse and content creation.

Large archives like NAVA usually do not participate in any P2P network. However, NAVA takes part in a very interesting experiment, an EU-funded project, P2P-Fusion that aims to develop a new software system called Fusion (P2P-Fusion site 2006). The Fusion software enables and encourages creative reuse of audiovisual content. This audiovisual content has two different content sources. One is the home-made videos, for instance, audiovisual cooking how-to clips. Besides ingesting, audiovisual archives also inject content into the P2P network of Fusion users. The roles of the audiovisual archives in this P2P Fusion project are the following:

1. They export audiovisual content into the P2P network.
2. They import user-produced metadata related to the corresponding audiovisual content.
3. They import user-produced audiovisual content as well.

It is an important issue, how to choose the audiovisual documents to import into the archives. One approach is the family archive approach. A small community, like a family, creates its best-of movie and they would like to archive it without any server hosted at home. What can they do? They upload their favourites into the archive, they tag it with the family name, but do not associate any passwords with that. Later, for instance, after ten years they can view and download all the materials they produced earlier. The questions of these issue are the following:

1. How to protect uploaded sensitive data
2. How to control the reuse of uploaded sensitive data

Another approach is to archive the contents, which are ranked high by the entire community. This involves some kind of overview over the network. This overview is still an issue. The third approach is that mainframe servers of the archive play the role of a superpeer on the network and provide a cache for the recently demanded documents.

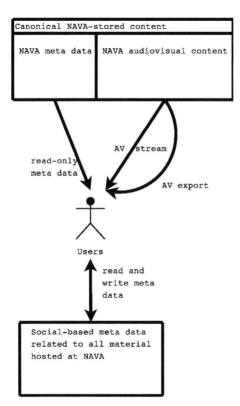

Fig. 3. NAVA stores and seeds user-generated content

4.3 User Authentication

The new functionalities described earlier requires the implementation of an extended user authentication process in NAVA. User-contributed data import requires new content policies. First of all, rules must be set to define the access rights to the resources. Furthermore, user's identity should be maintained between logins because all community benefit functions are based on virtual entities. Finally, users might want to use different services, hence the user session should be maintained while the user uses different NAVA or P2P-Fusion applications.

5 Conclusion

As web technology evolves and more and more users are involved in content creation and sharing, digital archives face new challenges. NAVA faces them too. Traditional ways of ingest and annotation can hardly be maintained because of the large amount of data and content, and the limited amount of human resources. Alternative methods and systems have to be implemented that exploit the developed techniques. So, we suggest a semi-structured file-based system with appropriate processing methodology and a software toolkit using inverted index-based free text search. Besides, controlled, experimental user contribution is planned. Users are involved in order that they annotate existing audiovisual content and furthermore create and upload new content.

References

Berners-Lee, T. 1998. Semantic Web Road map [online] [Accessed 5th April 2007]. Available from World Wide Web: <http://www.w3.org/DesignIssues/Semantic.html>

Wikipedia. 2007. *H.264/MPEG-4 AVC* [online] [Accessed 27th March 2007] Available from World Wide Web: <http://en.wikipedia.org/wiki/H.264>

DCMI Grammatical Principles. 2003. [online] [Accessed 20th March 2005] Available from World Wide Web: <http://dublincore.org/usage/documents/principles/>

The Dublin Core Metadata Element Set. 2006. [online] [Accessed 18th March 2007] Available from World Wide Web: <http://www.dublincore.org/documents/dcmi-terms/>

Lagoze, C., Van de Sompel, H., Nelson, M. and Warner, S. 2004. The Open Archives Initiative Protocol for Metadata Harvesting [online] [Accessed 23rd March 2007] Available from World Wide Web: <http://www.openarchives.org/OAI/openarchivesprotocol.html>

Tribler: A social based, BitTorrent powered p2p network. 2006. [online] [Accessed 2nd April 2007] Available from World Wide Web: <http://torrentfreak.com/tribler-a-socialbased-bittorrent-powered-p2p-network/>

P2P-Fusion. 2007. [online] [Accessed 12th October 2006] Available from World Wide Web: <http://arki.uiah.fi/p2p-fusion/>

Wikipedia. 2007. *Single Sign-On* [online] [Accessed 17th February 2007] Available from World Wide Web: <http://en.wikipedia.org/wiki/Single_sign_on>

Integrating Requirements Specifications and Web Services Using Cognitive Models[1]

Joe Geldart and William Song

Department of Computer Science, University of Durham, UK,
j.r.c.geldart@dur.ac.uk, w.w.song@dur.ac.uk

Abstract Modern telecommunication providers are under increasing competition in their markets due to deregulation and merging of previously separate domains. In order to maintain a competitive edge, providers are looking to allow an increase in the flexibility of their offerings without substantially increasing costs. This position chapter sets out a scheme for allowing the automation of the processing of customer requirements to give an executable service specification. This scheme involves the recognition of requirements as cognitive artifacts and the containment of the uncertain reasoning; this entails to a single level in a three-tier processing model.

1 Introduction

The modern telecommunication market is more competitive than ever before with deregulation leading to a massive increase in the number of service providers. Exacerbating this, previously separate markets have merged with telecommunication and new technologies have allowed alternatives to the traditional telephone system. It has become vital for telecom companies to seek new ways to give themselves an edge over their competition and to exploit the new technologies to reduce costs whilst improving their customers' experiences.

Many companies have looked to web services, e-business and related technologies to allow them to leverage the Internet, not merely as a data transfer system, but as a means to redesign their core infrastructure with flexibility in mind (Hayzelden and Bigham 1999). Such work has often focused upon using Semantic Web technologies, such as OWL and its service-oriented sister OWL-S (previously known as DAML-S), to describe such semantic web services with the hope of performing automated matchmaking and planning with a given requirement specification (Bansal and Vidal 2003; Sheshagiri et al. 2003).

---

[1] The authors' work presented here is supported by British Telecom plc and EPSRC grant EP/D/504376/1

C. Barry et al. (eds.), *Information Systems Development: Challenges in Practice, Theory, and Education, Vol.2*, doi: 10.1007/978-0-387-78578-3_34,

Such work often requires the description of complex and poorly understood domains in terms of a precise and formal language. This can take a considerable effort and background knowledge on the part of the formalizer and so research has been done into mapping natural language service descriptions into a form suitable for processing by Semantic Web reasoning systems (Simonov et al. 2004). These languages are often highly restricted to allow the precision they require in order to map onto formal languages like OWL. There is a natural tension between the precision of web services, and computations in general, and the ambiguity that is rife in human communication and reasoning.

The ambiguity in requirements specifications is most obviously seen in the specification of non-functional requirements. It has been known for some time (Ebert 1997) that non-functional requirements contribute considerably to the customer's perception of software quality. However, these requirements are also the greatest source of "soft requirements" (Sommerville 2001); requirements which are hard to manipulate in model-theoretic logics such as first-order predicate logic and its fragments, including OWL.

This position chapter lays out a scheme for the processing of requirements based upon research into cognitive semantics. A framework is outlined, which allows the uncertain world of cognition to be used to constrain a standard crisp model of services such as described by Broy et al. (2007). By using insights from cognitive science, and a processing model which effectively contains the uncertainty, it is posited that customers' natural requirements specifications will be able to be used to describe software systems composed out of standard web services.

2 Requirements Specifications as a Cognitive Artifact

The act of imagining one's needs and wants is an undeniably cognitive act. It occurs through the action of processes within the mind to produce a description, which is based upon evaluation processes amongst others. The act of describing these needs and wants is likewise a cognitive act. One takes the imagination, and through a process called language serializes it into a linear sequence of signals, which can be reassembled by a competent listener into a close facsimile of the original mental image. The serialized stream, which represents the model describes a set of constraints and it is by propagating and simplifying these constraints together with those provided by the communication context and background domain that the listener may recover a close analogue to the originally conceived model. This process of imagination, expression, and regeneration forms the basis of a cognitive account of language and, more generally, communication. It is the communication of detailed, yet partial, models of a customer's desires, wants, and their subsequent integration and reification that underpins the idea of requirements interpretation whether that is performed by human or machine. It is thus contended that to properly account for the range of requirements specifications that humans can generate, one must view the process of requirements analysis as an essentially cognitive one in order to be able to properly reason with the ideas, which are expressed and the form in which they are represented.

This section focuses on three of the more important aspects of cognitive semantics: stories, radial categories, and conceptual metaphor. This selection is not meant to define the sum total of cognition, but rather shows the general nature of cognitive accounts. For fuller accounts of the issues involved one is directed to the references.

2.1 Stories

A tale told is often seen as something special, a side-benefit of our reasoning processes used for our entertainment. In recent years, however, the idea of a story has been recognized as fundamental to how we structure and understand the world. In "The Literary Mind", Turner (1996) gives a detailed account of the nature of stories and how they underlie our descriptions of processes, causality and planning.

Through stories, humans can compactly and precisely express complex physical, mental, and social processes. These vary from exemplary tales, examples of a more general sequence of events, all the way to the most condense form of story-based communication; the parable and the proverb. Turner shows that every sentence is a story, as is every discourse. To automate the understanding of what humans are expressing, one must understand the importance of story. Recently, Englmeier et al. (2006) have described the use of "storybooks" as part of a requirements engineering methodology for web services orchestration. Their approach is, however, manual whereas it is hoped that the techniques described here will open the door to more automated processing.

2.2 Radial Categories

It has long been recognized, ever since Plato and Aristotle, that much of the high-level human reasoning is predicated upon a model of categorization. Such a perspective has, in more recent decades, motivated the use of connectionist models of classification, and the creation of complex symbolic ontologies. Cognitive science early on asked the question as to whether human categorization is the same as the classical, binary classifications found in most reasoning schemes. In the 1980s, Lakoff (1987) built upon the experimental work of Rosch (1973, 1975) to produce a description of the requirements of a cognitive model of categorization answering the aforementioned question in the negative.

Rather than being a crisply defined set of members, a cognitive category's membership and properties are defined by degree. Many categories admit no precise description in terms of necessary or sufficient properties. An example of this is the category "bachelor," which many would take as easy to completely characterize as an "unmarried man." However, there are many situations where this description does not properly represent what it means to be a bachelor; is the Pope a bachelor, for example. The surfeit of exceptions, and the general feeling that one thing can be "a better example" of a category than another (so-called exemplar theory) is a strong indication that the classical model of categorization is not sufficient for modeling the world how humans express it. In addition, what is taken to be a member or property of a category can vary from situation to situation depending upon the context and history; the category of mother admits many different situations and the context can influence which is taken or are taken to be the exemplars and prototypes for the given discourse or thought train ("Not my birth mother, my actual mother"). A cognitive account of requirements must be capable of representing and reasoning with such radial categories (as they are known) if it is to be able to cope with the range of inferences implied in natural communications without a vast list of exceptions and conditions. The radiality of human categorization has also been held in Lakoff (1987) and subsequent literature as the source of soft and uncertain reasoning. As such, it is even more imperative to provide a model, which admits radial categories if one is to deal with soft descriptions such as typically found in non-functional requirements.

2.3 Conceptual Metaphor

When one thinks of metaphor, one generally thinks of "flowery" literary devices for making text less dull. One of the first demonstrations of the burgeoning subject of cognitive science was to show that metaphor (generally distinguished from the everyday conception of the term as conceptual metaphor) was a fundamental operation in the brain's repertoire. Conceptual metaphor, as first defined by Lakoff and Johnson (1981) is responsible for the understanding of more abstract concepts in terms of more directly understandable and concrete domains as a semi-structured mapping. When we say "I went through the article with her," we are expressing an abstract domain (that of proof reading) in terms of the more concrete domain of a path intersecting a container. It was the identification of conceptual metaphor as the source and method of expression of abstract reasoning, and that metaphors are not arbitrary, but principled, that helped bring cognitive science to prevalence as a subject.

Since requirements specifications are generally describing fairly abstract domains, an account of metaphor is essential in any model of natural requirements interpretation. When the customer requires that "voicemails are sent to the user by email using MP3," the metaphors of "communication is transport along a conduit," "media are places on a conduit," and "encodings are tools" are being invoked. These metaphors are instances of more general metaphors, and the original utterance can only be accurately interpreted in terms of this background set of conceptual metaphors.

3 A Logic of Cognitive Requirements

The core of the scheme in this chapter is the interpretation of requirements and background knowledge as constraints expressed in terms of a cognitively based logical language. Each requirement is viewed as a story, and the set of all requirements is interpreted by trying to find a general story consistent with the knowledge base.

The cognitive logic must admit stories and thus have some notion of events occurring through time. That is, the logic adopted must have a temporal component. The requirement that it must be possible to express radial categories gives us a requirement of uncertain reasoning, whilst the added requirement of integration of inconsistent knowledge as a prerequisite of the other requirements ensures that the uncertainty that can be expressed must be second-order uncertainty. In addition, the typical devices of describing a more general event in terms of a more or less specific one (so-called hyponymy/hypernymy) and allowing generalization/specialization into the desired form requires that the logic admits abduction and induction as inference rules under uncertainty. The prolific use of metaphor in human conceptualization further adds the requirement that the logic be capable of expressing semi-structured mappings between terms, again under uncertainty.

Several candidate logics have been considered in the past year of this project. Firstly, connectionist schemes, such as self-organizing maps (Kohonen 2001) and fuzzy evidential logic (Sun 1992) were considered, but rejected on the basis that they rarely admit higher-order uncertainty such as required here. Many do not even admit first-order uncertainty in classification, producing a Boolean response as output from an uncertain process. This need for higher-order uncertainty also rules out many classes of possibilistic logics, such as classical fuzzy logic (Straccia 2005). Currently, the most promising family of logics are the interval logics (Rasmussen 2001), especially when extended with a probabilistic semantics (Gillet et al. 2007; Nguyen et al. 2001), and the non-axiomatic logics of Wang (2006). It is along these lines that current research is focusing.

4 The Interpretation Process

The act of interpretation of a set of cognitively expressed requirements is seen as the top level of a three-tier model called the RSA model. Figure 1 shows the basic form of the RSA model.

Each tier represents a stage in the life cycle of the system. The requirements tier contains the customer's requirements expressed in the form of a cognitive logic. The result of processing is a set of elementary stories, which represent the semantics of the system's provided services in the services tier. Composition is then used to produce a linear action plan in the actions tier, which may be executed. Significantly, all uncertainty is contained within the requirements tier. The

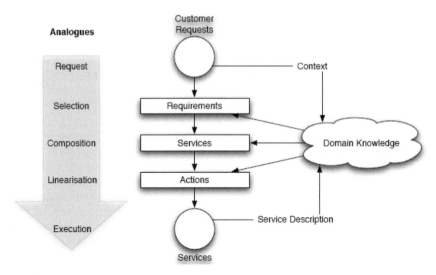

Fig. 1. The RSA model of requirements interpretation

services, which are selected by the reasoning at this level are crisp and therefore have a standard composition, linearization, and execution semantics. This will enable easy integration of the cognitive level with existing web services frameworks and methodologies for the remaining two tiers.

The role of the RSA model is to provide a conceptual framework within which uncertain reasoning about requirements specifications may sit. It is a contention of this research that any practical system for requirements interpretation and integration under uncertainty will have to specify a similar model as to how the uncertain and crisp processes interact.

Throughout there has been an unstated assumption that natural language engineering techniques would be used to turn the customer's prose into a description in an appropriate logic, but little has been said for reasons of exposition since the parsing technique to be used depends greatly upon the model that is adopted. Since our reasoning process is intended to work upon cognitive descriptions, the parser itself should produce such descriptions. The current position of this research is to adopt a frame-representation parser such as that described by Giuglea and Moschitti (2006), which is designed to produce cognitive semantic descriptions. This parser could also be used to turn prose descriptions of the semantics of the web services into a cognitive representation suitable for use in the integration process.

5 Further Research

The adoption of a cognitive approach – that requirements are best modeled using the tools of cognitive science – provides significant constraints upon the reasoning system used to interpret and integrate the provided requirements specifications. The current direction of research is looking at what impact these constraints have upon the semantics of the reasoner and attempting to produce a formal description of the logic's semantics. It is intended to implement the experimental reasoner in terms of some constraint handling system, although this is not the most efficient way, for the purposes of exposition and exploration. It is anticipated that a production system would use a hand-tuned reasoning algorithm.

Although there have been many attempts at integrating functional and non-functional requirements in both automated and manual fashions, it is felt that the approach here is unique in viewing the source of uncertainty as being the cognitive models which humans use to conceive of and express their needs. It is believed that by adopting a cognitive approach it will be possible to cleanly integrate competing requirements to produce a bespoke customer solution.

References

Bansal, S. and Vidal, J. (2003) Matchmaking of Web-Services Based on the DAML-S Service Model. In: *Proceedings of the AAMAS Workshop on Web Services and Agent Based Engineering.*

Broy, M., Meisinger, M. and Krüger, I. (2007) A Formal Model of Services. ACM Transactions on Software Engineering and Methodology, 16(1).

Ebert, C. (1997) Dealing With Non-Functional Requirements in Large Software Systems. Annals of Software Engineering, 3, 367–395.

Englmeier, K., Pereira, J. and Mothe, J. (2006) Choreography of Web-Services Based On Natural Language Storybooks. In: *Proceedings of the 8th International Conference on Electronic Commerce: The New E-commerce: Innovations for Conquering Current Barriers, Obstacles and Limitations to Conducting Successful Business on the Internet.*

Gillet, P., Scherl, R. and Shafer, G. (2007) A Probabilistic Logic Based on the Acceptability of Gambles. International Journal of Approximate Reasoning, 44, 281–300.

Giuglea, A.-M. and Moschitti, A. (2006) Semantic Role Labelling Via FrameNet, VerbNet and PropBank. In: *Proceedings of the 21st International Conference on Computational Linguistics and the 44th Annual Meeting of the ACL*, pp. 929–936.

Hayzelden, A. and Bigham, J. (1999) Agent Technology in Communications Systems: An Overview. Knowledge Engineering Review Journal, 14(3), 1–35.

Kohonen, T. (2001) *Self Organizing Maps*, 3rd ed. Springer, Berlin.

Lakoff, G. (1987) *Women, Fire and Dangerous Things: What Categories Reveal About the Human Mind.* University of Chicago Press, Chicago, IL.

Lakoff, G. and Johnson, M. (1981) *Metaphors We Live By.* University of Chicago Press, Chicago, IL.

Nguyen, H., Kreinovich, V. and Longpre, L. (2001) Second-order Uncertainty as a Bridge Between Probabilistic and Fuzzy Approaches. In: *Proceedings of the 2nd Conference of the European Society for Fuzzy Logic and Technology EUSFLAT'01*, England, pp. 410–413.

Rasmussen, T. (2001) Labelled Natural Deduction for Interval Logics. In: *CSL'01*, 2142 of LNCS. Springer, Berlin, pp. 308–323.

Rosch, E. (1973) Natural Categories. Cognitive Psychology, 4, 328–350.

Rosch, E. (1975) Cognitive Representation of Semantic Categories. Journal of Experimental Psychology, 104, 573–605.

Sheshagiri, M., des Jardins, M. and Finin, T. (2003) A Planner for Composing Services Described in DAML-S. In: *Proceedings of the AAMAS Workshop on Web Services and Agent Based Engineering*.

Simonov, M., Gangemi, A. and Soroldoni, M. (2004) Ontology-Driven Natural Language Access to Legacy and Web Services in the Insurance Domain. In: *BIS 2004: Proceedings of the 7th Business Information Systems Conference*.

Sommerville, I. (2001) *Software Engineering*, 6th ed. Addison-Wesley, Reading, MA.

Straccia, U. (2005) A Fuzzy Description Logic for the Semantic Web. In: Sanchez, E., ed., *Capturing Intelligence: Fuzzy Logic and the Semantic Web*. Elsevier, Amsterdam.

Sun, R. (1992) Fuzzy Evidential Logic: A Model of Causality for Common-sense Reasoning. In: *Proceedings of the Fourteenth Annual Conference of the Cognitive Science Society*.

Turner, M. (1996) *The Literary Mind: The Origins of Thought and Language*. Oxford University Press, Oxford.

Wang, P. (2006) Rigid Flexibility: The Logic of Intelligence. Springer, Berlin.

Semantic Service Description Framework for Addressing Imprecise Service Requirements

Xiaofeng Du, William Song and Malcolm Munro

University of Durham, Computer Science Department, UK, {xiaofeng.du, w.w.song, macolm.munro}@durham.ac.uk

Abstract   For the last decade, the study on semantic Web Services has become an important research topic in the fields of the Service-Oriented Architecture (SOA) and Grid computing. The key objective of semantic Web Services is to achieve automatic Web Service discovery, invocation and composition. There are several existing works that have proposed some semantic description frameworks such as OWL-S, WSDL-S and WSMO. However, these works are only focusing on ontology-based data-type semantics of the service capabilities and have not considered making use of contextual information about Web Services, which we believe more effective and natural for describing Web Services. Based on the existing work, the requirements have to be precise to locate services, which is difficult in most of the cases because if a service requester is not an expert in the required service's domain, it is impractical to provide a precise requirement. To address these problems, a context-based semantic service description framework is proposed in this chapter. This framework focuses on not only the capabilities of Web Services, but also the usage context information of Web Services so that the service requester can locate services by specifying how they want to use them rather than the type and interface of the services when they are not sure about it. We combine the conceptual graphs (CGs) and non-monotonic logic technologies into the framework for addressing the imprecise requirement issue.

1 Introduction

For the last decade, the study on semantic Web Services has become an important research topic in the fields of the Service-Oriented Architecture (SOA) (Huhns & Singh, 2005) and Grid computing (Foster et al., 2001). Web Services as a new paradigm of distributed system is used to solve the existing problems in the traditional distributed systems, such as platform-dependent, programming language-specific and security risks on opening extra communication ports on the firewalls. However, people have found out that Web Services can achieve much more than just solving the existing problems in the distributed systems. The platform and

C. Barry et al. (eds.), *Information Systems Development: Challenges in Practice, Theory, and Education, Vol.2*, doi: 10.1007/978-0-387-78578-3_35,
© Springer Science+Business Media, LLC 2009

programming language-independent and loosely coupled features enable Web Services to be able to be bound and invoked on demand. Based on these features a software application can be constructed in a very flexible and dynamic way. This is the fundamental idea of SOA. In order to achieve automatic or semi-automatic service discovery, invocation and composition, the semantic web technologies have been taken into account in the service description and service registry. The reason for involving semantics is that the current syntactical-based WSDL (Christensen et al., 2001) service description and keyword match-based UDDI (UDDI, 2002) service registry and search engine are not suitable for achieving automation. The Semantic Web Services seems to be the most promising way towards achieving automatic or semi-automatic service discovery, invocation and composition.

Enormous research efforts on Semantic Web Services have been spent on semantic services description and discovery (Ludwig & Reyhani, 2005; Paolucci et al., 2003; Song & Li, 2005) and semantic composition of services (Agarwal et al., 2005; Du et al., 2006). There are several existing works that have proposed semantic service description frameworks, such as OWL-S (Martin et al., 2004), WSDL-S (Akkiraju et al., 2005) and WSMO (Roman et al., 2005), to semantically describe Web Services. Puder et al. (1995) propose a new service-type notation based on conceptual graphs (CGs). Song (2006) proposes a business process and integration model for the purpose of guidance of service composition and service flow formation, and an extended architecture for Web Services. The main idea of the existing work is to build a semantic layer either on the top of WSDL or integrated into WSDL to semantically describe the capabilities of Web Services so that a software agent can reason about what a Web Service's capabilities are and how to interact with it. However, there are still some problems exist in current semantic service description and search:

- Insufficient usage context information: The current works are focusing on ontology-based data-type semantics and do not sufficiently address how a service is fitted into its usage context, i.e. a service's applicability/usability, which we believe is more effective and natural for describing Web Services because a service requester cares more about how a service can be used than the type of the service.
- Precise requirements required to locate services: In order to locate the required services, the current work requires precise service requirements which are difficult to be specified at the preliminary stage of the service discovery.
- Insufficient information about interrelationship among service: The current work has not addressed the interrelationships among services sufficiently, which makes the service discovery in an isolated manner.

In order to address the remaining issues discussed earlier, we proposed a Context-based Semantic Description Framework (CbSDF) for service description. Apart from the capabilities, this framework also takes into consideration the usage context information about Web Services. The contexts we focus on here are the information that can help to understand the usage of a service and the relationships with other services. The framework contains four parts: the definitions of atomic service and composite service, a set of service conceptual graphs, a Semantic

Service Description Model (SSDM) and a set of non-monotonic rules (Antoniou et al., 2004). By having clear definitions of atomic and composite services, we can identify the kind of information that is relevant to describing a service, which should be addressed in the Semantic Service Description Model. The service conceptual graphs give an overall and abstract description of the relationships between services and their related concepts. They are represented using conceptual graphs (Sowa, 1984). The non-monotonic rules are used to describe the preconditions and effects of services and the conditions for service composition. These rules are important in validating service discovery results and correctly constructing composite services. There are two kinds of rules: general rules and domain-specific rules. The non-monotonic rules are represented using Defeasible Logic (Nute, 1994).

Based on our framework, we develop a two-step service discovery mechanism. When a service requester proposes a service requirement, it is first converted into conceptual graph and then matched with the service conceptual graphs to locate the relevant services. In the second step, based on the service requirement, the Semantic Service Description Model and the non-monotonic rules, the results from the first step are validated and composite service is constructed if there is any possibility. Then, the result services are ranked according to their similarity degree to the requester's demands and returned to the service requester.

The rest of this chapter is organized as follows. In Section 2, we give a detailed discussion on the Context-based Semantic Description Framework. Then, we discuss the two-step service discovery mechanism in Section 3. Finally, the summary of the chapter and conclusion are given in Section 4.

2 The Context-Based Semantic Description Framework

The proposed Context-based Semantic Description Framework (CbSDF) follows the belief that the identification of meaning of a concept mainly stems from its contexts (Guha et al., 2004), i.e. its relationships to other concepts. To fully express the meaning of a concept, simply using its dictionary definition is not sufficient. For example, in a dictionary a hammer is defined as 'a hand tool with a heavy rigid head and a handle; used to deliver an impulsive force by striking' (WordNet Search – 3.0, http://wordnet.princeton.edu/perl/webwn). If a person has never seen a hammer, he/she will not get much impression on what a hammer is from the definition because that definition is a type definition (Sowa, 1984), i.e. the vertical relationships between the concept and its supertype/subtype concepts, which does not describe how the hammer can be used, i.e. the horizontal relationships between the concept and other types of concepts. If we say 'a hammer is a tool that can strike a nail into wood', then the person will know at least one way of hammer's usage by understanding the relationships among 'tool', 'nail', and 'wood', although he/she will know more ways to use a hammer after he/she really understands what a hammer is. Following this idea we propose the CbSDF that defines and describes services in both vertical and horizontal relational context in order to improve the efficiency and effectiveness of service discovery and composition. The context-based semantics is addressed by the components in the framework, such as the service conceptual graphs, the Semantic Service Description Model (SSDM) and the non-monotonic rules. Sections 2.2–2.4 explain each of them in detail.

2.1 Definitions of Atomic Service and Composite Service

Based on the model introduced by OWL-S (Martin et al., 2004), we give the definitions for both atomic and composite services, which are important concepts for later discussion. By these definitions we can clearly identify what should be addressed in describing a service.

Definition 1: An atomic service is a 7-tuple, denoted as:
$$AS =< N, \; Ipt, \; Opt, \; P, \; E, \; T, \; B >$$
where

N: The name of the service

$Ipt = \{Ipt_1, Ipt_2, ..., Ipt_n\}$: A set of inputs

$Opt = \{Opt_1, Opt_2, ..., Opt_n\}$: A set of outputs

$P = \{P_1, P_2, ..., P_n\}$: A set of preconditions to trigger the service execution

$E = \{E_1, E_2, ..., E_n\}$: A set of effects after the service execution

T: The type of the service

B: The binding information for interacting with the service

Definition 2: A composite service is a 10-tuple, denoted as:
$$CS =< N, Ipt, Opt, P, E, T, AS, DS, CtrlS, B >$$
where

N: The name of the service

$Ipt = \{Ipt_1, Ipt_2, ..., Ipt_n\}$: A set of inputs.

$Opt = \{Opt_1, Opt_2, ..., Opt_n\}$: A set of outputs.

$P = \{P_1, P_2, ..., P_n\}$: A set of preconditions to trigger the service execution.

$E = \{E_1, E_2, ..., E_n\}$: A set of effects after the service execution.

T: The type of the service.

$AS = \{AS_1, AS_2, ..., AS_n\}$: A set of atomic services used for composing the service.

$DS = \{(o, i) \mid o \in AS.O \wedge i \in AS.I\}$: The data flow of the service, which is a set of arcs, where each arc connects one atomic service's output to the other atomic service's input. $AS.I$ and $AS.O$ are the sets of inputs and outputs of AS.

$CtrlS =< stmt, cdt >$: The control structure of the service, where $stmt$ is a set of control statements and cdt is a set of conditions.

B: The binding information for interacting with the service.

2.2 Service Conceptual Graphs

In order to capture the semantics of imprecise service requirements, we create a set of service conceptual graphs. A service conceptual graph is a conceptual graph (Sowa, 1984) that is used to represent the conceptual relationships between a service and its relevant concepts or the relationships among services. The reason we choose conceptual graph is that it can define a concept not only through a type definition, but also through a set of schemata of the concept. A type definition is so-called genus and differentia (Sowa, 1984). It tries to define a new type through the genus types (primitive types) and the differentia between the new type and the genus types. '*A schema represents a perspective on one way that a concept may be used* (Sowa, 1984).' Through a set of schemata, the semantics of a concept can be defined. The way to use schemata to define a concept is how a service should be described because only placing the services into ontologies is not sufficient. When users search for services, they pay more attention to how the services can be used and whether the usage of the services can be applied into their own scenarios rather than the type of the services. Also more often than not, the service requester cannot provide complete information about required services, so the service description should be able to tolerate the impreciseness of service requirements. Therefore, we create a set of service conceptual graphs, i.e. a set of schemata of services, which are used to describe the usage of services in order to match with service requester's scenario and locate relevant services based on both precise and imprecise requirements though full or partial conceptual graph match and conceptual graph supported reasoning and inference. Before discussing the service conceptual graphs in detail, we first introduce some basic concepts of conceptual graph.

A conceptual graph (CG) is a finite, connected, bipartite graph with nodes of one type called concepts and nodes of the other type called conceptual relations (Sowa, 1976). *Concepts* represent entities, actions and attributes. The label of a concept node consists of two fields separated by a colon [*type: referent*]. *Type* represents the class of a concept. *Referent* represents an instance of the class. The functions *type()* and *referent()* can be used to get a concept's type and referent. If the value of *referent(c)* is an individual marker (an identification of an instance, such as name or id), e.g. [Cat: Tom], then the concept *c* is an *individual concept*. If the value of *referent(c)* is '*', e.g. [Cat: *], then the concept *c* is a *generic concept*. A concept only with type label is equivalent to a generic concept, i.e. [Cat] = [Cat:*]. *Conceptual relations* represent the relationships between concept nodes. *type(r)* is used to get the type of the relation *r*.

Suppose that *u* and *v* are two CGs. *u* is called a specialization of *v* (or *v* is called a generalization of *u*), denoted as $u \leq v$, if *u* is canonically derivable (derived by applying a sequence of generalization rules [Sowa, 1984]) from *v*. In this case, there must exist a mapping $\pi: v \rightarrow u$, where $\pi_u v$ is a subgraph of u called a *projection* of v in u. The projection operator π has the following properties:

- For each concept c in v, $\pi_u c$ is a concept in $\pi_u v$ such that $type(\pi_u c) \leq type(c)$, '$\leq$' here represents the subtype relationship between concepts. If c is an individual concept, then $referent(\pi_u c) = referent(c)$.
- For each relation r in v, $\pi_u r$ is a conceptual relation in $\pi_u v$ such that $type(\pi_u r) = type(r)$. If the ith arc of r is linked to a concept c in v then the ith arc of $\pi_u r$ must be linked to $\pi_u c$ in $\pi_u v$.

Definition 3: A service conceptual graph G_s is a CG, denoted as:
$$G_s = <C, R, E>$$
where

  C: A set of concept nodes that are relevant to the described service, such as input, output, owner and location
  R: A set of relation nodes that represent the relations among the concept nodes
  E: A set of directed edges
  An example G_s *(address_lookup)* for describing an address lookup service is illustrated in Fig.1.,
  where

  C: {[Input: postcode], [Output: address], [Operator: RoyalMail], [Location: UK]}
  R: {(AGNT), (REQ), (GEN)}

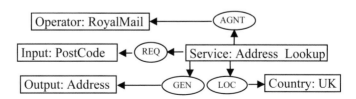

Fig. 1. An example of service conceptual graph

This example illustrates how an address lookup service or a service request can be described if the example conceptual graph is generated from a service requirement.

Here, we make a simple analysis of the relationship between the service conceptual graphs and the CGs generated from service requirements. Assume that we have a set of atomic services $S = \{S_1, S_2, ..., S_n\}$ and each service $S_i \in S$ is described by a service conceptual graph $G_s(S_i)$. Let R be a set of user's service requirements and each requirement R_i can be described by a CG $g(R_i)$. Then, we have the following definitions:

Definition 4: A (service) requirement R_i is *satisfiable* if there exists at least one service S_i that satisfy:

$$\exists S_i(S_i \in S \mid G_s(S_i) \le g(R_i))$$

In other word, if there exists a $G_s(S_i)$ that is identical to or a specialization of a requirement R_i's $g(R_i)$, then its corresponding service S_i is a candidate service that could satisfy the requirement R_i, otherwise the service is not a candidate.

Definition 5: If the service requirement R_i is *not satisfiable* we assume that it can be satisfied by a composite service CS_i which is a composition of the existing atomic services in S. A $G_s(CS_i)$ can be generated by joining the participated atomic services' service conceptual graphs. The $G_s(CS_i)$ is identical to or a specialization of $g(R_i)$.

$$S_i, S_j, ..., S_m \in S \mid (G_s(CS_i) = G_s(S_i) \oplus G_s(S_j) \oplus ... \oplus G_s(S_m)) \le g(R_i)$$

The $G_s(CS_i)$ can help to validate the composite services generated in later service discovery stage. The join operation used here for joining CGs is different from the join operation in the graph theory. Assume that we have two CGs, v and u, then the join operation can be described as: '*if a concept c in u is identical to a concept d in v, then let w be the graph obtained by deleting d and linking to c all arcs of conceptual relations that has been linked to d*' (Sowa, 1984) and at the same time, the duplicated conceptual relations have to be removed. '*Two conceptual relations of the same type are duplicates if for each i, the ith arc of one is linked to the same concept as the ith arc of the other*' (Sowa, 1984). We use symbol '$\oplus$' to denote the join operation here.

Each of the participated CG in $G_s(CS_i)$ must have a projection π in $g(R_i)$,

$$\pi_i : G_s(S_i) \to g(R_i) \wedge \pi_j : G_s(S_j) \to g(R_i) \wedge ... \pi_m : G_s(S_m) \to g(R_i)$$

The services selected by matching requirements with service conceptual graphs may not be the exact required services. However, it guarantees that only the services that are relevant to the requirements can be located for further validation and service composition.

2.3 Semantic Service Description Model

More often than not, a service requirement cannot be satisfied by a single service, but a composition of several services. How to correctly construct composite services is a major task in service discovery. In order to improve the efficiency and correctness of composite services and accuracy of the service discovery result, based on the definitions of atomic and composite services discussed previously, we propose the Semantic Service Description Model (SSDM).

Definition 6: The SSDM is a 7-tuple, denoted as:

$$SSDM =< IO, PE, M, O, S, R, B >$$

where

IO: The inputs and outputs of the service.

PE: A set of rules that describe the preconditions and effects of the service.

M: A set of metadata that describe the non-functional attributers of the service, such as time of execution, cost, rating and location.

O: A service ontology that defines the type of the service.

S: The internal structure of the service, which is a set of atomic services that used to construct the service. If the service is an atomic service, then the *S* is an empty set.

R: A set of resources that the service will consume when the service is executed, such as bandwidth, memory allocation and CPU usage.

B: The service-binding information for interacting with the service.

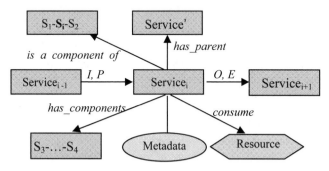

Fig. 2. A graphical illustration of SSDM

From the definition we can see that the semantics and the capabilities are addressed through components *IO*, *M* and *R*, and the structure of the service and how the service can interact with other services are addressed through components *PE* and *S*. A graphical illustration of SSDM is shown in Fig. 2. The notations used in Fig. 2 are:

1. S_i = Service$_i$
2. Service' can be either the parent or ancestor of Service$_i$
3. S_1, S_2, S_3 and S_4 are any services
4. *I, P* are the inputs and precondition, and *O, E* are the outputs and effects

2.4 Non-monotonic Rules

In order to validate the service discovery result and correctly construct composite services, and also successfully trigger the service execution, we propose a set of non-monotonic rules that are represented using Defeasible Logic (Nute, 1994). Defeasible Logic belongs to a class of non-monotonic approaches and is first developed by Nute (1987). A *defeasible theory DT* is a triple:

$$DT = (F, R, >)$$

where

        F: A set of facts

        R: A finite set of rules

>: A superiority relation on R

There are three kinds of rules:

Strict rules: the rules that are always true, denoted by $A \rightarrow q$, which reads as 'if A, then definitely q.'

Defeasible rules: the rules that can be defeated by contrary evidence, denoted by $A \Rightarrow q$, which reads as 'if A, then typically q.'

Defeaters: the rules that are used to defeat some defeasible rules, but not for drawing conclusions, denoted by $A \mapsto q$, which reads as 'if A, then may not be q.'

The superiority relation '>' defines when several rules have contrary conclusions, which one has the higher priority to be considered, e.g. $r_1 > r_2$.

The advantages of Defeasible Logic are computational efficiency and built-in superiority handling mechanism (Brewka, 2001), which are the crucial features when the number of Web Services is large. There are two categories of rules in our framework: the general rules and the domain-specific rules. The followings are some examples of the rules.

- **General rules examples**

    The general rules are normally used to construct and validate composite services and they are applicable to all the services, for example,

    r_1: If a service's precondition is satisfied, then normally it can be executed.

    $$satisfy(S.preCon) \Rightarrow executable(S)$$

    r_2: If a service is not available, then definitely it cannot be executed.

    $$\neg available\ (S) \rightarrow \neg executable(S)$$

    r_3: If two services are composed through input and output data flow, then normally the data types of the input and output are compatible, i.e. one is the same or subtype of the other.

    $$composable\ (S_1, S_2) \Rightarrow type(S_1.Opt) \le type(S_2.Ipt)$$

    The r_2 has higher priority than r_1.

    $$r_2 > r_1$$

- **Domain-specific rules examples**

    The domain-specific rules are normally used to describe the preconditions and effects of services and can only be applied to a specific domain. Here, we use the address lookup service as an example.

    r_1: If the service is supplied with a valid postcode, then normally the correct result will be returned.

    $$valid\ (postcode) \Rightarrow result(S)$$

    r_2: If the requested address is in UK, then this service is definitely applicable.

    $$location\ (UK) \rightarrow applicable(S)$$

Based on these rules, we can derive some conclusions, which can help us to validate the service discovery result. The result validation is performed from two aspects:

- Triggerable validation: A service that can satisfy the service requirement may still be an invalid service if the service's precondition cannot be satisfied.
- Composable validation: Two or more services may be syntactically composable to construct a composite service. However, the composite service may be logically incorrect.

3 A Two-Step Service Discovery Mechanism

Based on the CbSDF, we propose a two-step service discovery mechanism. The first step is the preliminary service discovery step using CG matching technique. At this step, the service requirements are converted into CGs and match with the service conceptual graphs to locate relevant services. The requirements do not have to be precise because an imprecise requirement still can locate relevant services by partial CG matching, CG reasoning and inference. The second step, validation and ranking step, is to refine the results from the first step based on the service requirements, the SSDM, and the non-monotonic rules. After this step the discovered services are ranked according to their similarity degree to the service requester's demands and returned to the requester.

3.1 CG Similarity Calculation

After converting a service requirement into a CG, we turn the search in the service conceptual graphs for matches to the requirement into the computation of similarity of CGs. We calculate the similarity between CGs using the method proposed by Montes-y-Gómez et al. (2001). According to them the similarity Sim between two CGs, G_1 and G_2, contains a concept similarity S_c and a relation similarity S_r. The concept similarity S_c is calculated using the Dice coefficient (Frakes & Baeza-Yates, 1992) similar expression:

$$S_c = 2\left(\sum_{c \in \bigcup O}(weight(c) \times \beta(\pi_{G_1}c, \pi_{G_2}c))\right)\bigg/\left(\sum_{c \in G_1}weight(c) + \sum_{c \in G_2}weight(c)\right)$$

where, $\bigcup O$ is the union of all of the common generalization graphs of G_1 and G_2; O is a set of the common overlaps graphs of G_1 and G_2, $weight(c)$ is the importance factor of the concept type c. We take $weight(c) = 1$ as we assume that all the concept types are of the same importance.

The $\beta(\pi_{G_1}c, \pi_{G_2}c)$ function is defined as follows to calculate the semantic similarity between the two concepts:

$$\beta(\pi_{G_i}c, \pi_{G_j}c) = \begin{cases} 1 & \text{if } type(\pi_{G_i}c) = type(\pi_{G_j}c) \text{ and } referent(\pi_{G_i}c) = referent(\pi_{G_j}c) \\ depth/(depth+1) & \text{if } type(\pi_{G_i}c) = type(\pi_{G_j}c) \text{ and } referent(\pi_{G_i}c) \neq referent(\pi_{G_j}c) \\ 2d_c/(d_{\pi_{G_i}c} + d_{\pi_{G_j}c}) & \text{if } type(\pi_{G_i}c) \neq type(\pi_{G_j}c) \end{cases}$$

The first condition indicates that the two concepts are exactly the same. The second condition indicates that the two concepts have the same type but refer to different instances. The *depth* represents the number of levels in the ontology. The third condition indicates that the two concepts have different types. The d_c represents the distance from the least common supertype of $\pi_{G_1}c$ and $\pi_{G_2}c$ to the root of the ontology; $d_{\pi_{G_i}c}$ represents the distance from concept $\pi_{G_i}c$ to the root of the ontology.

The relation similarity S_r is calculated using the following expression:

$$S_r = \frac{2m(G_c)}{m_{G_c}(G_1) + m_{G_c}(G_2)}$$

where, $m(G_c)$ is the number of the relation nodes in the common overlaps of G_1 and G_2; $m_{Gc}(G_i)$ is the number of the relation nodes of the common overlaps in G_i and the overlaps' adjacent relation nodes.

The overall similarity expression is shown below:

$$Sim = S_c \times (a + (1-a) \times S_r)$$

where, a is a value between 0 and 1 representing the impact factor of S_r. The impact factor can make sure that the overall similarity Sim will not be 0 unless both S_c and S_r are 0.

3.2 Semantic Similarity Ranking

In the second step of the service discovery, the located services from the first step are first validated using the non-monotonic rules. Then, according to the service requirement and the SSDM, the similarities between the services and the requirement are calculated. We develop a semantic similarity measurement method based on the SSDM. The measurement method is defined as:

$$sim(R, S) = \frac{\sum_{\forall a \in \lambda} \omega \times dist(\alpha(R), \alpha(S))}{max(\lambda(R), \lambda(S))}$$

where λ: A set of all the semantic characteristic functions
$\lambda()$: A function that returns the number of semantic characteristics

$\alpha()$: An element of λ that returns a semantic characteristic, which can be, e.g. an element of the metadata in the SSDM or the inputs and outputs of a service

$dist()$: A function that calculate the semantic distance between two semantic characteristics and its returned value is between 0 and 1

ω: A weight factor that specifies how important a semantic characteristic is to a service requester and its value is between 0 and 1

$max()$: A function returns the greater of its two arguments values

R and S: The service requirement and a candidate service

Through this method, we can get the similarities between the service requirement and the result services, and rank the result services according to their similarity degree to the requester's demands.

4 Conclusion

The Semantic Web Services has become an important research topic in the fields of SOA and Grid computing. How to semantically describe Web Services in order to achieve automatic service discovery, invocation and composition is a big issue. In this chapter, we proposed a Context-based Semantic Description Framework (CbSDF) for service description and a two-step service discovery mechanism for service search. The work proposed in this chapter aims to provide a service description framework and a search mechanism that can tolerate imprecise specified service requirements. The key technologies used to capture the semantics from imprecise requirements and validate the service discovery results are the CG and the non-monotonic logic, i.e. Defeasible Logic.

However, the attempt has been made to integrate CG and non-monotonic logic into service description and discovery in this chapter is only at a preliminary stage. We believe that if we dive into these two areas deeply, we can benefit more in service description, discovery and composition.

References

Agarwal, S., Handschuh, S., & Staab, S. (2005) Annotation, Composition and Invocation of Semantic Web Services, Journal of Web Semantics, 2(1).

Akkiraju, R., Farrell, J., Miller, J., Nagarajan, M., Schmidt, M., Sheth, A., & Verma, K. (2005) Web Service Semantics – WSDL-S, A joint UGA-IBM Tchnical Note, version 1.2, April 18, 2005, http://lsdis.cs.uga.edu/projects/METEOR-S/WSDL-S

Antoniou, G., Bikakis, A., & Wagner, G. (2004) A System for Nonmonotonic Rules on the Web, Rules and Rule Mark-up Languages for the Semantic Web, LNCS Vol. 3323, pp. 23–36, Springer, Berlin/Heidelberg.

Brewka, G. (2001) On the Relationship between Defeasible Logic and Well-Founded Semantics, Proceedings of the 6th International Conference on Logic Programming and Nonmonotonic Reasoning, Vienna Austria, September 2001, LNCS 2173, pp. 121–132.

Christensen, E., Curbera, F., Meredith, G., & Weerawarana, S. (2001) Web Services Description Language (WSDL) 1.1, http://www.w3.org/TR/wsdl

Du, X., Song, W., & Munro, M. (2006) Using Common Process Patterns for Semantic Web Services Composition, to appear in Proc. of 15th International Conference on Information System Development (ISD2006), Budapest, Hungary, August 31–September 2, 2006

Foster, I., Kesselman, C., & Tuecke, S. (2001) The Anatomy of the Grid: Enabling Scalable Virtual Organizations, International Journal of Supercomputer Applications, 15(3).

Frakes, W.B. & Baeza-Yates, R. (1992) Information Retrieval: Data Structures & Algorithms, Prentice-Hall, Englewood Cliffs, NJ.

Guha, R., McCool, R., & Fikes, R. (2004) Contexts for the Semantic Web. In Proceedings of the ISWC'04, Hiroshima, Japan, November 2004, Lecture Notes in Computer Science, Vol. 3298, pp. 32–46, Springer.

Huhns, M.N. & Singh, M.P. (2005) Service Oriented Computing: key concepts and principles, IEEE Intelligent System, January–February 2005, pp. 75–81.

Ludwig, S. & Reyhani, S. (2005) Semantic Approach to Service Discovery in a Grid Environment, Journal of Web Semantics, 3(4).

Martin, D., Burstein, M., Hobbs, J., Lassila, O., McDermott, D., McIlraith, S., Narayanan, S., Paolucci, M., Parsia, B., Payne, T., Sirin, E., Srinivasan, N., & Sycara, K. (2004) OWL-S: Semantic Mark-up for Web Services, http://www.daml.org/services/owl-s/1.0/owl-s.html

Montes-y-Gómez, M., Gelbukh, A., López-López, A., & Baeza-Yates, R. (2001) Flexible Comparison of Conceptual Graphs, Proceeding of 12th International Conference and Workshop on Database and Expert Systems Applications. LNCS 2113, Springer, 2001, pp. 102–111.

Nute, D. (1994) Defeasible logic, in Handbook of logic in artificial intelligence and logic programming (vol. 3): Non-monotonic Reasoning and Uncertain Reasoning, Oxford University Press, Oxford.

Nute, D. (1987) Defeasible Reasoning, 20th International Conference on Systems Science, Hawaii, IEEE Press, pp. 470–477.

Paolucci, M., Sycara, K., & Kawamuwa, T. (2003) Delivering Semantic Web Services, in Proceedings of WWW2003, pp. 829–836, May 20–24, 2003, Budapest, Hungary.

Puder, A., Markwitz, S., Gudermann, F., & Geihs, K. (1995) AI-based Trading in Open Distributed Environments, In: Proc. IFIP International Conference on Open Distributed Processing, Brisbane/Australia.

Roman, D., Keller, U., Lausen, H., Bruijn, J., Lara, R., Stollberg, M., Polleres, A., Feier, C., Bussler, C., & Fensel, D. (2005) Web Service Modelling Ontology (WSMO), WSMO Final Draft, April 13, 2005, http://www.w3.org/Submission/WSMO/

Song, W. (2006) A Semantic Modelling Approach to Automatic Services Analysis and Composition, in proceeding of the IASTED International Conference on Web Technologies, Applications, and Services (WTAS), Calgary, Canada, July 17–19, 2006.

Song, W. & Li, X. (2005) A Conceptual Modeling Approach to Virtual Organizations in the Grid to appear in Proceedings of GCC2005 (eds. Zhuge and Fox), Springer LNCS 3795, pp. 382–393.

Sowa, J.F. (1976) Conceptual Graphs for a Data Base Interface, IBM Journal of Research and Development, 20(4), 336–357.

Sowa, J.F. (1984) Conceptual Structures: Information Processing in Mind and Machine, Addison-Wesley, Canada.

UDDI 3.0 Specification (2002), http://uddi.org/pubs/uddi-v3.00-published-20020719.htm

Automatic Generation of Executable Code from Software Architecture Models

Aristos Stavrou and George A. Papadopoulos

Department of Computer Science, University of Cyprus, {cs98sa2,george}@cs.ucy.ac.cy

Abstract   Our effort is focused on bridging the gap between software design and implementation of component-based systems using software architectures at the modeling/design level and the coordination paradigm at the implementation level. We base our work on the clear support of both software architectures and event-driven coordination models for Component-Based Software Engineering and the similarities we have identified between the fundamental concepts of software architectures and the event-driven coordination model. Exploiting the improvements realized by the latest version of UML towards the support of software architecture descriptions, we present a methodology for automating the transition from software architecture design of component-based systems described in UML 2.0 to coordination code. The presented methodology is further enhanced with a code generation tool that fully automates the production of the complete code implementing the coordination–communication part of software systems modeled with UML 2.0.

1 Introduction

Our effort is focused on bridging the gap between software design and implementation of component-based systems using software architectures at the modeling/design level and the coordination paradigm at the implementation level. Our choice was based on the clear support of both software architectures and event-driven coordination models for Component-Based Software Engineering and the similarities we have identified between the fundamental concepts of software architectures and the event-driven coordination model. In Papadopoulos et al. (2006) we have presented a methodology for mapping ACME (Garlan et al. 2000), a generic language for describing software architectures, down to event-driven coordination code in the Manifold (Arbab et al. 1993; Papadopoulos and Arbab 2001) language. The reason for using ACME was precisely in order to show the generality of our approach: since ACME embodies the core features that any state-of-the-art Architecture Description Language (ADL) would support, by mapping ACME to Manifold we effectively provide the core of an implementation route for any other ADL (Medvidovic and Taylor 2000).

C. Barry et al. (eds.), *Information Systems Development: Challenges in Practice, Theory, and Education, Vol.2*, doi: 10.1007/978-0-387-78578-3_36,
© Springer Science+Business Media, LLC 2009

Based on the results and experiences of our first work and exploiting the improvements realized by the latest version of UML towards the support of software architecture descriptions, we propose a new methodology for modeling the software architecture of a component-based system in UML 2.0 (OMG 2003) and the automatic transition of this model to event-driven coordination code in Manifold. Our latest work targets an improved support for the dynamic aspects of the software architecture exploiting the powerful tools of UML for dynamic behavior. Furthermore, we use the standards (UML2.0, XMI) and approach proposed by the new software development discipline, which promises to be the next big step in software development, similar to the move from machine language to compilers 40 years ago, namely the Model-Driven Architectures (OMG MDA Website 2006). The presented methodology is further supported by a code generation tool that fully automates the production of the complete code implementing the coordination–communication part of software systems modeled with UML 2.0.

2 From UML 2.0 Software Architectures to Coordination Code

Our methodology addresses the challenging task of automatic code generation. The task of automating the translation of a system high-level model described in a general purpose modeling language, such as UML, to executable code has nothing to do with magic, but with:

1. The methodical construction of this high-level model using the proper constructs provided by the modeling language having in mind the target programming model. This means that the modeler (in our case the software architect) should be guided on the way that he/she will use the modeling language according to the desired goal. Modeling languages such as UML are not associated with a specific methodology, but they just provide the constructs and notation to model systems of different domains. Our models must adequately describe all aspects of a system's software architecture and provide all necessary details to our code generation tool in order to produce complete and functional codes.
2. The accurate and clear mapping of these constructs to the lower-level constructs used by the target programming model.

Satisfying the first requirement, our methodology defines, at first stage, the constructs to be used to model both static and dynamic aspects of a component-based system's software architecture and then guides the software architect on how to use these constructs. The static aspects of a component-based system's architecture include the definition of the components (and subcomponents) that the system is composed of the functionality provided and required by each of them as well as the definition of all possible interactions realized between components to accomplish the tasks that the system is supposed to implement. In UML 2.0, these are adequately described by the constructs provided for architecture modeling such as components, classes, ports, interfaces and connectors. Architecture modeling in UML 2.0 is realized by component diagrams (also called architecture diagrams).

The dynamic aspects of a component-based system's architecture include the setup of the software architecture under certain execution scenarios. This includes the subset of interactions taking place between components, realized by messages or events exchanged between them. The dynamic aspects may also include the activation or deactivation of component instances (and subsequently the new setup of interactions between them) in response to changing factors of the system's execution environment such as the load of the system at a specific time. The order in which the above actions may take place in response to the dynamic behavior of the system is very important and it has to be precisely defined in our model in order to produce the corresponding coordination code. The constructs provided by UML 2.0 for scenario (or interaction) modeling can adequately describe the above actions and the specific order in which they might occur.

From diagrams provided by UML 2.0 for scenario modeling, we choose sequence diagrams as the most suitable for precise and detailed description of a system's actions and behavior. Sequence diagrams are used to define:

- Messages and events exchanged between specific component and class instances under certain scenarios
- Details of other actions that may occur in a system such as activation/deactivation of component and class instances
- Conditions under which such actions might take place
- Specific sequences in which these actions will take place

The two types of diagrams that are used in our methodology are perfectly interrelated, thanks to the new feature of UML 2.0 for structure and behavior gross integration. This means that the model elements specified in the architecture diagrams such as components, classes, connectors, and interfaces are then directly associated with the model elements included in sequence diagrams. For example, each lifeline of sequence diagrams is directly associated with a component or class defined in architecture modeling, and the messages associated with this lifeline realize the interactions that have been specified for this component or class in architecture diagrams through connectors. The "call" type messages included in sequence diagrams invoke operations defined to be provided or required by components through interfaces and ports in architecture modeling. This useful feature of UML 2.0 not only provides us with the ability for consistency checking between elements specified in different diagrams, but also makes the process of automatic translation of diagrams to programming constructs easier since we do not have to proprietary define the relationship between the model elements of the different diagrams that we will use. However, although the specific feature is provided by UML 2.0, this does not mean that it will be used by the software architects. We give general guidelines to software architects for the way that they use this feature during modeling in order to take advantage of it. Furthermore, we define constraints in the way that they will use the different constructs of diagrams.

Satisfying the second requirement mentioned earlier, our methodology defines an accurate and clear mapping of the higher-level constructs of UML 2.0 to lower-level constructs provided by our programming model. Our construct (or concept) mapping is aided by the precise and unambiguous semantic definitions of UML 2.0 (an improvement made to satisfy one of the main requirements for Model-Driven Development) and the explicit relationship realized between the constructs of UML 2.0 and Manifold, the formal representative of control-driven coordination model that will form the target programming language of our methodology. Unlike our previous methodology (Papadopoulos et al. 2006) where we had to define events, interaction ordering, and all other aspects related to the dynamic behavior of the system in the form of proprietary properties, UML 2.0 provides us with not only first-class constructs that explicitly model these aspects, but also the semantic meaning of these constructs, as this is defined in UML 2.0 superstructure (OMG 2003), is very similar (in most cases identical) to the constructs realized by control-driven coordination models and Manifold for implementing the same aspects. This explicit mapping of high-level model element to control-driven coordination elements enable us to extract specific coordination constructs from each element included in our model diagrams, rather than proprietary extracting specific programming code parts out of specific pieces of a modeling language notation.

In Sections 2.1–2.4, we present an overview of the steps defined by our methodology to create the architecture and scenario model of a component-based system in UML 2.0, as well as the general rules followed to map these models to coordination code in Manifold. Due to space limitations, a detailed description of the steps and mapping rules of our methodology cannot be included in this chapter and will appear in an extended version of it for a journal submission.

2.1 Creating the Architecture Model of a System's Architecture

Architecture modeling is realized by a number of component (or architecture) diagrams describing the static aspects of a component-based system's architecture, which include:

- Definition of all different (types of) components, subcomponents, and classes that the system is composed of
- Functionality provided and required by each of them, realized by provided and required interfaces of components and classes
- All possible interactions between components and classes realized as connections between ports of them

For the construction of architecture diagrams the UML 2.0 constructs that are used by our methodology are: *components, classes, ports, interfaces (operations, signals, attributes), and assembly/delegation connectors.*

Apart from the clear semantics given by UML 2.0 for each construct of architecture modeling, the software architect has to be guided on the way that he/she will use these constructs to create appropriate architecture diagrams that will adequately describe the required information of the system under development and enable the automatic transition of these diagrams to the target programming model which is Manifold.

Our methodology satisfies this need by defining a number of constraints on the use of the UML 2.0 architecture constructs. Some of the constraints defined by our methodology on the use of the above constructs are the following ones:

- Only one operation per interface is allowed. This helps us to clearly define the connections between ports that interfaces are attached to and internal parts that implement the functionality defined by this interface.
- Each port must be attached to either a required or a provided interface. This enables us to easily and explicitly model the relationships between the ports and the internal parts of the component.
- Both a name and a type must be defined for each attribute of an interface.

A number of general guidelines on the way that architecture diagrams will be constructed are also defined. Generally speaking, the software architect will have to follow the principles of component-based development to identify the components, subcomponents, and classes of the system, and describe the functionality provided and required by them, but the target programming model also has to be considered. The general steps for the construction of the diagrams are the following:

1. Identify the top-level components of the system architecture. Create a top-level diagram and add a special *Main* component. (This will represent the special manifold process that every system in manifold should include). Add the top-level components of the system as subcomponents of the Main component.
2. For each component identify the different operations that are provided by this component.
3. For each operation identify the different parameters that are needed to be given to the component to execute this operation and the possible values returned by this operation. Create an interface for each operation and add the specific operation with its parameters and return values.
4. Identify the possible signals sent by the component providing this operation to its environment in response to a call on this function. Add the signals to the created interface.
5. Identify possible main variables related to the operation that can be identified at this stage and may affect the setup of the architecture. For example, a variable with name "requests_rate" that counts the number of requests per minute that is used by the component to instantiate a new instance of a subcomponent or class if the rate exceeds a certain number. Add these attributes to the created interface.
6. Identify the required operations and create an interface for each of them in a similar way as above. For each required interface add a signal sent by the component requesting the call of the related operation to its parent component that coordinates it in order to create the needed setups (connections).
7. For each component add a port for each provided or required operation of the component and attach it to the corresponding required or provided interface.

8. Identify all possible connections between the subcomponents of a first-level component. Create an assembly connector for each connection between the ports that the related, provided, and required interfaces are attached to.
9. Identify all possible connections from the top-level component to its parts (subcomponents and classes). Create a delegation connector for each such connection.
10. Decompose each of the subcomponents to another diagram. Add in the new diagram the specific subcomponent as the top-level component and add all subcomponents and classes that this component is composed of. Follow the steps above to add the ports, required/provided interfaces, as well as the connections.

2.2 Mapping an Architecture Model to Equivalent Manifold Constructs

The translation of the architecture model constructs will give us the manifold coordinator (manager) and atomic (worker) processes that the system will be composed of, the input and output ports of each process, as well as the possible events that are raised by each process to its environment. Furthermore, all possible streams created between ports of system processes will be extracted from the architecture model. Finally, some local variables used by processes for specific operations as well as extra control ports and guards installed on these ports to notify the receipt of an operation call will be created. More to the point:

A *Component* can be exactly mapped to a *Manifold coordinator process*. An *Active Class* is mapped to a *Manifold atomic process. Passive Classes* will be used in our architecture modeling to represent the different data types supported by Manifold such as *string, integer, and tuple*.

An *interface* is not directly mapped to a specific Manifold construct, but the set of operations, attributes, and signals defined for the specific interface are separately mapped. For every *operation* that is defined in a provided or required interface attached to a port, we create an *input port* for each input parameter and an *output port* if the specific operation returns a value. A special *input control port* is also created for each operation and a *guard* is installed on this port to notify the owning manifold process for requests received for the specific operation. The set of *signals* defined in provided and required interfaces attached to a component's or class' ports are defined to be the *events* that can be raised by the corresponding manifold or atomic process. *Attributes* of an interface attached to a component or class are mapped to *local variables* of the corresponding Manifold coordinator or atomic processes. The variables will be assigned an initial value if the corresponding interface attribute is assigned a value.

Connectors are mapped to the streams required to pass the related parameter values during an operation call and streams to pass the return values of an operation.

2.3 Creating the Scenario Model of a Software Architecture

Scenario modeling is realized by a number of sequence diagrams describing the dynamic aspects of a component-based system's architecture, i.e., the setup of the software architecture under certain execution scenarios. Specifically, sequence diagrams describe:

- Interactions taking place between components, realized by messages exchanged between them
- Activation/deactivation of component and class instances
- Conditions under which the above actions take place
- Sequence within which the above actions take place

For the construction of sequence diagrams the following constructs provided by UML 2.0 will be used by our methodology: *lifelines, messages (operation calls, signals, create, destroy, display, set), timers, inline frames, message groups, and gates*. The goal of the software architect during the creation of the sequence diagrams is to describe all possible execution scenarios of the system. As soon as the different scenarios are identified, the software architect can create in a hierarchical top-down approach the sequence diagrams of each scenario as follows:

1. Create a top-level sequence diagram and includes a lifeline for the "Main" component and a lifeline for each instance of the first-level components/classes that are involved in the execution of the first execution scenario.
2. Use the constructs for scenario modeling described above to define the interactions – messages taken place during the execution of the first execution scenario. Bear in mind that this sequence diagram will describe the interactions–actions from the perspective of the parent component, i.e., this sequence diagram will produce the events received by a parent component from its parts and the actions that the parent component has to make during the execution of the current scenario for coordinating its parts.
3. Decompose every decomposable lifeline to another sequence diagram, describing the message exchanges taking place for the current scenario at a lower lever (i.e., between the specific component and its part's instances). In the new sequence diagram, add a lifeline representing the component that is decomposed (i.e., the parent component) and then a lifeline for each instance of the component's parts.
4. Add all "signal" and incoming "operation" call messages of the higher level sequence diagram that are attached to the lifeline currently being decomposed.
5. Between the already created messages, add all message exchanges taking place between the decomposed lifeline (i.e., the parent component) and the other lifelines.
6. For each component, create a new sequence diagram with a special name "Component name – Init" in order to describe the initialization process of the component such as the creation of process instances. The same diagram can include any finalization process that may exist or any other scenarios that have not been described in diagrams before, e.g., the activation of a new component/class instance when the load of the system is high.

2.4 Mapping a Scenario Model to Equivalent Manifold Constructs

A scenario model describes the dynamic aspects of the system architecture. In the "world" of Manifold this is translated to a number of states for each component and a number of actions (such as the creation of new instances, the creation of streams, and raising of events) executed by the specific component when it is in this state. Mapping of a scenario model is performed after the mapping of architecture diagrams since the mapping of a scenario modeling builds upon (uses) the Manifold constructs extracted while mapping the architecture model. In the architecture model we have extracted the definitions of manifolds and atomics (i.e., names, events raised by them to their environment, ports, and local variables) of our system architecture and the hierarchy between them, i.e., which manifold coordinates which other manifolds or atomics. We have also extracted all possible streams to be created between instances of specific manifolds and atomics during operation calls in order to carry the needed data (needed input parameters and possible return values). Guards for receiving operation calls were also extracted. In the sequence diagrams we will:

- Define specific instances of manifolds and atomics and specify when and by which process these are activated/terminated.
- Put previously created streams in proper states of manifolds and specify the sequence of them in a state. Before adding created streams to states we define the specific names of source and target process instances, since during architecture modeling mapping instance names are not available.
- Specify when and under what conditions or in which state events previously defined by manifolds/atomics are raised.
- Identify which manifolds/atomics receive these events and what are the reactions to a specific event.
- Specify additional actions taking place under specific scenarios (and their sequence) using special messages provided by sequence diagrams such as the writing to ports by a manifold/atomic, the installation of a timer, and the assigning of a local variable.

The general steps for mapping sequence diagrams are the following:

1. Identify sequence diagrams of each component. These are the sequence diagrams in which the parent lifeline represents an instance of this component.
2. Map one by one the sequence diagrams of each component in the following way:
   (a) Order the messages/actions contained in the specific diagram from top to bottom irrespective of the lifelines that are attached to.
   (b) Group messages to states as follows:
       – Starting from the first message get all messages in order until next "state transition message" where a "state transition message" is: the next "signal" message sent by a lifeline other than a parent component OR the next "signal" message sent by the lifeline of

a parent component to itself OR next "operation call" message received by a parent component from its outside environment OR next timeout event of a timer installed by a parent.

- Create a state with *label="name of first message"* and put all messages until (excluding) the "state transition message".
- Get the next message from the diagram. IF this is NOT a "state transition message" then go to step "a" setting the label of the next state, i.e., name of first message="name of state transition message". *ELSE* get all subsequent messages until you find a message that is not a "state transition message". Then go to step "a" setting the label of the next state, i.e., name of first message="name of state transition message1 & name of state transition message2 & .. & name of last transition message found".

(c) Map messages of each state to Manifold constructs using our mapping rules (due to space limitations the mapping rules are not presented here).

3 The Code Generation Tool

Based on our methodology, we have developed a tool that automatically generates the Manifold code implementing the coordination–communication part of software architectures modeled with UML 2.0. Our code generation tool takes as input an XMI document describing the architecture model of a system and outputs the full Manifold code implementing the coordination part of the system. The full route of creating and transforming a software architecture model to Manifold code is shown below.

The creation of the software architecture of the system forms the first step. For the modeling of the software architecture we use the Sparx Enterprise Architect modeling tool (Sparx Systems Website 2006). Using the "export" function of Enterprise Architect we then export the modeled software architecture to an XMI (v.1.1) document. Since the latest version of XMI (v.2.1) that corresponds to UML 2.0 has recently been released, the few tools that provided support of UML 2.0 after its official release on 2003 have used previous versions of XMI format to export the models and added custom extensions to cover the needs not supported by these versions. Additionally, since XMI has to be general enough to represent not only UML models, but also every kind of model, there are specific needs of UML tools that may not be supported. As it is stated in Laird (2001) "the XMI standard itself doesn't support all that is needed, and vendors unfortunately implement it differently". In order to make our code generation tool more independent from specific UML modeling tools we first parse XMI generated by Enterprise Architect and create an intermediate, tool-independent representation of the model. The intermediate representation consists of generic UML 2.0 Java classes that represent the elements of our software architecture model.

For parsing the XMI document and creating the UML 2.0 object model we use Apache Commons Digester (Jakarta Commons Digester Website 2006). Having an intermediate representation of the software architecture enables the support for additional modeling tools in the future with minimum effort. If we wanted to add support for a modeling tool other than Enterprise Architect that has a different implementation of XMI format, then we would only have to add another set of digester rules for parsing the XMI document exported by this tool (or just the rules for parsing the XMI parts that are implemented differently in this tool) and transform it to the common UML2.0 object model. The next step is the transformation of the UML2.0 object model to the equivalent Manifold object model by applying the mapping rules of our methodology. The Manifold object instances are finally processed to generate the Manifold code by applying the syntax rules of Manifold.

4 Evaluation-Contribution, Limitations, and Future Work

The general approach of the work presented here, as well as the work presented in Papadopoulos et al. (2006), is the integration of software architectures and coordination models, which enables us to derive the advantages that both of them provide in reducing the costs of the software development process. The modeling of system architectures enables developers not only to define the more important properties and constraints of the system under development, but also to detect errors early at the design time, thus saving development time. The generated code, which is consistent with the previously modeled architecture, clearly separates the communication from the coordination parts of the system, making the system maintenance much easier. Furthermore, the integration of software architectures for specification, with coordination models and languages for implementation, has a number of advantages for both software architectures and coordination models as these are elaborately described in Papadopoulos et al. (2006). In summary: (a) coordination models offer to software architecture an alternative approach to code generation, which enjoys the fundamental advantages of coordination models, such as programming language independence (components may be written in different languages even within the same application), and higher degree of component reusability (because of the clear separation of the coordination code from the computational one). (b) Software architectures offer to coordination models a way of modeling and analyzing a system well before its implementation begins. This work enhances the coordination languages with a GUI front end, which can easily be learned and facilitated to generate most of the coordination-related codes.

In our first work we use ACME, a generic ADL, in order to show the generality of our approach. In this way we provided a general route for mapping any particular ADL to coordination code. However, this choice had led us to some limitations. Our first methodology cannot generate the code implementing the dynamic configuration of a system. We added a limited support for dynamism by defining the *active_on* property that specifies which event triggers the construction of each possible connection of a system's software architecture.

Based on the results and experiences of our first work and exploiting the improvements realized by the latest version of UML towards the support of software architecture descriptions, we have built our second methodology, which automates the transition from software architecture design of component-based systems described in UML 2.0 to coordination code. Our second work provides an improved support for the dynamic aspects of the software architecture exploiting the powerful tools of UML for dynamic behavior descriptions as well as the improved support of UML 2.0 for interrelating structure and behavior-centric diagrams. Our second methodology is also supported by an integrated code generation tool that fully automates the production of the complete code implementing the coordination–communication part of software systems modeled with UML 2.0. Other advantages introduced by our latest work are the following:

- The way that the dynamic parts of a software architecture are described by software architects in the latest methodology (i.e., by describing execution scenarios using sequence diagrams) is much closer to their way of thinking than the definition of the active_on property previously used. The methodology makes this process easier by giving guidelines to software architects for identifying all possible execution scenarios and describing them in a hierarchical way.

- The use of a standard, broadly accepted, and established modeling language for describing software architectures. Although ADLs have evolved and matured considerably over the last few years, UML is the standard notation language for analysis and design of a system. UML is more familiar to software developers and the one that is supported by many commercial tools. UML 2.0 and XMI standards that we use in our latest work are also two of the main standards proposed and broadly used by the new general software development approach of MDA.

- The two types of diagrams that are used in our methodology can be perfectly interrelated, thanks to the new feature of UML 2.0 for structure and behavior gross integration. The model elements specified in the architecture diagrams such as components, classes, connectors, and interfaces are then directly associated with the model elements included in sequence diagrams. This provides us with the ability for automatic consistency checking between elements specified in diagrams, and also makes the development of our tool easier since we did not have to proprietary define the relationship between the model elements of the diagrams that we use.

- By virtue of XMI, the software architecture descriptions can be exchanged and used/edited by many modeling tools. Although we used a specific modeling tool for software architecture design, we have designed our code generation tool in a way that additional modeling tools can be supported in the future.

- Adhering to the main principles of the MDA approach, we tried to keep the software architecture model constructed by our methodology "platform" independent. A "platform" is meaningful only relative to a particular point of view. Since the underlying implementation paradigm that our work is based on is the coordination paradigm and specifically the IWIM coordination model, we define as "platform" a specific coordination language that implements the IWIM model, such as Manifold. The constraints defined by our methodology on the use of certain UML 2.0 constructs were based on the IWIM principles and not specifically on the Manifold language. In this way the same model can be used to generate code in another language implementing the IWIM coordination model.

The software developer that will use our methodology and the associated code generation tool will face a common problem in the field of automatic code generation: the maintenance of the generated code. Although in our latest methodology the coordination code that can be generated is more complete limiting the need for the programmer to manually add missing bits of coordination code, if the software architecture of the system changes in a subsequent stage (e.g., the system is extended with new functionality and subsequently new components) the code has to be generated again. However, the problem is limited to the atomics files that the tool generates for the coordination-related code and where the programmer manually adds the computational code. Our future work involves the enhancement of our code generation tool by:

- Addressing the problem of code maintenance; we are currently in the process of considering code-block recognition methods used in other code generation tools
- Supporting additional modeling tools apart from Sparx Enterprise Architect
- Adding enhanced mechanisms for consistency checking and validation of the imported software architecture model

Acknowledgments   The authors of this chapter would like to thank their partners in the MUSIC-IST project and acknowledge the partial financial support given to this research by the European Union (6th Framework Programme, contract number 35166).

References

Arbab F., Herman I., and Spilling P. (1993) An overview of manifold and its implementation, *Concurrency: Practice and Experience* 5(1), 23–70.

Garlan D., Monroe R.T., and Wile D. (2000) ACME: An Architectural Description of Component Based Systems, *Foundations of Component-Based Systems*, Cambridge University Press, Cambridge, pp. 47–68.

Jakarta Commons Digester Website (2006) http://jakarta.apache.org/commons/digester

Laird C. (2001) XMI and UML combine to drive product development, IBM Whitepapers, available at: http://www-128.ibm.com/developerworks/xml/library/x-xmi/

Medvidovic N. and Taylor R.N. (2000) A classification and comparison framework for software architecture description languages, *IEEE Transactions on Software Engineering* 26(1) 70–93.

OMG (2003) Unified Modeling Language: Superstructure version 2.0.

OMG MDA Website (2006) http://www.omg.org/mda/

Papadopoulos G.A. and Arbab F. (2001) Configuration and dynamic reconfiguration of components using the coordination paradigm, *Future Generation Computer Systems* 17(8), 1023–1038.

Papadopoulos G.A., Stavrou A., and Papapetrou O. (2006) An implementation framework for software architectures based on the coordination paradigm, *Science of Computer Programming* 60(1), 27–67.

Sparx Systems Website (2006) http://www.sparxsystems.com.au/

Automating Software Processes

**Peter Killisperger[1], Georg Peters[2], Markus Stumptner[3]
and Beate Nothhelfer-Kolb[4]**

[1] Munich University of Applied Sciences, Competence Center Information Systems;
University of South Australia, Advanced Computing Research Centre,
Peter.Killisperger@postgrads.unisa.edu.au

[2] Munich University of Applied Sciences, Department of Computer Science and
Mathematics, Georg.Peters@muas.de

[3] University of South Australia, Advanced Computing Research Centre, ms@cs.unisa.edu.au

[4] Siemens Corporate Technology, Software and System Processes, Beate.Nothhelfer-
Kolb@siemens.com

Abstract   Successful software development is still a challenge. Siemens has
therefore started research projects aiming to improve Siemens' software process
models and their application. This chapter gives an overview of these projects and
presents first results. In particular, findings of research mainly dealing with challenges of the application of instantiated software processes in projects and requirements for software processes are described. In addition, demand for further
research in evolving a standardized and process-oriented adaptation process for
developing project-individual software process models is identified and motivated.

1 Introduction

Although software engineering has a long history, any larger software project remains a challenge with a significant risk of failure. For instance, the Chaos Report
2004 of the Standish Group shows that only 29% of all software projects were finished successfully as planned (Hartmann 2006).

To improve software project practice, a number of software process models
have been suggested in the literature and tested in practice. According to ISO/IEC
15504 (1998) a software process is "the process or a set of processes used by an
organization or project to plan, manage, execute, monitor, control, and improve its
software related activities". Some of the best known software process models are
the waterfall-model (Royce 1987), the spiral-model (Boehm 1986), V-Model
(Broy and Rausch 2005) or agile approaches such as Scrum (Schwaber 1995).

However, no model has achieved the status of de facto standard so far. This
can be regarded as an indicator for the challenges and risks that are still inherent in

C. Barry et al. (eds.), *Information Systems Development: Challenges in Practice, Theory,*
and Education, Vol.2, doi: 10.1007/978-0-387-78578-3_37,
© Springer Science+Business Media, LLC 2009

software projects today. Therefore, many organizations developing software choose one software process model as their internal standard or even develop and define their own standard (e.g., V-Model for German government or the Hermes model in Switzerland).

In this chapter we deal with the software process model(s) used at Siemens, which are embedded in a more general framework, the Siemens Process Framework (SPF). Due to Siemens' diversity and size, the company has no enterprise-wide standard; instead particular models are used by different business units. These unit-specific reference software process models need to be adapted to the special context of a particular software project. Only if the reference model is well designed so it can be optimally aligned to the particular software project, will the instantiated software process provide a good basis for project execution. Research projects at Siemens Corporate Technology have the goal to improve Siemens software process models, as well as their adaptation and application in projects. We present results of the first improvement project, mainly dealing with challenges of the application of the instantiated software process and the derivation of requirements for the software development process. The main focus of this chapter is to provide an analysis of past experience, a conceptual framework, and research agenda for the current projects dealing with the standardization and automation of the process of adapting reference processes to project contexts.

The chapter is structured as follows: The next section gives an overview of related literature. Section 3 introduces the current process modeling approach at Siemens and identifies key areas of further research. Section 4 offers an approach for improving Siemens' software process models by analyzing the application of instantiated software processes and defining requirements on instantiated software process models. Furthermore, we demonstrate the demand for a standardized and process oriented adaptation of reference software process models including tool support.

2 Related Literature

Processes are used to generalize problem solving by describing the essence of a solution approach in a model in order to apply it to a variety of problem cases. The description of a general solution (i.e., the reference software process model) is adapted in order to be applicable to individual problems. Already in 1987 Osterweil stated that one significant danger of this approach is that software process models are static but the actual software process is dynamic (Osterweil 1987). Therefore it is difficult to map the general and static guidelines of software process models to the dynamic and individual characteristics of real world projects. Several publications discussing approaches to improve software processes in theory and their application in practice have been released. They can be categorized according to whether they focus on process execution or outcomes.

Improvement approaches have been defined primarily to enhance process productivity and quality of the process outcome, i.e., the software product. Methods like CMMI (Chrissis et al. 2006) and Spice (Loon 2004) define guidelines to measure the maturity of software processes in organizations and their application in projects and thus can be used to reveal necessity of improvement. However, these approaches only define what has to be covered by software processes, but do not give any recommendation how this is achieved best. Consequently, they do not define any guidelines or requirements for the process of adapting a reference software process model to be applicable in a project.

As a counterpoint to these improvement approaches, research in *process-centered software engineering environments* (PCSEE) deals with the actual application of software processes in practice. The key idea is to use an instantiated software process model as input for a software engineering environment. This environment then executes the process according to the model (Balzer and Gruhn 2001). An example of such a system is MELMAC (Deiters and Gruhn 1998). Most of these solutions have not had much economic success until now. The main reasons are the limited number of process types they support and their rigid, workflow-like execution of processes which clashes with the creative and flexible characteristics of software development (Gruhn 2002). Research in PCSEE does not provide a solution for the issue of adapting software process models either. Instead, manual adaptation and deployment of processes is necessary which is cumbersome and in practice not feasible due to tight time frames and limited budgets of today's software development projects.

The concept of tailoring of the V-Model (BMI 2004) addresses the issue of adapting an abstract process model to the needs of individual projects. According to the type and the size of a project, process modules and an execution strategy can be selected to form the individual software process to be applied in a project. Process modules consist of related activities (e.g., project management or software development) and define work products, activities, and roles. The execution strategy defines the chronological and organizational flow. In addition to the tailoring at the beginning of a project it is also possible to add or remove modules during the project if necessary. Although the tailoring mechanism of the V-Model addresses the issue of adapting a reference software process model to individual project requirements, it does not individualize a process model to an extent which makes it applicable in a project.

3 Process Modeling at Siemens

3.1 Siemens' Corporate Policy for Modeling Processes

Software engineering and design within Siemens is nested into a more general framework, the Siemens Process Framework (SPF). The SPF is a company-wide framework for designing business processes within Siemens. Its purpose is to standardize the management and structure of these processes. The main components of the SPF are the Siemens Reference Process House (RPH), the roles of individuals, and committees in process management and methods of process management (see Fig. 1).

The RPH describes the hierarchical structure of Siemens' business processes. It covers all processes regarding the relationship to costumers (i.e., CRM, SCM, and PLM) as well as internal processes (i.e., management and support processes). The RPH provides only the structure of the top four levels. The structure and appearance of lower levels is determined by the business units according to their individual needs (Schmelzer and Sesselmann 2004).

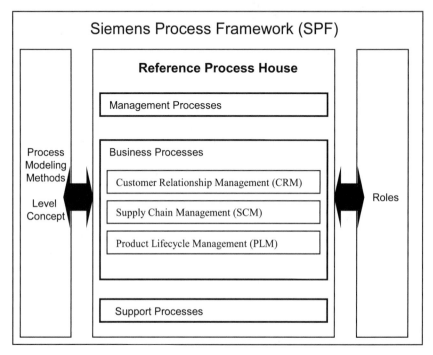

Fig. 1. Siemens Process Framework (Schmelzer and Sesselmann 2006)

3.2 Software Processes of Siemens

Software developing business units model their software processes according to the SPF. The software processes are part of the process group "Product Lifecycle Management" (PLM) and are further detailed on the lower levels. They function as reference processes for any software project within the particular Siemens business unit and therefore cannot be applied in software projects as they are. Instead, they are intended to be a guideline and basis from which the actual (instantiated) process model for a specific project can be derived. We call this step *process adaptation* (see Fig. 2).

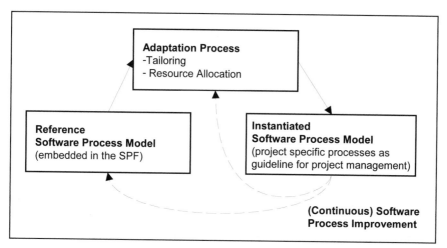

Fig. 2. Software Process Model

To obtain an improved adaptation process as described above the following key areas for detailed further research have been identified by Siemens so far:

- **Application of Instantiated Software Processes.** How can the application of instantiated software processes be better standardized in projects?
- **Requirements on Instantiated Software Process Models.** What requirements do instantiated software process models have to fulfil to enable improved application?
- **Standardized and Process-Oriented Adaptation.** How can standardized and process-oriented adaptation of software processes be enabled?
- **Tool Support.** How can tools be used to support adaptation?

The first two of these areas have been already addressed in a research project. The preliminary results are detailed in Sections 4.1 and 4.2. The remaining two questions are the focus of a current research project at Siemens Corporate Technology Group.

4 Improving the Siemens' Software Process Model

4.1 Application of Instantiated Software Processes

After manual adaptation to the individual characteristics of a project, the software process is used to organize work in the project at Siemens. The application typically does not occur in standardized fashion and the actual work often does not conform to the instantiated process. Therefore automation and support by information technology is desired to facilitate the application and tracking of instantiated software processes in projects.

Compared to the area of software processes, there are many areas within the field of business processes which are already supported by process automation such as production processes. These approaches can be used as a foundation for the support of software processes by information technology. However, software processes feature characteristics which are not common to business processes. "Software processes encompass parts which are similar to production processes. Other parts are engineering like processes and some parts are so closely depending on human creativity that they could be considered as essentially creative processes" (Gruhn 2002).

Workflow systems suitable for automating production processes can be used to guide agents through parts of the instantiated software process. Production processes are well-defined and stable. They are repetitive, predictable, the process is routine-based and changes are rare (Stohr and Zhao 2001). Some parts of software processes such as configuration management, quality management, error-handling management, or change request management often conform to the characteristics of production processes. Therefore workflow systems offer an instrument for supporting or even enforcing the execution as specified in the instantiated process model.

Contrary to that, there are also parts of software processes that are highly dynamic. It is not reasonable to automate them by workflow systems due to the restrictive character of these systems. Immediate changes can occur during the whole project's lifetime, e.g., by late requirements, feedback, delays, or by bottlenecks which force shift of work. It can be even impossible to concretize all parts of the process prior to its execution (Becker et al. 1997). Here systems that guide the process agent rather loosely are more suitable.

The idea is to offer each agent or role a customized view on the parts of the instantiated process he is involved in. Processes are often very complex and for most agents only small fractions of the whole are of actual interest. If several levels of these customized views are maintained, they can provide process agents with both detailed information as a step by step guide and a high-level overview of the activities in a part of a process. Higher levels are an aggregation of more detailed ones. Process agents are guided along the process, but they can also divert from it if necessary. Process conformance can be achieved by inspecting whether the defined deliverables of the activities have been created.

In order to implement the idea of supporting software processes by different kinds of systems, future research has to analyze which parts of software processes are best supported by either workflow systems or systems that guide the user rather loosely. In addition, it has to be investigated how such systems could look like in detail and restrictions of these systems have to be highlighted.

4.2 Requirements on Instantiated Software Process Models

In order to enable support of information technology as described in the last sub-section, instantiated software process models have to possess certain qualities. Five requirements have been defined.

- **Control Flow of Instantiated Software Processes.** The control flow of instantiated software processes has to be defined by the flow of information.
- **Assignment of Substitutes.** Substitutes for human agents have to be assigned to activities.
- **Limited Number of Human Agents.** Only a limited number of human agents can be involved in a single process activity.
- **Responsibility of Execution.** Assignment of responsibility for execution of process steps to human agents.
- **Estimating Duration of Execution.** Estimating the duration of execution of activities to enable improved project controlling.

The requirements are based upon the "Guidelines of Modeling" (Becker et al., 2000) and work on automating workflow models by Frank (1994), Oberweis (1996), and Galler (1997) and extend their findings. We now examine the requirements in more detail.

Control Flow of Instantiated Software Processes. Using the current control flow in Siemens' process models would mean that an activity cannot be started before the prior activity was executed completely. However, the ability to execute activities in software processes mostly depends on the availability of information. Work can be started even if only a subset of the information necessary for executing the whole activity is available. Therefore it is desirable to know what information is already on hand. It would be preferable to define the control flow of software processes by the flow of information.

Assignment of Substitutes. Every human process agent has to have a substitute. Software projects are often long-running projects. Therefore process agents will not be on site at all times, e.g., due to leave periods. In case of a bottleneck the activity has to be automatically forwarded to a defined human agent. Even if the agent cannot carry out the activity, he can at least ensure the execution by another process agent.

Limited Number of Human Agents. The number of human agents involved in a process step has to be rather small. The more people are involved in an activity, the higher the need to coordinate its execution. The goal of supporting software processes by information technology (reducing the coordination overhead) would be undermined.

Responsibility of Execution. For every activity executed by human process agents there has to be one responsible person even if several process agents execute the process step together. Thereby it is guaranteed that one person coordinates work and it is avoided that agents accidentally rely upon each other in cyclic fashion.

Estimating Duration of Execution. Software projects commonly run under time pressure. Therefore, effort of execution must be estimated for every activity. This allows calculation of the total time necessary for completing a project. It enables project management to identify delays early and offers the chance to respond to problems at an early stage.

Satisfying these five requirements accommodates the special needs caused by the characteristics of software development. However, there are drawbacks. The extension of instantiated software process models by additional information and the restructuring of the control flow result in higher complexity. Manual application of the adaptation process will be time-consuming and expensive if even feasible. Therefore future research has to develop an approach for automating the process of developing instantiated software processes.

4.3 Standardized and Process-Oriented Adaptation

The adaptation process[1] consists of two steps:

- **Tailoring.** Tailoring includes exclusion of unnecessary process steps, selection of pathways, and others.
- **Resource Allocation.** Assignment of resources (due to the nature of software projects, in most cases humans) to activities.

Up to now, at Siemens, the obtained instantiated software process model is intended to provide a knowledge base for the software project management and members. It serves as consulting tools forming the basis for organizing work in projects. Its purpose is not to be supported or automated by any kind of information technology such as workflow systems. Process agents interpret the given processes and try to apply them in projects. Because the current models are used by humans and not by machines, their focus is to be easily read and understood by humans.

Siemens has identified the following significant disadvantages of the manual execution of the adaptation process of the reference software model:

- Manual adaptation is time-consuming and expensive.
- Since the adaptation process is not standardized it depends on the experience and preference of the experts performing it and thus leads to non-standardized instantiated software process models.
- Due to the lack of a standardized adaptation process, the instantiated software process models vary widely. This reduces the effectiveness and efficiency of the software project due to limited learning effects and restricted possibilities of having the project members adopt a "standard project".

---

[1] We refrain from calling this process "tailoring" since this term, among others, is related to V-Model and does not describe our approach exactly.

- Lack of standardization means that improving the reference software process model as well as improving the adaptation process is very difficult if not impossible.

In contrast to that, a standardized or even automated adaptation process would lead to the following distinct advantages or goals in comparison to the current manual approach:

- Standardization and in particular automation should reduce costs and time for the adaptation process significantly.
- Standardization enables traceable adaptation processes.
- A standardized adaptation process leads to similar instantiated software process models for similar projects. So the efficiency of project management will, possibly, increase.
- Due to standardization, optimizing the reference software process model as well as the adaptation process becomes possible (CSPI = Continuous Software Process Improvement).

4.4 Tool Support

The possibility of tool support will be examined in a later part of the project.

5 Conclusion

In this chapter we have given an overview of research projects of Siemens Corporate Technology for improving software process models and their application at Siemens. We have introduced Siemens' current approach for modeling and applying software processes, and have identified some issues with the approach. A research framework was derived from the identified problems of the current approach, enabling improvement of Siemens's software process models and their application. We have presented the first outcomes of the improvement projects primarily dealing with challenges of the application of instantiated software processes in practice and requirements on the quality of instantiated software process models. We highlighted demand and motivation for a standardized and process-oriented adaptation process for developing instantiated software process models and stressed the necessity of tool support for this process.

Future research will address in particular the question which parts of instantiated software process models can be best supported by which type of system and what such systems could look like in detail. Furthermore the gap between reference and instantiated software process models has to be bridged both in theory and by support of tools.

References

Balzer, R. & Gruhn, V. (2001), Process-Centered Software Engineering Environments: Academic and Industrial Perspectives, *in* Proc. ICSE, pp. 671–672.

Becker, J.; Rosemann, M. & Uthmann von, C. (2000), Guidelines of Business Process Modelling, *LNCS* **1806**, 30–49.

Becker, U.; Hamann, D. & Verlage, M. (1997), Descriptive Modeling of Software Processes, *in* Proceedings of the Third Conference on Software Process Improvement (SPI'97).

BMI (2004), The new V-Model XT - Development Standard for IT Systems of the Federal Republic of Germany, URL: http://www.v-modell-xt.de (accessed: 08.04.2007).

Boehm, B. (1986), A spiral model of Software development and enhancement, *SIGSOFT* **11**(4), 14–24.

Broy, M. & Rausch, A. (2005), Das neue V-Modell XT: Ein anpassbares Modell fuer Software und Systems Engineering, *Informatik Spektrum* **28**(3), 20–29.

Chrissis, M.; Konrad, M. & Shrum, S. (2006), CMMI. Guidelines for Process Integration and Product Improvement, Addison-Wesley.

Deiters, W. & Gruhn, V. (1998), Process Management in Practice Applying the FUNSOFT Net Approach to Large-Scale Processes, *Autom. Softw. Eng.* **5**(1), 7–25.

Frank, U. (1994), Multiperspektivische Unternehmensmodellierung - theoretischer Hintergrund und Entwurf einer objektorientierten Entwicklungsumgebung, Oldenbourg.

Galler, J. (1997), Vom Geschaeftsprozessmodell zum Workflow-Modell, Gabler.

Gruhn, V. (2002), Process-Centered Software Engineering Environments, A Brief History and Future Challenges, *Ann. Software Eng.* **14**(1–4), 363–382.

Hartmann, D. (2006), Interview: Jim Johnson of the Standish Group, URL: http://www.infoq.com/articles/Interview-Johnson-Standish-CHAOS (accessed: 11.12.2006).

ISO/IEC 15504-9 (1998), Information Technology –Software Process Assessment – Part 9: Vocabulary. Technical Report.

Loon, H. (2004), Assessment and ISO/IEC 15504. A reference book, Springer.

Oberweis, A. (1996), Modellierung und Ausfuehrung von Workflows mit Petri-Netzen, Teubner.

Osterweil, L.J. (1987), Software Processes Are Software Too, *in* ICSE, pp. 2–13.

Royce, W.W. (1987), Managing the Development of Large Software Systems: Concepts and Techniques, *in* Proc. ICSE, 328–339.

Schmelzer, H. & Sesselmann, W. (2004), Geschaeftsprozessmanagement in der Praxis: Produktivitaet steigern - Wert erhoehen - Kunden zufrieden stellen, Hanser.

Schmelzer, H. & Sesselmann, W. (2006), Geschaeftsprozessmanagement in der Praxis: Produktivitaet steigern - Wert erhoehen - Kunden zufrieden stellen, Hanser.

Schwaber, K. (1995), Scrum Development Process, OOPSLA'95 Workshop on Business Object Design and Implementation.

Stohr, E.A. & Zhao, J.L. (2001), Workflow Automation: Overview and Research Issues, *Inf Syst Front* **3**(3), 281–296.

Ontology Transformation to Conceptual Data Model Using Graph Formalism[1]

Justas Trinkunas and Olegas Vasilecas

Information Systems Research Laboratory, Vilnius Gediminas Technical University, Lithuania, justas@isl.vgtu.lt, olegas@fm.vgtu.lt

Abstract The important requirement for developing conceptual data models is to reduce efforts, costs and time. This requirement can be implemented by the explicit use of enterprise knowledge for automatic or semiautomatic generation of conceptual data model. The enterprise knowledge can be represented using ontology. In this chapter we analyse graph-oriented ontology transformation to conceptual data model. We present a formal approach for automatic ontology transformation to conceptual data model.

1 Introduction

Conceptual data modelling methodologies became well known and quite successful because of their methodological guidance in building conceptual models of information systems. Moreover, they provide a graphical representation of a model.

Conceptual data models, also called semantic data models, were developed to capture the meaning of an application domain as perceived by its developers (Meersman, 1999).

But there are the following main problems concerning conceptual modelling. Firstly, as discussed in Wand et al. (1999), meanings of conceptual modelling constructs have to be defined rigorously to employ them effectively. Often, however, rigorous definitions of these constructs are missing. Secondly, in general, most conceptual schemas are developed from scratch, which means wasting previous efforts and time (Palol, 2004). Thirdly, domain knowledge acquired in the analysis of some particular domain is not used for conceptual modelling.

Because conceptual models are intended to capture knowledge about a real-world domain, the meaning of modelling constructs should be sought in models of reality. Accordingly, ontology, which is the branch of philosophy dealing with

---

[1] The work is supported by Lithuanian State Science and Studies Foundation according to High Technology Development Program Project "Business Rules Solutions for Information Systems Development (VeTIS)" Reg. No. B-07042

models of reality, can be used to analyse the meaning of common conceptual modelling constructs.

Companies install information systems to increase the effectiveness of activities, to get more profit and to increase the value of the company. However, to develop a database today is hard and involves much time-consuming work. When a database designer creates a new database he has to solve the same analytical problems every time:

- Every Application domain has a lot of terms and business rules which a database designer has to understand.
- A database designer may not have knowledge of the domain that is being modelled, and thus he must rely on the user to articulate the design requirements.
- One term can have many titles and meanings. This could be a very aggravating circumstance for getting requirements for database.
- A database designer has to anticipate what will be the cycle of existence of the system, how it can change in the future, what are the threats and weaknesses of the system and how to avoid them.
- The fast-changing requirements are the main problem of creating and/or modifying applications. Most of these requirements are related to business rules.
- In a case of change of application domain, a database designer has to adopt the database quickly and effectively.

To solve all these problems and to facilitate the job of a database designer, databases, which are based on knowledge bases and their management systems, such as domain ontology, began to be used. Ontologies began to be used for classification and formalisation of business rules. Ontology is a particular kind of knowledge base that describes the facts which are considered always right by some group of users. Ontologies are used to capture knowledge about some domain of interest. They describe the concepts in the domain and also the relationships that hold between those concepts.

The main goal of this work is to improve the process of transformation from application domain ontology to entity relational model.

This kind of database design method is not used frequently, because it is in the early stage of evolution. This work shows how domain ontology can be used for eliciting business rules and speeding up the design stage of information systems. It describes how the work of a database designer could be facilitated and suggests how the process of ontology transformation to conceptual data model could be improved.

In this chapter we present an approach for knowledge represented by ontology automatic transformation to conceptual data model. The metamodels of ontology and conceptual data model are analysed and the method of automatic transformation is proposed. The developed prototype OntEr, which realises the proposed method, is described in the case study section.

We can use ontology for conceptual data modelling at least for three different purposes. Firstly, ontology is a source of knowledge and an inexperienced designer can use ontology to get initial domain knowledge. Secondly, some parts of ontology can be used for conceptual data model development. For example, we can adapt several concepts from the ontology to our needs and transform them to conceptual data model. And finally, all ontology after adaptation can be used for the conceptual data model.

The advantage of using ontology for conceptual data modelling is the reusability of domain knowledge. As a result, the conceptual data model will be made faster, easier and with fewer errors than creating a conceptual data model in the usual way.

In earlier works we already demonstrated the benefits of knowledge reuse for conceptual modelling (Vasilecas et al., 2006). We also carried out ontology representation language analysis and conceptual modelling language analysis (Trinkunas et al., 2007). According to these analyses we decided to use OWL DL as an ontology representation language and ER for data modelling. Consequently, Protégé 3.3 tool was chosen for ontology creation and Sybase Power Designer 12.0 tool was chosen for data modelling. In this chapter we continue our work.

The work is organised as follows. Firstly we give a theoretical background on ontologies and conceptual data models, then we present transformation of ontology to conceptual data model based on graph and finally we describe our proposed method.

2 Theoretical Background

In this section we briefly present theoretical background. Firstly, we begin with ontologies and ontology languages, then we move on to conceptual data model and finally we present formal transformations.

2.1 Ontology

Many authors in their works propose different ontology definitions. We accept the proposed ontology definition in OMG (2006). Ontology defines the common terms and concepts (meaning) used to describe and represent an area of knowledge. Ontology can range in expressivity from a taxonomy (knowledge with minimal hierarchy or a parent/child structure), to a thesaurus (words and synonyms), to a conceptual model (with more complex knowledge), to a logical theory (with very rich, complex, consistent and meaningful knowledge).

The structure of ontology can be defined mathematically. However, different authors provide different definitions which can vary from 3-tuple definition where ontology is defined as O=(Concepts, Relations, Axioms) to 10-tuple definition, where ontology is defined in more detail (Motik et al., 2002).

Mathematically we define ontology using graph formalism. In their work Mitra et al. (2000) define ontology O as a directed labelled graph $G_O = (N, E)$ where N is a finite set of labelled nodes and E is a finite set of labelled edges. An edge e is written as a triplet (n1, α, n2) where n1 and n2 are members of N and α is the label of the edge. The structure of graph consisting of (Davies et al., 2006):

1. A set of concepts (vertices in a graph)
2. A set of relationships connecting concepts (directed edges in a graph)
3. A set of instances assigned to a particular concepts (data records assigned to concepts or relation)

2.2 Ontology Languages

In this chapter we briefly review ontology languages. According to Xiaomeng et al. (2002) ontology languages can be divided into two categories. The first category is traditional ontology languages. The languages can further be divided into four groups. The first group is an enriched first-order predicate logic (KIF, CycL). The second group is frame-based languages (Ontolingua, F-logic and OCML). The third group is description logic-based language (Loom). And the last group are the other languages. The second category is the Web standards which are used for facilitating interchange on the Internet, and ontology languages which are compatible to Web standards are named Web-based ontology specification languages. More details about other ontology languages can be found in Xiaomeng et al. (2002). We will pay more attention to the second category of ontology languages.

An RDF graph is a set of RDF triples (OMG, 2006). The set of nodes of an RDF graph is the set of subjects and objects of triples in the graph. A subgraph of an RDF graph is a subset of the triples in the graph. A triple is identified with the singleton set containing it, so that each triple in a graph is considered to be a subgraph. A proper subgraph is a proper subset of the triples in the graph. A ground RDF graph is one with no blank nodes.

A name is a URI reference or a literal. These are the expressions that need to be assigned a meaning by an interpretation. A set of names is referred to as a vocabulary. The vocabulary of a graph is the set of names which occur as the subject, predicate or object of any triple in the graph. The assertion of an RDF triple says that some relationship, indicated by the predicate, holds between the things denoted by subject and object of the triple. The assertion of an RDF graph amounts to asserting all the triples in it, so the meaning of an RDF graph is the conjunction (logical AND) of the statements corresponding to all the triples it contains.

OWL graph is an RDF graph. Not all RDF graphs are valid OWL graphs, however. The OWLGraph class specifies the subset of RDF graphs that are valid OWL graphs.

An OWL ontology contains a sequence of annotations, axioms and facts. Annotations on OWL ontologies can be used to record authorship and other information associated with ontology, including importing references to other ontologies. The main content of an OWL Ontology is carried in its axioms and facts, which provide information about classes, properties and individuals in the ontology.

Names of ontologies are used in the abstract syntax to carry the meaning associated with publishing ontology on the Web. The intent is that the name of the ontology in the abstract syntax is the URI where it can be found, although this is not part of the formal meaning of OWL. Imports annotations, in effect, are directives to retrieve a Web document and treat it as OWL ontology.

OWL ontologies may be categorised into three species or sublanguages: OWL-Lite, OWL-DL and OWL-Full. A defining feature of each sublanguage is its expressiveness (Brockmans et al., 2006). OWL-Lite is the least expressive sublanguage. OWL-Full is the most expressive sublanguage. The expressiveness of OWL-DL falls between that of OWL-Lite and OWL-Full. OWL-DL may be considered as an extension of OWL-Lite and OWL-Full an extension of OWL-DL.

The OWL language provides mechanisms for creating all the components of ontology: concepts, instances, properties (or relations) and axioms. Two sorts of properties can be defined: object properties and data-type properties. Object properties relate instances to instances. Data-type properties relate instances to data-type values, for example text strings or numbers. Concepts can have super and subconcepts, thus providing a mechanism for subsumption reasoning and inheritance of properties. Finally, axioms are used to provide information about classes and properties, for example to specify the equivalence of two classes or the range of a property.

The most important elements of the ontology are: classes (OWLOntology, OWLClass, ComplementClass, EnumeratedClass, DisjointClass, IntersectionClass, EquivalentClass, RestrictionClass, UnionClass), properties (Property, OWLAnnotationProperty, OWLOntologyProperty, FunctionalProperty, OWLDatatypeProperty, OWLObjectProperty, InverseFunctionalProperty, SymmetricProperty, TransitiveProperty), restrictions (OWLRestriction, HasValueRestriction, AllValuesFromRestriction, SomeValuesFromRestriction, CardinalityRestriction, MaxCardinalityRestriction, MinCardinalityRestriction) and data types (OWLDataRange).

2.3 Conceptual Data Model

The ability of the language to capture the domain knowledge is a very important criterion (Xiaomeng and Lars, 2002). Two major criteria are: the perspectives that the language can cover and the expressiveness of that language. Since different languages may focus on different perspectives, they may provide constructs for only some perspectives. Seven perspectives will be used to describe how well the languages provide constructs that cover them:

- Structural perspective, the static structure (entities and relationships)
- Functional perspective, the processes, activities and transformations
- Behavioural perspective, the states and transitions between them
- Rule perspective, the rules for certain processes, activities, etc.
- Object perspective, the objects (methods and attributes), processes and classes
- Communication perspective, the language actions, meaning and agreement
- Actor and role, the actor, role, society and organization

The structural perspective is the most important part of a conceptual data models, and will be discussed mostly here.

A conceptual data model provides the overall logical structure of a database, independent of any software or data storage structure considerations (Sybase PowerDesigner, 2002).

A conceptual data model represents the overall structure of an information system. It describes the conceptual relationships of different types of information rather than their physical structures. A conceptual data model is independent of a particular database management system (DBMS).

For a detailed conceptual data model analysis we choose entity-relationship (ER) language.

An ER diagram is a graphical modelling notation that illustrates the interrelationships between entities in a domain. ER diagrams often use symbols to represent three different types of information.

Basic components of the ER language are (Chen, 1976):

Entities. An entity is a phenomenon that can be distinctly identified. Entities can be classified into entity classes.

Relationships. A relationship is an association among entities. Relationships can be classified into relationship classes.

Attributes and data values. A value is used to give value to a property of an entity or relationship. Values are grouped into value classes by their types. An attribute is a function which maps from an entity class or relationship class to a value class; thus the property of an entity or a relationship can be expressed by an attribute-value pair.

Additionally, we include domains and data-type elements. And finally, ER model can be defined as quintuple:

$$ER = (E, A, D, R, DT) \tag{1}$$

where E – set of entities, A – set of attributes, D – set of domains, R – set of relationships, DT – set of data types.

ER model can be represented as a graph. We define ER model using graph formalism. ER model is a directed labelled graph $G_{ER} = (N, E)$ where N is a finite set of labelled nodes and E is a finite set of labelled edges. An edge e is written as a triplet $(n1, \alpha, n2)$ where n1 and n2 are members of N and α is the label of the edge.

The most important elements of the ER metamodel according to OMG (2003) are Model, Entity, Attribute, AternateKey, ForeignKey, InversionEntry, Key, PrimaryKey, Domain, AtomicDomain, DomainConstraint, ListDomain, UnionDomain, EntityConstraint, Relationship, Inheritance (Generalization), Association, Association Link and Link/Extended Dependency.

2.4 Metamodel-Based Transformations

The notion of model transformation is central to Model Driven Engineering. Model transformation takes as input a model conforming to a given metamodel and produces as output another model conforming to a given metamodel. Model transformation may also have several source models and several target models. One of the characteristics of model transformation is that a transformation is also a model, i.e., it conforms to a given metamodel. More information can be found in Kanai et al. (2000).

Levendovszky et al. (2002) and Gogolla et al. (2002) describe metamodel-based transformations. The authors argue that metamodel-based transformations permit descriptions of mappings between models created using different concepts from possibly overlapping domains and the transformation process facilitates the reuse of models specified in one domain-specific modelling language in another context: another domain-specific modelling language. Without the ability to perform model transformations, every existing model must be developed and understood separately, and/or has to be converted manually between the various modelling formalisms. This often requires as much effort as recreating the models from scratch, in another modelling language. However, when automatic model trans-formations are used, the mapping between the different concepts has to be devel-oped only once for a pair of metamodels, not for each model instance.

Metamodel of ontology and conceptual data model should be based on meta-meta-model, defining all necessary constructs.

Model Driven Architecture (MDA) (Miller et al., 2003) defines three view-points (levels of abstraction) from which some system can be seen. From a chosen viewpoint, a representation of a given system (viewpoint model) can be defined. These models are (each corresponding to the viewpoint with the same name): Computation Independent Model (CIM), Platform Independent Model (PIM) and Platform Specific Model (PSM). MDA is based on the four-layer metamodelling architecture, and several OMG's complementary standards. The layers are: meta-metamodel (M3) layer, metamodel (M2) layer, model (M1) layer and instance (M0) layer.

The mapping from OWL to ER was described in the OMG (2005) document. However, this document was just a proposal and in the final version of the docu-ment (OMG, 2006) OMG group did not leave the OWL mapping to ER. However, this mapping is incomplete and it is not clear which elements from the OWL on-tology are not transformed into ER model. As a result, some information from OWL ontology cannot be used in ER model.

3 Proposed Approach

In this section we describe how ontology can be transformed into conceptual data model using graph formalism based on metamodelling.

Many authors work in the field of transformation of ontology (Vysniauskas et al., 2006; Sugumaran and Storey, 2006; Conesa et al., 2003). However, pro-posed transformation methods are informal and used for different purposes.

We have adopted a graph transformation language used in the works of Mitra et al. (2000) and Gyssens et al. (1994). The language consists of the five basic operations: node addition, edge addition, node deletion, edge deletion and abstraction. Currently we need only two operations (node addition and edge addition).

Node Addition. Given the graph G, a node N and its adjacent edges $\{(N, \alpha i, mj)\}$ to add, the node addition results in a graph G' = (M', E') where M' =M $\cup$ N and E' = E $\cup$ $\{(N, \alpha i, mj)\}$.

Edge Addition. Given a graph G and a set of edges SE = $\{(mi, \alpha j, mk)\}$ to add, the edge addition operation EA [G, SE] results in a graph G' = (M,E') where E' = E $\cup$ SE.

The node addition operation can be used to introduce new objects into ER model from the ontology. The edge addition operation is needed to build relationships between the ER objects.

We adapted the schema of models transformation from Levendovszky et al. (2002) for ontology transformation into conceptual data model.

Transformation from ontology G_O into conceptual data model G_{ER} can be presented as:

$$G_O \rightarrow G_{ER} \tag{2}$$

where G_O is an ontology represented as a graph which is based on OWL metamodel, GER is ER model represented as a graph based on ER metamodel and $\rightarrow$ is transformation of the elements of the graph.

Ontology G_O transformation into ER model GER consists of a set of elementary transformations which can be presented as:

$$G_O(OWLElement) \rightarrow G_{ER} (ERElement) \tag{3}$$

where OWLElement is an element from OWL metamodel, ERElement is an element from ER metamodel and $\rightarrow$ is simple graph transformation which consists of Node Addition and Edge Addition operations defined above.

4 Case Study

We have chosen Protégé 3.3 for the development of the ontology. A free version of the software provides all features and capabilities required for the present research. Protégé 3.3 can be downloaded from the site http://protege.stanford.edu. In this ontology we describe main concepts and relationships which describe domain area of salaries.

4.1 Payroll Ontology

After deep analysis of types of contracts in Lithuania the following diagram was created. Figure 1 represents logical structure of types of contracts in Lithuania.

Briefly we describe the proposed method of building a conceptual model from the OWL DL ontology. The method consists of four main steps:

1. The first step is knowledge acquisition from the word, documents, people, conceptual data models, ontologies and other sources. All extracted knowledge is written in the domain ontology in OWL DL format. We use the Protégé 3.3 tool; however, other tools could be chosen for ontology development. Domain ontology is created manually. But we are expanding our work and in the near future we will propose a semiautomatic method for ontology development from existing conceptual models, ontologies and other sources.

2. The second step is the transformation of domain ontology into conceptual data model with our plug-in OntER. Created conceptual data model can be opened with Sybase Power Designer 12.0 tool and adapted for your needs.

3. The third step is verification of conceptual data model. If we made changes with Power Designer 12.0 we need to verify if conceptual data model is valid. The conceptual data model is compared with the domain ontology.

4. The last step is the generation of physical data model with Power Designer 12.0 for a particular DBMS. This feature is already implemented in the original version of Power Designer 12.0.

Through a simple generation procedure, you can transfer the solid design framework of the conceptual data model to the physical data model. The physical data model adapts your design to the specifics of a DBMS and puts you well on the way to complete physical implementation.

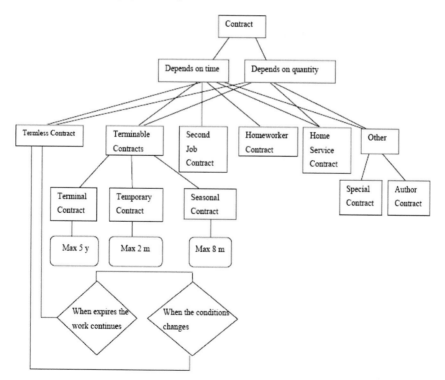

Fig. 1. Logical structure of types of contracts in Lithuania

The ontology was created with Protégé 3.3 tool. The knowledge was extracted from Lithuanian Work Codex and other documents.

The main concepts described in Salary ontology are: wage, taxes, employment contract. The employment contract type can be terminable, not terminable or other. Terminable contracts are those which have validity date. Terminable contracts can be seasonal, temporary or terminal.

4.2 Developed Plug-in OntER

OntER is the plug-in written in Java. A conceptual data model is built from the set of patterns which are filed with the needed data. Below we give the example of the attribute pattern. To build a conceptual data model, using patterns is very convenient. In case the conceptual data model of Power Designer will be changed in the future, we can change the patterns and update the plug-in.

```
<c:Attributes>
<o:EntityAttribute Id=Value>
<a:ObjectID>Value</a:ObjectID>
<a:CreationDate>Value</a:CreationDate>
<a:Creator>Value</a:Creator>
<a:ModificationDate> Value </a:ModificationDate>
<a:Modifier>Value</a:Modifier>
<c:DataItem>
<o:DataItem Ref=Value/>
</c:DataItem>
</o:EntityAttribute>
</c:Attributes>
```

5 Conclusions

We presented a graph-oriented model for ontology transformation to a conceptual data model based on metamodels. The advantage of the proposed method is formally defined as transformation of ontology into a conceptual model. However, it is not possible to transform all elements from OWL DL ontology into a conceptual data model because OWL DL is semantically richer.

After deep analysis of types of contracts in Lithuania the Payroll ontology was created. Later, we transformed Payroll ontology to a conceptual data model using plug-in OntER. And finally, the physical data model was generated with Power Designer 12.0.

References

Brockmans S., Colomb R. M., Kendall E. F., Wallace E. K., Welty C. & Xie G. T. (2006) A Model Driven Approach for Building OWL DL and OWL Full Ontologies. *5th International Semantic Web Conference*, Athens, GA, LNCS 4273, 187–200.

Chen P. P. (1976) The entity-relationship model: Towards a unified view of data. *ACM Transactions on Database Systems*, 1(1), 471–522.

Conesa J., Palol X. & Olive A. (2003) Building Conceptual Schemas by Refining General Ontologies. *14th International Conference on Database and Expert Systems Applications - DEXA '03*, LNCS 2736, 693–702.

Davies J., Studer R. & Warren P. (2006) Semantic Web Technologies Trends and Research in Ontology-Based Systems. Wiley, Chichester.

Gogolla M., Lindow A., Richters M. & Ziemann P. (2002) Metamodel Transformation of Data Models. In Bezivin, J., France, R. (eds.), *Proc. UML'2002*. http://citeseer.ist.psu.edu/gogolla02metamodel.html (2007-03-20)

Gyssens M., Paredaens J., Bussche J. V. & Gucht D. V. (1994) A Graph-Oriented Object Database Model. *IEEE Transactions on knowledge and Data Engineering*, 6(4), 572–576.

Kanai S., Kishinam T. & Tomura T. (2000) Object-oriented Graphical Specification and Seamless Design Procedure for Manufacturing Cell Control Software Development. *Proc. of the 2000 IEEE International Conference on Robotics & Automation,* San Francisco, 401–407.

Levendovszky T., Karsai G., Maroti M., Ledeczi A. & Charaf H. (2002) Model Reuse with Metamodel-Based Transformations. In C. Gacek (ed.), *Proc. of ICSR-7*, Springer, LNCS 2319, 166–178.

Meersman R. (1999) The Use of Lexicons and Other Computer-Linguistic Tools. In Zhang Y. et al. (eds.), *Proc. of the International Symposium on Cooperative Database Systems for Advanced Applications (CODAS 99)*, Heidelberg, Springer Verlag, 1–14.

Miller J. & Mukerji J. (eds.) (2003) MDA Guide Version 1.0. OMG Document: omg/2003-05-01. http://www.omg.org/docs/omg/03-05-01.pdf (2007-03-20).

Mitra P., Wiederhold G. & Kersten M. (2000) A graph oriented model for articulation of ontology interdependencies. *Proc. Extending DataBase Technologies*, Springer, Berlin Heidelberg, LNCS 1777, 86–100.

Motik B., Maedche A. & Volz R. (2002) A Conceptual Modeling Approach for Building Semantics-Driven Enterprise Applications. *Proc. of 1st Int'l Conf. Ontologies, Databases, and Application of Semantics (ODBASE-2002)*, Springer-Verlag, 1082–1099.

OMG (2003). Ontology Definition Metamodel. Preliminary Revised Submission to OMG RFP ad/2003-03-04. http://www.omg.org/docs/ptc/03-03-04.pdf (2007-03-20).

OMG (2005). Ontology Definition Metamodel Preliminary Revised Submission. http://www.omg.org/docs/ptc/05-08-01.pdf (2007-03-20).

OMG (2006) Ontology Definition Metamodel Specification. Adopted Specification 2006-10-11. http://www.omg.org/docs/ptc/06-10-11.pdf (2007-03-20).

Palol, X. (2004) A basic repository of operations for the refinement of general ontologies. Research Report LSI-04-26-R, UUPC.

Sugumaran V. & Storey V. C. (2006) The role of domain ontologies in database design: An ontology management and conceptual modeling environment. *ACM Transactions on Database Systems (TODS)*, ACM Press, 31(3), 1064–1094.

Sybase PowerDesigner (2002). Conceptual Data Model Version 9.5. http://download.sybase.com/pdfdocs/pdd0950e/cdgs.pdf (2007-03-20).

Trinkunas, J. & Vasilecas O. (2007) Ontologijos vaizdavimui ir koncepciniam modeliavimui skirtų kalbų analizė (Analysis of Ontology and Conceptual Modeling Languages). *Informacinės technologijos*, Kaunas: Technologija, 217–221.

Vasilecas O., Bugaite D. & Trinkunas J. (2006) On Approach for Enterprise Ontology Transformation into Conceptual Model. In B. Rachev, A. Smirkarov (eds.), *Proc. of the International*

Conference on Computer Systems and Technologies "CompSysTech'06", Varna, Bulgaria, IIIA.23-1- IIIA.23-6.

Vysniauskas E. & Nemuraite L. (2006) Transforming Ontology Representation from OWL to Relational Database. *Information Technology And Control*, Kaunas, Technologija, 35A(3), 333–343.

Wand Y., Storey V.C., Weber R. (1999) An ontological analysis of the relationship construct in conceptual modeling. ACM Transactions on Database Systems (TODS), December 1999, 24(4), 494–528.

Xiaomeng S., Lars I. (2002) A Comparative Study of Ontology Languages and Tools. Advanced Information Systems Engineering: 14th International Conference, CAiSE 2002 Toronto.

Definition Metamodel of ITIL

Vjeran Strahonja

Faculty of Organisation and Informatics, University of Zagreb, Croatia,
vjeran.strahonja@foi.hr

Abstract   The implementation of an adequate service management system for information technologies (IT) requires recognition of business needs, current level of maintenance, better insights into available approaches and tools, as well as their comparison, interoperability, integration and further development. The approach we are proposing and elaborating in this chapter lies on the construction of the Definition Metamodel (DMM) of the Information Technology Infrastructure Library (ITIL). The metamodel is derived from the ITIL glossary and other specifications and presented in an object-oriented fashion by using structure diagrams conform to UML notation. ITIL DMM is divided into a set of Component Metamodels (CMM). Some are briefly discussed, as well as their application in the field of evaluation of consistency, correctness and completeness of ITIL definitions and evaluation of ITIL-based tools.

1 Introduction

Safe and continuous performance of information technologies (IT) is one of the most important links in the modern business. As IT environments become more complex, the effective management of IT services plays a critical role. Taking into consideration different and sometimes divergent IT service and maintenance management models, companies that provide IT services are trying to turn to the industry-proven and standards-based approach to the IT Service Management (ITSM). ITSM is an approach that combines proven methods such as process modelling and management with industry's best practices, to enable the service provider delivery of IT services that satisfy customer business needs and achieve performance targets specified within service level agreements.

In line with this trends, the UK Office of Government Commerce (OGC) and the IT Service Management Forum (itSMF) provide a collection of best practices for IT processes in the area of IT service management, which is called IT Information Library (ITIL) (OGC 2002). Nowadays, ITIL is a respected and widely used collection of guidelines for IT service delivery and support. Because of its wide acceptance, the most important contribution of ITIL could be the convergence of

C. Barry et al. (eds.), *Information Systems Development: Challenges in Practice, Theory, and Education, Vol.2*, doi: 10.1007/978-0-387-78578-3_39,
© Springer Science+Business Media, LLC 2009

approaches and applications of leading vendors and motion towards the ITIL compliant solutions.

The aim of ITIL is to facilitate improvements in efficiency and effectiveness in the provision of high-quality IT services and the management of the IT infrastructure within any organisation. ITIL provides publicly accessible documentation written by specialists involved in service management activities. The service management is described by 11 modules, which are grouped into Service Support Set (provider internal processes) and Service Delivery Set (processes at the customer–provider interface). Each module describes processes, functions, roles and responsibilities, as well as necessary databases and interfaces. In general, ITIL describes contents, processes at a high abstraction level and contains no information about management architectures and tools.

Likewise to other 'best practices' and standards, the ITIL indicated some weaknesses:

1. Lack of holistic visibility and traceability from the theory (specifications, glossary, guidelines, manuals, etc.) to its implementations and software applications
2. Frameworks, best practices and standards are focused on logical level of processes, which instruct *what* should be done, but not *how*
3. Poor definition of information models corresponding to process descriptions

ITIL is a commonly accepted reference for many industrial implementations and applications, but they handle the ITIL's concepts differently and have their own conceptual world. It is thus interesting to bring up a universal medium, adequate for better insights, comparison, interoperability, integration and further development. Following this link, we are proposing a development of the ITIL Definition Metamodel (DMM), as elaborated below in this chapter. Analogue to definition metamodels of other domains, the role of the ITIL DMM is:

1. Definition, representation, diagrammatical visualisation and gaining of understanding of concepts, structure and behaviour of the ITSM problem domain
2. Evaluation of consistency, correctness and completeness of ITIL definitions
3. Comparison, evaluation and benchmarking of different ITIL-based applications and tools
4. Organisation- and technology-independent platform for development of ITIL-based models and applications
5. High-level conceptual model for integration of ITSM components and systems
6. Integration platform for the exchange of ITSM models that are specified in different languages
7. Extending the environment into other domains

2 Related Works

Services and IT service management are hot topics and attract researchers and practitioners from all around the world. Most of them are focused on development of particular services or modelling specific service scenarios. There are a few academic or professional publications concerning the conceptual modelling or metamodels of IT services. They are mostly process-oriented and describe how to generalise service processes into universal patterns or conceptual models.

Böhmann et al. (2003) have proposed a modularisation approach based on a conceptual model of IT services. Heiskala et al. (2005) have presented a conceptual model for modelling configurable services. Jäntti and Eerola (2006) have proposed a conceptual model of the IT service problem management, which clarifies the concepts and connects these concepts to traditional software engineering tasks, such as testing and defect management. Betz (2003) has analysed and demonstrated the convergence of metamodelling, based on the approach and standards of the Object Management Group (OMG) and the IT service management, especially along with the ITIL. He has elaborated some possible future directions for alignment of these areas.

One of the most comprehensive works in this field is the Munich Network Management (MNM) service model (Garschhammer et al. 2001). The MNM service model 'provides a generic model defining commonly needed service-related terms, concepts and structuring rules in a general and unambiguous way'. The MNM team demonstrated the application of MNM model on concrete service desk scenarios and also discussed the service modelling in general.

Some ideas for the research presented in this chapter have been found in the management of the product engineering process, as treated in the OMG's Product Data Management Enablers Specification (OMG 2000).

3 ITIL Metamodelling Framework

Scientific and professional papers are overloaded with discussions of models, metamodels and meta-metamodels. The aim of this section is not to give a profound explanation of this domain, but rather to describe the approach and some conventions as applied in this chapter.

Business and information system models are abstract representations of the problem domain. They represent different components: data and process, structure and behaviour, requirement and transaction, etc. While a model is an abstraction of phenomena in the real world, a metamodel is an abstraction of the model itself. A metamodel is the underlying model of all models, which are further developed and represents concepts, relations between concepts, rules, constrains and other theories applicable and useful for modelling in the predefined class of problems. The metamodel comprises an explicit description of constructs, rules and notation for building domain-specific models.

Metamodelling is the application of some valid abstract framework to describe the semantics of one or more problem domains. It addresses the problem of different abstraction mechanisms concerning information at different abstraction levels and transition from one abstraction level to another. Metamodelling generates metadata, which are considered as a classifier for a concept and its instances. A classifier can in turn be an instance of a higher-level classifier, which is a part of the higher-level meta-metamodel. The difficulty of conceptualisation and building of metamodels lies in multiple aspects, first of all in different semantic framework (terminology, definitions, rules, etc.) and notions and documentation of different systems. Therefore, the methods of information abstraction and conceptualisation play the main role in the context of designing of metamodels.

Following the metamodelling approach, we have proposed the ITIL Metamodelling Framework and developed the Definition Metamodel (DMM) of the Information Technology Infrastructure Library (ITIL). We took into consideration the ITIL DMM in a relation to the OMG's Meta Object Facilities (MOF), which is an abstract framework for defining and managing metamodels, neutral of any technology (OMG 2006). MOF is designed as a four-layered architecture. This architecture is applied on the abstraction hierarchy of the Unified Modelling Language (UML) and presented on the left side of Fig. 1. The highest layer, denoted as M3, provides a meta-metamodel. In the context of the OMG, a meta-metamodel is an MOF model of the language. It describes the structure and semantics of the abstract language used by MOF to build metamodels, at M2 layer. The MOF M2 layer is the UML metamodel, the model that describes the UML itself. The model layer M1 contains a particular model, for example, models written in UML. The lowest layer is M0 or data (information) layer, containing the implementation entities of the real world (officially "data").

Unfortunately, the rigid perception of 'four-layered metamodel architecture' may cause confusion, as has been warned in the official OMG MOF specification (OMG 2006). According to the MOF 2.0, any number of layers (metalevels) is possible, but it must be higher than two. The key modelling concepts of the OMG suite of standards are *Classifier* and *Instance* or *Class* and *Object*, and the ability to navigate from an instance to its metaobject (its classifier). These concepts and navigation from class to its instance and vice versa can be used across any number of layers.

The right side of Fig. 1 presents the ITIL Metamodelling Framework. The primary objective of the ITIL Definition Metamodel (ITIL DMM) is to provide all stakeholders, who have an interest in the field of information technology service management and delivery, with a technology-independent representation of ITIL concepts, their relationships and interpretation.

Arrow (1) presents that the ITIL DMM is in fact the MOF M1 layer. Its object of modelling, i.e. MOF M0, are ITIL definitions, glossary and other theory.

Arrow (2) represents that the ITIL DMM is a baseline of ITIL-based models. These models are specialisations and extensions of the ITIL DMM and baseline for development of ITIL-based systems, i.e. ITIL-based software systems (computer applications) and business models. Recursively, ITIL-based models are MOF M1 and the ITIL-based systems are on the MOF M0.

According to the theory of model engineering, a *model* can be also treated as an object. It can also be modelled. From the point of view of modelling theory and system engineering ITIL DMM is:

1. A generic model for it describes the entire family (class) of modelling instances in more general terms
2. A conceptual model for it describes the functional information and other relevant aspects of the problem (business domain) on a high abstract level, suppressing non-critical details
3. A business-oriented model for it is a software-independent description of the model that is to be constructed and meaningful to business, not just software people
4. A vertical model since it is focused on the specific range of services concerning IT
5. A reusable model since it can be reused and transformed into explicit models
6. A business pattern since it is based on best practice and it can be relevant to multiple contexts

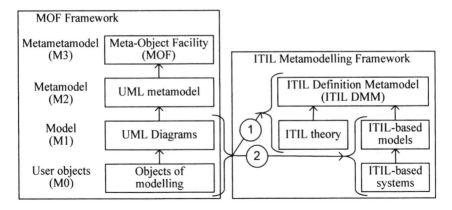

Fig. 1. The abstraction hierarchy of the MOF and the ITIL Metamodelling Framework

4 The ITIL Definition Metamodel and Its Components

Earlier in this chapter we have briefly introduced the ITIL Metamodelling Framework, which has been used as the conceptual base for the ITIL Definition Metamodel, elaborated below. ITOL DMM is derived from the original ITIL glossary (OGC 2006) and other specifications. As stated earlier, the ITIL DMM is presented in an object-oriented fashion by using structure (class) diagrams conform to the OMG's Unified Modelling Language (UML) notation (OMG 2005). As compared with software development, metamodelling efforts usually need a reduced set of concepts and notation. Therefore, it is a necessity to point out the naming and style conventions of UML, as applied in this chapter. All models presented in this chapter comprise only class names. The full model developed comprises also attributes and operations. Relations between UML classes and their multiplicity are drawn according to the common UML notation standard. Associations are bidirectional, drawn without arrow-ends. To improve the readability, names of relations are presented only in one direction. UML offers a variety of 'special' relations, but we used only aggregation (composite and shared) and generalisation.

ITIL is a highly complex domain. To resolve the problem of complexity and to support an incremental model development the ITIL DMM is divided into a set of Component Metamodels (CMM) as follows:

1. Core components (Service component; Process component; Information component; Organisation component; Responsibility component)
2. Service Support domain component (Service Desk; Incident Management; Problem Management; Configuration Management; Change Management; Release Management)
3. Service Delivery domain component (Service Level Management; Capacity Management; Continuity Management; Availability Management; IT Financial Management)

All these CMMs are just views of the common ITIL DMM.

In the rest of this section the examples of core and domain component models are presented, together with corresponding definitions of some concepts, as defined in the ITIL glossary (OGC 2006).

ITIL definitions are classified as follows:

1. Explicit definition, fully and clearly defined or formulated in the original source, i.e. the ITIL glossary
2. Implicit definition, implied or understood though not directly expressed
3. Derived definition, neither explicit nor implicit, but stemming from the original source and consistent

Keywords, i.e. terms that are explicitly defined in the ITIL glossary are marked in *italic*.

Figure 2 presents the Process CMM and basic relations to the Responsibility CMM and the Service CMM.

The Process CMM defines a structure of functional components (e.g. how an Activity is a part of a Process, and an Action is a part of an Activity). *Explicit definitions* concerning the Process CMM are:

1. *Activity* – A set of actions designed to achieve a particular result. Activities are usually defined as part of *Processes* or *Plans*, and are documented in procedures.
2. *Process* – A structured set of *Activities* designed to accomplish a specific *Objective*. A *Process* takes one or more defined inputs and turns them into defined outputs. A *Process* may include any of the *Roles*, responsibilities, tools and management controls required to reliably deliver the outputs.

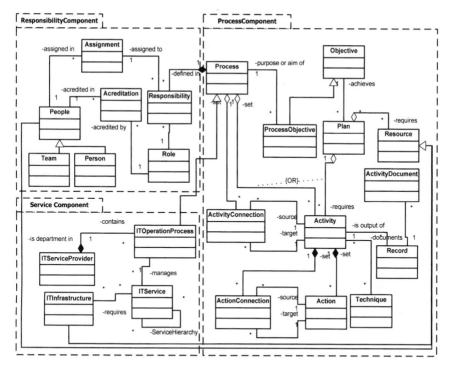

Fig. 2. The Process CMM

3. *Objective* – The defined purpose or aim of a *Process*, an *Activity* or an *Organisation* as a whole. Objectives are usually expressed as measurable targets. The term Objective is also informally used to mean a *Requirement.*

4. *Plan* – A *Document*, which identifies a series of *Activities* and the *Resources* required achieving an *Objective.*

5. *Record* – A *Document* containing the results or other outputs from a *Process* or *Activity.*

6. *Resource* – A generic term that includes *IT Infrastructure*, people, money or anything else that might help to deliver an *IT Service.*

Shared aggregation, represented on class diagram by a line with a hollow diamond, indicates that some classifier (*Process* or *Plan*) cannot be performed without another classifier (*Activity*).

ITIL *implicit definitions* concerning the Process CMM are:

1. *Technique* – A specific way of performing an *Activity*, including a specific approach, methods and skills.

2. *Action* – A constitutive part of some *Activity.*

Composite aggregation, represented with a full diamond, defines a relation between composite and composed objects. The composite object consists (or is made up) of smaller "composed" objects. In our case an *Activity* is composed of *Actions*.

It creates, modifies and destroys them. An *Action* exists only as a part of some *Activity*.

ITIL-*derived definitions* concerning the Process CMM are:

1. *Activity Connection* and *Action Connection* – Both provide relationships between the instances of the same class, i.e. up and down a composition hierarchy. These also define relations between entities at the same level of decomposition, e.g. that one *Activity* or *Action* relates with other (sequence, parallelism and other temporal or causal dependencies).

Figure 3 presents the structure of the component metamodel concerning ITIL Problem Management domain and basic relations to the Incident and Change Management domains. Definitions of basic concepts are as follows (OGC 2006):

2. *Change* – The addition, modification or removal of anything that could have an effect on *IT Services*.
3. *Error Control* – The *Activity* responsible for managing *Known Errors* until they are resolved by the successful implementation of *Changes*.
4. *Incident* – An unplanned interruption to an *IT Service* or reduction in the *Quality* of an *IT Service*. Any event which could affect an *IT Service* in the future is also an *Incident*.
5. *Incident Record* – A *Record* containing the details of an *Incident*. Each *Incident record* documents the life cycle of a single *Incident*.
6. *Known Error (KE)* – A *Problem* that has a documented *Root Cause* and a *Workaround*. *Known Errors* are created by *Problem Control* and are managed throughout their life cycle by *Error Control*.
7. *Known Error Record* – A record containing the details of a *Known Error*. Each *Known Error Record* documents the life cycle of a *Known Error*, including the status, *Root Cause* and *Workaround*.
8. *Proactive Problem Management* is the part of the *Problem Management Process*.
9. *Problem Control* – Part of the *Problem Management* Process responsible for identifying the *Root Cause* and developing a *Workaround* or structural solution for a *Problem*.
10. *Problem Management* – The *Process* responsible for managing the life cycle of all *Problems*.
11. *Problem Record* – A *Record* containing the details of a *Problem*. Each Problem Record documents the life cycle of a single *Problem*.
12. *Resolution* – Action taken to repair the *Root Cause* of an *Incident* or *Problem*, or to implement a *Workaround*.
13. *Root Cause* – The underlying or original cause of an *Incident* or *Problem*.
14. *Workaround* – Reducing or eliminating the *Impact* of an *Incident* or *Problem* for which a full *Resolution* is not yet available.

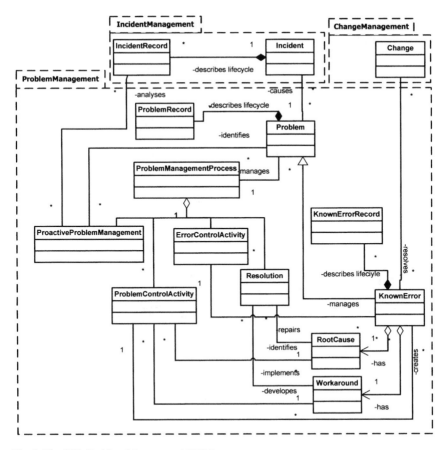

Fig. 3. The ITIL Problem Management CMM

5 Application of the Framework

This section presents some results of the application and evaluation of the proposed ITIL Metamodelling Framework.

The first application of the ITIL DMM was a recursive evaluation of consistency, correctness and completeness of ITIL definition itself. Namely, one of the motivations for development of metamodels is to move the object of validation and verification (V&V) from the textual description of some problem domain to its metamodel, which is a more structured, expressive and formalised representation of domain knowledge. Objectives of the validation and the verification are the same, i.e. detection of absence of completeness, consistency and other desirable properties. However, the approaches to validation and verification differ in their orientation. V&V originated in the fields of software engineering, but can be also applied on metamodels.

Table 1. Example of ITIL definitions and their semantic anomalies

IT Operation: The *Process* responsible for the day-to-day monitoring and management of one or more *IT Services* and the *IT Infrastructure* they depend on. The term is also used to refer to the group or department within an *IT Service Provider* responsible for *IT Operations.*   *Homonym:* Is the *IT Operation* a *Process* or an organisational unit?
Alert: A warning that a *threshold has been reached, something has changed* or a *Failure* has occurred. Alerts are often created and managed by *System Management* tools and are managed by the *Event Management Process. Event* – An *Alert* or notification created by any *IT Service, Configuration Item* or monitoring tool.   *Synonym:* Are *Alert* and *Event* synonyms?

Resolution: Action taken to repair the Root Cause of an Incident or Problem, or to implement a Workaround. In ISO/IEC 20000, Resolution Processes is the Process group that includes Incident and Problem Management.
    Completeness of decomposition: Is Resolution also an Activity or just an Action?
    Homonym: Is *Resolution* a part of the *Problem Management* or a complex composite?

Business Relationship Manager: A *Role* responsible for maintaining the *Relationship* with one or more *Customers*. This *Role* is often combined with the *Service Level Manager Role.*   *Dangling reference: Service Level Manager Role* is not defined as a keyword
Procedure: A Document containing steps that specify how to achieve an *Activity. Procedures* are defined as part of *Processes.*   *Consistency of Decomposition:* Is the *Procedure* always defined as a part of an *Activity* or can also be defined on a higher level of a *Process*?

For the purpose of our research a high-level checking of correctness, consistency and completeness of ITIL metamodels has been performed, in both syntactic and semantic dimensions. Consistency of the metamodel implies that there are not conflicting statements, rules or definitions of the same fact or situation. Some of the appearances of inconsistency are redundancy, unnecessary conditions, logical contradiction, subsumed and circular rules, naming conflicts (synonyms, homonyms), inconsistent generalisation/specialisation and other logical or semantic contradictions. Completeness means that there is no one relevant statement that could be added to the metamodel without creating inconsistency. Incompleteness issues are: missing concepts and rules, dead-end rules, unreachable concepts, dangling references, unreferenced attributes and other unintentional non-determinism. Correctness means both completeness and consistency and has syntactical and semantic aspects.

Table 1 provides an abstract of the cross reference between the ITIL definitions, as stated in the ITIL glossary, and the corresponding semantic anomalies.

The second practical application of the proposed framework was the comparison and evaluation of two different ITIL-based tools (Sys. 1 and Sys. 2 in Fig. 4.).

The *Supported concepts* criterion is the ratio between the total number of ITIL DMM and ITIL-based tool classes and associations. *Semantic and syntactic correctness* of two applications is a result of a subjective one-to-one comparison with the ITIL DMM. Evaluation of other software quality criteria is out of the scope of this chapter, but these criteria are evaluated in a case-study fashion, by using the software quality metrics (ISO 9126). Results of assessments are collected by using a simple spreadsheet application and presented in a form of radar graph.

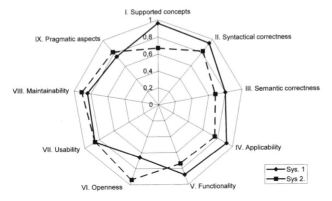

Fig. 4. Comparison and evaluation of two different ITIL-based tools

Practical application not only confirmed the presented evaluation method, but also highlighted some topics for future research and development. First of all, quantification, formalisation, metrics and decision-making methods should eliminate subjective assessment, wherever possible.

6 Conclusion

This chapter proposes and elaborates the construction of a metamodel of ITIL in an object-oriented fashion by using structure diagrams conform to UML notation. This metamodel provides an abstract representation of ITIL concepts and interpretation, as well as enables better insights into available approaches and tools, their comparison, integration and further development. Some important approaches to the metamodelling in software development and IT-related services have been referenced.

According to the approach given earlier in this chapter, the ITIL Definition Metamodel (ITIL DMM) is an abstract model of the theory of ITIL (ITIL specifications), and also a common model of all ITIL-based models. Recursively, an ITIL-based model is an instance of the ITIL metamodel, and also a representation of all corresponding ITIL-based systems and computer programs built upon it. To resolve the problem of complexity and to support an incremental model development, ITIL DMM is divided into a set of Component Metamodels (CMM).

Based on two applications of the ITIL DMM, we conclude that it enables recursive evaluation of consistency, correctness and completeness of ITIL definition itself. It also provides a mechanism for compliancy assessment of ITIL compliant models and applications.

7 References

Betz, C.T. (2003) The convergence of metadata and IT service management. University of Minnesota, http://erp4it.typepad.com/erp4it/uploads/MetadataITSM.pdf

Böhmann, T., Junginger, M. and Krcmar, H. (2003) Modular Service Architectures: A Concept and Method for Engineering IT Services. Proceedings of the 36th Annual Hawaii International Conference on System Sciences (HICSS-36), Big Isl., Hawaii, January 6–9.

Garschhammer, M., Hauck, R., Kempter, B., Radisic, I., Roelle, H. and Schmidt, H. (2001) The MNM Service Model – Refined Views on Generic Service Management. Journal of Communications and Networks, 3(4).

Heiskala, M., Tiihonen, J. and Soininen, T. (2005) A Conceptual Model for Configurable Services. IJCAI 2005 Workshop on Configuration, Edinburgh, Scotland, July 30.

Jäntti, M. and Eerola, A. (2006) A Conceptual Model of IT Service Problem Management. Proceedings of the IEEE Conference on Service Systems and Service Management (ISSSM'06), University of Technology of Troyes, France, pp. 798–803.

OMG (2000) Product Data Management Enablers Specification, version 1.3, OMG – Object Management Group.

OMG (2005) Unified Modelling Language (UML): Superstructure, version 2.0, OMG.

OMG (2006) Meta Object Facility (MOF) – Core Specification, version 2.0, OMG.

OGC (2002) ITIL Service Delivery and ITIL Service Support. OMG, The Stationery Office Books, ISBN 0113300174 and ISBN 0113300158.

OGC (2006) ITIL Glossary of Terms, Definitions and Acronyms, Baseline v01, Office of Government Commerce.

An Approach for WSDL-Based Automated Robustness Testing of Web Services

Samer Hanna and Malcolm Munro

Department of Computer Science, Durham University, UK,
{samer.hanna, malcolm.munro}@durham.ac.uk

Abstract Web Services are considered a new paradigm for building software applications that has many advantages over the previous paradigms; however, Web Services are still not widely used because service requesters do not trust services that are built by others. Testing can be used to solve part of this problem because it can be used to assess some of the quality attributes of Web Services. This chapter proposes a framework that can be used to test the robustness quality attribute of a Web Service. This framework is based on analyzing the Web Service Description Language (WSDL) document of Web Services to identify what faults could affect the robustness attribute and then test cases were designed to detect those faults. A proof of concept tool has been implemented and experiments carried out that show the usefulness of this approach.

1 Introduction

Web Services (W3C, 2004b) are considered a new paradigm in building software applications; this paradigm is based on open standards and the Internet. Web Services facilitate the interconnection between heterogeneous applications since it is based on XML open standards that may be used to call remote services or exchange data. Web Services are considered an implementation or realization of the Service-Oriented Architecture (SOA) (Singh & Huhns, 2005), which consists of three roles: *Service Requester* (Consumer), *Service Provider*, and *Service Publisher* (*Broker*). To implement SOA, Web Services depend on a group of XML-based standards such as Simple Object Access Protocol (SOAP), Web Service Description Language (WSDL) and Universal Description, Discovery and Integration (UDDI). A problem that limits the growth of Web Services is the lack of trustworthiness by the requesters of Web Services because they can only see the WSDL document of a Web Service, but not how this service was implemented by the provider.

An example of using a Web Service is when building an application that needs to get information about a book (e.g., price and author) given the book's ISBN.

C. Barry et al. (eds.), *Information Systems Development: Challenges in Practice, Theory, and Education, Vol.2*, doi: 10.1007/978-0-387-78578-3_40,
© Springer Science+Business Media, LLC 2009

Amazon provide a Web Service (see Cornelius, 2003) to fulfill this requirement and using the approach in this chapter it can assess how robust the service is before using it.

Software Testing is mainly used to assess the quality attributes and detect faults in a software system and demonstrate that the actual program behavior will conform to the expected behavior. Testing techniques can be divided into black box and white box depending on the availability of the source code; if test data are generated depending on the source code, then a testing technique belongs to white box, while if the source code is unavailable, then a testing technique belongs to black box.

This chapter's approach of Web Services testing assumes that the tester only have the WSDL document of the Web Service under test and not the source code, for this reason black box testing techniques will be used. Testing can be used to solve part of the problems of Web Services trustworthiness; by assessing the quality attributes of a Web Service under test, the confidence of the requesters of this Web Service will increase or decrease according to the test results. It will also help the requesters to choose between Web Services doing the same task. However, Web Services testing still face many problems like unavailability of the source code to the requesters and that the traditional testing techniques do not cope with the new characteristics introduced by Web Services standards (Zhang & Zhang, 2005). This chapter introduces an approach to solve part of these problems, which is based on analyzing WSDL documents in order to generate test cases to test the robustness quality attribute of Web Services.

Testing has special importance for systems that are assembled from many components (Dix & Hofmann, 2002), Web Services application are dynamically assembled or composed from many different Web Services, which makes testing very important in Web Services application in order to gain more confidence of the quality attributes to each Web Service in the composition. This chapter focuses on testing the robustness quality attribute of Web Services only and it solves the problem of unavailability of the source code to the application builder by making the testing process depends on WSDL only. Robustness is a sub-attribute of reliability, and to assess how reliable a Web Service is, other sub-attributes of reliability such as fault tolerance should also be assessed.

This chapter has the following main contributions:

- Finding a method for automatic generation of test cases to assess the robustness of Web Service. This method can also be enhanced to assess other quality attributes.
- Finding how WSDL can help in detecting faults that may affect the robustness quality attribute of Web Services.
- Analyzing what traditional black box testing techniques can be used to test a Web Service' robustness depending on WSDL only.

This chapter is organized as follows: Section 2 discusses the related work. Section 3 will introduce a model for Web Services robustness testing, Section 4 will describe the process of test data generation, Section 5 will discuss how the tool for

Web Services robustness testing was implemented and also the evaluation of this tool, and finally Section 6 discusses the conclusion of this research and provide future research paths.

2 Related Works

There are many research papers concerning Web Services testing, but the closest to the research presented in this chapter are summarized below.

Zhang and Zhang (2005) stated that there is lack of technologies for Web Services verification and that the current testing techniques cannot merely be applied to Web Service. They discussed an approach to test the reliability attribute of a Web Service.

Bloomberg (2002) lists a variety of desirable capabilities for testing Web Services, such as:

- Testing WSDL files and using them for test plan generation: using the information in WSDL files to generate black box test plans.
- Web Service requester emulation: emulating the requester of a Web Service by sending test messages to another Web Service and analyzing the results.

Offutt and Xu (2004) used data perturbation, which is considered a black box testing technique to generate test cases for Web Service. They stated that most of the current testing tools for Web Services focus on testing SOAP messages, WSDL files, and requester provider emulation.

Looker et al. (2005) used fault injection to assess the dependability of Web Services.

Bai et al. (2005) used WSDL for test case generation.

After analyzing how researchers tackled Web Services testing, we noticed that they focused mainly on testing the composition of Web Services using integration testing and few considered testing a single Web Service. Few researchers discussed the quality attributes and faults of Web Services.

3 A Model of Web Services Robustness Testing

The approach proposed in this chapter for Web Services robustness testing depends on analyzing:

- WSDL documents to identify what faults may affect the robustness quality attribute of Web Services
- What testing techniques can be used to detect those faults
- How test data can be generated based on specific information inside WSDL

This analysis is then used to build rules for test data generation for Web Services. Table 1 shows the schema for specifying these rules. Figure 1 describes the model of this approach to Web Services testing. The model describes all the components that participate in testing the robustness quality attribute of Web Services and also how they are related to each other. Next, a brief definition of those components and their relationships are given.

Web Service is the service under test. *WSDL* is the contract or the specification of the Web Service under test. *Operation* is the *operation element* of the specific operation under tests. *Input Message* is the input message of the operation under test. *Input Parameter* is the parameters of the input message of an operation inside WSDL. *XML Schema Datatype* is the datatype specification of the input parameter to the WSDL operations. *Middleware* is an integration or connectivity software (Vinoski, 2002), using a middleware enables processes or services on different places (machines) to communicate. *Fault* is a defect or malformation in the system that may lead to a failure (Osterweil, 1996). *Quality Attribute* is the product characteristics that meet the user needs or expectations whether explicit or not (Garvin, 1984). *Robustness*, for the purposes of this research is defined as: *the quality aspect of whether a Web Service continues to perform despite some violations of the constraints in its input parameters specification. Testing technique* is a Software Engineering Technique that is used to detect faults and assess some of the quality attributes of a software system or application. After a survey of the traditional testing techniques it was found that the testing techniques that can be used to assess robustness of Web Services and that can be applied to the information inside WSDL include: *boundary value analysis* (Jorgensen, 2002), *equivalence partitioning* (Myers, 1979), *robustness testing* (Jorgensen, 2002), *syntax testing* (Beizer, 1990), and *mutation testing* (Voas & McGraw, 1998). *Test Data Generation Rules* are the rules that will be used for the test data generation for Web Services. *Test Case*, when the Web Service under test is invoked for the purpose of analyzing its response, then test data together with the response become a test case. *Client Generator* is the component that is responsible for building a client to the Web Service and invoking it using the test data. *Response* represents the reply from the Web Service, which is either a SOAP response or a SOAP fault message. *Analyzer* is the component that compares the response of the Web Service with the expected response that can be taken from the test case. *Test Report* is the result of the test.

Researchers in the field of Web Services testing proposed other models for verification and test case generation for Web Services (Tsai et al., 2005). The model in Fig. 1 is different to these models in that it relates faults, quality attributes and the WSDL components in the rules for Web Services testing.

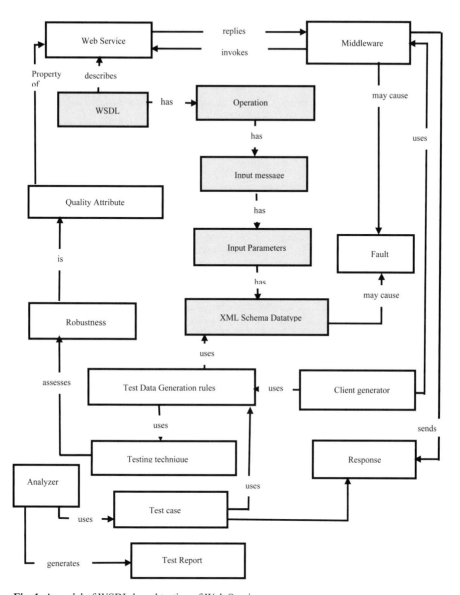

Fig. 1. A model of WSDL-based testing of Web Services

Table 1. Schema for the test data generation rules

Attribute	Type	Description
ID	String	Identifier or reference of the rule
Fault	Enum	The fault that the test data suppose to detect
Traditional Testing Technique	Enum	The traditional testing technique used in the rule,
		Testing_Technique::= BVA | EP | RT | MT | ST
		Where BVA = Boundary Value Analysis
		EP = Equivalent Partitioning
		RT = Robustness Testing
		MT = Mutation Testing
		ST = Syntax Testing
Traditional test data generation rule	String	Description of how the test data is generated using the traditional testing technique choose
Valid/Invalid	Enum	Whether the test data chosen are valid or not
WSDL Component test data is based on	Enum	The WSDL component test data is based on which could be the input parameter datatype or the constraining facets for the input parameter datatype
WS Datatype	Datatype	Defines the Web Service datatype of the input parameter tested. Where
		WS_datatype:: = String | Integer | Date and Time | Real | Boolean | null
WS Test Datatype	Datatype	Defines the Web Service datatype of the test data which might be the same as the Web Service datatype or different
WS test data	Depends on WS Test Datatype	Defines the actual data used for testing
Expected output	String	Defines what is the expected response of SOAP message of the Web Service under test
Quality attribute(s) assessed	Enum	Defines the quality attribute this test data aims to assess

4 Test Data Generation

Test data generation depends on the input parameters datatype and this section will explain how these datatypes and their constraints can be used to generate test data. XML Schema datatypes can be categorized as: *built-in primitive (or derived from built-in primitive)* simple datatypes, *user-defined* datatypes, and *complex* datatypes. Test data will be generated depending on which of these categories an input parameter belongs.

4.1 Generating Test Data for Simple Datatypes

Designing test data for simple datatype is more difficult than designing test data for user-derived and complex datatypes because there are no constraining facets (CF) or other schema components that can help in designing the test cases. After analyzing the simple XML Schema datatypes that are used inside WSDL it was found that they can be categorized as: *integer* or derived from *integer*, *string or derived from string*, *real (float, decimal, double)*, *date and time* or derive from *date and time*, boolean. Table 2 describes the test data generation process for simple datatypes, based on the rule schema in Table 1.

4.2 Generating Test Data for User-Derived Datatypes

User-derived datatypes are created by restricting a built-in (or derived from built-in) datatype using constraining facets. The approach here for test data generation for this kind of datatypes depends on the base type (the datatype from which this datatype was derived) and the constraining facets (CF) (W3C, 2004a). Table 3 shows the rules for generating test data for a combination of base type and their CF. For

Table 2. Test data generation for simple datatypes

ID	WrongInput1	WrongInput2	WrongInput3
Fault	Wrong input datatype → Null replacement	Wrong input datatype → Integer replacement	Wrong input datatype → Real replacement
Traditional Testing Technique	EP & MT	EP & MT	EP & MT
Traditional test data generation rule	Replace the input parameter with Null	Replace the input parameter with Integer	Replace the input parameter with Real
Valid/Invalid	Invalid	Invalid	Invalid
WSDL Component test data is based on	Operation input message parameter's datatype	Operation input message parameter's datatype	Operation input message parameter's datatype
WS Datatype	String/Integer/Date and Time/ Real/ Boolean	String, Date and Time, Boolean	Integer, String, Date and Time, Boolean
WS Test Datatype	Null	Integer	Real
WS test data	Null	Random Integer	Random Real
Expected output	Fault message with proper fault string	Fault message with proper fault string	Fault message with proper fault string
Quality attribute(s) assessed	Middleware/Service Robustness	Middleware/Service Robustness	Middleware/Service Robustness

Table 3. Test Data Generation for User-derived datatypes

ID	WrongRange1	WrongRange2	NotInList1
Fault	Wrong range → Below lower bound	Wrong range → Above upper bound	Item not in list
Traditional Testing Technique	RT	RT	EP
Traditional test data generation rule	Select test data below lower bound	Select test data above upper bound	Select item not in the list of expected values
Valid/Invalid	Invalid	Invalid	Invalid
WSDL Component test data is based on	Operation input message parameter's datatype and its minInclusive CF	Operation input message parameter's datatype and its maxInclusive CF	Operation input message parameter's datatype and its enumeration CF
WS Datatype	Integer/Date and Time/Real	Integer/Date and Time/Real	All
WS Test Datatype	Same as WS DataType	Same as WS DataType	Same as WS DataType
WS test data	minInclusive value − 1	maxInclusive value + 1	Random item not in the enumeration list with same datatype
Expected output	Fault message with proper fault string	Fault message with proper fault string	Fault message with proper fault string
Quality attribute(s) assessed	Middleware/Service Robustness	Middleware/Service Robustness	Middleware/Service Robustness

each CF and for each of the datatypes an analysis has been carried out on what faults may be caused by violating the datatype's CFs and also what test data should be used to detect these faults. (Table 3 shows only few of these test data for space limitation.)

4.3 Generating Test Data for Complex Datatypes

Complex datatype consists of a group of Simple and User-derived datatypes. If the input parameter to a Web Service is of complex datatype, then for each of the Simple and User-derived datatype of its sub-elements, the relevant test data rules are chosen as given in Sections 4.1 and 4.2 and then the cross product for the test data of each of those parts are computed.

5 Implementation and Evaluation

This section firstly describes the tool that implements the automatic test data and test cases generation process and then evaluates the efficiency of the proposed approach of test data and test case generation in Web Services testing.

5.1 Implementation

A proof of concept tool WSTF (Web Services Testing Framework) has been implemented and has the following functionality:

- Generate test data for a certain Web Service depending on its WSDL only and by using the rules described in Section 4.
- Store the resulted test data in an XML file so that it can be used by any requester or provider regardless of the platform or the middleware being used. List 1 shows only part of the test data that was generated using the WSTF tool for an input parameter of type integer.
- Automatically build a requester or client to the Web Service under test using the test data XML file generated in the previous step.
- Generate test cases by using the test data in the XML file to invoke the Web Service using the client generated and then store the response together with the test data used in a new XML file. List 2 shows a portion of a test cases XML file generated for a Web Service operation that accepts two input parameters of type integer, the output element represents the response of the Web Service. The first test cases send two *null* value for the Web Service, the second test cases send *null* and *random string* to the Web Service.

```
<input_part>
<part_name>first</part_name>
<part_dataType>int</part_dataType>
<testings>
  <testing>
    <test_datatype>null</test_datatype>
    <test_data>null</test_data>
    <expected_output>Fault message with proper fault string</expected_output>
    <quality_assessed>Middleware/Service robustness</quality_assessed>
  </testing>
  <testing>
    <test_datatype>String</test_datatype>
    <test_data>tjjzdim</test_data>
    <expected_output>Fault message with proper fault string</expected_output>
    <quality_assessed>Middleware/Service robustness</quality_assessed>
  </testing>
```

List 1. An example of a test data for an input parameter of type integer

5.2 Evaluation

To evaluate the approach of this chapter, the WSTF tool was used in a series of experiments.

```
   <test_case>
   <first>null</first>
   <second>null</second>
            <output>Fault SOAP message sent with fault string: No such operation
'getGreaterNumber'</output>
   </test_case>
   <test_case>
    <first>tjjzdim</first>
    <second>null</second>
            <output>Fault SOAP message sent with fault string: org.xml.sax.SAXException:
  Bad types (class java.lang.String -&gt; int)</output>
   </test_case>
```

List 2. Test cases example

1. Experiments on a Web Service that accepts three integer input values and returns a String. The experiment was to assess the robustness against each of the following faults (null replacement, String replacement, Real replacement, Date-Time replacement, Boolean replacement, empty String replacement, and maximum allowed Integer). The experiments used Axis middleware and Tomcat web server. An interesting robustness failure was found in the Axis middleware when sending an SOAP message with *null* value as a parameter. Axis generated a fault response message with fault string "No such operation" as can be seen in List 2. This is considered a robustness failure because the tool invoked the correct operation and the fault message should be either "Bad type" or "Null value was sent as a parameter" or any other exception handling message that tells the requester of a Web Service that *null* value was sent to an operation inside this Web Service. Another interesting result was that Axis generated a fault message for the first parameter if that parameter was false and ignored the other parameters. For example, the second test case in List 2 contains *random string* for the first parameter and *null* for the second parameter, but Axis did not care for the *null* and generated a fault message because a string was used for the first parameter and not integer as expected by the operation. However, Axis was robust for all other faults in our test data.

2. The same experiments in 1 was conducted again, but after modifying the types of the input parameters inside WSDL by adding constraints to those parameters in order to apply test data rules for User-derived datatypes. The robustness faults that were tested depended on the constraining facet for the input parameter, for example, for the *minInclusive* facet (below lower bound, at lower bound, and just above lower bound) and the same for the faults that can be associated with the other types of constraining facets (minExclusive, maxInclusive, maxExclusive, totoalDigits, fractionDigits, enumeration, pattern, length, maxLength, and minLength). Eleven experiments were carried out, one for each constrain. WSTF was able to assess how robust the Web Service was and revealed what operations inside the Web Service should be modified to handle the invalid input.

6 Conclusion and Future Work

Web Services are considered a new paradigm of building software application that depends on the reusability of services that can be integrated with applications using open standards such as XML and the Internet. Testing Web Services is important because it increases the confidence and trustworthiness of the requester and the provider of a Web Service.

This chapter proposed a novel approach of testing the robustness quality attribute of a Web Service that can be easily extended to test other quality attributes. This approach is based on analyzing the WSDL document that describes the Web Service and then using the description of the input parameter to generate test data depending on the expected faults that might be introduced to the Web Service based on those parameter datatypes and their constraints.

Future work is needed in the following directions:

- Assessing other quality attributes using WSDL, such as the vulnerability to wrong input, which is one aspect of security testing.
- Since testing Web Services is expensive we want to find a way to reduce the number of test cases, but without compromising the robustness assessment.
- Analyzing how other elements of WSDL may affect the robustness quality attribute, such as the binding element, for example.
- Analyzing if there exist other faults that also may affect the robustness quality attribute of Web Services.

References

Bai, X., Dong, W., Tsai, W. & Chen, Y. (2005) WSDL-Based Automatic test case generation for Web Services testing. Proceedings of the 2005 IEEE International Workshop on Service-Oriented System Engineering (SOSE'05), 20–21 October, China, pp. 215–220.

Beizer, B. (1990) Software Testing Techniques. Second Edition. Van Nostrand Reinhold, New York. ISBN 0-442-20672-0.

Bloomberg, J. (2002) Testing Web Services Today and Tomorrow. Rational Edge E-zine for the Rational Community.

Cornelius, B. (2003) Web Services Using Axis. Computing Services, University of Oxford, http://www.barrycornelius.com/papers/web.services.using.axis/onefile/

Dix, M. & Hofmann, H. (2002) Automated Software Robustness Testing, Static and Adaptive Test Case Design Methods. Proceedings of the 28th Euromicro Conference.

Garvin, D. (1984) What does "Product Quality" Really Mean? Sloan Management Review, USA, pp. 25–45.

Jorgensen, P. (2002) Software Testing – A Craftsman's Approach, Second Edition. CRC, Boca Raton, FL. ISBN 0-8493-0809-7.

Looker, N., Gwynne, B., Xu, J. & Munro, M. (2005) An Ontology-Based Approach for Determining the Dependability of Service-Oriented Architecture. 10th IEEE International Workshop on Object-oriented Real-time Dependable Systems, Sedona, USA.

Myers, G. (1979) The Art of Software Testing. Wiley, New York. ISBN 0-471-04328-1.

Offutt, J. & Xu, W. (2004) Generating Test Cases for Web Services Using Data perturbation. ACM SIGSOFT, Software Engineering Notes, 29(5), September, 1–10.

Osterweil, L. (1996) Strategic Directions in Software Quality. ACM Computing Surveys, 28(4) December, 738–750.

Singh, M.P. & Huhns, M.N. (2005) "Service-Oriented Computing". Wiley, England. ISBN 978-0470091487.

Tsai, W.T., Cao, Z., Chen, Y. & Paul, R. (2005) Web Services-Based Collaborative and Cooperative Computing, Proceedings of the IEEE 7th International Symposium on Autonomous Decentralized Systems (ISADS) China, 4–8 April, pp. 552–556.

Vinoski, V. (2002) Where is Middleware? IEEE COMPUTING. 6 March, April, pp. 83–85.

Voas, J. & McGraw, G. (1998) Software Fault Injection – Inoculating Programs Against Errors. Wiley, New York. ISBN 0-471-18381-4.

W3C (2004a) XML Schema Part 2: Datatypes, Second Edition. W3C Recommendation 28 October 2004, http://www.w3.org/TR/xmlschema-2/

W3C (2004b) Web Services Architecture. W3C Working Group Note, 11 February 2004, http://www.w3.org/TR/ws-arch/

Zhang, J. & Zhang, L.-J. (2005) Criteria Analysis and Validation of the Reliability of Web Services-oriented Systems. Proceedings of the IEEE International Conference on Web Services (ICWS'05), pp. 621–628.

Events Propagation from the Business System Level into the Information System Level[1]

Diana Bugaite and Olegas Vasilecas

Information Systems Research Laboratory, Vilnius Gediminas Technical University, Lithuania, diana@isl.vgtu.lt, olegas@fm.vgtu.lt

Abstract   Active database systems (ADBS) have been developed for applications needing an automatic reaction in response to certain event occurring. The desired behaviour is expressed by event-condition-action rules (ECA rules), which have been proposed by HiPAC as a formalism for active database capabilities. A set of rules, implemented in active database management systems (ADBMS), is taken from the particular application domain. However, in the application domain or ontology, to which the rules belong, they are not always expressed in terms of ECA rules. This chapter covers how events, as an important part of ECA rules, are modelling in the process of rule-based systems development. Section 1 describes the main problem, which is going to be analysed in this chapter. Section 2 reviews related works on events modelling in the process of systems development. Section 3 details events propagation from the business system level into the information system (IS) level. Section 4 presents a case study and Section 5 concludes the paper.

1 Introduction

Active database systems (ADBS) have been developed for applications needing an automatic reaction in response to certain event occurring. The desired behaviour is expressed by event-condition-action rules (ECA rules), which have been proposed by HiPAC (Dayal et al., 1996) as a formalism for active database capabilities. Generally, ECA rules are represented by rule language, for example, SQL triggers in an active database.

Once a set of rules has been defined, the ADBS monitors the relevant events. Whenever it detects the occurrence of a relevant event it notifies the component

[1] The work is supported by Lithuanian State Science and Studies Foundation according to High Technology Development Program Project 'Business Rules Solutions for Information Systems Development (VeTIS)' Reg. No. B-07042

C. Barry et al. (eds.), *Information Systems Development: Challenges in Practice, Theory, and Education, Vol.2*, doi: 10.1007/978-0-387-78578-3_41,
© Springer Science+Business Media, LLC 2009

responsible for its rule execution. Subsequently, all rules which are defined to respond to this event are triggered or fired and must be executed. Rule execution incorporates condition evaluation and action execution. First, the condition is evaluated and if it is satisfied, the active database management system (ADBMS) executes the action.

A set of rules, implemented in an ADBMS, is taken from the particular application domain. However, in the application domain or ontology, to which the rules belong, they are not always expressed in terms of ECA rules. Some of these rules have explicit or implicit condition and action parts. The missing condition can always be substituted with a default condition state as TRUE. Some rules may have no explicit action since they can state what kind of transition from one data state to another is not admissible. But the majority of these rules do not define explicitly or implicitly the event.

An event is an important component of an ECA rule, since event denotes a particular occurrence in a database or outside database. Events specification and linking them to corresponding rules enable us to automate rules triggering. Moreover, system is not overloaded during the rule execution every time when an event occurs.

The objective of this chapter is to investigate how events, as part of ECA rules, are modelling in the process of rule-based systems development.

2 Related Works

The development of an enterprise system requires that systems operating at all enterprise levels (business, information and software) would share a common conceptualisation (Caplinskas, 2003). A business system of an enterprise depends to a large extent on the supporting information system (IS) and a software system. Therefore, changes in the business system result in the changes of the IS and the software system.

In an ADBMS context (Dittrich et al., 1996), an event type describes situations to which a reaction must be shown. An event type can be primitive or composite. Primitive event types define elementary occurrences that are of interest; possible primitive event types are method invocation, data item modification, transaction operation, abstract and time event types. The event types supported should at least subsume the data manipulation language (DML) operations and transaction statements. This means that, e.g. the update of a specific relation can be defined as an event of interest (Dittrich et al., 1996). Composite event types are defined as combinations of other primitive or composite events using a set of event constructors such as disjunction, conjunction and sequence.

Event occurrences are the instances of event types (Dittrich et al., 1996). Such an occurrence is conceived as a pair (*<event type>*, *<timestamp>*) where *<event type>* denotes the event type of the occurrence, and *<timestamp>* represents the point in time when the occurrence actually took place. In general, the point in time when an event occurs is a parameter of the event occurrence. Further parameters are possible, such as the transaction in which an event occurs or the name of the user who has started this transaction.

An event-driven system is a system in which actions result from business events. Rules determine what these events are and under what conditions they can lead to some particular actions. Any action may constitute a new business event.

In Cilia (2005) events are classified as follows. *Database events* refer to the data modification (like SQL operations INSERT, DELETE and UPDATE) and data retrieval in the database (like selection in a relational database). *Transaction events* refer to the different stages of transaction execution, e.g. begin transaction, commit, and rollback. *Temporal events* refer to time. *Abstract events* or application-defined events are signalled explicitly by the application, e.g. AuctionCancelled.

According to Mahesh (1996) and Humphreys et al. (1997) knowledge about events is represented by ontology as well. Events are modelled by the terms defined in the domain ontology. Sometimes, special event ontologies are created for events in a certain application domain modelling. But these so-called event ontologies do not exist alone. They usually are related to term (or so-called context) ontologies of the same domain (Yu et al., 2001).

According to Michelson (2006), each event occurrence has an *event header* and an *event body*. The event header contains elements describing the event occurrence, such as the event specification ID, event name, event type, event timestamp, event occurrence number and event creator (like applications, services, business processes, data stores, people, time and automated agents that generate events and/or perform an event-driven action). These elements are consistent, across event specifications. Event types are simple or primitive events and complex events (Michelson, 2006; Adaikkalavan et al., 2003; Rules Manager Concepts, 2005). The event body describes what happened. For example, if a customer reserves a flight, the event body should contain the information about customer, airlines, from-city, to-city, departure time and return time. The event body must be fully described so that any interested party could use the information without having to analyse all domain ontology. To ensure events are understood by all consumers, clear business terms or domain ontologies should be used (Michelson, 2006).

Sowa and Zachman (1992) describe a Zachman's framework for information systems architecture (ISA), which provides a systematic taxonomy of concepts for relating things in the world to the representations in the computer. The world contains entities (data), processes (function), locations (network), people, times and purposes (motivation). Those aspects of the world are analysed from the perspectives as follows: scope (Ballpark view), model of a business (Owner's view), model of the information system (Architect's view), technology model (Designer's view), detailed representations (Builder's view) and functioning system.

As discussed in Hay (1997) the fifth column of the Zachman's Framework describes the effects of time on the enterprise. It is difficult to describe or address this column in isolation from the others (data, function, network, people and motivation), especially column two (function). At the strategic (row 1) level, this is a description of the business cycle and overall business events. In the detailed model of the business (row 2), the time column defines when functions are to happen and under what circumstances. Row 3 defines the business events, which cause specific data transformations and entity state changes to take place. In the technology model (row 4), the events become program triggers and messages, and the information processing responses are designed in detail. In row 5, these designs become specific programs. In row 6 business events are correctly responded to by the system.

According to Hay (2003) data flow diagram, which presents activities of an enterprise in terms of the events that trigger them, and entity life history, which describes the structure of the events and activities that affect each entity type, are used in the events modelling. An 'event/entity type' matrix shows all of the events affecting each entity type. It helps to classify events in terms of *create, read, update* and *delete* and can be used in the mapping of events of an information system level into software system events.

However, while there are a number of methods and languages for ECA rules modelling and their implementation into ADBMS (like Dynamic Relation Nets [Allain and Yim, 2000], a Structural Model of ECA Rules [Li et al., 2002], Petri Nets [Li et al., 2004; Cilia et al., 2005] and Conceptual Graphs [Valatkaite and Vasilecas, 2003]), it is not yet clear how they should be modelled and mapped at different abstraction levels of an enterprise.

3 Events Propagation from the Business System Level into the Information System Level

In the related works, the majority of authors analyse events of the software system level, e.g. of the lowest level of abstraction. Since events same as rules are taken from the particular business domain, they should be analysed and modelled from the highest level of abstraction – business system level – and then appropriately extended at and propagated into the lower levels of abstraction – IS level and consequently software systems level.

The structure of an enterprise system (Fig. 1) from Vasilecas and Bugaite (2005) shows the propagation of rules and events to lower levels of enterprise system and the formation of rules and events in different levels of abstraction.

Executable rules implement information processing rules, and the information processing rules implement business rules. Software events implement events in an IS, and the events in an IS implement business events. Therefore, the business rules should be mapped into information processing rules (like ECA rules), while the information processing rules should be mapped or transformed into executable rules (like SQL triggers in an ADBMS). The business event should be mapped into events in an IS, while the events in an IS should be mapped or transformed into software events.

According to the levels of abstraction all events can be classified into business events, events in an IS and software events. The main point of this chapter is that it is necessary to distinct business events, events in an IS and software events to ensure consistent and complete modelling and implementation of these events. It is necessary to start analysis and modelling of events in the business system level and consequently follow to IS and then to the software event.

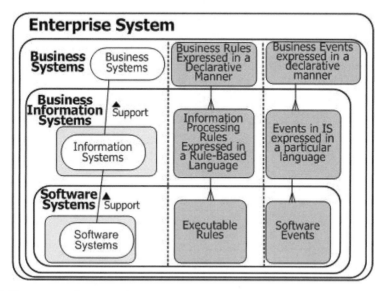

Fig. 1. The structure of an enterprise system

According to the related works presented in Section 2 business events, events in an IS and software events are defined in the following way.

A business event is a significant occurrence of a happening of interest in the application domain. A business event matches something that happens in the real world within the universe of discourse. An example of a business event can be customer order, the arrival of a shipment at a loading dock or a truck breakdown. A business event activates a business process and/or a business rule. In particular situations the ending of a business process and/or a business rule can cause a new business event.

An event in an IS is generated by an IS. It is the implementation of the business event. One business event can be implemented by one or several events in an IS. An example of an event in an IS can be a method execution by an object.

A software event is generated by a software system. It is the implementation of the IS event. An example of a software event can be SELECT, CREATE, UPDATE, DELETE and others.

In the business system level, to which events belong, they are expressed by natural language and/or concepts from the business domain or ontology. In the IS level, events together with rules are defined by a particular language, like rule-based language, where events are part of rules. In the software system level or execution level, events are defined in terms of DML operations.

To summarise statements of the authors about events of different abstraction levels, events of the higher level (e.g. concepts of a business domain) should be mapped into events of the lowest level (e.g. DML-operations in relational DBMS). The main question should be answered – how are business events translated into events in IS and consequently into software events? Moreover, not all events in an IS level come from the business system level. Some of them originate in the IS level.

The schema of events propagation from the business system level into the IS and software system levels is presented in Fig. 2.

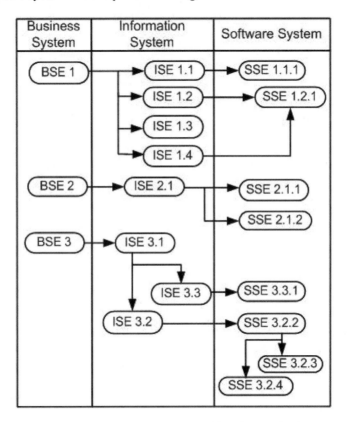

Fig. 2. Events propagation from the business system level into the IS and software system levels. BSE – Business System Event; ISE – Event in Information System; SSE – Software System Event

As shown in Fig. 2, there are several cases of events propagation from the business system level to the lower levels. They are the following:

- One-to-one – one higher level event is implemented by one lower level event (e.g. BSE 2 → ISE 2.1)

- One-to-many – one higher level event is implemented by several lower level events (e.g. BSE 1 → {ISE 1.1, ISE 1.2, ISE 1.3})
- One-to-none – one higher level event is not implemented by a lower level event for some reasons (e.g. ISE 1.3)
- Many-to-one – two or more higher level events are implemented by one lower level event (e.g. {ISE 1.2, ISE 1.4 → SSE 1.2.1)

Moreover, for the sake of simplicity, an event of the same level can be replaced by two or more events of the same level (e.g. ISE 3.1 → {ISE 3.2, ISE 3.3}).

4 A Case Study on Events Propagation from the Business System Level into the IS Level

A particular business enterprise was chosen for the detailed study of events propagation from the highest level of abstraction into the lower levels of abstraction. The domain knowledge of this business enterprise is presented by the ontology, which was developed in the outgoing research project AGILA (Caplinskas, 2003).

Events of an enterprise are described by a special class *Event*, which has the structure as follows:

$$event := \text{<}evheader, evbody\text{>}, \tag{1}$$

where *evbody* is a body of an event and *evheader* is a header of an event, which can be expressed as follows:

$$evheader := \text{<}evname, evtype, evtimestamp, evcreator, evocnum\text{>}, \tag{2}$$

where *evname* is a name of an event, *evtype* is a type of an event, *evtimestamp* is a timestamp of an event, *evcreator* is a creator of an event and *evocnum* is an event occurrence number. An event occurrence number is optional in this case. A body of an event depends on a particular event.

A frame (or header) for the Making_Contract event follows:

```
Making_Contract (name      String,
    creator      Instance of Enterprise,
    timestamp    String,
    evocnum      Integer,
    subrelated_event Instance of Event,
    description String,
    contract            Instance of Contract)
```

where related *Contract* has the following frame (or body):

```
Contract (contract_code   String,
    contract_data     String,
    expiry_date String,
    customer    Instance of Customer,
    supplier    Instance of Supplier,
```

```
contract_product  Instance of Contract_Product,
discount     Float,
%sum_to_pay_after_delivering Float,
%sum_to_pay_before_delivering Float,
payment_term      String,
penalty      String,
transport_type     Symbol)
```

Customer, *Supplier* and *Contract_Product* are related classes, which are presented in the ontology tree too.

Another important events analysed in this research are: *Renew_Contract*, *Break_Contract*, *Delivering_New_Product*, *Selling_Product* and *Delivering_Existing_Product*.

The schema of events *Making_Contract* and *Renew_Contract* propagation from the business system level into the IS level and the software system level is presented in Table 1 and Fig. 3.

Table 1. Events *Making_Contract* and *Renew_Contract* propagation from the business system level into the IS and software system levels

Business system	Information system	Software system
1. *Making Contract* between two Parties	1.1. *Checking* the possibility of make a contract	1.1.1. *Select*
	1.2. *Checking* if the client is an old or a new one	1.2.1. *Select* Client From Client where Client = Current Client
	1.2a. *Registering* a new client	1.2a.1. *Insert Client*
	1.3. *Preparing* a new contract	1.3.1. *Insert Contract*
2. *Renew Contract* between two Parties	2.1. *Checking* if the contract is in the system	2.1.1. *Select* Contract From Contract where Contract = Current Contract
	2.2. *Checking* conditions of the contract	
	2.3. *Renewing* contract if it is possible	2.3.1. *Update* Contract From Contract where Contract = Current Contract

Let us suppose that in the business system level an event '*Making Contract*' (1) exists. It is implemented as '*Checking* the possibility of making a contract' (1.1), '*Checking* if the client is an old or a new one' (1.2) and '*Preparing* a new contract' (1.3) events in the IS level. '*Registering* a new client' (1.2a) event is optional. It is originated if a client is a new one. All *Checking* events are implemented as *Select* events in the software system level. *Registering* and *Preparing* events are implemented as *Insert* events in the software system level.

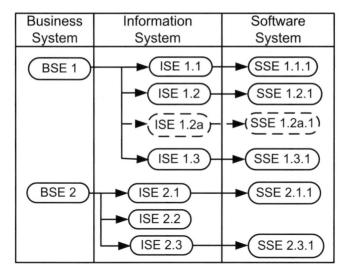

Fig. 3. Events *Making_Contract* and *Renew_Contract* propagation from the business system level into the IS and software system levels

Let us suppose that in the business system level an event '*Renew Contract*' (2) exists. It is implemented as '*Checking* if the contract is in the system' (2.1), '*Checking* conditions of the contract' (2.2) and '*Renewing* if it is possible' (2.3) events in the IS level. *Checking* (2.1) event is implemented as *Select* event in the software system level. Second *Checking* (2.2) event is not implemented in the software system, since the following action '*Checking conditions*' is manual. *Renewing* event is implemented as *Update* event in the software system level.

The detailed study of *Making_Contract, Renew_Contract, Break_Contract, Delivering_New_Product, Selling_Product* and *Delivering_Existing_Product* events shows that:

- *Making, Delivering_New* events are implemented as several *Checking, Registering* and *Preparing* events in the IS level.
- *Renewing, Delivering_Existing, Selling* events are implemented as several *Checking* and *Renewing* (*Inserting*) events in the IS level.
- *Breaking* events are implemented as several *Checking* and *Breaking* (*Deleting*) events in the IS level.
- *Checking* events are implemented as *Select* events in the software system level.
- *Registering, Preparing* events are implemented as *Insert* events in the software system level.
- *Renewing* (*Inserting*) events are implemented as *Update* events in the software system level.
- *Breaking* (*Deleting*) events are implemented as *Delete* events in the software system level.

According to this observation authors conclude that business and IS level events are not defined by *Insert, Update, Delete* and *Select* terms. They are defined using business or application domain terms, like *Making_Contract*. Therefore, the adaptation is necessary to convert them into *Insert, Update, Delete* and *Select* events.

Authors suggest to classify business system level events according to *Insert, Update, Delete* and *Select* classifiers. For this purpose the events classification ontology is developed (Fig. 4). It helps to show and classify a big variety of business and IS level events according to *Insert, Update, Delete* and *Select* events. Figure 4 presents *Delete* events in detail. Each class of events (*Insert, Update, Delete* and *Select*) can be extended by new events.

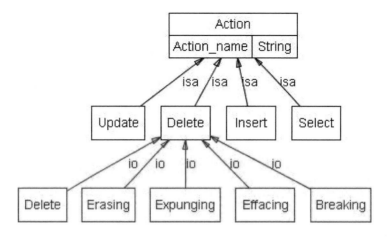

Fig. 4. The hierarchical tree of the events classification

It is necessary to note that one business event can be implemented as several events of an IS, and consequently each event of an IS can be implemented as several software system events. The events classification ontology shows only main events. For example, the main implementation of a business event *Making_Contract* is *Insert* event. Additional events, like *Select*, are not presented in the ontology.

The events classification ontology is used in the outgoing research project AGILA for the automatic transformation of ontology axioms into formal rules presented in the form of SQL triggers. For more details see Vasilecas and Bugaite (2006).

The next step of the research is extending the developed ontology by additional events. Also the full case study of events propagation from the business system level into an IS level and consequent software system level is necessary.

5 Conclusions

The analysis of the related works on events modelling in the process of active database management systems development shows that it is necessary to distinct business events, events in information systems and software events to ensure consistent and complete modelling and implementation of these events in active database management systems.

The business events should be mapped into events in information system, while the events in information system should be mapped or transformed into software events. Business events and events in information systems are not defined by *Insert, Update, Delete* and *Select* terms. They are defined using business or application domain terms. Therefore, the adaptation is necessary to convert them into *Insert, Update, Delete* and *Select* events.

The events classification ontology according to *Insert, Update, Delete* and *Select* classifiers developed were applied in the frame of the outgoing research project AGILA for the automatic transformation of ontology axioms into formal rules presented in the form of SQL triggers.

References

Adaikkalavan, R., Chakravarthy, S. (2003) SnoopIB: Interval-Based Event Specification and Detection for Active Databases. *Springer-Verlag.* LNCS 2798, 190–204.

Allain, L., Yim, P. (2000) Specification of an Active Database System Application Using Dynamic Relation Nets. In: Lloyd, J. et al. (eds.) *CL 2000, Springer-Verlag.* LNAI 1861, 1197–1209.

Caplinskas, A. (2003) An Ontology-based Approach to Enterprise Engineering. Computer Science Reports, 14/03. *BTU Cottbus* 22–30.

Cilia, M., Bornhovd, C., Buchmann, A.P. (2005) Event Handling for the Universal Enterprise (to appear). *Information Technology and Management (ITM)*, Special Issue on Universal Global Integration (June 2005), http://www.dvs1.informatik.tudarmstadt.de/staff/bornhoevd/ITM-journal.pdf

Dayal, U., Buchmann, A.P., Chakravarthy, S. (1996) The HiPAC Project. In: Widom, J., Ceri, S. (eds.) *Proc. of Active Database Systems – Triggers and Rules for Advanced Database, Springer,* 177–206.

Dittrich, K., Gatziu, S., Geppert, A. (1996) The Active Database Management System Manifesto: A Rule-base of ADBMS Features. A Joint Report by the ACT-NET Consortium. *SIGMOD Record.* 25(3), 40–49.

Hay, D.C. (1997) The Zachman Framework: An Introduction. In: Seiner, R.S. (ed.) *The Data Administration Newsletter* (April 2007), http://www.tdan.com/i001fe01.htm

Hay, D.C. (2003) *Requirements Analysis: From Business Views to Architecture.* Prentice Hall, Upper Saddle River, NJ. ISBN 0-13-028228-6.

Humphreys, K., Gaizauskas, R., Azzam, S. (1997) Event Coreference for Information Extraction. *In: The Workshop on Operational Factors in Practical, Robust Anaphora Resolution for Unrestricted Texts. 35th Annual Meeting of the Association for Computational Linguistics.* Madrid, 75–81.

Li, X., Medina, J.M., Chacarria, L. (2004) Composite Event Specification in Active Database Systems: A Petri Nets Approach. In: Jensen, K. (ed.) *Fifth Workshop and Tutorial on Practical*

Use of Coloured Petri Nets and the CPN Tools (CPN'04) (April 2007), http://www.daimi.au.dk/CPnets/workshop04/cpn/slides/x_li.pdf

Li, X., Medina, J., Chapa, S.V. (2002) A Structural Model of ECA Rules in Active Database. In: Coello Coello, C.A. et al. (eds.) *MICAI 2002, Springer-Verlag*. LNAI 2313, 486–493.

Mahesh, K. (1996) Ontology Development for Machine Translation: Ideology and Methodology. *In: Technical Report MCCS 96-292* (September 2005), http://www.fdi.ucm.es/profesor/vaquero/DOCT/MikroKosmosOnto(MCCS-96-292).pdf

Michelson, B.M. (2006) Event-Driven Architecture Overview. Event-Driven SOA Is Just Part of the EDA Story. Patricia Seybold Group (November 2006), http://www.psgroup.com/detail.aspx?ID=681

Rules Manager Concepts (2005) Rules Manager and Expression Filter. *Oracle Database Application Developer's Guide* (October 2006), http://dba-services.berkeley.edu/docs/oracle/manual-10gR2/appdev.102/b14288/exprn_brm_intro.htm

Sowa, J.F, Zachman, J.A. (1992) Extending and Formalizing the Framework for Information Systems Architecture. *IBM Systems Journal*. 31(3), 590–616.

Valatkaite, I., Vasilecas, O. (2003) A Conceptual Graphs Approach for Business Rules Modeling. In: Kalinichenko, L., et al. (eds.) *Proc. of Seventh East-European Conference on Advance in Databases and Information Systems* (ADBIS'2003), *Springer-Verlag*. LNCS 2798, 178–189.

Vasilecas, O., Bugaite, D. (2005) Events modelling in the process of business rules based information systems development. *Lithuanian Mathematical Journal*. 45 (spec. No. of Proc. of XLVI Conference of Lithuanian Mathematical Society), 167–173.

Vasilecas, O., Bugaite, D. (2006) Ontology-based Information Systems Development: the Problem of Automation of Information Processing Rules. In: Neuhold, E., Yakhno, T. (eds.) *Proc. of the Fourth International Conference Advances in Information Systems* (ADVIS'2006), *Springer*. LNCS 4243, 187–196.

Yu, J., Hunter, J., Reiter, E., Sripada, S. (2001) An Approach to Generating Summaries of Time Series Data in the Gas Turbine Domain. *In: Proc. of ICII'2001 (Beijing). IEEE Press*, 44–51.

An Evaluation of the State of the Art in Context-Aware Architectures

Pyrros Bratskas, Nearchos Paspallis and George A. Papadopoulos

Department of Computer Science, University of Cyprus
P.O. Box 20537, 1678, Nicosia, Cyprus, {bratskas, nearchos, george}@cs.ucy.ac.cy

Abstract Mobile computing is an innovative field gaining increasing attention as many new systems are designed towards that direction. Among these systems, many are desired to be context-aware, with the aim of optimizing and automating their offered services. Such systems provide components whose main feature is to manage the context information, which is communicated between sensors, actuators and applications. In these systems the use of middleware is a solution to the need for detecting and adapting to the changing context. In mobile computing, factors such as scalability, support for distribution, self-adaptivity, support for mobility and modularity/plugability are of particular interest. Many attempts have been documented in the literature concerning systems aiming to address some or all of these requirements and which are used for the implementation of context-aware systems. The scope of this chapter is to study and present the current state of the art in context-aware system architectures. These are evaluated and compared, based on a set of characteristics such as support for distribution, privacy, mobility or fault tolerance. Finally, we document our current results and initial decisions concerning the design of a context management middleware system enabling the design and deployment of adaptive applications in mobile and ubiquitous computing environments.

1 Introduction

Mobile computing is an innovative field gaining increasing attention as many new systems are designed towards that direction. Among these systems, many are desired to be context-aware with the aim of optimizing and automating their offered services. Such systems provide components whose main functionality is to manage the context data, which is communicated between sensors, actuators and applications. Furthermore, mobile computing environments include a huge spectrum of computation and communication devices that seamlessly aim to augment peoples' thoughts and activities with information, processing and analysis. Devices such as Personal Digital Assistants (PDAs) and mobile phones have gained a lot

C. Barry et al. (eds.), *Information Systems Development: Challenges in Practice, Theory, and Education, Vol.2*, doi: 10.1007/978-0-387-78578-3_42,
© Springer Science+Business Media, LLC 2009

of popularity and are increasingly being networked. On the other hand, people use different software development platforms to create applications for this type of devices. These applications must be context-aware to meet the requirements of the highly distributed environment. This kind of context-aware systems adapt not only to changes in the environment, but also to user requirements. But even though the devices' capabilities are becoming more and more powerful, the design of context-aware applications is constrained not only by physical limitations, but also by the need to support a plethora of features such as distribution, scalability, modularity, mobility, privacy and fault tolerance. Indeed, mobile devices will continue to be battery-dependent and operate in an environment where more and more devices will be present and will need to communicate or share resources. Wide-area networking capabilities will continue to be based on communication with base stations and with fluctuations in bandwidth depending on physical location and mobility.

In order to provide a fair quality of service to the users, applications must be context-aware and able to adapt to context changes, something that renders the development of context-aware applications an increasingly complex task. A solution to managing this complexity is the use of a middleware layer, which is now becoming a common requirement. Many middleware solutions are proposed in the literature with the aim of addressing requirements, which are normally addressed by middleware for distributed systems. They include support for sensing, gathering and managing context information in order to simplify application development through sharing this information among middleware components. However, as stated by Henricksen et al. (2005) many additional requirements are not met. In this chapter we evaluate and compare a set of popular approaches for implementing context-aware architectures. This is done with respect to a set of characteristics that were detected.

The rest of this chapter is structured as follows. Section 2 briefly introduces an overview of the architecture of the examined systems. Section 3 evaluates and compares the examined architectures based on a predefined set of desired features and characteristics. Following that evaluation, Section 4 describes the current state of our work, which aims at designing and implementing a context management system targeting adaptive applications in mobile and ubiquitous computing environments. Finally, Section 5 closes with conclusions.

2 Context-Aware Systems

Context-aware computing is an area, which studies methods and tools for discovering, modeling and utilizing contextual information. Such information may include any information affecting the interaction of a user with a system, such as user location, time of day, nearby people and devices, user activity, and light or noise conditions. A more formal and widely used definition by Dey (2000, 2001) specifies context as "*any information that can be used to characterize the situation of an entity; an entity is a person, place or object that is considered relevant to the interaction between a user and an application, including the user and application themselves*".

Context can also be classified in more fine-grained categories: *physical, computing* and *user* context information types, as it is described by Chen and Kotz (2000). The physical context type is related to environmental factors, which can be usually evaluated by specialized hardware mechanisms. The light, noise, and temperature are examples of physical context data types. The computing context refers to the information, which describes the resources available by the computing infrastructure. This includes information such as the network connectivity and its characteristics (e.g., bandwidth and latency), nearby resources (such as printers and video projectors), and details concerning its own memory availability, processor use, etc. Finally, the user context refers to the user's profile by focusing on the user needs, preferences, mood, etc. For instance, these can include information concerning the user's occupation (e.g., driving or studying) or the user's choice for preferring, say, to use a desktop computer rather than a PDA while at work.

Furthermore, as it is argued by Satyanarayanan (2001), any system that aims to be minimally intrusive must be context aware, in the sense that it should be conscious of its user's state and environment. In other words, context-aware mobile systems are expected to utilize such information in order to adapt their behavior, based on a predefined set of adaptation rules. These rules are usually monitored by a system, which dynamically adapts the system's operation based on the contextual information sensed.

In this section we present and review popular, middleware-based solutions, which are used for enabling context-aware systems. This review primarily aims to evaluate a number of desired features for context-aware systems, as they are discussed in Section 2.1.

2.1 The Context Toolkit

The Context Toolkit, introduced by Dey et al. (2001), assists software developers by providing them with a set of abstractions, which enable them to build context-aware applications. These abstractions include: widgets, aggregators, interpreters, services, and discoverers.

A widget is a component that is responsible for acquiring context information directly from a sensor. The aggregators can be thought of as meta-widgets, taking on all capabilities of widgets. They also provide the ability to aggregate context information of real-world entities such as users or places and act as a gateway between applications and widgets. Interpreters transform low-level information into higher-level information that is more useful to applications. Services are used by context-aware applications to invoke actions using actuators, and discoverers can be used by applications to locate suitable widgets, interpreters, aggregators, and services.

The toolkit is implemented as a set of Java APIs that represent its abstractions and use the HTTP protocol for communication and XML as the language model.

Components implemented in other languages can also interoperate through the use of Web standards. An extension to the Context Toolkit was proposed by Newberger and Dey (2003) for providing user control of context-aware systems using an approach called end-user programming.

2.2 The Context Fusion Networks

The Context Fusion Network (CFN) approach was proposed by Chen and Kotz (2004). It allows context-aware applications to select distributed data sources and compose them with customized data-fusion operators into a directed acyclic information fusion graph. Such a graph represents how an application computes high-level understandings of its execution context from low-level sensory data. The CFN aims to address four challenges: flexibility, scalability, mobility, and self-management.

CFN was implemented by a prototype named Solar, a flexible, scalable, mobility-aware, and self-managed system for heterogeneous and volatile ubiquitous computing environments. Solar consists of a set of functionally equivalent nodes, coded Planets, which peer together to form a service overlay using a distributed hash table (DHT)-based P2P routing protocol such as Pastry. This approach is described by Rowstron and Druschel (2001). A Planet has two kinds of message transports: normal TCP-/IP-based and DHT-based services. Solar does not restrict the syntax of its events, as long as it follows a hierarchical attribute structure. Thus, it is easy to incorporate XML events into the Solar system. Sensors and applications may connect to any Planet. Planets are execution environments for operators and they cooperatively provide several operator-management functionalities, such as naming and discovery, routing the sensory data through operators to applications, operator monitoring and recovery in face of host failures, and garbage collecting operators that are no longer in use. Each one of the Planet functionalities is considered a service. Thus, mobility service tracks clients (sensors or applications), which may detach from a Planet and reattach to another one.

2.3 The Context Fabric

The Context Fabric (Confab), a toolkit for facilitating the development of privacy-sensitive, ubiquitous computing applications was proposed by Hong and Landay (2004). Confab focuses on privacy rather than on context sensing and processing. From a software architecture view, Confab provides a framework of privacy mechanisms that allow developers and end users to support a spectrum of trust levels and privacy needs. Privacy and security are supported by the fact that personal information is captured, stored, and processed on the end user's computer as much as possible.

Context information is modeled as Infospaces, which can contain both context data and sources of the context data, such as sensors. Infospaces contain tuples that describe individual pieces of contextual data. These tuples are implemented as data-centric XML documents, that is, context tuples consist only of XML tags and XML attributes, with no text between tags. XPath is used as the query language for matching and retrieving XML tuples. Confab is implemented in Java and uses HTTP for network communication. It does not address traditional distributed system requirements such as mobility, scalability, component failures, and deployment/configuration.

The core services include the Context Event Service, which provides a universal event system for context events, the Context Query Service, which provides a universal interface by which applications can synchronously check context state, the Automatic Path Creation Service, which takes a directive in the Context Specification Language (CSL) and then processes it to the best of its abilities, and the Sensor Management Service, which registers all local sensors and provides a uniform data format for sensors for the Context Event Service and the Context Query Service. The Context Specification Language is a simple XML-based language, which provides a flexible way of specifying context needs.

2.4 Gaia

Roman et al. (2002) have proposed Gaia, which is designed to support the development and execution of portable applications for active spaces, which are programmable ubiquitous environments in which users interact with several devices and services simultaneously. Gaia manages the resources and services of an active space and has three components: the kernel, the application framework, and the application. It offers five basic services: the *event manager*, which distributes events in the active space and uses the CORBA event service as the default event factory, the *context service* through which applications query and register for context information (several components named context providers offer information about context), the *presence service*, which detects and maintains information about software components and devices, the *space repositories*, which store information about the entities in the space and lets applications browse and retrieve them based on specific attributes, and the *context file system*, which is a context-aware file system and uses properties and environmental context information to simplify many of the tasks that are traditionally performed manually or require additional programming

Gaia uses XML to describe the resources of active spaces and LuaOrb, a high-level scripting language, to program and configure them. Corba services are widely used, however, active spaces require extensions to handle fault tolerance and dynamic resource detection. Gaia supports direct communication similar to synchronous low-level operating system (OS) communication, and indirect communication similar to asynchronous low-level OS inter-process communication.

Gaia does not address scalability and privacy is not addressed by any of the basic services, but can potentially be provided by additional services. Heterogeneity, mobility, and component configuration can all be supported by Gaia, but in limited forms.

2.5 Reconfigurable Context-Sensitive Middleware

The *Reconfigurable Context-Sensitive Middleware* (RCSM) is a middleware proposed in Yau et al. (2002) and designed to provide two properties to applications: context-awareness and ad hoc communication. This is done not in an independent way, but in a way that allows RCSM to provide another property named context-sensitive ad hoc communication. RCSM provides an object-based framework for supporting context-sensitive applications similar to middleware standards and prototypes such as CORBA, COM, and TAO for fixed networks.

Thus, RCSM provides application developers with a context-aware Interface Definition Language (CA-IDL) that can be used to specify context requirements, including the types of context that are relevant to the application, the actions to be triggered, and the timing of these actions. Ad hoc communication support is provided by a context-sensitive object request broker (R-ORB). This communicates at runtime with the skeletons produced by the compilation of the IDL interfaces, provides device and service discovery and use a symmetric communication model to allow ad hoc and application-transparent information exchange between a pair of remote objects.

The prototype described by Yau et al. does not satisfy the heterogeneity requirement, as it supports C++ applications only, for the Windows CE platform. However, the IDL compiler could potentially be modified to produce skeletons for a variety of platforms and communication protocols. In addition, the context discovery protocol is not flexible enough to support mobility or component failures, the RCSM authors do not attempt to address scalability, privacy, traceability, or control.

2.6 The PACE Middleware

The PACE middleware consist of a set of components and tools that have been developed according to three design principles: First, the model of context information used in a context-aware system should be explicitly represented within the system. Second, the context-aware behavior of applications should be determined, at least in part, by external specifications that can be customized by users and evolved along with the context. Third, the communication between application components and between the components and middleware services should not be tightly bound to the application logic. The components and tools that are part of the middleware include: a *context management system*, which provides aggregation and storage of context information and performs query evaluation, a *preference management system* that provides decision support for context-aware applications, a *programming toolkit*, implemented in Java and using RMI for communication, that facilitates interaction between application components and the context and preference management systems, *tools* that assist with generating components and with developing and deploying context-aware systems, starting from context models specified in the context management system, and finally a *messaging framework* for remote components to communicate. The PACE middleware provides support for heterogeneity, mobility, traceability, control, deployment, configuration, and decision support. Requirements like scalable deployment, configuration, and management of sensors have not been addressed.

Hardian (2006) has enriched the middleware developed by Henricksen et al. (2005) by providing traceability and control to facilitate user understanding and feedback. This includes selectively exposing various components (context information, preferences, and adaptation rules and logic) to users. The new functionality can be viewed conceptually as an additional layer above the context and preference management components, providing logging and generation of explanations/feedback for users.

2.7 The MADAM Context System

The main concept of the MADAM context system's architecture is the separation of concerns between context clients and context providers, as it is hinted by Satyanarayanan (2001) and discussed by Mikalsen et al. (2006). In this respect, all nodes act as both context providers and context consumers, as part of a membership group, which is formed using a loosely coupled protocol. Furthermore, while individual nodes are free to access context information from any possible provider it is nevertheless assumed that in most cases context sharing is limited to a local area only. In this respect, the locality refers to groups formed by nodes, which can directly communicate with each other, e.g., over a wireless link by forming an ad hoc WiFi or Bluetooth networks.

The MADAM context system architecture is built around a centralized context repository, where the context information is modeled and stored. Special entities are then used to populate the repository with context information (i.e., context sensors) and for registering and receiving notifications when certain context elements change (i.e., context listeners). In addition, specially designed components (i.e., membership managers) are designed and implemented with the aim of enabling distribution of context information between different computing models.

This approach has the important advantage of assigning higher importance to local context and consequently enabling localized scalability. The first one refers to the fact that it is more likely that two neighboring nodes will share a common interest on the same context as opposed to nodes at different geographical locations. This is true, for example, in most pervasive computing applications where applications aim to utilize the infrastructure, which is embedded in the surrounding environment. Second, localized scalability is achieved by preferring local sources (and respectively consumers) for sharing context information. In this approach, the use of backbone links is avoided as most of the communication is carried out over local (i.e., direct) network links.

3 Evaluating and Comparing the State of the Art

In this section we compare and analyze the context-aware systems presented in Section 2 in terms of their architecture. When designing a middleware system, many of the requirements of the classic distributed systems must also be taken into consideration: mobility, scalability, fault tolerance, and/or heterogeneity. But additional requirements are also needed when designing context-aware systems.

Support for distribution. When dealing with context, the devices used to sense context most likely are not attached to the same computer running the application. The sensors may be physically distributed and cannot be directly connected to a single machine. In addition, multiple applications may require use of that location information and these applications may run on multiple computing devices.

Modularity/plugability. Modularity makes the system easy to extend through the introduction of new sensors, new devices, and new services. This feature is crucial due to the dynamic nature of context and in particular of user preferences. On the other hand, plugability concerns the feature of the system to support the ability to develop and/or easily install new context and sensor components like plug-ins, and eventually to combine them in complex hierarchies to support new context features, and offer new services as well.

Support for privacy/security. The use of distributed resources provides a huge potential for expanding the way that people communicate and share data, provide services to clients and process information to increase their efficiency. This broad access has also brought with it new security and privacy vulnerabilities.

Technology used for context modeling. Context modeling is about providing a high-level abstraction of context information. Context information can be originated from a wide variety of sources, leading to extreme heterogeneity in terms of quality. In our analysis of the systems we focus on the technology they use, e.g., XML as the interface description and encoding language or simple textual key-value pairs, to model the context information.

Technology used for communication. We refer to this requirement in our review to define which protocols are used for communication between components.

Support for mobility. All components (especially sensors and applications) can be mobile, and the communication protocols that underpin the system must therefore support appropriately flexible forms of routing. Context information may need to migrate with context-aware components.

Tolerance to failures. Sensors and other components are likely to fail in the ordinary for operation of a context-aware system. Disconnections may also occur.

The system must continue operation, without requiring excessive resources to detect and handle failures.

Support for decision making. This requirement refers to tools that help applications to select appropriate actions and adaptations based on the available context information.

The Context Toolkit defines a distributed architecture supporting context fusion and delivery with three notions of widget, aggregator and interpreter based on an object-oriented architecture. These are implemented as Java objects, which communicate using a protocol based on HTTP and XML. However, there are a set of limitations of the context toolkit architecture. The main ones are the nonsupport for continuous context, unreliable data and context privacy, scalability or tolerance to failures, and decision support.

The Context Fusion Network was implemented as a prototype infrastructure named Solar. This infrastructure supports scalability and mobility and uses a P2P routing protocol for communication. Solar provides an XML-based composition language for application, identifying context-fusion operators and name queries that select sources. The language allows components to be connected using pull or push channels. However, Solar does not address privacy and decision support.

The Context Fabric has a decentralized architecture whose primary concern is privacy. This is done with several customizable privacy mechanisms. Context fabric also comes with extensions for managing location privacy. Combined, these features allow application developers and end users to support a spectrum of trust levels and privacy needs. While mobility, scalability, tolerance to failures and decision support are not addressed. Context fabric provides a framework and an extendable suite of mechanisms that application developers and end users can use for managing privacy. From this point of view, there is a kind of modularity supported by the Context Fabric.

Gaia is a system built as a distributed middleware infrastructure that coordinates software entities and heterogeneous networked devices contained in a physical space. Gaia provides a framework to develop user-centric, resource-aware, multi-device, context-sensitive, and mobile applications. It supports mobility, but does not address scalability, privacy, and decision support.

RCSM tries to provide a balance between awareness and transparency, and support for ad hoc communications. RCSM allows addition or deletion of individual active object containers (ADCs) during runtime (to manage new or existing context-sensitive application objects) without affecting other runtime operations inside it. RCSM does not address scalability, privacy, and decision support.

PACE Middleware offers support for mobility through the use of Elvin by Segall et al. (2000) a content-based message routing scheme, which facilitates component mobility. Privacy is addressed by providing access control to sensitive information. PACE, unlike the other solutions presented earlier, provides also decision support. On the other hand there is no support for scalability and tolerance to failures is not fully supported.

The evaluation results are summarized in Table 1. Although there are no definite answers as per the optimal solution to specific requirements (e.g., we cannot argue for sure whether XML-based modeling is preferable to Object-based modeling), however, it is possible to argue that some approaches are more *complete* as per the predefined requirements as compared to others. For example, the Context Fabric approach appears to satisfy only a few of the requirements that we have predefined, which is natural observing that the main direction of its designers was to achieve privacy and security-related characteristics. On the other hand, approaches such as the PACE and the MADAM projects appear to be more promising with respect to the prospects they offer for inspiring a new approach for which these requirements are important.

Table 1. Comparing the studied context management systems

Requirement	Context Toolkit	CFN	Context Fabric	Gaia	RCSM	PACE	MADAM
Support for distribution	Yes	Yes	No	Yes	Yes	Yes	Yes
Modularity/ plug-ability	No	No	No	No	No	No	Yes
Privacy/security	No	No	Yes	No	No	Yes	Low
Mobility	Low	Yes	No	Low	No	Yes	Yes
Tolerance to failures	No	Yes	No	Low	No	Low	Yes
Scalability	No	Yes	No	No	No	No	Low
Decision support	No	No	No	No	No	Yes	No
Technology for context modeling	XML	XML based	CSL (XML-based)	XML, Lua ORB	CA-IDL	CML (XML-based)	Object-based
Technology for communication	HTTP	TCP/IP	HTTP	CORBA	R-ORB	HTTP	Java RMI

4 Towards a New Context Management System

The review of context architectures in this chapter was undertaken as part of our effort to define the architecture of the MUSIC middleware system. This system aims at providing software engineers with appropriate methods and tools for the efficient development of context-aware, adaptive applications. Because MUSIC primarily targets at applications that are deployed in mobile and ubiquitous computing environments, we started quite early by trying to detect the most important requirements, which are critical for these environments.

For example, the fact that some of the involved applications and devices are expected to be embedded in the infrastructure, as per the ubiquitous computing paradigm, imposes the requirement for efficient, small-footprint context management systems. In addition, as other devices might be expected to require more function-alities, and consequently more complex systems, the designed architecture should be as modular as possible. For instance, target devices include smart-phones, PDAs, and laptops. The first devices are small and require efficient, small-footprint applications. The latter are typically very powerful devices and thus should not limit their functionalities simply for efficiency reasons. This validates our decision to set scalability and plugability as a high priority in our approach.

For the future, we have started working on three primary directions. The first one is the design of an appropriate context model, which can be expressed by pro-grammatic Objects (at runtime), by XML artifacts (during communication and while stored on disk) and by UML artifacts (during design time). Furthermore, we are working on studying different approaches for distribution of context informa-tion on top of several existing technologies such as WiFi, Bluetooth, JXTA (i.e., peer-to-peer), Jini, and UPnP. Finally, we are working on defining special languages for enabling context querying and context accessing. These languages are signifi-cant as we are aiming to provide a complete methodology for enabling developers to design the context-awareness aspect of their applications in an automated way, as per the MDA approach.

5 Conclusions

The main goal of this chapter was to research and evaluate existing context man-agement architectures, as they were proposed and presented in the literature with the aim of assisting and directing the design and implementation of a novel con-text management system. The newly designed system aims at providing support for designing and engineering adaptive applications targeting mobile and ubiqui-tous computing environments. For this reason, we extracted a set of important fea-tures that we wanted to compare these projects on, and we extracted results that are currently used while we are designing the MUSIC context system.

Although a number of existing approaches appear to be quite suitable and effi-cient, none of them appears to be a perfect match for the detected requirements. Nevertheless, we have scheduled a design and implementation process, which lev-erages on the knowledge extracted by these systems so that we avoid solving problems that have already been tackled. Finally, we have presented our current work and described our plans for future work, in the frame of the MUSIC project. These plans include research in the areas of modeling, managing, and distributing context information, which was also partly faced by the studied approaches.

Acknowledgments The authors of this chapter would like to thank their partners in the MUSIC-IST project and acknowledge the partial financial support given to this research by the European Union (6th Framework Programme, contract number 35166).

References

Chen, G., Kotz, D. (2000) A Survey of Context-Aware Mobile Computing Research, Technical Report: TR2000-381 Dartmouth College, Hanover, NH.

Chen, G., Li, M., Kotz, D. (2004) Design and implementation of a large-scale context fusion network. 1st Annual International Conference on Mobile and Ubiquitous Systems (MobiQuitous), IEEE Computer Society, pp. 246–255.

Dey, A. (2000) Providing Architectural Support for Building Context-Aware Applications, Ph.D. thesis, College of Computing, Georgia Institute of Technology, pp. 170.

Dey, A. (2001) Understanding and Using Context, Personal Ubiquitous Computing, 5(1), 4–7.

Dey, A.K., Salber, D., Abowd, G.D. (2001) A conceptual framework and a toolkit for supporting the rapid prototyping of context-aware applications, Human-Computer Interaction, 16, 1–67.

Hardian, B. (2006) Middleware support for transparency and user control in context-aware systems. 3rd international Middleware Doctoral Symposium, Melbourne, Australia, Nov. 27–Dec 1, 2006. MDS'06, vol. 185. ACM Press, New York, p. 4.

Henricksen, K., Indulska, J., McFadden, T., Balasubramaniam, S. (2005) Middleware for Distributed Context-Aware Systems, International Symposium on Distributed Objects and Applications (DOA), Ayia Napa, Cyprus, Oct. 31—Nov. 4, 2005, pp. 846–863.

Hong, J.I., Landay, J.A. (2004) An Architecture for Privacy-sensitive Ubiquitous Computing, 2nd International Conference on Mobile Systems, Applications, and Services (MobiSys), Boston, MA.

Mikalsen, M., Paspallis, N., Floch, J., Stav, E., Papadopoulos, G.A., Ruiz, P.A. (2006) Putting Context in Context: The Role and Design of Context Management in a Mobility and Adaptation Enabling Middleware, International Workshop on Managing Context Information and Semantics in Mobile Environments (MCISME'06), Nara, Japan, May 9–12, 2006, IEEE Computer Society Press, pp. 76–83.

Newberger, A., Dey, A. (2003) Designer Support for Context Monitoring and Control, Intel Research, Berkeley, CA.

Rowstron, A., Druschel, P. (2001) Pastry: Scalable, Decentralized Object Location, and Routing for Large-Scale Peer-to-Peer Systems, International Middleware Conference, Heidelberg, Germany, pp. 329–350.

Roman, M., Hess, C., Cerqueira, R., Ranganathan, A., Campbell, R.H., Nahrstedt, K. (2002) Gaia: A middleware infrastructure for active spaces. IEEE Pervasive Computing, Special Issue on Wearable Computing 1, pp. 74–83.

Satyanarayanan, M. (2001) Pervasive Computing: Vision and Challenges, IEEE Personal Communications Magazine, pp. 10–17.

Segall, B., Arnold, D., Boot, J., Henderson, M., Phelps, T. (2000) Content based routing with Elvin4, AUUG2K Conference, Canberra.

Yau, S.S., Karim, F., Wang, Y., Wang, B., Gupta, S. (2002) Reconfigurable Context-Sensitive Middleware for Pervasive Computing, IEEE Pervasive Computing, pp. 33–40.

The Development and Validation of Data Transformation Functions in Educational Assessment Data

Phelim Murnion and Claire Lally

School of Business, Galway Mayo Institute of Technology, Ireland
Phelim.Murnion@gmit.ie, clairelally@hotmail.com

Abstract　The core functions of information technology – data storage, data processing and data retrieval – have become part of the basic infrastructure of business. Justification for the advantages of computing technology has moved from a data processing approach to a business-driven approach. Data Warehousing is a concept that supports this business-driven approach. The primary objective of a data warehouse is to facilitate management in the decision-making process. This is achieved by turning raw operational data into strategic information for decision making. Quality assurance is an important area of decision making in higher education. Data warehousing offers the possibility of utilising the large quantities of detailed student data held by institutions of higher education to support decision making in the quality assurance area. This chapter (the major thesis for a Masters Degree in Information Systems) describes work in progress on an investigation into data warehousing using student data.

1 Introduction

The core functions of information technology – data storage, data processing and data retrieval – have become available and affordable to all; they are part of the basic infrastructure of business (Carr 2003). Justification for the advantages of computing technology has moved from a data-processing approach to a business-driven (Devlin 1997), information management (Dyché 2000) approach. Data warehousing is a concept that supports this business-driven approach. The primary objective of a data warehouse is to facilitate management in the decision-making process (Shahzad 2003; Inmon 1996). This is achieved by transforming data in operational systems into information in a data warehouse (Hoffer et al. 2001). An important area of decision making in higher education is quality assurance. Data warehousing offers the possibility of utilising the large quantities of detailed student data held by these institutions to support decision making in the

C. Barry et al. (eds.), *Information Systems Development: Challenges in Practice, Theory, and Education, Vol.2*, doi: 10.1007/978-0-387-78578-3_43,
© Springer Science+Business Media, LLC 2009

quality assurance area. This chapter describes work in progress on an investigation into data warehousing using student data (the major thesis for a Masters Degree in Information Systems).

2 Data Warehousing

Data warehousing is an approach to data management that separates informational from operational requirements (Devlin 1997) and provides a foundation for effective decision support (Inmon 1996). Organisations can use data warehousing techniques to extract meaning and inform decision making from their informational assets (Barquin 1996).

A data warehouse is a database that stores high-level historical data used to support management decision making and provides an integrated view of high-quality information (Hoffer et al. 2001)

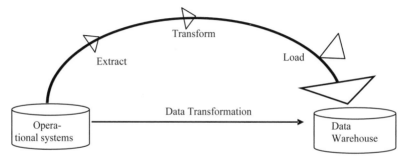

Fig. 1. Steps in data warehousing

A data warehouse is built by extracting data from operational data sources and loading it into the data warehouse (Inmon 1996). The process of extracting data from the operational systems to the data warehouse is known as data transformation (Devlin 1997), sometimes described using the abbreviation ETL, after the three main steps: *Extracting, Transforming* and *Loading* (Fig. 1, based on Hoffer et al. 2001). Data is extracted from operational data stores, transformed into the format for the data warehouse and loaded into the data warehouse.

Beyond the basic model described above (and Fig. 1), there are a variety of data warehouse architectures (Hoffer et al. 2001), varying on two axes: how many layers (between raw data and final warehouse); and breadth across the organisation. A full-scale organisational data warehouse would generally have three layers: (i) the operational data layer, (ii) a reconciled data layer where data from across the organisation is integrated, and (iii) a derived layer, where reconciled data is further transformed into the final format of the data warehouse (Devlin 1997). Smaller scale functionally based data warehouses (known as data marts) do not require a reconciled data layer and thus use a two-tier architecture: (i) operational data and (ii) derived data (Devlin 1997).

Data transformation is at the heart of data warehousing (Hoffer et al. 2001). It converts data from the format of the capture component (operational systems) and changes it to the format of the target (data warehouse) (Devlin 1997). This transformation process differentiates data warehousing from traditional extract and load processing (Inmon 1996). Despite the centrality of data transformation to data warehousing there has been much confusion about the best way to accomplish data transformations (Bischoff et al. 1997). A generic list of transformation functions has been described (Devlin 1997; Hoffer et al. 2001) and there have been attempts to generalise data transformation through a standard transformation language (Zamanian and Diaz 2002). However, these generalisations are at a "lower technical level" (Devlin 1997) dealing with basic record structures and do not address the ultimate purpose of a transformation function, i.e. 'to meet a business need' (Devlin 1997).   Despite the emphasis in theory on the need for data warehousing to support decision making, most descriptions of data transformation functions emphasise functions that integrate data across the organisation. For example, of ten practical examples of transformation functions in standard texts on the subject, nine are related to integration of disparate data and only one is related to converting data to information for decision making (Hoffer et al. 2001; Inmon 1996; Devlin 1997). The question is this. What guidelines does the designer use to ensure that the transformation functions are selected and developed in an objective manner? One approach is to examine existing models of data, information and decision making.

3 Data, Information and Decision Making

The process of transforming raw data into information for decision making has been examined within several disparate fields, from psychology to management theory to the information sciences. Two well-established approaches are described here.

3.1 Management Theory and Decision Making

The first approach, from management theory, is based on organisational context. Decision making is examined in the context of managerial activities. Decisions within an organisation are categorised into separate levels: Operational Control, Tactical Control and Strategic Planning (Fig. 2). Operational control represents decisions that concern day-to-day tasks. Management control concerns the effective use of resources in the accomplishment of the organisation's objectives. Strategic planning deals with organisational policies and objectives (Anthony 1965). The information required for higher-level managerial decisions is more than a mere aggregation of operational data (Gorry and Scott Morton, 1989).

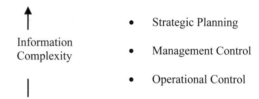

Fig. 2. Managerial activities (Adapted from Gorry and Scott Morton 1989)

This approach to decision making, based on organisational context and managerial activities, provides what might be called a 'top-down' method of devising transformation functions and designing the data warehouse. Start by selecting a defined area of managerial activity which includes a significant element of both strategic planning. Secondly, benchmark transformation functions against decision-making processes in the defined area.

3.2 Educational Psychology and Information

The second approach, based on research into cognition (Bloom 1956), categorises a spectrum of cognitive processes or information processing steps that 'refine' data in a stepwise fashion from its raw state into a final state of complex knowledge for decision making. An example of this approach describes the transformation of raw data into knowledge involving six steps (Fig. 3). It entails collecting and organising data, summarising, analysing and synthesising information prior to decision making (Light et al. 2004). Data is collected and organised before it can constitute information. Information can be summarised, analysed and synthesised for decision making. Then, after decision making, information becomes knowledge.

This approach to information based on a hierarchy of complexity provides what might be called a 'bottom-up' method of devising transformation functions and designing the data warehouse. Starting with the original data, any transformations must incorporate some form of **analysis** and/or **synthesis** in order to generate real information. Analysis can be characterised as categorisation or separation (of parts of a whole) while synthesis represents the integration and origination of new information from data (Bloom 1956).

The combination of the two models provides a basis for developing transformations required for the data warehouse using the combination of a top-down and a bottom-up approach. The next step is to apply these very general principles to a practical situation.

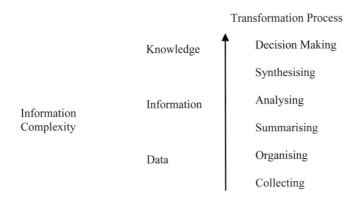

Fig. 3. Data transformation process (Adapted from Light et al. 2004)

4 Strategic Decision Making in Higher Education

Compared to the business world, higher education has a low rate of adoption of data warehousing for decision making. A recent study of higher education institutions identified seven broad subject areas where data warehousing is used; Academic, Alumni/Development, Enrolment, Finance, Financial Aid, Human Resource and Student Services. Despite the obvious importance of the academic function in higher education, this subject area recorded the second lowest use of data warehousing. Furthermore, data warehouses in the Academic area were more likely to be used for operational purposes as opposed to strategic decision making (Heise 2006).

One important area in higher education is academic quality assurance. Quality assurance is a key tool in educational management. It refers to the mechanisms and procedures adopted by educational providers to assure a given quality of service or the continued improvement of service. The strategic importance of quality assurance in the higher sector in Ireland (and in particular in the IOT sector) is indicated by the major recent changes in the national legislative and regulatory environment, for example the Qualifications (Education & Training) Act 1999, and the foundation of both the Higher Education and Training Awards Council (HETAC) and the National Qualifications Authority of Ireland (NQAI) in 2001. To meet quality assurance standards in the Institutes of Technology (IOT) sector the educational provider must monitor the effectiveness of the services delivered to the learner. For quality assurance purposes the main services delivered to learners are educational programmes and modules (HETAC 2002).

Data warehousing has been applied to the problem of supporting quality assurance procedures. It can provide an organised infrastructure to track, monitor and enforce parameters of operations to comply with quality assurance standards (Gould 1998). Academic quality assurance has tended to be process-based (e.g. ensuring that appropriate procedures are carried out) and input-based (e.g. ensuring that staff and facilities are adequate for a programme) but has included some outcome-based objective measures (e.g. measurement of student retention rates). However, the main recorded outcome from academic programmes is student results. Academic decision making based on outcomes (evidence-based decision making) has been extensively studied and advocated in research into student learning programmes (Pellegrino et al. 2001). The problem for decision makers is that student results are stored and processed at an operational level while institutional quality assurance is executed at the strategic level of decision making. Some method of linking the strategic level to the operational level is required.

5 Analysis and Synthesis in Educational Data

The bottom-up method defined in Section 3 requires that transformation functions incorporate some kind of analysis and synthesis. The obvious place to look for existing methods of analysis and synthesis of educational data is within the educational literature. Much of educational research has focussed on individual student learning (Gagné et al. 1992) or on the context of assessment (Black and William 1998). However, researchers working on educational measurement have developed a range of data analysis techniques including descriptive, correlation and other psychometric statistics (Hsu 2005; Cronbach 1984; Thorndike 1971). In addition, classical test theory describes a number of data analysis techniques that can assist in educational decision making (McAlpine 2001). These techniques have both analytic and synthetic functions. A traditional analytical objective of test theory has been to assign a measure to an individual test item, i.e. one question in a test, describing the ability of that item to discriminate between 'weak' and 'strong' students (McAlpine 2001). Educational measurement techniques have also included synthetic tasks: the creation of new information from aggregate data, for example, describing a range of expected outcomes for students based on past student performance data using a structure known as an Expectancy Table (Thorndike 1971, p.493).

In summary, the area of quality assurance in higher education provides a well-defined set of strategic decision-making problems. Institutes of higher education contain large volumes of student assessment data which represent outcomes of processes that are central to these institutions. A number of analytical techniques are available which provide a basis for transforming raw student data into information for supporting higher-level decision-making processes.

6 Methodology

6.1 Operational Data

The Galway Mayo Institute of Technology (GMIT) has implemented an information system for the processing of educational data. An Chéim, a national Management

Information Systems (MIS) project, is a collaborative project between the Institutes of Technology and the Department of Education and Science. One component of this project is the Banner system. This computer system centrally stores all academic records in an Oracle relational database management system (managed by An Chéim in Dublin) including student, examination and assessment data. Currently, GMIT uses the Banner system for operational processing of student examinations data and has recently begun creating ad-hoc queries for management reporting purposes using Oracle Discoverer. Sungard, the company that provides the Banner product, has, as part of its product suite, a set of tools for providing data warehousing and business intelligence on top of the Banner platform (www.sungardhe.com) but these are not in place in GMIT.

The existence of the Banner system at GMIT was the trigger for this project, providing ready access to a large body of raw operational data for research into data warehousing.

6.2 Project Concept/Research Question

The initial project concept was to investigate data warehousing using educational data using the data from the Banner system. This concept was supported by a recent study (Heise 2006) reporting that data warehouses in educational institutions were still concentrated in traditional business functions rather than in the academic function. A parallel element of the project was to investigate the possibility of using educational theories as a basis for any complex information/knowledge in the data warehouse. Essentially the project is exploratory in nature. At this stage two interim outcomes have been achieved and three final outcomes are expected.

Interim Outcomes (achieved)
1. A defined area of management decision making has been identified for the project
2. A defined subset of the educational theory (specifically educational measurement/psychometrics) has been identified

Final Outcomes (work in progress)
1. A set of transformation functions/data warehouse for academic data
2. A method of using educational measurement theory in information system that could be generalised a number of research areas outside of data warehousing:
    (a) Business intelligence
    (b) Data mining
    (c) Educational technology

6.3 Literature Review

The first step in the project was a two-part literature review. The first part consisted of a review of the literature on data warehousing to identify a particular area in data warehousing to investigate that which suited this project. This literature is described in Sections 2 and 3 and resulted in the focus on transformation functions related to decision support of strategic decision making. The review also led to the focus on quality assurance as the area of strategic decision making that the warehouse will support (Section 4).

The second part of the literature review involved an examination of the educational literature. The aim of this review was to identify frameworks, theories or models that would provide a basis for any transformation functions to be developed. The result of this review was the decision to focus on the literature on educational measurement described in Section 5 above.

6.4 Initial Review of the Raw Data

A sample of the data has been obtained from the Banner system. This consists of two text dumps of student and examinations data in the form of spreadsheets, generated by the MIS department in GMIT using Oracle Discoverer (65,000 student results across 240 programmes in 10 Schools over 4 years). The data was anonymised prior to the text dump. These text dumps have been loaded into an Access database management system and restructured into a sample database. Currently this Access platform is being used to store the sample data (as a virtual Banner) as one set of tables, to start on the first drafts of the data transformation functions (using SQL and Access query methods) and to store the data warehouse as a set of separate tables.

The next stage in the physical implementation will be to port the operational data and the data warehouse to an Oracle platform using Oracle tools to implement the transformations.

6.5 Data Warehouse Design & Design of Transformation Functions

Although the data warehouse has not yet been designed a number of features are already clear.

6.5.1 Architecture

The architecture of any data warehouse is a key design decision (Devlin 1997). The data warehouse envisaged will be a data mart supporting a particular set of decision-making functions (quality assurance) rather than an enterprise-wide data warehouse. The architecture will be two-tier rather than three-tier since the reconciled layer of three-tier systems is not appropriate for a functional data mart style system. This also matches well with the raw data which is all stored in a single large operational data store (Banner) and therefore does not require the construction of an intermediate layer of reconciled data.

6.5.2 Granularity of the Data Model

A key feature of any data warehouse is the granularity (Inmon 1996) or level of detail of the units of data in the warehouse. In this instance the decision to focus on quality assurance defines a level of granularity based on academic programmes and modules. The data warehouse model will therefore consist initially of two core subjects (entities): Programmes and Modules. This determines a certain level of aggregation in the transformation functions since the raw assessment data is at a much finer level of granularity (results of individual students on individual modules). Other supporting entities to describe dimensions of the data have yet to be identified but candidates exist, for example, administrative entities such as Departments or Schools and conceptual entities such as programme levels (e.g. honours versus ordinary degrees).

6.6 Transformation Functions

The specific transformation functions are the final physical output of the project and have not yet been designed and developed. However, the secondary research has provided a framework for their development following a stepwise process:

1. Identify algorithm/computation from educational measurement theory
2. Modify algorithm to transform existing raw data into new attributes/ entities at the specified granularity of the data warehouse
3. Implement the transformation function in SQL
4. Evaluate modified transformation in terms of contribution to quality assurance processes

As stated, this step of the project has not yet commenced. However, examples of transformations have been identified for illustrative purposes

Illustrative Transformation 1

Compute the discrimination (ability for a test item to separate weak from strong students) for a module from student results (in that module and in the entire programme). Assign this computed value to a new attribute of the Module entity. A quality assurance process could then involve the extraction of all modules in rank order of discrimination with low-discrimination modules subject to further scrutiny.

Illustrative Transformation 2

Compute correlation statistics for all modules on a programme for a given stage (year). The aggregate statistic would be assigned to a new attribute of the Programme entity. This attribute would indicate a level of heterogeneity/homogeneity in Programme results. Quality assurance processes might compare the score on this attribute to other qualitative characteristics of the programme. For example an Accounting degree with few electives might be expected to very homogenous compared to a general Arts degree.

Illustrative Transformation 3

Programmes consist of modules built on each other over several years/semesters using a prerequisite structure. Generate a tree structure (a completely new entity or set of entities) of modules on a programme based on relationships between module results. Quality assurance could compare this outcomes-based tree structure with the module structure described for that programme.

7 Conclusion

Data warehousing is a technology that can support management decision-making processes by providing an organisation-wide view of high-quality information and by transforming operational data into information for decision making. The introduction of new large-scale operational computer systems in the higher education sector, such as the Banner system in the Institutes of Technology in Ireland, provides the pool of raw academic data which is the basis for data warehousing. While data warehousing technology has been gradually adopted in higher education it has tended to be in the traditional business functions rather than in the core academic functions. An examination of the information requirements for decision making and of the steps required in processing complex information suggests a method for creating transformation functions for a data warehouse in an academic environment. Quality assurance of program offerings is identified as an appropriate area of strategic decision making. Educational measurement theory provides a variety of analytic and synthetic tools for designing and developing new transformation functions to populate an educational data warehouse. The expected outcomes of the completed project are a set of transformation functions for an educational data warehouse and a way of using concepts from educational measurement theory in an information system that could be generalised to other research areas such as data mining, business intelligence and educational technology.

References

Anthony, R. (1965) *Planning and Controlling Systems: A Framework for Analysis.* Harvard Business School Division of Research Press, Boston.

Barquin, R. C. (1996) 'On the First Issue of the Journal of Data Warehousing.' *Journal of Data Warehousing,* 1(1).

Bischoff, J., Alexander, T., Foreword by Zachman, J. A. (1997) *Data Transformation, Data Warehousing, Practical Advice from the Expert.* Prentice Hall, New Jersey.

Black, P., Wiliam, D. (1998) 'Inside the Black Box: Raising Standards Through Classroom Assessment. *Phi Delta Kappan,* 80(2): 139–148.

Bloom, B., Englehart, M. Furst, E., Hill, W., Krathwohl, D. (1956) *Taxonomy of Educational Objectives: The Classification of Educational Goals. Handbook I: Cognitive Domain.* Longmans/Green, New York/Toronto.

Carr, N. G. (2003) IT Doesn't Matter. *Harvard Business Review.* May 2003, 5(12).

Cronbach, L. J. (1984) *Essential of Psychological Testing,* 4th Edition. Harper, New York

Devlin, B. (1997) *Data Warehouse from Architecture to Implementation.* Addison-Wesley Professional, Reading, MA.

Dyché, J. (2000) *E-data: Turning Data into Information with Data Warehousing.* Addison-Wesley Information Technology Series, Reading, MA.

Gagné, R. M., Briggs, L. J., Wager, W. G. (1992) *Principles of Instructional Design,* Harcourt Brace College Publishers, Fort Worth.

Gorry, A. G., Scott Morton, M. S. (1989) 'A Framework for management information systems.' *Sloan Management Review,* 13(1): 55–70.

Gould, L. S. (1998) 'What you need to know about data warehousing.' *Automative Manufacturing & Production,* 64(4). Retrieved February 18, 2007 from InfoTrac OneFile.

Heise, D. L. (2006) 'Data Warehousing and Decision Making in Higher Education in the United States'. Andrews University

HETAC (2002) Guidelines and Criteria for Assurance Procedures in Higher Education and Training, Higher Education and Training Awards Council, Dublin.

Hoffer, J. A., Prescott, M. B., McFadden, F. R. (2001) *Modern Database Management,* 6th edition. Prentice Hall, New Jersey

Hsu, T. (2005) Research Methods and Data Analysis Procedures Used by Educational Researchers. *International Journal of Research and Method in Education* 28(2): 109–133.

Inmon, W. H. (1996) *The Data Warehouse Environment, Building the Data Warehouse,* 2nd edition. Wiley, New York.

Light, D., Wexler, D. H., Hienze, J. (2004). 'Keeping Teachers in the Center: A Framework of Data-Driven Decision Making' http://cct.edc.org/report_summary.asp?numPublicationId=195

McAlpine, M. (2001) Workshop on Computer Assisted Assessment: Issues in the Large Scale Use of Multiple Choice Questions. Robert Clark Centre, University of Glasgow.

Pellegrino, J. W., Chudowsky, N., Glaser, R. (2001) *Knowing What Students Know: The Science and Design of Educational Assessment.* National Academy Press, Washington, DC.

Shahzad, M. A., (2003) 'Data Warehousing with Oracle.' Retrieved March 5, 2007 from www.oracular.com/white_paper_pdfs/DataWarehousingwithOracle.pdf

Thorndike, R. L. (1971) *Educational Measurement.* American Council of Education, Washington, DC.

Zamanian, K., Diaz, N. (2002) 'Apparatus and Method for performing Data Transformations in Data Warehousing.' United States Patent, Patent No. US 6,339,775 B1. www.freepatentsonline.com.

Index

Printed in the United States of America